The Loss of Happiness in Market Democracies

The Institution for Social and Policy Studies at Yale University
The Yale ISPS Series

ROBERT E. LANE

The Loss of Happiness in Market Democracies

Yale University Press
New Haven &
London

Set in Postscript Sabon type by Keystone Typesetting, Inc. Printed in the United States of America.

Library of Congress Cataloging-in-Publication Data
Lane, Robert Edwards.
The loss of happiness in market democracies / Robert E. Lane.
p. cm.
Includes bibliographical references and index.
ISBN 0-300-07801-3 (alk. paper)
1. Economics—Moral and ethical aspects. 2. Economics—Sociological aspects. 3. Quality of life. 4. Money—Moral and ethical aspects. I. Title.
HB72.L364 2000
330.1—dc21 99-29817

A catalogue record for this book is available from the British Library.

The paper in this book meets the guidelines for permanence and durability of the Committee on Production Guidelines for Book Longevity of the Council on Library Resources.

10 9 8 7 6 5 4 3 2

This book is dedicated to all unhappy people, especially to the lonely and those who have lost their children, their parents, or their spouses, wherever they may be.

Contents

Acknowledgments

Earlier versions of the following chapters have appeared elsewhere: chapter 9 as "The Joyless Market Economy," published in Avner Ben-Ner and Louis Putterman, eds., *Economics, Values, and Organization* (Cambridge: Cambridge University Press, 1998), 461–88; chapter 10 as "The Road Not Taken: Giving Friendship Priority Over Commodities," *Critical Review,* 1994, 8: 521–54. Chapters 12 and 15 borrow from "The Joyless Polity: Contributions of Democratic Politics to Ill-Being," presented to the Conference on Citizenship Competence sponsored by the Committee on the Political Economy of the Good Society, University of Maryland; Washington, D.C., February 10–11, 1995, published in *Citizen Competence and Democratic Institutions,* edited by Stephen Elkin and Edward Soltan (Penn State University Press, 1999). Also in chapter 15 are selections from "Diminishing Returns from Money, Companionship—and Happiness," paper presented at the first annual meeting of the International Society of Quality of Life Studies, Charlotte, N.C., November 1997; chapter 16 of this work borrows from chapter 27 of my *The Market Experience* (Cambridge University Press, 1991).

I wish to thank Ed Diener for permission to use figure 1.1 (private communication) and for an invitation to attend the Conference on Enjoyment and Suffering, Princeton University, October 31–November 2, 1996. The papers of this conference proved especially useful in chapter 3 in this work.

I am grateful to Soo Yeon Kim of the Yale Social Science Statistical Laboratory for her help in analyzing the NORC and NES data and for creating the figures from these sources.

I gratefully acknowledge permission by the Los Angeles Higher Education Research Institute to reprint figure 8.1; by Russell Sage to reprint figure 9.1; and by McGraw-Hill for permission to reprint figure 17.1.b

PART I

Introduction

I

Shadow on the Land

Amidst the satisfaction people feel with their material progress, there is a spirit of unhappiness and depression haunting advanced market democracies throughout the world, a spirit that mocks the idea that markets maximize well-being and the eighteenth-century promise of a right to the pursuit of happiness under benign governments of people's own choosing. The haunting spirit is manifold: a postwar decline in the United States in people who report themselves as happy, a rising tide in all advanced societies of clinical depression and dysphoria (especially among the young), increasing distrust of each other and of political and other institutions, declining belief that the lot of the average man is getting better (see chapter 2), a tragic erosion of family solidarity and community integration together with an apparent decline in warm, intimate relations among friends (see chapter 6).

We are not the first generation to be suspicious of each other (in spite of Ferdinand Tönnies, gemeinschaft revealed plenty of that) and certainly not the first to distrust institutions (currently Russia and recently Weimar are and were more suspicious), but we may be the first to monitor these disturbances with such care—and idly watch them accumulate. The current unhappiness and malaise are not marked by revolutionary sentiments, for the ethos of modern market democracies is characterized by strong beliefs in the legitimacy, if not the practices, of its institutions. But in subterranean ways the modern era may be languishing while another is struggling to be born.

Have we not traveled this route before: the prolonged whingeing, to use a British expression, about alienation in the 1960s? Not only the Frankfurt School (Max Horkheimer, Theodor Adorno) and its diaspora (Erich Fromm, Herbert Marcuse, Leo Lowenthal); not only the antimodernists (Hannah Arendt), the aesthetic critics (Lewis Mumford, Theodore Roszak), the existentialists (Jean-Paul Sartre), the neo-Marxists (Lewis Althusser), the psycho-Marxists (Hendrik Ruitenbeek), the street people and their minstrels (Allen Ginsberg). Not just these: in 1968, 45 percent of the U.S. public (especially radical rightists) said we are a sick society. I do not wish to return to the themes of these curdled imaginations.

How account for this combination of growing unhappiness and depression, interpersonal and institutional distrust, and weakened companionship in advanced market democracies, in which people are, with important exceptions, reasonably well-off? The populations of these countries do not press against their resources; they can expect to live longer than their parents, and their old age is reasonably protected; there is (still) a safety net to catch them if they lose their jobs or become ill; their children are not likely to die in childhood, and these children have available to them more educational facilities than were available to their parents. Politically, they are endowed with rights unknown to their parents; they do not live in police states but rather have some assurance of due process of law; and they are offered reasonably adequate opportunities to participate in political decisions affecting their own fates. Moreover, it is a hedonic gain, I think, to substitute ecological doomsday for theological doomsday — because it is less invidious and less guilt-ridden.

The paradox of apparently growing unhappiness in the midst of increasing plenty is illustrated in figure 1.1, which shows the strange, seemingly contradictory pattern in the United States of rising real income and a falling index of subjective well-being (people reporting themselves as being "very happy"). Later (see chapters 8–10) I will show in some detail why in advanced economies income does not buy happiness.

This book is a preliminary effort to explain why there is so much unhappiness and malaise in market democracies, when the very purpose of markets is to maximize utility (whose meanings will be analyzed later) and "satisfaction of wants in human societies," which Tjalling Koopmans said was the subject of positive economics;[1] and when the very purpose of democracies is to facilitate the pursuit of happiness — James Madison's and Thomas Jefferson's agenda for the American democracy. My focus is not on the origins of depression and unhappiness, although I will necessarily treat this question along the way, but

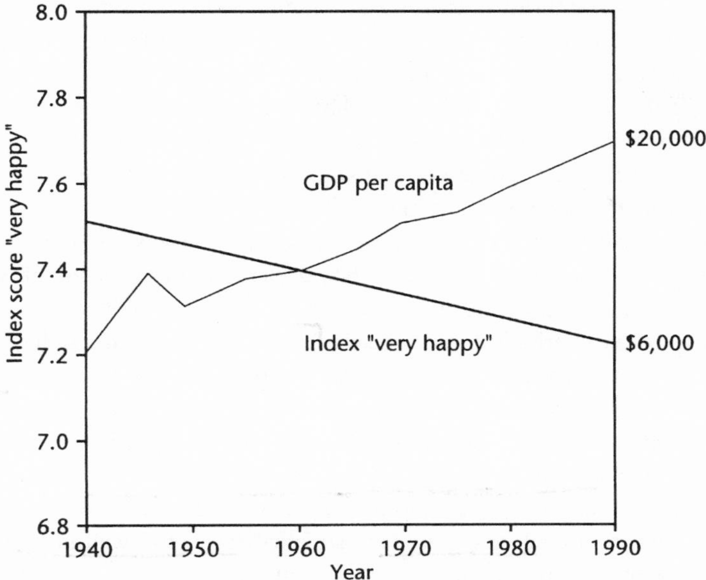

Figure 1.1. Index of "Very Happy" Responses in U.S. National Surveys and GDP per Capita, 1946–90

Sources: Fitted line of index "very happy" scores in various surveys, courtesy of Ed Diener. GDP per capita in constant 1987 dollars: U.S. Bureau of Economic Analysis; *Statistical Abstract of the United States, 1995*. Washington, D.C.: Bureau of the Census, 1995.

rather on the contributions of our major institutions, markets and democracies, to both happiness and unhappiness. My argument does not depend on the evidence of growing unhappiness in the postwar period (which may be a mere blip in a long-term curve); even if that infelicity were not growing, there would be enough misery to make an accounting necessary—in spite of the fact that in the United States today most people say they are happy.[2]

Happiness as a Good

Happiness is a strong candidate for an ultimate good or, in a pluralist system, one of several coordinate ultimate goods: for example, Aristotle, Epicurus, John Stuart Mill, the intuitionist David Ross, and, of course, Jeremy Bentham and his latter-day interpreters, including the modified utilitarian Nicholas Rescher, who requires happiness to be merited. But Bentham alone makes happiness a single unconditionally supreme good. Economists are more circumspect, but they are lodged in the same utilitarian tradition, in the post-

Marshallian version disguising the idea of happiness in the term *utility*.[3] Actually, by *utility* economists now mean that a person's preferences have been met, a concept some distance from happiness. (Would I prefer to die by hanging or by lethal injection?) In the next chapter I will examine the meaning of happiness in a little more detail, but here I want to consider whether the commonsense meaning of happiness (or satisfaction with one's life, the main alternatives in the literature on subjective well-being) can stand alone as the ultimate good toward which people strive and which markets and democracies should favor above all else. I will treat the problem of plural coordinate goods in chapter 15, but let me state at the outset that I do not think hedonic criteria are enough for evaluating the good society. For one thing, pursuit of happiness without pursuit of another goal is impossible or at least self-defeating. The very logic of happiness, then, implies that there is something else worth pursuing whose pursuit or attainment is itself the source of happiness.

It follows that happiness cannot be the only good to be pursued. Others may have different candidates, but I find it convenient and fruitful to think of the following coordinate, ultimate goods as a trinity: subjective well-being (SWB), human development (including virtue), and justice, no one of which may be resolved into or subordinated under another. In my opinion, the ultimate goals that people actually pursue are embraced by these three, although others might think of a group of goods different from mine.

For those who believe there is already a satisfactory philosophy of happiness and that it is utilitarianism, I beg leave to defer the reasons why this is not so until chapter 15.

From Income to Companionship

If, as suggested by figure 1.1, income is not the most important direct source of happiness or of life satisfaction (see chapter 4), what are the important sources? The first answer is simple and obvious: we get happiness primarily from people; it is their affection or dislike, their good or bad opinion of us, their acceptance or rejection that most influence our moods. Income is mostly sought in the service of these forms of social esteem, as Adam Smith reported long ago.[4] To make this view plausible, there are evolutionary principles, theological arguments, and social science studies to support the priority of what I shall call companionship. The evolutionary principles will be given in chapter 4 and the social science studies in chapters 5 and 6, but here I want to digress into the theological argument.

God said to Adam, "It is not good for man to be alone" (Genesis 2:18). Then, in testing Adam, God asked, "What thinkst thou of me, and this my state / Seem I to thee sufficiently possessed / Of happiness, or not? Whom am alone / From all eternity. . . . / How have I them with whom to hold converse?" (*Paradise Lost,* 403–05). Adam says he is only an imperfect mortal and needs companionship. Then God, who says he knew this all along, puts Adam to sleep and, as is well known, creates a companion from his rib. But the Christian god was not finished testing his creatures: Among Job's sufferings, the most hurtful was the estrangement of his family and his friends; Job says of God, "He has removed my brothers far from me, / And my acquaintances are completely estranged from me. / My relatives have failed, / And my close friends have forgotten me" (Job 19:13–14). Loneliness, deserved or not, is God's punishment.

Two alternative versions also emphasize companionship as the reason for the Creation. An anthropomorphic version says that in his loneliness, Man created God to befriend him ("Oh, what a friend we have in Jesus"). And the Hindu myth of creation echoes the Christian god's complaint: because of his own loneliness, the Original Being created the world for his companionship.[5]

The studies to be reported in chapters 5 and 6 support God (and Milton and Job); they create a strong presumption that the way to increase SWB in the United States and probably in all advanced Western societies is to move from an emphasis on money and economic growth toward an emphasis on companionship. Of course, people need and want both material resources and companionship, but the needs vary with the relative supplies of these two goods. In rich societies, for people above the poverty line, more money, as compared with friendship and community esteem, a loving spouse and affectionate children, quickly loses its power to make people happy. That is why satisfaction with one's family life contributes more to SWB in the United States than does satisfaction with one's standard of living and why satisfaction with friends is a more powerful contribution in individualistic societies than in the familistic societies of Asia. In contrast, in developing countries, where money is scarce and family life usually strong, more money makes a larger contribution to SWB.[6] Does this not seem to reflect the basic principle of declining marginal utility, which says that as a person acquires relatively more of one kind of good, that good loses value compared to another, relatively scarcer good, with the scarcer good in each case gaining in relative value (see chapter 15)? At least, that is the way I interpret the data presented in this book.

Contribution of Markets and Democracy to Well-Being

In this book I ask how the great institutions of market democracies contribute to (subjective) well-being. The large and growing literature on well-being inevitably has direct relevance to the study of markets and democracies. What is it?

MARKETS

The reason markets in advanced economies fail to do much to promote, let alone maximize, well-being is that the things that contribute most to well-being, especially companionship and family life, are market externalities (see chapter 9). And commodities, it seems, are poor substitutes for friends (see chapter 10). Our accounting systems reflect this bias: they have tracked individual and national income over the years with meticulous care—but not companionship. Following the lead of Henry Maine, Tönnies, and Max Weber, who noted a marked change in personal relations in the late nineteenth and early twentieth centuries (from status to contract, from gemeinschaft to gesellschaft), I have tracked visiting patterns in families and communities and among friends for the past quarter century (see chapter 6). The decline of family and community is almost as dramatic as the increase in disposable income noted in figure 1.1. This, I think, is a useful clue to understanding the decline in happiness in the United States and the rise in depression in most advanced economies.

DEMOCRACY

The other great institution that governs our lives, democratic government, gives us the freedom to vote as we please: why not vote for a share of happiness? Here is where malaise, as contrasted to unhappiness, is most clearly reflected: we do not trust our government, we do not believe it is responsive to our wishes. The instrument itself is tainted (see chapters 11, 12). And when we do participate, it is more out of a sense of duty than because we anticipate benefits to flow from our acts of voting; indeed the very acts of voting or other participation give no pleasure and some pain (see chapter 13). Democracies *must* inflict pain to perform their functions, but is there surplus pain in modern democracies?

Why Do Individuals Not Choose Paths to Their Well-Being?

This account of the agencies that might promote happiness is incomplete: the whole idea of markets and democratic governments is not that of their own accord they will guarantee happiness but that they will respond to the demands of their publics to relieve their miseries. Why, then, do the constituent individuals not make better use of these instruments and choose paths that will maximize their well-being? The short answer is that people are not very good judges of how, even within the private spheres of their own lives, to increase, let along maximize, their happiness (see chapter 16). It is not just that they are embedded in an economistic culture that misleads them, or even that they are governed by misleading ideologies; rather, the problem is that people often choose of their own accord paths that do not lead to their well-being: they escalate their standards in proportion to their improved circumstances, choose short-run benefits that incur greater long-term costs, fear and avoid the means to their preferred ends, infer from early failures an unwarranted and disabling incompetence (see chapter 17). Western individualism, treasured among westerners' cultural endowments, presents a thoroughly mixed account of benefits and losses.

This view is heresy in a society whose economic and political institutions depend on individual choices and in which self-reliance and the belief that the individual *should* control his or her own destiny are canonical. The heresy seems to invite what Immanuel Kant anathematized as paternalism.

The Malnutrition Model

Searching for sources of rising dysphoria, I will look for evidence of rising known causes of unhappiness: increasing unemployment, increasing poverty, epidemics of illnesses and of addictions, breakdown of social norms, and the loss of the things that give security and meaning to our lives. During most of the postwar period one will not find these objective causes; often, indeed, the sources of pain have been ameliorated. I propose a model that may help to account for this puzzle.

Let us suppose a two-stage process: debilitation followed by disease. I call it the malnutrition model, in which people are first weakened by hunger and then die, not of malnutrition but, say, of influenza or infections to which they are made vulnerable by their malnutrition. Then rising incidence of death from influenza can be explained not by some new and more virulent strain of flu but by the debilitation of the population. In the malnutrition model people have increased vulnerability to a low or even declining incidence of the usual traumatic and stressful experiences of life.

My hypothesis is that there is a kind of famine of warm interpersonal relations, of easy-to-reach neighbors, of encircling, inclusive memberships, and of solidary family life. There is much evidence that for people lacking in social support of this kind, unemployment has more serious effects, illnesses are more deadly, disappointment with one's children is harder to bear, bouts of depression last longer, and frustration and failed expectations of all kinds are more traumatic. Thus, the malnutrition model explains why the search for increases in objective hardships will fail, for the causes lie not in the rise of objective traumas but in the increased vulnerability of the public. A weak version of the metaphoric flu will then do the damage of a more virulent strain because people without social support are less resistant.

Can Unhappy Cultures Save Themselves?

Each culture selects among what Ruth Benedict called a "rainbow of possibilities." As we know from studies of Alor and Dobu, Greek and Mexican villages, *La Vida* in New York and San Juan, some peoples possess and retain cultural traits that make them unhappy. It has long been thought that Americans had forged for themselves a happy pattern (because, it is said, they never knew tragedy—this in spite of slavery, genocide, and the Civil War). Nature favored (some of) them, and the opportunities thus presented gave scope to the spirit of enterprise brought by those who migrated from unhappy situations to try something new. Perhaps, compared to others, Americans were once a happy people, although Alexis de Tocqueville and some contemporary historians have thought not.[7] In 1946 the United States was the happiest country among four advanced economies; in the late 1970s it ranked eighth among eleven advanced countries; in the 1980s it ranked tenth among twenty-three nations, including many third world countries. It has been said, therefore, that the United States is not as happy as it is rich.[8] Something has gone wrong. The economism that made Americans both rich and happy at one point in history is misleading them, is offering more money, which does not make them happy, instead of more companionship, which probably would. Over the long term, persistence forecasting (tomorrow will be like today) is not working.

In making this observation, I merely repeat a well-known fault of nations and cultures. Following G. W. F. Hegel's lead, A. L. Kroeber, a German-American anthropologist, discovered a useful metaphor for the kind of social change I am addressing. He speaks of the life cycles of great civilizations—Babylonian, Grecian, medieval Christian. Kroeber speculates on how great artists and thinkers develop the potential of the distinctive "configurations" of each culture and how that greatness passes away when its possibilities have been exhausted. The end comes when a theme is simply repeated without innovation or experiment.[9] The death of a culture is not usually encountered by cataclysmic events, not by either a bang or a whimper, but by failure to adapt, a monotonous repetition of what it had done before. This is a very different view of "the end of history" recently said to characterize the triumph of market democracies.[10] Is that where Americans are now?

PART II

Well-Being and Depression

2

Unhappiness in Our Time

Sigmund Freud once asked whether whole epochs of civilization, perhaps civilization itself, might have "become neurotic under the pressure of civilizing trends."[1] Twenty-five years later Fromm offered a kind of answer: "The world in the middle of the twentieth century is mentally sicker than it was in the nineteenth century."[2] Freud found the sources of mental illness in family relations, but Fromm found the answer in social institutions, especially the market. I do not want to return to either tradition, but I think they were each partially right: The sources of our unhappiness and depression certainly include the tragic loss of family solidarity and other human ties, a loss which is, I think, exacerbated by the market economy and made no better by political institutions.

In a moment I will present the substantial evidence of declining happiness and of increasing clinical depression, at least since the 1970s. But in the meantime notice the paradox in my proposed thesis: the economic and political institutions of our time are products of the utilitarian philosophy of happiness, but they seem to have guided us to a period of greater unhappiness. This is partly because they have been influenced by Bentham's philosophy of money: "Money," he said, is "the most accurate measure of the quantity of pain or pleasure a man can be made to receive."[3] But it is the nature of "utility functions" to change with changes in the supply of a good. All I want to do for the moment is to note that what seems to be a paradox and is certainly ironic is a familiar predicament in other spheres of life: the desire to be invited to a party that, once a person has been invited, loses its value; the belief in Eastern Europe that as soon as they have markets, all will be well—only to find that all is not well when the markets come. Albert Hirschman's belief that changes in preference ordering come as much from disappointment as from satiation is well taken.[4]

In this chapter I will first describe what we are talking about when we refer to happiness and depression. Then, I give a portrait of the recent decline in happiness, marital satisfaction, work satisfaction, financial satisfaction, and satisfaction with one's place of residence. These infelicitous trends are partially parallel to the trends in other advanced economies: although there is no evidence of increases in unhappiness in Europe similar to those in the United States, Europe shares the rising tide of depression characteristic of many advanced economies. In this analysis, the important point, again, is the waning power of income to yield that ephemeral good utility. Getting away from happiness—but not very far away—I will take up the associated declines in mutual trust, belief in progress, and confidence in public authorities. Together these have been associated with the concept of anomie, a general distemper often treated as a form of alienation or *ressentiment.* As one would expect, loss of optimism about the future is a feature of depression, but strangely, it seems, relative pessimism about a country's future can survive in the same mind with happiness. Finally, I will look at cross-cultural studies of happiness and depression, studies which have the great advantage of dealing with societal phenomena like the presence of individual rights and democracy (see chapters 11–15). But it is time to specify what I mean by happiness and satisfaction with one's life (jointly, along with "affect balance," captured by the abbreviation SWB).

The Meanings of Happiness and Depression

Sparing you a discussion on the dimensions of happiness (for example, intensity, duration, affect balance, and so on) and sparing myself a review of the long history of what philosophers have meant by happiness,[5] I must nevertheless alert the reader to the rich new biomedical research on enjoyment and suffering,[6] pleasure and pain—the two sovereign masters which Bentham thought were beyond measurement. I shall refer to this research below and in chapter 3 and later chapters, but here I turn to a more topographical issue: In the many empirical studies on happiness or subjective well-being (SWB), what do respondents have in mind when they address questions about their satisfaction with their lives-as-a-whole or with their happiness?

SOME PLAIN MEANINGS OF HAPPINESS AND UNHAPPINESS

For Frank Andrews and Stephen Withey, the matter is commonsensical; in their informed opinions the dream of happiness is a "dream to be loved, liked and accepted, responsible, respected, somewhat independent, somewhat secure, interested in life, comfortable, successful, and to have fun. . . . We suspect," they say, "that people diverge more in how much of these attributes they want, and in what domains they want them, than in what the criteria mean to them."[7] This will do for a starter, although I think people do want different things or at least place different emphases among the things mentioned, for instance, some crave love and others financial success.

Jonathan Freedman's imaginative study of many thousands of magazine readers gives more vivid, personalized responses. What do people say when they describe their meanings? Freedman divides the responses into the two basic dimensions (1) fun, pleasure, excitement, and (2) peace of mind. These two dimensions are almost identical with those that Mill used.[8] First, excitement:

> "Enjoying myself," "things going well," "pleasurable experiences." These people focus on the active enjoyment of life. They use the term pleasure frequently . . . from all sources — sex, a good meal, a successful tennis match, a "fun" movie, a good party, and so on. [This dimension also includes] acts of creativity, helping a friend, being loved, doing something nice for people you love or having them do so for you, and sharing in the success and satisfaction of loved ones. A clear theme . . . is that pleasure and good times, whatever their sources, involve mostly active, dynamic experiences.[9]

And then there is what Freedman calls peace of mind and Mill calls tranquillity:

> "Self-satisfaction and equilibrium," "happiness is being satisfied," "peace of mind," "ability to cope," "feeling content with myself," "being secure in my feelings about myself," "feeling fulfilled and worthwhile." This view often focused on the absence of negative feelings or "not being unhappy," "being free of worries about things I can't control." Happiness [in this view] is more peaceful, quiet, passive, and perhaps internal. It involves satisfaction rather than thrills, contentment rather than fun, peace instead of pleasure . . . and "a feeling of having done well."[10]

Freedman explains that references to excitement and peace of mind occur with about equal frequency in his interviews and, most important, must both be present in a person's life for the person to consider himself or herself happy.

Without being invidious, one may consider how empty are the criteria of utility or even the external criteria of welfare considered by economists to represent well-being: income, education, and health.[11] In fact, education, good for other reasons, has no consistent relationship to SWB.[12] Neither has income, whose interpretation suffers from the economistic fallacy (to be discussed in chapter 4), namely, that beyond the poverty level higher incomes increase SWB. All the evidence shows that although more money to the poor decreases their unhappiness and also increases their satisfaction with their lives, in advanced countries, above the poverty line this relationship between level of income and level of SWB is weak or nonexistent. Thus, the rich are no more satisfied with their lives than the merely comfortable, who in turn are only slightly, if at all, more satisfied with their lives than the lower middle classes[13] (see chapter 4).

But people in richer nations are happier than people in poorer nations: the so-called affluence effect; but here again, among richer, advanced nations the power of gross domestic product (GDP per capita) to predict average happiness is weak, indeed. Reporting on cross-national studies, Ruut Veenhoven, the Dutch archivist and analyst of world happiness data, comments, "In fact, a curvilinear relationship appears: the correspondence between average happiness and gross national product being more prominent in the poorest part of the world than in the richest one. As such, it neatly reflects the law of diminishing returns."[14] But I am dealing with individuals.

There are other plain meanings of happiness. For example, one might ask a series of questions that have a commonsense currency for sense of well-being: (1) Do you enjoy your daily life so that you generally welcome each new day? Andrews and Withey's question "How much fun are you having?" taps this arena, as do questions about hassles in daily living. Hassles have a devastating effect on SWB.[15] (2) The more traditional questions about meaning and purpose lead to assessments of, for example, whether John Rawls's "life plans" are on their way to fulfillment (which he says *is* happiness but which is conceptually and empirically different from pleasure). More specifically, meaning often comes from religion, which, as we shall see, is generally associated with high SWB. (3) Does the future seem hopeful? Not only is it the case that "without hope, the people will perish," but depression is defined as a condition of hopelessness (see below). (4) Do you feel competent in coping with the things you have to do? This is a matter of general attribution: Do you control events in your life or are you a pawn of fate? Self-attribution, believing that you are in control of events in your life, is highly related to SWB. (5) As one would expect, a sense of one's worth, self-esteem, is almost a surrogate for SWB. (6) Even though a person can be both happy and worried, anxiety is the enemy of well-being—just as it is a companion to depression. In studies too numerous to mention, all of these commonsense aspects of life have been measured and all have been found to be a cause or part of the syndrome of SWB or its opposite.

A rich array of complexities is suggested by language and its differentiated meanings. In current economic theory, *utility* means satisfaction of preferences, not just satisfaction itself. In my opinion, we would not care about preference satisfaction if we did not think it had hedonic value. Daniel Kahneman has sorted out these meanings as "liking," which is satisfaction from consumption experience; "wanting," which is "decision utility" and has been shown to have quite different properties from immediate satisfaction or pain; and "remembering/anticipating" pleasure, which again has been shown to be different from the immediate experience.[16] Much of our positive feeling has to do with remembering past and anticipating future events. Pleasure itself is different from happiness and life satisfaction; according to many psychologists and physiologists, pleasure is related to physical enjoyments, but others refer to the pleasure of the mind. Bishop Berkeley found three types of pleasure: pleasure of reason, pleasure of the imagination, and accomplishment. The evolutionary psychologist Randolph Nesse thought that the variety of kinds of sadness were each specific products of specific experiences: grief comes only from the loss of someone you loved, disappointment from lost opportunities, shame from loss of status, jealousy from the threat of loss of a partner's fidelity, and so forth. The fact that pleasure and pain derive from different parts of the nervous system suggests that they are not simply the opposites that Bentham thought they were and that ambivalence occurs when they compete for dominance. Nor is the pleasure coming from escape from pain easy to classify.[17] The scientific study of SWB occupies many psychologists, physiologists, neurobiologists, and medical doctors; in my societal focus, we shall have to be satisfied with simple indicators of happiness, sadness, and depression, with, in the psychologists' language, positive and negative affect.

Many issues are technical and are referred to in the Appendix, but one recent finding is important enough to mention here. Against the argument that happiness is only an unstable mood, Daniel Kahneman, a former critic of measures of SWB, now finds that people keep a kind of running account of their moods and then summarize them to give a meaningful report of these moods over a much longer period of time. Thus, responding to a question about their happiness, people can report their usual mood this week or this month or even over longer periods.[18] Nevertheless, in these reports there are many sources of distortion. People edit their judgments with moral criteria (for example, happiness because of drugs is depreciated); they employ conventional theories about what *should* cause happiness; they give more weight to losses than to gains of the same amount; they bias remembered experiences by remembering peaks and end points but not duration; they employ a positivity bias—and much more. Yet with all these faults, self-reports correspond fairly closely to reports about the respondents by teachers and friends who know them well and to the results of a variety of somatic tests.[19]

THE MEANING OF DEPRESSION

Major depression is not just a matter of mood, for among its symptoms are the following, taken from the recently standardized test used in the cross-national studies [DSM-III-R]. To qualify for "major depression," "at least four of the symptoms have . . . to be present nearly every day for a period of at least two weeks":

1. Poor appetite or significant weight loss (when not dieting) or increased appetite, or significant weight gain.
2. Insomnia or hypertension.
3. Psychomotor agitation or retardation.
4. Loss of interest or pleasure in usual activities or decrease in sexual drive.
5. Loss of energy, fatigue.
6. Feelings of worthlessness, self-reproach, or excessive or inappropriate guilt.
7. Complaints or evidence of diminished ability to think or concentrate, such as slowed thinking, or indecisiveness not associated with marked loosening of association or incoherence.
8. Recurrent thoughts of death, suicidal ideation, wishes to be dead, or suicide.[20]

One classic formulation focuses on the trinity hopelessness, helplessness, and worthlessness.[21] Although depression and anxiety are separate illnesses, most research reports find the two closely related. Hopelessness is said by Aaron Beck to be the key variable.[22] Another poignant insight is provided by the same author: "The depressive's view of his valued attributes, relationships, and achievements is saturated with the notion of loss—past, present, and future. . . . The term 'loser' captures the flavor of the depressive's appraisal of himself and his experience."[23]

For most psychiatrists and sociologists (and for the rest of us, too), depression is an unalleviated personal and social loss, but evolutionists, according to the habit of their trade, try to find some biological function or benefit in depression, such as the stimulus to examine one's life and try some other life-solution.[24] Our understanding of a pathology is aided by an understanding of the norm from which it departs.

MENTAL HEALTH

Here are two capsule definitions of mental health:

> It is the acceptance of one's own and only life cycle and of the people who have become significant to it as something that had to be and that, by necessity, permitted of no substitutions. . . . It is a sense of comradeship with men and women of distant time and of different pursuits, who have created orders and objects and sayings conveying human dignity and love.[25]

> In very simple terms, a mature and mentally healthy person is one who (1) respects and has confidence in himself and because he knows his true worth wastes no time in proving it to himself and others; (2) accepts, works with, and to a large extent enjoys other people; (3) carries on his work, play, and his family and social life with confidence and enthusiasm and with a minimum of conflict, fear, and hostility.[26]

To be sure, the first, by Erik Erikson, is an idealized version of mental health, and neither mentions the capacity for feeling pain, without which, at least in nature, life is very short. Notice, however, that both of the definitions are much more than the obverse of depression. One does not restore mental health by curing the symptoms of depression. And I cannot help observing the importance of "comradeship" and references to "enjoys other people" and to engaging in "family and social life with confidence" in these capsule views of mental health.

Decline in Happiness in the United States: 1972–94

Here are some typical questions used in measuring people's feelings of well-being: "Taken all together, how would you say things are these days—would you say that you are very happy, pretty happy, or not too happy?" And "How do you feel about your life as a whole?" (scored "delighted" to "terrible"). They are imperfect measures but quite good indicators of SWB and are supported by other measures with different wording.[27] (To avoid repeating the figure in chapter 1, to extend the period to 1994, and to make the time period correspond to the figures for domain satisfaction, I present in figure 2.1 a graph for happiness in this shorter but more recent period.) Does this series support the idea of declining SWB in the United States?

The variations from year to year conceal an underlying trend discovered by fitting a curve (fig. 2.1) to the 1972–94 data. The declining trend charting the "very happy" responses of the roughly one-third of the nation claiming this

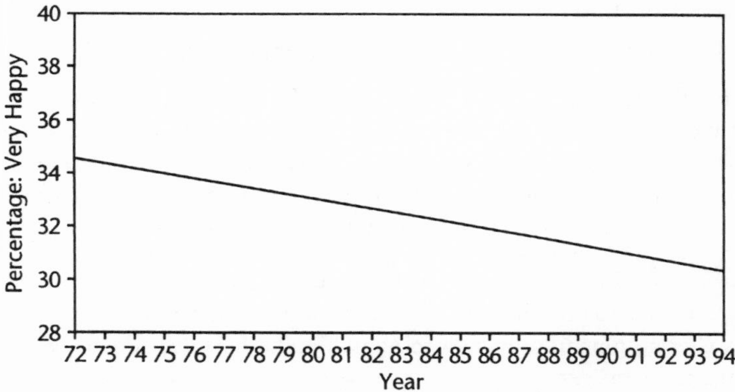

Figure 2.1. Percent of U.S. National Sample Reporting Themselves to be "Very Happy," 1972–94
Question: "Taken all together, how would you say things are these days—would you say that you are very happy, pretty happy, or not too happy?"
Source: General Social Survey (NORC).

positive mood does, modestly, support the claim that in this market democracy fewer people think of themselves as being very happy than they did at the end of the war.[28]

The decline in "very happy" responses is only about five percentage points, but when one considers how these judgments are made, it is surprising that there is trend at all. People must seek anchors or standards for such evaluations, and it is natural for them to compare their current situation with their situation in the recent past: if last year was bad, then an average current year would appear to be good. Such annual corrections would tend to wipe out any trend. I called the trend modest; in truth, I was surprised to find any trend at all.[29]

This decline must be accounted for as a departure from a norm. Ed and Carol Diener explain this norm in the following terms:

(a) There is a positive, biologically based set-point for the emotion system;
(b) People are motivated to experience pleasant affect and therefore to adjust their cognitions to maximize it;
(c) Most individuals possess adequate resources to make progress toward their goals; and
(d) Westerners are socialized to be happy[30] (although when cross-national studies compare happiness responses to responses in a "value hedonism" scale, they find little correlation: cultural prescriptions of what one ought to feel seem not to make much difference).[31]

"It is concluded," say the Dieners on the basis of the four points they propose, "that in order to fully understand and prevent problems such as emotional disorders, marital distress, work dissatisfaction, and alienation, we must understand why the majority of people in the West are satisfied and happy most of the time." I agree. But it is also important to ask why the unhappy are unhappy and why, at least for the past quarter or half century, Americans are decreasingly happy and increasingly depressed.

Before looking for major differences in SWB among the various social groups, I note that, at least in the past, these differences have been minimal.[32] Nevertheless, women, the young, African Americans, and certain immigrant groups are unhappier than others. I will take up their special circumstances in the context of particular issues in which the differences among subgroups help to explain the issues.

For theories of both American exceptionalism (supported) and a countertheory of cross-national modernity (not supported), it is important to note that, unlike depression, the decline in happiness is largely an American phenomenon. For example, from 1981 to 1990 among the ten European nations on which I have data, "judgments of happiness have changed little between the two surveys." The same body of data over the same period shows that those who were predominantly satisfied with their lives increased four percentage points from 79 percent to 83 percent.[33] Partly because of stable cultural norms, relative rankings are fairly stable over decades, with Denmark and the Netherlands generally ranking first or second and France or Italy last.[34] In light of these cross-national data it is difficult to indict modernity for making people less happy; rather, it seems that in its declining SWB (but not its relative happiness or life satisfaction) America is exceptional.

Rise in Depression in Advanced Countries

Consider some evidence of a rising tide of depression in economically advanced democracies. In 1992 Daniel Goleman wrote in the *New York Times,* "In some [advanced] countries the likelihood that people born after 1955 will suffer a major depression—not just sadness, but a paralyzing listlessness, dejection and self-deprecation, as well as an overwhelming sense of hopelessness—at some point in life is more than three times greater than for their grandparents' generation."[35] Referring to the same data, Martin Seligman wrote, "We are in the midst of an epidemic of depression, one with consequences that, through suicide, takes as many lives as the AIDS epidemic and is more widespread. Severe depression is ten times more prevalent today than it was fifty years ago. It assaults women twice as often as men, and now it strikes a full decade earlier in life on average than it did a generation ago."[36]

A nine-nation study under the direction of Myrna Weissman found that the epidemic is characteristic of most of the advanced countries included, but much less so among the rapidly modernizing Asian countries like Taiwan and South Korea, which revealed the fewest symptoms of depression in the sample.[37] Other studies report similarly disturbing incidence and prevalence. In London (1978) a research team estimated that during the three-month period of their study about 15 percent of the women in their sample suffered from "definite affective disorders" with another 18 percent labeled borderline cases. Overall, they estimated that about a fifth of the female population had clear symptoms of depressive illness.[38] A World Health Organization study reports, "Each year at least 100 million people in the world develop clinically recognizable depression and for several reasons the number is likely to increase."[39]

Although the United States is among the least depressed countries in the world,[40] it may be rising in that infelicitous ranking. On the basis of two earlier (1982, 1985) epidemiological studies in the United States involving a total of about twelve thousand people, a rate of increase much higher than the rates of other countries seems evident: "People born after 1945 were 10 times more likely to suffer from depression than people born 50 years earlier."[41] Weissman and her associates, reporting research covering five sites in the United States, found "an increasing risk of depression at some point in life for younger Americans. For example, of those Americans born before 1955, only one percent had suffered a major depression by age 75; of those born after 1955 six percent had become depressed by *age* 24."[42] Weissman also suggests that now about a quarter of the population experiences some of the clinical symptoms of depression during some portion of their lifetime;[43] another study reports that almost half of the population (48 percent) has suffered from depression severe enough to inhibit functioning for two weeks or more, and nearly 20 percent qualify for a lifetime diagnosis of major depression or dysthymia.[44]

Studies of mood disorders in children are even more disturbing. For example, one study in Britain found a 42 percent increase of mood disorders from 1985 to 1990 among children under ten years of age.[45] Reports from the United States indicate similar increased childhood rates, adding that childhood depression is a strong indicator of depression in adulthood.[46] Because children of the depressed are much more likely themselves to be depressed,[47] a malign, self-reinforcing cycle seems to envelop us.

Given the fallibility of surveys, some support for this tragic rise in youthful depression is available in increasing rates of adolescent suicide in advanced countries (table 2.1).

Table 2.1. Increase in Adolescent and Youth (Ages 15–24) Suicides per 100,000

	1970–87	1990
Australia	8.6	16.4
Norway	6.2	16.3
Canada	10.2	15.8
Switzerland	13.7	15.7
USA	8.0	13.2
Sweden	13.3	12.2
France	7.0	19.3
W. Germany	13.4	9.6
UK	4.3	7.2
Japan	13.0	7.0
Italy	2.9	3.2

Source: UNICEF. 1993. *The Progress of Nations.* New York: United Nations, 45.

Rising depression of this magnitude is a tragedy for any civilization, but the epidemiological study of these tragic phenomena is dependent on measurement instruments that are being perfected, and the longitudinal data are in their infancy. Consequently in most of the analysis to come I rely on the studies going under the name of quality of life, whose main explicandum is SWB.

Decline in Satisfaction by Domains of Life

The early (1976) quality of life studies found that satisfactions in certain specific domains of life (family, work, leisure, and so on) sum in a straight linear fashion to whatever measure of overall SWB was used in each study.[48] Thus, one would expect that satisfaction with marriage, work, finances, and one's community would move in the same direction as the overall measure of well-being. They do, as may be seen in figures 2.2, 2.3, 2.4, and 2.5—whose time range is limited to the General Social Survey's (GSS) 1972(3)–94 coverage.

Satisfaction with circumstances in the various domains of life should also correlate with criterial indicators of overall well-being: they do, but in line with my theory that it is people, not money, who make people happy, a happy marriage is by far the best indicator of happiness with life as a whole (table 2.2):

The obvious fact that correlations do not necessarily imply causation leaves open many interpretations. Does overall SWB cause people to be more satisfied with, say, their jobs and finances in what is called a top down pattern of

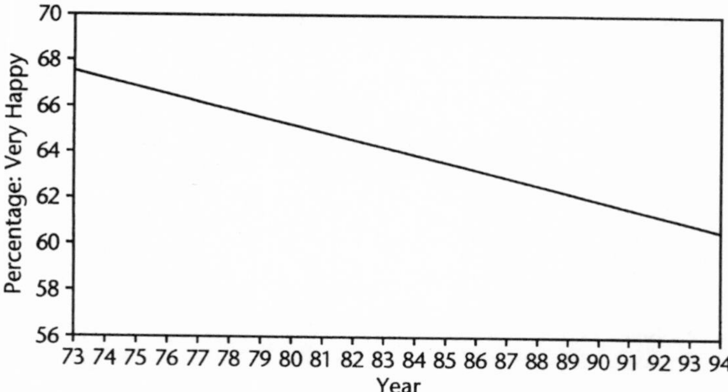

Figure 2.2. Percent of U.S. National Sample Saying Own Marriage is "Very Happy," 1973–94
Question: "Taking all things together, how would you describe your marriage? Would you say that your marriage is very happy, pretty happy, or not too happy?"
Source: General Social Survey (NORC).

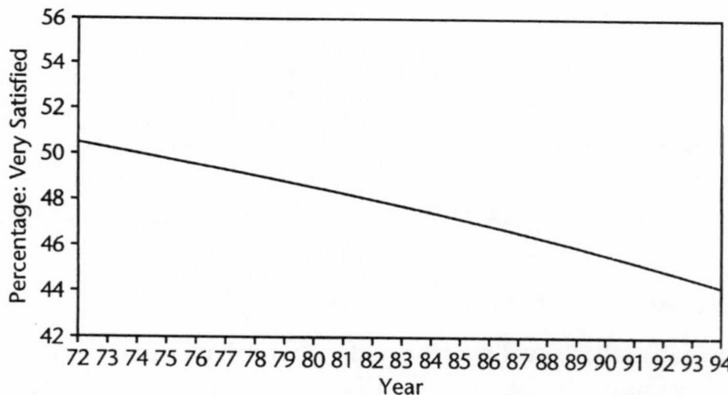

Figure 2.3. Percent of U.S. National Sample Saying They Are "Very Satisfied" with Their Jobs or Housework, 1972–94
Question: "On the whole, how satisfied are you with the work you do—would you say you are very satisfied, moderately satisfied, a little dissatisfied, or very satisfied?" [Asked only if currently at work, temporarily at work, or keeping house.]
Source: General Social Survey (NORC).

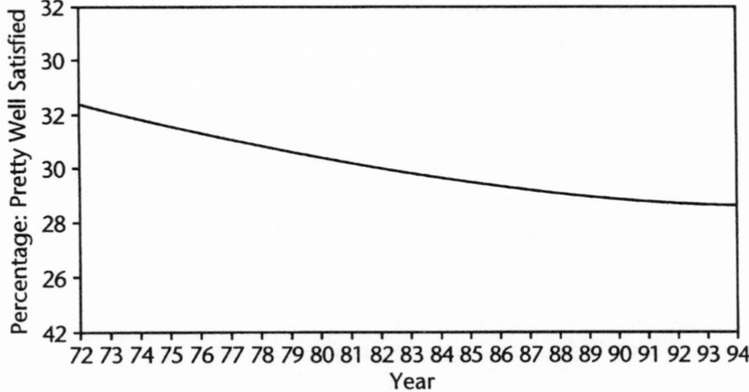

Figure 2.4. Percent of U.S. National Sample Saying They Are "Pretty Well Satisfied" with Their Financial Situation, 1972–94
Question: "We are interested in how people are getting along financially these days. So far as you and your family are concerned, would you say that you are pretty well satisfied with your financial situation, more or less satisfied, or not at all satisfied?"
Source: General Social Survey (NORC).

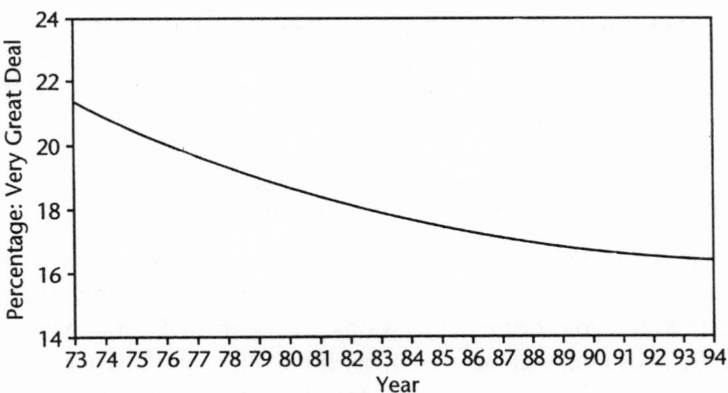

Figure 2.5. Percent of U.S. National Sample Reporting a "Very Great Deal" of Satisfaction from Their Place of Residence, 1973–94
Question: "For each area of life I am going to name, tell me the choice that shows how much satisfaction you get from that area. . . . The city or place that you live in. . . . [A very great deal; a great deal; quite a bit; a fair amount; some; a little; none.]
Source: General Social Survey (NORC).

Table 2.2. Correlations Between Domain Satisfactions and Happiness

1. Happy with marriage	.469
2. Satisfaction with job	.290
3. Satisfaction with finances	.288
4. Satisfaction with friends	.288
5. Satisfaction with city or place	.275

Source: General Social Survey (NORC) survey data for either 1972–94 or 1973–94.

well-being, or do the satisfactions with particular parts of a person's life cause a person to be happier and more satisfied with life, the bottom up theory.[49] Most probably, they are interactive. Thus, Veenhoven finds that "having a partner" is a strong cause of happiness and that happiness makes having a partner more likely.[50] Finally, does some exogenous factor, such as a personality predisposition, greatly influence both the domain and the overall feeling of well-being? That is also true: extroverts are happier in most situations but being with others further enhances their happiness. The quality of life studies support all four possibilities: top down, bottom up, interactive, and exogenous factors.[51] But they do not support an economic explanation of the evident decline (see fig. 1.1).

Mutual Distrust, Anomie, and Pessimism

Shall one include evidence of malaise, if not, perhaps, actual dysphoria, as evidence of declining well-being? Three such items are of interest: mutual distrust ("Would you say that most people can be trusted or that you can't be too careful in dealing with people?"), belief that "the lot of the average man is getting worse, not better," and belief that "most public officials are not really interested in the problems of the average man." One needs to know two things: have these distressed (and distressing) beliefs increased? And are they related to unhappiness, enlarging the dysphoria syndrome? On the first point, their change in the 1972–94 period, the answer is yes, especially distrust, as may be seen in figure 2.6. Evidence of similar, if more modest increases in the beliefs that people are untrustworthy, the lot of the average man is getting worse, and public officials are indifferent to the ordinary person is strong (figs. 2.7, 2.8). At least coincidentally, malaise has increased along with unhappiness.

Inclusion of these items in this roster of modern distempers would give a unity to my presentation if these beliefs were closely related to happiness. But

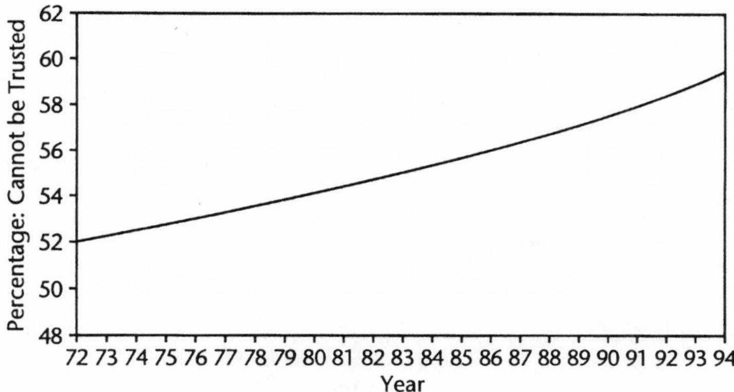

Figure 2.6. Percent of U.S. National Sample Saying, "You Can't Be Too Careful in Dealing with People," 1972–94
Question: "Generally speaking, would you say that most people could be trusted or that you can't be too careful in dealing with people?"
Source: General Social Survey (NORC).

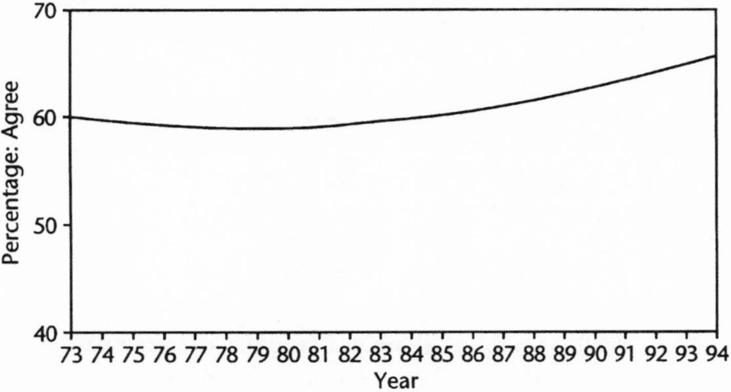

Figure 2.7. Percent of U.S. National Sample Agreeing that "the Lot of the Average Man Is Getting Worse," 1973–94
Question: "Do you agree with the following statement? In spite of what some people say, the lot [situation/condition] of the average man is getting worse."
Source: General Social Survey (NORC).

the relationships are weak or mixed (table 2.3). To borrow a distinction I shall turn to later, the criticality of these beliefs, their criticism of people, trends, and institutions, is not painful for those who believe them: believing these critical things is not aversive; it does not make a person unhappy.

To take the important item on trust first, it seems that one can distrust

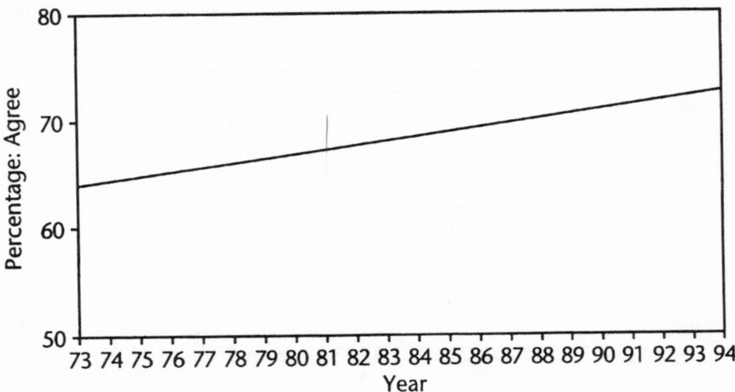

Figure 2.8. Percent of U.S. National Sample Who Agree that "Public Officials Are Not Interested" in the Average Man, 1973–94
Question: "Please tell me whether you agree or disagree with this statement: Most public officials [people in public office] are not really interested in the problems of the average man."
Source: General Social Survey (NORC).

Table 2.3. Correlation of Happiness with Interpersonal Trust, Belief that Average Man Is Worse off, and Official Indifference

People can be trusted	+.09
Lot of average man getting worse	-.16
Public officials not interested in average man	-.13

Source: General Social Survey (NORC). 1972–94.

people without feeling unhappy about it. Given the attention paid to interpersonal trust in recent analyses,[52] it is remarkable that distrust of one's fellows is not a more important source of unhappiness. Nevertheless, from other data, it seems that interpersonal trust is associated with satisfaction with one's job and one's friendships.[53] Furthermore, if we collectivize the relationship between trust and happiness so that we examine how a higher average level of happiness in nations, not individuals, relates to average levels of trust, the expected relationship is restored, for at that level the relation is strong, positive, and fairly significant (+.61, $p > .05$).[54] Taking a plunge into these murky waters, one might say that living in a nation in which people trust each other is a source of hedonic relief, but to be distrusting oneself is not painful.

The belief that the lot of the average man is getting worse is an affront to the American belief in progress and, one would think, would cost the holder of

Table 2.4. Evidence of Increased Powerlessness and Alienation

Question	1966	Intermediate	1986
"Most people with power try to take advantage of people like myself."		33% (1971)	66%
"What I think doesn't matter any more."	36%		60
"The people running the country don't really care what happens to me."	26	64 (1976)	55
"I feel left out of things going on around me."	09	45 (1983)	37

Source: Louis Harris. 1987. *Inside America.* New York: Random House/Vintage, 35–36.

such an opinion some pain, that is, it would be aversive. It is (or at least the correlation with happiness is negative and significant), but only modestly so. What is surprising in figure 2.7 is not so much the slope (which increases modestly only after 1982—when Americans were all supposed to be sitting tall in the saddle) as the level: even in the best years about half of the population agreed to this most unprogressive belief, and by 1994 that proportion was almost two-thirds. On the other hand, the belief that public officials are not really interested in the problems of the average man chimes with traditional skepticism, some say negativity, toward politicians and government (see chapter 11). Less surprising, then, is that two-thirds of the population in the early period are skeptical that public officials have the public welfare in mind, though it is somewhat surprising that three-quarters should agree in 1994. Skepticism about politicians, too, is modestly costly in happiness (or at least modestly related to happiness), but, like other conventional beliefs, not very.

I will show other evidence of a rising sense of futility in chapter 13, where the declining sense of political efficacy further illustrates this pathology. In the meantime, the responses to a set of questions revealing the sense of powerlessness and alienation in the 1966–86 period are reported in table 2.4.

This is the "little man" expressing his sense of insignificance, not members of the sovereign public aware of their ultimate power. It is a subject mentality, not a citizen mentality. Is this a set of aversive opinions? Political philosophy says yes, but, to tell the truth, we do not know.

One further related set of indicators of malaise, this time from Germany, helps to fill out the picture. Wolfgang Glatzer gathered data on changes in German estimates of current progress and expectations of the future over the 1978–84 period. As shown in table 2.5, in the 1980s Germans increasingly saw their recent (five-year) past as better than their present and their future as

Table 2.5. German Evaluations of Current Satisfaction Compared to Past and Future

	1978	1980	1984
5 years ago to now			
Increase	41%	34%	31%
Constant	44	48	46
Decrease	14	18	23
Now to 5 years future			
Increase	24	21	19
Constant	64	54	56
Decrease	12	25	25

Source: Wolfgang Glatzer. 1991. "Quality of Life in Advanced Industrialized Countries: The Case of West Germany." In Strack, Argyle, and Schwarz, eds., *Subjective Well-Being,* 261–75 at 276.

somewhat darker than their present. What makes this study so interesting is that this pessimistic pattern of changing personal situations is consistent with a fairly constant evaluation of their current well-being (on a ladder scale: 1978 = 7.3; 1980 = 7.1; 1984 = 7.3). There are many dimensions to perceptions of well-being not captured by simple questions on happiness or satisfaction with life as a whole.

An earlier (1975) study in the United States, the country of boosters and optimists, showed a somewhat similar pattern: although people tended to think of themselves as a little better off now than five years earlier, they believed that in five years they would be worse off.[55] Several cross-cultural studies have found that, unlike trust, optimism about one's own and one's nation's economic future tends to decline with economic advancement.[56] Although this is a narrow range of expectations, this decline may be important in explaining the rise of depression in advanced countries because of the centrality of hope in the depressive symptomology. And finally, optimism is closely related to personal control (self-attribution), which is a central feature of the personality of happy people.[57] Lack of personal control (the belief that one is not in charge of one's life) is also a central feature of psychological distress: in the words of two researchers, "Of all the things that might explain the social pattern of distress, a sense of control over one's own life stands out as a critical link. The patterns of distress reflect the patterns of autonomy, opportunity, and achievement in America."[58]

In later chapters I will examine the relative weights to be assigned to various features of life in explaining both unhappiness and depression, but now I turn to some cross-national studies of happiness and depression.

Happiness in Nations

National differences in average happiness always interest people—who are nevertheless usually ready to dismiss them on the grounds that responses are merely reflecting cultural norms and do not reveal whether people in one culture actually feel happier or unhappier than other peoples. These cautions have some limited merit: the Japanese are rarely very happy or very anything, for it is bad form to stand out; and among the nations of northern Europe, the French tend to report themselves as being among the least happy—but they are said to enjoy reporting miseries and holding a sardonic view of life. The Swiss report guilt feelings and self-reproach much more (68 percent) than the Iranians (32 percent), who in turn reveal more psychomotor agitation.[59] And in the Hindu culture of India, about a third (34 percent) agreed that "whether or not an outcome of an action will be pleasant or unpleasant for me is not an important consideration." Only 12 percent of a comparable U.S. sample agreed.[60] To conform to one's cultural values in these respects reduces pain.

In this context, does the alleged U.S. focus on happiness[61] bias cross-cultural comparisons of self-reported SWB? In a colloquial phrase, is America happiness happy, that is, does the United States rank high among nations because of the high value placed upon being happy? Actually, among twenty-three countries for which there were comparable data (circa 1980) the United States ranked tenth, below Denmark, Sweden, the Netherlands, Britain, Australia, and so on, and just ahead of Norway, France, and Germany. Commenting on this modest U.S. ranking, Veenhoven says, "Average happiness in the USA appears to be slightly lower than the quality of living conditions would justify."[62] In this he confirms Tocqueville's and David Potter's observations.[63] So much for the persistent belief that Americans are the happiest nation and that this is because they value happiness more than others. They are not and do not. (Cross-cultural validity of questions on SWB is a technical matter treated in the Appendix.)

Table 2.6 represents correlations between average self-reported happiness and various indicators of economic, political, and social forms of modernization: increased GDP per capita, the equality of women, provision for old age, a free press, democratic processes, education, and even exposure to mass media. At first glance, the table seems to offer felicific endorsement of the liberal agenda for modernization, but in my opinion the second column, giving the correlations of the "causes" of average national happiness with "economic

Table 2.6. Happiness and Living Conditions: Correlational Analysis, 23 countries ca. 1980

	Correlation with Happiness	
National characteristic	Zero order	Economic prosperity controlled
Material comfort		
Real national income	.69*	
Nutrition	+.50 *	-.19
Social equality		
Women's emancipation	+.75*	+.64*
Social security	+.57*	+.20
Freedom		
Freedom of the press	+.55*	+.27
Political democracy	+.54*	-.02
Access to knowledge		
Education	+.82*	+.60*
Media attendance	+.54*	+.07
R^2	+.77*	

*$p < .01$

Source: The measures are: *Nutrition* = daily calorie supply per capita (evidently, the rich countries eat too much); *Women's emancipation* = educational participation of women and women's suffrage; *Social security* = social security coverage and/or proportion of the government budget (minus defense) spent on social security; *Freedom of the press* = an unexplained measure borrowed from G. T. Kurian. 1979. *The Book of World Rankings*. London: Macmillan; *Political democracy* = an index of country's independence, a functioning parliament, and absence of military coups; *Education* = school enrollment, proportionate expenses on education; *Media attendance* = summed scores of daily newspaper circulation and number of radios per capita. Veenhoven, *Happiness in Nations,* 50.

prosperity controlled," undermines some of these inferences. Only two of the seven correlations in this second column are statistically significant, that is, economic growth is capturing almost all of the variance. As we shall see in a later chapter, without economic gain, political democracy in this analysis contributes nothing to happiness. But in other studies limited to advanced countries (Europe and the United States) number of years of continuous democracy does predict happiness.[64] Not long ago many studies found that communications were the most important feature in modernization.[65] That may be true but, according to table 2.6, once economic development is controlled, "media attendance" contributes almost nothing to well-being. One additional point not mentioned in the table: Gini-coefficients of inequality/equality also contributed nothing to happiness, although measures of income dispersion did relate to dispersion measures of happiness.[66] As I said long ago, income equality is not generally desired by most people,[67] and there is no reason to believe that it would increase happiness.

CROSS-NATIONAL PREVALENCE OF DEPRESSION

Although earlier studies in the 1950s found few differences in clinical depression or mental illness (except for different symptoms within similar degrees of severity),[68] across the rich–poor divide, recent cross-national studies with better instrumentation and agreed concepts have found many. As mentioned, major depression and dysphoria have increased dramatically in economically advanced countries, with the incidence highest among younger age cohorts: Where did these increases occur? And crucially, did they also occur in the less developed countries? As a first step, notice the ranking of prevalence in developed compared to developing nations (table 2.7).

If one sets aside Lebanon because of its civil war, the first striking finding is that the two recently modernizing, industrializing countries of Asia have by far the lowest rates of major depression. Except for Puerto Rico, they were also the poorest nations in the group. In that respect, this ranking of nations is very different from cross-national ranking by income showing a direct correlation between income and average level of SWB[69]—attenuated as wealth increases. Some force other than income must be at work.

That other force is most likely to be the continuing (but waning—see chapter 6) integrity of the Taiwanese and South Korean family and the close friendship bonds associated with collectivist societies (in which group goals take precedence over individual goals).[70] Just as family and friends facilitate happiness, so they are the very greatest protectors against depression and other forms of psychological distress.[71] It is still uncertain whether these collectivist Asian societies can retain enough of their companionable tradition to protect them from distress in the face of the market onslaught, but scattered evidence suggests that recent (1997–98) economic adversity had driven these nations back to *greater* reliance on the family. The outcome of this titanic conflict between the oldest human institution and the newest, the market, will likely resolve how these nations emerge from their bout with major depression. (In this conflict, one cannot help but recall Freud's cosmic conflict between Eros and Ananke [external necessity] as in *Civilization and its Discontents.*)

Average income in Puerto Rico in constant 1993 dollars is $6,241—the lowest of the group. Being Hispanic (like the Mexicans, who have been intensely studied),[72] Puerto Ricans share some of the collectivist culture of the

Table 2.7. Lifetime Rates of Major Depression per 1,000 population, Mean Age at Onset (1980s) and GDP per capita

	Lifetime rates per 1,000 for Major Depression	Mean age at onset*	GDP per capita†
Lebanon (Beirut)	19.0	25.2	—
Paris region	16.4	29.2	$21,530
Florence, Italy	12.4	34.6	16,800
New Zealand (Christchurch)	11.6	—	—
Canada (Edmonton)	9.6	24.8	18,940
W. Germany (Munich)	9.2	—	21,020
U.S. (5 sites)	5.2	25.6	24,500
Puerto Rico	4.3	29.5	6,241‡
S. Korea	2.9	29.3	7,360
Taiwan	1.5	29.3	10,460

*For comparative purposes, standardized for age and sex.

†Constant 1993 dollars. Source: *Statistical Abstract of the United States, 1995*. Bureau of the Census, Washington, D.C. September 1995, 855.

‡Per capita income 1993.

Source: Myrna M. Weissman and 17 others. July 24–31 1996. "Cross-National Epidemiology of Major Depression and Bipolar Disorder." *Journal of the American Medical Association* 275: 293–99, table 2, p. 296.

Asian nations, although not the Asian sense that fate is controllable.[73] In any event, the Puerto Ricans' relative freedom from depression also violates the economic ordering of the SWB studies but in an attenuated sense supports the hypothesis that collectivist cultures are more resistant to depression. This modest confirmation is supported by a study comparing Hispanics with Anglos in the southwestern United States: "The best adjusted subjects were bicultural, although oriented more toward the Latino than the Anglo culture."[74]

But perhaps relative poverty in other countries which are less endowed with the protections of a collectivist culture encourages high, if not necessarily rising, rates of depression comparable to those in Europe and the United States. Concerning other undeveloped, even primitive societies, Seligman holds that depression is not nearly so frequent in poor countries as in developed countries. "On the whole," said Seligman, "you do not find much in the way of depression as we know it—suicide, hopelessness, giving up, low self-esteem, passivity, and the like—in nonwestern cultures before they are modernized." But this crucial observation is supported only eclectically by references to one study (1984) of New Guinea and another of the American Amish.[75] More recent and systematic evidence suggests that mental illness is increasing in third world countries, but for reasons irrelevant to modernity, namely, the displacement and uncertainty "caused by political violence."[76] More relevant are studies of Nigeria and Uganda showing rates of depression among village women quite as high as in the advanced countries, or at least as high as were found in the inner suburbs of London.[77] Perhaps another reason for doubting the effect of modernity on rising depression is that less developed nations do not show the higher prevalence of that disease among women that characterizes advanced countries.[78] Although we shall see a strong case for market erosion of familistic values in Asia, in my opinion, Freud's hypothesis that "civilization, itself" makes people mentally ill or depressed has not been subject to the appropriate comparative research.[79]

Unhappiness and depression are tragedies whenever and wherever they occur, but in a world in which the idea of progress is bred in the bone, the significance of the decline of happiness and the rise of depression deserves special attention. Have we traveled this far only to continue our journey on a hedonic treadmill? Or, to change the metaphor, if we need to change course, must the crew be a new cohort brought up in peace and prosperity? How much unhappiness and depression must we bear before a new light dawns on the unhappy world? If the market is useless in any dematerialization of culture and if democracy is hedonically ineffective (see chapters 11–15), what agency can one rely on for the changes needed? I turn to these questions in chapter 19.

Citing Richard Baxter, an influential eighteenth-century Protestant theologian, Weber said, "The care for external goods should lie on the shoulders of the 'saint like a light cloak' which can be thrown aside at any moment. But fate decreed that the cloak should become an iron cage." And referring to the Reformation, he continued, "The rosy blush of its laughing heir, the Enlightenment, seems also to be irretrievably fading."[80]

3

Happiness as an Endowment: Evolution, the Fall from Grace, and Devalued Children

We all know some happy people who cope well with adversity and swim through their troubles with minimal distress. They have a sunny disposition. We also know people who always look on the dark side, for whom nothing is a source of joy, nothing consoles, and everything is fraught with danger. They have one of the original (Greek) temperaments: they are melancholic. In explaining who is happy and who is depressed, endowment theories go a long way, but they are an embarrassment in explaining individual changes in mood, cross-cultural differences, and especially the decline in happiness and the rise in depression since World War II that concern us. Endowment theories make explanations based on events and behavior difficult. But not all endowment theories rely on what individuals are given by nature.

There are three principal sources of what I shall call fixity of mood or SWB. The first is a genetic or biological source: people are born with dispositions that tend to make them happy or unhappy, cheerful or depressed throughout their lives.[1] Call these inherited dispositions temperament; my discussion of them will occupy the first half of this chapter. But, second, early socialization also shapes an adult's happy and sad dispositions. Together, temperament and socialization create diverse personalities differentially receptive to good and bad moods. Third, there are enduring circumstances (for example, social class, family connections, national culture, and inherited wealth) that affect the kind of experiences a person has, experiences that give a constancy to mood because they are, for better or worse, repeated again and again. Among these givens are certain resources (intelligence, good looks, social and occupational skills) that can influence how one copes and how one is received by others, resources that do not change quickly over time. But these more or less fixed resources do not explain the decline in happiness and rise of depression. For that explanation, I will offer two hypotheses: we have violated evolutionary instructions and we have devalued our children.

Some Implications of Fixity of Mood

Before I describe these relatively fixed qualities, let me suggest why they are important in interpreting the roles of democracy and markets in encouraging well-being. Most obviously, they suggest limits to what markets and governments can do to make current populations happier. In a study to be discussed below, after these stocks were taken into account, the events in people's lives accounted for only 8 percent of the variance in their happiness.[2] To make a difference, governments and markets would have to enter the struggle at an early stage, influencing family socialization, school policy, the way populations are stratified, and the value of children. This is not easy, for intervention in family matters is regarded as intrusive, and relieving poverty without creating dependency has proved difficult where it has been seriously tried.

Fixity of mood also has implications for the assessing of distributive justice. Philosophers wrestle (unsuccessfully, in my opinion)[3] with problems of justice when the outcomes of behavior are fixed by such genetic endowments as intelligence and beauty. If happiness is at least partly given by nature, philosophers like David Ross and Nicholas Rescher, who make happiness an ultimate good only when merited, are in trouble.

There is a third consideration. Not only are institutional reforms and assessments of justice thrown off balance, but the value of individual pursuits of happiness takes on a new aspect. The evidence of fixity does not justify it, but one could say, Why *pursue* happiness? It is like Calvin's predestination: I am either born happy (saved) or I am not, and there is nothing I can do about it. Here is an irony: Passivity is a known source of melancholy, so perhaps this line of reasoning would be self-correcting. Or people might say, If I am unhappy, it is not my fault; it is the fault of my parents, who did not train me for happiness or who gave me a bad start in life. Either way, individual responsibility for one's own happiness is discouraged. Another irony: In most (but not all) circumstances, believing that one is in control of one's fate is closely associated with happiness and satisfaction with one's life. Early, perhaps prenatal, determination of one's hedonic fate would deprive people of the sense that they are in control.

These are but some of the implications of a fixity hypothesis. With them in mind, let us look at some findings on the degree to which a person's hedonic fate is fixed.

Genetic and Biological Influences: The Genetic Endowment

Some clues to the physiology of happiness set the stage.[4] One author writes, "In the normal range of behavior, 30 to 50 percent of the variance (diversity in the general population) can usually be assigned to genetic factors."[5] Much of the evidence for fixity of moods comes from studies of monozygotic (identical) and dizygotic (fraternal) twins. Thus, A. Tellegen et al. found that "even when monozygotic twins grew up in different homes, they are extremely similar in SWB; whereas dizygotic twins who were raised within the same homes were on average less similar." In some longitudinal studies, "genes account for 80% of the stable variance in long-term reports of well-being."[6] But, as we shall see, the interaction between mind and body gives a little more space to volition, behavior, and changing circumstance.

The nature–nurture relationship is complex. For one thing, our genes often influence our choice of environments; what is nurture is then something shaped by nature. If people choose their own environments, they make socialization a two-way process. As one group of researchers has written, "Whatever effects parents, schools, and neighborhoods may have had, they were either quite different in different children or [were ephemeral and] did not persist until the children grew up."[7] Given the tendency of children to differentiate themselves so as to occupy special niches in families and schools, and given the consequent lack of the same environment for children in the same family, it is not surprising that socialization effects "were quite different in different children." The bright child pleases her father, the musical child her mother: parental treatments of the two children follow from the children's respective endowments.

Also, genetic influences sometimes increase with age. This would follow in part from the influence of genes on intelligence, which is substantial and is revealed by the fading resemblance of the IQs of adopted children to the IQs of their adoptive parents.[8] The idea that siblings do not share the same environment is now standard doctrine and seems to add more weight to nurture in accounting for these differences, but why, for example, did a certain father treat one child worse than another? Some research suggests that the way a child is treated is itself heavily influenced by the child's genetic propensities—

and how they match the adult's propensities.[9] In chapter 17 I will discuss how people influence their own well-being (blame the victim?), but in the meantime I note that in addition to these interactive nature–nurture relationships, there are also purely environmental influences; for example, the loss of a parent during childhood is directly correlated with alcoholism of daughters, irrespective of their genes.[10] The complexity of the nature–nurture relationship has roots in our evolutionary histories.

THE EVOLUTIONARY SOURCES OF WELL-BEING AND ILL-BEING

The genetic endowment mentioned above has a source: evolution. In contrast to cognitions, the emotions are closer to our animal origins. Edward Wilson asks rhetorically about the sources of the emotions, "What [evolutionary pressures] made the hypothalamus and limbic system?" The answer, of course, is a natural selective process that favors proliferation of the genes.[11] In this connection, consider the comments of two informed interpreters of the relation of evolution to happiness. After reporting on the discovery of a short gene that predisposes to anxiety and pessimism (see below), Una D. McCann of the National Institute of Mental Health says, "Anxiety is there for a really good reason. . . . It's one of the things that is part of our genes because it's protective."[12] Nevertheless, the processes of evolution have endowed us with capacities for happiness as well as for anxiety and sadness and with various response patterns that favor one or the other of these "two sovereign masters." In this section I will explore how this evolutionary heritage both promotes and hinders our pursuits of happiness.

Robert Wright, the author of *The Moral Animal,* comments, "We are built to be effective animals, not happy ones. . . . The frequent *absence* of happiness is what keeps us pursuing it, and thus makes us productive."[13] But nature is wiser than that, for happier animals are more *re*productive, which, after all, is nature's sole concern. Partly, or perhaps solely, for that reason we are social animals, bonding in families and communities (or troops, if we happen to be apes), and, as we shall see in chapter 5, made happy by the companionship of others. In spite of Thomas Hobbes and John Locke, the "state of nature" is social.[14]

Such emotions as anxiety and fear, guilt and shame, happiness and sadness were learned over the course of our evolutionary history. "Emotions had their origins in the evolution systems that enable the animal to perceive the outcomes of actions as affects or feelings, pleasurable or painful, i.e., the 'reward' and 'punishment' effects. These percepts provided a mechanism for the evolution of associative learning and were also the precursors of emotion which emerged as a later evolutional development."[15] Having this advantage, humans learned to regulate their emotions to a moderate degree, bringing some of them some of the time under conscious control (but see chapter 16 on our woeful ignorance of why we feel happy or sad). The aim is reproductive fitness: "Thus it is not surprising that good food, good company, and good sex are sought after, and, when achieved, bring pleasure if not happiness [a longer term mood]."[16] Randolph Nesse lists the assets that favor reproduction and therefore tend to give us pleasure: the personal qualities of health and good looks (they are not related), skills and knowledge; such tangible assets as money, jobs, certificates of learning; obviously mates and sex; children and other kin; and such social resources as group membership, status, reputation, and friendships. Devoting time and effort to these resources is, Nesse says, relevant to reproductive fitness.[17] In my opinion, this makes the concept of reproductive fitness so broad that, like its predecessor, libido, by explaining everything it explains nothing.

Without reference to reproductive fitness, however, it is certainly true that pain and sadness come from the loss of the resources Nesse mentions. Pain, a universal capacity in all normal animals (when it is pathologically missing, the animal dies young), is local to a part of the brain different from that whose activity is stimulated by good feelings. Nesse writes, "The experience of pain indicates a situation that harms fitness, but the lack of capacity for pain is even worse.... In humans, this resource [capacity for pain] is more likely to be social than physical. . . . Certainly the capacity for sadness [as well as pain] is adaptive" because of its role in preventing similar losses.[18] Thus, according to Nesse, sadness is part of the solution, not part of the problem—a point of view that utilitarians, never concerned about reproductive fitness, might well ponder.

The way evolution prepares us for bonding is an important part of the story of this book. There is a body chemistry to guide bonding activities. In one account, developed at a conference on the integrative neurobiology of affiliation (1996), there is a conflict for dominance between two hormonal systems: on the one hand, the fight or flight system, producing cortisol and epinephrine and "breaking down . . . the body's energy stores for the business of attacking an enemy," and, on the other hand, an affiliative circuitry whose main hormonal product in women is oxytocin (a peptide originating in the hypothalamus deep within the brain), which acts as a muscle contractor and is especially important for lactating women (the "calm madonna" syndrome). Oxytocin is a hormone that helps "nearly every type of animal bonding: parental, fraternal, sexual, and even capacity to soothe one's self." According to Susan Carter, one of the organizers of the conference, this hormone has "played an essential role in the evolution of social animal behavior, particularly for mammals."[19] Carter also emphasized that the capacity to affiliate with others increases both the quality and length of life: "Animals that live in groups enhance each other's chances of survival, for social behavior contributes to both individual survival and reproductive fitness."[20]

But given that the populations of modern market democracies are failing to reproduce themselves, something about these social systems seems inimical to reproduction. Can it be that one reason increased income in developing countries increases happiness (see chapter 4) is that it increased reproductive fitness, whereas in advanced economies, where reproduction is inhibited by social factors and perhaps by low blood serotonin due to the prevalence of the stress-response, it did not.[21]

THE BIOLOGY OF HEDONIC ENDOWMENTS

As we have seen, the biology of mood and affects deals, among other things, with hormones, neurotransmitters, and neurological networks. Too much or too little of such hormones as the endorphins or of such neurotransmitters as serotonin or some slight difference in wiring of the brain can affect moods. Like the basic experiences of pain and pleasure, moods are associated with hormonal changes.[22] Serotonin deficiency is a strong indicator of anxiety, a source of misery in itself and often linked to depression: "Scientists have discovered a modest but measurable link between anxiety-related behavior and the gene that controls the brain's ability to use an essential neurochemical called serotonin. They have found that individuals who have a slightly abbreviated version of the gene for the serotonin transporter rate higher in negative thoughts and feelings than those with a relatively longer rendition of the gene."[23] The effect of this abnormality is likely to be small (about 4 percent of the variance) because it is part of a multigene complex involving between nine and fourteen other genes as well as many environmental factors.

A morphinelike substance, the endorphins, protects the human system from feeling pain, a faculty that is especially useful in periods of crisis and may also play a role in producing feelings of well-being.[24] In addition to hormonal differences, neurological factors affect mood. When rats are permitted to stimulate by electrical charges certain portions of the brain, they will do so (if only in that setting) to the exclusion of all else.[25] And when male humans in hospitals are wired to stimulate the same brain centers, they report pleasant ideation and become flirtatious with female nurses. It is thought that these external stimuli somehow mimic natural processes, which are known to rely on substances like dopamine and noradrenaline that facilitate the work of the neurotransmitters.[26] Right- and left-lobe dominance is also related to mood. Nathan Fox of the University of Maryland reports that "less cheerful infants and adults have greater right frontal EEG activation and happier infants and adults have greater left frontal activation."[27] And lobe dominance is difficult to change, as every left-hander who has tried to change handedness knows.

The biological origins of well-being are, of course, not limited to direct physiological relations, but also are greatly modified by genetically influenced patterns of behavior. There are many of these genetically influenced behavior patterns, but one will illustrate the point. If companionship and active participation in life's activities are important sources of good moods, shyness and fear of novelty will inevitably cast a shadow across one's path. These two qualities have recently been found to be traceable to a specific gene. Robert Emde of the University of Colorado Health Center reports, "The temperament characteristics found to be significantly influenced by genes were shyness and [response tendencies toward] anything unfamiliar."[28] Although tracing a given trait to a specific gene is extremely rare (genetically influenced traits are usually the product of clusters of genes),[29] these particular findings on responses to the unfamiliar seem to indicate biological bases for two of the aversive feelings I examine: loneliness and depression, the latter because of its close association with friendlessness and withdrawal. Aversion to the unfamiliar also influences risk aversion and risk seeking (arousal), as among compulsive gamblers.[30] The claim by economists that risk preferences are substantially within our control is not well founded.

This illustrative review of cases of apparent biological fixity is impressive but not determinative. It does not explain why people are happier when they marry rather than live with an unmarried partner, why certain kinds of precipitating events should plunge people into depression, why the death of a daughter's mother before but not after age eleven should predict depression,[31] or why happy childhoods do not predict happy adulthoods. But it is compatible with the set-point model of SWB (see below) and the theory that predisposing dispositions must be present to precipitate depression as outlined in the classic study of depression by George Brown and Tirril Harris replicated in several countries.[32] Biology is not destiny.

THOUGHT AND BEHAVIOR INFLUENCE PHYSIOLOGY

Without eroding the idea that we are unhappy because we violate (often for the very best ethical reasons) the instructions of evolution, one can still believe that as conscious members of *Homo sapiens* we influence or even override those instructions. After the Fall, Adam and Eve still had free will.

The main point here is that physiology is influenced by experience. We know that from the stress-response studies, but it is more broadly true than these studies indicate. Take the study on serotonin levels mentioned above. Recent research on serotonin shows that it is itself influenced by early experiences.

"Monkeys reared without their mothers—and with only their peers for support—had low 5-HIAA [a measure of serotonin levels]."[33] Hamsters that early in life had traumatic experiences which reduced their serotonin levels were unable to cope with territorial threats to them later in life.[34] In studies on yet another species, "blood serotonin levels in vervet monkeys differ depending on rank, *change dramatically with changes in rank,* and . . . drugs that influence serotonin dramatically influence the outcomes of status competitions."[35] "The most important message our research can make," said Steven Suomi, chief of the laboratory which did the research on serotonin in monkeys, "is that experience is as strong or stronger than anything that's inherited."[36]

In connection with Suomi's emphasis on the mutual roles of environment and genetic endowment, take the remarkable case of the reciprocal causal relationship between dominance behavior (and inferred feelings) and changes in the size of the part of the hypothalamus that influences mating. Although the discovery was in fish, the human analog to this process has been pointed out by Russell Fernald, who "suggests that the architecture of the human brain may also be affected by a person's behavior." The relevant portion of the hypothalamus of aggressive, dominant males is six to eight times larger than "equivalent cells in mild-mannered males with no social clout." The remarkable part of this study, however is that, as with the vervet monkeys, the size of the relevant brain cells can be changed by manipulating the social rank or dominance of the male fish—and then reversed. Fernald and his colleagues believe that an animal's body, its behavior, and its social milieu very likely "represent interdependent points on a giant feedback loop, with one alternately affecting the other." In this research, when the behavioral changes come first, they "spur dramatic growth in brain cells responsible for producing a compound called gonadotropin-releasing hormone."[37]

If we are given free will, that gift is revocable: *akrasia,* or loss of will, characteristic of depressive patients, may also be reciprocally influenced by physiology, which in turn influences mood. When rats are given uncontrollable electric shock, the release of norepinephrine is such that the brain cannot use it, a situation resulting in deficits of that hormone. This is relevant because under shock, rats' behavior "is similar to human clinical depression in etiology, symptoms, and responsiveness to treatment."[38] Thus, traumatic experiences among humans may create depression through the mediating influence of failure of supplies of usable norepinephrine in the brain—and then be reflected in associated feelings of helplessness.

Finally, the biological rhythms of hunger, thirst, sex, and cycles of arousal and fatigue imply corresponding cycles of dissatisfaction and satisfaction. Eating and drinking and sexual activity follow the physiology of appetites which have innate connections to pleasure centers.[39] To that limited extent learning theory's idea of satisfaction as "drive reduction" has merit—although the implication that happiness represents some state of drive reduction or wantlessness is wrong.

Capital Stocks Yielding Psychic Income

The capacity for experiencing pleasure is a personality trait,[40] but one also needs the right kind of life experiences, the kinds of stimuli and situations which make these happy responses easier: growing up in a family that gives one emotional security and a good start (education and connections), living above the poverty level, companions and friends to provide fun, consolation, and help if need be. All this seems obvious enough, but one does need a model.

Bruce Headey and Alexander Wearing developed the appropriate model: Such stable characteristics as social background, personality traits, and social networks may be regarded as stocks (the capital account), whereas the satisfactions and distress arising from life events in a particular time period may be regarded as flows of psychic income (the current account).[41] In their four-wave (1981–87) panel study of Australian adults the stocks were social background characteristics like social class, age and sex, social networks, and several long-term personality characteristics known to influence SWB. In addition to stocks, Headey and Wearing recorded life events, life satisfaction, and positive and negative affect. Their theory was that the stocks would influence the kinds of events experienced, and this would in turn influence people's affects and satisfaction with their lives. They found that the stocks showed "moderate stability over time," that higher levels of stocks predicted higher levels of SWB but that this relation was attenuated by adaptation and lower expectations by those with lower stocks. Because of the relative fixity of stocks "levels of psychic income are also fairly persistent over time. People who experience favorable/satisfying life events in one time period are likely to experience favorable/satisfying events in subsequent periods." And the same for distressing events: "As a result of stable stocks each person has a level of psychic income which represents his/her own 'normal' *equilibrium* level."[42] The findings also confirm Michael Argyle's proposition that to a considerable extent people "determine their own events"[43] (see chapter 17).

Of the various stocks, SES (without differentiating the poverty group) did not influence life satisfaction but did influence positive and negative affect; youth (because of their vulnerability to untoward events) and several of the stable personality variables (extroversion, neuroticism, and openness to experience—see below) were the most important. Events (for example, family

not easily resolved, but for now the circumstance → disposition → circumstance sequence at least gives some play in the middle term to individual choice. And if the disposition is one that fosters adaptation, a leading theory accounting for the constancy of SWB, the second set of circumstances will foster a higher level of well-being than the first.

Yet the decline in happiness and the rise of major depression after World War II cannot be explained by adaptation to increasingly perverse circumstances. Rather, it must have been that some crucial circumstances changed: perhaps we violated the evolutionary instructions discussed above.

The Descent of Man and the Fall from Grace

Those values and ethics that effectively served our ancestors, whose genes we carry, remain in some fashion encoded in our cognitive and behavioral apparatus. —Lionel Tiger[55]

Adam fell from grace because he disobeyed God; have we incurred a pestilence of depression and unhappiness because we disobeyed the instructions encoded in our brains and hormonal system over eons of evolution? Are unhappiness and depression the punishment for disobedience? One relatively clear act of disobedience is our abuse of the stress-response system.

THE STRESS-RESPONSE

"The stress-response is a set of hormonal and neural events that are fairly stereotyped among vertebrates," Sapolsky writes.[56] It is the fight or flight response designed to save an organism from injury during crisis. It activates the sympathetic nervous system, induces secretion of adrenaline and noradrenaline, glucocorticoids (also from the adrenal glands), and other hormones, while suppressing the hormones related to sexual behavior, body growth, and tissue repair. It increases heart rate and mobilizes energy from fat; it inhibits the immune system, pain perception, digestion, growth, inflammation, and sexual urges and activity. In animals the stressors are physical or status threats and opportunities for prey; it is episodic and usually brief. Under these circumstances, the stress-response saves lives by facilitating escape or victory in combat; it yields such rewards as status and sex and food—and life itself.

In modern humans the stressors are less often physical threats and more often social, occupational, and internally generated mental anguish or worry. The stress-response is "pathological when mobilized chronically, and much of Westernized disease consists of diseases caused or worsened by overactive stress-response."[57] That response both inhibits well-being and is caused by the loss of well-being: "Insofar as chronic unhappiness, anxiety, and depression cause sustained overactivation of the stress-response, they increase the risk of diseases" such as heart disease, hypertension, ulcers and colitis, adult-onset diabetes, infectious diseases, and even the defeat of immune defenses, as in cancer.[58] And depression! Recently David Kupfer, chairman of the psychiatry department of the University of Pittsburgh Medical School, observed that "whatever the source of life stress, it makes the body increase levels of cortisol, a stress hormone that ripples through your neurodendocrine and neuropeptide systems, leading to changes that are precursors to depression."[59]

Among nonhuman primates, subordinates in a hierarchy have higher symptoms of stress-response (elevated levels of glucocorticoids in the blood). Like other evolutionists, Sapolsky applies these lessons of primate society to human society, in which subordinates (low SES) live more unpredictable lives, are more subject to bouts of unemployment, and are markedly more likely to be ill from stress-related diseases (more than other diseases) and to have shorter life spans. "With the invention of societal stratification," says Sapolsky, "humans have come up with a form of subordination whose impact is unprecedented in the primate world."[60]

Evolutionary Instruction Versus Instructions of Modern Life

When the brief, physically prompted episodes of stress-response that protected our ancestors are adapted by *Homo sapiens* to life in modern circumstances, the consequences are maladaptive. What lessons can we learn from our primate ancestors' adaptative solutions? One of the ways nonhuman primates reduce their stress-response is by fighting, a counterproductive solution in modern society. A second lesson is the value of stable hierarchies, which are less likely than unstable ones to produce such stress-response illnesses as those produced by the Western doctrine of equality of opportunity. Neither ethical principles nor economic efficiency would be served by eroding that doctrine. A third primate solution was "cooperative breeding," whereby subordinates help to bring up the troop's young and move up in the status hierarchy only as vacancies occur, the resulting stratification by age and position being wholly ascriptive with no room for merit. Neither market nor democratic doctrine would be satisfied through stable hierarchies or the cooperative breeding solution; they are resolutely on the side of chronic stress-responses that seem to make us both ill and unhappy.

So far, so bad. Albert Somit and Steven Peterson report that "evolution has given our species an inherent preference for hierarchically structured social and political systems."[61] "Inherent" is uncertain, for nature may come to the rescue, especially of females. Some studies of chimpanzee behavior show that although the alphas are always males, females can manipulate the alpha male to their needs.[62] This is not primate democracy, but neither is it patriarchy or tyranny. Furthermore, research on the bonobos, formerly called pygmy chimpanzees and as close to the human species as any primate, reveals that females can have an alpha structure parallel to that of males and can form coalitions to prevent male aggression.[63] And there is relief of a kind in the findings that achieved rank can change hormonal balance just as hormones can determine and fix rank.

The question of hierarchy leads straight to the question of equality, a theme that may imply disobedience to our evolutionary instructions. Political as well as evolutionary history indicates a general preparation for hierarchy, and when societies are in trouble, they do revert to the hierarchical mode. It is relevant but also possibly misleading to note that "almost without exception, studies [of child ethology] point to the spontaneous emergence of dominance structures among even very young children."[64] Furthermore, it is known that "firm limits" on tolerable behavior imposed by the reigning authorities of the family give children both greater self-esteem and greater SWB.[65] Recognition of authority—without authoritarianism—seems to be the prescription.

On the other hand, among families, where strains are most likely to appear, those that are authoritarian do not fare well. Moreover, the encoded instructions of evolution are by no means clear: not only are chimp societies known to allow females to manipulate (male) leaders, but baboon societies are matriarchies[66]—but they are not egalitarian. Furthermore, the spread of education among subordinates may make obsolete what instructions we have; these instructions are not imprinted in the brain in any clear fashion. If pain is a clue to the violation of evolutionary instructions, note that there is no evidence whatsoever that people are happier in hierarchical society—but there is no contrary evidence either. Leave a marker on this page of history; the ethics of equality is clear and often commanding, but we do not yet know the evolutionary psychology of hierarchy and relative equality.

Role insecurity and ambivalence, especially among women, is another area in which the evolutionary patterns of our primate and hunter-gatherer antecedents provided instructions for a certain specificity of roles which we do not follow. Again, our moral codes and our evolutionary heritages are at odds—a possible source of chronic pain.[67]

Evolutionary instructions on companionship and familism are clearer. Sapolsky writes, "For social primates, such as we are, isolation appears to be an aching and potent stressor."[68] In gemeinschaft, kin and neighbors fill that aching void (incurring other pains), but in metropolis, even though relatively few people are isolated (see chapter 7), many are without kin and do not know their neighbors.

"In many groups of organisms, from the social insects to the primates," says Wilson, "the most advanced societies evolved directly from family units."[69] If we abandon that line of evolution, do we not create strain—perhaps the stress-response again? The hormonal and sympathetic nervous systems will not tell us why we are unhappy, but they will follow ancient instructions to let us know that something is wrong, and those instructions are experienced as unhappiness or depression.

If genetic factors determine 40 percent of the variance in mood, 60 percent is vulnerable to environmental manipulation. Some causes are purely environmental, as in the case of early parental death—a matter partially dependent on public health. If companionship (bonding) is a neglected route to well-being, we can work with, not against, evolution by promoting companionship. If chronic stress-response is an important source of disease and unhappiness in modern market democracies, public health can pay as much attention to stress as to infection. And if subordinates suffer more from the stress-response than elites, the hedonic and physical benefits of reducing life's uncertainties among low SES members must be weighed against the cost of providing greater security. Richard Wrangham's solution to family and community violence based on his study of the bonobos is intriguing: more power to women.[70] For good reasons, evolution has given us exaggerated beliefs in our power over our destinies: let us take advantage of those beneficent (if often erroneous) beliefs. Society as well as nature plays an important role in determining our well-being.

The Value of Children

This section and the next depart from the fixity hypothesis by treating the very process of changing the human personality, a process that itself has changed since the war—and not for the better. Has something happened to socialization and the underlying value of children to help account for the rising tide of depression and loss of joie de vivre? Or even ignoring such a rising tide, can one identify in socialization practices those features that tend to make children, and the adults they become, unhappy?

SOCIALIZATION

Avoiding the familiar clichés about the value of warm maternal relations—"the mutual delight that [mothers and babies] take in their transactions with each other"[71]—I will develop four themes: (1) nature masquerades as nurture—and vice versa; (2) culture primes hedonic responses; (3) interpersonal relations masquerade as economics; and (4) moral doctrine in socialization risks unhappiness.

The Interaction of Nature and Nurture

Long before Freud, mothers took credit for happy babies and blamed themselves (or their neighbors) for unhappy ones. But babies do not come from the womb in a happy state: without much regard to nurturance, from age 2½ months to 7½ months infants show linear increase in positive affect and decrease in negative affect.[72] Children, however, start at different places on this mood chart: Studies of twins have found not only that heredity explained about half of the SWB effects among children, but that for these twins institutionalization of the child, divorce of the parents, and socialization experience in early childhood had little effect on hedonic development.[73] The other 50 percent of the variance is, of course, socialization, which provides "the building blocks for adult personality dimensions."[74] These proportions are crude estimates; using an arboreal image that appealed to Aristotle, one might say that it is true both that happy acorns grow to be happy oaks and that as the twig is bent, so grows the tree.

Culture Masquerades as Nature

Cultural differences in values are so locally ubiquitous that they masquerade as nature, but in fact they give nurture more weight. Thus, cross-cultural studies show that cultural preferences for certain kinds of emotions are reflected early in infancy and childhood: "Latin nations deplore negative emotions compared to Confucian nations in the Pacific Rim, where they are viewed as neutral. Similarly, different religious cultural traditions teach that suffering is either something to be avoided, or has redemptive and transformative value. . . . In the socialization approach, variations in SWB may result from the differential importance afforded SWB in different cultures."[75] "Affective neutrality," which Talcott Parsons associated with modernity and Freud with inhibition, meant to Abraham Maslow a less happy culture.

The Hidden Hand of Interpersonal Relations in Economic Explanation

In the manifest economic accounts of people's fortunes, there is a hidden force, even a hidden hand at work: it is the hand of human relations. Working-class children do indeed suffer from privation, but the long-term source of their disadvantage is substantially cognitive. Class differences in IQ don't begin to show up until age eighteen months, after which time the lower-class children's scores tend to drift downward for about four years while the middle-class children tend to remain constant or rise.[76] These class differences are largely caused by "lack of intellectual stimulation, inferior language background, lack of parental interest in education, poor schooling."[77] During the first three years of life the brain grows through verbal stimulation, which is directly proportionate to parents' economic status.

A second example is represented by Glen Elder's studies of children of the Great Depression of the 1930s, which revealed that the main deprivations of children of the depression were not material but the effects of unemployment on family relations, effects that differed by social class. In working-class families, family disorganization and father demoralization deprived the children of social adjustment and happiness in later life. "By comparison, family deprivation in the middle class is associated with psychological health among men and women. . . . The same stressor can have both pathogenic and salutary effects."[78] In comparative studies of Berkeley and (older) Oakland cohorts, the older Oakland cohort did better, partly because the adolescent boys (but not girls) were able to assume new family responsibilities which "enhanced the social independence of boys" and partly because they could escape the pathogenic family crucible by entering the army as World War II approached. Thus, "the costs of family deprivation among Berkeley males were matched in some respects by the developmental gains of older boys in the Oakland cohort. In the latter group, boys from deprived homes were judged even more resilient and resourceful than the nondeprived."[79] These studies were not devoted to SWB, but I think it is a fair inference that young men who had overcome grave handicaps and showed resilience and resourcefulness would be more satisfied with their lives than others. At least it has been shown that those with more occupational success than their education would predict are generally happier.[80]

I would like to contrast this picture of how "pain and suffering can have a steeling—hardening—effect on some children, rendering them capable of mastering life with all of its disadvantages,"[81] with Ronald Inglehart's belief that cohorts brought up in peace and prosperity are better off because they develop certain liberal and humane values.[82] That account of value changes may be true, but Inglehart's "postmaterialists" (see chapter 8) are not happier than others, whereas at least some of those who grew up in the Great Depression and entered the army at an early age seem (the evidence is incomplete) to have achieved positions in life that would lead to happiness or at least to great life satisfaction.

Moral Claims and Child Labor

Child labor is known to be an immoral use of children, is it not? Yet another longitudinal study of a sample of working-class youth interviewed first at age fourteen and again (1981) at age forty-seven found that "the willingness and capacity to work in childhood is the most important forerunner—more important than native intelligence, social class, or family situation—of mental health."[83] The criticism that such work interrupts and may prevent school achievement is partly forestalled by the fact that hard work at school—indicated by academic achievement beyond that predicted by intelligence scores—also qualified as adolescent labor. Again, although mental health is not a measure of happiness, it is a measure of lack of depression and is probably a condition for happiness.

As a codicil to this account of moral judgments and the conditions of well-being, consider the fact that although one study, entitled *Happy People,* found that retrospective accounts of happiness in childhood were quite irrelevant to happy adulthoods, recollection of feeling guilty as a child was associated with unhappiness later in life.[84]

In review of this section, I would like to emphasize how economic hardship in childhood does its socializing work not so much through material deprivation as by its effect on the family. In childhood as in adulthood, money is not a good predictor of SWB. And as a subordinate theme, note how moral first principles can lead to failed human development and unhappiness.

The Declining Value of Children

In *The Wealth of Nations,* Adam Smith speaks admiringly of the economic value of children in North America, where, he said, "the labor of each child, before it can leave [the parents' house], is computed to be worth a hundred pounds' clear gain to them." For widows with children there was an added advantage: "The value of children is the greatest of all encouragements to marriage."[85] As has often been observed, children have now lost much of their value as human capital and are, instead, rather expensive consumer goods. Have Americans accordingly devalued their children?[86]

Birthrates have fallen below the replacement rate in France and Germany, but that could be partly for technological reasons. In the United States over the past thirty years fertility has dropped 40 percent, although the number of children born out of wedlock has quadrupled while the number of children living in single-parent homes has tripled. Perhaps the opprobrium connected with bastardy has deservedly been laid to rest, but even in the absence of opprobrium, the evidence of damage to children caused by these developments remains: "Young people from single-parent families or [with] stepfathers were two to three times more likely to have had emotional or behavioral problems than those who had both of their biological parents present in the home. . . . Delinquency, teen-age suicide, child abuse and other problems are demonstrably worse in families without a mother and a father." David Popenoe, the author of this statement and cochairman of the Council on Families in America, continues in this fashion: "Several commissions have compiled evidence showing that we may have the first generation of children in history who are worse off in important behavioral and psychological respects than their parents were at the same stage of life. These facts lie behind a growing belief that America is suffering not only from an economic recession [1991] but from a social recession as well—a decline in social order and civic virtue and a rise in psychological impairment."[87] The "psychological impairment" is evident in the studies of rising clinical depression, especially among the young, reported in the previous chapter. To this, two specialists who have followed child welfare in the United States for thirty years add (1990), "In the past 30 years of monitoring the indicators of child well-being, never have the indicators looked so negative."[88] And the First Lady of the time, Hillary Clinton, said, "The present state of children and families in the United States represents the greatest domestic problem our nation has faced since the founding of the Republic. It is sapping our very roots."[89]

The decline in time spent on family care reveals another facet of this same problem. In a longitudinal (1965–75) time budget study, all groups of women, employed and not employed, single and married, "report less family care in their 1975 than 1965 diaries." Although men reported slightly more time devoted to their families, the "total decline of 20% in family care is unparalleled in modern history."[90] Nor does the provision of child care support for the poor improve the time parents spend with their children. In their time budget study, Russell Hill and Frank Stafford report, "We were unable to discover any obvious relation between income support (alimony, ADC, Social Security) and levels of child care. . . . Among those women with educational attainment of high school or less, there was no significant relation between these support payments and child care."[91] Ronald Cohen, reporting on the message of a new study by the National Commission on Children, said, "Probably the central message would be that there has been a tremendous erosion of the role of parents in the lives of children."[92]

Perhaps it is gratuitous to ask what this has to do with happiness, but for the record, across cultures, unstable families, conflict in families, divorce, death of a parent, and less affectionate parents are reliably linked to lower levels of average happiness and life satisfaction.[93]

Health statistics for children tell a similar story. Referring to both "Under 5 Mortality Rates" and infant mortality rates (death in the first year), James Grant, the executive director of UNICEF, said in 1994, "We have seen a vast deterioration in the condition of the American child in the 1980s and the cost of pulling them back into the mainstream now will be mammoth. . . . Three million American children a year are neglected or physically or sexually abused. The U.S. shows a significant under-performance in the records for children reaching the fifth year of schooling."[94]

When economic capacity to help children is factored into the account of under age five mortality, the United States ranks dead last.[95] Why? One clue is the group with which the United States shares this dismal record. Grant said the condition of children in virtually all English-speaking industrialized countries had worsened in the 1980s, while it improved steadily in continental Europe and Japan.[96] Put differently, the absence of nursery care and health provisions is greatest in the countries which rely on market forces to solve their problems as contrasted to countries which permit the state to assume responsibilities where market forces are unable to pick up the burden.

PART III

Income versus Companionship

4

Why Money Doesn't Buy Happiness for Most of Us

If prosperous market democracies are so hospitable to unhappiness, perhaps they and their populations are pursuing the wrong goals. Perhaps, indeed, beyond a certain point, prosperity does not have much to do with happiness. The hungry person seeks food until she is sated (and possibly obese), but then she wants something else or, not recognizing satiety, *needs* something else.

In this chapter I will ask whether prosperity, for societies and individuals alike, leads to happiness and protects against depression. Does economic growth make people, on average, happier and less depressed? Within countries, are richer individuals happier than poorer ones — and if so, is the power of money to buy happiness a constant across the economic spectrum or does it stop as one crosses the poverty line? In each case the important point is the obvious one: when money is relatively scarce, money buys happiness; when it is relatively plentiful, it ceases to do so. Although money seems to people in a market culture to be a congealed source of all pleasures, convertible into anything one wants, that is not the case. As Tibor Scitovsky said more than twenty years ago, many, perhaps most, of the pleasures of life are not priced, are not for sale, and therefore do not pass through the market.[1]

Why should this obvious fact be so opaque? Why do we believe that ever greater per capita GNP for society or ever higher income for oneself should yield ever greater utility? I have little patience with conspiracy theories: "the executive committee of the ruling class," the *Hidden Persuaders,* and so forth. Rather, it seems to me that the belief that more money and goods will make us happy is a product of cultural lag. Like other successful societies, market democracies must, by the logic of their own success, continue to emphasize the themes that have brought them to their current eminent positions. In these circumstances, individuals are not, in any practical sense, free to go against the culture that nurtures them. What Christian or Muslim or Buddhist in a country of Christians or Muslims or Buddhists is free to be an agnostic? Furthermore, there are immediate rewards for working within a system which, in the long run, is not working to most people's benefit. Market economies present the kind of learning situation familiar to all learning theorists: the immediate rewards (reinforcements) of more income are persuasive, even captivating, so much so that they discourage a peek over the wall of the maze to see what else is there.

In the next chapter I shall take a peek over the wall of the maze, but before doing so I must look at the anomalous relation between collective and individual prosperity. The policy implications flowing from this heresy are so great that they upset both traditional conservatives and traditional liberals, especially liberals who have invested their souls in the hope that income equality means greater happiness.

Economic Growth and Happiness

The relation between measures of SWB and income takes a curvilinear path through history: climbing toward modernity for a long (or sometimes brief) period and then, after a little plateau, turning down again. The ascending part of this path is indicated by table 4.1.

The relation is strong: across levels of development people are happier as per capita GDP increases. What happened to the felicity that Tönnies thought characterized traditional society, or gemeinschaft? and, for that matter, what happened to the happy South Sea islanders that Capt. Louis de Bougainville reported in the eighteenth century (and which so misled Jean Jacques Rousseau about the "state of nature")? After surveying happiness in various corners of the world, George Gallup reported, "Although one could probably find isolated places in the world where the inhabitants were very poor but happy, this study failed to discover any area that met this test." "Poverty," he said, "adversely colors [all] attitudes and perceptions."[2] In the most probing cross-national analysis so far, Alex Inkeles and Larry Diamond examined eight cross-national studies using ten different measures of well-being and, most important, controlling for occupation so that the effects of income and oc-

Table 4.1. Correlations with SWB of Measures of Economic Development

Economic Development	Zero order Correlation	Source
GDP per capita	+.58**	Diener
GDP per capita "real national income"	+.69*	Veenhoven
Purchasing power	+.61**	Diener
Equality of income (gini coeff.) (low score = more equality)	−.43†	Diener

† = $p > .05$; * = $p > .01$; ** = $p > .001$

Sources: Ed Diener, Marissa Diener, and Carol Diener. 1995. "Factors Predicting the Subjective Well-Being of Nations." *Journal of Personality and Social Psychology* 69: 857, 859; Ruut Veenhoven. 1993. *Happiness in Nations.* Rotterdam: Erasmus University Press, 50. (Compare table 2.6.)

cupation could be examined separately. Their analysis, they said, provides "a strong indication . . . that personal satisfaction rises with the level of economic development of the nation."[3] For most of modern history (if we can take a cross section of development as a kind of historical profile), economic development did buy happiness, a fact that I have called the affluence effect.[4] The price was high, as the many accounts of family disruption, frustrated expectations, lost ancestral rights, fractured social life, wasted skills, and broken cultures all report. Leonard Doob said that in Africa neither the traditional nor the modernized people suffered so much as those in between, the changers;[5] and assorted reports from Korea[6] (a success story), from Africa[7] (not yet successful), and from the tragic course of Native Americans[8] all tell how painful and uncertain this route to greater happiness can be. Across fifty-five nations, when the influence of increased income is removed, growth itself has a slight (nonsignificant) negative correlation.[9] It is the increased income, not the process of increasing income, that makes people on average happier.

Nothing could be more satisfying to economists and unreconstructed utilitarians than the robust correlations between GDP per capita and measures of happiness. Bentham would be pleased if not surprised.[10] So would Francis Fukuyama, who announced in the mid-1990s that in the institutions of market democracies we had found "the end of history."[11]

But history does not end with the progression from what we are now pleased to call underdevelopment to advanced status. As mentioned in chapter 2, there is a curvilinear relationship between average SWB and GNP such that in the very wealthiest nations increased income buys very little, if any, increased SWB.[12] The declining hedonic return on national income, says Veenhoven, "neatly reflects the law of diminishing returns."[13]

Most specialists in European and American values and moods agree about the law of diminishing returns: Among the advanced nations of Europe, there is, indeed, a slight positive relationship between per capita GDP and happiness (or satisfaction with one's life), but "the linkage is surprisingly weak."[14] Across the Atlantic, the United States was in the 1980s and still is the richest country in the world (as measured by purchasing power of average wages—excluding the oil states), but among advanced countries it ranks only in the middle in happiness (and the two relatively poorer Irelands rank at or near the top!). Incidentally, the United States is notable as a place where money buys less happiness than in other advanced countries.[15] Americans work hard for their higher incomes—but find them less rewarding.

Much of the variance in cross-national studies is caused by cultural differences,[16] so studies of the effects of wealth within a culture might tell us more about these wealth effects. In this connection, it is significant that even within political units whose cultures are as homogeneous as certain U.S. states, level of regional income does not predict level of average SWB.[17] For example, people in a prosperous area of Wisconsin are no happier than those in the least prosperous areas, and in Oklahoma those living in the most prosperous areas are actually less happy than those in the poorer areas.[18] Although he has been challenged, I believe Veenhoven is right: as countries become richer, their increased income buys smaller and smaller increments of felicity. As mentioned in chapter 1, as per capita income increased in the United States over the postwar period, the proportion of the population feeling "very happy" modestly declined.

I speak of economic development as though it were a one-way street. Aside from Argentina, it is true that few advanced nations have gone into a long-term economic decline, but all have had those temporary declines called recessions. By and large, national well-being is not greatly sensitive to short-term ups and downs—there is mixed evidence on the effect of unemployment on the self-reported happiness of the general public[19]—but there are exceptions: the Belgians responded to the recession of the 1980s with despair, dropping from second or third place among European nations to next to the bottom.[20] Thus economic reversals, if sufficiently marked, do have a serious effect, indicating again that sharp changes and losses make a difference in well-being, even if gradual improvements do not.

WHY DOES ECONOMIC GROWTH BUY HAPPINESS IN POOR SOCIETIES BUT NOT IN RICH SOCIETIES?

Why does economic growth have a curvilinear relation to happiness such that the effect is large at the earliest stages of development and wanes as development progresses? One explanation relies on the difference between meeting basic needs for food and shelter and meeting social needs for goods that are valued chiefly because of the esteem or status they confer on their possessors.[21] This is seen most vividly when basic needs are separated from other things money buys. In Ed Diener et al.'s cross-national study, happiness rose sharply as GDP per capita increased to take care of basic needs up to about 40 percent of the purchasing power of the United States — and then rose much more slowly, with a barely significant correlation (+.05) between growth and happiness beyond that point.[22]

But at the modern end of this curvilinear route, isn't it still true, as Diener and his associates claim, that, having more resources, people can pursue their goals, whatever they may be, with greater success?[23] This conjecture is correct under two circumstances: (1) that people's goals are to acquire purchasable things, and (2) that purchasable things yield happiness. But, as the evidence in this chapter strongly implies, the richer the society and its individuals become, the less purchasable are the goals that bring them happiness — although they may still pursue greater wealth with their accustomed vigor. We are still materialists at heart (see chapter 8) — but the heart is unfulfilled.

A poignant report confirming this interpretation of the effect of increasing income on well-being comes from Australia, where, after more than a decade of modest growth and increased reliance on market forces, 64 percent of a middle-class sample reported feeling that "the incomes and prospects of middle-class Australians were falling," and 51 percent said that their "quality of life is declining." As the author of this study recommends, "This seems to point to some kind of contradiction and mismatch between economic measures of progress and the *experience* of ordinary people."[24] A similar report from Italy on declining SWB in recent years supports the general idea of rising economic malaise in the face of objectively rising per capita income.[25]

Nevertheless, for two reasons the power of economic development to foster happiness is not exhausted in rich societies. First, economic growth generally increases the income of the poor, and for them money does buy happiness. And second, a higher GNP per capita is a kind of collective good in the sense that when people enjoy the many benefits of national wealth (such as the higher general levels of education and health that collective wealth makes possible) their enjoyment does not detract from the enjoyment of others. The particular afflictions of the poor, such as high rates of infant mortality, are reduced by the public health provisions bought by collective wealth. Along the same lines, rich countries have (or had) better welfare systems than poor countries. Thus, increased collective wealth buys both objective and subjective well-being for the poor. Or, more accurately, it buys relief from sorrow, a relief that fosters well-being more than any similar increment of joys.

There is irony in this interpretation of growth as a collective good created by the market, for it is an accepted principle that, because of the free rider problem, markets cannot foster collective goods! Without exploring this irony, are there other reasons the collective good of collective wealth increases the sense of well-being of those who participate in those societies?

A rising tide in the bay may lift all boats, but, curiously, if the tide is the green tide of money, some boats will rise higher than others. This might invite envy, but comparisons with one's own experience or expectations is more often the standard. Using a different metaphor, I found in some earlier research that if a person climbed a little higher on his own ladder, he did not care if another person climbed even higher on another ladder.[26] And we know that social comparisons, as contrasted to self-comparisons, are less likely to favor well-being[27] (unless these are "downward comparisons," which cheer some unhappy people).[28] When the economy grows, people attribute their rising incomes to their own efforts and derive great satisfaction from these alleged achievements. That is, the contribution to happiness made by doing something for yourself is common to both earned wealth and to participation in a rising national income that individuals cannot be said to have earned for themselves. As I note in chapter 13, the illusion of control benefits as it misleads individuals who share that common illusion—an illusion, incidentally, more common among happy people than among the depressed. The illusion has effects which are not illusionary, however, for merely striving for personal goals of almost any kind increases the sense of well-being.[29]

In Any Society, Are Rich Persons Happier than the Less Rich?

Comparisons of the rich with the poor and with the not-so-rich within a society tell a story quite compatible with these cross-national accounts, and yet one that challenges some of our basic, commonsense assumptions. The story is this: in poor societies there is a strong relationship between individual income and happiness, but in rich societies that relationship wanes, sometimes to the vanishing point. I have called the common belief that happiness is in some sense proportionate to income the economistic fallacy.[30] That belief is widespread through all societies and is almost universal among economists, for whom money is a fungible source of both preference and Benthamite utility. But in advanced societies, that belief is genuinely erroneous (if not exactly a fallacy).

The belief is not wrong in poor nations. Thus, in Greece, "by far the poorest nation in the European Community, we find a relatively strong relationship between income and subjective well-being."[31] In the old days of the command economies, this income–happiness relationship was also quite strong in Hungary—it is not a capitalist product.[32] In contrast, in the United States (1972) the relationship between individual income and happiness has been very weak. In perhaps the best of the many single-country quality of life studies, Andrews and Withey found that "the groupings by socioeconomic status show very meager differences [in sense of well-being] . . . and no significant single steps for [satisfaction with] Life-as-a-Whole." These authors commented, "One tends to note the smallness of differences because many observers of the American scene would have expected larger ones."[33]

A few years later, in his study *Happy People,* Jonathan Freedman reported that "the rich are not more likely to be happy than those with moderate incomes: the middle class is not more likely to be . . . happy than those with lower incomes. . . . For the majority of Americans, money, whatever else it does, does not bring happiness." But the poor are different: "Fewer of them say that they are very happy or moderately happy and more of them say that they are very unhappy than people with higher incomes."[34] I will return to this question of the poor in a moment. A few years later still Angus Campbell reported his findings from extensive American data: "Knowing people's incomes does not tell us a great deal about their general satisfaction with life."[35] It is no different in Europe: on the basis of a huge cross-national sample stretching over many years, Ronald Inglehart and Jacques-René Rabier found that "when we analyze satisfaction with one's life as a whole, the variance explained [by level of income] is very modest indeed."[36]

Commenting on this weak or even nonexistent relation between income and happiness in the United States, Argyle pays tribute to the theory of declining marginal utility of money: "The reason for the rather weak effect of income [on happiness] in the USA may be that many Americans are above the level at which income affects happiness." But this relative wealth may, in turn, be vulnerable to rising expectations: "Lack of response to prosperity in America may be due to rising expectations and an American optimistic belief that things will keep on improving."[37] Note the two conflicting principles: diminishing returns conflicting with rising expectations. Also notice the irony: optimism is generally associated with happiness, but call it rising expectations and it seems to be a setup for frustration.

This analysis is about unhappiness and depression, both of which are apparently increasing in the American market democracy, but if that increase flattens out, Americans remain at a level of unhappiness that progress theories would not have predicted. I do not achieve my purpose, however, by exaggerating the situation. Although higher level of income has been associated with a fairly steady postwar decline in happiness in the United States, in 1976 it could be said that Americans "are generally a happy culture, lacking in anxiety, satisfied with our jobs, happy in our marriages, armed with positive orientations to ourselves, and buttressed by social support for problems we encounter."[38] And twenty years later, in 1996, after the sizable erosion of happiness in marriage and of satisfaction with work, community, and finances reported in chapter 2, it could still be said that "most people are happy."[39] For those who wish to see it that way, the glass is still at least half full.

The Erratic Application of the Economistic Fallacy

As mentioned, Freedman's qualification is crucial: among the poor, money does buy happiness and a greater sense of well-being. But the poor are not the only people for whom increased income buys happiness. As I have pointed out elsewhere, when money takes on symbolic value and is an intimate part of a person's identity, its acquisition does much more than increase goods and services, it validates the person.[40] In this line of thinking, there is nothing special about money; friends, honors, favoritism at court, and recognition of piety would all do just as well. It is the dominance of the market that makes money so special in advanced market democracies. Thus, studies show that for those who invest their striving in athletics, athletic achievements are most closely related to SWB, while "having a lot of money most influenced SWB among individuals who had personal strivings that involved acquiring wealth."[41]

"Having a lot of money" is the dominant goal of many people in all market societies (see chapter 8) but not for a lot of others; at least it is not acknowledged by a lot of people. Thus, a Lutheran poll taken in the United States finds that in response to a question on "the most important things in life," 56 percent said, "relations with family and friends" and 21 percent said, "religious faith and spirituality," but only 4 percent said, "monetary success."[42] When a general U.S. sample was asked to agree or disagree with the statement, "Money is one of my most important concerns," 60 percent disagreed.[43] In a variety of countries many disclaim any desire "to be rich." Thus, only 9 percent of a national British sample acknowledge that this ambition is "their main goal in life," while 15 percent of the Americans and 38 percent of the Japanese made similar claims. The British support the modesty of their financial ambitions by greatly preferring a situation in which they have "enough money to be free of financial worries" (61 percent) compared to having "plenty of spare money in the bank" (16 percent) or "a great deal of money" (2 percent).[44]

There are two lessons here: desire for security and freedom transcend avarice in Britain, and, in line with my thesis that experience with relative wealth leads people to desire other things, the oldest industrial nation (Britain) was least avaricious, the second oldest—and richest (the United States)—came second, and the newest rich nation (Japan) was the most avaricious.

I have found that most of my friends, on reflection, agree that it is not the things they buy or own that make them happy or the lack of these things that depresses them. As I show in the next few chapters, it is their relations with their spouses and colleagues, the well-being of their children, their sense of achievement, and their exercise of skills at work that give them genuine utility (in the Benthamite sense). I invite my readers to engage in similar introspection. For, unless people think about it a little bit, they tend to measure themselves by their income levels and what they call their standard of living—the conventional but misleading standard in a market economy.

WHY DOES MONEY NOT BUY A SENSE OF WELL-BEING IN ADVANCED SOCIETIES?

The reason the economists' formula greater income equals greater utility (where *utility* means the satisfaction of preferences—which has significance only if that preference satisfaction implies a more general satisfaction)[45] is so persuasive is that for most people it seems to correspond to both experience and common sense. As noted, the formula does correspond to the experience of the poor, but for the nonpoor money still seems to buy many estimable things. For example, it should buy social esteem. Adam Smith thought this was the case: "It is chiefly from this regard to the sentiments of mankind that we pursue riches and avoid poverty,"[46] but he had not reckoned with the variability of social esteem whose reference points change with each escalation in standing. The Joneses, after all, may also be moving up, and, more important, one may move from keeping up with the Joneses to keeping up with the van Schuylers, should they be one's new neighbors. A partially confirming study by Mark Stein shows that middle-class people who improve their incomes are not likely to be happier in their higher bracket—unless they also increase their subjective status.[47] It is higher status, not higher income, that increases well-being.

Then, too, the increments that money buys of what is usually called the sense of personal control, that is, the belief that one controls one's fate, are precarious. In their longitudinal analysis of the effects of work on workers' personalities, Melvin Kohn and Carmi Schooler found that the higher people rose in an occupational hierarchy, the less control they believed they had over their work life.[48] As with personal control, so with promotion in a hierarchy. George Homans found that the effect of a recent promotion on a worker was to make her less satisfied: the experience of one promotion simply led to the expectation of further promotions—and therefore to dissatisfaction with her relative status.[49] In this case, adaptation to one's improved work status merely raises the stakes (see chapter 17). Thus many of the good things that money seems to buy are evanescent, disappearing with the new circumstances created by higher salary or greater power.

In an earlier exploration of the hedonic purchasing power of money, Richard Easterlin gave an answer that embraces many of the above anomalies: people adapt to their circumstances so that each increment of money soon creates a new standard against which they measure themselves. This partially explains, for example, why people's happiness did not rise with their higher income in the postwar period.[50] Although there is something to these theories of adaptation and escalating social comparisons, they confront intense opposition from market doctrine. Although adaptation makes the well-being of the elderly relatively high, general adaptation to one's standard of living is antithetical to market doctrine. Aspiration, not adaptation, is what makes markets dynamic and profitable.

In any event, there is evidence that many other forces are at work, some of which are income inelastic, that is, situations in which income has no effect on moods and other situations which incur their own self-limiting forces. First, it isn't just adaptation or problems of social comparison that limit the power of money to buy self-esteem or personal control for, strangely, these highly desired goods are not related to level of income.[51] Of course, more money should increase one's sense of power over one's environment — but apparently it doesn't. As I will point out in chapter 13, the illusion of control is so built into people's systems that higher income is often irrelevant to one's sense of personal control.

The power of social comparison to influence and undermine well-being (see chapter 17) works through a sense of fairness, beliefs about what a person ought to get. A sense of being fairly treated is important: Andrews and Withey's study of the quality of life (1976) showed that a sense of being treated unfairly lowered people's sense of well-being. In that study, however, people's assessment of unfairness had more to do with interpersonal relations than with income[52] — as one would expect from the finding that it is relations with people, not with money, that most influence well-being. But of course there are some income comparisons. A long history of research on self- and social comparisons shows that people are more aroused if they think their group is unfairly treated than if they think that they themselves are so treated.[53] Furthermore, in these group comparisons (as in individual comparisons) people compare themselves to similar others, the relevant reference group, rather than to groups much richer or poorer than they are. (It is just as well: people ranking high on a materialism scale tend to compare themselves to remote and richer others, which then contributes to their general unhappiness.)[54] Thus the national distribution of income is largely lost from sight — one reason Marxist predictions of class conflict failed: people do not relate their discontents to the larger question of the social distribution of income. Indeed, as Sidney Verba and Gary Orren report, except for the high salaries of film stars and sports heroes, leaders of many socioeconomic groups, including labor and ethnic groups, approved something very close to the actual distribution of income by occupational classifications.[55] And, as reported by other studies, the status quo is generally approved by people very close to the bottom of the heap.[56] Finally, at least in the late 1970s, in the United States there was little resentment of people's wages relative to others'.[57]

These interlocking findings help one to understand the lack of relation between income and well-being: (1) the sense of being fairly treated makes an important contribution to well-being but applies mainly to how people treat a person; (2) at least in the United States, social comparisons of wages by individuals are minimal, and comparisons of groups or occupations do not, with certain exceptions, create any large sense of unfairness; and (3) people tend to think that the current distribution of income is about right. All these things tend to minimize the relationship between level of income and well-being.

Then there is the biological fixity of moods discussed in the previous chapter: people are born with happy or unhappy dispositions. Jan Fawcett says of joylessness, "We seem to be measuring a biological characteristic, like blue eyes, that doesn't change,"[58] although, for the reasons given in chapter 3, biological fixity does not preclude an income–well-being relation; it is only a limiting condition. In any event, the "blue eyes" wear rose-tinted glasses, for people are generally endowed with a positivity bias that, for example, leads them to check the positive, agreeable items in questionnaires more than the negative, disagreeable ones and to choose "happy" words over "unhappy" ones; and, for a variety of reasons, people quite unreasonably believe that objectively improbable good things will happen to themselves, if not to others: the illusion of control that I mentioned earlier.[59] Level of income does not influence most of these in-built human characteristics.

Daily pleasures are different from other sources of satisfaction with one's life as a whole, but they follow much the same pattern in their lack of any significant relation to income. When Gallup asked Americans, "What gives you the most personal satisfaction or enjoyment day in and day out?" family activities ranked first, but then, in order of preference, television (but see below), friends, music, reading books and newspapers, house or apartment, one's work, meals, one's car, following sports, and the "clothes you wear."[60] Few of these things and activities require expenditures that those above the poverty line cannot afford, even cars. The pleasures yielded by many of the others, especially housing, are largely comparative or, as Thorstein Veblen would say, invidious, but perhaps more invidious in midscale or upscale than in downscale households.

Possessions may be important — in another study, a sample of primary grade schoolgirls identified with "the clothes that you wear" more than with their fathers![61] — but, at least above the poverty line, enjoyment of these activities is not income-dependent, for, as the law of diminishing returns suggests, the small possessions of the less well-off yield as much gratification as the larger possessions of the rich.[62] Moreover, as a society Americans have focused so much on possessions that they forget that it is not so much what one owns as how one is treated by others that gives pleasure.

What about enjoyment of working activities, which surely must be related to income because the higher paid jobs afford more power, discretion, challenge — and therefore pleasure? In 1985 Thomas Juster reported on several surveys (in the 1970s and early 1980s) of the activities that people said gave them the greatest pleasure; he found again that family activities (playing with one's children) and friendship (socializing with friends) were most enjoyed. But most striking about this study was the high rank given to "the actual work that you do," which was ranked right after family and socializing activities and well ahead of watching television, sports activities, going to movies, gardening, reading, and shopping. And, strangely, he found that "there is virtually no association between the process benefits from work [enjoying work activities] and the intrinsic characteristics of the job as reflected by its occupational status."[63] Other studies would dispute the independence of occupational characteristics and enjoyment of working activities, but we may assume that the relationship is much looser than middle-class intellectuals imagine. (I once interviewed a wallpaper-hanger who found his skill in handling corners a source of great delight.)

Well-being has as much to do with relief from pain as with pleasure, indeed, more so, because losses hurt more than gains please — and pain is remembered longer than is pleasure.[64] Take the question of worries, which surely must be more frequent among the less well-off than the better-off. Not so. Andrews and Withey's surveys in the early 1970s found that when it comes to worrying "there are virtually no differences associated with socioeconomic status. . . . Higher status people apparently did not reduce the frequency of worrying."[65] For those above the poverty line, money does not reduce worrying; it simply changes the subject. But for the poor, "economic hardship, the sense of not having enough money to provide food, clothing, shelter, and medical care for one's family, is profoundly distressing for both husbands and wives." At this level "it is the hardship, not the injustice, that is most distressing."[66]

Of course, worries about security of income are important for well-being (see chapter 9), but they vary with level of income less than one would think. For example, a study of workers in Baltimore and Detroit (1976) showed that whereas the income levels of blue-collar workers and white-collar workers were almost identical, the blue-collar workers worried more about security of income than did white-collar workers.[67] Experience with corporate "downsizing" in the 1990s suggests that security of income and status is not guaranteed even at their higher levels.

I have been reporting the relation between money and well-being as though people were not themselves involved in the process of self-placement. What do people do when they are faced with adversity? Thomas Langner and Stanley Michael's study (1963) in social psychiatry related social stresses that reduce well-being—for example, physical illness, loss of spouse, lack or loss of close friends, and failure to "get ahead"—to coping strategies. They found that the actual incidence of social stressors did not differ much by social class (the working class scoring 5.7 on the stressor index, the middle class 5.3, and the upper class 4.7), but that the coping strategies differed greatly. Whereas the middle- and upper-class strategies were often to plunge into work, a strategy that had a therapeutic effect on some sources of misery, the working-class strategies more often employed expressive acts like drinking and aggression, acts which only made matters worse.[68] Thus, the relation between money and well-being is mediated by the superior coping strategies of those with more education and more money. Here, as is so often the case in studies of well-being, the less well-off get worse while the better-off get better. It would be a pity if in our concern for well-being we were to forget that we are dealing not with anvils struck by repeated blows but with tissue cut by an upper blade of circumstance and a lower blade of human disposition and skill.

Why Do People Believe Their Well-Being Depends on Their Incomes?

Most people believe that a 25 percent pay increase would make them much more satisfied with their lives[69]—but those whose incomes are now at that higher level are not, in fact, happier or more satisfied with their lives. Why are we so easily deceived about something that is central to our happiness?

One general reason is that we are all self-centered, not selfish but, as Jean Piaget said, "egocentric" in the sense that what is salient in our own minds is the essence of reality.[70] In spite of Veblen, we are much more aware of our own feelings than of the feelings of our richer or poorer neighbors. But supposing each of us did a comparative analysis, asking, What is the relation between my neighbor's greater wealth and his happiness? As it turns out, we are relatively poor judges of people's moods. When the neighbors of respondents in one study were asked about the respondents' happiness, they were rarely even approximately correct: "Even people who the respondents felt knew them pretty well were in fact relatively poor judges of the respondents' perceptions. . . . The inference is strong that we as a people do not really know how each other feels."[71] Thus, assessing the happiness of a richer (or poorer) neighbor would not help to moderate the belief that a little more money would make a person happier.

Earlier in this chapter I compared the belief in economic growth to religious beliefs and to the pain of being agnostic in a religious culture. The weight of culture also applies to beliefs in the healing power of individual wealth. People believe that a little more money would make them happier, and, lacking privileged knowledge of the causes of their feelings, people accept conventional answers.[72] In spite of Kant and Mill, people's basic premise is that they are much like others—they have no great desire to be unique.[73] The market culture teaches us that money is the source of well-being. Many studies show that people are not very good at explaining why they feel good or bad (see chapter 16), and, accepting the conventional market ideology, they believe that the source of their happiness (or misery) is money.

A further reason we believe that our well-being depends on our income is that we always have before us images of things or a lifestyle that is designed to tempt. Less than half of the population believes they have enough money to "lead the kind of life [they] want to,"[74] although, as mentioned above, a surprisingly large number disclaim any desire to be rich. In a monastery no monk will claim he has all the sanctity he might wish for. In a market culture it is hardly possible to believe that one has all the income one could wish for—a failure of imagination more than a measure of materialist discontent.[75] The imagination, of course, is stimulated by "media images of remarkably successful people, often portrayed as idealized objects without troubles or limits, [which] may make any actual life seem pallid and unsuccessful by comparison."[76]

Perhaps the most important cause, however, is that we experience moments when money does give us great happiness. These moments come when there are changes in income that do briefly influence our sense of well-being—and decreases make us more miserable than increases make us happy. But as the recently promoted person in Homans's study experienced, even the happiness that comes with an increase in income does not last long, for very soon the new level of income becomes the standard against which we measure our achievements: the adaptation process that haunts all studies of the causes of happiness (see chapter 17). It haunts the poor as well, for the phenomenon that Gallup could not find, happy poor people, does exist, in foreign areas as well as in the United States. Thus, "the happy poor has been interpreted as a state of adaptation and learned helplessness produced by long experience of being unable to do anything about it."[77] Here is another reason that so slight a relation exists between income and well-being: the poor have given up and are, so to speak, insufficiently discontented if not insufficiently unhappy.

Other reasons follow: Americans' belief (stronger than that of Europeans) that whatever income is received is earned and therefore deserved. Although probably not influential with the average consumer and worker, market economics teaches the same message: the definition of the right wage is the wage that the (perfect) market pays—a case of pure procedural justice and, like psychoanalysis, wonderfully self-confirming. But it is also the message of a popular theory of substantive justice: "the just world theory," which says that people get what they deserve.[78] For the successful (and most people at all levels of income define themselves as successful, that is, two-thirds of the people think they have above-average earnings), just world thinking is a way of bolstering people's images of themselves. It is partly for this reason that those who believe in a just world are more satisfied with their lives than are those who tend to see injustices in the world.[79] C. E. Lindblom, referring to the strategic superiority of a capital strike over a labor strike, once called the market economy a "fiendishly clever" device for justifying and maintaining an economic elite in power.[80] Similarly, and without prejudice, it seems to me that the market ideology is a kind of codification of many of the common beliefs of humankind, especially a preference for the justice of deserts compared to the justices of need and equality.

There is one final reason people believe that it is money from which all happiness flows: official economic doctrine denies them the belief that many of their main pleasures in life come from their work. Economists call work a disutility, the pain necessary to earn the pleasures of money and leisure. In this they are strict Benthamite utilitarians: "Desire for labor *for the sake of labor*—of labor considered in the character of an *end*, without any view to anything else—is a sort of desire that seems scarcely to have a place in the human breast. . . . *Aversion*—not *desire*—is the only emotion which labor, taken by itself, is qualified to produce . . . ease, not labor, is the object. Love of labor is a contradiction in terms."[81] Aside from wondering how much pleasure Bentham derived from writing this passage (and of course wondering how economic journals could afford to pay their authors amounts sufficient to compensate them for their time), I must refer readers to the section on intrinsic rewards in *The Market Experience*.[82] Or consider that in one of Andrew and Withey's arrays, the "sense of efficacy" (for example, "What you are accomplishing in your life?") contributed six times as much to people's satisfaction with their life as did the "money index."[83] Remember, too, that in my reference earlier to Juster's study of what people actually enjoyed doing (not earning), working activities came well before all leisure activities except for playing with one's children and socializing with friends.[84] Beyond a rather low level of skill and discretion, work itself is not just the pain for which income is the compensating pleasure. The economists have their pain–pleasure calculus all wrong.

What is so strange is that conventional beliefs about the relation between money and happiness are almost beyond debate. As Karl Polanyi once said, if you question the money–happiness nexus people think you are not so much dangerous as mad.[85]

TWO TESTS OF THE INFLUENCE OF INCOME ON HAPPINESS IN ADVANCED COUNTRIES

If the law of diminishing returns were at work eroding the power of money to yield happiness as countries became richer, what evidence, beyond the weakening correlations between wealth and happiness reported above, would one expect to find? I will offer two tests: (1) a weakening power of money to buy happiness among the rich but not the poor; and (2) a decline in materialist values in the richest countries. For the first test, consider that in the United States between 1957 and 1972 the self-reported happiness of an upper income group showed a fairly sharp decline while the reports from a lower income group remained fairly constant over the period. The consequence, of course, was that the two groups came closer together in their estimates of their well-being: money (being rich) bought less happiness in 1972 than in 1957.[86] The first test confirms the declining marginal utility of money hypothesis.

But I do not think the second test is so successful. In the 1970s there was a widely reported drift from materialist to "postmaterialist" values by youth brought up in peace and prosperity after the war.[87] By the measure used, postmaterialists give priority to such values as self-determination (including self-direction at work) and cultural expression. Postmaterialists are relatively prosperous, and for them, money does not buy happiness, thus weakening the income–happiness relationship. If it had thrived, postmaterialism would have contributed to the evidence of the diminishing happiness yield of money. But it did not, partly because the prosperity that nurtured it in Europe waned and unemployment grew.[88] Better measures of materialism and its alternatives now show that at least in the United States materialism among youth is not declining but rather is historically high after rising steadily for the fifteen years from 1972 to 1987 (see chapter 8).[89] Curiously, however, even in the presence of this apparent increase in materialist values, money does not buy any more happiness now than it did a quarter of a century ago—at least happiness has declined while per capita income has risen, if slowly, even during the relatively stagnant 1970s and 1980s (see fig. 1.1). As money buys less and less happiness, materialist ambitions rise and flourish!

DISAPPOINTMENT WITH THE FRUITS OF PROSPERITY

When people arrived at this stage of relative affluence, were they disappointed? I have suggested some of the pains of the process of economic development, but there are pains associated with being developed or advanced that might account for the downturn of felicity in the United States.

One popular theory relies on the frustrations arising from expectations that one's achievements will give one a relative advantage—only to find that the same hope stimulated others to attain the same achievements. One works hard to gain a level of education higher than one's parents—only to find that others, too, have higher education. The advantage disappears. This is the theory of "positional goods" whose enjoyment depends on relative advantage.[90] This theory of disappointment inherent in positional goods is reminiscent of the economic principle that entrepreneurs and inventors rarely enjoy the full economic returns of their work because of competitors and imitators. Market societies are more dynamic than they are fair (they do not value sunk costs)—but which of us wants to return to patents royal or restricted enrollments?

Can this disappointment be blamed on the media? With some plausibility, the rising political malaise that I shall report in chapter 11 is attributed to the media.[91] But happiness is a much more intimate feeling than political malaise and has its genesis in experience rather than in observation or secondhand reports. Nevertheless, if the drumbeat of bad news on corruption, crime, foreign disasters, adolescent pregnancies and delinquency, pollution, and so forth is sufficiently insistent, chronic, and dramatic, people might think they ought to be unhappy or, more likely, inferring an unhappy mood from the news, then fitting their own mood to what they see as the national mood. Is self-reported happiness responsive to news stories? The apparent effect of peace in Vietnam (both the cease-fire and the Paris conference) was a very brief blip in mood—followed by unhappiness; Watergate had transient and almost imperceptible influences on mood; the Cuban missile crisis seems to have made people a very little bit *happier* for a brief moment.[92] But the test is the effect of media reporting on ordinary, chronic ills and malfeasance day in and day out, not on the dramatic events of war and peace and presidential resignation. But notice that while self-reported unhappiness may be responsive to the news, depression is not. The coincidence of the two trends leads me to think that it is not the news but the unsatisfying nature of people's lives that accounts for much of the dysphoria of the postwar period. Life satisfaction drives political satisfaction, not vice versa (see chapter 11).

The point is not that events and trends can justify good or bad moods, but that their discussion creates an impression of life among the ruins. For the most part, our increased wealth seems irrelevant to many of these news reports. (A headline in August 1997 for a story reporting on then-recent poll responses reads, "America's Blues: Prosperity Is No Cure.")[93] As the journalist Robert Samuelson commented on another occasion, "Wealth will not bring love or civility. It will not make the dishonest honest. It will not mend broken families or stifle crime."[94] If these ills are related to market culture — a disputed point — then it seems that many people both want the market for its economic benefits and dislike the culture it produces: a genuine dilemma, as some Asian leaders have pointed out.

THE HEDONIC TREADMILL

If desires, expectations, and standards of comparison increase as rapidly as achievements, or at least attainments, no increase in income, no matter how large, will increase SWB. This process leads to what two psychologists, Philip Brickman and Donald Campbell, have called the "hedonic treadmill."[95] Is there no escape? In the next chapter I will explore a plausible escape, but let us see who is destined for the hedonic treadmill. At the bottom, the poor and the near poor will profit from economic growth because for them increased income, whether collective or individual, does buy happiness. And for the better off and better educated, two growing groups, there is at least the possibility of a postmaterialist path of self-directed work and even, it may be hoped, "a society where ideas count more than money." But for the materialist middle, who are quite indifferent to whether or not ideas count, more money will not buy greater well-being: the hedonic treadmill lies before them.

5

Companionship or Income?

The bird, a nest; the spider, a web; man, a friend.
— *William Blake*

If money does not contribute to the happiness of those above the poverty level, what does? The main answer is companionship, an inclusive term I use to mean both family solidarity and friendship (social support, to social scientists). There is a painful obviousness about this answer — but there is more to it than Love Conquers All. There is, for example, a blunt challenge to the way we live. The novelty of the message is the comparative advantage of companionship over income. But first I will seek to explain why companionship is so good for well-being and why it is so costly to violate the drives that impel us toward it. Then the comparative analysis: What are the respective yields in well-being of companionship and income? Finally, if this is clear to us, as I think it is, how will people choose? and what inhibits a fruitful choice?

Does Companionship Make Us Happy?

One way of testing whether companionship is a major source of well-being is to see if satisfaction with family life and with friends is associated with the kinds of overall measures of well-being discussed in chapter 2.

SATISFACTION WITH FAMILY LIFE AND FRIENDS

In each of the two massive pioneering studies of quality of life published in 1976, satisfaction with family life was the second most important predictor of well-being and of satisfaction with one's life. In these two studies, satisfaction with family life made more of a contribution to SWB than satisfaction with standard of living, work, "the fun you are having," religious life, or any of the numerous other areas of life measured.[1] Literature reviews report the same general findings.[2]

In both of these major studies, the contribution to well-being of satisfaction with one's friends (for example, feelings about "the people you see socially" and the "things you do with them") is much smaller,[3] but cross-nationally satisfaction with one's friends is a better predictor of life satisfaction than is satisfaction with one's family.[4] When people in the United States assess their feelings about friends and "the people [they] see socially" the appraisals tend to be "delighted," a category rarely used in other domains.[5]

Also, acquiring a new friend or doing new things with old friends greatly improved people's moods.[6] If this is the consequence of attachment, the reverse, loss (in John Bowlby's paired terms), tells the same story, this time as tragedy. The most powerful cause of depression is disruption of family and friendship relations. Being widowed or divorced or separated is associated with higher levels of depression[7]—as it is with unhappiness. Studies of depression over time tell the same story: when a person's loneliness is relieved, his or her depression is also relieved.[8] Basically, feelings of well-being are interactive with other, more specific feelings, thus combining the top-down (overall SWB determines domain satisfaction) and bottom-up (domain satisfaction determines overall feelings about one's life and mood) influences.

Cross-national studies universally find that married people are happier than the unmarried, and regular contact with friends and relatives increases happiness.[9] Depression, like unhappiness, is directly related to lack of emotional support.[10]

PEOPLE'S OWN REPORTS ON THE SOURCES OF THEIR HAPPINESS

Although their views are quite fallible, people have their own views on what makes them happy. For example, weighting the correlational measures mentioned above by people's estimates of the importance of the various sources of satisfaction actually makes for worse predictions.[11] But in market democracies great importance is placed on what people *think* they want. In the previous chapter I noted that when the pollster Louis Harris asked a national sample about the most important things in their life, they gave overwhelming

Table 5.1. Self-Reported Sources of Happiness and Unhappiness, 1957 and 1976

Sources	Sources of Happiness		Sources of Unhappiness	
	1957	1976	1957	1976
Economic and material	35%	28%	27%	20%
Children	29	24	7	7
Marriage	17	15	5	5
Other interpersonal	16	18	3	13
Job	8	9	11	20
Respondent's health	9	11	7	9
Family's health	8	6	5	3
Independence, absence of burdens	8	16	—	—
Personal characteristics, problems	2	5	13	8
Community, national, & world problems	—	—	13	24
TOTAL	132	126	91	109

Source: Joseph Veroff, Elizabeth Douvan, and Richard Kulka. 1981. *The Inner Americans: A Self-Portrait from 1957 to 1976.* New York: Basic Books, 57.

priority (56 percent) to "relations with family and friends."[12] But because the "things that are important in your life" are not necessarily the things that make you happy, one may not be persuaded by this poll. Earlier, for the period 1957–76, a team headed by Joseph Veroff sought to probe the changing circumstances that contributed to mental health in the United States. The self-reports in this study are more qualified endorsements of the hedonic fruitfulness of companionship (table 5.1).

The reports on children and marriage as sources of happiness reflect conventional values and, if you will permit the phrase, "faking good." Allowing for that, it is still important to note that the two family items (children and marriage) taken together are considered overwhelmingly more important as self-reported sources of happiness (1957 = 46 percent, 1976 = 39 percent) than anything else. One must not take this table too literally, but one might still wonder why people shifted from believing that their unhappiness was due to something within themselves in 1957 to believing that their unhappiness had its source in their friends and relatives twenty years later. (In chapter 7 I will note that people stopped seeing so much of their relatives—but not of their friends—over this period and thereafter.)[13]

The point, however, is not that either friendship or marriage is an unfailing contribution to happiness but that, even discounting the social approval and self-approval motives, people do tend to believe that it is their family and friends that make them happy. Indeed, in the above data, they believe these interpersonal relations are much more important to their happiness (if not their unhappiness) than their incomes and work lives—and more so in 1976 than in 1957.

NETWORKS OR CONFIDANTS

If one relates measures of well-being to actual number of friends or to being married (rather than to satisfaction scores), an even stronger case emerges. Actual number of friends turns out to be a better predictor for SWB than any other resource (income, attractiveness, intelligence—see below).[14] Moreover, "if all kinds of social support are combined and scores on a social support factor obtained, this is found to have an unusually strong correlation with happiness" (.50).[15]

Networks or Intimacy?

Intimacy clearly is more important for better mental health for the depressed,[16] but for the ordinary run of young people one suspected that "being popular" would prevail. Not so. As we shall see in a discussion of warmth in chapter 6, students want confidants, people in whom they can confide, more than friends with whom they can "hang out."[17] Is that because they are young? Not at all: the importance of intimacy actually increases from youth to middle life.[18] To return to my central theme: it might be that market relations increase networks (they are so useful), but it is doubtful that they encourage intimacy (partly because it is so time-consuming).

HAPPINESS ALONE AND IN THE COMPANY OF OTHERS

Do people report themselves to be happier when in the company of others or when they are pursuing happiness alone, perhaps reading a book or listening to an opera? (As we shall see, achievement and personal control contribute as much to well-being as do companions.) At first, the evidence is just what the above analysis suggests it would be: "People are in a more positive mood when with friends compared to being with family or alone."[19] But "being with" family or friends is different from living with them.[20] While the elderly are much less happy when living alone than when living with others, among the general public, a study reported (1986), the live-alones had at least as many social contacts with others as did those living in group situations.[21] Nevertheless, "people who live alone are more likely to die after a heart attack"[22]—the body has information that our conscious minds overlook. In leaving gemeinschaft behind, we increased choices about companionship—and created some casualties, including heart attacks, in the process.

But if the elderly are different, so are adolescents, both in Italy and the United States. True, adolescents are unhappiest when alone (partly because when alone they suffer the adolescent's disease, self-focus), but they (especially the Italian youth) are not happy when they are with their families, either. They are happiest when they are with their friends, whether working or playing or doing nothing in particular.[23] Here again is a reversal of the priority of family solidarity over friendship affiliation—but still a confirmation of the importance of companionship to happiness.

Why? One has fun doing things with one's friends—and many of these things could not be done alone: tennis, bridge or poker, and of course conversation.[24] Much is at work in this simple observation. Participation in almost any group activity (dancing, sports, even work) contributes to SWB partly because it is active and therefore enlists the physiology of good feelings and partly because it is social, enlisting the pleasures of belonging. As we know from other studies, even the enjoyment of work is heavily colored by whether or not one enjoys the company of workmates.[25] It is well known that when others are having a good time and are happy, then we all are more likely to have a good time and be happy. If laughter is infectious, so are moods, both good and bad. "Laugh and the world laughs with you; weep and you weep alone."

One other aspect of companionship is often mentioned: companions reduce the pain of stress. Affiliation provides "information leading the subject to believe that he is cared for and loved, that he is esteemed and valued, and that he belongs to a network of communication and mutual obligation, [and] appear[s] to reduce the levels of stress experienced, improve health, and buffer the impact of stress on health."[26]

SELF-ESTEEM AND PERSONAL CONTROL

People's most treasured possession is their self-esteem, something intimately related to social esteem: "Good name in man or woman, dear my lord, / Is the immediate jewel of their souls," says Iago. Reputation and popularity, or the illusion of popularity, are food for self-esteem: "If anyone can bolster one's feelings of self-worth," say Andrews and Withey, "friends should have a share in providing such support."[27] Here we enter the domain of "reflected appraisal," the doctrine of the Chicago School to the effect that we know ourselves as we imagine others know us. In the familiar jingle:

Each to each a looking glass
Reflects the other that doth pass.[28]

It has been said that Americans, more than others, feed each other benign self-images—and become greatly concerned when these are insufficiently reassuring. They are also more concerned about being liked than are those in other nations.[29] Being in love is good for self-esteem, for it tends to bring self-concept into harmony with the idealized self.[30]

The second most precious self-perception is the sense that one can control one's fate or at least is influential in one's own small environment. This is because occupational and marital success as well as success in games hinges on one's general or specialized effectiveness. In its contribution to happiness, the sense of personal control ranked only after self-esteem in a roundup of American quality of life surveys.[31]

The Drive for Companionship

If people get such pleasure from companions, isn't that enough to explain why people seek companionship? No, because it does not explain the sources of either the pleasure of companionship or the pain of being deprived of it.

RECIPROCAL HELP

One set of benefits (and therefore of pleasure) is wholly prudential, while others deal with the very constitution of the personality and the process of making and keeping friends. On the first of these, Michael Argyle and Adrian Furnham asked people what they had found to be the benefits of companionship of all kinds, and then extracted three independent clusters of answers.[32] The first was "instrumental and material help from another person." These are the prudential aspects of companionship or, to use the social science term where it is most appropriate, social support.[33] When I asked a sample of working-class men what friendship meant to them, they tended to say, "Someone you can count on when you need help."[34] Relatives are enlisted on many occasions for this kind of support; workmates help on the job; neighbors, who contribute least to happiness, are useful for minor help[35]—they supply the proverbial cup of sugar—as well as the occasional gossip. It is here the social exchange theory of companionship has its most literal application, for such help is thought to be reciprocal, each person keeping a more or less accurate ledger of who owes what to whom.

Of course parents help their children during their nonage, but do they continue to help them when the children are grown? And do children help their parents when they need help? The decline of the family (see chapter 7) suggests that this help ceases when the children are on their own, and the help is never returned, not even when the parents are old and infirm. As it turns out, this version of family decline is partly wrong. In the early 1990s, 30 to 40 percent of American parents in their fifties helped their children as needed, about a third of the middle-aged children helped their parents with household chores, and about 10 percent of the children helped them financially as well. In fact, "family members are the most important source of help for older people."[36]

THE EVOLUTIONARY BASIS OF COMPANIONSHIP

People are made for companionship and group living. Before entering on the evolutionary argument, I want to suggest a caveat: the fact that primates live in troops and reveal instinctual bonding behavior does not prove that humans are under a similar influence. For one thing, some monkeys, like the baboons, live in matriarchal societies composed entirely of adult females and their young; the males are out in the bush and return only for intermittent mating.[37] Evolutionary accounts are more persuasive when supplemented by two additional kinds of evidence: (1) studies of human twins that suggest the force of common genetic inheritances, and (2) discovery of the genes and hormones governing bonding behavior: when the genes are present the behavior occurs; when absent, it does not. Fortunately, where bonding is concerned, sometimes all three of these kinds of evidence exist.

As mentioned in chapter 3, all primates live in groups and suffer pain when separated from their groups, especially from their kin. Isolation is painful: "Rhesus monkeys, like other higher primates, are intensely affected by their [social] environments — an isolated individual will repeatedly pull a lever with no reward other than the glimpse of another monkey."[38] Bonding starts as family cohesion. In most primate troops, not only is there good maternal care of offspring but also, at least among our nearest relatives, the chimpanzees (but not gorillas), fathers often reveal their "genetic investment" by parenting behavior. Among some subspecies, females other than the mothers (called aunts — without the genetic connection — by their observers) seek and are usually allowed to fondle the offspring of a mother in the troop, sometimes serving as baby-sitters.[39] Thus, the "selfish gene" favors both nuclear family bonding and an extended family or community bonding.[40]

Supplementary evidence that this pattern is not wholly learned by humans but is, indeed, genetic comes from a study of social support that adds twin studies to the primate bonding studies. In these, it was found that "relations with family members were influenced by both heredity and family environment, but heredity accounted for *all* twin resemblances with respect to *all* forms of social support." Moreover, "a measure of social integration, based on number of friends, frequency of contact with them, and attendance at meetings of clubs and other organizations, was under the strongest genetic influence of all" even though these data were least influenced by subjective perceptions.[41]

The hormonal supplements mentioned above make the case for physiological influences stronger. As mentioned in chapter 3, affiliation has a biochemical base (oxytocin)—and so does cooperation. At least some research has "found that players [who were administered] librium, in contrast to those with placebos, scored higher on prisoner's dilemma games because they were more relaxed" and hence more cooperative.[42] Furthermore, social discord and isolation incur the stress-response, which over the long term impairs sexual activity, growth, and tissue repair (see chapter 3).[43] Conventional explanations of family bonding relying on the prolonged helplessness of offspring and the noncyclical sexual drive in humans are also important.

Finding companionship, then, contributes to happiness because it is a genetically programmed behavior which we violate at risk of pain and deteriorating functioning: the blood chemistry of affiliation and cooperation is congenial to our physiological constitution. The alternative, the fight or flight response, may or may not be the default constellation of the body, but it leads to all the illnesses associated with chronic stress-response (see chapter 3).

ATTACHMENT AND LOSS

If humans learned attachment behavior in childhood they might be miserable when the attachments were broken, whether or not close infant–mother relations were programmed by evolution. The theory would then say that as adults we are made unhappy by separation because it was a learned human disposition. The evidence of innate bonding between parents and offspring, however, is reinforced by primate studies. When separated from their mothers at an early age, infant monkeys behave like human infants. Martin Reite and his associates examined the influence of ten days of maternal separation on behavior and physiology in eight social, group-living pigtailed macaque monkey infants. As in human studies, maternal deprivation led to symptoms of depression in the infants: slowness of movement, decreases in play, and "assumptions of a characteristic slouched posture, sad facial expression, . . . decreases in heart rate and body temperature, sleep disturbances, and changes in EEG."[44]

This and other primate studies reinforce Bowlby's theory of attachment and loss, stemming from the need of infant for mother. The original theory followed from observation of the sickening and death of infants when their primary caregiver departed, especially in institutional settings. From an elaboration of these observations, Bowlby devised a general theory of the need for attachments in human life and the suffering caused by loss of these attachments. Bowlby claims that "attachment behavior in adult life is a straightforward continuation of attachment behavior in childhood . . . [and that] no form of behavior is accompanied by stronger feelings than is attachment behavior. The figures towards whom it is directed are loved and their advent is greeted with joy."[45] There is enough research on the attachment and loss theory to lead us to believe that one reason family and friends are sources of happiness is that they derive support from early attachments which were nurturant and satisfying.[46] In my opinion, the devaluation of the child in contemporary advanced societies (see chapter 3) is a direct cause of the rise of depression in these societies. Brown and Harris agree: "Loss and disappointment are the central features of most events bringing about clinical depression."[47]

RELIEF OF LONELINESS

The case for a companionship deficit would be stronger if there were evidence that many people actually felt lonely in the United States and other advanced countries suffering from unhappiness and depression. As it happens, there is such evidence: about a quarter of a national U.S. sample (26 percent) reported that they were lonely—about the same as the Germans and the French—and more than half (54 percent) of the French say that they have suffered from loneliness at some time. Some of the causes of loneliness can be inferred from the demographics: the poor suffer more than the middle classes, women more than men, and, of course, those who move are more lonely than those who remain in the same neighborhood for a long time.[48] Whether the anonymity of big cities[49] is worse than the isolation of farm areas is uncertain, but—communitarians please note—loneliness seems to be least often experienced in suburbs of big cities, rather than in villages beloved of small communities advocates.[50]

But, demographics aside, loneliness has a more specific and subjective cause: A study based on reports of all social encounters lasting more than ten minutes found that the absence of intimacy was the strongest determinant of loneliness.[51] It is the lack of someone to confide in and with whom to share one's feelings and thoughts that is experienced as loneliness.[52] These are not momentary episodic symptoms, for loneliness has been found to be fairly stable over periods of several months.[53] Studies of retailing also find quite a few lonely people,[54] and anecdotal evidence suggests that people relieve their loneliness by seeking the social encounters involved in shopping, even in supermarkets (but see chapter 10).

Is loneliness increasing? If the category "interpersonal problems" in Joseph Veroff et al.'s study (1981) includes loneliness, one sees a sharp increase in loneliness between 1957 (3 percent) and 1976 (13 percent).[55] And in surveying the prospects for mental health across the world, the authors of a study for the World Health Organization expressed their fears in this fashion: "Traditional protective mechanisms of social groups are breaking down, and many people are exposed to the unsettling effects of uprooting, family disintegration, and social isolation; the prevalence of depressive disorders arising as a response to stressful psychosocial factors is likely to increase."[56] This increase fits well into the pattern of declining family and neighborhood visiting over the past quarter century (see chapter 7).

THE NEED FOR AFFILIATION

There is a cognitive analog to the evolutionary biological sources of companionship, one that is often stated as a need for meaning in one's life. The absence of meaning tends to be expressed as cynicism and has been found to be associated with unhappiness.[57] Usually, too, this phrase refers to religion or ideology, but I think people are more likely to find meaning in persons for whom they care, chiefly, people in whom they can confide. The notion of a lineal family in which grandparents watch over their descendants with pride and anxiety is one elaboration of this idea (Tocqueville found such families sadly absent in America), while Joseph Schumpeter's fear that capital accumulation would dry up without a family to inherit wealth is the capitalist version.

More conventionally, there is another approach that is based on projective measures of motivation. The motive of interest here, the need for affiliation, may or may not rely on either evolutionary or childhood experience. It is measured by tests showing a tendency to see ambiguous situations in terms of the relationships among people.[58] And it is defined as "concern . . . over establishing, maintaining, or restoring a positive affective relationship with another person(s) [and is] illustrated by themes of friendship threatened, lost, or won."[59] Unlike the evolutionary and the attachment theories, theories of the various psychological needs (including, in addition to the need for affiliation, the need for achievement and the need for power) vary greatly among individuals and cultures, giving us a possible handle on family and especially friendship problems in contemporary market democracies. Because a need can represent a response to either a deficit (as David McClelland seems to think) or a desire for more of what one already has and because the need for affiliation is positively and quite strongly related to happiness,[60] one may infer that it represents either an innate or a learned taste whose satisfaction is associated with and reinforced by happiness. Have market democracies subordinated the need for affiliation to, say, the needs for achievement and power? or, alternatively, have they made the need for affiliation greater because of their overemphasis on the needs for power and achievement?

Although McClelland has succeeded in using his theory of the need for achievement actually to change productive behavior in India,[61] the scholarly world has generally been skeptical of his projective measures of needs, especially historical measures based on content analysis of children's stories, hymns, folk tales, and texts or even nonprint artifacts.[62] In spite of these doubts, I find McClelland's hydraulic equilibrium theory of three main needs interesting: the three needs, he says, are in such balance that when a society overemphasizes achievement and power, people want more emphasis on family and friends, and the need for affiliation rises. McClelland found some evidence for his theories[63] but others have not. When themes of power and achievement increased in American short stories between 1901 and 1960, there was no change in their themes of affiliation; when themes of achievement in Egyptian stories and folk tales increased, themes of affiliation did not change.[64] Nevertheless, the sketchy data above on a possible rise in Americans' loneliness and unhappiness about interpersonal problems and the evidence of greatly reduced neighboring and visiting of parents and relatives (see chapter 7) leave open the possibility that their emphasis on achievement, wealth, and power has increased their desire for, as the postmaterialists say, "a more friendly and less impersonal world," that is, for affiliation. This theory, then, adds the satisfaction of a need for affiliation as a supplement to, or substitute for, such other needs as achievement and power.[65]

THE LACK OF DEMAND FOR FRIENDS

Needs and wants (or demands) are different. Is there a demand for more friends? Not really. When, in the early 1970s, Angus Campbell and his associates asked people about their interest in making new friends, the answers were ambiguous. Although the surveys of the early 1970s found that those with the most friends were the most satisfied with their lives and that a large majority expressed some interest in making new friends, the urgency of this desire was minimal: only one-half of one percent said they were "very interested." As might be expected, those who had the fewest friends were the most likely to be "very interested"; those with the most friends were the most likely to show only a modest interest in making new friends.[66] This pattern suggests the causal influence of individual differences, of personality, and, as mentioned in chapter 3, extroversion has been found to be both directly associated with general cheerfulness and also productive of friendships that add to a person's happiness[67] (although extroverts are also happier than introverts when they are all by themselves). It is the introverted, the socially awkward, and those for whom friendship is a problem who would benefit from any institutional or cultural pattern that changes priorities among commodities and friends.

Whatever else may be said about the popular demand for friendship, it does not represent a demand for affiliation comparable to the demand for more income and more commodities. Although having a lot of friends contributes to a sense of well-being, demand for new friendships more closely resembles the demand for replacing a car or a refrigerator than the more elastic demand for other commodities. This view is reinforced by studies of depression. Among the depressed, it is the loss of a friend that serves as a "provoking agent" for the onset of the illness, rather than the unacknowledged pain of general absence of friends. Adaptation is the key. If people can adapt to the chronic absence of their arms and legs—as they do[68]—they will also adapt to absence of friendship, and it is this adaptation that accounts for the lack of demand by the lonely for friends. But, as with the elderly, this adaptation may have a hidden cost, for "the presence of a familiar person lowers blood pressure under stress, [and] . . . people whose heart rates rise more in [certain] experiments have high blood pressure two to 15 years later, *whether or not they acknowledge being under stress or feeling intense emotion.*"[69]

Companionship is almost a condition of happiness; there is considerable loneliness in advanced societies, and families are disintegrating; the loss of a friend or other human attachment is sharply painful; it seems that the need for closer companionship is apparent. But the demand for more companionship is weak while the demand for commodities is strong. Ask the sorcerers of Dobu what they want and, even with the help of their shamans' most rational calculations, they will not tell you relief from sorcery.

What Will Companionship Cost Us?

One may think of all of life as a set of tradeoffs, if only trading one opportunity for another. This section is about the costs of trading income for family solidarity and friends. First, I need to show in a little more detail the relative contributions of money and companionship to SWB.

RELATIVE CONTRIBUTIONS TO HAPPINESS OF INCOME AND COMPANIONSHIP

Recall that the comparison in chapter 2 of the contributions to happiness made by people's satisfaction with five domains of life (marriage, job, finances, friends, and the place one lives) showed that people's satisfaction with their marriages made by far the greatest contribution to SWB: .47 compared to about .29 for finances and most of the other kinds of satisfaction.[70] That is, compared to one's satisfaction with, say, one's finances, if one is happy with one's marriage one is much more likely to be happy with one's life.

The two major studies (1976) of the quality of life in the United States cited previously establish the greater contribution to well-being of companionship compared to income. For example, Andrews and Withey's "family index" (feelings about one's children, one's spouse, and one's marriage [r = .19] made a stronger contribution to life satisfaction than "the money index" (feelings about one's family income and, confounding meanings I would like to keep separate, with feelings on "how secure you are financially" [r = .15]). This hedonic dominance of people over money is reinforced by adding (such summing is legitimate with beta scores) the fifth largest contributor (.11) to life satisfaction, "the things you do with your family"; with this addition, the balance tips even more toward family.[71]

In Campbell and associates' study *The Quality of American Life,* satisfaction with "family life" (r^2 = .28), with marriage (.16), and with friends (.13) seems to dominate satisfaction with "standard of living" (.23) and with "savings and investments" (.15). Again, one gets the impression that feelings about people contribute more to SWB than feelings about money, whether spent or saved.[72] To repeat, the main sources of enjoyment do not pass through the market.[73]

In turning to depression, I want to make a different point: the interaction of income and companionship in precipitating or relieving distress. We know that poverty leads to circumstances that promote unhappiness and depression, but above the poverty line this interaction is less evident. I will illustrate this relationship with the evidence at hand (table 5.2): the immediate provoking agents of depression in Camberwell, a suburb of London (leaving out of account the dispositions that made these events so traumatic). Are these troubles economic or interpersonal? The list is helpful because it shows so plainly and painfully the interaction of human relations and their economic contexts. Housing is a frequent problem and so are jobs, as I shall note in chapter 9, but who knows why the depressed housewife had to leave her laundry job? was *she* delinquent? Overall, however, family problems seem central (husband coming home or released from prison or loses his job because of a row at the plant; must take care of son; daughter takes an overdose). Can these family problems be blamed on relative lack of income? Not entirely because, at least above the poverty line, family problems are not closely related to income[74]—although poverty does increase the likelihood of divorce.[75] (As an aside, note that if the insecurity created by markets is to be blamed for these precipitating events, then the market's contribution to the decline of poverty must be credited—even though poverty in poorer societies is not an important source of depression.)[76] Because of these complexities, I focus on the sources of happiness/unhappiness in the studies of quality of life.

There is a caveat to any sweeping claim that the pursuit of money does not make people happy. Although it seems often to be the case that people pursue

Table 5.2. Household Events Precipitating Depression in a London Working-Class Sample

- Given notice must leave long-term laundry job
- Long-estranged husband coming home to live
- Leaving job in order to look after son
- Arrangement about new flat falling through
- Threatened with eviction by landlord
- Court appearance for not paying rent (husband out of work)
- Because of housing, must have unwanted abortion
- Husband sent to prison
- Move to escape difficult neighbors
- Left alone after move of daughter
- Notice to quit flat
- Husband released from prison
- Overdose by school-age daughter
- Husband row at work, lost his job

Source: George W. Brown and Tirril Harris. 1978. *Social Origins of Depression: A Study of Psychiatric Disorder in Women.* London: Tavistock, 160.

money as compensation for something they want more of but cannot get,[77] it can be shown that material gain for some nonpoor people is a genuine source of SWB; for them (only 6 percent of a national sample), a higher level of income is indeed the source of well-being.[78] Moreover, for some people the pursuit of money is greatly satisfying. It gives them a life purpose and, indeed, a sense of meaning to their lives. But in general materialists of this kind are not a happy lot (see chapter 8).[79] Because people's goals differ, one should attend to the fit of personality dispositions and the environmental goals of a society such that there is a better Personality/Environment Fit.[80] But what is a good P/E Fit when what people think makes them happy does not have that effect, and what does make them happy is alien to their culturally shaped desires? Are they not like the people of Dobu, who are miserable because their belief in sorcery poisons their relations with each other and yet are unable to see the sources of their unhappiness?[81]

POSSESSING SOMETHING AND BEING SATISFIED WITH SOMETHING

More detail on the predictive power of sheer numbers of friends is offered in table 5.3, which elaborates the relationship to SWB mentioned above. These findings are confirmed and slightly modified by a later study which also

Table 5.3. Prediction of SWB *by Various Resources*

	Eta coefficients	Beta coefficients #1	Betacoefficients #2
Family income	.17	.19	—
Personal income	.07	.04	—
Number of friends	.27	—	.24*

*The table deals separately with the contributions of "achieved resources" and "other current resources." The Eta coefficients are in an array that includes both of these kinds of resources and such "ascribed resources" as intelligence, health, and attractiveness (age controlled). The amount of variance explained by number of friends, time pressure, and religious faith (13.5%) is more than five times the variance explained by family income *and* personal income *and* education (2.5%).

Source: Angus Campbell, Philip E. Converse, and Willard L. Rodgers. 1976. *The Quality of American Life: Perceptions, Evaluations, and Satisfactions.* New York: Russell Sage, 368.

found that happiness was a close correlate of number of friends and frequency of seeing them.[82]

Now I wish to draw attention to the difference in relationships between being satisfied with something (money or friends) and possessing that something. Satisfaction with income is minimally related to actual income and contributes much more to SWB than does actual income.[83] This is possible because actual level of income and satisfaction with one's income are two very different things. A person with a low income can be quite satisfied with what he or she is paid, whereas a person with a much higher income is not. On the other hand, satisfaction with friends contributes only a little more to SWB than does the number of friends one has (or claims to have—see above). For friendship, satisfaction follows possession rather closely.

From these differences between money and friends in their relations to well-being, I draw two important inferences. As Easterlin argued,[84] increasing income for everyone has little effect on SWB because income satisfaction is not closely related to actual income. But with friendship, satisfaction from having and being with friends *is* closely related, so that increasing friendship would have a substantial effect on SWB. Think of this difference in terms of the hedonic treadmill. In the economic relationship, "*Here,* you see," said the Red Queen, "it takes all the running you can do to stay in the same place." But the Red Queen does not rule over friendship. Because one's attitudes toward one's friends are closely linked to the number of friends one has, if one takes the trouble to gain a friend, one is very likely to find that one's new friendship contributes to one's life satisfaction. The friendship route is less invidious, less vulnerable to escalation of standards to match any improvement of circumstances, and therefore farther from that utilitarian hell, the hedonic treadmill.[85]

THE VALUE OF COMPANIONSHIP AND THE VALUE OF "A COMFORTABLE LIFE"

What we call values are ambiguous constructs of the desired, what one wants, and the desirable, what one thinks one ought to want. Milton Rokeach has developed a set of measures of eighteen "terminal values"—for example, such end states as "a world at peace," "wisdom," and "a comfortable life (a prosperous life)"—and a comparable set of eighteen "instrumental values" or qualities of persons—for example, "honest (sincere, truthful)," "responsible (dependable, reliable)" and "ambitious (hard-working, aspiring)." I want to use these data for two purposes: first, to compare the terminal values with the relevant contributions to well-being set out above, and, second, to see if the instrumental values are such as to lead to the terminal values people claim to have. Is there a clue here to our ambivalence about the values of money and of companionship? The relevant terminal values (whose ranking is quite stable) are given in table 5.4.

Although the items in table 5.4 do not serve my purpose very well ("family security" confounds family felicity and economic security), the relative ordering of these three values (1981) is parallel to the ordering in the quality of life studies a few years earlier: family, prosperity or material well-being, and friendship—in that order. Note, too, how much lower in this materialistic society is the value of "a comfortable life" compared to the higher ranking values (not shown): "a world at peace," #2; "freedom (independence, free choice)," #3; and "self-respect (self-esteem)," #4. Again notice how easy it is for people to rank their preferences without the aid of a common currency. (How much material comfort would they trade for peace, freedom, and self-respect?) Is it unfair to say that what economists call value is only a modest portion of what we think of as value, even without including moral value or what Kant says is beyond value, dignity.

The three most highly ranked instrumental values (in the two years for which I have measures) are presented in table 5.5. "Ambition" trumps "loving" by a very wide margin, and both are outranked by "honesty" and "responsibility". Again, we might understand the low demand for more friends by the kind of values prized: apparently, a "loving (tender, affectionate)" quality is not the kind of quality people consider especially valuable in others—or themselves.

Note the disharmony between ends and means in tables 5.4 and 5.5 taken together. Among end states, "taking care of loved ones" comes first, but the

Table 5.4. Relative Ranking of Material Values and Companionship Values, 1968–81

	1968	1971	1974	1981
Family security (taking care of loved ones)	2	2	1	1
A comfortable life (a prosperous life)	9	13	8	8
True friendship (close companionship)	11	10	9	10

Source: Milton Rokeach and Sandra J. Ball-Rokeach. 1989. "Stability and Change in American Value Priorities, 1968–1981." *American Psychologist* 44: 775–84 at 778.

Table 5.5. Relative Ranking of Ambition, Loving, and Self-sufficiency

Value	1968	1971
Ambition (Hard-working, aspiring)	2	3
Loving (Affectionate, tender)	11	8
Independent (Self-reliant, self-sufficient)	13	15

Source: Milton Rokeach. 1978. "Change and Stability in American Value Systems: 1968–1971." *Public Opinion Quarterly* 38: 222–38 at 226–27.

qualities that make families successful (loving) are not highly valued. On the other hand, wealth (a comfortable life) is ranked quite low, but the qualities required to attain that wealth (ambition and hard work) are ranked very high. Do we value wealth because, in the popular mind, it seems to be the product of ambition and hard work — which, as character, is the truly valuable end state? In contrast, apparently we do not value hard work because it promises wealth. Much literature and the relative ranking of wealth and hard work suggest that we value qualities of persons, including ourselves, more than their (our) circumstances.[86] Where the values of ends and means are out of harmony, change is more likely. But if we value the quality of persons more than material wealth and "ambition" dominates "loving," we are likely to move in the wrong direction.

Individual Choices Between Income and Companionship

What happens when individuals must choose between companionship and income? That choice need not be conscious or reflect rational calculation. Does a person ask, "Am I lonelier than I am poor?" From the lives of the depressed, one gets a sense that the choices are guided more by the adventitious arrival of opportunities for the relief of loneliness or of poverty than by consulting a latent preference schedule. The supply side, so to speak, guides the choices. Or, to change the metaphor, where the road forks, "The Road Not Taken," as I have called the companionship road,[87] is not so much rejected as overlooked, passed by on the busy highway of modern urban life. Just as gemeinschaft makes clear all turnings to and from companionship but may not give signposts for Wall Street or, as the British say, the High Street (where all the shops are), so, in contrast, our current market democracies have manuals and schools and multiple signs for maximizing wealth but little or none for increasing the benefits of companionship.

This biased information network is especially characteristic of the workplace. For one thing, the market offers better information on pay than on congenial workmates and generally makes income more salient than friendship. Thus, people applying for jobs are guided by pay schedules, but people appraising jobs they currently hold give more weight to the congeniality of their workmates.[88] Under these circumstances, people in the labor market will tend to fall back on their interpretation of cultural values[89] like those revealed in Rokeach's study above ("a comfortable life" dominates "true friendship"). They will probably base their job selections, to the extent they are able, on higher pay rather than on more congenial friendships[90] even though giving up friendship at work for higher pay probably means that people will achieve less overall life satisfaction. Furthermore, the satisfaction achieved through higher income may be more chimerical than that gained through friendship, since, as mentioned, actual pay is less closely related to income satisfaction than actual number of friends is to friendship satisfaction.[91]

Even though price is not usually the most important dimension in economic choice,[92] the common measuring rod of money helps the harried housewife in the supermarket while the constraints of her budget polices her exuberant desires. In choosing between time invested in companionship or in income producing activities, a financial budget limits (or stimulates) only one side of the choice. The other side is more like a career or marital choice, in which most of the consequences are hidden from view. In these limited senses, the market frustrates the satisfaction of human wants.

In addition to problems of biased information and the influences of common measurements and constraining budgets, a further problem emerges: How to think about a choice that may be classified as money versus companionship but is actually one between money and Tom or Dick or Harry? In asking how much companionship we would exchange for how much income, we are often asking people to generalize about particularistic goods. Any one of us might ask ourselves if we are willing to give up our regular Thursday evening poker game in order to earn a little extra money by giving an extra lecture. We have to make these choices, and we do make them all the time, but the more we think about them, the harder they are. As "cognitive misers," we will probably do what George Katona says we do with most purely economic choices: we follow habit.[93]

THE MARKET'S INDIFFERENCE TO PERSONS

The search for our lost companions is further frustrated by the market's indifference to persons. This indifference, I think, is not due to the impersonality of transactions, the treatment, as Frank Knight said, of others as "slot machines."[94] Neither do I think it is the popular (and Marxist) reason that markets evaluate people by the "measuring rod" of money (Arthur Pigou's term), or at least that is true only in a derivative sense. The reason for this indifference to persons, I believe, is that the market is an ecology with properties very like a Darwinian system that is indifferent to individuals but is designed, if that is the word, to protect species. Just as in nature the system may be profligate of individuals, arranged, for example, so that the sacrifice of a third of the individual birds in winter will preserve the gene pools of those best fitted to survive and propagate in that wintry environment, so the market is arranged in such a way that many individuals or firms may be lost but the fittest will survive. This is neither cruel nor compassionate toward individuals; it is merely indifferent. Like nature, the market is a winnowing process. This, of course, creates difficulties if people in a market economy want to shift their priorities from money to persons.

One of these difficulties is the substitutability of each individual for other comparable individuals in the market. Without much evidence, this substitutability has been said to lead to the neutralization of personality, to "moral neutralization."[95] I know of no evidence showing more amorality in market than in household or command economies, and some evidence going the other way, but there is abundant, if casual, evidence that individual members of the labor force are treated as hands rather than persons—at least until they become in some way uniquely valuable to the production process. Moreover, marginal analysis, at least in economics and very likely in the market, too, treats the last hired as representative of the set of workers to which he or she may belong, partly because pay schedules are classified by sets in which the individual's characteristics are lost.

Another cause for indifference to individuals is the substitutability of capital, or land and resources, for individuals. This familiar criticism often leads to the assumption that, if workers and things are substitutable for each other, the worker is no more than a thing. But since substitution of this kind has occurred in command economies (which, by definition, are guided by human purposes in a sense not true of market economies) as much as in market economies, one must look to technology rather than to the market for the more fundamental sources of this machine-for-man substitution.

We come now, third, to a consideration that may have more to do with market economics than with markets. Marshall reports that economists are concerned with the "desires, aspirations and other affections of human nature. . . . But the economist studies mental states rather through their manifestations than in themselves, and if he finds they afford evenly balanced incentives to action, he treats them *prima facie* as for his purpose equal."[96] Thus, "desires, aspirations and other affections of human nature" are dropped from sight and represent only a particular set of forces in a larger field of forces. Because ecologies are, indeed, fields of forces, niches, and balances, it is not necessary to ask what it is in people that helps to explain why they behave the way they do. In the familiar psychological formula, we see S → O → R (stimulus → organism → response) without any content to the O. Companionship without attending to the organism or person is not possible.

FRIENDSHIP AND INCOME AS COMPLEMENTARY GOODS

The reasons friendship is not a market commodity are so obvious that they will not bear repeating.[97] When friendship and income are complementary, not substitute, goods, it would seem to be a matter of indifference whether one pursues satisfaction in the friendship market (receiving income along the way) or income in the labor market (receiving an incidental bonus of friendship). But common sense and research both suggest that the world is not so constructed. Why?

The reason is that making friends in order to make more money and making money in order to "buy" friendship both spoil the friendship relation. Friendship as exploitation does not work: "People who simply try to maximize their rewards are liable to lose their friends; socially isolated adolescents have been found to have such childish ideas, and fail to realize that friendship involves loyalty, commitment and concern for the other."[98] Making friends in order to make more money instrumentalizes the friendships; it is a form of interpersonal relations, called Machiavellianism in some studies, which leads to many acquaintances but few friends.[99] And Machiavellianism tends to lower life satisfaction.[100] On the other hand, making money in order to buy friendships often inhibits the friendship relation because of the nature of the proposed exchange. Only friendly acts and feelings create enduring friendships. They cannot be bought with any other currency.[101] Thus, complementarity does not relieve us of concern over the incapacity of the market to facilitate an exchange of commodities for companionship and vice versa.

INVESTING IN COMPANIONSHIP OR INCOME

A further general property of the two goods friendship and money is said to influence the nature of choices between them: the comparative time schedules of their yielding up their utilities. How long does it take to get the expected yield from the investment? Although we cringe at applying this calculating language to friendship, we nevertheless do assess our friends, although with less attention to "value for money" and less concern for whose ledger shows a credit and whose a debit. It is for reasons like this that moral philosophers claim (a little too glibly) that the question of justice does not arise among friends.

Maturation of an Investment

Among the few scholars who have compared investments in friendship and in money-denominated goods, there seems to be a consensus that it takes longer for friendship to pay off than it does for money investments to pay off.[102] I disagree. Consider the timing of payoffs for initiating a friendship. One invests time and effort in an encounter only if it offers immediate rewards—if you do not like a person, the relationship will not continue. Norman Bradburn and David Caplovitz's early study showed that "making a new friend" added substantially to "positive affect."[103] As for the argument that old friends are the best, it seems that it takes only a short time before new friends receive the same intimacies as old friends, are as available for social support, and are considered as close.[104] In the case of marriage, most studies report that, at least for women, the hedonic return of the marriage is at its greatest in the honeymoon period and usually lasts until the children come, when marital felicity dips until they leave the nest. I do not think that the delay or waiting period explains the relative failure of investment in companionship.

There is more to investment than time and effort: (a) one invests self-esteem by risking immediate rebuff, but, if successful, one gains the immediate gratification of being liked; and (b) conquering one's shyness and inhibitions is painful, but the very conquest of inhibitions is an immediate reward. Thus, we encounter situations in which, strangely, costs may at the same time themselves be benefits or are succeeded promptly by benefits. The strange behavior of costs in friendship is revealed in a study by R. B. Hays showing that although there were more rewards in close relationships (compared to those among acquaintances), "the best predictor was rewards *plus* costs, perhaps because close friends do a lot for each other."[105] I know of no money investments in which costs are treated as part of the profits.

For these reasons and the general argument of this chapter, I conclude that investment in companionship is not so costly as alleged and, compared to money, is more likely to be rewarding in this low friendship/high income society. There is a further supportive argument, one that challenges the general thesis of declining marginal utility. Instead of the declining marginal utility common among market goods, for a considerable period of time companionship usually has a rising marginal utility. This is so because companionship is a learned skill which, like other skills, enhances enjoyment as the skills are mastered. If there is an adaptive learning process of this kind, every new friend makes the process of companionship easier. But of course at some point, as other interests become salient, the general law of diminishing marginal returns will set in. Yet because so many of life's other rewards involve the company of people, satiation with companionship comes later than satiation with commodities.

6

Searching for Lost Companions in Market Democracies

> *Through [market] anonymity the interests of each party acquire an unmerciful matter-of-factness; and the intellectually calculating egoisms of both parties need not fear any deflection because of the imponderables of personal relationships.*
> — *Georg Simmel*

How and why has companionship changed in the United States in the postwar period? If the unhappiness and depression and other forms of malaise described in chapter 2 are caused by failures of companionship, then it must be that the health-giving qualities of companionship have also declined in some manner during this period. It is not easy, but I think I can show just such a decline, at least for many of the ways in which companionship is normally expressed.

I want to link this analysis to the ideas of gemeinschaft and gesellschaft mentioned in the previous chapter and give them greater specificity. Like Sir Henry Maine, Tönnies thought the transition from the one to the other was inevitable. I call the change described by Maine, Tönnies, and Weber the first bend in companionship, to be compared at the end with a possible reverse bend back to some elements of gemeinschaft — made less promising in the late 1990s by the Fall of the collectivist, mostly Asian, pattern.

Like similar concepts, companionship has two important dimensions:

extension, represented here by the data on visiting patterns, and intension, the warmth and intimacy of a relation. The main empirical analysis is devoted to the extension dimension, in which I will analyze the pattern of affiliation in the United States over the past twenty-five years. This will be supplemented by an effort to see if it is urbanism, rather than (or in addition to) the commercialization of society, that accounts for changes in visiting patterns. These two sections include the main original findings of this chapter. Then I will examine the intensional dimension, the issue of the warmth and intimacy of the relationships—well explored in psychological experiments but lacking the historical data that I would find useful. As it happens, a remarkable historical experiment has taken place in many Asian collectivist societies to see whether the two great institutions, strong families and strong markets, are compatible. I explore the current outcome of this experiment as it unfolds at the end of the twentieth century.

Gemeinschaft and Gesellschaft: The First Bend in Companionship

Like "punctuated evolution," historical change seems, at least to post hoc observers, to have been marked by periods of rapid, momentous change, climacterics in the lives of societies. Sometimes these climacterics have been assigned to military victories: Thermopylae, defeat of the Turks at Vienna, defeat of Philip's armada. More cogently, the turning points have been represented as changes in the way we think or in what we believe: in the West these are, epigrammatically, the Renaissance, the Reformation, the Industrial Revolution, and, less bounded by time, the Scientific Revolution. As Alfred North Whitehead points out, the Reformation was a local phenomenon, but the rise of science since, say, Newton and Galileo has shaken the foundations of thought and action around the world. And, of course, the Industrial Revolution and its sequelae in postindustrial society are still transforming the way we live.

Many of these changes altered the way people relate to each other, but there came a point in the mid nineteenth and early twentieth centuries when this matter of human relationship was seen as the crucial aspect of multiple and accelerating changes in society. Although Tocqueville, Auguste Comte, and Émile Durkheim were major interpreters of this change, I will focus on Maine, Tönnies, and Weber, who represent heralds of the triumph of economic relations over social relations. Speaking of an inevitable and benign tendency (rather than a sharp turn in history) among what we call advanced economies but which he called "progressive societies," Sir Henry Maine (1861) was the first:

> The movement of the progressive societies has been uniform in one respect. Through all its course it has been distinguished by the gradual dissolution of Family dependency and the growth of individual obligation in its place. The individual is steadily substituted for the family, as the unit of which civil laws take into account. . . . We seem to have steadily moved toward a phase of social order in which all these relations arise from the free agreement of Individuals. . . . If then we employ Status . . . to signify these personal conditions only, . . . we may say that the movement of the progressive societies has hitherto been a movement *from Status to Contract.*[1]

Some twenty-six years later, Ferdinand Tönnies, often citing Maine, developed an equally familiar contrast between traditional agricultural communities, gemeinschaft, and modern urban, capitalist societies, gesellschaft. This is explicitly a theory of human relations ("the relationship of human wills"), and it is equally a theory of inevitable change: "Wherever the urban culture blossoms and bears fruit, Gesellschaft appears as its indispensable organ."[2] Gemeinschaft is analogous to the family, but it extends from ties of blood (kinship) to ties of place (community) to friendship based most usually, said Tönnies, on common religion and common or related occupations. Anticipating our discussion on SWB, Tönnies says, "The ordinary human being . . . feels best and most cheerful if he is surrounded by his family and relatives. He is among his own (*chez soi*)."[3]

Gesellschaft, on the other hand, is industrial capitalist society. In gesellschaft, "everybody is by himself and isolated, and there exists a condition of tension against all others. . . . [People have a] negative attitude toward one another."[4] The tension of "the war of all against all" (he borrows Hobbes's phrase) is modified only by each person's need to maintain commercially profitable relations with others and by the conventions of society, never by any kind of fellow feeling.[5]

No friend of modernity, Max Weber also finds distressing the change in the way people associate with one another. Whereas formerly their associations were communal, "based on subjective feelings of parties that they belong to each other, that they are implicated in each others' total existence," human groups had become associative, resting on a "rationally motivated adjustment or interest or a similarly motivated agreement." For Weber, the problem for human comity is not so much the dominance of self-interest as the emphasis on rational calculation, a rationality that scorns spontaneous affections. The market, said Weber, is "no respecter of persons"—a good epigram for law (the law that Maine extolled), but a bad one for human companionship.[6]

Were Maine, Tönnies, and Weber right about the trends in our relations with each other: less frequent association, from affectionate to contractual relations, from warmth to coldness? And was Tönnies right about people, especially women, being happier when "surrounded by . . . family and relatives"?

Erosion of Family and Friendship in Postwar American Society

In 1976 it was said that consistent evidence "indicates that the prevalence of significant informal social relationships, networks, and supports has been declining over the last quarter century while people are increasingly calling on those same sources of support for help in dealing with personal problems."[7] That is partly right. Much of what follows is based on the changing visiting patterns among family members and friends. But readers will be quick to point out that instead of visiting each other, people now telephone each other or "visit" on the Internet. There is something to this criticism: average daily calls increased from 225 million in 1960 to 10,665 million in 1993 — of which a large but unknown proportion was business calls.[8] But, as we shall see, at the same time that people saw less of their neighbors and family, they continued to visit their friends at the same or even increasing levels of frequency. If, in the postwar period up to about 1994, people visited less with their families and neighbors because they substituted the telephone for visiting, why would they not have done so with their friends? Furthermore, communication among intimates relies substantially on nonverbal communication not conveyed by phone: "proximity, gaze, facial expressions, touch, and paralinguistic cues."[9] But I do not mean to brush aside this criticism of the data; it will have to remain unresolved.

There is another reason for the decline in visiting: the advent of television. By a wide margin, television watching increasingly (up to a plateau) absorbed the free time of the public during this period. As Robert Putnam has argued, television watching robbed the public of its civic culture, especially that aspect of it that involved joining and working in intermediate organizations that link the public to the polity.[10] For the same reasons and for the sheer logic of time budgets, one can assign considerable responsibility for the decline in private socializing to the ascendance of television — which is not thought to promote socializing but rather to take its place.[11]

FAMILIES AND FRIENDS

In gesellschaft, Tönnies said, people distrust each other. As we saw in chapter 2 (see fig. 2.6), increasingly they do, although this is contrary to the usual pattern of increasing trust along with economic development.[12] Over this period the young, marked by unprecedented increases in unhappiness and depression, increased their distrust more than others.[13] Furthermore, in response to the question, "Do you think most people would try to take advantage of you if they got a chance, or would they try to be fair?" there was a modest decline over this period (1972–94) in the belief that people would try to be fair: from 61 percent in the 1970s to 56 percent in the early 1990s. Declining interpersonal trust and increasing fear that others will take advantage of one portend an increasingly dismal social world. Are these symptoms of distrust influenced by rising urbanization—urban cynicism? No, at least not systematically; as may be seen in table A.6.1 (see Appendix to this chapter), distrust is influenced by poverty (which did not rise during most of this period) but not by urbanism.

VISITING PATTERNS AMONG NEIGHBORS, FAMILY, AND FRIENDS

Again drawing on the GSS historical data, one can analyze the record of visiting patterns among family members, neighbors, and friends—and the satisfactions derived therefrom. These visiting patterns tell us that Tönnies is partially right: we have certainly diminished our ties of community or place; ties of blood have, indeed, become weaker; but ties of interest and affection, that is, ties of friendship, do not seem to have weakened at all. Let us look at the evidence. The difference between these ascriptive and achieved forms of companionship is a puzzle which I seek to disentangle in chapter 7.

The GSS questions were, "How often do you spend a social evening with friends?. . . . With someone who lives in your neighborhood?" and so forth. Because trends sometimes reveal a bifurcation, changes in frequent visiting diverging from those reflecting infrequent visiting, both kinds of data will be reported. *Socializing* refers to visiting "almost every day" or "several times a week," and *isolation* or neglect means "several times a year" or "about once a year" or "never."[14]

Neighbors

Summarizing much data, one can say that visiting of neighbors has fairly sharply and continuously declined over the twenty-two-year period from 1972 to 1994, with socializing falling off and isolation increasing. Whether cause or effect or common response to something else, the decline in neighboring corresponds to a substantial decline in satisfaction with "the place where you live" (figs. 6.1 and 2.5). The falling off of neighboring has been much greater among women than among men, no doubt because the increased number of women with market work spend less time at home; sadly, they have had no compensating increase in such friendships as might be made at the office

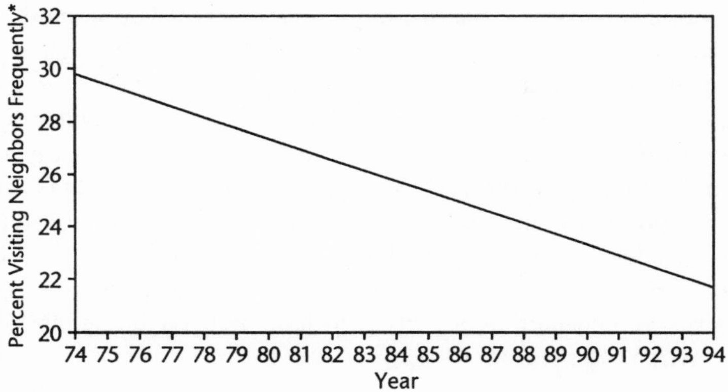

Figure 6.1. Frequent Visiting with Neighbors, 1974–94
Question: "How often do you spend a social evening with someone who lives in your neighborhood?" [Almost daily; a few times a week; several times a month; once a year; never.]
*"Frequently" = almost daily or several times a week
Source: General Social Survey (NORC).

or plant. Looking for sources of greater unhappiness and depression among women, one might start here.[15]

Parents

The increase in divorces by parents makes parental visiting a two-pronged affair, perhaps more easily accomplished by a phone call. And yet in the absence of a spouse, an older parent will want to see a departed child more often; thus parental visiting becomes more difficult as it becomes more urgent. From 1978 to about 1986 parental visiting increased, whereupon it declined (fig. 6.2), but the more serious and hurtful isolation (or neglect) increased monotonically over the period. The GSS also separately provides a comparison between people visiting their mothers in 1986 and 1994, a comparison that shows a clear decline in frequent visiting and an increase in isolation/neglect for this most recent eight-year period.[16] Much has been made of the economic protection of the elderly in the postwar period by Social Security and Medicare; would it be wrong to say that many of these protected elderly would give up some of what is called their standard of living for a visit or two from their grown children?

Relatives and Siblings

Visiting with relatives suggests the ties of an extended family, more characteristic of Eastern and southern Europe than of northwest Europe, espe-

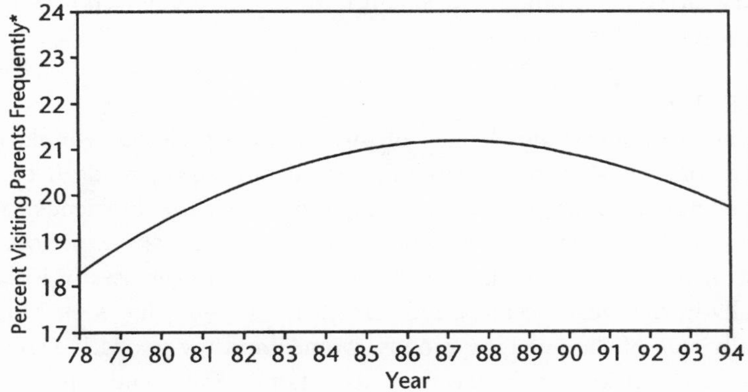

Figure 6.2. Frequent Visiting with Parents, 1978–94
Question: "How often do you spend an evening with your parents?" [Almost daily; a few times a week; several times a month; once a year; never.]
*"Frequently" = almost daily or several times a week
Source: General Social Survey (NORC).

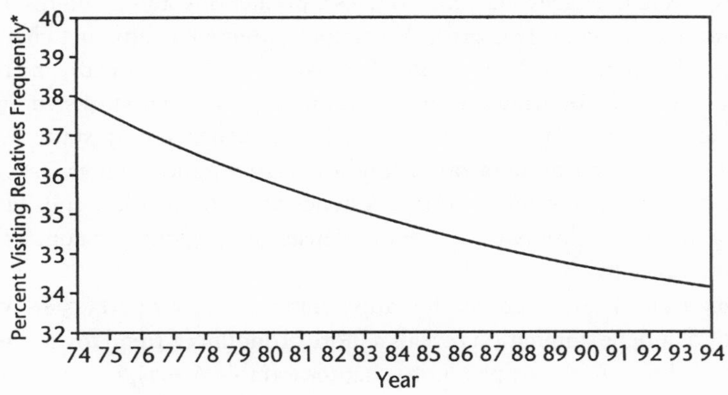

Figure 6.3. Frequent Visiting with Relatives, 1974–94
*"Frequently" = almost daily or several times a week
Question: "How often do you spend a social evening with relatives?" [Almost daily; a few times a week; several times a month; once a year; never.]

cially Britain. Lacking information on ethnicity, however, I note that over the twenty-year period 1974 to 1994 a very modest decline in visiting occurred, due largely to a falling off of socializing (fig. 6.3), especially by women, and a more pronounced increase in both men's and women's isolation from their relatives. These changes unfavorable to affiliation are more apparent among the young (less socializing and more isolation) than among other age groups.

(A brief analysis of visiting among siblings, which also declined, is presented in the Appendix to this chapter.)

Friends

The most surprising element of these visiting patterns, I think, is the resistance of friendships to these isolating and demoralizing trends. In contrast with the findings on neighbors and family visiting, visiting of friends has not declined but rather has (slightly) increased over the 1974–94 period, with modest increases in socializing and more substantial decreases in isolation, especially in the most recent period recorded, 1989–94 (fig. 6.4). This was especially true of the unhappy groups, women and the young.[17] Figure 6.5 reveals the sharp contrast between trends in family and friendship visiting in the general population, a contrast reflecting the low but significant correlation (+.08, $p < .001$) between these two types of interpersonal relations. We may assume, therefore, that we are not dealing principally with general dispositions whose influence would extend across family and friends.

To summarize these indigestible data: neighboring has the clearest and sharpest decline, suggesting that Tönnies's predictions about the decline of community of place were correct. Visiting of parents has little net change in 1978–94, but in the 1986–94 period there was a decline (especially in visiting mothers), a weak confirmation of the decline of ties of blood, depending on the period chosen. The decline of what Maine called family status is also modestly supported by data on visiting of relatives and siblings, especially among the young. And finally, the persistence of visiting with friends falsifies the idea that in gesellschaft "everybody refuses to everyone else contact with and admittance to his sphere."

As one scans the fitted curves, it is apparent that the later part (1986–94) of the period under examination reveals a more pronounced trend toward weakening social ties. In the Appendix to chapter 6 (table A.6.2), I summarize the pattern for this period for the general population with a record of which hypotheses are confirmed and add the concept of a cold society when both socializing declines and isolation increases. Only one of the hypotheses of a cold society is disconfirmed. But the record of confirmation for the specific groups that are most vulnerable to unhappiness and depression, women and the young, confirms the cold society hypothesis somewhat less successfully (see table A.6.3 in the Appendix).

If we recall that the period witnessed a substantial increase in level of education, which normally increases socializing behavior, an increase in household income, and a more modest increase in individual income—and increased income tends to reduce isolation (but apparently not for women)—the overall pattern suggests that in some respects the cold society hypothesis has merit.

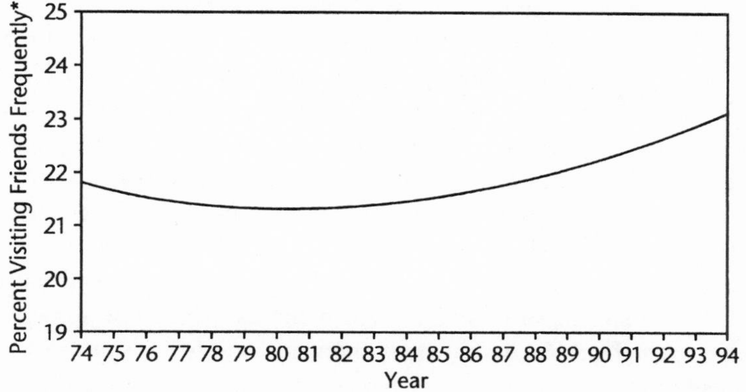

Figure 6.4. Frequent Visiting with Friends, 1974–94
Question: "How often do you spend a social evening with friends?" [Almost daily; a few times a week; several times a month; once a year; never.]
*"Frequently" = almost daily or several times a week
Source: General Social Survey (NORC).

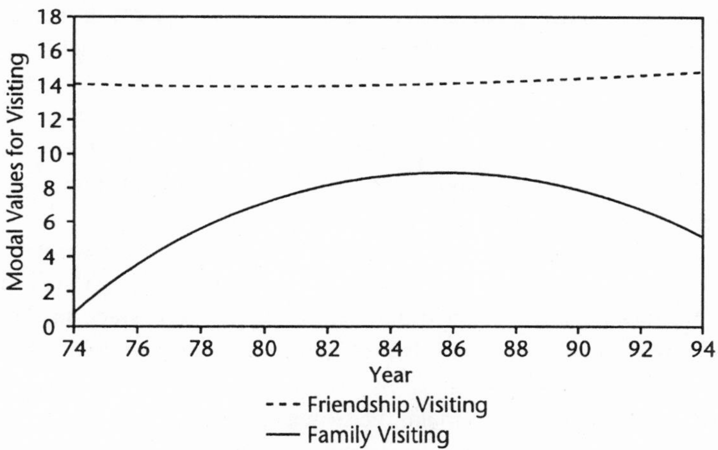

Figure 6.5. Visiting with Family and Friends (Modal Values), 1974–94
Source: General Social Survey (NORC).

SATISFACTION WITH FAMILY RELATIONS AND FRIENDSHIPS

Interpreting of the satisfaction data presents problems: Should one expect growing satisfaction from family and friends on the grounds that what is increasingly scarce is more highly prized? This might represent the pattern that Christopher Lasch has called "Haven in a Heartless World."[18] Or should one expect declining satisfaction because, in an impersonal world, opportunities for affiliation are inevitably insufficient? In that kind of a world, people's genetically given bonding instinct is frustrated (see hydraulic theory in chapter 5). Or, again, should one expect that adaptation to the norms of the time would inoculate one against disappointment with one's associational life, suggesting constant satisfaction no matter what happens to friendship and family relations—possibly with the result that one is unhappy without knowing why?

Given rising divorce rates, it comes as no surprise that people are decreasingly happy with their marriages (see chapter 2, fig. 2.2). Given, too, that pleasure in family life is the most important contribution to happiness and life satisfaction, here lies a major explanation of Americans' current and rising sorrow. Widely shared sorrows have social causes. Is this one somehow attributable to the fact that two breadwinners in a family is a source of strain? Society has ceased relegating women to the role of housewife? Good, but does this act of justice make us, especially women, unhappy and depressed (see chapter 9)? The matter is beyond our capacity to resolve, but as a caution, note that in some less advanced societies in which women still play conventional roles the rates of depression in women are about the same as in the West.[19] An earlier twenty-year analysis (1957–76) hinted at some other causes of dissatisfaction with the family: growing dissatisfaction with one's children, a decline in positive attitudes toward parenthood and marriage, and a general increase in anxiety about the future.[20]

Friends continue to visit each other, but the direction of change in their satisfaction with their friendships is uncertain.[21] Assuming no great decline in friendship satisfaction, however, note that this apparent constancy conceals two diverging patterns: men take decreasing pleasure in their friendships (decline in satisfaction and increase in dissatisfaction) while fewer women in the later years are dissatisfied with their friendships, a pattern giving the illusion of no change, masking a sex-linked difference in friendship satisfaction.[22] In both the 1957–76 and 1972–94 periods there developed a pattern which has long been familiar: what was once *given* by neighborhood and work now must be achieved; people have had to make their own friends (as in urban networks) and actively cultivate their own family connections. Part of this shift was due to the increasing impersonality of the workplace, for men, at least in the earlier period, found decreasing satisfaction in their relations with their work colleagues.[23] Failed social support in the 1957–76 period represents a powerful drag on SWB, for, say the authors of the relevant study, "we are a very social people who rely on interpersonal contacts with others to help us cope with life's problems."[24] Gesellschaft, market societies, makes friendship hard work (see below).

The consequence of this increasing separation from our families, including parents, relatives, and brothers and sisters, is that Americans' recreation is

Table 6.1. Recreation at Home and Outside the Home

Watching movies at home	71%
Going out to a theater to see movies	23
Getting together with friends in your home	62
Going out with friends to a restaurant, bar, or club	28
Watching a sports event at home on TV	51
Going out to a sports event	22

Source: Roper. Oct. 15–22, 1994. *Public Perspective* 6 (Aug.–Sept. 1995), 43.

increasingly solitary. The title of Robert Putnam's article on lower participation gives one clue: "Bowling Alone: America's Declining Social Capital."[25] Do we increasingly seek recreation at home (often in solitude) or outside the home (usually with others) (table 6.1)? In his account of changes in the use of time over the decade from 1965 to 1975, John Robinson finds a decline in visiting and informal social life.[26] That is, the decline in visiting, at least among family members, is not only a source of unhappiness in itself, but also a cause of the decline in the fun that comes from doing things with others.

But perhaps the cause is to be found in the rise of urbanism. I present the evidence in detail in the Appendix to this chapter, but in summary: (1) density of population does not generally reduce visiting (but may affect intimacy); (2) neighboring is less common in big cities but visiting with friends is *more* frequent; (3) visiting with parents is more common in the smallest places, but across all sizes of place urbanism has no systematic influence.

Happiness by Size of Place

The GSS data permit one to assess general happiness (1994) by size of place. The responses noted in table 6.2 are "Very Happy" (VH) and "Not too happy" (NH), the latter representing the least happy. First, but only as an aside in this analysis of urbanism, note that the modest relation between income and happiness (see chapter 4) shrinks to a vanishing point in those groups below the richest quartile when urbanism is controlled (the economistic fallacy, again). The same pattern holds for the unhappy. But my main concern here is with the influence of urbanism or size of place. Controlling for income, there are consistent differences in SWB by size of place: for example, in every income group there is a larger proportion of "very happy" people in the smallest places than in the largest places and a larger proportion of unhappy people in the

Table 6.2. Happiness by Size of Place and Income

	Size of Place by Quartiles							
	Smallest		2d smallest		2d largest		Largest	
Income quartiles	VH	NH	VH	NH	VH	NH	VH	NH
Richest quartile	46%	6%	38%	6%	28%	8%	34%	11%
2d richest	30	11	23	9	31	9	18	24
2d poorest	33	8	31	8	28	11	27	14
Poorest quartile	29	11	21	16	23	12	23	15
Average percent	34	9	28	10	27	10	25	16

Sources: General Social Survey (NORC); basic data were extracted from the GSS files and served as the basis for the creation of related figures (not shown) by Soo Yeon Kim of Yale's Social Science Statistical Laboratory. Substantive analysis here is my responsibility.

largest places than in the smallest places (although the intermediate size places are less regular in this latter respect).

These findings are inconsistent with the findings of cross-cultural studies presented first in chapter 3. Across nations, with income controlled, the relationship between density (a surrogate for size of place) and SWB disappears.[27] A different analysis of the same or similar data shows that in poor countries urban dwellers are happier than rural or village dwellers, but in rich countries, there is no difference.[28] (Since rural–urban differences in depression are even more complex and less consistent, I must relegate them to a footnote.)[29] If across cultures among advanced countries there is no difference in SWB by size of place, but my data show that there are such differences in the United States, one can conclude only that what Lewis Mumford once called *The Culture of Cities* differs across nations. Given the nature of American cities (and the fact that in the United States the poor are concentrated in the center of cities while in France and elsewhere in Europe the poor tend to be concentrated in the suburbs), this cross-national difference is not surprising. In the United States it does seem that fewer people are unhappy and more people happy in smaller places — a score for the American communitarians.

Another Dimension: Warmth

I now come to the other main dimension of affiliation: intension, or the quality of family and friendship relationships. Something more than frequency of social contact is at stake in an explanation of the decline in happiness and the rise in depression. In their analyses of human relations, most psychologists[30] have treated levels and kinds of affectivity as separate from frequency of contact.[31] In these treatments, intimacy is defined as a process of engagement with another in which the partners reveal themselves to each other and find in the other an understanding, validation, and solicitude that meet their needs.[32] The crucial point about intimacy, however, is how much intimate relations are preferred to a wider but shallower set of relationships. For example, one study found that in a college population "73 percent of the men and 83 percent of the women said they prefer a few intimate friends . . . to many good but less intimate friends."[33] The results of another study indicate that the absence of intimacy was the strongest determinant of loneliness.[34]

I will refer to this affective dimension as warmth, a little broader denomination than intimacy because it can be conveyed by acquaintances. It is a crucial quality in interpersonal perception. According to Solomon Asch and Harold Kelley,[35] warmth is associated in people's minds with mostly positive qualities: generosity, happiness, humor, sociability, and also, on the margin of the positive, "with a certain sense of easy-goingness, or a lack of restraint and persistence." It is contrasted, of course, with coldness, which is associated with satirical comment, restrictive communication, hostility, shrewdness, and, above all, self-centeredness. The warm–cold dimension is important because it changes perceptions of other aspects of personality. Like Tönnies, many critics of modernity (for example, Louis Wirth, Fromm, Mumford, Simmel) claim that social relations in modern society are characterized by coldness, impersonality, treatment of each other as numbers, as machines, on the surface, without self-disclosure.

Warmth and feelings of intimacy do more than cement relations: they buffer stress.[36] Other studies have shown the greater value of emotional support as contrasted to instrumental support in developing close and mutually beneficial ties.[37] When these ties are absent, they are sorely missed: at least in the 1957–76 period there was a "growing desire for warm interpersonal relations."[38]

I believe that individualism (defined as pursuit of one's own goals rather than of group goals) partly explains why relationships have become more shallow and impersonal over the years. In this connection, recall that the American society has, by a variety of measures, been found to be the most individualist of all societies, including the advanced societies of Western Europe. Individualism expresses itself in at least three ways: (1) Yearning for greater warmth, as mentioned above, people nevertheless seek greater self-sufficiency and regard this as a "crucial element in well-being";[39] such ambivalence is psychologically costly. (2) Unlike the patterned nature of relations in collectivist societies, in individualist societies people are unguided by controlling protocols and "tend to develop skills for effective superficial relations with others." They have to improvise as they go along.[40] (3) Compared to less modern societies, social exchanges in modern society are more a matter of dyadic exchanges enforced by fairly precise reciprocity.[41] The British anthropologist Geoffrey Gorer says this reciprocal "grooming" is the accepted convention among American males; reciprocity is also marked by deference for favors; (disguised) material exchanges; assurance of help in time of need, and so forth.[42] In contrast, social exchanges in the collectivist societies rely on chains in which *A* does a favor for *B* who does a favor for *C*[43] who, more or less unconsciously, returns the favor to *A*. The exchange here is between individual and community, whose members understand the protocol and complete the circuit.[44] Whereas the dyadic exchanges of the West require some trust in others, their main enforcement comes from the ability of each party to withhold favors, flattery, or whatever the desired good may be. On the other hand, the extended exchanges of the collectivist societies require a great deal of trust in unspecified others and are enforced by the solidarity of the community, that is, by norms and conventions. Solidarity implies a degree of emotion, of warmth; reciprocal favors do not. This is in line with Harry Triandis's concept of an important difference between the two kinds of culture: "An emphasis on relationships, even when they are disadvantageous, is common in collectivist cultures. In individualist cultures, the emphasis is on rational analysis of the advantages and disadvantages of maintaining a relationship."[45]

The influence of urbanism on human relations is another matter. Although the density of big cities may not be generally detrimental to human welfare, the isolation from neighbors and the loss of family solidarity in big cities seem to take their toll. Each person has an optimal level of stimulation, and for some, big cities are overstimulating (just as villages are boring for others). In general, however, stress and feelings of insecurity, probably more common in big cities, inhibit friendly relations; for example, men working in stressful environments tend to be less companionable at home.[46] Recent increases in economic insecurity in the middle class may have the same effect (see chapter 9).

Partly as a consequence of this combination of market forces, urbanization, and increased time constraints, the Machiavellian syndrome mentioned in chapter 5 is apparently growing. This syndrome of manipulative attitudes toward others includes "a relative lack of affect in interpersonal relations, . . . and a lack of concern with conventional morality."[47] The syndrome is associated with the rise of industrialism in developing countries and is more prevalent among modernizing than traditional peoples.[48] Machiavellianism (derived from *The Prince*) produces a relatively enduring, cross-situational pattern of behavior marked by many acquaintances who are frequently visited, but relatively few close, affectionate confidants. And it is — or was in the 1950 to early 1970s period — increasing rapidly among student and other populations in the United States and in selected European and Asian societies (for example,, Portugal and Hong Kong).[49] Everywhere it is more prevalent among the young than among older people. With the rise of Machiavellianism, affection and warmth decline. Whether this is a peculiarly American problem is uncertain: Kurt Lewin once commented that whereas in Europe people had relatively few acquaintances but several close friends with whom they could share their most intimate confidences, Americans shared something of themselves with many people but had few intimate friends.

The change in patterns of social exchanges from those based on solidarity to those based on reciprocal favors, the less intimate social encounters of individualist societies, the rising syndrome of manipulative behavior that produces many acquaintances but few close friends — all suggest that the continued frequency of contact among friends may mask significant changes in the emotional content of companionship, the decline of warmth. Hence the craving among students and the depressed for greater intimacy. (But the argument is ad hoc and awaits confirmation.)

The decline in visiting of neighbors, parents, and relatives together with evidence that intimacy and warmth are, at least, lagging (the evidence is weak) suggests that, indeed, market democracies do not facilitate companionship. Now I come to a very different kind of evidence, the monumental conflict between familism and markets in the Asian collectivist countries.

The Triumph of the Market over the Family

Here I want to turn to whole societies, comparing those that historically have put a premium on companionship with those that have been more individualist and given priority to wealth. First, I will give an account of what happens to companionable societies when they adopt market institutions in their search for wealth. Second, I will outline some costs in any possible return to some of the practices of gemeinschaft. In the next chapter, I will discuss the "hedonic perversity of culture," the failure to adapt to changing hedonic returns of the two goods companionship and wealth.

FAMILY VALUES OR MARKET SUCCESS?

I must offer first a brief account of recent studies of individualism and collectivism (interdependence having nothing to do with collective ownership of the means of production). Triandis and Geert Hofstede have defined these two kinds of societies according to the priority given to individual values: in one, people pursue their own interests (self-reliance, self-esteem, self-interest) without much regard to the goals of their groups, whereas in the other the group's interests and values come first.[50] By and large, Asian societies rank high on collectivism and the West ranks high on individualism, the United States, as noted, ranking as the most individualist of all nations.

If the triumph in the West of the market individualist pattern over the companionable gemeinschaft pattern was a nearly total rout, the apparent Asian collectivist pattern of market success *and* the retention of companionship in family and neighborhood seemed to promise a reconciliation of the two values. It is a fascinating story, fully as important as the argument over the relationship of democracy to economic development and relatively unrestrained markets. Social and economic theory said the reconciliation was impossible: familism and markets were incompatible because efficient markets required (a) contracts won by the least cost bidder, uncontaminated by friendship and family considerations (Maine's "from status to contract"); (b) meritocracy uncontaminated by cronyism and nepotism; (c) rational choices made with a single eye to profitability; (d) banking in which risks were always proportionate to probable money rewards and not to payoffs in friendship; and (e) these various constraints to be policed by arm's-length competition—in which any priority given to friends fatally undermined market efficiency. Bribery was acceptable, as always, but only as a fee system compatible with maximizing profitability and increasing market share. The cost of market efficiency, and therefore of wealth, was the sacrifice of family and friendship relations in economic affairs.

Not long ago, it seemed that the theory was wrong: certain Pacific Rim and Southeast Asian societies had, the world thought, developed flourishing market economies and yet had retained strong familistic patterns and group loyalties. At least in Asia, history, culture, and human ingenuity had taken strides toward solving the problem by combining the two. The problem has two aspects: familistic values in economic life, that is, public familism, and retention of intact and cohesive families in private life, private familism.

Public Familism

How might these familistic societies combine their collectivist cultures with the requirements of competitive markets? The answer was that they had (but to a limited extent—see below) a within-firm gemeinschaft combined with external relations more closely resembling what the theory said was necessary: profit maximizing impersonality. If one thinks this odd, one should recall that all species divide the world into we and they—and treat the two groups differently. It seemed to work: composite rates of change (averaged year over year) from 1980 to 1994 were South Korea, 7.6 percent; Taiwan, 8.5 percent; Japan, 4.5 percent (but through 1990 they were 9.3 percent, while from 1991 to 1994 they were −5 percent). During this 1980–94 period the U.S. economy grew, on average, 3.8 percent. Thus, except for the recent Japanese figures, the Asian familistic societies grew more than twice as fast as the individualist U.S. rates.[51]

Public familism and rapid economic growth are related: during periods of growth employers can afford to give a semblance of familistic tenure to their employees; the illusion of the firm as family could be persuasive, at least to familistic (and increasingly prosperous) employees. Ironically, the larger the firm (*zaibatsu*), the more familistic it could be. But during this period another kind of familistic and friendship standard in banking was undermining the economy.

Just as American individualism differs from, say, Scandinavian and Dutch individualism, so Asian familisms differ from each other. In Japan, "the decision-making unit is the group, and command is exercised not by fiat but by consensus. . . . South Korean firms, on the other hand, reflect the expression of a patrimonial principle, . . . organizations dominated by a patriarch and his children, but extending beyond them to include professional managers from outside the family." In contrast, Taiwanese firms operate by "familial network[s] . . . [which] express the interests of an extended family where divisions of financial holdings on the death of the patriarch is the rule." These firms have prospered, said Marco Orrú and his associates in 1991, because "they have successfully institutionalized the principles of market activity suited to their [familistic] sociocultural environment and to their strategies of economic development."[52] But even as these authors announced the triumph of economic familism, the tension between market and family values was growing.

Private Familism

Seeking to explain the low rate, compared to other economically advanced countries, of clinical depression in Taiwan and South Korea, a multinational team emphasizes the integrity of the family in these countries.[53] Rates of divorce (highly correlated with other measures of individualism)[54] are, as one might expect, low in the Asian collectivist societies. For example, in the early 1990s Japan had five divorces per one thousand married women, whereas in the United States the figure was twenty-one, more than four times as large. Markets and family integrity, encompassing the implied better childcare stemming from two-parent families, seemed compatible. But note that, ominously, rates of divorce were also low (by modern standards) in the nineteenth-century gemeinschaft days in the West—before Fukuyama's postwar "end of history."

In the end, market values seem to have triumphed over family values. Even in China, divorce rates are rising and recently have doubled in Thailand, Malaysia, and Singapore[55] (see below).

There were cultural explanations of why market success was compatible with familistic values and practices. All of the collectivist societies have had their within-group mutual assistance patterns influenced by the quasi-religious Confucian code: "Neighbors should help each other in time of need." Weber claimed that the superior economic and technological performance of the West was due to a transcendental religion that gave perspective as well as instruction on human affairs, thus helping to break the mold of tradition.[56] For a time it seemed that Eastern immanent religions, hewing to and cherishing tradition, might inform economic development with equal success and (perhaps) with greater compassion. But in the end, Weber may be right, at least temporarily: one must break the mold of mutual obligation to establish a successful market.

In a detailed analysis of the development of a market economy in the collectivist society of South Korea, Yun-shik Chang explains the retention of collectivist norms in impersonal markets: "The emphasis on close personal ties is [retained in urban market settings and is] often expressed as *uiri,* the concept more widely known in the Japanese context as *giri.*" It is an insult to say a person did not know his *uiri.* "To ignore human feelings for impersonal ends is likely to be frowned upon"; and people are expected to "share their feelings with others." In general, "the collectivized orientation has been deeply embedded in the traditional cultural pattern and appears to have adapted itself rather successfully to the new market situation that arose in the process of development in South Korea."[57] Even after the Fall, that is true of Korea, which is, in its embarrassment, still a rich nation, but the uses of *uiri* in banking are not compatible with profit maximization—and in this conflict, it will be *uiri* and *giri* that yield. In passing, I note that, as agents of the collectivity, governments in all three Asian societies examined here take active roles in promoting economic development. Familistic collectivism seems to invite government intervention to preserve both restraints on competition and cultural protectorates (such as highly inefficient rice farming in Japan).

The Cost of Rapid Economic Development

In the understandable drive for greater GDP per capita, quality of life has suffered in Asian collectivist societies. For example, in South Korea, Shin's measures of some noneconomic dimensions of welfare give a partial and suggestive account: although there was continuous, uninterrupted growth of per capita income for the twelve-year period measured, "both the interpersonal welfare and personal growth dimensions declined by 20 percent. This means that economic growth not only contributed to but also detracted from welfare."[58] Throughout the world, the main cost of the imposition of modern market and technological patterns on traditional patterns has been the disruption of interpersonal, especially family, relations.[59] The cross-cultural study by Ed Diener, Marissa Diener, and Carol Diener reveals the difference between the effects on happiness of higher levels of income and, separately, of growth: whereas the correlation between SWB and GDP per capita was an impressive .58 ($p < .001$), correlation with rate of growth was a nonsignificant −.08.[60] On the other hand, the nine-nation cross-national study mentioned above found that the two collectivist Asian economies included, South Korea and Taiwan, had much lower lifetime rates of major depression than any of the individualist nations measured. They also had the lowest rates of divorce.[61]

THE FALL

Now, to modify this picture further: market success deteriorated in Japan in 1990 in part because of the familistic standards of banking, and in other Pacific Rim and Southeast Asian countries in 1997 (but also because of world overproduction of the goods they specialized in). Running throughout the accounts of this collapse are stories of favoritism to friends and family, monarchical family commercial fiefs not subject to market discipline in Southeast Asia, personalistic standards substituting for meritocratic, impersonal standards, bank loans to friends in which the only collateral was friendship, opaque transactions by insiders, and so forth. From June 1997 to June 1998, GDP fell in Indonesia by 6.2 percentage points, in South Korea by 3.8 points, in Japan by 3.7 points, in Hong Kong by 2.0 points, and in Thailand by 0.4 points.[62] The remarkable growth of the previous decade(s) had been led principally by capital formation; when the currencies were regarded as overpriced, foreign capital withdrew, bursting the bubbles and exposing these familistic economies to the withering power of efficiency sensitive market forces.[63]

Exaggeration and Erosion of Public Familism

Even before the Fall, there were many reports of the weakness of within-firm familistic standards. Although some analyses of Asian development in the 1960s concluded that individualism actually retarded Western economic development,[64] observations of later developments have been less certain. First, at least in Japan, the familistic concern for employees is more limited than Orrú and his associates suggest. By Western measures unemployment is much higher than acknowledged by the official Japanese statistics. Also, "Japan's quasi-mythical lifetime employment only ever covered 15 percent to 20 percent of all workers. . . . [And] big firms pay pensions (at much less than full wage) when men take early retirement, as they are encouraged to do."[65] Market pressures prevent small firms from implementing their family responsibilities, and large firms often contract out the more volatile elements of their businesses (compare Maine on the substitution of contract for family status).[66] Although the principle of promotion by seniority provides some security, women and contract workers are especially "vulnerable to buffeting by market forces."[67]

Private Familism

Like other traditional institutions, the "family, too . . . appears to be weakening. As wage earners migrate to the city, often leaving children behind; as both parents work more often; as old people live longer and find the family a less reliable source of social services, family networks are breaking down." In Japan and South Korea, "some middle-class parents are raising their children increasingly by cellular phone or pagers."[68] I spoke above of the lower divorce rates as indicating two-parent care of children, but cross-cultural polls find that "a father in Japan spends on average 36 minutes a day with his children compared with 56 minutes in the United States." At the other end of the age spectrum, in the Asian cultures people were supposed to take care of their aged parents. Perhaps they did so prior to the market experience but apparently not after that exposure: "When asked 'Will you take care of old parents by all means?' respondents in three countries replied 'yes' as follows: the United States, 46 percent; China, 66 percent, and Japan, 16 percent."[69] Finally, recall the discussion of the declining value of children in market societies (see chapter 3). One would not expect to find such a decline among the Chinese, but, comparing the marketized Hong Kong Chinese with Chinese on the mainland, research finds that although parents in Hong Kong acknowledge the value of children, "a majority also perceived that parenthood was associated with increased financial burden and personal sacrifice. In contrast to the heavy emphases on the traditional Chinese values of security and posterity, these Hong Kong Chinese parents did not seem to emphasize such values strongly."[70]

The conflict between familistic traditions and market requirements seems, on this account, to take a toll on both. Although one must recognize that the Asian economies, even after their post-1997 decline, are still successful relative to their historical pasts and to other LDC and still treasure family life and have warmer friendships than does the individualist West, the costs of the tension have been revealed with stark clarity.

The collectivist symbiosis of family and market may turn out to have been a transient experience, but the inevitability of the triumph of contract relations and gesellschaft patterns asserted by Maine and Tönnies seems, even in the promising Asian culture, to have prevailed. It is fair to ask: Can an economy preserve the advantages of warm and mutually caring relations and pursue market shares (often instead of current profit)? Can people employ the rational calculations that Weber found so preemptive in industrial society and employ the appropriate emotional spontaneity at home? Can people treat each other as merchants treat clients outside the firm and as members of a family within it, as being individually responsible for their separate fates in the labor market and as reciprocally responsible for a collective fate within the firm, as rivals for advantage in exchange relations and as "belonging to each other" (Weber) in within-firm relations? Market forces, as Maine, Tönnies, and Weber all said, are destructive to familistic cultures. On another continent, among African societies, the family has been the last institution to change — but it is changing.[71] Is there no hope for a familistic culture to survive in a market society? Perhaps; research finds that in contrast to firms, families are not wholly the creatures of economic systems, but rather have an autonomy of their own.[72] But the Asian experience does not promise much autonomy of this kind.

Perhaps one should take a Marx-like dialectical position: he said (and later recanted) that economies must pass through the triumph of capitalism before they can achieve socialism. Similarly, in order to achieve a decent symbiosis of companionship and market-generated wealth, societies may have to go through a phase of individualism to achieve the necessary level of prosperity before they can, once again, discover the benefits of family and friends. Tönnies and Weber were prescient only after the fact. In the next chapter I will report on both the forces at work and the costs of the kind of culture change proposed.

Appendix to Chapter 6

Community Characteristics by Size of Place

INTERPERSONAL TRUST

Table A.6.1. "Most People Can Be Trusted" by Size of Place and Income

	Size of Place by Quartiles			
Income quartiles	Smallest	2nd smallest	2nd largest	Largest
Richest quartile	28%	53%	48%	48%
2nd richest	38	30	30	19
2nd poorest	32	37	47	24
Poorest quartile	31	34	28	27
Average percent	32	38	38	29

Sources: General Social Survey (NORC); basic data were extracted from the GSS files by Soo Yeon Kim of Yale's Social Science Statistical Laboratory. Substantive analysis here is my responsibility. The question was, "Generally speaking, would you say that most people could be trusted or that you can't be too careful in dealing with people?" The answers were dichotomous, although a very few respondents volunteered, "It depends." Cells are percent of the public saying most people can be trusted.

Higher income generally (but not in the least urban areas) makes people more trusting; and poverty in most places (but not in the largest cities) tends to make people less trusting. But our concern is with size of place where, disregarding wealth, the relationship is curvilinear with the least trust in the largest places. In these metropolitan areas, only the rich are relatively trusting. And only the "bourgeoisie" (2nd richest quartile) show anything like a regular descent of trust as size of place increases. Thus, with income controlled, the failure to find a consistent influence of urbanism on trust leads us to anticipate minimal effects of urbanism on social visiting patterns.

VISITING SIBLINGS

Visiting patterns specifically among siblings (not shown) reveals a modest tendency (accelerated at the end of the period) for socializing to fall off, and this was accompanied by a more substantial and linear trend toward isolation. Having more recently left the family, the youngest group socializes more than other age groups with siblings. Even though the number who "never" visit their siblings is small, what is distressing about the pattern of change among the young is the large increase (25 percent) in that young group of isolates.

Record of Confirmation of Cold Society Hypotheses

As in the text of chapter 6, socializing represents frequent visiting (daily or weekly) and isolation represents "once a year" or "never." Where socializing declines and isolation increases, we have what might be called a cold society. For my purposes in finding sources of unhappiness, increasing isolation is more important than declining socializing.

*Table A.6.2. Visiting Patterns, General Population, 1986–94**

Visiting with:	Socializing	Isolation	Cold Society
Parents	Decline	Increase	Confirmed
Relatives	Decline	Decline	1/2 confirmed
Siblings	Decline	Increase	Confirmed
Neighbors	Decline	Increase	Confirmed
Friends	Increase	Decline	Disconfirmed

*The abbreviated time period reflects the limitations of some of the time series.

Three of the five visiting patterns suggest the growth of a colder society, one is ambiguous, and one, friendship, unambiguously contradicts and reverses the hypothesis.

DO WOMEN AND THE YOUNG LIVE IN A COLD SOCIETY

One other attempt to discern patterns in this thicket of observations: Compared to others, are women and the young, the two groups most vulnerable to unhappiness and depression, losing their nurturing relations with family and friends? Using the same concepts of socializing and isolation, Table A.6.3 assesses this possibility.

Table A.6.3. Visiting Patterns, Women and Young, 1978–89

	Women			The Young (18–23)		
Visiting with:	Socializing	Isolation	Cold S.	Socializing	Isolation	Cold S.
Parents	Increase	Increase	1/2	Increase	Decline	No
Relatives	Decline	Increase	Yes	Decline	Increase	Yes
Siblings	Decline	Decline	1/2	Increase	Increase	1/2
Neighbors	Decline	Increase	Yes	Decline	Increase	Yes
Friends*	Increase	Decline	No	Increase	Decline	No

* = 1973–94

For these vulnerable groups, the case for a cold society hypothesis receives only modest support. The cold society hypothesis fails for women in only one case, is confirmed in two, and is partially confirmed (or partially disconfirmed) in two others, of which one represents the more benign pattern of declining isolation. The most distressing pattern for women is the increase in market work with no increase in friendships outside the home. For youth, there are only two full confirmations and two disconfirmations, with partial confirmation (or disconfirmation) in one case. I estimate that if socializing and isolation were fully independent of each other (because of the large middle term, they are partially so and do move independently) that the probability of this pattern is about .03.

URBANISM AND VISITING PATTERNS

If urbanism proved to be the cause of less frequent socializing, we would still be faced with its possible consequences in unhappiness and depression, but some of the blame would be deflected from immediate market forces. In addition to the lore identifying small places with close human relations, there are claims that the sheer human density of big cities takes a toll in interpersonal relations, for it tends to foster more anonymous relations.[1] Also, the greater the bustle on a street, the less willingness to help a stranger.[2] On the other hand, some studies show that urban life does not tend to isolate people from one another,[3] and yet other studies present fairly conclusive evidence that "the cities' problems are not due to high density; . . . for the high density will enhance the positive aspects of city living and the cities can continue to be what they have been in the past — dynamic, vital forces."[4]

What the GSS evidence on the effect of urbanism on visiting patterns in 1994 shows can be summarized as follows: In general, the larger the place, the less frequently people visit their neighbors, both because of greater mutual isolation and because of a falling off of high frequency socializing. But when these visiting patterns are controlled for level of income, the relationship is greatly attenuated and loses its statistical significance ($p < .12$, NS). For example, the allegation that, compared to the middle class, poorer people are more reliant on neighbors (and kin) for companionship seems to be true for small cities but not for large ones, where the class pattern is reversed. But, as figure 6.1 above shows, neighboring in general has itself declined, partly because the poorer half of the population visit their neighbors less often in big cities than in small towns — and the population in metropolitan areas (though not in big cities, themselves) has greatly increased. (References to "poor" and "rich" here and in the next few paragraphs refer to the poorer and the richer *halves* of the population.)

Visiting friends shows a reversed overall pattern: the larger the place, the more frequently people visit their friends and the less often are people isolated from each other. And for friends, the overall visiting relationships hold with income controlled ($p < .0001$), in fact, in both small and large places, the poorer half of the population does *more* visiting with friends than the richer half — although in all places there are also more isolated "poor" than isolated "rich." The pattern of persistently high friendship visiting, then, could be due in part to population movements to metropolitan areas.

Finally, while it is clear that people visit their parents less often in the largest places than in the smallest ones, there is really no systematic decrease in visiting by size of place. That is, degree of urbanism has no overall effect ($p < .15$, NS) — and this holds true with income controlled.

These data suggest that although urbanism (size of place) does play a part in the visiting patterns of contemporary American society, it is not systematic and often, although not always, that difference is an artifact of different levels of income in places of different sizes.

Do Visiting Patterns Help Explain the Greater Happiness in Smaller Places?

Now, can one say that the greater happiness in smaller places is in part due to the different visiting patterns in large and small places? Let me simplify:

For neighboring: compared to smaller places, big cities seem to encourage isolation; if people have to depend on their neighbors for companionship, there will be more lonely people in big cities than in villages and small towns. This isolation is not class bound: the richest half of the population are just as isolated from their neighbors as the poorest half. (Socializing is really not much different in big and small places.) To the extent that happiness depends upon social engagement with one's neighbors, the difference in neighboring does help to explain the happiness of the villages.

For friendship: compared to smaller places, big cities seem to discourage isolation and encourage socializing. And here, the poorer half are the victims (and perpetrators) of the relative isolation. Whatever may be the differences by income, we cannot explain the greater happiness of villages by their solidarity with their friends: in smaller places, they see them less often and are isolated from them more often.

For parents: people visit their parents a little more frequently and neglect them a little less frequently in villages and small towns than in big cities, but there is not much difference by size of place. Neither are the differences by income level as great when it comes to visiting parents as they are for neighbors and friends. There is an underlying cause: relations with parents are influenced more by things internal to the family (and internal to the psyche) than by external things, like income and size of place. We can say, however, that if visiting parents adds to happiness (it does not among adolescents), to that extent the greater happiness in villages is enhanced by that parental visiting. More plausibly, visiting frequency is a symptom of feelings of greater family solidarity, and it is these feelings, rather than the actual visiting, that makes villages happier places than big cities.

7

Gaining Felicity While Losing Income?

How can it be that people pursue income at the cost of the SWB offered by families and friendship? One answer is that we are witnessing only the most recent phase of a centuries-old conflict between family and markets. In a sense, the long-delayed victory over feudalism was a victory over a familistic system (Ernst Bloch); the exploitation and reinforcement of individualism by markets were a blow against familism (Maine, Alan MacFarlane); the change in the form of wealth from land to money and personalty liberated people from ties of kin as well as of place (Simmel); and the victory of factory organization in a commercial setting over cottage industry in the family setting (William Parker), together with the quasi-voluntary drift to factories (sometimes with their own regulated dormitories for women) from family and village surveillance of a more informal nature (Edward Shorter), may only have changed the form of indenture, but in the process it weakened families. Marx and Engels's hyperbole captures the theme: "The bourgeoisie . . . had put an end to all feudal, patriarchal, idyllic relations . . . [and] has torn away from the family its sentimental veil and has reduced the family relation to a mere money relation."[1]

So the account of changes in Asian collectivism records only the most recent battle in a long war fought by the market and its advocates to convert all spheres of society to an economism in which neither government nor family interrupts the play of market forces. The end of history, indeed!

The rewards were enormous: decline of poverty, protections against the deprivations of old age, support for democracy (a willing ally), assault on ill health, a wild expansion of education (if not art), some erratic growth in equality, and freedoms the world had rarely known. So why are we not happy? Well, most people are, and, as J. H. Plumb said, we hardly know the miseries we have been spared. But something is missing: warm companionship has been partly lost, and family felicity is declining. The collectivist societies of Asia tried to combine these things, but, at least in their recent experiments, they failed.

What Will Companionship Cost Us?

At this stage in the evolution of our civilization, what would we gain in well-being for what we lose when we change priorities and sacrifice *some* of our actual or potential gain in income for *some* new feelings that we are, if not bands of brothers (the phrase, of course, is a Nazi slogan), at least embraced in our families and communities. The italicized "some" is intended to indicate a kind of marginal evaluation, that is, an assessment of incremental movements toward a more felicitous balance of the two goods. Moving in that direction, we should staunch the erosion of happiness and reverse the rise of depression.

COSTS AND BENEFITS OF SACRIFICING INCOME FOR FRIENDS

Following are some of the economic implications of giving up money and income-producing activities for friendship and friendship-producing activities:

1. Increasing productive efficiency in the workplace at the expense of reducing its sociability seems to be hedonically counterproductive, at least in the short run.[2] That is, in order to gain utilities from more commodities made cheaper by industrial efficiency, we sacrifice what are probably greater utilities yielded by sociability at work. If one were to think of workers who give up companionship as selling companionship for higher earnings in the market, one might paraphrase Omar Khayyam: "I often wonder what the consumer buys one half so precious as the stuff the worker sells." But the (contested) evidence from the United States (where, compared to other countries, relatively fewer friendships are made at the workplace) suggests that congenial relations at work have more influence than income levels over people's job satisfaction.[3]
2. The substitution of sociability at the office or plant for money income in the form of take-home pay seems ex parte: it appears to benefit only the worker

and not the family of the worker. But consider another commodity, good will or warmth (see chapter 6). Many families might prefer to have the breadwinner bring home more tension-free warmth (in what is called spillover) than more money. We know that when the breadwinner is unemployed, the family, especially the children, suffers—not from material deprivation so much as from the distemper of the breadwinner.[4] In the same way, it may be that both spouse and children benefit from a happy breadwinner sharing his or her happiness with the family. Realistically, utilities from companionship at work might easily dominate the utilities from a shared higher standard of living—as Tibor Scitovsky once suggested.[5]

3. The above income–companionship tradeoff refers to market income and workplace companionship. But in fact (at least in Britain), with conservative assumptions, "household production . . . adds just over half to disposable income for all families and about two thirds for families with children."[6] Under these circumstances, two forms of companionship ([1] within the family—like workmate companionship—and [2] external companionship—social life of spouses and children separately) and two forms of productivity ([a] what might be priced were it contracted out, and [b] the productivity of children's development and their—usually uncounted—"utilities") emerge. Without accounting for all the cells in the implied fourfold table, note just the one, 1b, in which intrafamily relations combine to increase the productivity that matters most: child welfare and well-being. Companionship and productivity are symbiotic. That is, if one counts the utilities of children, household production by parents, including child care, may be much higher for the household than the official statistics, imputing prices of goods and services at market value, imply. Because they are not themselves market consumers, small children's utilities are not recorded in economists' calculations based on consumption—by which they usually mean demand.

People have plural desires; they do not want or need only income, or only intrinsic work enjoyment—or only companionship. What, then, is the cost of companionship?

PAINS AND COSTS OF COMPANIONSHIP

There are five parts to the question of pains and costs of companionship. One has to do with the positive dislike of some form of companionship, the cloying sense of too much God-damned love, the feeling of constraint by all the social obligations, the intense desire to be alone, the loss of control over one's agenda, perhaps over one's life. I call these decrements of pleasure companionship pains. The affiliative process is costly in another way: because of fear of rejection or actual rejection, companionship has its risks and affiliative costs. The third kind of loss of pleasure through companionship is different in that the pleasures of companionship are gained at the expense of the community. These are community costs. A fourth kind of pleasure loss has to do with lost opportunities to do something else, perhaps something desired but less preferred. One may love one's friends and cherish one's family but nevertheless recognize that time spent with them robs one of a chance to finish one's book (sermon, organization chart for tomorrow's meeting, or to close a money-making deal): opportunity costs. And this sense of companionship as the wrong priority tends to increase with the availability of friends and family: companionship has declining marginal utility. That is, its opportunity costs change with the availability of the various alternative goods. One of the principal opportunity costs is human development and social reform. And finally, the terms on which one gains membership in a companionable group are crucial: one may give up one's freedom and dignity by unfavorable terms.

Companionship Pains

Inevitably, group membership is constraining. In their study of psychological distress, John Mirowski and Catherine Ross explain that although social support is necessary for mental health, "responsibility to the group places constraints on the individual, who must take into account the expectations, desires, and well-being of family and friends. These constraints produce a sense of not being in control of one's own destiny, which increases depression."[7] The same reasoning applies cross-nationally; Ed Diener and Eunkook Suh report that "the same extended family that offers support in the collectivist culture also serves to limit freedom. Thus, the collectivist is less able to follow his or her own personal desires, and is less likely to experience high life satisfaction in good times."[8] Comparing the gemeinschaft of a Scottish community to a London community, Brown and Harris note that " 'integration' into the small-scale community in the Outer Hebrides is not, apparently, without cost in terms of psychiatric disorders other than depression."[9] Turning back to the industrial world, one finds that for women, interpersonal conflict in work groups is worse than marital or housewife strains at home, with "strains deriving from interpersonal conflicts [at work] making the strongest contribution to role-specific stress."[10] Nor is the family free from pain, for, as mentioned, adolescents are often positively uncomfortable in family situations, and the presence of children in the household actually reduces the happiness of the parents.[11]

Affiliative Costs

Another kind of pain from companionship is fear of rejection or, less obviously, striving too hard to make friends. People possessed by the need for affiliation (mentioned in chapter 5) tend to be disliked because they are animated not by affection for another but by a drive that has nothing to do with particular others.[12] As Maslow points out, needing others, as contrasted to wanting to be with others, is a form of incomplete personality development[13] and is painful because one is often denied the fruits of one's aspirations and best efforts.

Community Costs

Dyadic friendships, especially in individualist societies, may come at the cost of wider community affiliation. Finding companionship in each other's company, couples or friends can be as withdrawn as individuals. In addition, there is another way whereby group affiliations can be at the cost of the community. The good fellowship of the adolescent gang and the bonhomie of youthful experimenters in drugs and alcohol are types of companionship that bring the young people and their larger communities pain. Thus, one study of youthful drinking in Israel, France, and the United States found that "in all three countries, the drinking behavior of parents and peers was a more powerful predictor of alcohol use than the subjects' personal attributes, such as attitudes, behaviors, and demographic characteristics." Whereas in Israel parents were more important influences, in the United States and France peer group pressure was.[14]

Opportunity Costs

Opportunity costs are not strictly painful except as one may be reluctant to give up even an inferior pleasure for a superior one. This problem surfaced in chapter 6 in my comparison of the utility of money and companionship, but I briefly note here that all economic exchange involves opportunity costs: for example, gaining more desired economic benefits in exchange for desired—but less desired—benefits.

Opportunity Costs in Human and Social Development

The good ol' boy syndrome of the southern small town may be a symphony of warm human relations, at least for the initiates. But it retards both individual and social development.[15] Pressures to conform inhibit individual differences and heterodoxy: inventors and entrepreneurs, for example, come from marginal peoples who have group histories of education and prideful independence:[16] Scots (Britain), Ibo (Nigeria), Jews (Europe and the United States), Huguenots (France), and so on. Social development and reform require heterodoxy and the will to try something different.

Freedom and Dignity Costs

Like communities, groups are stratified: their elites gain status and prestige while their more humble members may give up dignity and pride in exchange for group membership bought by a humbling servility.

SOCIAL COSTS OF GEMEINSCHAFT

If Western individualists returned to their familistic traditions, they might sacrifice some of the (now discounted) pleasures of foregone commodities whose comparative yield in happiness has been shown to be low. But that is not all they would lose. Even in the imagination, the temptation to return to small town values and ways of life is not great. Alternatively, if they followed the path of the (still and, after reform, probably once again) economically successful Asian collectivist and increasingly urban societies, the costs would also be substantial for, as we shall see in chapters 14 and 15, they would include a universalistic ethics, impartial justice, relief from favoritism, and much more. Would people brought up in an individualist Western culture be happier in friendship-friendly, reciprocally respectful (because of socially enforced *giri*), familistic culture? Perhaps not. In this contemplated tradeoff, it is not so much commodities that we would be giving up as a set of cultural patterns that have become, rightly or wrongly, highly moralized. Marginal adjustment is the key, for it is direction, not destination, that one seeks to foster.

The Painful Transition: Hedonic Perversity of Culture

There is a perversity to the process of changing priorities that characterizes all kinds of societies. For advanced Western countries, the perversity comes from the fact that their current prosperous societies are driven by the traditions, institutions, and norms that made them rich in the first place. These forces then give enhanced value to the pursuit of wealth, and they devalue the companionship given up in the interests of wealth. Gemeinschaft, or traditional, agricultural village society (and, mutatis mutandis, the Asian collectivist societies) suffered from the same kind of perversity. For example, the banker is a villainous figure in *Middlemarch,* and merchants and moneylenders fare no better in *Père Goriot.* The strains are found everywhere: Leonard

Doob found that Africans greatly valued the wealth of the advanced countries but detested the methods necessary to achieve that wealth; in the 1970s a Polish survey found that a majority of the population wanted a market economy but did not trust merchants to set their own prices; in the Middle East, Daniel Lerner found that members of those hierarchical cultures were contemptuous of the "grocers" who were producing the wealth that they envied.[17]

The problem is clarified by three points: (1) as mentioned, companionship and money income have a value relative to each other; (2) if choosing between these goods followed economic rules of utility maximization, each good would drop in value as it became more common relative to the other; but (3) because the culture that prompts the relative bounty and dearth of these supplies will give the bountiful good an artificial value, this value will be out of harmony with its hedonic yield. Thus, both friendship cultures and income cultures will fail to maximize their members' utilities. The potential hedonic yield of each good is known to the majority, if at all, only after a long, dysfunctional delay by the members of the laggard culture. This perverse hedonic lag, the tendency of every culture to persist in valuing the qualities that made it distinctively great long after they have lost their hedonic yield, explains a lot of the malaise currently afflicting market democracies. I will return to this point in the concluding chapter.

In our market society, economics is the discipline that instructs us on maximizing well-being through maximizing income. We have turned over to that discipline the study of the nature and development of welfare, utility, and well-being. How the gods must laugh!

Trading Companionship for Income

It is always convenient to rely upon a single explanatory device—for example, rational choice or maximizing reproductive fitness—but explanatory theories bear fruit only when they match the various things they are trying to explain. As Thomas Nagel once observed about values, "Not all values represent the pursuit of some single good in a variety of settings."[18] Thus, there are several prototheories available for interpreting change from economic priorities to sociability priorities, but, regrettably, they are somewhat incoherent.

Consider the relationship among five candidates for this explanatory office: declining marginal utility (DMU), adaptation level theory (AL), dialectical theory, motivational hydraulic theory, and learning generalization. I will add a sixth theory of a framework within which these other theories must now work: laissez-faire.

1 and 2. DMU (explained in chapter 4 and further treated in chapters 8 and 15) yields outcomes radically different from those of AL), which says that all pleasure and pain is relative to what one has known before.[19] The standard analogy is psychophysical: a ten-pound weight seems heavy after one lifts five-pound weights and light after one lifts twenty-pound weights. As people's experience in a given domain improves, their expectations or aspirations adapt to that improvement so that a new level becomes the basis of their assessments, and the improvement brings no new long-term joy into their lives. But, similarly, when the benefit level of that experience declines, their pain is only temporary because the new lower level of benefits again becomes the basis of their assessments, and their disappointment wanes. The result is that increasing benefits do not improve SWB, and declining benefits do not decrease it. Readers recalling the set-point theory in chapter 3 ("Happiness as an Endowment") will recognize how AL gets to the same place by a different route. AL is a conventional psychological prototheory for explaining why, for example, after their accidents or their winning a lottery, paraplegics and lottery winners gradually return almost to the same level of well-being experienced before their accidents or winnings.[20]

Comparing DMU with AL, we observe that DMU predicts declining pleasure from a given amount of something as the supply of an alternative to that something increases; it does not predict a declining level of SWB. AL is more pessimistic; it predicts a constant amount of pleasure from a given experience when that experience itself gets better. AL might be said to be intrinsic to a given process while DMU is contingent on what happens to an alternative good. AL implies ceiling and floor effects not present in DMU, effects such that no long-term increases in pleasure are possible—but neither are decreases.

3. Dialectical theories have been applied to major institutions, not to individual choices. The theories say that the hypertrophy of institutions like markets and families (and states?) breeds counterforces to challenge and undermine the institutions, with, finally, a balance emerging to reconcile the two conflicting arrangements. In the case I am examining, a dialectical theory would say that a society relying too much on income (or companionship) would create forces undermining those institutions that are largely devoted to the production of income (or companionship) in order to institutionalize the production of the alternative good: companionship (or income). Dialectical theories are incompatible with DMU and AL because both of these processes are self-adjusting (if not self-correcting) by individual actions and do not contain implied demands for institutional change.

Two other prototheories focus, respectively, on individual processes of motivation and cognition:

4. The motivational theory is a hydraulic theory that says certain needs are so built into the human species (or so instilled by a given culture) that they either will find expression one way or another or, alternatively, as in Freudian theory, will cause unhappiness (or sublimation) in the host person. Evolutionary theory is also a kind of hydraulic theory: the pressure to reproduce is a given and if a species thwarts that pressure it is punished by extinction, while for individuals—and this is most speculative—it is punished by lack of fulfillment, at least for females. Hydraulic theories are compatible with DMU if the need is broad enough (recall the late, unlamented libido) to allow for substitutes, but it is not compatible with AL because the hypothesized need is a constant not yielding to adaptive adjustments.
5. Learning generalization is a cognitive process whereby what is learned in one domain or situation generalizes to other domains or situations as, for example, when what is learned in market practice is applied to interpersonal relations—or, as in the Asian familistic cultures, when favoring of family members is applied to market situations.
6. Finally, although not a theory of choosing or change, laissez-faire (LF) is a relevant theory accounting for relative imbalances of income and companionship in society. It says that society and its agent, the state, can (perhaps must) rely on individual choices for the maximization of well-being because each person is the best judge of his or her own self-interest (see chapter 16). LF is compatible with, indeed relies on, DMU for well-being maximization but is impotent in the face of AL, which may reduce well-being. LF is a substitute for dialectical processes because it does by individual choice what dialectical transformations do by institutional changes: when one's life is encumbered with too much of one good, one simply chooses another; lives are equivalent to institutions. The great puzzle for the problem of income versus companionship considered here is why, under laissez-faire, people do not choose to maximize their well-being.

It will be useful to elaborate how these prototheories work in the case of the income–companionship tradeoff.

DECLINING MARGINAL UTILITY

Why is it that people in individualistic societies derive more pleasure from their friends than people in collectivistic societies, in which companionship is thought to be more highly prized[21] and, in fact, in which friendship relations tend to be more intimate?[22] Although there is something to the view that individualism offers more choice among companions (but not, of course, more choice of family), I believe the main reason is that companionship is more scarce and therefore yields higher utility in individualistic nations. Similarly, income is more scarce in collectivist nations and therefore yields more SWB.

A complement not used by economists is the idea of increasing marginal utility. The rising marginal utility of the products of skill, including social skills, gives a boost to our evaluation of friends (although there does not seem to be much of a demand for new friends—see chapter 5). Note how increasing utility of friends makes the substitution of companionship for income easier and less likely for a period of time to be reversed.

ADAPTATION LEVEL THEORIES

The principal reason people like the Ojibwa and the Dobu do not change the practices that make them unhappy is that their peoples have adapted to the levels of anxiety and mutual suspicion that they have learned. Here is the dilemma: If they were more discontented, they might be even more unhappy, but that unhappiness might lead them to change their misery-making institutions. *Ad astra per aspera.* Another dilemma: Although happy people are more active and effective than unhappy people, they are also more satisfied with their situations (are more conventional and use more stereotypical thinking) and hence less likely to be motivated to contribute to reform. What AL theory tells us is that the tendency to adapt one's hedonic level to one's circumstances, accepting fewer objective benefits for any given set-point level of SWB, may increase current SWB at the cost of greater long-term SWB. Thus, AL theory is incompatible with dialectical theories of social change.

DIALECTICAL THEORIES

Dialectical theories have not fared well in the course of history: even the idea that every form of organization breeds its counterform has misfired, let alone the part about the culminating synthesis. But neither Hegel nor Marx had hold of good ideas about human motives that, failing to find satisfaction in one form of social organization, would lead them to develop counterorganizations wherein they might find fulfillment. Following this line of thought, one might say that because familistic societies could not fulfill their needs for material welfare, they created or borrowed markets, and then, because they could not fulfill their companionship needs in markets, they corrupted markets to express their affiliative needs—and collapsed (for now) from the incompatibility of the two.

In the United States the dialectic took another form: the market's "victims" created a religious revival. Then, relying on the resurgence of a "primordial" characteristic of gemeinschaft, ties of religion became the sources of many friendships. Robert Wuthnow reports that more than 40 percent of an American national sample belonged to small groups, of which about two-thirds were church related. Asked about the benefits they received from the groups, the two leading answers were, "made you feel like you weren't alone" (82 percent) and "gave encouragement when you were feeling down" (72 percent). In interpreting the place of these mostly religiously oriented groups in our (gesellschaft) society, Wuthnow says, "we may think [of small groups] as ways . . . of getting back some of the solidarity with other people that has been lost in our society, of combating some of the rampant individualism that has become so evident in our culture."[23] Through the gift of companionship, religion takes its revenge on the secularism of modernity.

HYDRAULIC THEORIES

As for the strange persistence of friendship while family relations decline, I suggested (see chapter 6) a hydraulic pattern. The need for affiliation, I hypothesized, is a constant, something biologically driven and unvarying over history. When family affiliation declines, the need for affiliation (McClelland) will express itself in the search for more friends. The evidence is only partially supportive (see chapter 5). But McClelland is not Darwin, whose evolutionary theory, at least in Edward Wilson's hands, suggests a better hydraulic drive: bonding.[24] Our brains and hormones drive us to companionship, whatever the market teaches. Failing to find the intimate relations that seem to be quite widely sought—and often sorely missed—we substitute more extensive networks of companions, and if they are unsatisfying, we become ill: "The price of progress in civilization," said Freud, "is paid in forfeiting happiness."[25]

GENERALIZED LEARNING

One final reason markets and familistic or intimate relations seem to be incompatible might be that what people learn in markets is inappropriately generalized to social situations. The Frankfurt school diaspora argued that because markets involve exchange for material benefits, so, in market societies, do our relations with each other. They might borrow Adam Smith's phrase, "every man a merchant" as evidence or, like Fromm, argue that in market societies each person puts himself or herself up for sale: "I am as you desire me."[26] The trouble with theories of generalized learning is that they must be selectively applied: for example, they do not apply to mother-child relations, and they do not explain why this mother-child relation, having been learned first, does not, in reverse, apply to market relations. In fact, people both generalize and compartmentalize, and the theory offers no clue regarding when one and not the other is applied. Thus, as noted in chapter 5, the paradigm case of mutually exploitative relationships inhibiting intimacy and confidential relationships is the pattern of disturbed adolescents—not, say, the pattern of market salespeople.[27]

The cross-domain generalization pattern nevertheless has distinguished antecedents in the Protestant ethic, embracing a set of attitudes and beliefs learned in religious domains and applied to economic life. The "trait–state" distinction helps: if a characteristic is a trait it applies cross-situationally, but if it is situationally specific, it is a state—and probably ephemeral. What traits does the market teach (or select for)? Internality, the belief that one is effective and in control of one's fate, is one and is known both to foster business success and to be related to social success as well.[28] Conscientiousness, a genuine and important trait with some affinity for the Protestant ethic, is another, and in one guise or another (as in Jencks's "industriousness")[29] is also related to market success as well as to SWB because, it is argued, people like reliable others whom they can count on. The drift is clear: although it may be that people learn attitudes and cognitions in the market that inhibit their social lives, the case for generalization that facilitates companionship is equally strong.

Values and goals are another matter: the evidence in chapter 8 will show dramatically how materialistic values inhibit social success. One might assume that the market teaches materialism, and I think it does, but why then are peasants so materialistic? Theories of generalized learning tend not to show that markets are either necessary or sufficient as tutors of traits that inhibit friendships, and I will not lean heavily on them here.

INDIVIDUALISTIC LAISSEZ-FAIRE

Explaining the unhappiness of the members of market democracies may, after all, be best accomplished by relying on the prevailing wisdom of the economists and political theorists: each person is exercising within his or her small world of experience that combination of income and companionship that best pleases that person—but they too often fail. One might say that there is enough happiness to balance the apparent unhappiness in any hedonic scale we might devise. Our ancestors fought for these choices, and their struggle to allow people to create their own economic fates in market societies and to give them the votes to pursue their own version of happiness in politics must count for something. In any event, as Kant said, each person must plot for himself his own individual route to happiness; it cannot be ordered by anyone else.[30] That is both freedom and individualism. But it is also complacency in the face of much more sorrow and frustration than we can be comfortable with. And, as the next two parts of this book will demonstrate, there are systematic forces and reasons why reliance on the market to restore our health and on democracy to come to our rescue must both fail.

Conclusion

The final account of these various prototheories has not been written. Referring to the effects of the dominant laissez-faire individualism on our sense of well-being, one can say only that the recent pages of that account are as Robert Bellah, Amitai Etzioni, and others have reported: whatever the interpretative theory employed, too much individualism is a source of deep unhappiness because it inhibits companionship. Few major historical turnings are reversible, but should we not, nevertheless, attempt to reverse that nineteenth-century bend in companionship that has led us to where we are? Perhaps like the Asian collectivist societies we can introduce more companionship in our economistic societies—but so far the record is unpromising. I shall not prescribe but rather offer a clue to successful reform.

In my opinion, moral and cautionary appeals to family values, to greater altruism, and to loving thy neighbor will be less persuasive than straightforward appeals to self-interest. For those above the poverty line, self-interest does not lie in increased income; that is the road to a hedonic treadmill. At the fork of the road marked out by Maine, Simmel, Tönnies, and Weber, there is a signpost for the road not taken: To Companionship.

PART IV

The Market Makes People Unhappy

8

Materialism in Market Democracies

Desire for self-preservation is well received and natural. The desire for gain is a propensity no less natural, but in this case, although more useful, it is not regarded with the same approbation. This is a mischievous prejudice. —*Jeremy Bentham*

Can a market economy maximize well-being? Perhaps there is something intrinsic to market economies that limits the ability of their participants to achieve that state of grace. The irony will not be missed: markets have been defended largely because of their capacity to maximize utility or well-being, that is, to permit one to pursue happiness in one's own way and thus, within one's budgetary constraints, find that road that leads to one's individualized well-being. Intrinsic limits in the system would spoil that idyll. Part IV of this book deals with how markets inhibit well-being: first, in this chapter, with the effects of materialism, then, in the next chapter, with how well-being is an externality for market processes, and third, with the failure of the market's consumer paradise to relieve unhappiness. If the very materialistic motives on which markets rely are sources of unhappiness, what is left of the claim that markets maximize utility?

Materialism

The concept of materialism branches into two main divisions: first, a metaphysical and often historical view of what is real and causally forceful, as in the materialist dialectic. These matters are not my concern here. The second main meaning of materialism has to do with values, motives, and goals. That dubious individual economic man, whose death is often proclaimed but then ignored, is, of course, a materialist. But in what sense? Does materialism refer to the practicality and tough-mindedness that William James found characteristic of one kind of person? Or the reliance on sensory information such that only the tangible, auditory, and visible are real? I must also omit most of these cognitive issues[1] here and confine attention to motives and values: What moves a person to pursue happiness by pursuing wealth? Not Marxism but, so to speak, vulgar Marxism.

Research on materialism employs two main kinds of measures: (1) Inglehart's extensive cross-cultural research on materialist values refers to policy preferences and will here be called policy materialism; (2) research and theory on individual goals and values, the main concern in this chapter, will be called goal materialism.

Policy materialism and postmaterialism. Appropriately, policy materialism is assessed through questions dealing with preferred public policies: if a person places priority on fighting inflation and on maintaining order, that person is a policy materialist; if priority is placed on increasing participation in decision making at work or in elections or protecting freedom of speech, that person is a postmaterialist.[2] For assessing the effects of materialism on well-being, Inglehart's concept is not very useful: postmaterialists, by individual (not cross-national) measures, are only slightly happier than materialists.[3] Moreover, postmaterialism is relatively silent on the central values and goals that generally guide a person in private life.[4] Thus, in a U.S. sample of students, postmaterialists and materialists were no different in their satisfaction with their incomes, no different in their memory of material deprivation as children, and no different in the perceived materialistic values of their parents. In fact, "life satisfaction for postmaterialists is actually *more* dependent on satisfaction with income than it is for materialists. In sum," say Aaron Ahuvia and Nancy Wong, "this research has provided reason to doubt the primary theoretical mechanism proposed by Inglehart to explain his findings."[5]

Nor, in the United States, are postmaterialists particularly philanthropic: compared to others, they are not much more likely to trust people or to believe that people are helpful when they can be, and are only a little more likely to

Table 8.1. Richins and Dawson's Items Measuring Materialism

Success
"I admire people who own expensive homes, cars, and clothes."
"Some of the most important achievements in life include acquiring material possessions."
Centrality
"I usually buy only the things I need." (reverse scoring)
"I enjoy spending money on things that aren't practical."
"Buying things gives me a lot of pleasure."
Happiness
"I have all the things I really need to enjoy life." (reverse scoring)
"My life would be better if I owned certain things I don't have."
"I wouldn't be any happier if I owned nicer things." (reverse scoring)
"I'd be happier if I could afford to buy more things."
"It sometimes bothers me quite a bit that I can't afford to buy all the the things I'd like."

Source: Richins and Scott Dawson. 1992. "A Consumer Values Orientation for Materialism and Its Measurement: Scale Development and Validation." *Journal of Consumer Research* 19: 303–16 at 310. I have oversampled the happiness questions because of my interest here in the effects of materialism on well-being.

believe that people will not take advantage of one if they have a chance.[6] For obvious reasons, therefore, I will concentrate on goal materialists.

Goal materialism. In contrast to the policy focus of policy materialism, the orientation focused on here is goal materialism, the centrality and direction of the values that inform career choices and personal striving. Along these lines, Marsha Richins and her associates have developed measures of materialism which they characterized as follows: "We considered materialism to be a set of centrally held beliefs about the importance of possessions in one's life and measures the three belief-domains: acquisition centrality, the role of acquisition in happiness, and the role of possessions in defining success."[7] One grasps these principles better when the actual questions that measure these values and beliefs are given. A sample from Richins and Dawson's eighteen-item measure is given in table 8.1.

Although this scale (the three sections of the questionnaire form separate factors) is more extensive than others, other studies tap the same main dimension: "Materialists place possessions and their acquisition at the center of their lives."[8]

A second kind of research links materialism ("I must admit I put a pretty high value on material things") with normlessness or anomie. The remaining items in this "anomia scale" are measures of cynicism, for example, the undependability of friends, lack of mutual helpfulness, and the principle that the ends justify the means.[9] The interesting point here is that in a society in which a high value is conventionally placed on material things, people who admit to (or perhaps claim) that value tend to be cynical and normless in other ways.

A third approach, supplementing the Richins and Dawson questions above, is to ask people what they would sacrifice to be rich, a "put up or shut up" kind of question. This elicits a kind of denial, a tribute to the lack of cultural support for admitting that one cares that much for money. Although we know that many people work at jobs that prevent them from seeing much of their family, only 4 percent of a Gallup poll admitted that they would do that; similarly, many dislike their work, but only 8 percent said that they would work at a job they disliked even if they were guaranteed riches from that work.[10] In other answers to Gallup's poll (1990) there was little evidence people thought that wealth brought happiness: while half thought that the rich were about as happy as others, only 11 percent thought the rich were happier, compared to 36 percent who thought they were unhappier. From my own studies many years ago, I would guess that this was because they thought that wealth brought more cares than benefits.[11] For this and other reasons, Gallup found that 82 percent of an American national sample claimed that they did not envy the rich, and only 38 percent said they wanted to be rich themselves. There is a sour grapes as well as a social desirability flavor to these answers that requires some discounting,[12] but at the same time we are reminded that in their daily jobs, most people are seeking to get along, to be liked by their workmates, to keep out of trouble, to get promotions and pay rises—but hardly to be rich. That is the world of lotteries and the dreams of avarice. In fact, as in most preference orderings, the problem is ambivalence—discussed below.

Does Materialism Make People Unhappy?

Although, in their search for parsimony, economists limit the human qualities allowed for market participants to greed and rationality, markets themselves invite every conceivable motive and emotion.[13] Others have interpreted market thinking more broadly: for example, Weber's Protestant ethic,[14] and Robert Frank, Howard Margolis, David Collard, and others on altruism, of all things, in market calculations.[15] It is time to examine what economists have always assumed, namely, that greed (or material self-interest) is both the motive that makes the market work (which is partly true) and the motive that leads to maximum individual well-being (which is false, as I will show).

Richins and Dawson, whose questions on materialism I illustrated above, also included questions on people's satisfaction with their lives, the amount of fun they were having, family life, friends, and their standards of living. As it turned out, "materialism was negatively related to satisfaction in all aspects of life measured," the strongest relationship being satisfaction with standards of living (−.39), closely followed by the fun people were having (−.34) and their friendship satisfaction (−.31). The weakest relation was with their satisfaction with family life (−.17),[16] always the most autonomous area of any of the domains of life. Taking up a causal ordering question, the authors present evidence that materialism is not the *effect* of unhappiness, but rather is more likely its cause.

Tim Kasser and Richard Ryan's several studies are totally supportive. Using tested measures of psychological adjustment, vitality, depression, and anxiety, they found that "placing money high in the rank ordering [of goals] was associated with less vitality, more depression ($r^2 = .28, p < .01$) and more anxiety ($r^2 = .22, p < .05$)." In contrast, "the relative centrality of self-acceptance and affiliation [value of good relations with others] was related to less anxiety and depression."[17]

A study of college alumni (not students) helps to confirm the relationship between materialism and unhappiness: "Among 800 alumni of Hobart and William Smith Colleges, those who preferred a high income and occupational success and prestige to having very close friends and a close marriage were twice as likely as their fellow alumni to describe themselves as 'fairly' or 'very' unhappy."[18]

Following economic theory, I have from time to time referred to material self-interest but have not introduced any evidence that materialists are more self-interested than others. In fact, they are. Asked how they would spend a windfall of twenty thousand dollars, materialists, according to the data, would spend three times as much as nonmaterialists on themselves, would contribute less to charity or their churches, and give less than half as much to friends and family. There is a negative correlation of −.21 ($p <$ 01.) between materialism and giving to environmental organizations. Materialists also say, "I don't like to lend things, even to good friends" and resent "having guests stay in my home."[19] Although there is no logical reason idealists, salvationists, and "self-actualizers" should not be as selfish as materialists, empirically that is not the case. Materialist *self*-interest is a fair description.

Not surprisingly, materialists make the same assumptions that are made by economists: they "see possessions and acquisition as essential to their satisfaction and well-being."[20] And, from a different study: "Too much emphasis on this [materialist] aspect of the American dream may be a . . . nightmare."[21]

Why are the materialists wrong? Why is it that materialism in a materialist, consumer driven society is associated not with well-being but with ill-being?

Why Are Materialists Unhappy?

In capsule form we can say the following:

> (a) When income is plentiful compared to companionship, people who (b) believe that income and wealth are the primary sources of well-being, (c) see themselves and others primarily in terms of income and wealth, (d), engage disproportionately in activities they think will bring material success (rather than activities that are intrinsically enjoyable), and (e) derive their life satisfaction from their success or failure in materialist pursuits—will (f) enjoy relatively lower well-being than others.

Why do elements of this mnemonic (a) through (e) lead to the result (f)?

Materialism is a set of values and, perhaps, a set of personality traits; it is not a description limited to those in materialistic occupations, that is, businessmen, merchants, salespeople, and so forth. Many of the studies of materialism deal with students who have no other settled occupation; many of the qualities described can be found in the professions, the arts, and among intellectuals. Nevertheless, what a person does for a living inevitably influences values and what a person thinks is important. But one thing seems clear: the unhappiness of materialists does not stem from poverty. In the Richins and Dawson study, the correlation of materialism with income was .04 (NS), and in the Kasser and Ryan studies it was almost 0.[22]

Materialists tend to be less happy than others (1) because something about their values and practices is unsatisfying; or (2) because the kinds of people who choose materialist values carry within them the seeds of unhappiness. Both hypotheses are plausible.

MATERIALIST VALUES AND PRACTICES PROMOTE UNHAPPINESS

Extrinsic rewards. Materialists are said to pursue goals that have an inherently weak capacity to generate happiness. These are contrasted to intrinsic goals, which are characterized by less reliance on the approval of others: by self-acceptance, good relations with others, a desire to help the community, and physical fitness and good health. Kasser and Ryan found that the general class of extrinsic goals, of which material possessions is one, does not generate feelings of well-being. In contrast, the intrinsic goals were positively related to well-being and negatively related to symptoms of psychological distress.[23]

Loss of self-determination. Because their activities rely on extrinsic rewards, materialists are inevitably dependent on rewards controlled by others.[24] Thus, they lack the benefits of self-rewards and self-direction that come from reliance on intrinsic, noncontingent pleasures.[25] The argument has research support, but we should not forget that one of the reasons possessions are gratifying is that they enhance a sense of control.[26]

Loss of process benefits. People who work for money may enjoy outcome satisfactions without process satisfactions, that is, pleasure in doing the job itself—process benefits (see chapter 4). For example, people who work primarily for pay are somehow marked by low self-esteem and anxiety and have lower job satisfaction than those with mixed motives.[27] In my opinion, it is not the activities themselves that are less rewarding; it is the exclusive focus on outcomes that deprives the materialist of feeling pleasure along the way.[28] That is the aspect of materialism devoted to earning; as we shall see in chapter 10, pleasure in shopping, in acquiring commodities, is also generally low.

Competition and rivalry. Is it the case that market work involves more interpersonal competition and rivalry than other kinds of work? Here, I think, the economists' distinction between competition and rivalry is useful: for the economist, competition is defined as the presence of alternatives, whereas interpersonal competition is defined as rivalry. It is rivalry that is unpleasant, not the presence of alternatives, and rivalry surely is at least as common in bureaucracy as in markets.

Money is not a goal yielding satisfaction. This is a restatement of the thesis of the economistic fallacy described in chapter 4. Unlike other goods, such as glory (athletes and warriors), piety, a satisfied conscience, and companionship, money and commodities have limited powers to yield pleasure. Is the appetite for material goods less satiable than other appetites? As Durkheim, Friedrich Lange, and Samuel Pufendorf all believed, the appetite for material goods is more insatiable than the desire for these other kinds of goods. Commenting on materialists' general disappointment with their "lot in life," Richins and Dawson explain, "The lust for goods can be *insatiable:* the pleasures of a new acquisition are quickly forgotten and replaced with a desire for more. This cycle leads inevitably to dissatisfaction and discontent. . . . Empirical tests using earlier measures of materialism support this hypothesis."[29]

The reason for this distinction between the power of money and other goods to yield pleasure is not self-explanatory. The cause of the difference, I believe, is not so much insatiability per se, as that, unlike other goods, money is both an input (earned) and an output (spent). Consequently, it is possible to want to spend more than one earns—a sure prescription for misery, as Micawber once explained to David Copperfield. Thus, M. Joseph Sirgy suggests that "this proclivity to overconsume and underproduce may be partly responsible for materialists' inflated and value-laden expectations of their standard of living."[30] Furthermore, money is thought to offer a passport to all other pleasures—to piety, a good conscience, and gratifying companionship—but it does not.

Finally, many Americans are ambivalent about their values and goals.[31] For example, it was possible (1973) for American students simultaneously to "welcome less emphasis on money (80%)" and to list "the money you earn" among their most "important objectives (61%)." It is a strange combination, perhaps handled through compartmentalization but also, I think, implying a degree of internal conflict.[32] Just being rich is not quite good enough for self-presentation. Thus, it is the *priority* given to material things more than their lack of value that makes materialists' lives unrewarding.[33]

If the values and practices of materialists provide us with a clue to their relative unhappiness, the character of materialists may offer further clues: Why do they choose materialist values?

THE CHARACTER OF MATERIALISTS

As soon as one moves from values, which can be held by a variety of kinds of people, to personality traits and types, one risks analytical problems—but some research has done this with modest success. For example, Russell Belk and his associates have found a syndrome of envy, nongenerosity, and possessiveness that withstands a variety of psychometric tests.[34] Other evidence suggests that a person who places special value on material things ranks lower on a measure of ego development.[35]

How do materialists differ from others? Materialists are socially awkward, that is, "materialists have poorer social adjustment and mental health" than others.[36] This weakness follows from an unusual preoccupation with the self—narcissism.[37] The unhappiness of materialists, therefore, is explained not only by their unrewarding values, but also by their low social skills and psychological distress.

Materialists are less effective than others in their life pursuits. Here is a further curious twist to this study of economic man: he has a lower sense of efficacy than his soft-headed brothers and sisters.[38] Low efficacy tends to find expression when people set goals that are either too easy, lacking challenge, or so difficult that failure is not a defect. So it is with materialists, who set standards of wealth for themselves that they cannot reach.[39]

Materialists' activities are more passive than those of others. A major reason for examining the characters of materialists, and not just their values and activities, is that student subjects are not involved much in making money;

rather, the activities that distinguish them are those that have little to do with making money: materialists watch a lot more television than others, an activity that most studies show is not really enjoyed very much (for example, less than gardening or cooking).[40] In contrast, nonmaterialists are more likely to spend time socializing with others or planning for their futures, activities that are usually (but not always) more enjoyable.[41]

Materialists are more concerned about being treated fairly than are others. Materialists are quick to perceive discrepancies between what others get and what they get.[42] As Belk said, the materialist syndrome embraces envy. But the reference groups of materialists are not their neighbors and friends or people like themselves (with whom they have no rapport) but rather remote others, perhaps those portrayed on the television shows they watch with such attention.

How Is Materialism Learned?

There are three interrelated theories of how materialism is learned and reinforced: socialization, market experience of contingent reinforcement (plus ideology), and evolutionary theory. They are interrelated: the relative importance of socialization depends on what the market teaches everyone in market societies, which, in turn, depends on the nature of humankind—evolutionary theory.

Socialization hypotheses. Compared to the parents of nonmaterialists, the parents of materialists have been found to be less nurturant, less democratic and warm, and more controlling.[43] This suggests that materialism thrives in an atmosphere of control and domination whose very nature is, at least for a child, an unhappy one. Beyond this indirect route, the children of parents who emphasize materialist values are, not surprisingly, more likely to be materialists.[44] Those surrogate parents television sets portray the goods that money buys as the epitome of life itself; protecting children from pornography, we carelessly expose them to the vivid lessons of materialist appeals.[45]

Although materialism is not related to level of income among adults, young adults from poor homes were especially likely to emphasize attainment of wealth among their values.[46] Growing up in a poor society, however, *is* different from growing up under more favorable circumstances. One of Inglehart's studies makes the change in the wealth of society particularly vivid. Over many years Japanese polls have asked, "In bringing up children of primary school age, some think that one should teach them that money is the most important thing. Do you agree or disagree?" From 1953 to 1978 the "agree" answers declined from 65 percent to 45 percent. An average of only 6 percent of the people changed their minds each year, whereas the difference between cohorts varied by year from eighteen percentage points in 1953 to forty-four points in 1978, when Japan was a relatively rich nation; the change was almost entirely due to replacement of old cohorts by new ones.[47]

Such emphasis on childhood experiences and cohort changes minimizes the experiences of people themselves and assigns their responses to what can only be habits or traits learned at an early age. This must be partly wrong. Every day in the market people are learning that the object of work and the very condition for life itself is to earn money. And, of course, parents learned the same way and conscientiously taught their children what they had learned.

Contingent rewards in the market. The contingent reward system of the market is the greatest teacher of materialistic striving that could be imagined—a perfect Skinner box.[48] But what do people learn from their reinforcement by pay? The evidence on payment by results (PBR) and token economies in asylums and schools suggests that payees learn exactly what they are rewarded for learning and nothing more: they learn to work for pay and that pay is the value of work. Whether the materialism they learn in the market is likely to affect cross-situational dispositions, that is, whether they develop a materialistic trait, is uncertain. For example, in matters of work discipline and responsibility no genuine dispositional set is created in the token economies. So little was internalized, indeed, that when these institutions are made into more rational and orderly places, the measured character structures (cross-situational dispositions) of their populations seem to remain unchanged.[49]

But in the actual market something else is taking place: materialist rewards are moralized and become part of participants' ethical systems as well as part of their operational codes. And according to one persuasive theory of behavior, the worker will first see what he does and then discover why: "I must like money because I have been working for it."[50] In my opinion, people do learn materialistic values in markets, but to a lesser extent than has been attributed to the market process by its critics.

This learning and reinforcement process may be effective, but nonmaterialists experience it as well. One needs something to differentiate between the two. Whereas the differential socialization discussed above may be one answer, experiences on one's first job lead to another. For example, although individual values steer people into their first jobs (working for money, with people, or for the public good), from then on the values inherent in those jobs become self-reinforcing. Work experience in jobs in which making money is the goal reinforces goal materialism, but working in jobs in which good social relations are both the method and the goal reinforces that kind of nonmaterialistic motivation as well.[51] It is not quite the case that one becomes what one does, but there is some (Aristotelian) process of that kind at work.

Of the many social changes that might increase or decrease materialism, the increased work roles of women and adolescents and the role of religion are obvious candidates. If working for money encourages the idea that money is the goal of life, then when more women enter the workforce, they and the children whose values they influence at an early age should foster a rising materialism in the population.[52] The same is true of the increasing employment of high school students.[53] Similarly, rising or declining focus on religion might offer alternative goals and values. It has been said, for example, that the decline of religion in Europe has paved the way for the rise of materialism,[54] but there has been no such decline of religion in the United States.

Evolutionary Inheritance of Acquisitiveness and the Love of Possessions[55]

As noted in chapter 3, if some 40 percent of our traits are influenced by our genetic inheritance, one might well search the record for the influence of that inheritance on, if not materialism, at least acquisitiveness. One approach to evolutionary theory is through the behavior of very young children. Lita Furby reviewed the evidence in the Human Relations Area Files[56] and concluded the following: "The large majority of references stated or implied that children are naturally possessive and acquisitive and that society must inculcate something different if so desired." But she was skeptical: "Most of the material was too general and fragmented for solid conclusions."[57] On the other hand, there are certain repeated and possibly universal experiences that might make the appreciation of "what is mine" and what is not mine (theirs) a universal culturally learned disposition.[58]

Ernest Beaglehole searched for animal behavior that might suggest acquisitiveness and found that except for hoarding for nest-building and food, there was no evidence of cross-species acquisitiveness that matched the human pattern.[59] Similarly, laboratory experiments with animals show that they do work for "pay," but they increase their work as pay is decreased—hardly a pay maintenance behavior.[60] In another approach, Lawrence Becker, a property lawyer, searched for the origins of individual possessiveness in territoriality and was equally dismissive of any evolutionary foundations for human acquisitiveness and possessiveness. Among other points, Becker found that territoriality was a group and not an individual claim—territoriality worked through bonding.[61]

Buried in the theories of socialization and contingent reinforcement is a further theory of the nature of humankind: in the absence of these influences children will grow up to want something other than money and material goods. This idea, explicitly borrowed by Inglehart, is a Maslovian "need-hierarchy" theory and although suggestive has not fared well in subsequent research.[62] I know of nothing in the theory of human development that draws that Maslovian picture of what people are like when they are not taught otherwise; quite the contrary.[63] That is, although we have not found the evolutionary links to prove the point, some aspects of materialism may be the natural tropism of humankind.

Materialism Increases from Primitive to Traditional Society—And Then Declines

Although the increased proportions of the population exposed to the contingent reinforcement of the market suggest an increase in materialism in postindustrial society, the cross-cultural evidence tentatively suggests a curvilinear pattern of materialism (acquisitiveness and love of possessions) across levels of development. In simpler societies, anthropologists report, people are much less materialistic than in the advanced societies of Europe, Asia, and North America: "The characteristic feature of primitive economics," said Richard Thurnwald (1932), "is the absence of any desire to make profits from production and exchange"; Bronislaw Malinowski wrote (1922), "Gain, which is often the stimulus for work in more civilized communities, never acts as an impulse to work under the original native conditions"; and Karl Polanyi: "If so-called economic motives were natural to man, we would have to judge all early and primitive societies as thoroughly unnatural."[64]

They do not trade to make profits, but are they less possessive? Perhaps, since so much of wealth is communally owned. Comparing urbanized workers with peasant or cattle-tending villagers in third world countries, Alex Inkeles and David Smith found that the villagers were more likely to think of their possessions as sources of happiness.[65] But they are vulnerable to materialistic appeals. Doob points out that in Africa, at least, the desirability of material goods is the first thing learned on the way to civilization.[66]

Moving up the developmental scale (a haughty Western concept), one finds many developing (and sometimes preindustrial) countries in the cross-national study of SWB by Diener and Diener. They found that materialism (measured by the relative contribution to SWB of income and wealth) is more characteristic of poorer countries than richer ones: "Our findings do not support the contention that wealthier nations are more materialistic, valuing material good to the exclusion of all else. . . . This set of findings supports the idea of a post-industrial society in which attention turns from the acquisition of material goods to self-development and other pursuits."[67]

Within the developed countries, should variation in materialism be related to level of wealth (the variable explaining the effect of income on well-being) or to the number of years a country has been relatively wealthy (as is the case for the influence of democracy on well-being — see chapter 15)? The evidence presented in chapter 4 showing that the percentages reporting "getting rich" to be their most important goal in life were lowest in Britain and highest in Japan, with the American in between, suggests that the time a nation has been relatively prosperous has at least some small support. If one followed Inglehart's theory of the importance of age cohorts and of lengthy socialization during periods of peace and prosperity on materialistic values, one would expect just such an influence of generational experience with affluence.

Cutting across the levels of wealth and income is marginality. Aborigines living in advanced economies (for example, Maori in New Zealand, Native Americans in the United States) are more materialistic than the dominant majority, but not just because of their relative poverty. Wherever people are marginalized they become materialistic,[68] for financial success, being an achieved good, is the "ethnic's" end run around the barriers of status and ascription.

Which societies are likely to be the most and the least materialistic? I suggest that primitive societies are least materialist, then the postindustrial societies in which we are living,[69] then peasant or traditional societies (Tönnies's gemeinschaft!); and most materialist would be industrializing societies whose members have just discovered they can influence degrees of wealth (as Montesquieu said). One is reminded of John Maynard Keynes's belief: "The love of money as a possession — as distinguished from the love of money as a means to the enjoyments and realities of life — will be recognized [when we are rich enough] for what it is, a somewhat disgusting morbidity, one of those semi-criminal, semi-pathological propensities which one hands over with a shudder to the specialists in mental disease."[70]

POSTMATERIALISM AND GOAL MATERIALISM IN MODERN SOCIETIES

For a time, following Inglehart's hopeful account, people thought that policy postmaterialism was winning over policy materialism. But later inquiries have come to three conclusions: (1) policy materialism is less the product of socialization in peace and prosperity than simply of increased levels of education.[71] (2) After the long economic recession of the late 1980s and 1990s, policy postmaterialism began to decline in Europe in the 1990s.[72] As we shall see, this decline is not (yet) characteristic of the United States. And (3) by some measures, policy materialism is inversely related to the goal materialism that is my primary concern.[73]

Changes in materialism, of course, are only part of broader changes in values and ideology. The best way to think of changes in both policy materialism and goal materialism is as part of a general process of value change. Elinor

Scarborough puts it this way: "The fading of religious orientations, the weakening of social bases of left-right materialism, the emergence of feminist, 'green' and 'postmodernist' outlooks are all indicative of a general process of value change. . . . The less advanced countries seem to be different only in coming later to these processes."[74]

If this is true of policy materialism, goal materialism should also be vulnerable to a variety of contemporary ideologies (religious, feminist, ecological) which are partially incompatible with materialist values.[75] As we shall see, these influences, different in their religious complexion in the United States, have not yet eroded the materialist values of the American public, perhaps because the reinforcing ideology and practices of the market are so much stronger in the United States. In the early 1970s and again in 1980, among eleven advanced Western nations the United States was among the less materialist nations, ranking in the bottom quarter of the roster of policy materialist countries and in the top half of the postmaterialist roster.[76] Where overall attitudes about materialist values clash with specific preferences for materialist goals (see below), some ambivalence is again suggested.[77]

The conflict between trends in Europe and the United States, the ambivalence people have about money and materialism more generally, and the loose relation between policy materialism and sense of well-being all lead to uncertainty about trends for both policy and goal materialism in the United States.

IS MATERIALISM RISING OR DECLINING IN THE UNITED STATES?

To repeat: My premise is that diminishing marginal utility for any value or good in relative abundance implies that materialism will contribute less and less to happiness as a society becomes richer. If people are rational, materialism will decline. We have two tests of this thesis, one from a remarkable long series on personal goals and values of first-year students in American colleges and another from the National Election Studies dealing with policy materialism. The account of the change in student values pairs two values: materialist desire to seek wealth as a career and a value "to develop a meaningful life philosophy" (fig. 8.1). Note, first, the gradual decline of materialism and the rise of a meaningful philosophy for a decade to about 1978, then the reversal of these trends for a ten year period until about 1987, followed by a high plateau for the next seven years to 1994.[78] Among American college freshmen over this period materialism has certainly not declined.

A simultaneous rise occurred in both policy materialism and postmaterialism from 1972 to 1992, postmaterialism rising more rapidly than materialism and passing it after 1988 (fig. 8.2). In some ways, however, these rises were artifacts of the computer-generated graph, for the dispersion is greater than

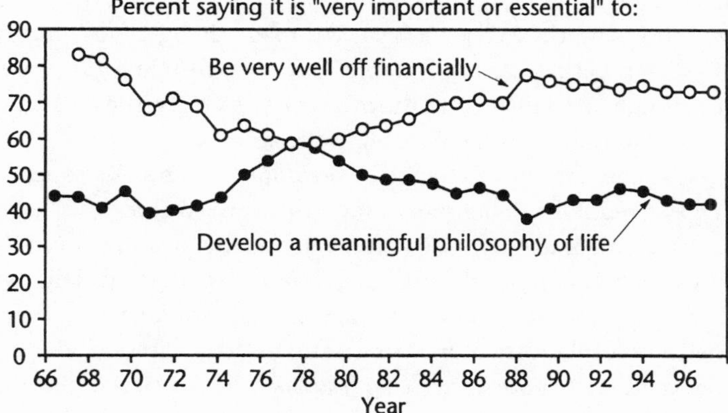

Figure 8.1. Goal Materialism among U.S. College Freshmen: Percent Saying It Is "Very important or essential" to "Be very well off financially" or Saying to "Develop a meaningful philosophy of life," 1966–96
Source: Annual surveys of 200,000+ entering American colleges annually as published in *The American Freshman* (Los Angeles: Higher Education Research Institute, UCLA). Figure created by David Myers and reproduced with his kind permission.

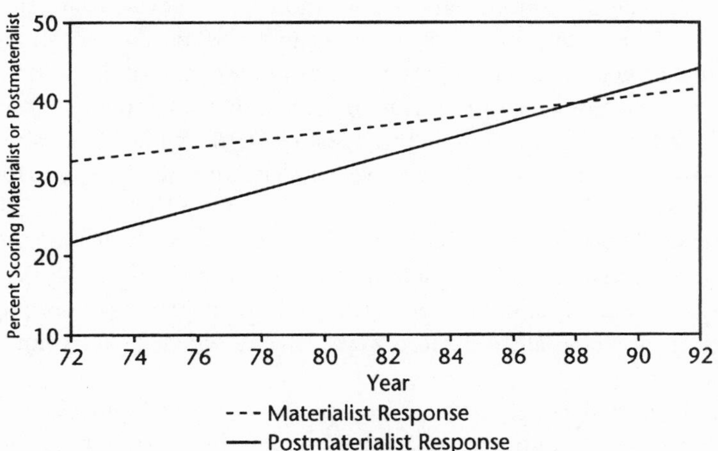

Figure 8.2. Policy Materialism–Postmaterialism as "Goals of the Nation," 1972–92
Question: "For a nation, it is not always possible to obtain everything one might wish. [hands card with various goals] If you had to choose among them, which one would seem most desirable to you? Which one would be your second choice?" 1. "Maintaining order in the nation" [scored materialist]; 2. "Giving people more say in important political decisions" [scored postmaterialist]; 3. "Fighting rising prices" [scored materialist]; 4. "Protecting freedom of speech" [scored postmaterialist].
Source: National Election Studies [NES].

the central tendency. A closer look shows policy materialism rising rapidly in the 1970s and, with the exception of 1984, maintaining a fairly high plateau in the 1988–92 period. In both graphs the 1972 to mid-1980s period is a period of rising materialism, and the mid-1980s to early 1990s is a period of high, stable materialism. Is there a ceiling effect?

Looking at the pattern of change of postmaterialism in Europe, Scarborough suggests that when materialists (and their mixed categories in the four-question scale) fall to about 75–80 percent (still, obviously, the overwhelming majority of the population), their decline is somehow arrested. This pattern of change, says Scarborough, "suggests that some ceiling effect is at work: below the 20 per cent level, postmaterialism continues to progress; above a level of 20–25 per cent, further advances seem fragile."[79] The pattern is just the opposite of the one I am suggesting: at a high level of affluence and education (and the materialism that produced it) satiation with materialism sets in, and then, and only then, do the alternatives to materialism seem widely attractive. If both theories—of a satiation effect and of a ceiling effect—are at work, one would expect unhappiness to follow: materialists do not enjoy the fruits of their efforts but something blocks substituting goods that would be more satisfying.

Some further support for the ceiling effect is suggested by comparison of Japanese changes mentioned above with those of American youth shown in figure 8.1. The Japanese analysis shows a substantial decline in a straightforward test of goal materialism, the value of money as a guide to life, and it shows that the younger were less materialistic than the older in every time period. As we have seen, comparable questions in the United States found an actual rise in materialism among first-year college students from 1970 to 1987. The postwar decline of Japanese materialism and the rise and continuously high materialism of the U.S. youth (fig. 8.1) do not intersect: the Japanese are still more materialistic ("most important thing in life") than the British or Americans. There does seem to be a ceiling effect: later stages of development tend to erode materialism up to a point beyond which that erosion is discouraged. Why?

One suggestion noted above is the rise of women and adolescents in the labor force, where contingent reinforcement and the value of money in what they do increase their materialism. That is, as countries become richer they once again enlist women and youth in the work process. Or perhaps the occupations in which nonmaterialists are happiest (teaching? social work? civil service? research and development? the performing arts [outside of Hollywood]?) are in limited supply.[80] Perhaps it is not possible to find round holes for the round-pegged nonmaterialists, but the alternatives are not promising: Shopkeepers and small businesspeople are less happy than people in other similarly rewarded occupations,[81] and managers are more anxious about their futures than are professionals.[82]

I suspect that market economies simply require that most of the population enter careers that demand for their gratification some love of money; that is how they are designed and regulated. As Frank Knight observed, however, many participants "do not like the [market] game at all and rebel against being compelled to play it and against being estimated socially and personally on the basis of their success or failure."[83] So the materialist is a realist and adopts the values that he thinks must be adopted to play the game—and doesn't, in the end, find satisfaction. Realism of this kind takes the form of searching for happiness where it is least likely to be found.

Materialism and Companionship

As we move from an industrial to a postindustrial society, our values should shift from money to companionship, which yields greater utility or SWB. The idea has some resonance with various indicators of change. Postmaterialists, for example, emphasize "being esteemed by others, getting along with friends," but they also shift "out of the family toward broader social and leisure activities." It is the policy materialists who "are much more likely to emphasize the importance of marriage, family life, children."[84] From my perspective, the postmaterialists are trendy, New Left apostles whose decline in Europe in the 1990s and flattened profile in the United States may be part of the general decline of the ideologies of the 1960s. Postmaterialists may not be representative even of European trends. In the 1980s, although two-thirds of a sample of Europeans wanted "less emphasis on money" almost nine out of ten wanted a society with "more emphasis on family life," and this must have included many of the postmaterialists.[85]

Part of the materialist syndrome is the crowding out of companionship because of the precedence given to material pursuits. Materialists do, in fact, want "warm relationships with others"—they just do not give this goal a high priority.[86] The proposed change in priorities, then, does not require the introduction of a new and uncongenial value, but a relaxing of the dominance of an old and unfruitful value to permit the expression of a genuine but currently subordinated one.

There is an infelicitous cycle here: (1) materialism does not lead to life satisfaction or happiness; (2) unhappiness, and especially depression, leads to withdrawal and tends to alienate people; (3) lack of companionship—and companionship is a genuine, if subordinated, value for materialists—contributes further to the materialist's unhappiness. Should we pity the self-made businessman who sacrifices so much for his success? Well, his achievements console him, but at a cost whose sources he may never know.

Political Economy of Materialism

The materialist is economic man, endowed with all the qualities that are said to be necessary for market economies to do their work. If he were also endowed with rationality (which is itself negatively related to well-being),[87] the market would then maximize his well-being—would it not? Consider the following paradox: market rationality leads the materialist to pursue wealth; more wealth (beyond the poverty level) has little effect on well-being. Furthermore, something about the kind of people who choose (if that is the verb) to be materialists is associated with low life satisfaction. Materialists, economic men, endowed with the qualities that economists assume are the characteristics of winners, tend, in fact, to be losers from the start.

9

Is Well-Being a Market Externality?

> *The measure of success in economic activity is the welfare experienced by human beings, in the broadest sense of the term. It is not just material things that affect persons, but the qualities of their relationships with each other.*
> — *Randall Bartlett*[1]

Do markets make for happy societies? If materialists are not a happy lot, is there something about the market itself that inhibits joy or at least reduces life satisfaction? This chapter and the next offer some tentative answers to this question: this chapter briefly reviews the general problem of income and the labor market, and the next deals with the consumer market; both chapters deal with the friendship–income tradeoff. I hope to avoid the clichéd indictments of poverty-in-the-midst-of-plenty, exploitation (whatever that may mean), greed and avarice, and so forth. These indictments may all be true; but I want to say something different.

The thesis of this chapter is twofold: First, the one source of happiness that it is within the power of markets to give, money, is losing its power to make people happy. By now this point is thoroughly familiar and will merit only a brief reminder. And second, the principal sources of happiness and unhappiness are market externalities, things that markets may casually ignore, make better or make worse without endogenous correction. In dealing with the labor market, I will take up such questions as the relation of level of income to security of income, enhancement of intrinsic work enjoyment, and the market's treatment of those special spheres of felicity, family solidarity, social inclusion, and sociability at the workplace. In these several respects markets often inhibit rather than facilitate the maximization of utility.

Money and Well-Being: A Review

We have seen that in the postwar period (1) happiness has declined in the United States while per capita income has grown—and psychological depression has grown in advanced countries throughout the world; (2) although the process of economic growth is an unhappy experience, the new income more than compensates people in developing countries for that wrenching process;[2] (3) in the United States the hedonic yield of increased income has declined at least since 1957, with the consequence that beyond the poverty level higher levels of income yield either no or at most trivial increases of SWB; (4) as a consequence there seem to be diminishing hedonic returns to income such that the returns are great in the poorest countries, modest and erratic among the relatively rich countries of Europe, and offer even smaller and apparently declining yields in the United States. Americans are not alone: as Japan increased its per capita income fivefold during the postwar period, its measured SWB changed hardly at all.[3] We have also seen (5) that in rich countries, especially in the United States, companionship consistently yields greater hedonic returns than any other good; and (6) that the greatest fatality in the modern marketizing process is the value of children, an apparent cost of the erosion of family life. In contrast, countries that have preserved relatively strong—albeit weakening—families (for example, South Korea and Taiwan) are uniquely resistant to the epidemic of major depression that infects economically advanced countries everywhere else.[4]

Observe the dilemma: rich nations, made richer by their focus on productivity, have happier citizens than poor nations, but at the same time those persons who dedicate their lives to getting richer are likely to be unhappier than others. One might say that the sacrifice of well-being now for the well-being of our children is, like saving for our children, a generous act. But three considerations intrude: first, a small proportion of these dedicated entrepreneurs gain satisfaction from their achievements; but, as Schumpeter said, they do not care much about money but rather pursue a vision of a "private kingdom" which they may create and then rule over.[5] They are not materialists in the sense described in chapter 8. Among ordinary mortals, the hedonic yield of money varies with the priority given to material success.[6]

But, second, there is no evidence that the hard work of the parents in the 1940s to produce economic growth (if their hard work had anything to do with growth) made the children's generation any happier. Indeed, the level of well-being for children and youth entered a precipitous decline in the 1960s and 1970s. Children have no direct way of knowing that they live in a society in which they have been devalued (see chapter 3)—but in growing up they will have experienced the pains of that devaluation.

Third, comparing rich and poor countries, one will conclude that the sacrifices and effort of economic growth are worth the costs—even though, by itself, growth of per capita GDP adds nothing to SWB.[7] In poor but not in rich societies, the stresses of growth seem to be counterbalanced by the pleasure of increasing income. Comparing the differences in wealth within the rich countries, one might well wonder whether the grinding struggle to maximize economic growth is worth the pain, and one might settle, instead, on some optimizing strategy, some better mix of economic growth and, say, more *gemütlich* rendezvous in a café or more mateyness in the local pub (to enlist three cultures in a mixed metaphor of experience).

As I turn to the second main thesis, the market externality of the principal sources of unhappiness, I shall focus in this chapter on the labor, not the consumer, market. Nevertheless, one must bear in mind that unhappiness has many origins in the values of the consumer market. It is difficult to tell whether this is due to the market or the ideology of the market, with its definition of what is worth doing and where, in a noneconomic sense, value lies.

Two fundamental questions emerge: (1) given the fact that the market was a thriving institution long before we became relatively unhappier and depressed, can we explain this variable mood by reference to an antecedent institution? The answer to this question is central to my argument: declining marginal utility of money and commodities relative to companionship gives the constant market presence a variable effect. And (2) given both the perils of materialism and the greater materialism of peasant societies (love of possessions but not profit maximization—see chapter 8), how much can we fault the market for our growing unhappiness? One answer is that earlier household (or other) economies embedded in their societies do not fracture social relations when their members pursue material wealth.[8] But there are other answers, which I will now explore.

The Sources of Happiness Are Externalities in Labor Markets

Marx's belief that the circumstances of work are the principal sources of ill- and well-being and Durkheim's belief that insatiable demands for ever more commodities destroy contentment are both right and both support the arguments in this and the next chapters. But, following Marx (and extending his immiseration thesis by a different route), here I will focus on work and the labor market. First, I wish to draw attention to how certain differences between the consumer and the labor market influence well-being. The feedback in the consumer market is direct and rapid, giving consumers more control over the sources of their well-being (utility). They may want things that, in the end, do not make them happy, but, within their budget constraints, they have a fair chance of getting what they want. In labor markets, workers have far less choice, for their skills are not fungible, as is money; they are often faced with a monopsony, whereas consumers are less often faced with monopoly; exit as a means of control is far more costly to the worker than is exit for the consumer, and many of their choices are in internal labor markets under tight control by their employers. Moreover, the choices of rewards in the labor market are more constrained; it rarely offers employees choices between, for example, job security and level of pay.[9] The two are usually related, but they may not be.

There is a deep reason for the undervaluation of the psychic income and enjoyment of work: in market accounting work is a cost, whereas consumption is a source of benefit. Making workers happier and work more pleasing is likely to be a charge on profits, whereas making goods pleasanter and consumption more pleasing is probably a source of profits.[10] The underlying assumption is that people work in order to earn in order to consume; work is a disutility for which income and consumption are the compensating utilities. But even in a market economy, this is often, perhaps usually, not true.[11] In the studies of intrinsic work enjoyment (to be treated shortly), it is clear that work is often not a disutility at all, but rather work and work mastery are the sources of very great pleasure, as most professionals and artisans intuitively know. The sense of mastery is especially important, as indicated by the priority given to the "sense of efficacy" in Andrews and Withey's study reported in chapter 4. Finally, for workers, competition among firms—made worse by globalization—is the enemy. Where competition among firms is limited by market power, firms are more indulgent to such worker benefits as in-house training, job security, and other amenities. (Contrary to economic theory, when it can, management has a record of sharing firm profits with workers.)

There are two good reasons for claiming that the pleasantness and security of work are externalities: first, worker satisfaction has almost no effect on productivity (see below). And second, although Adam Smith thought that wages would reimburse workers for such unpleasant features of work as hazards and dirtiness, in fact, they are rarely reimbursed by the market; they are true externalities.[12] It does not pay to devote resources to benefits accruing to workers but not to the firm's net income.

I now turn to more detailed examination of some of these unacknowledged market pains and pleasures.

LONGER HOURS AND GREATER STRESS?

First, I want to raise a candidate for explaining unhappiness—in order partially to dismiss it. In her book *The Overworked American*, Juliet Schor presented a forceful argument that the American worker is overworked and severely stressed. She says that although for a hundred years up to 1940 hours of work had declined, from that time forward (a little earlier than the rise of clinical depression and the decline in happiness) hours of work have generally increased.[13] The stress comes from the "time squeeze" rather than from what people actually do at work or greater responsibilities thrust upon them. I do not doubt that Americans and others in advanced economies are stressed, but I do doubt that their stress comes from working longer hours and overwork.

As to the longer hours, Schor discounts official data and various time studies, but their cumulative weight does not indicate that many people have increased their work hours in recent decades. The matter is technical (and Schor might be right), but two sets of figures suggest caution: U.S. Bureau of Labor statistics show almost no change in average work time over the twenty-eight years from 1960 to 1988 (38.3 versus 39.1). As recently as March 1995, Federal Reserve Board officials said that in the previous month the "average length of the workweek fell by 24 minutes to 34.5 hours."[14] And second, comparison of hours worked (1993) in different countries shows the United States to be about in the middle (40.0 hours), with Britain at 43.6 and France at 39.0. (I will turn in a later section to some of the injuries to families and children that are clearly related to the time squeeze people often suffer.)

I am also skeptical about the nature and meaning of work stress. In an impressive ten-year longitudinal study of the effects of work on personality and attitudes, Kohn and Schooler report, "Working longer hours tends, in the long run, to be reassuring. Certainly one cannot conclude that job pressures, as we have measured them, are uniform in their psychological import. . . . Since all . . . job pressures might be regarded as 'stressful,' these findings cast doubt on any interpretation that the effects of stress are necessarily deleterious."[15] Moreover, the time squeeze has a double-sided relation to well-being. If people "always feel rushed" *or* if they report that they "never feel rushed" and agree that they have "time on [their] hands," in either case they are very likely to be unhappy and dissatisfied with leisure time (fig. 9.1).[16] Note that there are (or were in 1976) at least twice as many people who have "time on their hands" as "always feel rushed."

Granted that Schor shows that "workers' compensation claims related to stress have tripled during the first half of the 1980s,"[17] in light of the fact that

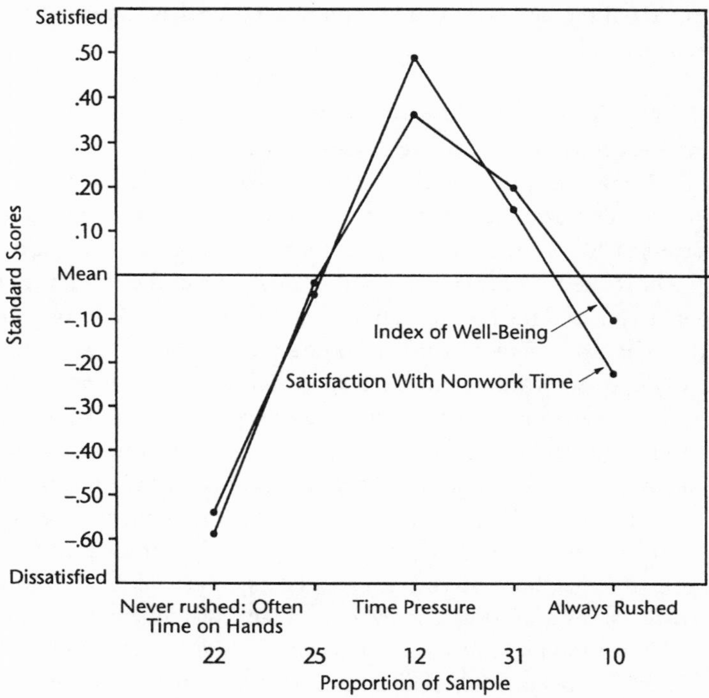

Figure 9.1. Variations in the Index of Well-Being and Satisfaction with Nonwork Time as a Function of Reported Time Pressure
Source: Angus Campbell, Philip E. Converse, and Willard L. Rodgers.1976. *The Quality of American Life: Perceptions, Evaluations, and Satisfactions.* New York: Russell Sage, 357. © Russell Sage Foundation. Used with permission of Russell Sage Foundation.

from 1960 to 1988 the rate of "workers killed or disabled on the job" has declined from twenty-one to nine per one hundred thousand, the increased claims for compensation are very likely to be related to other features of work, especially job insecurity, or to greater health consciousness in the population. There are more serious reasons to indict the market.[18]

STRESS AND UNHAPPINESS

Recall from chapter 3 how the stress-response "increases heart rate and mobilizes energy from fat; it inhibits the immune system, pain perception, digestion, growth, inflammation, and sexual urges and activity." People under stress are more susceptible to illness, depression, anxiety, low self-confidence, and dissatisfaction than people not experiencing stress.[19] Along with reported symptoms of depression, stress is the best predictor of low evaluations of quality of life.[20] Is stress increasing? In Britain, more than 80 percent of medical practitioners reported that "the number of patients treated for stress-related problems has risen significantly since 1979."[21] In the United States, polls find 59 percent reporting "great stress" at least once or twice a week,[22] and Schor reports evidence of a "dramatic rise" in reports of feeling stressed, with 30 percent of the population saying that they experience high stress nearly every day.[23] "In 1986," said Louis Harris, "the U.S. is a stressful society."[24]

The causes are multiple and not wholly clear; they include sources similar to those of depression mentioned in chapter 2: marital discord, children in difficulty, job loss or threat of loss, chronic financial insecurity, long-term conflict with others — and the work demands that Schor finds excessive. The labor market demands skills and performances that are rewarding only after they are painfully learned. Also, there is overstimulation by the pervasive and intrusive media (in an interview many years ago, a working-class man complained to me of "the many tiny messages" that bombarded him daily); there are too many life choices — the very thing on which both the labor and consumer markets pride themselves without concern for the resulting overload; and lack of constraint by custom, demands for self-actualization, that is, demands to discover or create an identity rather than to accept a given identity, and, as mentioned, the requirement to make friends rather than relying on kin and neighborhood for companionship all add to the stress. Women's dual roles (women's liberation?) are especially stressful, as we shall see below. If we are programmed to prefer the familiar and the similar, cosmopolitanism is stressful at the same time that it is ethically rewarding. Aspirations and expectations are too high for peace of mind; that is, of the two qualities, excitement and tranquillity, that Freedman (and John Stuart Mill) said comprised happiness, there is too much excitement and not enough tranquillity.[25]

The point is not that these sources of stress are attributable to the market but that they are market externalities for which the market has no cure or whose market remedies would only make matters worse. They are not solved by economic growth but rather may be the consequences of later stages of that growth once it has done its work of providing for basic needs — and for the surplus that we call civilization.

UNEMPLOYMENT

Because the sequence of rising and falling unemployment and inflation bears no close relation to the rising tide of unhappiness and depression, it is difficult to blame these economic maladies for the increase in infelicity. Moreover, following patterns of adaptation familiar in other areas of life, it seems that living in a society with relatively high unemployment does not cause the employed to be more unhappy.[26] Indeed, some evidence suggests higher work satisfaction for the employed in areas with higher unemployment compared to areas with lower unemployment.[27] Nevertheless, *being* unemployed is excruciating. As Argyle has pointed out, among the unemployed, "depression increases and becomes worse with time. . . . Alcoholism increases; there are twice as many heavy drinkers [among the unemployed]. Attempted suicide is 8 times more common, especially during the first months. In several of these studies it was possible to demonstrate that unemployment caused the mental ill health rather than vice versa."[28] A German study found that "prolonged unemployment or re-unemployment led to depression, reduced hope, and financial problems. . . . Being employed or retired led to a reduction of depression and financial problems."[29] Unemployment drastically impairs physical well-being: "Results [of several studies] show that loss of job or the prospect of becoming jobless has been found to cause elevated blood pressure and serum cholesterol, increased concentration of blood catecholamine and elimination of noradrenaline, an increase in the frequency of stress, and psychosomatic diseases." And these damaging effects were not limited to the unemployed, for the spouses and children of the unemployed have increased somatic disorders and higher rates of admission to hospitals.[30]

Finally, a disturbing study from Australia suggests that those unemployed who were more motivated to find a job were also more likely to suffer depressive symptoms.[31] One is tempted to attribute this pattern to the Protestant work ethic and its associated guilt for failure, but these highly motivated persons were not more likely to blame themselves for their predicaments, but rather the system. This is just as well, for the Protestant ethic has been found, at least in the United States, not to be related to economic success.[32]

Making a distinction between economic costs (operating the economy below the production possibility frontier) and market costs (costs that invoke homeostatic tendencies to maintain or return to equilibrium), one can say that unemployment incurs high economic costs. Paul Samuelson and William Nordhaus wrote, "The losses during periods of high unemployment are the greatest documented waste in a modern economy. They are many times larger than the estimated inefficiencies (or 'deadweight losses') from monopoly or of waste induced by tariffs and quotas."[33] But is unemployment a market cost as well as an economic cost? Apparently not, for there is no endogenous tendency for markets to maintain full employment, and there is reluctance by human agents in central banks to encourage it lest inflation accelerate.[34] Unemployment is a market externality.

I have found no evidence that inflation has any effect on clinical depression, dissatisfaction with life as a whole, or unhappiness. Thus, one study finds that "while unemployment was found to be significantly related to both mood and stressful life events, inflation was related to neither."[35] Cross-nationally, "there is at least no correspondence between average happiness and inflation rates."[36] Nevertheless, the public does fear inflation and believes it reduces people's standard of living.[37]

I conclude that unemployment certainly adds to the prevalence of unhappiness, though not to a rising tide of it, and that, in spite of public fears, creeping inflation is innocent in both respects. By increasing unemployment to control inflation we are apparently increasing misery for no direct (though possibly some indirect) gain in well-being.

ECONOMIC SECURITY

While the economistic fallacy deals with levels of income, it does not at all apply to the security of one's income or, more especially, the security of one's job, which does have an effect on SWB in every bracket. The fact that money (sometimes) buys security as well as goods and services obscures many interpretations of people's desire for money.[38] But two tests help to clarify the matter. In the early 1970s Andrews and Withey asked national samples to rate their satisfaction with various aspects of their lives: 49 percent ranked their feelings about their pay as "delighted" or "pleased," whereas only 26 percent ranked their feelings about "how secure you and your family are" at the same level.[39] An even simpler way of sorting out these meanings is to ask people what money means to them. In a 1993 poll, people were asked, "Money represents different things to different people. I'd like to find out what it represents to you personally. Here is a list. For each item, please tell me if it is a very important aspect of what money represents to you, a somewhat important aspect, or an unimportant aspect." The percentage of respondents citing the various aspects of money as "very important" is given in table 9.1.

The estimates of people about what is important to them is often an unreliable indicator of the contribution of that feature of their lives to their overall sense of well-being. Fortunately, a study of the quality of life helps to settle that question. Reporting on his study of a Michigan sample (1983), Alex Michalos found that "of the 12 domains, satisfaction with *financial security* has the greatest relative impact on satisfaction with life as a whole." In accounting for this priority, Michalos develops his concept of how people establish their standards of well-being by observing certain "gaps: the gap between what one has and wants, between what one has and thinks others like oneself have, and between what one has and the best one has had in the past." He finds that "fifty four percent of the variance in satisfaction with financial security can be explained by [these] three perceived gaps." Of these, the burden of explanation

Table 9.1. "Very Important" Aspects of Money

Security	78%
Being able to help your children	63
Comfort	62
Freedom	58
Pleasure	45

Source: Roper Starch Worldwide Inc. May 15–22 1993, reported in *American Enterprise,* Nov./Dec. 1994, 98.

falls first on "the gap between what one has and wants."[40] People tend to want security more than they want higher income, and, in contrast to level of income, the absence of such security has a powerful effect on their well-being.

There can be little doubt that, after the great gains in economic security brought about by the New Deal and the Great Society, the American public has grown increasingly insecure in the past several years—too recently to account for the rise in depression but nevertheless reflected in the continuing decline of SWB. The press has not neglected this growing economic insecurity, as the quotations from interviews and survey reports in the *New York Times* sampled in note 41 indicate.[41]

What is the market's role in coping with this insecurity? *Cui bono?* Well, the consuming public is saved from price increases, but managers and shareholders profit from insecurity: "Worker insecurity may well be the flip-side of the American economic success. Workers who feel insecure are less likely to demand pay increases."[42] Worker insecurity is good for profits. At this point, one wants to say more than that job insecurity is a market externality, since the most powerful players benefit from it.

WORK AND LEISURE SATISFACTION

The fundamental point here is again that work satisfaction of all kinds is a market externality. The significance of this point emerges when one examines how various facets of work contribute to SWB. First, one should note that in general most people like their jobs and that job satisfaction contributes substantially to overall life satisfaction—and vice versa.[43] But my concern at the moment is in changes in work satisfaction: there was a steady drop in work satisfaction of about 5 percentage points over the 1972 to 1994 period (a decline more marked among women than men) (see fig. 2.3). The decline is not new: a literature review in 1979 found that in the twenty years from 1959 to 1979 there had also been a decline in satisfaction with the intrinsic qualities of work, and in that period no objective change in the nature of the work could account for it. The implication was that people's standards had changed.[44]

*Table 9.2. Declining Preferences for Work Compared to Leisure, 1955 and 1991**

"Which do you enjoy more, the hours when you are on your job, or the hours when you are not on your job?"

	1955	1991
Hours on the job	38%	18%
Hours off the job	49	68
No opinion	13	14
	100	100

*We cannot attribute this difference between pleasure in work and pleasure in leisure to a relative increase in leisure satisfaction, for the General Social Survey [not shown above] shows that from 1973 to 1994 there was almost no change in leisure satisfaction—even though there was, it is often said, a decline of leisure time over this period.
Source: The Gallup Monthly, September 1991, 2.

A Gallup poll in 1991 revealed a different aspect of the decline in work satisfaction (table 9.2). There is an interesting corollary to this apparent trade-off: by ordinary economic theory, if one values work more (putting a higher price on it), one should also value leisure more—because of the higher opportunity costs of leisure.[45] That seems not to be the case: at least valuing leisure more is apparently associated with valuing work less.

On the job, lack of close supervision, absence of routine and repetitive work, and the presence of substantive complexity in what one does contribute most to work satisfaction.[46] By and large, Frederick Herzberg is right: the intrinsic features of work (largely unpriced by the market) make the most important contributions to satisfaction with one's work: pleasure in what one actually does, the congeniality of colleagues, and the sense of making a difference.[47]

With this in mind, we can examine several potential explanations of the decline in work satisfaction and the growing sense that one would rather be elsewhere: changes in the nature of work itself, in sense of fairness, in feelings about companionship at work, and in the belief that the work is intrinsically interesting. Two of these can be dismissed rather easily: changes in what one does at work and sense of being treated unfairly.

Changes in the nature of work. The main argument about changing work demands is the deskilling thesis that Harry Braverman has put forward,[48] but I think it has been conclusively shown that although there was a period of deskilling when assembly lines were introduced, the postwar trend has been to increase the substantive complexity of work.[49]

Fairness. Briefly, in contrast to other forms of work satisfaction, there is little evidence that people feel either that they are unfairly paid[50] or that they are individually discriminated against because of their sex (but this does not apply to feelings of general sex discrimination).[51]

One other point about market fairness: growing inequality of income over the past twenty years might have, but has not, roused a storm. Why not? Because the fairness of one's treatment is evaluated by comparing one's own treatment to that of similarly paid others, the relevant reference group, rather than to groups much richer or poorer than oneself. Thus, the national distribution of income is largely lost from sight. This pattern of within-group comparisons is one reason Marxist predictions of class conflict failed. Indeed, as Verba and Orren report (see chapter 4), except for the high salaries of film stars and sports heroes, something very close to the actual distribution of income by occupational classifications is approved by leaders of many different groups, including unions, farm groups, and cultural associations.[52]

Companionship. For those seeking jobs, pay may be the most important consideration,[53] but for the employed, enjoyment of companionship at work is more important.[54] Unfortunately, for at least part of the postwar period that concerns us, enjoyment of companionship at work has declined,[55] contributing to the decline in work satisfaction shown in figure 2.3. (I will turn to this more fully below in discussing the question of sociability at work.)

Intrinsic work enjoyment. As Scitovsky pointed out, intrinsic work enjoyment is a major source of unpriced well-being: "The difference between liking and disliking one's work," he said, "may well be more important than the differences in economic satisfaction that the disparities in our income lead to."[56] If *utility* means life satisfaction and not just preference ordering satisfaction, intrinsic work enjoyment is an unpriced means of maximizing utility. It is a market externality. How, for example, does the market appropriately reward the 68 percent of the American workforce who say, "I'm fully committed to my work and often do more than I have to. My job is important to me and I sacrifice a lot for it"?[57] How does the market deal with the process benefits ("the joy of the working" — Kipling) discussed in chapter 4? As is the case with hazards, the market does not usually compensate people for doing things which most people dislike doing or reduce their pay because they are doing what they enjoy[58] (except, for example, lower pay for actors, musicians, and college teachers?). Demand for intrinsic qualities at work has increased with rising education — and its absence in many of the jobs offered partially accounts for declining work satisfaction.[59]

Work life is not unrelated to the second broad topic I wish to treat as a market externality: the effect of the market on family and friends. Often, indeed, both the quantity and quality of work life are major determinants of family life (as is shown in the studies of the relation between work and family)[60] and the pleasure one takes in one's friends.

Market Externalities: Friends and Families

Having followed Scitovsky to the point of saying that the market is not the most important source of most of our utilities (neither as pleasure nor as preferences), should one embellish this point by saying, somewhat hyperbolically, that pleasure itself is a market externality? (How F. Y. Edgeworth would squirm!) After all, it is not commodities but our social relations that contribute most to our well-being, and only a small proportion of these relations go through the market. And since, by some definitions, society *is* our network of social relations, should we say that society is a market externality? Polanyi is the great pioneer in this area, but I do believe he was wrong in this respect: "Instead of the economic system being embedded in social relationships," he said, "these relationships are now embedded in the economic system."[61] Not at all. Most of our social relationships in the family, the pub, café, and restaurant, the carpool and the train, the stadium and the grandstand, even in front of the television (during one-fifth of their viewing time people are talking to each other) are conducted without the hint of a transaction or the mention of price. Society, or at least that portion comprising social relations, is a market externality in the sense that there are no homeostatic tendencies for markets to return to any one of their many equilibria according to how these social relations are conducted. Except as they may influence prices, these relations simply do not figure in market calculations. But the reverse is not true, for, as we shall see, market behavior is not an externality for social relations.

Here I would like to reinstate the time squeeze, not as it may affect stress at work but as it relates to family felicity. Work satisfaction, as might be expected, is closely related to marital satisfaction, for strain at work inevitably spills over into strain in marriage and, even worse, stressful childhoods. Job insecurity is a major source of family strain, and unemployment for the breadwinner, of course, is a disaster. (As mentioned in chapter 3, the worst effects of the Great Depression on children had little to do with material deprivation and much to do with parental stress.)[62] About half of the working population reports that they now have less time for their families, and working mothers, surely the most overworked part of the population, report "a lot" or "extreme" stress from their dual roles.[63] That is one horn of the dilemma; the other horn transfixes housewives, who are generally less happy than working mothers.[64] If a dilemma can have three horns, children occupy the third: women, whether engaged in market work or not, report an average decline (1965–75) of more than 20 percent of their time devoted to "family care."[65] Inevitably, this strain has an influence on the well-being of children, a strain that is not captured in the surveys of adult happiness but, as noted in chapter 2, is revealed in the epidemiological studies of depression in which children are found to experience a rising tide of depression that is even greater than that of adults.[66]

If work time dominates family time in market economies, the absence of work, unemployment, can have even worse effects on children. A Finnish study found that "children and members of families of the unemployed suffer from various somatic and psychosomatic disorders, take a less active part in various health education promotion programs, and have a much higher admission rate to hospitals than children of employed families."[67]

These familial costs are externalities to the generation of employers whose decisions count, but they are family internalities and may imply actual money costs to a future generation of employers. Thus, to relate the theme of insecurity and lack of work enjoyment to the hypothesis that the breakdown of family (and warm friendship) relations is a principal cause of the rise of depression and unhappiness, it seems that the labor market's tendency to externalize these costs to workers and their families is a major source of people's dysphoria, not because work is a disutility, often quite the opposite, but because the practices of the market rob workers of time for family life. Family life is a market externality.

I have suggested that market economies can no longer count on increased income to maximize or even promote utility and have no endogenous interest in or power to cope with many of the sources of unhappiness and, in more extreme cases, of depression. Now I turn to another aspect of labor market effects on companionship, this time at the workplace.

SOCIABILITY IN MARKET WORK

It has been said that capitalism unites people as it divides them: the bourgeoisie in ever more monopolistic corporations and the working class in ever larger factories (and unions?). Solidarity forever! Had it developed, that solidarity might not have yielded well-being, dividing families across class lines, at the workplace making management, however selected, an alien force, and, like nations, uniting masses of people by use of symbols rather than friendship. We may never know how class solidarity would have affected SWB. But we might at least inquire about how market forces influence companionship in both internal and external labor markets. These forces operate within the context of things I have already discussed: the choice between investments in companionship or income producing activities, the market's indifference to persons, the effect of economically induced mobility on family and neighborhood, and chilling aspects of "the cold society" discussed in chapter 6.

The basic principle that influences all internal (within-firm) relations between workers and their firms is the conflict between agent (employee) and principal (employer). By increasing productivity (the efficiency directive), the firm benefits, the benefits being shared first by owners and managers and second by employees, whose jobs are made more secure when the firm thrives. The relationship is not reciprocal: when workers thrive (increase *their* incomes), neither management nor owners are better off and possibly worse off. More surprisingly, when workers are more satisfied with their jobs, the firm is not better off except in a tight labor market, for, as mentioned, there is no consistent relationship between worker satisfaction and productivity or profitability.[68]

Market encouragement or discouragement of companionship, therefore, has nothing to do with worker satisfaction, only with the effect of companionship on productivity and profitability. One indication of market hospitality to companionship is whether people who behave in a companionable way are rewarded. Whereas "friendliness" and "respect for others" are rewarded, "gregariousness" and behavior prompted by the "need for affiliation" are not.[69] Conflict among workers inhibits productivity; friendship may not foster it, but some fellow feelings may help. At very early stages in variously repeated industrial revolutions, when third world migrants go from village life to factory life, they learn to treat women and apprentices with a little more compassion and empathy.[70] In market firms, workers guided by the bonding instinct walk a narrow line.

Management is not exempt from these market constraints. One study reports, "It is hard to escape the inference that men who wanted to keep their shops small and friendly, as in face-to-face working groups, were less likely to do the things that would lead to rapid expansion in their business."[71] Managers endowed with the need for achievement, on the other hand, tend to emphasize growth of the firm (although more in size than in profits), but measures of the need for affiliation are generally negatively related to the need for achievement. The market is choosy about how much and what kind of companionship will be encouraged by management as well as by workers.

Why do market principals not enlist the power of community and fellow feeling in motivating their employees? In Asian collectivist societies familistic behavior was at the expense of meritocratic efficiency, but in primitive societies this solidarity is a powerful force for productivity. Thus, the anthropologist Raymond Firth observes, "Powerful incentives to work lie in the individual's membership in a social group. He dare not relax lest he lose the benefits of membership."[72] Marx was expecting from the industrial era in the West something more natural to primitive and archaic societies: in the West, the agent–principal differences in interests intervene, and worker solidarity is not solidarity with managers but against them. As Michael Buroway documents so well, small-group solidarities are often conspiracies to sabotage the efficiency imperative that drives the system.[73] Management, then, also treads a narrow path: to promote the profitability of the firm, neither their own needs for affiliation, nor their workers' affiliative tendencies, especially should they lead to worker solidarity, can be given extensive license.

Conclusion

Is there no escape from the hedonic treadmill implied by market imperatives? In chapter 3 I suggested that although the poor do advance in well-being as income increases and the educated classes might escape into a so-called postmaterialist world of friends and ideas, the materialist middle, just as the ghost of Hamlet's father is doomed for a certain time to walk the night, is condemned to walk the treadmill until redeemed.

But escape into companionship is available to all, and escape into intrinsic work enjoyment could be facilitated. True, companionship may cloy and invade privacy (the diminishing returns to companionship), but we are not there yet, and, from research on the intrinsic pleasures of challenging work, at least when it is self-directed, we know that intrinsically interesting work is characterized by the desire to continue working in "free time." Rather than being satiable, that kind of work is addictive.[74]

Market economies have made us prosperous, but they do not maximize utility or the satisfaction of human wants. If made with skill and restraint, government policy might convert markets to that purpose (see chapter 18). To this end governments must, so to speak, go off the gold standard and treat increased per capita GNP as a useful but inadequate means to the principal end of both governments and markets: maximizing well-being.

Returning to Keynes's advice to his grandchildren, we find him once again transcending the limits of his discipline. He urged these "grandchildren," now adult inhabitants of a future he envisioned quite differently, to try "encouraging, and experimenting in, the arts of life as well as the activities of purpose [earning a livelihood]." "But chiefly," he said, "do not let us overestimate the importance of the economic problem, or sacrifice to its supposed necessities other matters of greater and more permanent significance." Keynes thought that "the permanent problem of mankind" is learning to live well,[75] or, as we would say, learning to maximize well-being in its broadest sense.

10

Pain and Loneliness in a Consumers' Paradise

The consumer market is supposed to be the place where people reap their rewards for the "pain" of working. And of course, they do. Whatever we may think of commodities and their touts, advertisers and salespersons, shopping malls, mail order catalogs, and corner grocery stores are all places where people generally get what they want and generally (four-fifths of the time) are satisfied with what they get. By and large, this plethora of goods and services is what attracts people to market economies from third world and former communist countries, their noses pressed against the display window of television dramas and advertisement spreads.

In this chapter I will address mainly two questions: How do buying and consuming contribute to well- and ill-being? And: How do buying and the consumer culture influence that major special source of well-being, companionship?[1] We live in a consumers' paradise; what devil has come to disturb us in this Eden? Is that throng in the mall a "lonely crowd"?

The Consumer Culture

One well-known text on consumer behavior imagines what Rip Van Winkle's observations would be on waking from his very long sleep: he would "come to the conclusion that selling, buying, and consuming lie at the very core of life in most of the developed countries of the world."[2] An anthropologist calls this preoccupation a "rage to consume" and attributes it to the synthetic "logic of scarcity" of the capitalist system.[3] Calling modern man *Homo consumens,* Erich Fromm claims that "we, as human beings, have no aim except producing and consuming more and more."[4]

Many observers find in the United States the apotheosis of shopping and consuming; consumerism shapes "the totality of American life in a very profound manner."[5] And "we live in what may be the most consumer-oriented society in history."[6] Consider three indicators of the consumer culture: time spent on and enjoyment of shopping, exposure to advertising, and proportion of income spent rather than saved. Americans spend more time shopping than members of any other society—and save a smaller proportion of their incomes. Women spend more time shopping than men (in a middle-aged group, about 4 percent of their time, compared to about 2 percent for men),[7] but men share the same consumer culture. Is this a bourgeois culture? Perhaps, but the working-class members have absorbed it through television and, in the United States, because of their drift to the partially mixed-class suburbs, where they pick up from their neighbors the ingredients of the consumer culture.[8] African Americans are full-fledged members of the consumer culture: "Black consumers appear to react more favorably to advertisements than do white consumers." With the exception of housing, in which residual limitations constrain purchases, African Americans tend to buy more status products than whites.[9] The consumer culture is universal in the United States. And for some, but not all, it is a source of great happiness.

One researcher has written, "Americans go to shopping centers on average once a week—more often than they go to church or synagogue. . . . We have more shopping centers than high schools." These are external indicators; but closer to my concern here are attitudes toward shopping: "Some 93 percent of American teenage girls surveyed in 1987 deemed shopping their favorite pastime."[10] Mature women also report that, on average, they enjoy shopping, although this enjoyment differs by class (upper-class women like the exciting displays and elegance of their shopping venues, while working-class women like shopping for bargains). But for women with jobs outside the home, shopping has become a hassle and decreasingly pleasurable. Men, never very high on most shopping (their specialties are cars and consumer durables), are also finding shopping less enjoyable.[11]

The Hedonic Unfruitfulness of Commodities

Following the lines of thought of the economistic fallacy, which claims that above the poverty level, higher income does not increase SWB, one is prepared for evidence that the things income buys will not be hedonically very fruitful. Furthermore, as we saw in chapter 8, the people whose goal it is to accumulate commodities and wealth are not themselves happy people. Thus, in Andrews and Withey's classic study of the contributions of various activities and domains of life to life satisfaction, a consumer index including "the goods and services you can get when you buy in this area—things like food, appliances, and clothes" ranked only twelfth (beta .06) among thirty possible domains, behind even political attitudes (which are usually tangential to feelings of well-being) and totally swamped by feelings about recreation, family, and, of course, the self.[12] The Andrews and Withey question is not ideal for my purposes, but the answers do suggest that buying and commodities generally are not a major source of SWB.

How does enjoyment of shopping compare with enjoyment of other activities? Not very well. Referring again to Juster's account of what people like doing in and of itself, we find that of twenty-two activities, grocery shopping was next to the last in both 1975 and 1981, while "other shopping" ranked seventeenth, or fifth from the last, in both years, just ahead of repairing the house. Note, too, that shopping enjoyment declined in this six-year period.[13] Other studies confirm this ranking.[14] The pleasures of shopping are certainly muted in accounts of what people enjoy doing, and the decline in enjoyment of nongrocery shopping seems to confirm other reports that adults like shopping less than they used to. Why should it be that what pleases teenage girls does not please most people?

PLEASURES AND DISPLEASURES OF THE CONSUMER CULTURE

The problem here is to assess whether and why people are or are not made happier by the consumer culture in which they live. Given the proportion of our lives spent buying and consuming, the matter has a bearing on our well-being: "As consumption forms a continuous and important part of everyday life, satisfaction with consumption is a crucial aspect of general well-being."[15] Of course acquiring the food, clothes, housing, and recreation that we want does give pleasure, just as being deprived of them gives pain. In this book, however, I am not talking of the pains of deprivation but of the pains or reduced pleasure from acquiring and consuming the goods and services that we can pay for.

The first point is to notice that the happiness of the consumer is a reflection of the happiness of the person: the top-down theory of well-being. Alice Isen waylaid people in a shopping mall and gave some of them small, unexpected favors. The trivial act put them in a good mood. A little farther on in the mall these same people were asked by someone else about their satisfaction with the maintenance and repair of their appliances. Those in a good mood were more likely than others to say their appliances were in good working order.[16] Satisfaction with one's goods is dependent on much more than the quality of the goods; it depends at least as much on the mood of their owner. It is not so much that people are made happy or unhappy by their shopping and consuming as that happy people like what they are doing, eating, and wearing. Later we will see how satisfaction with one's life drives political satisfaction; in the same way it also influences consumer satisfaction.

Similarly, whereas many feel controlled or victimized by market pressures, people who feel that they can control the events in their lives also feel that they are in control of their shopping experiences. For most people possessions are empowering, and possessing money especially so, whether or not people are endowed with internal locus of control. The fungibility of money is a special advantage in this respect for it permits a wide variety of empowering acts.[17] For individuals, this is the meaning of consumer sovereignty; it is experienced at the point of purchase, not in the abstract. Joan Robinson may be right when she says, "Consumer sovereignty can never be established so long as the initiative lies with the producer. For the general run of consumer goods the buyer is necessarily an amateur while the seller is a professional."[18] But, as in the case of popular sovereignty (see chapter 13), it is the experience of contingent reinforcement and the immediacy of choice that confer the sense that I am sovereign in this encounter. As an experience of positive freedom, this feature of the consumer culture is, as Milton Friedman says, a strong recommendation for the market.[19]

Beyond the pleasures of freedom and control are pleasures of self-expression in shopping and consuming, pleasures in providing for others, and all the other pleasures mentioned above. When "traditional homemakers," say, "I like to make my cakes from scratch" or "I like to go grocery shopping . . . [and] arrange for children's convenience,"[20] they reflect anticipatory pleasures in creativity and motherly responsibility. The bitter taste of the sovereignty of a consumer *culture* need not prejudice our recognition of the pleasures of buying and shopping.

As contributions to people's well-being, advertising may help individuals to create and manage satisfactory identities: macho images for beer drinkers, feminine images for perfume buyers, and so on.[21] It may also be true that self-images are increasingly taken from the world of consumption rather than from the world of work, modeled, it is said, on the "heroes of consumption," the movie stars and the jet set, rather than on the "heroes of production," people like Andrew Carnegie, Henry Ford,[22] and, perhaps in the 1990s, Bill Gates. Sometimes this process of image-making may, indeed, represent an "enlargement of the self"[23] and hence more than a simple answer to the question of identity. In this sense, consumer identities may be a "solution to the existential problem of alienation"[24] and thus be given a Sartrean quality that we may not like — but we are not called upon to comment on such identities; if they help to answer existential questions, they contribute to well-being.

The dark side of defining the self in terms of consumer goods is, of course, that the purpose of advertising is to make people feel inadequate if they do not have certain image-enhancing products — even laundry products that add the "final touch . . . [associated with] effusive love and approval of husband."[25] Obviously, the purpose of advertising is to create not satisfaction, but dissatisfaction, including dissatisfaction with the self. In this respect, advertising's emphasis on status and upward comparisons does not make people happy; people are made happy, if by comparisons at all, by downward comparisons.[26] Indeed, the attempt to give a product status appeal has an implicit message: "You are inadequate without product X," surely a painful message, especially if you cannot afford product X.[27]

There is a hidden agenda in the consumer culture: ever greater consumption implies longer hours at work and more intensive attention to earning, including working second jobs and overtime. It is this feature that Schor finds offensive.[28] But while hard work done to achieve a purpose is not in itself a hedonic loss, the stress and worry that may accompany it is — as pointed out in chapter 9. Does the hidden agenda imply a hidden hand as well? Bernard de Mandeville thought so: "luxury / Employ'd a million of the poor, / And odious pride a million more: / Envy itself and vanity / Were ministers of industry." Over the first three-quarters of the twentieth century, advertising appeals to luxury (as contrasted to meeting needs) increased.[29]

One general point helps to explain the particular pains I will briefly mention: Although it is said that the function of the market is to satisfy human wants and so to maximize various satisfactions, it is not true that the function of advertising is to maximize satisfaction; rather, its function is to increase people's dissatisfaction with any current state of affairs, to create wants, and to exploit the dissatisfactions of the present. Advertising must use dissatisfaction to achieve its purpose.

Finally, although I believe that materialism (love of possessions) is stronger in peasant cultures than in consumer cultures, it is quite likely that consumer cultures do contribute to the materialism that is associated with lower SWB (see chapter 8). Would dissatisfaction with the results of what might be called the incontinence of buying characterizing these cultures make post- or nonmaterialists of us? An originator of studies of consumer behavior, George Katona, thought not: "Dissatisfaction with the quality of consumer goods . . . contributes to societal discontent, but not to a revolt against material values."[30]

THE OPPROBRIUM ATTACHED TO CONSUMER CULTURES

In many ways, the problem is not so much that people are made unhappy by the consumer culture as that they are happy with it all! Much has happened since "asceticism was carried out of the monastic cells into everyday life, and began to dominate worldly morality."[31] As mentioned, in the United States today there are more shopping malls than churches, and the malls are far more popular. This story of the opprobrium attached to consumer culture has many facets: it fosters hedonism and a "rage to consume" (Marshall Sahlins); it undermines its own work ethic by replacing it with a consumer ethic (Daniel Bell); it encourages invidious comparisons (Veblen); it makes a fetish of money (Marx); because a consumer's happiness is thought to be purely relative, it leads to insatiable striving (mutatis mutandis, Hobbes, Machiavelli); and it stimulates the appetites by each increase in wealth (Durkheim, Lange). Pleasure, unlike happiness, has no philosophical support (outside the utilitarians), and indulgence is associated with weakness of will. In religion, gluttony, like lust, is a cardinal sin. The hidden hand argument has its ethical parallel: consumption is self-serving, narcissistic, and egoistic and of no visible public benefit (except as Mandeville found public virtue in private vice). Consumption invites debts, far more in the United States than in Europe, where people are more likely to save to spend rather than to incur debt to spend. If saving is a virtue in most societies (but not in Japan in the 1990s), then spending is the denial of virtue, an indulgence. Where, in Robert Kuttner's phrase, "everything is for sale,"[32] all intrinsic values are foregone, including the relations among people. (It was Carlyle who invented the term "cash nexus," but Marx and Engels applied it to family relations.) And: "A society obsessed with consumption cannot at the same time be cultured or produce a culture."[33] But this is too elitist for an account of popular responses to advertising.

How do people respond to the saturation of the airwaves, newspapers, and billboards with appeals to consume? Early in the development of advertising on television, the American public seemed at least resigned to watching advertisements as a price for watching the programs that the advertisements made possible.[34] Was this because private advertising was the main source of funding for popular programs? In Britain, where British Broadcasting Corporation programs are paid for from funds generated by the taxing of television sets, it was reported in 1983 that some fifteen studies found only about 5 percent of the population objected to advertising on ITV (Independent Television) and other commercial channels.[35]

DECISION-MAKING PAINS IN THE CONSUMER CULTURE

For some prospective buyers it may be true that the "search is part of a larger information-gathering activity *enjoyed both for its own sake* and because consumers are *intrinsically* interested in particular products."[36] But for others, especially those with other things on their minds, the pains of making buying decisions are substantial. Among these are the following:

Ambivalence. Following the literature on rational choice, one does not encounter the concept of ambivalence; but following actual studies of decision making in consumer markets, one finds it cited as one of the most common problems of decision making. According to this research, we "simultaneously want and do not want an outcome, experience it as both pleasure and pain, love and hate."[37] That experience of uncertainty is itself a pain. Worse, it exemplifies our divided selves, our multiple identities: saver and spender, bon vivant and prudent family provider.

Regret. Although postdecision dissonance reduction (reassuring ourselves that what we bought is, after all, better than what we did not buy) is a chronic, if irrational, protection against regret, there remain many shopping and consumer regrets: guilt for the way we overspent our budget, shame for purchasing a jacket that does not fit well, regret that we did not take advantage of a sale, anger with ourselves for what we did not buy.

Cognitive Overload

Choices proliferate beyond our pleasure in choosing and our capacity to handle the choices.[38] The consumer market is the venue for cognitive overload—or would be if we did not adopt shortcuts that make resolution of doubt possible. But the love of the search mentioned above is partially belied by the fact that fewer than one-tenth of consumers in one sample checked the advertisements before shopping for shoes and other personal accessories, and only one-half did so when shopping for large appliances. In two-thirds of the cases the buying spouse failed to check with the other when buying major appliances. In general, there was "a major disinclination to seek out information."[39] Or, if they get relevant information, "most consumers don't know how to process or use the little factual information they get from advertising."[40] Most distressing are reports that increased information about products both increased satisfaction with the information and decreased the ability of consumers to select the goods with the characteristics they had previously said were what they wanted.[41] But this is the application to consumer behavior of problems of cognitive overload well documented elsewhere—including the findings that cognitive complexity increases with challenge up to the point of overload, when it falls back to a very simple level.[42] For better decision making, the advantages of information are curvilinear: both too little and too much are disadvantageous.[43]

Choices That Do Not Satisfy

People like what they have chosen *because* they chose it; in this respect the market and its culture have inherent advantages. This is the theme of mastery and personal control mentioned above plus the theme that whatever is mine is more likeable (as William James once noted). And it is also true that people have better opportunities in markets than in politics to test the merits of their choices, a point so important to Schumpeter.[44] But when shoppers do not use the information available to them, do not buy the product with the characteristics they specify as most desirable, do not plan for major purchases, let adventitious commentary take precedence over solid information, are vulnerable to salesmen's ex parte remarks, are swept away by symbolic but not product-relevant appeals, and let price represent quality (frustrating market analysis of the function of price),[45] it is little wonder they often do not get what they want, even though they may have gotten what they asked for. As Kahneman and his colleagues have demonstrated empirically, wanting and liking are different aspects of gratification.[46]

Now or Later

How does advertising influence the capacity for deferred gratification? We know that deferred gratification is impeded by the visibility of the rewards to be earned by holding off consumption. In experiments that became famous, Walter Mischel and his associates varied the visibility of the reward (candy bar) offered to children if they delayed their requests: if they could see the reward they were more likely to break discipline and consume it on the spot.[47] But isn't it the function of advertisements to make visible and urgent the appeal of some attractive object? Quite apart from advertising, the impulse to buy can be exigent and have unhappy consequences. "The impulse to buy is hedonically complex, may stimulate emotional conflict, and is prone to occur with diminished regard for its consequences" — which are often quite unfortunate.[48] Moreover, there is a special problem of overeating by those who are stimulated by external sensory stimuli, eating whenever they see or smell food, rather than by internal stimuli such that when they have had enough they lose their appetites. It is characteristic of the market to offer visual temptations at every turn, making self-control a special problem for a consumer culture.

As a consequence of these appeals to consume now, in the United States "the desire to save is frequently pushed into the background and saving becomes residual. Some people wait to see how much remains after diverse other wants have been satisfied before they save."[49] And is it an accident that the country that spends the most per capita on advertising has the lowest savings rate among advanced economies? On economic grounds we may regret the encouragement given by the consumer culture to spend and enjoy ourselves beyond our means (yet recall Keynes's diagnosis of the 1930s depression as partially due to oversaving!), but on hedonic grounds we must reserve judgment.

Optimal Arousal

A cognate problem is the level of arousal people need or enjoy: gamblers appear to have special appetites for arousal, appetites which override normal restraints[50] and which are made worse by temptations—the very function of advertising. In general, people perform best at moderate levels of arousal. For example, "children manifest their highest level [of performance] at an intermediate degree of arousal and lower levels as arousal increases or decreases from that point."[51] Effective advertising follows this code of modest arousal,[52] but what is modesty on Madison Avenue may be experienced as lustful or exigent in other quarters: "I must have Lady Chantilly shampoo to attract my lover." The pain is twofold: the lovers of those who buy the shampoo have other things in mind and do not respond as predicted (but does the very belief that I am loveable make me loveable?); and those who cannot afford the shampoo believe that their lovers will not love them.

Self Versus Others

While the burden of ethics is to make the consideration of others at least as important as the consideration of the self, market economics has no such bias. Remember the familiar lines from Adam Smith: "It is not from the benevolence of the butcher, the brewer, or the baker, that we expect our dinner, but from their regard to their own interest."[53] True enough, but we are nevertheless confronted daily in the small decisions of life, as well as the large ones, with self–other dilemmas, and here, I think, advertising and the consumer culture more generally reinforce our bias to put ourselves before others. In this respect, we might say that advertising relieves pain by licensing our preference for ourselves; it does not abolish conscience but merely applies it exclusively to the duty one owes to oneself and others for whom one buys things.[54]

Limited Capacity of Commodities to Gratify

Compared to human beings, commodities do not love or of themselves confer esteem (which is a social experience) or make a person feel appreciated or worthy, although they may, indeed, confer a sense of mastery (as my computer does so well). The products may taste good and save trouble and relieve pain, but, as mentioned in the report on Andrews and Withey's study, these experiences rank low in the roster of things that predict SWB.

Companionship in a Consumer Culture

In this section I want briefly to take up some of the common allegations of the generalization of market mentality to personal relations and to put this in the context of the errors of generalization across domains mentioned in chapter 9.

MARKET COGNITIONS AND COMPANIONABLE RELATIONS

Markets Erode Trust in Others

Whereas Tönnies and Fromm speak of the universal suspicion engendered by market relations, Kenneth Boulding argues that "without an integrative framework, exchange cannot develop, because exchange . . . involves trust and credibility."[55] In spite of the extensive humanistic criticism of the market as the source of distrust, Inkeles and Diamond's comparison of human traits in modern and less modern countries finds "a strong positive association between economic development and a psychological disposition to trust other people."[56] But, as we saw in chapter 2, at least for a quarter of a century, in spite of greatly increased levels of education, interpersonal trust has declined. Can it be that, like so many other qualities, the relation of trust to markets is curvilinear: whereas early marketization encourages trust, late marketization discourages it? I doubt it. I believe rather that interpersonal trust is first a function of rising education and affluence, and its subsequent decline has to do more with television (see below), crime, and the increasing proportion of the population living in metropolitan areas.[57]

Commodification of Persons

The claim is that in market societies people come to see others as market objects to be exploited and manipulated. In violation of Kant's categorical imperative, markets encourage people to treat others as means to their own ends—and teach the value of people as mere instruments. Marx and György Lukács, Fromm and Marcuse believe in this commodification theory. But are people treated less as means to one's own end in bureaucracies? Rivalry and exploitation of juniors in bureaucracies may be just as great as in markets. Impressionistically, it is not clear that markets instrumentalize human relations more than other contemporary institutions.

Money Is the Measure of All Things

The claim is that in market societies money becomes an obsession and everything, including people, is evaluated in money terms. "How much do you make?" becomes a question of individual worth or, more likely, a criterion for how to treat another. I believe that the evidence for this allegation is supportive, but the use of a dominant value for how to classify or treat others is general across all kinds of societies. Although we deprecate assigning value to individuals on the basis of their economic status,[58] it is nevertheless true that the default values of information on income extend to concepts of people's other qualities: their honesty, responsibility, even good looks.[59] In this market society, most people's money schemas are indeed uniquely, if mistakenly, informative. But market societies at least avoid ascriptive values, like lineage and family.

Unidimensionality of assessment has a social base: multidimensionality occurs in communities in which there are repeated encounters among people who know each other in many roles, whereas unidimensionality occurs in cities, where people know each other more superficially and only in single roles. This is the difference between gemeinschaft and gesellschaft and the difference between village and city rather more than between market and nonmarket societies.

The Imperialist Market Encroaches On and Corrupts Roles and Activities That are Better Guided by Their Own Values

This claim is the general form of the more specific questions I have been exploring: Can we insulate families and friendship from market influences? In 1997, the issue emerged in reverse form in the emerging collectivist Asian economies that have been so much admired: they failed to insulate their markets from familistic practices—nepotism and cronyism. Familism has its own imperium. So does the polity, not as regulation and control but as the practice of populism (every goal is tested first for the political support it promises to elicit) and the ubiquitous exchange of favors.[60]

The most effective argument against the marketization of everything is Kuttner's treatment *Everything for Sale*.[61] Writing against the then-current (1997) tendency to rely on market forces to solve all social problems, he shows that the criteria of what is called economic efficiency tend to depreciate the worth of the clients, patients, or employees involved. When strict market norms are imposed on any area of life, the chronic confounding of maximizing profits with maximizing well-being is imported along with the market institutions.

In a reversed variation of the separate spheres, or "wall," argument, Adam

Smith and David Hume argued that markets free human relations from instrumental calculation by separating instrumental, self-interested relationships from what they called the sympathetic relationships in which people had previously been entangled. "If that is correct," writes Allen Silver, "commercial society promotes rather than discourages personal relations that are normatively free of instrumental and calculative orientations."[62] But we have seen in chapters 6 and 9 that instead of freeing individuals for companionship, market demands seem rather to encroach on the time that might otherwise have been spent with family and friends — and, as in Asia, to corrupt family values as well.

Two examples help to illustrate, but not to resolve, the problem of generalization of market transactions to interpersonal relations. In an experimental setting, Leonard Berkowitz found that the children of businessmen helped others only in exchange for help to themselves, but the children of bureaucrats helped others because they thought that it was the right thing to do or that helping others represented a general social rule.[63] But in his study of close friendships mentioned at the end of chapter 5, Robert Hays found that the best predictor of closeness was not benefits minus costs, as exchange theory predicts, but benefits plus costs or sacrifices.[64] There is similar folk wisdom: one loves someone whom one has helped. In contrast to the generalization of market attitudes by children of businessmen, in the Hays study the values and behavior of friendship dominate the situation. Other inferences about cross-domain influences illustrate the power and fragility of this style of thinking.

The Generalization of Rationality

In Simmels's view, the cold rationality of market transactions transfers easily to other situations, like family life, with different roles and requirements (see chapter 6).[65] I am skeptical. People compartmentalize their thinking so that they learn to behave one way in their consumer roles and another in, say, their social roles. For example, Gorer says of Americans that they are generous in social situations but that as soon as a situation is defined as commercial, they become hard and shrewd.[66] On the other hand, parents whose occupations require mainly obedience teach their children the virtue of obedience, whereas parents who must employ critical thinking on their jobs teach their children the value of critical thinking.[67] Behavior does generalize, but each class of cases needs separate examination.

Looking back over these arguments, one sees the importance of the extent and limits to learning generalization (see chapter 7). Until we know whether or not types of thinking, moral norms, degrees of trust, the instrumental use of others, and the monetization of value are generalized to social relations, we cannot judge the effect of market norms and practices on companionship. The effectiveness of barriers to these generalizations is not yet clear, but it does appear that something like the more or less "total communities" of the military may be the most effective barrier to the market—and that alternative will not appeal to many.

There are other ways to assess the influence of markets on companionship: uses of time, the impact of alternative seducers like television, and the possible symbiosis of shopping and consuming with companionship. I turn, then, to the way in which shopping and consuming may serve companionship.

BUYING AND CONSUMING ARE SOCIALLY CONDITIONED

The first point I wish to make is that buying and consuming are not influenced only by market terms but are in several senses socially conditioned activities: (1) tastes are shaped, if not determined, by the tastes of others in one's social group; (2) one of the rewards of buying is the esteem of others, that is, consumers frequently see their possessions as social communication tools;[68] (3) the availability of goods depends on the preferences of others—shops will not store and often manufacturers will not make products to suit idiosyncratic tastes of the nonrich; (4) transportation grids determined by the preferences and needs of others influence the locations of the shops and services that one uses; (5) prices are socially determined by the preferences of others; (6) governments will not provide infrastructures (roads and schools) unless people want them; and finally, (7) reliance on markets for products instead of on households and governments is the consequence of a shared ideology explained by the sociology of knowledge as well as by the market's technical advantages. The influence is reciprocal, of course: "Advertising works not by its impact on specific individuals but by influencing the social climate in which action takes place. Advertising affects the shared ideas, common understandings and the social meaning of acts. Advertising does not change individuals as much as the social world in which they operate."[69]

DO CONSUMPTION AND BUYING CROWD OUT COMPANIONSHIP?

The crowding-out hypothesis says that, given limited amounts of time and attention, people must choose between devoting these resources to companionship and devoting them to commodities. For each of these two goods (companions and commodities) there is a level of supply necessary for good health, including mental health, but beyond that level individual choices can mix the two goods in different bundles according to taste. The specific allegation of the crowding-out thesis is that for many people in modern market economies, the hypertrophy of time and attention devoted to commodities has reduced the time and attention devoted to companions below the level necessary for both happiness and mental health.

Were less time devoted to market work, more might be available for either shopping[70] or social activities. Yet might the newly available time be devoted instead to watching television? In order to be sure, we need data on work time, television-watching time, shopping time, and time spent in socializing with others. I know of only two studies that give these data. The first shows that from 1965 to 1975, when there was a decline in time spent on the job, the newly available time was devoted almost entirely to watching television (men by thirty-five minutes and women by forty-seven minutes), but that both men and women decreased their shopping (men much more than women) while they increased the time spent on such activities as visiting, letter writing, and informal social life.[71] The crowding out was mostly done by television, but in the remaining time, socializing increased while shopping decreased.

A second study, using comparable methods but with a better breakdown of activities, covered 1975 to 1981. Although both men and women spent about three times as many minutes watching television as socializing, the time spent on socializing increased slightly, and "the overall impression is that uses of leisure time were slightly more interactive in 1981–82 than in 1975–76."[72] (Compared to the quarter-century decline in visiting with family and neighbors, this increased socializing between 1965 and 1975 and between 1975 and 1981 seems to have been a countertrend exception.)

By these (inadequate) tests, the hypothesis that a "rage to consume" crowds out socializing fails. If the market has a destructive influence on friendship (and I think it does), it must be, as discussed above, through the elevating of instrumentalist and materialist values over social values, the eroding of communities and neighborhoods, and the intermittent increasing of the demand for overtime labor—as in the mid-1990s. In my opinion, a nonmarket influence, television watching, is mainly responsible for the decline in families and communities.

TELEVISION AS A NEW SOURCE OF FRIENDLY INTERACTION?

Television watching, the principal activity showing increased time use for most of the postwar period, may bring family members together and could be an occasion for social interaction, especially since it is often desultory and itself can be a secondary activity. But equally, television watching may be a substitute for friendly intercourse. Given the sharp rise in divorces occurring at about the same time as the rapid spread of television in the 1950s, one would not expect television watching to favor family felicity. The microscopic view, however, is more ambiguous. One study reports, "It is evident that TV harmonizes with family life, and has indeed become a central part of it."[73] The set is usually in the living room, and therefore many of the hours spent watching are also being spent with the family. About 20 percent of the time, viewers are also talking to each other. Another study observed that television gave family members "something to talk about and in several ways made a positive contribution to family social life. . . . More than this, TV gives the whole nation a shared set of experiences, by participating live in major political or historical events, major sporting events, and sharing the day's news."[74] Like a pet, the television set and its programs represent a form of companionship, explicitly so for about a quarter of the population.[75] Friendships with television characters (for example, those on the *Cosby Show* or *Coronation Street*) have been said to give companionship to television viewers,[76] but they are not interactive, and, as with children (see below), television friends are more important to people who have fewer friends.

Two facets of the darker side of television are important: isolation from others and commercialization of viewers' attitudes. As one would expect from the inelasticity of time, compared to those who watch less frequently, heavy watchers spend more time at home. Television watching is a cause of isolation as well as an effect, for acquiring a television set results in a decline of social contacts outside the home (equivalent to two to four weeks of visiting annually): "TV watching comes at the expense of nearly every social activity outside the home, especially social gatherings and informal conversations."[77] Television watching is also associated with lower interpersonal trust, a sense of being victimized, and (with demographics controlled) seeing the world as relatively more dangerous.[78]

There are more subtle mood effects. Although the effect of television watching may be favorable for experiencing feelings of sociability, it is not favorable for extensive or active socializing. According to one study, compared to the effects of other activities like reading, watching television tends to make people "more relaxed, cheerful, and sociable"—but also "more drowsy, weak, and passive."[79] Television watching is a kind of anodyne that probably prevents active social interaction more than it stimulates it.

The commercialization of the viewing process is of special interest to us. By the time American children have reached first grade, they "will have soaked in 30,000 advertisements."[80] They learn consumer values, of course, but they also learn something about honesty: children have great difficulty in distinguishing between advertising puffing (lying, in children's interpretations) and presentation of the news, a problem for their mothers: if advertising cannot be believed, why should newscasts be believed?[81] Children become early postmodernists.

The concern about children's heavy watching is well taken: in 1994 the average time children spent watching was about twenty-one and a half hours a week. As with adults, children's heavy viewing is isolating and unwholesome.

Thus, one study finds that "children with few friends, with restricted peer mirrors [*sic*], identified with television heroes almost half as often again as did children with plentiful peer[s]."[82] When the television is turned off by parental fiat (aided by a national campaign during TV Turnoff Week), children socialize more: Instead of watching a baseball game on television, an eight-year-old Red Sox fan and his friend went to see the game in Fenway Park and described the experience in glowing terms. A younger group "played in their sandboxes, drew chalk pictures on the driveway, looked for salamanders, and dressed up as pirates." Another eight-year-old "socialized with her hamster — but also played baseball and visited her public library."[83] Children's viewing habits, however, are heavily influenced by their parents' habits: they are natural imitators.

As we have seen, shopping and consuming may also crowd out socializing, but it is mainly television that obstructs the sociable life which usually increases happiness and the recruitment of confidants who tend to reduce depression.

Shopping as a Social Experience

Has shopping become less of a social experience, more solitary, impersonal, and friendless? The days are long gone when there were counter clerks instead of checkers-out, when a neighborhood store was a social center and the storekeeper was everyone's friend. The decline of community in which recommendations by friends were the main source of product assessment has made advertising, a colder and less personal agent, more important.[84] Can this change in the human relations of shopping serve to increase the sense of isolation experienced by depressives and the unhappy?

Some families make of shopping an intrinsically rewarding family experience.[85] In other cases the circle of companionship is more extended. A "family gatekeeper" (a psychographic marketing category) revealed a source of pleasure in her role as an opinion leader: "People come to me more often than I go to them for information on brands." As a way of keeping her supply of information up to date, she says, "I shop a lot for specials."[86] Because it takes time to shop for specials and to do comparative shopping, working-class shoppers rely more on advice from family and friends, familiar stores, and what is called face-to-face shopping. In the working class, too, husband-and-wife shopping teams are more common.[87]

Recent emphasis on economic efficiency influences the interpersonal relations in commercial transactions, for the busier the store, the less "eye contact, smiling, thanking, pleasantness, and attending to the customer."[88] And the increase in automated outlets deprives people of what little human contact there has been in supermarkets and discount stores, with particularly unfortunate effects on lonely persons, who are deprived of what is often their only daily human contact.[89]

The demise of the neighborhood store, the colder relations between shopkeepers and their clients, and the modesty of the growth of husband–wife shopping all suggest an increasingly unsociable climate for consumers. Because shopping is still divided along sex lines, women doing most of the everyday shopping, the loss of socializing is borne mainly by them.[90] Shopping is decreasingly a social experience.

Consumption as a Social Experience

The tentative hypothesis in this section is that there has been a shift from collective to individual consumption, with a consequent loss of social interaction.[91] Beyond the family, people talk about their various consumption experiences among their friends. Elihu Katz and Paul Lazarsfeld's early analysis of "opinion leaders" found that women talked much more — and much more democratically — about articles of purchase than about politics.[92] The expertise becomes shared, for members of friendship networks tend to use the same brands — a form of symbolic socializing.[93]

A variety of goods may invite or require social participation for their enjoyment: food and drink, playing baseball and playing cards, bingo and bowling, attending sporting events, theater, and concerts. In each case the enjoyment of the company of others is almost a condition for enjoying the experience. The idea that consumption is primarily a solipsistic experience in which only one's own utilities count, and not a collective experience dependent on the utilities of others, could be entertained only by economists. Inevitably, a large part of the pleasures of consumption is social.[94]

Is consumption more or less social than it once was? I suggest the following proposition: Beyond a certain level, increased disposable income is more likely to be spent on goods consumed individually than on goods consumed collectively by households. From the gross data it is not easy to know exactly how the greater disposable income over the past quarter century was consumed, but we know that the proportion of income spent on food, which is often consumed in groups, and on housing declines as income rises. And there are suggestive items in recent accounts of household budgets: between 1985 and 1988, household expenditures for food and housing increased about 2 percent, while expenditures for "personal care" increased about 6 percent. (Time spent on personal care has also increased in recent years.)[95] Similarly, between 1988 and 1989 the expenditures for food, housing, and household operations and furnishings each increased by less than 4 percent, while expenditures on the more individualized items in "apparel and services" increased 7.4 percent.[96]

To make the point more vivid, consider how the category of things associated with home, for example, the house itself and certain familiar rooms, is uniquely capable of enhancing a sense of well-being, especially among children. These things are often cherished and are four times as likely to be positively than negatively toned, a higher positive loading than any other set of objects.[97] Family objects also have evocative power, as Peter Laslett observes in *The World We Have Lost:* "Time was when the whole of life went forward in the family, in a circle of loved, familiar faces, known and fondled objects, all to human size. That time has gone for ever. It makes us very different from our ancestors."[98] Does it also make us less happy and more depressed?

In the welter of alleged causes for the decline in family integrity and community solidarity, I have found some ambiguous evidence that markets themselves are an inherent cause of social isolation; I have questioned the idea that attention to buying and consuming necessarily crowds out the time and attention available for companionship, suggesting instead that television is more likely to have this isolating effect; and I have proposed that the increased impersonality of shopping and the increased use of individually, as contrasted to socially, consumed goods have played modest roles in the loss of a therapeutic community of friends.

One other conclusion: In chapter 5 I pointed out that although all the quality of life studies strongly indicate that companionship makes a larger contribution than higher income to the well-being of the nonpoor, nevertheless, there is little evidence of a strong *demand* for more friendship. If, therefore, one were to use the test that Richard Musgrave suggests for the right level of public goods (what people would pay if the goods were priced),[99] one would come up short on companionship (as public goods). In contrast, there is a strong demand for more commodities. In my opinion, this pattern is another indication that people have trouble, especially in a consumer culture, knowing where their best interests lie (see chapter 17).

PART V

Is Democracy a Source of Unhappiness?

11

Rising Malaise at Democracy's Feast

If market forces do not promote well-being, we are likely to turn to government for help. That is what democracies are for — the redress of grievances. But in the United States (more than elsewhere) democratic institutions are often viewed with mixed contempt and hostility. Turning to democracy for help, we find a kind of political malaise (to use President Jimmy Carter's term), a disappointment or weariness with democracy reflected in what observers variously call alienation, cynicism, and, more generally, negativity. In this chapter I will look at the meanings and scope of this negativity, its causes and symptoms, and ask how political negativity is related to the unhappiness and depression found in the United States and other advanced countries. Are these negative symptoms only a continuation of a long history of critical comment, perhaps only the undertone of conventional, although often scurrilous, observations on politicians irrespective of regime? Or are they something more deep-seated and serious?

Or, again, is the apparent dissatisfaction with government part of a worldwide postmodern movement to shrink governments down to human size and to find, if possible, substitutes for the welfare state? This movement has already gone some distance in the United States and Britain and has been influential in other countries,[1] and, like any major transition, it has incurred considerable human costs. I do not want to present as a pathology a genuine and well-defended social movement—but well-defended movements, from the Crusades to Marxism, often appear pathological in retrospect. First, however, what is the contrasting background for these symptoms of negativity?

THE POSITIVITY BIAS

The evidence of political negativity in market democracies is all the more remarkable because of a more general "positivity bias,"[2] a tendency to look on the bright side, to endorse positive more than negative wording in survey questionnaires,[3] to reconstruct events and memories so as to emphasize their positive features, and to employ what Margaret Matlin and David Stang called the "Pollyanna Principle."[4] There are both good causes and good reasons for this positivity: the mind is wired to think positively, negation requiring an additional step and additional effort.[5] "In the human brain more areas seem to produce positive experiences than negative ones" (25 percent to 5 percent),[6] and positive thoughts make people happier, more productive, and more helpful to others.[7] The average set-point (see chapter 3) is positive, most people in the United States are happy,[8] and most people (or at least most college students) rate their lives as very, but not quite perfectly, satisfying.[9] The positivity bias applies to most areas of life, but not to political institutions. Why?

Political Alienation and Negativity

The meaning of political negativity is not self-evident and has been given several meanings.

THE VARIOUS MEANINGS OF POLITICAL AND OTHER NEGATIVITY

Richard Brody and Paul Sniderman report that in a U.S. sample they "do not find a positivity bias in assessing government as a rule." Rather, on general, somewhat stereotypical questions they find a "negativity bias" and define this as "a tendency to respond unfavorably when asked global and affect-laden questions about 'officials in Washington.'"[10] Other definitions emphasize cognitive sets, as where "greater weight [is] given to negative information relative to equally extreme and equally positive information in a variety of information processing tasks."[11] The result is often the use of negative stereotypes.[12] Definitions of political negativity may also focus on the functioning of a regime: "a statement of the belief that government is not functioning and producing outputs in accord with expectations";[13] or may simply stress the suspicion and distrust or lack of confidence that it implies.[14] As mentioned, President Carter introduced the broader public to the concept of malaise, which I have used as a covering term for both unhappiness and negativity. To some extent, political negativity changes with the party in power, but to an even greater extent it reflects more general cultural patterns that are slow to change. The stability of a democracy, however, is more related to average life satisfaction than to political satisfaction.[15] It is life satisfaction that drives political satisfaction and not the other way around.

Thus chronic, generalized, pervasive negativity toward government may be understood as a historically influenced, largely culturally (not politically) determined set of affects and cognitive dispositions that are expressed in general criticism and derogation of politics and government. By this definition, there is not much that governments — or constitution drafters — can do to prevent or reduce political negativity: it is a reflection of broader forces in society.

SCOPE OF CURRENT DISTRUST OF DEMOCRATIC INSTITUTIONS

First I will present some data on the simple question of confidence (or trust) in political institutions and their leaders (table 11.1).

The lack of political trust is not marked by general partisan differences, although, of course, trust in the opposition tends to be less than trust of fellow partisans.[16] Political distrust has historically been correlated with unemployment and inflation[17] and modified by victory in war, but this kind of distrust appears to be immune to the prosperity of the late 1980s and early 1990s and even to the remarkable victory in the Gulf War of 1991 (see table 11.1). The highest trust for both the executive branch and Congress occurs in the earliest period recorded, that is, during the Vietnam War, the urban riots, and the student protest movements, while the lowest trust is in the most recent period reported. One important inference emerges: although vulnerable to history and economic cycles, political negativity is not just a transient phenomenon; it is a persistent characteristic of post-1966 culture. And it is significant that its origin dates from about the same period as does the epidemic of depressive symptoms in America and, it seems, most advanced countries.

From 1958 to 1992 (and probably later) the National Election Studies (NES) asked the question, "How much of the time do you think you can trust the government in Washington to do what is right — just about always, most of the time, only some of the time, or none of the time?" There was a dramatic decline in those answering, "most of the time" and a corresponding increase in those answering, "only some of the time" (fig. 11.1).[18] Note that this decline in political trust is parallel to the decline in interpersonal trust shown in chapter 2.

Because of my belief that these responses are products of a larger malaise, I am reluctant to draw attention to the effects of political events on institutional trust but observe that the point at which trust crosses distrust is during the period the Watergate scandal and questions of Richard Nixon's credibility were in the news.[19]

The discussion of political distrust (sometimes called cynicism) marks out

*Table 11.1. Percent Reporting "A Great Deal of Confidence in" the Leaders of Political Institutions, by Year**

Institution	1966–1967	1971–1973	1973–1974	1974–1977	1977–1980	1980–1984	1985–1989	1990–1992	Change 1971–73 1990–93
Executive Branch Fed. Government	39	26	15	18	17	21	18	14	−12
Congress	42	21	21	15	16	19	18	10	−11

*In 1937 in the midst of the Great Depression 44 percent of the public thought Congress "as good a representative body as is possible for a large nation to have," whereas in 1990 only 17 percent held these sentiments. Burns Roper. 1994. "Democracy in America. How Are We Doing?" *Public Perspective* 5: 3–5 at 4.

Sources: Data up to 1980 from Seymour M. Lipset and William Schneider. 1983. *The Confidence Gap: Business, Labor, and Government in the Public Mind.* New York: Free Press, 48–49; data for 1980–92 from Humphrey Taylor. 1992. "The American Angst of 1992." *Public Perspective* 3: 3.

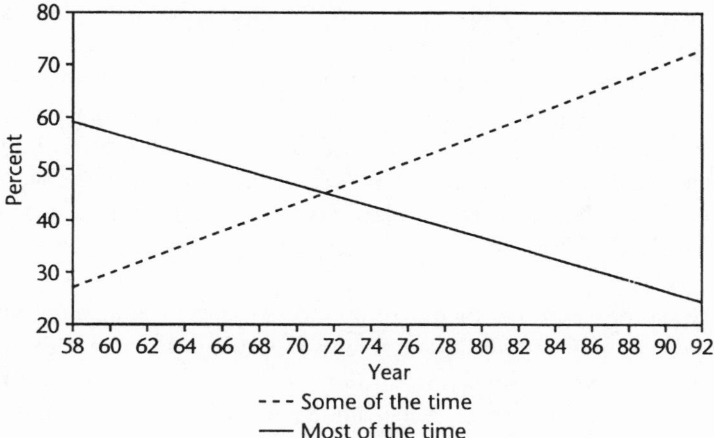

Figure 11.1. Percent U.S. National Sample Trusting Government "Most of the Time" or Only "Some of the Time," 1958–92
Question: "How much of the time do you think you can trust the government in Washington to do what is right—just about always, most of the time, only some of the time, or none of the time?"
Source: National Election Studies [NES].

two schools: some, like Arthur Miller and E. J. Dionne, hold that the expressions of distrust represent a new and disturbing political cynicism or alienation from political life.[20] Others, like Jack Citrin, Everett Ladd, and S. M. Lipset and William Schneider,[21] point to the expressions of faith in the political system and hold that these criticisms are merely "verbalizing a casual and ritualistic negativism rather than an enduring sense of estrangement that influences their beliefs and actions."[22]

The positivists might support their views by reference to a long record of similar criticism and alarm. Thus, not only did Paine and Jefferson want minimal government because of their distrust of government, but other observers of the American scene found the public equally or more distrustful. Tocqueville commented that Americans "are prone to despise and hate those who wield [power and to] elude its grasp" as best they can.[23] Just before the First World War, James Bryce observed that Americans tended to believe most legislation was presumptively bad and as many bills as possible should be killed.[24] In 1913 A. Lawrence Lowell held that the "recent distrust of legislatures [was characteristic of all democracies, and] the American people are drifting towards a general loss of faith in representative government." This failing support, he thought, was less marked in America than elsewhere because the founders "foresaw abuse on the part of legislatures, and strove to prevent it by limiting their power."[25] In 1948, Gorer said, "With practically no exceptions, Americans regard their own governments as alien; they do not identify themselves with it, do not consider themselves involved in its actions, feel free to criticize it and despise it."[26] Thus, in the revolutionary period, in the early nineteenth century, before the First World War, during the 1950s, and, as mentioned, in the alienated 1960s, American distrust of government was widely exemplified and reported. So far as one can tell from elite opinions, American political criticality lived happily with general feelings of optimism and good cheer.

Before accepting current themes of political distrust as political rejection, I want to enter some caveats. Asked about the principles or the legitimacy of democracy, an overwhelming proportion of Americans endorse them;[27] in ranking occupational prestige, Americans assign eight of the top ten to political occupations;[28] attitudes toward electoral candidates, including the candidate a person will vote against, tend to be more positive than negative;[29] there are remissions in this negativity toward government leading to an occasional observation that antagonism toward big government and high taxes has declined.[30] These kinds of data invite the disagreement on the meaning of American negativity mentioned above.

Two kinds of tests might help to resolve the controversy over the meaning of American political negativity: Does political negativity extend to other democratic societies? And does negativity extend to nonpolitical domains?

IS THERE MALAISE IN OTHER DEMOCRACIES?

Like the rising tide of clinical depression, the rising tide of political negativity is common in other advanced countries of the world. (Before that depression occurred, in 1913 Lowell saw a "world-wide loss of confidence" in democratic legislatures.)[31] For example, at the meeting of the Group of Seven (G7) in 1993, all of the political leaders had low confidence ratings in their respective countries. Great Britain has a long history of what seems to be political negativity. In his *Life of Samuel Johnson,* James Boswell reports on a conversation in 1777 "in which I alleged that any question [in Parliament], however unreasonable or unjust, might be carried by a venal majority." Johnson replied, "The British Parliament was not corrupt, [because] there was hardly ever any questions of great importance before Parliament, any question in which a man might not very well vote either upon one side or the other."[32] In contemporary times, too, British political criticality embraces political negativity. Hugo Young, a respected commentator, reported (1993) on the failings of Parliament in the following terms: "It deceives people as to what is possible; it makes our leaders say things they know to be untrue; it fathers false promises, especially in elections; it buys present comfort at the expense of future pain, [and it is] the disease of all politicians but none more easily infected than the British."[33] In 1989 a national sample in Britain was asked to register its satisfaction or dissatisfaction with twenty national institutions, and the results were that "the institutions which rank lowest in public satisfaction are all political."[34]

The rest of Europe is a little different, although of course there have been long-term reasons for concern. In the 1970s more people were dissatisfied than satisfied with the way their democracies were working, and the number of people subscribing to outright antidemocratic movements has always been higher in Europe than in the United States.[35] Nevertheless, after a period of rising political trust from 1959 to 1981, public trust in parliaments maintained a fairly steady level in the 1981–90 period.[36] The European picture for that period, however, is more complex than that: of eleven countries, the publics in six of them decreased their confidence in democratic institutions while five did not.[37] Comparing the United States with continental Europe, one cannot say either that it is exceptional or that it is similar to Europe, only that it is more like Denmark than like France. By this test of generality, arguments based on a unique American distrust of government or of unique American political institutions begin to fade. Something characteristic of the culture of modernity shared with at least some other market democracies seems to be at work.

But, as in the United States, in Europe there is a difference in responses to democratic institutions and to the democratic system. On the larger question of democratic systems, for a longer period (1976–91) the data indicate "an overall increase in satisfaction with democracy."[38] But after 1991, there was a "dramatic shift" down in satisfaction and shift up in dissatisfaction; it is an unfinished story.

In Asia, the picture is similar. In Japan, for example, a national poll (1995) found 67 percent reporting either hostility to the then-current cabinet or no interest in government.[39] Hostility and anger are mobilizing; indifference is the politically pathological side of malaise.

NEGATIVITY TOWARD OTHER INSTITUTIONS

If the negativity were only toward politics, as in the pre-Populist period of American history, it would be somewhat less plausible to link popular negativity to some underlying mood of unhappiness or depression. But, in fact, the American negativity is much more general (table 11.2). Again there is a sharp drop in the 1966–70s period and a variable but continuing decline in confidence after that time. And again the earliest period shows the greatest

Table 11.2. Percent Reporting "A Great Deal of Confidence in" the Leaders of Television and Business, by Year

Institution	1966	1971–1979	1980–1984	1985–1989	1990–1992	Change 1970s to 1990s
Television news	NA	36	26	26	23	−13
Major companies	55	22	17	18	13	−9

Source: Humphrey Taylor. 1992. "The American Angst of 1992." *Public Perspective* 3: 3.

confidence, and the most recent period reported the least. One cannot speak only of political negativity for both the once-trusted television news and major corporations have lost popular confidence as well.

One other feature of this generalized distrust is notable: whereas liberals and conservatives alike have seen government and business as alternative agencies for delivering goods, suggesting that as confidence in one of them decreases, confidence in the other should increase, in fact, the two indices of confidence move up and down together. This is important for two reasons: (1) It suggests that changes in confidence vary, not with alternating political or ideological preferences, as Albert Hirschman has suggested,[40] but with larger swings of a more generalized malaise, as I have argued.[41] And (2) the result of this parallel movement is increased difficulty in selecting between the two agencies according to some concept of which will do better in solving the problems at hand.

I believe that business and political negativity move together because people know only *that* they are unhappy, not *why*. A. D. Lindsay said the benefit of democracy stemmed from the public's knowledge of where the shoe pinches.[42] Perhaps, but I suspect the public knows only that its feet hurt. Whether the pain comes from a clot upstream, chilblains, or lack of exercise is mysterious to most people.

Why Has Political Negativity Increased in the Past Thirty Years?

All explanations of human behavior involve an interaction between the circumstances which prompt or constrain people's behavior and the qualities of the individual actors: stimulus and organism, circumstance and disposition, environment and person. To which shall we attribute causal force? In later chapters I will look at the properties of politics that may be said to stimulate negativity. Here I will focus on the beliefs of individuals, beliefs which, however, may be the consequences or symptoms of negativity as well as its causes.

EFFICACY

The sense of political efficacy is a belief that one has some influence over political events, that when one acts, the political system responds. For this influence to take place, two things are necessary. First, the individual must feel efficacious, a feeling called, in electoral studies, internal political efficacy. This concept is the political scientists' version of the psychologists' internal attribution and personal control: *I* am the cause of the events that affect my life (see chapter 13). The belief in personal control has been shown in one large study to be one of the two closest personality correlates of SWB;[43] it is also a very good predictor of turnout.[44]

Second, for people to believe that their political acts are effective, the political system itself must be thought to be responsive: external political efficacy. This duality reflects the importance of including perceptions of both the self and the environment; both aspects of efficacy are perceptions — something in the head of the political actor.

If either of these perceptions of efficacy has declined over recent history, we would have a clue to the rise of political negativity. And, in general, they have both declined.[45]

To test the changes in internal political efficacy over the thirty-two-year period from 1952 to 1984 we can monitor answers to the following question: "People like me don't have any say about what the government does. Please tell me whether you agree or disagree with this statement." The decline up to 1984 is straightforward with little variation around the central tendency (figure 11.2). For the decade following 1984 (not shown), gradually the disbelievers (efficacious) replaced the believers (inefficacious) so that, in contrast to earlier years, there was a net disbelief in 1990.

Because of its relevance to Arthur Miller's theory that the political agenda of the period of the Vietnam War could not reconcile bitterly opposing views,[46] it is interesting to note that in the mid-1970s both the extreme liberals and extreme conservatives felt less efficacious than others. At least up to the middle of the Reagan regime, people had decreasing faith that they could make any difference in political outcomes.

External political efficacy, the belief that the government *is* responsive to public opinion, is measured here by disagreement with the statement, "I don't think public officials care much about what people like me think." The picture of declining disagreement and rising agreement for the full twenty-one-year

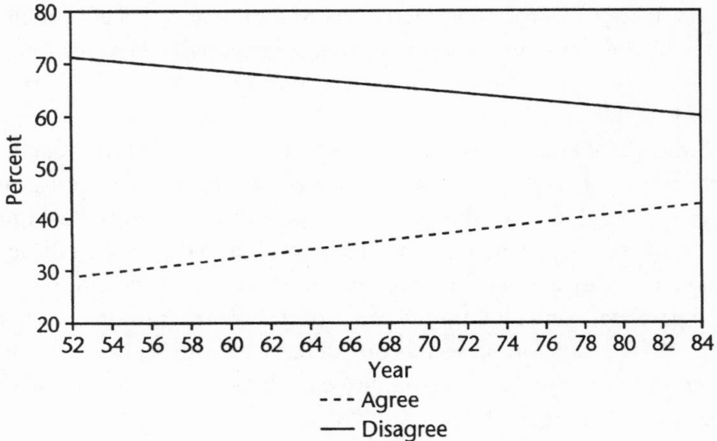

Figure 11.2. Percent of U.S. National Sample Who Believe People Like Themselves "Don't Have Any Say About What the Government Does," 1952–84
Question: " 'People like me don't have any say about what the government does.' Please tell me whether you agree or disagree with this statement."
Source: National Election Studies [NES].

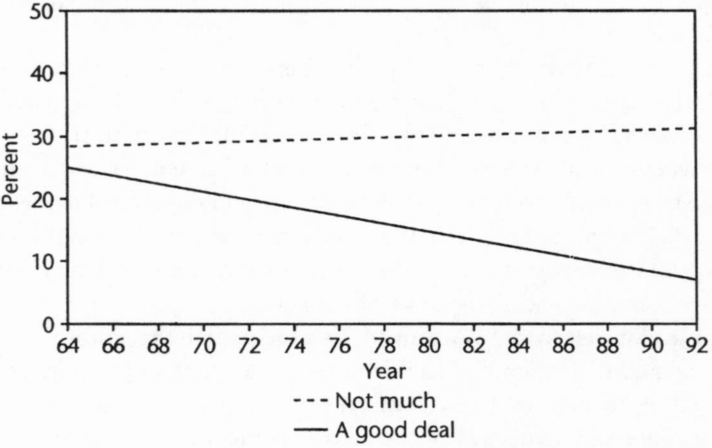

Figure 11.3. Percent of U.S. National Sample Who Believe the Government Pays "A Good Deal" or "Not Much" Attention to People, 1964–92
Question: "How much does government pay attention to people—a good deal, some, not much?"
Source: National Election Studies [NES].

period between 1973 and 1994 is shown in figure 2.8. For a shorter period (1964–92) a confirming trend is revealed by the pattern of answers to the question, "How much does government pay attention to people—a good deal, some, not much?" From 1964 to 1992 there was a declining proportion answering, "a good deal" (a belief in something that, after all, is thought to be the virtue of democracy) and a very modestly rising proportion saying, "not much" (fig. 11.3).[47] In general, the groups showing internal political efficacy also found the government more responsive (the indexes for internal and external political efficacy are highly correlated (r = .48).

Puzzled by the frequent failure of attitudes to predict behavior, psychologists have developed a formula to improve that prediction, a formula that includes a term for the perceived likelihood that the goal can be attained by the means available.[48] When the goal seems not to be possible—as in the current case, in which influencing policy is the goal—an attractive alternative is to change the value of the goal, that is, again in this case, to change one's opinion of the value of participatory democratic institutions: political negativity.

IN WHOSE INTEREST IS THE GOVERNMENT RUN?

A concept of political trusteeship says that representatives should be bound not by opinions or even the demands of their publics, but rather by their needs.

If, as the evidence suggests, people often do not know what makes them happy (see chapter 16), then, were they to have more information and access to better causal theories, representatives might serve as the trustees into whose care constituents temporarily entrust their welfare and even their well-being. Certain strands of democratic theory allow such an interpretation, taking a cue from Edmund Burke's speech to the Electors of Bristol (which ironically—in Burke's case—reflected Rousseau's concept of the Legislator and the General Will) and developed recently by such theorists as Virginia Held and C. R. Sunstein.[49] I find something to be said for the trustee theory of representation,[50] a theory which, in any event, informs much governmental action on safety, the ecology, and foreign policy. Could there be some such underlying understanding that keeps the public voting and loyal when they do not believe they are effective or that public officials care what they think?

Since 1964 the NES has asked the question, "Do you think the government in Washington is run for the benefit of a few big interests or for the benefit of all?" And since 1964 the proportion of the public answering, "a few big interests" has steadily risen, and the proportion choosing "benefit of all" has declined (fig. 11.4). Of all the trends presented, this one involves the largest changes, with "benefit of all" going from more than 55 percent in 1964 to below 20

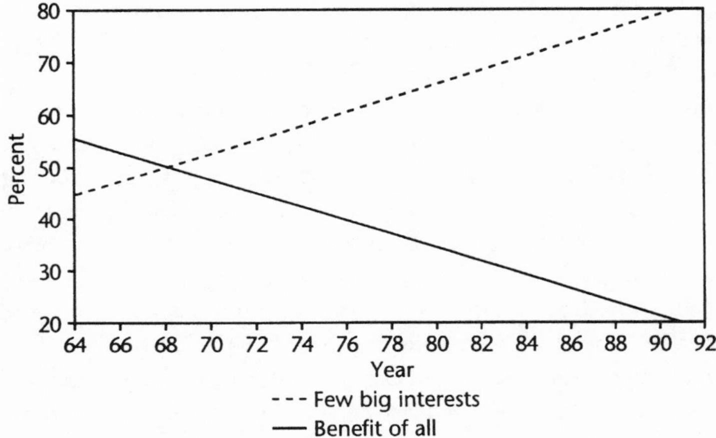

Figure 11.4. Percent of U.S. National Sample Who Believe Government Is "Run for the Benefit of a Few Big Interests" or "For the Benefit of All," 1964–92
Question: "Do you think the government in Washington is run for the benefit of a few big interests or for the benefit of all?"
Source: National Election Studies [NES].

percent in 1992. No trustee theory could survive this rising conviction that the public interest was not served by the government in Washington.[51]

CITIZEN DUTY

If the trustee theory fails, what about the theory that political participation is driven chiefly by moral considerations, by concepts of duty? Since 1952 the NES has asked people to agree or disagree with the statement, "If a person doesn't care how an election comes out, then that person shouldn't vote in it."[52] The (rather scattered) pattern of responses for the forty-year-period from 1952 to 1992 is revealing (fig. 11.5). Given the growing cynicism seen so far, one is astonished to find an increasing conviction that no matter what their personal beliefs may be, people should do their citizen duty and vote in elections. The power of a sense of citizen duty to mobilize the electorate has long been recognized, even by those eager to show that material self-interest dominates political behavior as it does market behavior.[53] What is so extraordinary is the tendency for the sense of citizen duty to hold up in the face of the political negativity that pervades public perceptions.

To caricature findings that, after all, are only tendencies and modest correlations, one might say that the main driving force for participation is decreasingly a sense that voting and other forms of participation might influence outcomes important to a participant, but rather to satisfy a sense of duty, to do what one ought to do. This chimes with other findings showing that people's

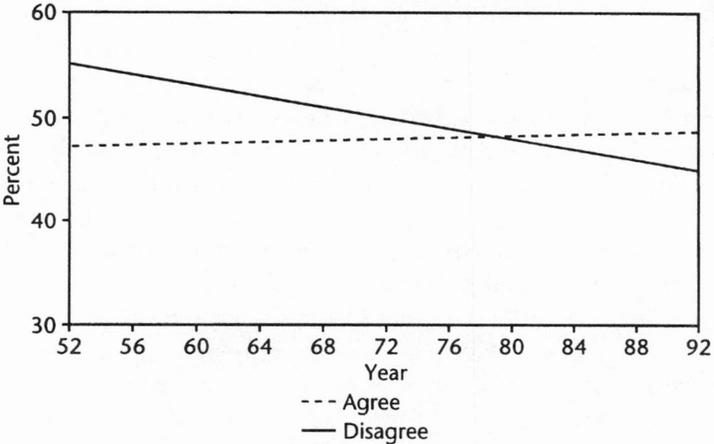

Figure 11.5. Percent of U.S. National Sample Who Agree that If a "Person Doesn't Care How an Election Comes Out that Person Shouldn't Vote in It," 1952–92
Question: "If a person doesn't care how an election comes out, that person shouldn't vote in it."
Source: National Election Studies [NES].

votes are not perceptibly influenced by concepts of self-interest (in the sense that those with personal or family stakes in an outcome like school busing or affirmative action are—except for tax and public employment—no different from those who have no such stakes). Instead they are motivated by their long-standing (if weakening) commitment to parties, race and ethnicity, nation, and, to a lesser extent, to symbols of liberalism and conservatism[54]—and also to judgments about the sincerity and effectiveness of the candidates.[55] What the findings on citizen duty add to this analysis is the importance of moral claims, the imperatives of what Freud called the superego. One need not borrow Freud's belief that the superego is the major source of unhappiness in Western society to understand the fragile hedonic payoff of behavior guided principally by the appeals of conscience—and the social esteem derived therefrom.[56] Others, too, have found that the "hyper-moralization of politics" is a source of political negativity[57] or malaise.

But is this political negativity aversive? Does it in any way contribute to or reflect the unhappiness and depression I discussed in earlier chapters?

Political Negativity and Unhappiness

However political negativity may harm the felicitous functioning of political systems (and there is a substantial literature on this),[58] at this point we want to know if it hurts the individuals who possess and exhibit it.

IS POLITICAL NEGATIVITY AVERSIVE?

For this purpose, I would like to distinguish several meanings among the various attitudes in this negative set. *Criticality* is largely cognitive and means a tendency to criticize some particular set of objects, in this case politics. As we have seen, America's most distinguished democratic founders surely exemplify it. *Negativity,* the term I have been using, is more affective and refers to a pervasive tendency to respond to the world in terms of critical, deprecatory, and even hostile opinions. Negativity has been defined as part of the "major depression" syndrome and is recognized in personality research as "negative affectivity" (see chapters 2, 3).[59] *Aversiveness* refers to the pain or hurt that is experienced by a person holding an opinion or expressing an attitude. Finally, *aversive weight* of an evaluation or an opinion is measured by correlations (or beta weights) between attitudes toward government and some criterial measure of well-being.

Cross-National Studies

From a global perspective, the evidence on relations between political negativity and SWB is mixed. In cross-national data covering nations at all levels of development, there is no relationship between political distrust and average happiness, although interpersonal distrust has a strong relationship to that felicitous state.[60] But in Europe the correlation between political satisfaction and life satisfaction is fairly high ($r = .41$). Indeed, "low levels of life satisfaction are linked with negative orientations toward one's entire society."[61] In my opinion, the explanation for this discrepancy lies in the fact that in poorer nations governments and ideologies are likely to be either conventional dictatorships (no help from that quarter) or only pro forma democracies, inducing hypocrisy rather than hope. Across nations at these lower levels of development happiness (or satisfaction with the lives people lead) will have no stable connection with trust in government.

Quality of Life Studies in the United States

Before turning to the aversive weight of political negativity in the American quality of life studies, I want to look at the evaluations themselves, which are instructive. In the verbal descriptors of the relevant questions (for example, "How do you feel about . . . 'the way our national government is operating'), "delighted" is almost exclusively employed to describe family life and friends, while "terrible" is used chiefly to characterize political and governmental life.[62]

The low evaluations seem at first to be only weakly related to these overall measures. Thus, in Andrews and Withey's study of the sources of "satisfaction with your life-as-a-whole," out of thirty sets of concerns, the index of concern with the national government ranked eleventh, contributing only 7 percent (beta) to the variance explained by the thirty items, but when the roster of concerns considered is reduced to twelve, the national government index ranks seventh and explains a little more of the variance (9 percent).[63] Thus, even though attitudes toward government are usually too remote from the self to have important consequences for most people's sense of well-being, negativity toward government does seem to reduce life satisfaction by some small margin.

Political Alienation and Psychological Distress

If political distrust is thought of as a form of alienation, especially the powerlessness component of alienation, it is relevant that American data show a close relation between alienation and psychological distress. A large empirical study by Mirowski and Ross of the causes of psychological distress finds alienation (helplessness, self-estrangement, isolation, meaninglessness, and normlessness) to be a principal cause. Of these, I examine two politically relevant aspects: helplessness, meaninglessness (isolation was treated in chapter 6, and normlessness seems not to apply because of the high citizen duty scores). To link this discussion to the theme of this section, I hardly need say that psychological distress is aversive.

Powerlessness and helplessness. "Of all the beliefs about self and society that might increase or reduce distress," say Mirowski and Ross, "one's sense of control over one's own life may be the most important. . . . Powerlessness is central."[64] Recall that in an earlier explication depression was diagnostically defined by feelings of helplessness. Because of my belief that what matters with regard to unhappiness and depression occurs in the microworlds of personal and family experience, I must also note that measures of (declining) internal political efficacy are, indeed, correlated ($r = .28$) with a general sense of personal control. The final link with well-being is found in the high correlation between well-being and personal control.

Meaninglessness. Another aspect of alienation that bears on my findings is meaninglessness, defined as the "sense that the world is unintelligible, and that life is without purpose." A meaningful existence is important, say Mirowski and Ross, because, among other things, "a world that cannot be understood cannot be controlled."[65] The NES internal political efficacy scale included the following item: "Sometimes politics and government seem so complicated that a person like me can't really understand what's going on." From 1952 to 1992 about 75 percent of the public agreed with that statement, but after a sharp dip in the late 1950s and an equivalent rise in the early 1960s there has been little secular change over the following thirty years. If unintelligibility in political matters were to contribute in this way to general unhappiness, one would have a clue to the prevalence of unhappiness. But because of the perceived marginality of politics to everyday life, I do not think these findings provide such a clue.

Meaninglessness has another significance: it leads to psychological distress because "people usually require a sense of purpose, significance, and value in their lives."[66] Does political negativity deprive people in stable democratic regimes of such a sense of meaning? Perhaps, but only when democracy is challenged or is doing the challenging. I know of no evidence showing that democracy yields more meaning to its believers than does, say, theocracy or, for that matter, communism or fascism. If SWB is associated with political meaning, then it is relevant to observe (again) that across nations with varying levels of development and controlling for per capita GNP, there is no relationship between degree of democracy and measures of happiness.[67]

It is challenge that gives a political regime meaning, for challenge provides the "sense of purpose, significance, and value" in people's lives. There are physical–perceptual principles enlisted here: contrast heightens perception and stimulates evaluation. And there are the familiar numbing effects of adaptation (chapter 17). But attachment to symbols, anticipation of restored equity, sense of (challenged) community may also play a part. For example, popular revolutions of almost any kind (Marxist or nationalist or communitarian) stimulate well-being—for a brief period.[68] It takes something like a revolution to make a form of government a source of either happiness or meaning.

Alienation as distancing and disowning. What is mine is a source of pride (pleasure) and shame (pain). But to some extent, Gorer is right: Americans do regard their government as alien. In discussing optimism, I will give below some empirical evidence supporting this view, for people's futures are sharply divorced from the future of the nation. The point here is double-edged: the loss of identification with what is in fact one's government may be painful, but, given the negativity toward government, emotional insulation from the government may relieve the pain.

FAITH IN PEOPLE

The reference in Mirowski and Ross's definition of normlessness to "faith in others" and to "mistrust" recalls the evidence, presented in chapter 2, showing a sharp decline in faith in others measured by the question, "Generally speaking, would you say that most people can be trusted, or that you can't be too careful in dealing with people." In cross-national studies, interpersonal trust strongly predicts happiness: with income controlled, distrust of one's fellow human beings is negatively correlated (−.61) with happiness,[69] and in the American case trust in others is strongly related to political participation.[70] Declining trust, therefore, makes the link between declining SWB and rising political malaise. Other measures of faith in people tell a similar story.[71]

Does support of democratic institutions depend on belief in the trustworthiness and fairness of others? One tangential clue is the fact that moderate liberals and conservatives trust people more than extreme liberals and conservatives. Because extremism and intensity go together, one might infer that in political matters at least, intense partisanship is an obstacle to political trust.[72] And it makes theoretical sense. Just as belief in the rationality of the ordinary person was a prerequisite for "licensing" the rise of the market,[73] so trusting others was a prerequisite for licensing the extension of the franchise beyond the propertied interests. Indeed, Hirschman's account of the demotion of the passions and promotion of the interests in economic affairs might equally be applied to politics — because conflicts of interests can be better accommodated than conflicts of passions.

Thus, another link has been forged between, on the one hand, symptoms of unhappiness, depression, alienation, and lack of faith in people and, on the other hand, political negativity. There is one other link: personal optimism and hopefulness and political optimism and hopefulness.

OPTIMISM AND PESSIMISM; HOPE AND DESPAIR

My concern is fourfold: (1) Is the American baseline of optimism unusually high? (2) Is hope or optimism a predictor of happiness? (3) Is personal optimism related to political optimism? (4) Have either or both personal and political optimism increased or declined over recent years?

America's "mental climate," said Harold Laski in 1948, "is one of discovery, expansion, *optimism*."[74] Twenty-five years later a national sample indicated that Americans were quite unsure that the future would be better than the past and that their children would be better off than they were. Reporting on 1972–73 data, Andrews and Withey point out that with respect to progress over the past, "Americans certainly were not perceiving overwhelming improvements in their global well-being over the past five years." And with respect to the future the "broad trend was toward optimism, but of a rather muted sort." One-third expected no change and 40 percent anticipated only slight improvement.[75] (Germans, too, experienced a decline in optimism in the 1970s and 1980s.)[76] In the postwar period, Americans neither prized happiness as much as was claimed (chapter 2) nor anticipated such rosy futures as others thought they did.

On the second question, Is optimism a correlate of happiness? there is conflicting evidence: individual optimism, yes; social optimism, no. In experimen-

Table 11.3. Personal and National Best and Worst Possible Lives

	Past		Present		Future	
Year	Self	Nation	Self	Nation	Self	Nation
1971	5.8	6.1	5.6	5.4	7.5	6.2
1972	5.5	5.6	6.4	5.5	7.6	6.2

Sources: William Watts and Lloyd A. Free. 1973. *The State of the Nation.* Washington, D.C.: Universe/Potomac Associates, 23.

tal work, hope is a robust predictor of happiness,[77] and in surveys hopeful responses to the question, "When I undertake something new, I expect to succeed" are positively associated with greater happiness.[78] But in a German survey, while hope for one's future life satisfaction declined from 1978 to 1984—that is, when perception that the future would bring less life satisfaction than the present more than doubled—ratings of present well-being remained constant. The explanation for this German phenomenon, answering the third question (relation between personal and political optimism), was that the estimates of the future were heavily colored by anticipating national social problems while the present ratings were based on current and personal feelings.[79]

This divorce between personal circumstances and feelings and national circumstances is vividly portrayed in similar studies in the United States. For example, in a study (1973) using a "ladder scale," in which respondents place themselves and their nation on a ladder scored from one to ten and are asked to rate the " 'best' and 'worst' possible life" for the self and for the nation—five years ago, now, and five years from now—an interesting pattern obtained (table 11.3): The present self is always better off than the present nation; compared to the past, the present self has always improved its circumstances whereas the nation has backslid; the future self is always substantially better off than the future nation; and, most important, the future self will be much (at least two points) better off than the present self, whereas the future nation will be only .7 or .8 points better off than the present nation. Optimism is a state of mind that applies mainly to the self and hardly at all to society. And one's destiny is thoroughly separate from the nation's destiny.

Above I found that political negativity, or lack of trust in government, has only a modest effect on a person's happiness. People's happiness, I said, comes from the microworlds of experience, not from respect for government. These data offer supporting evidence of the insulation of the private microworld from the political world. But the worldviews may be more accurate than estimates of personal futures, for most people, especially, until quite recently, the less educated, tend to be unreasonably optimistic about their own futures. This optimistic bias is not just wishful thinking but has a cognitive component: people perceive in exaggerated form the factors that would support their hopes while neglecting the same factors in other people's lives.[80]

The fourth question was, Has there been a rise or decline in optimism over the past quarter century? Perhaps one should not expect much change because optimism has a strong biological component.[81] On the other hand, perhaps one should expect declining optimism because, unlike trust, economic optimism, at least, declines with economic development.[82] And that is precisely what is revealed in recent American surveys. Two studies reflect the declining optimism.

First, over a short term, in 1975 (a recession year) a *New York Times* follow-up of the ladder study by William Watts and Lloyd Free cited above (1973) (and data from 1959 reported by Hadley Cantril)[83] found a decline in even the personal optimism shown in the earlier research: "For the first time since public opinion research began measuring such attitudes in 1959," reported the *Times,* "Americans believe they have lost substantial ground in their standard of living, and there has been a significant decline in their own expectations of what the future will bring." And, as in the earlier studies, there was a substantial gap between the expected future for the nation and the respondents' estimates of their own futures.[84] This pessimism corresponds with answers to the question, "Do you agree with the following statement? In spite of what some people say, the lot (situation/condition) of the average man is getting worse," whose graph (see fig. 2.7) showed a steady increase in agreement, with the latest figures available (1994) revealing decidedly the most pessimistic view.[85]

In summary, the American baseline of optimism is probably not higher than that in many other counties and certainly not as high as has been claimed; optimism and happiness usually, but not always, go together; personal optimism is not related to social optimism; and both personal and social optimism have declined in the past quarter century. Political negativity may well find a source in declining optimism.

DO POLITICAL NEGATIVITY AND UNHAPPINESS/DEPRESSION STRIKE THE SAME PUBLICS

The relationship between depression/unhappiness and political negativity may also be roughly assessed by examining the prevalence of the two pathologies in selected publics. Some correspondence is indicated: compared to men, women are more depressed, less efficacious (have lower internal political efficacy scores), have lower trust in government, and are less optimistic; low income and low education groups are also more depressed, less happy, and disproportionately less efficacious and less trusting in people and governments; African Americans, while not more depressed, are unhappier and more dysphoric than whites; they are also less efficacious, less trusting of people, and, by the 1980s, less trusting in government (in the Lyndon Johnson years they had greater trust in government).

Rising incidence of depression has hit young adults with special force. Compared to older people, the young are now (but not before 1960) more depressed and also less satisfied with their lives; they also feel less efficacious than others. Also, the young have lower feelings of citizen duty and have lower rates of turnout than older people; and along with others, they have become increasingly pessimistic about the lot of the average person. Although the young are not consistently less trusting in government, along with others, their trust in government has declined over the years.[86]

Concluding Observations

Take first the evidence that life satisfaction drives political satisfaction—and not the other way around. This supports my claim that well-being is generated in the microworlds of experience and not, in the first instance, in the public arena of politics. Insofar as researchers' tests for political evaluation turn on criteria of well-being, the merits of democracy rest on its influence over these microworlds. It is for this reason that across polities at all levels of development, the presence of democracy (functioning parties and parliaments and absence of military coups) is unrelated to average SWB—but poverty, a chronic feature of daily experience, is closely related. Political theorists and constitution makers might ponder this point to great advantage.

Second, by what standards shall one appraise political negativity? Suppose one cannot fine-tune positive and negative attitudes toward government and is confronted with only two poles, positive and negative. If strong positive attitudes prevail, is there not a risk of hypertrophy of government, with the dependency and sometimes the encroachments on freedom that government usurpation of private functions implies? Or if what one wants is a steady, informed debate between political negativists and political positivists, how many negativists are needed to give weight to the debate?

Third, how and in what ways is political negativity aversive? The answer lies in the kind of relations that exist between political and private worlds in individual minds. Consider three kinds of relationships: (1) Political efficacy and sense of personal control are related; if the causal order is wholly from personal control to political efficacy, well-being is not jeopardized by low political efficacy; if there is a feedback relation, well-being is jeopardized. (2) Personal optimism is not related to political optimism; therefore there is no risk of personal pessimism from political pessimism. (3) Negative affect as a personality attribute applies both to personal worlds and to political worlds; again, political negativity will not cause personal negativity, for they have a common source.

American democracy does many things very well, but it does not seem to make its citizens happy or do much to relieve their unhappiness.

12

Do Democratic Processes Contribute to Ill-Being?

Could the processes of democracy, themselves, be at least partially to blame for the rise or prevalence of unhappiness and malaise? But would it make sense to blame democracy for these infelicitous postwar trends where people have had relatively constant democratic forms for most of their history? It makes sense if one believes, as I do, that democracy is not the cause of political malaise but that it not only fails to relieve malaise but also represents a constant irritant that exacerbates the malaise arising from other sources.

The main hypothesis in this analysis of ill-being in the United States and other democracies is that democratic processes are generally painful, fail to contribute to good cheer in democratic publics, and contribute to an unhappiness–negativity syndrome. Note that I am not comparing democracy with other systems of government but rather examining processes more or less inherent in democratic systems. Democratic theorists and what I will call participationists (chapter 13) have amply explored the credit side of this hedonic ledger.

Why should it be that the very instrument that gives people a say in how they are governed seems not to cheer them? Of the two aspects to this question, the effect of democratic political processes on sense of well-being and the effect of political outcomes, in this chapter I will treat the processes. If, as is said of the labor market, the processes are the pain for which the outcomes are the reward (which, for the market, I deny), then the parallel analysis does not do justice to democracy.

In the following account I will first examine why negative attitudes toward democratic processes should dominate favorable attitudes toward political outcomes. Next I will look at certain reasons for expecting democratic processes to be painful, more painful, for example, than market processes. If a democracy is to do its job, it will, at least in the short run, hurt many, perhaps most, people. I look at these pains next, including the way people adapt to democracy, discounting the benefits and registering only the pains. Democratic processes are saturated with moral issues: consequently, the enduring problem of the relation of morals to happiness is inevitably part of my agenda. Finally, the role of pain in all human feedback systems is acknowledged.

Process and Outcome

Theoretically, people might be satisfied with democratic processes but not with the policy outcomes of the democratic governments they know. Or vice versa. Thus one might conceive of the four types satisfaction and dissatisfaction with outcomes and satisfaction and dissatisfaction with processes (table 12.1). By "Dissatisfied with democratic processes" I do not mean favoring one form of democratic process over another, say, proportional representation instead of first-past-the-post or parliamentary over presidential systems. I mean someone who holds elections, politicians, parties, legislatures to be objects of ridicule, derides them, and holds them in contempt even though maybe endorsing democratic systems in the abstract.

There are very few complacents (cell I) in our societies, for almost everyone who refers at all to politics has some policy preference which is unsatisfied. Complacency, therefore, is likely to mean apathy.[1] But in this chapter the concern is with those dissatisfied with the democratic process, the undemocrats (cell III) and the political negativists (cell IV).

The relation between outcome dissatisfaction and process dissatisfaction is as follows: (1) attitudes toward the (or a) democratic process dominate attitudes toward outcomes because: (i) bad outcomes will be more readily explained by bad processes than vice versa. As in other means–ends relations, processes come before their outcomes; (ii) processes are treated as morally sacred whereas outcomes are generally (though not always) treated as policy preferences; and (iii) processes are perceptually salient whereas outcomes are more opaque, diffuse, and obscure. As we have seen in earlier chapters, "the availability heuristic" says that whatever is vivid, immediate, and personal

Table 12.1. Satisfaction and Dissatisfaction with Political Processes and Outcomes

	(a) Satisfied with Outcomes	(b) Dissatisfied with Outcomes
(c) Satisfied with Democratic Processes	(I) *Complacents*	(II) *Political Critics*
(d) Dissatisfied with Democratic Processes	(III) *Undemocrats*	(IV) *Political Negativists*

dominates the more "pallid" background characteristics of a situation;[2] cognitive theory tells us that for most people perception dominates other kinds of cognition and the concrete dominates the abstract. Thus, rows (c) and (d) should dominate the conflicting feelings implied in cells (II) and (III), and it is easier to go across columns from (a) to (b) and back than across rows from (c) to (d) and back.

(2) Negative feelings dominate positive feelings: losses are feared more than gains are prized;[3] and pains are noticed more and remembered longer than are pleasures.[4] Thus column (b) should dominate column (a), and row (d) should dominate row (c), that is, undemocratic sentiments are more likely to invade complacency than vice versa, and political negativity is more likely to infect political criticality than vice versa. The dominance of process over outcome and of negative over positive pushes people toward the southeast quadrant, political negativity. The positivity bias then yields to superior force.

That process should dominate outcome is a familiar story. E. Allen Lind and Tom Tyler have shown how feelings about procedural justice often dominate feelings about substantive justice received;[5] I have found that in the conflict between how one is treated versus what one gets, the former tends to dominate the latter in a variety of evaluations;[6] Thomas Juster and Frank Stafford have demonstrated the importance of process benefits in allocating time;[7] and in attitudinal research, attitudes toward the means often decide whether the end is worth striving for.[8] The story I am telling is about processes; the effect of policy outcomes on feelings of well-being is a different story.

General Causes of Cheerlessness

Most aspects of democratic politics imply more pain and unhappiness than good cheer. Indeed, it may be said that democratic political systems are inherently painful and perhaps, therefore, unlikable. The first reason for this pain and dislike is obvious enough: All painful social problems are, in the end, political problems.

ALL PAINFUL SOCIAL PROBLEMS ARE POLITICAL

Facing social problems seems to be increasingly painful. Asked in 1957 what they thought the sources of their happiness and unhappiness were, only 13 percent of a U.S. national sample said that "community, national, and world problems" were sources of unhappiness. By 1976 this proportion had almost doubled to 24 percent—more than thought they were made unhappy by their economic or occupational problems.[9]

The problems are painful for several reasons: (1) thinking about them may create internal conflicts (both ambivalence and dissonance) and external conflicts, that is, quarrels; (2) the resolution of these quarrels will injure one side or another; (3) acknowledging the presence of these problems is painful because, as in the case of theodicy, to do so is to jeopardize some prized belief; and (4) the implied or open conflict of values is painful because it hurts to find one's values challenged or scorned. These pains emerge in political form partly because politics is the domain in which concepts of the good life and of justice are reflected. As Karl Mannheim and Harold Lasswell have both observed, politics is the place where ends or values conflict and, because conflicting ends do not lend themselves to ends–means rationality,[10] the "irrational" decisions in that domain are harder to justify to oneself and others. Such justification must come from the tacit agreement of others,[11] but political conflict challenges that agreement. When an earlier school of political scientists (for example, C. J. Friedrich) argued that democracy required "agreement on fundamentals," they misstated the case: it is not so much agreement (except for agreement on how to reconcile conflicts) as the papering over or concealing of fundamental disagreements that is required to make democratic or other ways of living together tolerable. When democratic debate opens old fissures (old wounds) democracy is painful. And (5), just as there can be cognitive overload, so, for some of the same reasons, there may be political overload: "Paradoxically, by expecting politics to settle too many issues, we have diminished the possibilities of politics."[12]

The shift from economic issues to so-called symbolic issues (abortion, prayer in the schools, work ethic among welfare clients) makes the conflict even more distressing. People care a great deal about the symbols that reflect on their own ways of life and touch chords of sympathy because they are validations of people's self-concepts.[13] And self-concepts are treasured more than material interests.

WHY POLITICS IS MORE PAINFUL THAN MARKETS

Although the gains from having markets take the load off governments are considerable, many of the pains of democracy are caused by its association with market economies, sometimes because democracies inappropriately borrow market thinking, sometimes because market failures are off-loaded onto politics, sometimes because of the sharp conflict over the meaning of *minimal government,* and sometimes because of the different ratios of winners to losers in the two domains.

The economistic fallacy (chapter 4) reaches the political domain without strain. Because level of income beyond the poverty level has such a trivial relationship to well-being[14] and because the insecurity of jobs and income associated with current market behavior is so much more important for well-being than level of income,[15] one can understand why efforts to redistribute income fail to make people happy. Above the poverty line, beneficiaries may be temporarily grateful (which might be all that is needed in an election year), but over a longer term they will not be any happier than they were before the redistribution. In any event, gratitude for favors received has little to do with voting.[16] Prospect theory has something to say here: those from whom something is taken will be hurt more than those to whom something is given will be pleased.

Is there a Left–Right dimension to happiness politics? On the one hand, happiness is associated with conservatism: happy people are "more attracted by the political right and the center than by the political left,"[17] but on the other hand, "political protest is an active response to one's environment and evidence suggests that happiness fosters rather than blocks active [protest] involvement."[18] Both Left and Right have stakes in happiness; but whoever is in power cannot be sure that their making people happier will yield supporting votes. (Although, perhaps fortunately, politicians believe otherwise.)

The economistic fallacy is reflected in two other political ways. One is in a fiscal policy by means of which the economy is reflated before elections. Although there is controversy on the effects of reflation on voting, I believe that those who, like Douglas Hibbs, find minimal evidence for the effects of fiscal policy on voting are likely to be right.[19] And the ingratitude of publics for favors mentioned above applies as much to economic favors as to any others. This is in line with David Sears and Carolyn Funk's analysis of the minimal effects of self-interest in elections.[20]

Market failures. A specific and crucial instance of the off-loading of pain onto politics follows from the principle *market failures become political responsibilities.* No matter how devoted to the principles of minimal government people may be, when the shoe pinches, they turn to politics. As Robert Dahl points out, it is not possible to solve economic issues in a wholly laissez-faire manner, for people *will* bring their economic grievances into the political forum.[21] Brody and Sniderman add to this the specification that personal problems become political not simply when people are in difficulty, for Americans, at least, tend to think that they themselves should solve their problems (self-reliance, self-attribution); rather, issues are politicized only when people think they ought to be helped by government and believe they are not. It is then that people become alienated from politics.[22] Similarly, in Australia it is those who believe their government could help who tend to find fault with political institutions.[23]

Charles Wolf, Jr., defining market failure as situations in which "total benefits do not exceed total costs," suggests a few such situations: failure to promote or use technology to lower costs or improve products, failure to improve organizational capability or individual incentives to increase productive efficiency (including Liebenstein's X-efficiency),[24] failure to accommodate to popular concepts of "distributive justice" (which tend to favor market principles of desert over political distributional principles [sometimes] of need),[25] high levels of externalities or spillovers that create unacceptable burdens on others, burdens which are not reimbursed by firms, economically rational behavior in the presence of decreasing marginal costs, and so forth.[26] The rectifying of market failures by political means implies both challenging the market ideology (which hurts many true believers) and damaging the interests of some parties involved in the failure. To cure inflation, current doctrine holds that one must raise interest rates (harmful to holders of variable rate mortgages) and, incredibly, increase unemployment! The tradeoff is hedonically costly, for (as mentioned in chapter 9) rates of inflation are not related to measures of SWB. In any event, policies that favor unemployment to prevent inflation are politically unprofitable, for "the personal impact of inflation quite consistently has had no influence on voters' choices."[27] Finally, perceptions of "what the government is doing about the economy . . . jobs, prices, and profits" are salient and very negative, although compared to concerns closer to the self, these political-economic concerns tend to contribute little to (or, in this case, detract little from) people's satisfaction with their lives.[28]

Yet even if some symptoms of political malaise do not greatly influence sense of well-being (and do not influence turnout), when they are expressed as unfairness, they are more corrosive. And this is where economic issues make their mark on politics. "One reason why so many Americans are alienated is clearly money. The biggest single contributor to the record high alienation index [of the late 1980s] is the 83% of the public who feel that 'the rich get richer and the poor get poorer,' "[29] a matter shown vividly in the ascending curve of beliefs that government favors the big interests (see fig. 11.4).

Growth of the economy is a source of rejoicing, whereas growth of politics and of government is frequently a source of distress. Economic growth is thought by most people to benefit most of the population, but, although the expansion of certain government functions is cheered by those who hope to benefit from those functions, the general growth of the public sector frightens many. The alarm arising from the expansion of the public sector reflects a variety of considerations: sometimes it is caused by the superior influence of advocates of minimal government, sometimes it is because of people's personal stakes in market activities, sometimes because of party partisanship, occasionally because of convincing evidence that public enterprises are, in strictly economic or technical terms, less efficient than private enterprises, and sometimes because the expansion of the public sector may lead to costs that people are unwilling to pay now and, if deferred, are said to burden the next generation. (It is notable that business borrowing occasions little public alarm while government borrowing, even for capital expenditures with demonstrable economic return, alarms many.)

The expansion of politics, as distinct from the expansion of government, may be opposed because, as we shall see in the next chapter, the processes of politics are not themselves enjoyed. Whatever the reason, there is no joy when either campaigning or the public budget expands, but there is joy in the expansion of the gross national product.

Whereas economic issues lend themselves to compromise, to splitting the difference, and to Pareto optimality, symbolic or moral or sacred issues are not so easily reconciled. Sacred beliefs are those for which no scientific evidence is available or at least none that is persuasive to nonbelievers, as in the case of beliefs about equality, freedom, democracy, the goodness or badness of human nature, as well as the nature of the supernatural. Because historical evidence has allegedly proven (provided evidence that convinced marginal believers as well as nonbelievers) that communism is an inefficient way of organizing an economy, over a relatively short period of seventy years communism has lost its persuasive power. But historical experience cannot prove that the pope is or is not the vicar of God, or that free speech is a condition of economic prosperity (for example, Singapore and the United States in the McCarthyite period), or that equality between whites and African Americans is better than inequality. Morals and religion are famously invulnerable to proof—so are many ideological issues which draw their strength from their moral content. Issues which cannot be settled by evidence arouse passions that, like other passions, have physiological symptoms. Arousal is based on the autonomic nervous system and involves such physical symptoms as sweating, increased pulse, gastrointestinal disturbance, preparing for a fight or flight response. Arousal flows from a perceptual or cognitive coding of a situation and informs the brain of the inner state which increases alertness. This process is not necessarily painful (there is a condition of optimal arousal), but it augments the pain arising from a challenge to cherished beliefs.

Compared to the markets, democratic politics yields more losers than winners. In a close two-party contest almost half of the voters will be losers (and in a multiparty contest in which pluralities create winners there may be even bigger proportions of losers), but there is no such ratio of losers to winners among the parties of market transactions. In that sense, although democracy is a long-term benefit to almost all citizens, in the short run electoral politics is more of a zero-sum game than is the market game. There is also a difference between the two systems in the benefits to third parties. In politics, almost everyone is a partisan and therefore a winner or loser in the competition among candidates and parties; few are third parties. In the consumer market, when firms compete, almost everyone is a third party for whom that competition is always a positive-sum game. Positive-sum games permit greater harmony (indeed, they facilitate Pareto optimality), while zero-sum games are patently antagonistic, for they encourage rivalry, competitiveness, reciprocal antagonism—all more or less painful emotions. If your gain is my loss, I will have trouble taking satisfaction in your good fortune. But of course, there are other satisfactions for losers in elections, not the least of which is participation in a ceremony that is laden with moral value (chapter 11).

What people receive from markets is thought to be earned; what they receive from government is only deserved. For very different reasons, Aristotle and Locke agree: we have greater affection for what we have earned than for what is given to us, and whatever we have mixed with our own labor we can appropriately regard as ours or, better still, mine. I will put a marker here to register this point developed in the next chapter on self-determination: *democratic processes yield little pleasure in controlling events in one's life.*

Because market systems have the maximization of consumer utility as their sole justification, and because political systems have other justifications (defense, police, protection of rights, and so forth), markets should be better agents than governments for making people happy and relieving their depression. In spite of massive research on the relative economic efficiency of private and public enterprises and of powerful arguments showing that public interference with market decisions must reduce economic efficiency, I know of no evidence comparing the utility generated by markets with that generated by democracy. In substantial part, the utility produced will depend on how each of these agencies facilitates or hinders companionship (see chapter 14).

PROCESSES INHERENT IN DEMOCRACY

Painful problems are inherent in the very nature of democracy, problems which cannot be avoided if the regime is to remain democratic.

Democratic governments often seem to be, and sometimes are, in opposition to their citizens. This oppositional principle has several sources. Politics, of course, is a domain in which people conflict with one another. When the government decides what to do, it sides with one of the conflicting parties. The other party (or parties) then finds itself (themselves) in opposition to the government, that is, the government is the opponent. Or suppose that the government does nothing: then all parties to the contest are in opposition to the government. Is this different from the market, which Tönnies describes in Hobbesian terms as "the war of all against all"? Yes and no. Yes, in the sense, as Adam Smith pointed out, that in the market there is a hidden hand that ensures that all third parties benefit from economic competition. No, in the sense that the loser of any particular economic conflict is not easily consoled by the fact that others benefit from the conflict in which she was defeated.

The opposition between citizens and governments stems also from certain duties governments are asked to perform, duties that require as a condition of their fulfillment that some, perhaps most, of the public will be offended. In protecting the rights of, say, homosexuals or, especially at an earlier stage in history, of African Americans, governments incur the anger, irritation, or hostility of more people than are mollified, pleased, or benefited. The government's police power protects some while angering others. NIMBY lives here, too: certain things must be done, but not in my back yard. The opposition of citizens to their governments and of governments to their citizens is a condition of the very processes of democratic government.

The administration of policies offends people even, or especially, when administrators follow principles of good government. Holding governments to account for their expenditure of public funds and for adhering to due process of law is widely endorsed and, when applied in any particular case, bitterly resented. *Good government* means, among other things, the rule of law, that is, a law that is no respector of persons. But the popular preference for special treatment that characterizes the particularistic ethos of the working class and village residents must be violated—to their pain.[30] People want to be treated as individuals, not merely as plaintiffs or defendants. Also, public policy generates and defends public goods, whose benefits are available to all without special effort or cost. But these are goods whose overuse may incur the tragedy of the commons and therefore the imposition of quotas and rationing, something that individuals accustomed to free choice will resent. An alternative problem for public goods is the alleged logic of collective action, by which individuals are tempted to enjoy their use without paying the cost, leading to imposed payments (for example, user fees or taxes) and again inviting resentment over the necessary coercion[31] (but see discussion of taxes below).

The subject role is painful. As the world becomes more complex, our bureaucratic encounters multiply. As it turns out, studies have found that the public's personal experiences with nonregulative government bureaucracies (health, welfare, pensions, and so on) are actually experienced by subjects as rather benign: there were usually agents available to handle a person's inquiry or complaint, the agents took personal responsibility for the case presented and pursued the matter to a conclusion, the agents were usually courteous and informed, and so forth. But do these favorable bureaucratic encounters change people's attitudes toward government bureaucracy? No. The default values of the familiar schemas of bureaucracy prevail: ideology triumphs over experience.[32] But of course any dealing with bureaucracy, public or private, is, in a literal and metaphoric sense, a pain. We are all made anxious by bureaucratic forms, and most of us by our dealings with authority.

Paying taxes may (or may not) be a source of discontent. The strategy of the New Deal was said by its critics to be "Tax and tax, spend and spend, and elect and elect." No longer. After hammering away at the "tax burden" for fifty years, conservatives have persuaded the American public (far more than European publics) that taxes are wasted, a drag on the economy, and burdensome to the public. The consequence has been a series of so-called tax revolts, the best known occurring in California in the early 1980s. In 1991 the *Los Angeles Times* commissioned a survey of attitudes toward taxes (table 12.2). Fewer respondents were angry about taxes than might be expected, but, still, over a third were angry. As we now know, anger and feelings of frustration have uncertain relations with both political behavior and feelings of well-being. In reviewing attitudes in several instances in which tax policies had become salient, Sears and Funk found that those with higher stakes were, indeed, more influenced than others by their "self-interest:" "In almost all these cases . . . taxpayers' self-interest in real ballot or legislative propositions has significantly influenced their support for them." But did these feelings influence their sense of well-being? Probably not, for there was only a trivial (.02) correlation between attitudes on taxes and "economic discontent,"[33] the form of discontent most relevant to tax payments.

The fact that opposition to taxes is greater in the United States than in

*Table 12.2. California Residents' Attitudes Toward Taxes**

Source of taxation	Very angry	Fairly angry	Fairly satisfied	Very satisfied	Don't Know
Federal income tax†	11%	28%	52%	8	1%
State sales taxes	12	23	54	10	1
State/local income tax	12	22	8	10	8

*The question was, "Are you very angry about the amount of (federal income taxes / state sales taxes and local income taxes) you or your family paid last year or fairly angry, fairly satisfied, or very satisfied?"

†Sample of respondents who filed federal income tax last year; includes 7 percent who said they did not pay local or state income taxes.

Source: Los Angeles Times April 1991.

countries where taxes are much higher suggests that the economic cost of taxes is not the main source of political malaise. Rather it is, itself, part of the malaise. This is suggested by the fact that of eight explanations for support of the California Tax Revolt the most predictive was the item noted in the previous chapter: "People like me don't have any say about what the government does" and another similar item ("Those we elect to Congress in Washington lose touch with the people pretty quickly") — tapping both internal and external efficacy. Noting that none of the eight relevant questions on the list accounted for much of the variance, the authors of a study (1981) say, "We believe that the symbolic politics interpretation of the tax revolt goes a long way toward explaining the inadequacies of the eight explanations considered here."[34] Supporting this view is the close relation between measures of trust in government and attitudes toward taxes.[35]

Like the subject role, *the citizen role is not a happy one,* but that treatment must be deferred to the next chapter.

Exercising rights does not lead to positive feelings toward government. Rights are unlikely to be enjoyed unless we claim them. They are not given to us by governments, but rather they are intrinsic to our status as persons or as citizens. In the United States people enjoy them because they are "endowed by our Creator with certain inalienable rights." Two considerations modify the benefits of rights. First, when the beneficiaries are socially denigrated, as in the case of welfare recipients, many people do not apply, and for those that do "the stance these recipients adopt is not that of a rights-bearing citizen claiming benefits to which he is entitled but that of a suppliant seeking in the words of a number of recipients, 'a little help to tide us over until we can get back on our own feet again'."[36] The second thing that happens in the case of rights is that because they are rights to which people are entitled, if the rights are protected or granted, their benefits are not credited to government although the government is blamed if the claims are not promptly answered. The crowning glory of democratic government, the protection of rights, is a perverse source of blame, of political negativity, and of pain.

Other processes intrinsic to democracy inhibit the maximization of well-being. At this point we see how difficult, perhaps impossible, it is for democracies directly to maximize SWB. As mentioned in the previous chapter, by their very nature democracies are constrained to give priority to demands rather than to needs,[37] to the sources of unhappiness that people can identify rather than the equally important sources that people cannot identify, to the relief of pain rather than the promotion of happiness (for example, negative utilitarianism). There are very good reasons for these priorities: if citizens relax their control of the public over policy, authorities will impose on their publics the authorities' own version of the sources of felicity, a hazardous process in which the loss of both present happiness and opportunities to redress grievances in the future is risked. As Popper has suggested,[38] governments that experiment with promoting happiness are very likely to want to control the circumstances of people's lives in order to make their experiments pay off—as Pol Pot did in his Cambodian experiment of 1975–79. The aggregation of interests in political parties does not easily aggregate publics with discreet, subtle, private ills. In the United States rather more than in Europe, democracy serves producer interests better than consumer interests (railroads instead of passengers, doctors instead of patients), so it would not serve beneficially the consumers of unhappiness if the producers of that unhappiness had conflicting stakes.

And the combined vested intellectual interests of market economists and democratic theorists give initially plausible reasons for market and democratic procedures necessarily being more or less as they are. The trouble is that these theories are based on two false premises: first, that demand reflects informed opinion on what would improve an individual's well-being, or at least that each person knows this better than anyone else (chapter 17), whereas the evidence shows that this is very often not the case[39]—although the remedy is far from clear. And second, is the economistic fallacy.

Erosion of sources of commitment to political contests. In addition to the general causes of the failure of political systems to give meaning to life that were mentioned in the discussion of meaninglessness in the previous chapter, there are causes in everyday politics that belong in a discussion of the effects of democracy on malaise. Some political scientists believe that the decline in party identification in the United States deprives people of a meaningful attachment to politics,[40] an argument that helps to explain the timing of the rise of political negativity in the 1960s and is congruent with Bowlby's attachment and separation argument.[41] Also, many have compared political ideologies, especially Marxism, to religion, which, as we have seen, is generally, though not universally, found to be a source of meaning contributing to well-being.[42] Is it the decline of ideology, so recently heralded and then abandoned, that makes politics devoid of meaning? Perhaps, for it is ideologies that give hope social meaning—in contrast to the personal meaning of hope which is currently the dominant one. As people begin to lose hope for their nation's future ("the lot of the average man is getting worse"—chapter 2), they express their disappointment in political malaise.

While democracy has an ambivalent relationship to nationalism and national pride, the decline in commitment to democratic institutions has been said to follow from the alleged decline in commitment to the nation.[43] In my opinion, this interpretation is wrong. Although I found in the previous chapter that people divorce their own futures from the nation's future, they do not lose their identification with their nation. Asked (1982) if they took "pride in their country," 80 percent of the Americans said yes, while only 55 percent of the British, 33 percent of the French, 30 percent of the Japanese, and only 21 percent of the Germans claimed such pride. One might say that the Europeans are exposed to institutions and ideologies that depreciate national pride ("in many European countries, pride in nationality is regarded as a rather outmoded concept"),[44] but the Japanese! I do not think that the rising political malaise of the American public comes from any failure of national pride. What are they proud of? Both in the late 1950s and in 1996 the answer is "the political system."[45]

Conflict between support for principles and negativity toward practices. If political beliefs were believed to be sufficiently important to people's lives, the conflict between support for democratic principles and opposition to political practices would have only one outcome: disappointment. This seems to have been the case in Russia, where people more or less eagerly supported the idea of an elected government, but in the 1990 November elections, "so few people actually could be bothered to exercise their democratic rights that all the 45 seats available at by-elections to the Moscow and Leningrad Soviets, and to the Russian Supreme Soviet, had to be left vacant."[46] Giving due credit to the superior practices in the United States, one can see something in the Russian case of the effects of disappointment when ideals outrun practices. By teaching only the ideals in schools we do not prepare the young to be committed to democracy as it actually works.

Is the U.S. political system inherently less likeable than other political systems? The arguments (made more by foreign than native observers) that malaise in the United States derives from the government's failure to enact popular measures — because of the weak parties and separation and division of powers[47] — are unpersuasive. If anything, American politics is all too responsive to popular pressures and public opinion. Up until 1994 if one party controlled the presidency and another the Congress, success in enacting legislation did not differ much from enactment during periods when the same party controlled both branches.[48] Great Britain, with its parliamentary and unitary systems, has suffered from political negativity very similar to that in the United States. And comparing the political responsiveness of the British and U.S. systems does not establish a clear difference in their meeting of social needs.[49] In any event, the features of the U.S. government that are alleged to cause political malaise have hardly changed since the Civil War, yet unhappiness, clinical depression, and political negativity rose sharply in the 1960s. To return to a European finding mentioned above: life satisfaction drives political satisfaction and not vice versa. It is the quality of American life, not of American politics, that is the source of political malaise.

The moralization of politics creates more pain than pleasure. The hypermoralization of politics, I said in chapter 11, is a source of both pain from a nagging sense of duty and of pleasure when one has done one's duty. Duty is the key, not other aspects of morality: benevolence (Kant), altruism (Richard Titmus), prosocial behavior (John Darley and Bibb Latané), moral reasoning (Lawrence Kohlberg), or morality as caring (Carol Gilligan). On the one hand, conscientious people, those sensitive to social norms, are in fact happier than others.[50] And so are benevolent people and those who engage in prosocial behavior. But, on the other hand, the questions defining citizen duty and philosophical discussions of civic obligation do not imply altruism or caring or moral reasoning. Rather they are about duties to society and as such do not suggest the forms of morality that are associated with happiness.[51] I do not want to overstate the case or to imply a Freudian tension between conscience and desire, but some empirical research finds, first, that people do experience the tension between duty and pleasure and, second, that the tension relaxes as people become habituated to performing their duties.[52] (Empirical moral philosophers rate the defense of an act on grounds of duty at a middle or conventional level, not at a principled level of moral reasoning.)[53]

Why are the demands of citizen duty moral demands? As the advocates of rational choice and so-called rational ignorance tell us, my vote will not change the outcome in an election. Indeed, if fewer people voted, the outcome would be about the same as it is now.[54] Russell Hardin gives one answer: acts which seem to have only the ad hoc moral status of convention derive their ethical standing from their proven value as coordinating principles for the society: "They may encapsulate the experience of society and take their [ethical] value from human experience."[55]

Legal philosophers assert that justice has nothing to do with happiness and much to do with obligation.[56] Democratic politics, it seems, is in the same boat.

PAIN IS A NECESSARY FUNCTION OF ALL SYSTEMS

Pain is functional in all systems, including democratic systems. Systems are governed by cybernetic processes in which pain and pleasure are, as Bentham said, "sovereign masters" (really only semisovereign, given that nature is indifferent to people's pain and concerned only with the multiplication of their genes). Of the many types of systems I will allude to four: species, individual lives, institutions, and societies. Whereas in this chapter I am asking about the functions of institutions in serving human well-being, physiologists and some evolutionary psychologists often reverse the question: What is the function of pain and pleasure in serving biological systems?[57] For example, instead of asking how economic systems maximize utility (greatest pleasure and least pain), Martin Seligman and J. L. Hager ask how the states of pain and pleasure help various species, including humans, to be fruitful and multiply.[58]

Unhappiness, an excess of pain over pleasure, also functions to serve individuals, as when their unhappiness is a kind of internal signal providing them with information on their capacities to cope with the situations that confront them and so to prepare them to meet the demands of these situations.[59] Similarly, the moods of their members serve institutions by facilitating the purposes of the institutions. For example, the function of the expression of dissatisfaction or pain in a democratic system is to make that system more responsive to popular needs and demands, that is, to fulfill its central purpose. To serve their own purposes, democracies do not invite pain, of course, but they do invite the expression of pain. Finally, democracies are not ends in themselves but must be judged by how they function to benefit the purposes of their societies, the latter being inclusive entities that embrace the purposes of the other three systems: survival of the members of the human species within their domains, flourishing lives, and responsive institutions. Pain in democracy has a societal function that embraces the pain–pleasure balance of all three.

If democracies, in spite of all their felicitous properties and recent triumphs over alternative political systems, contain within their systems the means of inflicting pain on their cheerless publics and benefiting therefrom, why do people not correct these faults by entering the political arena and voting away the sources of pain? One reason, of course, is that the pains are often inherent in the democratic process. Another reason is that participating in politics is itself a pain.

13

The Pain of Self-Determination in Democracy

People want to be self-determining and prefer to believe that they are. The desire to control one's environment seems to be part of our genetic endowment. The public value of self-determination is high and comes with a distinguished philosophical endorsement. The dominant economic ideology of the time assumes self-determination—and then reifies it, that is, sees its operation in the ambiguous circumstances of market transactions. By giving humankind free will, God seems to require of human creatures that they determine their cosmic fates for themselves. And democratic theory and institutions justify many of their practices by reference to the ideal of self-determination.

So how can it be that this eagerly sought, socially honored, gladly experienced, religiously and ideologically endorsed self-determination in politics is not a source of joy? One reason is that political participation is not experienced as self-determination and does not share its hedonic benefits. Another reason is that acts that are thought to be beneficial to society are not individually rewarding. To explicate this puzzle is the assignment for this chapter.

The Concept of Self-Determination

I shall not review the long list of philosophers who have paid tribute to self-determination and autonomy (for example, Kant, Baron D'Holbach,

Jefferson, Mill, Ralph Waldo Emerson, and many more). For most of these authors the benefits of self-determination are moral: self-determination enhances the dignity of humans. But there is an emptiness about the concept. What does it mean to be autonomous or *self*-determining in a world in which all human acts are subject to the constraints of circumstance and of social influences? "Kant's free individual is a transcendent being, beyond the realm of natural causality," said Isaiah Berlin.[1] An American critic says, "The problem with autonomy is that . . . the notion is substantively empty"[2] for it says nothing about how an autonomous person acquires opinions without being influenced by others. The criticisms are apt, for all acts are caused by an interaction between self and circumstance, as the familiar paradigm S → O → R (stimulus → organism → response) illustrates. Self-determination represents an emphasis on O, the organism or person, not because the stimuli were irrelevant or that in the accounting for variance the O accounts for more, but rather because philosopher critics believe the dignity of humans is enhanced if the O dominates the *S*.

Some of the enemies of self-determination are the approval motive, by which a person's responses are chronically calculated to elicit the approval or agreement of others,[3] conformism, habit, deference to authority, closing one's mind to new information whether religious or ideological (exclusive reliance on Piagetian assimilation),[4] custom, and so forth. "He who does anything because it is the custom makes no choice," Mill writes.[5] Self-determination requires a consideration of social influences, a knowledge of one's deepest preferences, and a synthesis that expresses the self's idiosyncrasies. It is a rare skill. Self-determination enters the argument between dispositional explanations and circumstantial explanations on the side of dispositions: "A rather general *'dispositional theory'* is shared by almost everyone socialized in our [Western] culture."[6] Certainly, it is a part of the worldview of the so-called Protestant ethic, which says that "one's fate will eventually mirror one's character, and one's personal traits and abilities will ultimately prevail over circumstances."[7] Self-determination is to be contrasted to a belief in fate or historical determinism or the inexplicable intervention of divine forces.

Tocqueville thought the idea of self-determination was particularly American: "They [Americans] acquire the habit of always considering themselves as standing alone, and they are apt to imagine that their whole destiny is in their own hands."[8] Even today, Americans, more than continental Europeans, believe their welfare is their own doing, not their labor union's and not their country's.[9] In contrast to Kant's and Mill's version, the dispositional attributions of the West have been called "the fundamental attribution error."[10]

Requirements for Self-Determination

For self-determination to work, people must want to be self-determining, must believe that they can be, and must find it rewarding. It helps if society values their efforts. Given the motive, if their efforts are frustrated or socially undervalued or unrewarded, they will suffer pains such as those we have seen.

THE MOTIVE TO BE SELF-DETERMINING

To a remarkable extent, philosophers and psychologists agree on people's desire for self-determination. Here is Berlin's version: the positive sense of the word *liberty,* he says, "derives from the wish on the part of the individual to be his own master. I wish my life and my decisions to depend on myself, not on external forces of whatever kind. I wish to be the instrument of my own, not of other men's, acts of will. I wish to be . . . self-directed and not acted upon by external nature or by other men as if I were a thing or animal."[11] The parallel psychological motives are the desire for "effectance" or "competence"[12] or "personal control"[13] and are given a cognitive dimension by the idea of "internal locus of control,"[14] meaning the belief that one can influence events in one's life. One might say that psychologists understand the processes better, but that philosophers like Berlin understand their social significance better.

In his original study of psychological competence, Robert White grounded the motive in evolutionary and biological research and hence gave it instinctual or, in the language of the Enlightenment, natural standing. "The motive," he said, "is capable of yielding surplus satisfaction well beyond what is necessary to get the biological work done."[15] It is gratifying in itself. As White suggested, the desire to be effective or competent, to produce an effect when one acts, has a deep biological underpinning. Seligman reports a series of experiments with the following outcomes: "It is highly significant that when rats and pigeons are given a choice between getting free food and getting the same food for making responses, they choose to work. Infants smile at a mobile whose movements are contingent on their responses but not at a noncontingent mobile. These activities, because they entail effective instrumental responding, produce joy."[16] In accounting for these responses, Seligman gives an evolutionary answer: joy in instrumental responses has reproductive value. In the absence of such effectiveness, "an aversive state arises, which organisms seek to avoid. It is called depression."[17]

The motive is strong enough that people *will* believe that they have caused such outcomes as winning a lottery (by drawing, instead of being given, a number) or a football victory by cheering their team. This illusion of control is widespread,[18] the default belief of the species and part of the evolutionary endowment that permitted the species to survive frequent and overwhelming threats to survival.[19] Children choose to join unrewarded groups, instead of groups in which they may earn rewards, if they are more free to select their activities in the unrewarded groups. Given alternatives between certain kinds of pleasurable but uncontrolled excitement and duller situations within their control, children will more often choose the duller, more controllable ones.[20] But there is a stronger motive for protecting familiar choices than for extending the range of choice.[21] At work, the frustrating of self-determination by close supervision undermines work satisfaction.[22] Finally, next to self-esteem, the belief that one is effective is more closely associated with happiness than anything else, especially level of income, to which so much attention is paid in the American market society.[23]

If the motive for personal control or self-determination is so strong, why did it take so long to create the institutions that facilitate such control and direction? One reason is that the personal control motive must often be subordinated to other motives addressed to the maintenance of life itself: food, shelter, sex, and companionship. When a motive is urgent, the learning and scanning behavior associated with satisfying that motive takes over. But controlling of one's environment, while gratifying in itself, is an instrumental motive that yields, when necessary, to more urgent motives.[24]

And, of course, there are competing motives like those that favor hierarchy and obedience that are also said to have strong evolutionary force.[25] Moreover, the burden of having autonomous, individual, rational free will is often too much for people.[26] In Fromm's graphic term, when the burden is too great there is relief in an "escape from freedom" — which means an escape from self-determination. In addition, for most of history authorities feared individual self-determination. Among many other advisors, Plato, Hobbes, and Burke recommended that ordinary people leave control of their collective destinies to their betters.

Desiring to control one's environment is said to lead inexorably to valuing the circumstances in which choices are favored, that is valuing freedom itself, at least the freedom one knows. But actually it is freedom of choice and control in the microworlds of experience that makes people happy or unhappy. To some extent, this discrepancy between small-world experience and claims about self-determination in politics explains the public malaise described in chapter 11. Democratic processes just don't feel like the self-determination of the private world.

THE BELIEF THAT ONE CAN CONTROL ONE'S DESTINY

When an overwhelming majority wants to control their own fates, something further is necessary: to avoid mental conflict, they must believe they *can* control the events that influence their lives. In a philosophical epigram: Ought implies can. W. E. Henley captured this belief in heroic, if extreme, form: "I am the master of my fate; / I am the captain of my soul." For Henley, the locus of control was wholly internal.

"Of all the beliefs about the self and society that might increase or reduce [psychological] distress, one's sense of control over one's own life may be the most important."[27] Internality is a condition for believing that one is effective, and its absence, powerlessness, is a principal cause of depression.[28] As mentioned in chapter 11, a sense of political efficacy is one of the three most important psychological determinants of participation (the others are sense of citizen duty and party identification).[29] And it is the general sense of powerlessness that influences feelings of political efficacy and not vice versa.[30]

PUBLIC SUPPORT FOR SELF-DETERMINATION

In his introduction to *The Enlightenment,* Peter Gay says, "In the West, the Enlightenment mainly sought ways of teaching people to take affairs into their own hands."[31] This teaching was responsive to the latent desire for self-determination described above. And in an associated message, the Enlightenment made articulate and licensed individual pursuits of happiness. Unhappiness, then, comes to people who seek to take control over their public and private affairs so as to pursue happiness as best they can and are disappointed and frustrated by their failure to control them. Although democratic politics was to have been the instrument, perceptually and to some inevitable degree in actual practice, it did not turn out that way.[32]

The American public's claimed values are in accord: in explicit rankings of values, the value of "freedom (independence, free choice)" is consistently ranked high (third in four surveys from 1968 to 1981—generally following only "peace" and "family security").[33] The value has American as well as Enlightenment roots, as Emerson's essay on self-reliance reveals;[34] it says that people *should* be self-determining in the sense of relying chiefly on their own resources and abilities in order to enhance their welfare and well-being. This value is operational for it influences behavior. The authors of a study of Americans' demands upon government (mentioned in chapter 11) reported that most rejected government help if they could cope on their own. "The ethic of self-reliance," they said, "is scarcely dead."[35] Moreover, the value placed on self-reliance seems not to have changed over the past half century or so: in both 1924 and 1977 exactly 47 percent of the high school students in that paradigmatically American community of "Middletown, agreed: 'It is entirely the fault of the man himself if he cannot succeed.' "[36] The constant, or even rising, belief that people get ahead by "hard work" rather than by "lucky breaks or help from other people"[37] makes this sweeping allegation of individual fault for economic failure plausible to those who believe this version of the Protestant ethic.

People in the West hardly realize how central to their society is the value of self-determination: but "its decline," says Berlin, "would mark the death of civilization, or an entire moral outlook."[38]

Societal and Individual Benefits of Self-Determination

Efforts to be self-reliant and self-determining must be rewarded, perhaps by societal benefits but in any event by individual rewards.

SOCIETAL BENEFITS

The "movement of progressive societies" from status to contract was at the same time a movement from ascription to achievement and from circumstantial determination to self-determination. In many ways, the market was the venue of this movement, and it worked well, for by individualized choices it gives individuals the sense that in choosing occupations (if less often discretion on the job) and in choosing the uses of their money (especially with the rise of what is called discretionary income) and, now, in the selection of a lifestyle, they were in fact self-determining. Iron laws of economics, such as they are, may have taken the place of the iron bonds of religious doctrines, but these economic laws were part of the "necessity" that was less minatory and more like the laws of nature than were religious injunctions. On the whole, societies benefited from releasing individuals to the fates they might determine for themselves. (Democracy was to have been the political instrument for self-determination, but, as we shall see, it is not experienced that way.)

If societies benefited from the rise of self-determination, how did individuals fare in the presence of new opportunities for exercising that universal, if often weak, motive in a climate of post-Enlightenment approval?

INDIVIDUAL BENEFITS OF SELF-DETERMINATION

For individuals, the sense of being self-determining (internal locus of control) is associated not only with happiness, as mentioned above, but also with many other good qualities: internals have a better sense of humor;[39] they are "more persistent, creative, logical, and coherent in task activity";[40] in problem solving, they seek relevant information and use it better than externals.[41] In general, "internals have been found to be more perceptive to and ready to learn from their surroundings. They are more inquisitive, curious, and efficient processors of information than are externals."[42]

More than externals, people who believe they can control the events in their lives resist conformity: "The internal resists being placed in positions where he is the pawn who is 'put down' so to speak, by the assumed knowledge of others [and], regardless of the style of influence (subtle or overt), externals are more compliant than internals."[43] Thus, in practice, the belief that one is the cause of one's outcomes is a bulwark against malignant obedience: Lt. William Calley (who, acting in the belief that he was following orders, shot women and children in a Vietnam village)[44] was apparently not an internal. Moreover, internals are also more helpful to others: in one experiment, "internals were more likely to help another individual than were externals despite the fact that they were penalized for doing so."[45] Self-determination is by no means selfish.

One remarkable experiment reflected the beneficial power of controlling some small portion of one's fate. In a nursing home members of an experimental group were given instructions on their responsibility for themselves while a control group was told how important it was for the staff to take good care of them. Each member of the experimental group was also given freedom to make choices and have responsibility in caring for a plant which had been the responsibility of the staff. "Questionnaire ratings and behavioral measures showed a significant improvement for the experimental group over the comparison group on alertness, active participation, and a general sense of well-being." The long-term effects were startling: Members of the experimental group not only were happier but actually lived several years longer than the control group.[46]

The triumph of belief in the causal force of one's actions over any tendency to see circumstances as dominant is, at least in the West, generally associated with feelings of well-being. But not always. Chronic self-attribution for failure (but not success) is a source of misery, especially if the attributions are both global (applying to a variety of situations) and stable (a permanent feature of the personality).[47] In short, the self-determination so admired by philosophers implies a complex theory of cognition of which they seemed to be unaware. And as the causal part of self-determination, self-attribution is by no means a four-lane highway to happiness.

Political Participation Is Not Self-Determination

Both societies and individuals benefit from the presence of widespread opportunities for exercising self-determination, but it is possible that societies will be better off if their members participate in democratic institutions when the participating individuals will not be. Two levels of analysis are required to cope with this conflict.

CONFLICT BETWEEN SOCIAL AND INDIVIDUAL BENEFITS

The prisoners' dilemma, the Arrow impossibility theory, the logic of collective action, the tragedy of the commons, and the conflict between agents and principals prepare one for recognizing a situation in which what is best for the individual is not best for the group and vice versa. But one always knew that. Anyone who has joined a queue realizes that it is often more advantageous to be an exception to a general rule than someone who abides by the rule — even though we approve of the rule and recognize that the societies and groups we belong to benefit from it.

The surprise, then, lies not in the divergence of individual and social benefits, but in the expectation of harmony between these two levels of benefits, an expectation no doubt stimulated by the metaphor of the hidden hand. To cope with their concern for self and society, people seem to need two rationalities (as Anatol Rapoport put it),[48] one whereby individuals maximize their individual welfares (and well-being) and another whereby people maximize what they consider to be the collective welfare. This is too formalistic: because every soldier and team member has faced just this kind of conflict and because self-esteem (the most sacred individual good) is dependent on social esteem, the tension is both familiar and often relieved by the very elements of the situation that created it. Identification with groups, as in patriotism, is not uncommon. Two considerations help to unite benefits to the self and benefits to the group: (1) people are made happier by being among happy people both because happiness is infectious and because happy people treat each other better. The pursuit of happiness is usually not a zero-sum game. (2) Nor is happiness a status good such that its benefits are greater when other people have less of it[49] — at least not usually, although downward comparisons sometimes help.[50]

The conflict between individual and social benefits, then, does not arise from the particular good of well-being but from the more common problem of social benefits derived from acts which do not benefit the individuals, or at least are not experienced by individuals as beneficial. This is said to be the case for political participation and self-determination. Widespread political participation may (we will see) be good for a society but costly for individuals, and collective self-determination (if that is not an oxymoron) may be the very stuff of democracy but may not be experienced as an attractive form of *self*-determination by the disparate selves involved.

SOCIETAL BENEFITS OF POLITICAL PARTICIPATION

The societal benefits of widespread political participation come, inter alia, from the reaffirmation of solidarity, implicit endorsement of the democratic process, identification of individuals with the political system, legitimation of both democratic outcomes and of the system that spawned them, encouragement to political minorities that they might win another time, and symbolic recognition of ethnic minorities. Participation and the moral code that it embodies police incumbents' uses of power to enrich or aggrandize themselves while giving guidance to leaders on the direction and force of constituency opinion. Only the last of these functions has much to do with self-determination. But, again, because it is collective opinion that gives guidance, giving that guidance may not feel like self-determination to each of the constituents in the collectivity.

But are these familiar arguments for participation valid? Finding answers to these questions would entail research projects in themselves, but I will try to offer clues (no more than that) from existing sources.

Stability of government can be best assessed cross-culturally. In the 1970s among developed countries (in a ranking including other countries as well) the proportion of adult population voting varied greatly: Italy, where there are penalties for not voting, ranked highest (fifteenth—the then-communist countries ranked higher!); other high-ranking countries were the Netherlands (twenty-first), Sweden (twenty-third) and Austria (twenty-fourth); West Germany is relatively high (thirtieth) and France is relatively low (sixtieth), while the United States is very low (seventy-third), just above Switzerland (seventy-sixth), which has the lowest rate of turnout of all advanced countries.[51] In my opinion, these examples do not suggest that high turnout is a clue to better government: two of the countries with the highest turnouts have recent histories of totalitarian government, while the two lowest are probably the oldest, most stable democracies in the world.

Wide participation in politics is also said to protect society from inequality because, at least in the United States (with its weak unions), it is the least-educated and poorest members of the population who tend to participate least. Cross-culturally, there is a hint of the validity of this inference about the turnout–inequality relation in the fact that the United States has both the greatest income inequality and the lowest turnout among advanced nations. A better, though still inadequate, test is possible using recent U.S. measures of income inequality by states and relating these data to turnout in these states. When education is controlled, there is indeed a correlation between turnout and equality, but it is not quite statistically significant (.068).[52] In my opinion, this test is not conclusive, but I think it fails to support the claim that high turnout has much causal influence on degree of inequality.

Participation in elections is said to be an inoculant against antidemocratic movements. That is, where conventional participation is high, votes from the radical Right, usually nationalistic and ethnocentric, and from the radical Left (usually communist in Europe) are fewer. People who are satisfied with their lives have higher turnouts (see below), and satisfied people are less likely to be radical Left or radical Right or radical anything. To repeat, life satisfaction drives political satisfaction rather than the other way around (see chapter 10), and in countries in which life satisfaction is high, choosing a revolutionary option for the relief of one's grievances is low.[53] On the other hand, in the United States with its low turnout, the revolutionary option is infrequently chosen, a fact that modestly damages the lower-turnout-equals-higher-radicalism thesis.

High turnout might reflect ethnic divisions and friction, but is there any evidence that high turnout by minorities increases ethnic divisiveness? After the Civil Rights Acts of 1964–65, African Americans greatly increased their turnout, but their increased participation seems to have improved race relations rather than to have made them more divisive.[54] Whatever may be said of the effect on government of generally high or low turnout, low rates by subordinate "ethnics" (more than by class) is not propitious for most democratic purposes.

Evidence on the more general question of the policy effects of lower participation is indeterminate. On economic issues, voters are more conservative than nonvoters, but on social issues (for example, affirmative action, abortion, prayer in the schools) there is little difference. On foreign policy, there is very little correspondence between congressmen's views and their constituencies' views whether or not the constituents vote.[55] More cogently, Raymond Wolfinger and Steven Rosenstone have found that policy outcomes following elections with low turnout would be no different if there had been higher turnouts,[56] and Peter Nardulli and his associates found that if all states had had the same rates of turnout, the outcomes of only two presidential elections would have been affected: Winfield Hancock instead of James Garfield (1880), Hubert Humphrey instead of Richard Nixon (1968).[57] But that small turnout effect is not so small in local elections, where authorities "are responsive to citizenry with high participation rates."[58] This greater influence over policy in local elections, however, does not lead to greater turnout in local elections; quite the reverse.

Consider two high turnout elections. When the Nazis won the election in 1933, Germany had relatively high rates of turnout.[59] Observing this, V. O. Key once referred to turnout as a kind of "fever chart" of a society. The high turnout, of course, did not cause the subsequent German disaster, but neither did it prevent a (large) minority of extremists from capturing the government.[60] And, as we shall see in the analysis of the U.S. election of 1840 below, at times high turnout may reflect a populist mood that has little to do with the issues that are relevant to the people's pain. The social benefits of widespread participation identified above are only the brighter side of the picture—the side put forward by such participationists as Benjamin Barber and Carole Pateman.[61]

INDIVIDUAL BENEFITS OF POLITICAL PARTICIPATION

If participation does not imply self-determination, why would individuals participate? Here I will change gears and offer some unpublished results of a study of the political attitudes of a small group of white, working-class, family men in an eastern industrial city in 1957. I asked them, "Think back to the last time you voted. You are standing in line; you approach the tables where they ask your street and number, and then your name. You go into a booth and pull the lever that closes the curtain. What do you think about and how do you feel when you are doing these things?" I think the mood has changed since 1957, but for these men the experience was, in retrospect, both anxious and positive. It mixes moral satisfactions with feelings of effectiveness.

Although in the previous chapter I noted the burdens of duty, here the gratifications from performing one's duty are evident: one of the participants said, "I feel as though I've been thinking, and I've done my duty." As always, the sources of this kind of gratification are complex, but at least in the case of another man who felt guilty because of his failure to serve in the war it seemed that his voting was an act of atonement: he was doing his duty to "those who died for their country." The source of another man's moral gratification was his voting without being paid to do so, something that he and others suspected was common.

There was gratification from asserting themselves in this political milieu, a form of control over their environment: "Nobody's going to tell me 'Well, you vote for this fellow'. . . . I am going in there and vote for who I want to. I feel pretty good when I come out." Exercising the right of a citizen is part of this gratification: "You have the right to do it and no one can say no"; and "I feel good because knowing that I'm a citizen and have the right to vote, I mean I feel good that I could vote"; or, from an enterprising machine tender: "Well, it makes you feel good. . . . The first time I voted I says, 'Ma, I done it.'" Another says, "You feel you've done something, taken part in something that's important." Turnout is not the puzzle that rational choice theorists struggle with: for many, voting has hedonic value in itself.

The reports from this small sample of white family men in 1957 can serve only as a partial corrective to the much larger and more recent body of evidence in chapter 11 showing the declining sense of efficacy in politics and the waning belief that politicians pay much attention to the public's wishes. In 1957 the public felt that the lot of the average man was getting better, that they themselves could influence political outcomes, and that government was responsive to their wishes. Today, only the sense of citizen duty remains.

It is hard to find anything in what the Eastport men say that refers to self-determination in the classical democratic sense: they are not anticipating any policy benefits from their participation. But perhaps their rewards follow a different theme; perhaps there is some reward in the process of voting not apparent when people review that process from a distance. One might call this ceremonial satisfaction.

The rewards for voting may not have anything to do with the inevitably remote victory of any given candidate, but rather stem from the responses to ceremonial rewards and from talking about these acts to others. As I once put the matter, people care more about "how they are treated than what they get."[62] It makes no more sense to apply a single contingent reinforcement theory to politics than to apply a single theory of rational choice. The rewards from voting may have little to do with self-determination.

COSTS TO INDIVIDUALS OF POLITICAL PARTICIPATION

Costs in time and effort versus probability of winning. The traditional way of assessing the costs or pains of participation is to compare the effort and time involved in voting with the likelihood that one's vote will make the difference between winning and losing and, in an extended comparison, the likelihood that one will actually receive the policy benefits from winning. It is no contest. As has often been noted, one is more likely to be run over on the way to the polls than to cast a winning vote. Hence the rational choice is to stay away from the polls. As revealed in the above analysis of the actual benefits in the act of voting, these rational considerations are quite off the mark.

The missing sources of well-being. Another way to approach this assessment of benefits in politics is to look, as we did in chapter 9, at the things that do make people happy. In the quality of life studies these are a sense of achievement, family felicity, financial security, enjoying one's leisure activities (of which "having fun" is the most powerful contributor to SWB), the feeling that one has a number of good friends (social support), and anything that contributes to self-esteem and belief in one's effectiveness.[63] How does political participation enlist or draw upon the pleasures of these activities? The answer box is almost empty.

Politics is not regarded as fun. Reporting on pleasurable uses of time, John Robinson and Philip Converse state, "Stimulating least enthusiasm (falling well behind 'sports,' 'relaxing,' 'one's car') were organizational memberships and following politics, pursuits which have little visibility in time-budget diaries."[64] Robinson's later evidence mentioned in chapter 10 on the satisfying uses of one's time found that of eighteen activities people enjoyed doing, "politics" was dead last (9 percent).[65] In *Homo Ludens,* Johan Huizinga deplores the twentieth-century loss of humor in politics and cites the American Log Cabin and Cider campaign of 1840 as a measure of what is lost. As it happens, in the midst of a serious depression, humor won. Turnout increased by 54 percent "in one of the most inane campaigns ever waged for the presidency."[66] Even if it increases turnout, electoral fun can be very costly.

The citizen's role is not a happy one. In the extended interviews mentioned above, I also asked the group of working-class men what it meant to be a good citizen and a good patriot. Being a good patriot was easy: one had only to be loyal and ready to fight for one's country. Being a good citizen, however, was difficult, partly because it had such ambiguous and extensive boundaries; good citizenship involved being a good parent and spouse, financially responsible, a good community member, a taxpayer, loyal to one's country, and, of course, a voter in elections. All Eastport men knew they were good patriots, but few thought they were "especially good" citizens. The citizen role is fraught with ill-defined moral demands, guilt, anxiety, and uncertainty.[67] Role ambiguity is a known source of unhappiness;[68] there is strain in the ambiguous citizen role.

In the interviews, these blue-collar workers variously said, "I hope I'm voting for the right man"; "I hope that I did it right"; "I feel sorry for the people I promised that I'd do one thing and didn't do it for them." A large, anxious former football player worried about his feelings of inadequacy and said he felt like a "midget among giants." He said he walked away confused and feeling that he is "just mechanically performing an act." Most of the men worried about what was demanded of them and then were gratified by the feeling of doing their citizen duty.

The high level of cognitive and moral demands (chapter 12) democracy makes on its citizens[69] contrasts sharply with the simplistic responses to these demands, not least in Converse's theory of the "non-attitudes" prevalent in political thinking.[70] One way to interpret this discrepancy is to think of it as cognitive overload with its attendant strain. If it is experienced that way one can easily see why, following well-tested theories, the strained person drops below his or her best level of thinking and reduces the complexity to manageable—and simplistic—responses.[71] Another way is to follow Mihalyi Csickszentmihalyi's research matching level of challenge with level of response capability; he finds that, in contrast to the ideal pattern of high challenge and high capability, a level of challenge higher than the level of skill creates anxiety.[72] People have ways to protect themselves from such anxiety, but we saw in the Eastport reports that people *were* made anxious by the demands of participation, and in chapter 10 we saw that about 75 percent of the public agreed with the statement, "Sometimes politics and government seem so complicated that a person like me can't really understand what's going on."

Self-determination does not meet the requirements of collective determination, for example, democracy. Oddly, the desire to control one's individual destiny frustrates collective efforts to control group destinies. Because, as Tocqueville said, Americans "are apt to imagine that their whole destiny is in their own hands," they are not disposed to join unions or political parties or engage with others in collective group-determination.[73] But, in spite of Madison, democracy requires political parties and group effort. In less individualistic Europe, unions and parties are stronger than in the United States—and, partly for that reason, turnout is higher and political malaise is less visible.

Thus, because of their rejection of collective means, self-determining individualists may forego actual control over their fates and the pleasure associated with it. In children's games in which winning depended on cooperation rather than competition, U.S. children were less successful than Mexican children because they were less cooperative.[74] The idea of self-determination may have served Western capitalism well, but Asian capitalism has thrived (at least until the summer of 1997) on norms of group-determination[75]—and may do so again. The irony of self-determination interpreted as isolated, individual action is the perverse frustration of actual self-determination in a society in which fates are intertwined.

Civic participation has rewards not present in political participation. The reason for the dislike of political participation is not a reluctance to participate in collective enterprises so much as the dislike of politics: participation in other kinds of acts of benefit to communities is, in the 1990s, widespread and growing and is "associated with fewer [than average] feelings of upset, loneliness, boredom, depression."[76] Comparing the accounts of voluntary community activities with political participation, it appears that this political aversion is colored by the absence of a feeling of making a difference. Fatalism, or a belief that one does not control one's life, is important, for, with fatalism controlled, the usual relationship between number of memberships in voluntary organizations and lack of psychological distress disappears.[77] Again, the belief that one is effective turns out to be the crucial mediating factor in the association between well-being and participation in all kinds of voluntary work. Except for what happens in the interstices of political life (see above), democratic processes do not encourage feelings of effectiveness.

As before, one must bear in mind that it is the microworlds of experience, not the larger political world, that most influence people's beliefs that they are effective. Thus, people are made happy by the belief that they control their immediate environment (mostly family, community, and work), but when asked, "How do you feel about your opportunities to change things around here that you don't like," satisfaction plummets — although the influence of this concern over measures of life satisfaction registered near the bottom of the list.[78]

CONTINGENT REINFORCEMENT IN POLITICS

The basic assumption of economics and learning theory alike is that people repeat acts they find rewarding and do not repeat acts that are not rewarding (the drive extinguishes). Of course, the rewards are not limited to the extrinsic rewards that these two theories postulate, for self-rewards, for example, a good conscience and feelings of inclusion, are important stimuli to participation. But are the rewards sufficient? Do people gain a feeling of effectiveness from political participation?

To experience self-determination, people must believe there is a coupling of actions and outcomes, or "contingent responses."[79] Over a lifetime people build up confidence that they can influence the outcomes from which they benefit or suffer if, in fact, they have been rewarded with favorable outcomes for effort. If they have not had favorable experiences, they may develop a pattern of learned helplessness[80] and give up self-determination as a goal.

Failed Reinforcement in Political Participation

"Man's primary motivational propensity is to be effective in producing changes in his environment," writes Richard DeCharms.[81] The condition for satisfying that propensity, that is, learning personal control, and, alternatively, for learned helplessness may be explicated in a simple fourfold table presenting the four possible relationships between action and response, in this case the act of voting. People learn that they are effective if cell (I) is more or less consistently *Yes,* cell (IV) is more or less consistently *No,* and the cross-diagonal cells (II) and (III) are consistently neither *Yes* nor *No*. Thus, the environment is seen to respond to one's acts when cells (I) and (IV) are consistent opposites. In that case, people experience the rare moments when their acts are a necessary and sufficient condition for something desired to happen. If they vote for their preferred candidate, their candidate wins; if they do not vote for that candidate,

Table 13.1. Individual Acts and Environmental Responses

		Environmental Response: Candidate Wins or Loses	
		Candidate Wins	Candidate Loses
Individual Act	Vote	(I) Yes	(II) Yes / No
	Not Vote	(III) Yes / No	(IV) No

he or she loses. Under these circumstances people learn that control is vested in themselves. If, on the other hand, when people act and there is no relation between their acts and environmental responses, they learn that they are ineffective; if generalized they develop learned helplessness.[82] Because, as rational choice tells us so often, the individual's vote will almost never decide a political contest and the history of his or her voting will (really) never show the pattern giving the pleasure of being a cause shown in table 13.1. Insofar as winning elections is the test of effectiveness, electoral participation does not offer contingent reinforcement and does not give that kind of pleasure.

Generalization and Trends

Is the industrial discipline (as contrasted to the market experience) a further source of learned helplessness, of being controlled by others but not by one's will?

INDUSTRIAL SELF-GOVERNMENT AND POLITICAL SELF-DETERMINATION

One test, but not a very good one, would be the effect of self-determination in industrial experiments. Quite contrary to the beliefs of G. D. H. Cole, Carole Pateman, and others who held that experience of self-government at work would create more efficacious citizens, worker self-management has had little effect on general attitudes. In one study of worker self-management there was apparently some generalization of attitude,[83] but in an even more participatory industrial setting in Norway what was learned was a generalizable skill but not a change in sense of efficacy or personal control.[84] Controlling one's job, discretion without close supervision, however, does seem to make for a desire for self-direction, at least in the workplace.[85] Again, it is not collective self-government but individual control over one's small domain that teaches self-direction and its value.

CHANGES IN SELF-ATTRIBUTION DO NOT IMPLY CHANGES IN TURNOUT

As countries advance economically, their citizens acquire the motives and beliefs and learn the skills for self-determination, especially self-attribution,[86] although this learning is largely owing to market experiences and higher levels of education rather than to their political experiences. But as we know from our analysis of SWB, such an increase in self-attribution could tail off among the advanced countries. Apparently, it does not. At least there are reported increases in self-attribution in both Europe and, for an earlier period, in the United States.[87] But on both continents political turnout declined during this same postwar period. One is reminded again that political participation is not closely related to feelings of self-determination, neither as a cause nor as an effect.

Self-Determination as a "Noble Lie"

Plato's "noble lie" was the instruction to restless silver and especially bronze members of the city-state that their statuses were more or less determined by birth—an attribution to the circumstances of their births. The modern noble lie is quite the opposite: each of us determines our status and success by our skills and efforts—an attribution to the dispositions and skills of persons.

The noble lie is a lie because, as mentioned, all outcomes are caused by some combination of circumstances and dispositions. Studies of occupational attainment are illustrative. In one study, occupational success was best explained by a set of dispositional variables (qualities associated with going from school to first job and rate of promotion thereafter), but the sum of circumstantial variables (father's education and income, son's education) explained more of the variance.[88] It would have been false to say that the son's occupational level was self-determined. While these findings give some weight to dispositional factors, they reveal the interaction of these dispositions with prior circumstances—ignoring that interaction is what makes purely dispositional explanations a lie.[89] But, however false, the belief that one is the master of one's fate usually has the individually beneficial consequences mentioned above, hence the lie is noble.

But there are also advantages in perceiving that the noble lie is, in fact, a lie. In the 1960s educated African Americans who believed that social norms were substantially responsible for their relatively lower status were happier and more effective than African Americans who believed that each person was individually responsible for his or her status in life.[90] In such situations the noble lie loses its nobility.

Democratic Politics Is for Happy People

A "negative mood," say Daniel Batson and his associates, "is likely to discourage action by leading one to believe the action will bring no good."[91] This chimes with the findings of many studies showing the relative passivity of the unhappy and the listlessness of the depressed,[92] who do less well at school,[93] do not act on their beliefs,[94] are unable "to behave autonomously, to assert themselves,"[95] have trouble delaying gratification,[96] and crumble under stress.[97]

Happiness has opposite effects: "Good feelings seem capable of bringing out our better nature socially and our creativity in thinking and problem-solving.... They are potential sources of interpersonal cooperativeness and... improve such cognitive processes as judgment, problem-solving, decision-making, and creativity."[98] The idea that happiness leads to political quiescence (which could include conventional voting) seems not to be supported.[99] The reason is the double effect of SWB: first, it encourages the sense of control that facilitates acting on one's beliefs, while, second, it stimulates conventionality and obedience to social norms.[100] Unhappy people (and especially depressed people) do not vote for the policies that would make their little worlds happier places because their unhappiness inhibits them from participating in the democratic process. The happy are twice blessed; the unhappy are doubly deprived. Democratic politics is for happy people.

It is ironic that the self-determination and sense of personal control generally associated with well-being should not find expression in the democratic practices which they are said to justify. This irony is a partial explanation of the failure of democracies to relieve unhappiness and depression. But perhaps the association of democracy with companionship can come to our relief.

14

Companionate Democracy

To what extent are democracy and companionship incompatible? The tension between the two has three parts. First, there is the normal, some would say instinctual, human tendency to focus affective energies on people rather than on principles, a kind of personalistic tropism. This gives companionship an edge where it conflicts with democratic principles.

Second, although democracy thrives on family stability and reciprocal support among friends, there is little in modern democratic theory or practice to acknowledge this dependence. Aristotle claimed that states "are created by friendship, for friendship is the motive of society,"[1] and there is something to it: democracy (which was not Aristotle's preference) needs affectionate relations not usually acknowledged, even by American pluralists and German romantics.

Third, there is a deep and often irreconcilable tension between the universalistic principles of democracy and the particularistic principles of companionship. The state is no longer what Aristotle claimed it was, "the union of families and villages" (nor was it simply that in the Greek gemeinschaft). A democratic state is also a body of principles that are not comfortable with familistic assumptions: the rule of law, enforceable contracts, security of property, inalienable rights, and control of rulers by their subjects or citizens. How can we resolve this tension between democracy's need for close friendship and family integrity, on the one hand, and its reliance on principles that inhibit, even exclude, familistic and friendship principles, on the other? That democracy depends upon but cannot itself employ these qualities of intimacy and friendship is the irony I shall examine.

Companionship is above all affective, whereas democracy requires at least some cognitive constraint. Companionship relies on the familiar and the similar; democracy must include strangers and the unfamiliar and dissimilar. Companions enlist anthropomorphic preferences, whereas democracy, while composed of people and often personalized, must rely on impersonal law. Companionship is a matter of bonding with specific, known others, whereas democracy enlists symbolic identifications and distant institutions. These antipathies are fundamental and mark the problems of a companionate democracy.

Democracies Need Family Solidarity and Companionship—But Not Too Much of Them

Democracies need voluntary groups for two functions: first, to aggregate interests, represent the concerns of individual members of the public to political bodies, and, in reverse, to interpret governments to their members. These groups are bound together by ties of interest. The second function is to bind people together with ties of affection, thus preventing anomie among isolated, unconnected individuals. The first function is thoroughly familiar to political specialists and most members of the public. It was the theme of the earlier pluralist school of politics, Pendleton Herring, E. E. Schattschneider, David Truman, William Kornhauser,[2] and others.The second theme, protection against anomie, is the one I wish to develop here.

With some overlap, especially in local politics, the two kinds of groups are quite different. Interest groups include unions, chambers of commerce, professional associations, and organizations of special interests: steel, groceries, sports, organized religion, education, and ethnic groups like the NAACP. Affectionate groups include families, neighborhood groups, individual churches, fraternal lodges, and so forth. Because they are small enough to permit face-to-face relations, affectionate groups offer companionship along with their more official business. Interest groups represent Weber's "associative" principle whereby people are bound together by "rationally motivated adjustment or interest or a similarly motivated agreement." The face-to-face groups are, to a greater extent, "communal . . . based on subjective feeling of parties that they belong to each other."[3] Affectionate groups (especially families) are rarely overtly political even though they influence political systems. Neighborhood groups once served these cohesive functions, but the dramatic and continuous postwar decline in neighboring (see chapter 6) may be one further factor accounting for lower participation in American local elections. Affectionate groups perform functions outside the range of things recognized by the political pluralists, but their functions are equally important to democracy.

Democracies, like markets, require fairly high levels of interpersonal trust to permit political rivals to alternate their command of governmental power. Measures of trust of this interpersonal kind are related to the reconciliation of differences in Congress[4] as well as in commerce. (It is ominous, therefore, that interpersonal trust has declined so dramatically in the United States over the past quarter century.) Also, bonds of family and friendship are inoculants against the kinds of alienation and anomie that curdle democratic politics. For example, one question in a measure of anomie deals with the undependability of friends, and another asks people to agree or disagree with the statement, "What is lacking in the world today is the old kind of friendship that lasted a lifetime." Both measures are strongly related to ethnocentrism and political hostility.[5]

When one distinguishes, as David Easton does, among support for a particular administration, for the regime (democracy, monarchy, dictatorship), and for the political community (the nation and its people),[6] one sees that the last of these is particularly vulnerable to the breakdown of social relations. Social support for each other is already a kind of "diffuse support" of national community, making tolerable the sacrifices required by all political systems and giving a certain leeway for a functioning, if often bumbling, democracy.[7] A society of detached and therefore often anomic people is sterile ground for democracy and fertile ground for its enemies.

More specifically, isolated and friendless individuals are less likely to participate in the elections which form such a central feature of democracy (see chapter 13). Indeed, the influence of friends and neighbors has been found to be more important than the political agenda in prompting voting and other forms of participation.[8] There is also a somewhat less obvious principle at work: compared to individuals, groups are more efficient transmitters of such national norms as citizen duty. As one study found, "The American turnout decline is [partially caused by] a weakening of social ties adversely affecting the socialization and enforcement of norms responsible for generating civic participation."[9]

Tenuously integrated individuals are not good material even for protest groups, for such individuals are anomic, protesting, if at all, in ad hoc fashion, rarely effective and perhaps even burning their own neighborhoods in a self-immolating moment of anger.[10] Furthermore, the person whose reference is mainly to his or her own self is subject only to the appeals of what W. G.

Runciman called "egoistic deprivation," not to the truly mobilizing force of "fraternal deprivation" which arouses people in the defense of their kindred sufferers.[11] (The appeal of the similar — see below.)

In caricaturistic form one might say that interest groups mobilize people while affectionate groups integrate them. Interest groups collectivize grievances and channel and give purpose to the emotions aroused by discontent following from failed group solidarity. Although it is surprising that the protestors are not recruited from among the unhappy, that surprise is reduced when one sees that anger and unhappiness are not only different emotions but are negatively related to each other.[12] Affectionate groups tend to reduce anomic anger, socializing people so that they can join interest groups while not themselves expressing any political views. They are prepolitical, but no less important to democracy for that.

PRIORITY OF AFFECTIONATE RELATIONS

Edward Wilson wrote, "In many groups of organisms, from the social insects to the primates, the most advanced societies evolved directly from family units."[13] Such kinship attachments are almost as important among humans as Wilson, Richard Wrangham, Frans de Waal, and many others have found them to be among other primates, a set of findings that accounts in substantial part for my basic premise that it is above all our relations with people that determine our feelings of well-being. Where attachments are close and person-related, participation in decisions affecting a group is highest and then becomes less so with socioeconomic development, returning to extended but relatively impersonal forms of participation only with the advent of democracy. (Democracy now does the work of governing performed by close, intimate groups in primitive societies.)[14] But even now in the Asian collectivist societies, and in simpler rural politics and in big city machine politics in the West, politics becomes again reliant on connections among family and friends. Localism in politics reflects this preference for the interpersonal. In spite of poorer levels of performance and less professional civil servants, leaders of local governments receive higher confidence ratings than do the leaders of the national government.[15]

Anthropomorphism

The dominance and priority of companions over principles and practices of democracy flows also from the preference people have for humans and humanlike objects compared to institutions, principles, print, and other inanimate objects. We respond more positively to persons than to other objects,[16] especially but not exclusively to persons we know: "Our emotions tend to seek a human object rather than an abstraction."[17] Perceptions of war share this priority of persons (for example, Wellington, Napoleon, Douglas MacArthur), and so do politics: "The assassination [of President John Kennedy] generally evoked feelings similar to those felt at the death of a close friend or relative; rarely was it compared to other times of national crisis."[18] Projective measures of the need for power find that the high scorers, like teachers and social workers, seek power over people rather than, like lawyers and politicians, over events.[19] And a wide range of our most important emotions apply only to people: jealousy, rivalry, empathy, pity (with some animal exceptions), and almost all sex-related emotions. Companions benefit from anthropomorphism while democracy does not.

INCOMPATIBILITY OF DEMOCRACY AND RELIANCE ON AFFECTIONATE RELATIONS

If affectionate groups are necessary to prevent the anomic individualism that threatens democracy, and if they dominate abstract thinking, as is implied by appreciation of democratic principles, one can understand why they are often incompatible with democratic norms and practices. What follows are specifications of this incompatibility.

Affective Versus Cognitive Processes

Robert Zajonc has found that humans have two partially independent judgmental systems, the affective system, which renders its judgment first and with which we are more comfortable, and a cognitive system, which weighs the evidence and consequences and is, in the end, probably more reliable.[20] Even more than other assessments, judgments of companions are inevitably assessed first and foremost by the affective system; after all, it is the liking of the person that is usually most important. Consequential weighing of costs and benefits is more appropriate to politics. Does an affective environment encourage more reliance on these initial affective judgments? Crucially, is there an affective/cognitive tradeoff such that friendliness of milieu undermines the cognitive factor in that tradeoff? Consider three possible outcomes, of which the first is conflict and pain. According to the classical sociologists Simmel and Tönnies, rationality and feelings of friendship are antithetical to each other, at least when simultaneously experienced. As a general account of mental processes, this antithesis is probably not accurate, but it is accurate to say that when our feelings and our cognitions are at variance, we experience the pain of cognitive dissonance.[21]

The second possible outcome is the use of affection to bolster individual decision making. Thus, the sure knowledge of inclusion (as in most families) licenses greater independence of thought. Along these lines, it has been found that the presence of one reliable confederate lets a person stand firm against the world.[22]

And the third is the triumph of group affection over independent thinking. Even though conformists tend to be happier than independent thinkers,[23] conformity has a bad name, and probably conformity is greater among friends—because the costs of defection are higher. Too much affection leads to group pressures for agreement—and "groupthink" does not make good decisions.[24] Along these lines, a marketing study found that conformity increases with group cohesiveness,[25] that is, affectionate relations probably make for less independent thinkers and voters. Studies of collectivist Asian societies report that "if necessary, individuals are expected to subordinate their personal feelings and wishes to the goals of their in-group."[26] The political expression of this tendency is not favorable to democracy.

The political machine offered political bonding, but at the cost of an ethical pollution one might find excessive.[27] A marginal fraction of Americans once joined the communist party because it was a source of dedicated companionship rather than because of its ideology[28]—but to suggest that political parties become the private therapy of the lonely is not a happy thought—nor good for politics. It has been suggested that politics has its moments of fraternal joy in Woodstock-like expressions like the various marches on Washington in the 1960s and the African-American march led by Louis Farrakhan in 1995. But one cannot make the governing of a country a series of peak experiences. Do you hear the magical beat of marching men with armbands proclaiming, "Strength through joy"?

DEMOCRACY AND IMPERSONALITY

The American Constitution guarantees to everyone, not just friends of friends, "the equal protection of the laws." Although people are admitted to citizenship in the United States because they are brothers, children, or spouses of current citizens, after admission their family relations are officially irrelevant—or almost irrelevant, for ethnic politics, more than class politics, makes a kind of kinship relevant once again. Consider the opposite of this politics of familiarity. Graham Wallas lays out the mental set of a member of (a somewhat idealized) parliament:

> Now the first virtue required in government is the habit of realizing that things whose existence we infer from our reading are as important as the things observed by our senses, of looking, for instance, through a list of candidates for an appointment and weighing the qualifications of the man

> whom one has never met by the same standards as those of the man whom one has met, and liked or pitied, the day before; or of deciding on an improvement with complete impartiality as between the district one knows of on the map and the district one sees every morning.[29]

Wallas is not asking citizens to adopt this kind of indifference to friends and neighborhoods, but rather to accept that their representatives must follow these codes if they are to serve democratic ideals, hard as it may be when that citizen is himself the "man whom [the representative] has met and liked . . . the day before." Unfortunately, the priority of persons outlined in the first section of this chapter works against that acceptance.

Do democratic governments borrow impersonality from their enveloping market environments and their own economic functions? Money is impersonal, of course; that is one of its advantages. But it is not easy to see why governments must foster impersonality because, perforce, they have budgets, hire people for wages, let contracts, tax and spend, and, in campaigns, raise money for election expenses. If dealing with money reduced companionship, one would expect brokers, bankers, and merchants to be less companionable than professors, soldiers, and artists. I do not think that is the case.

Three points are relevant. The unpleasant relations between politics and money are better if the money relation is impersonal. If the donor of funds claims friendship because of his donation, corruption is inevitable. The same is true of taxing policy, the letting of contracts, and appointment of officials and judges. Second, bureaucracy is intended to be impersonal so that policy and enforcement are not person-dependent; we are better off when people are more or less interchangeable in bureaucratic slots. And third, it is size and not money that makes democracy cold and incompatible with close companionship: Put another way, democracy permits large numbers to be governed by introducing a kind of accountability which in smaller communities is handled by face-to-face relations: "Let me put a word in your ear, Mayor [or more likely, 'Joe']." The history of participation across levels of socioeconomic development seems to bear this out: the smaller the society, the larger the proportion of the population participating in collective decisions.[30]

FRIENDSHIP AND JUSTICE

Contrasting companionship in politics and law. In contrast to the opprobrium associated with nepotism in government,[31] it is expected that one will try to get one's nephew to vote for one's favored candidate, certainly in the case in which the candidate is oneself. What is the difference? In the first place, there is a difference in the kind of exchange implied: generalized exchange (electoral support for policy returns) is accepted but without an explicit quid pro quo. People are expected to vote for the candidate who will foster policies beneficial to themselves, or at least to that set of people with whom they identify—working-class people, Polish Americans, farmers. Democracy embraces that kind of exchange without qualms. Why, then, in return for the nephew's vote, should winners not reward their nephews? The answer seems to be threefold. First, diffuse power such as is present in elections may be bartered, but concentrated power, such as that exercised by a government official, should not be. This is a sensible position and is reinforced by a second consideration, efficiency: nephews in government, as in business, are not selected for their competence; better to choose according to a merit system. But there is a third, moral consideration: in democracy everyone is supposed to be treated equally, a consideration that rules out benefits based on family connections.

The moral matter at issue is broader than that, enlisting the most general questions of the meaning of justice: justice whereby everyone is treated equally irrespective of the claims of particular persons (Kohlberg)[32] versus justice embracing caring for particular individuals involved (Gilligan et al.).[33] The first is favored by professionals and the better educated generally, and the second, often, by the working class, whose ties to kin are usually stronger than their appreciation of abstractions.[34] Whether favoring friends and family in politics is acceptable, then, depends on the kind of justice one prefers—and where one lives: in the individualistic West or the collectivist East.[35]

As noted in chapter 6, the collectivist or interdependent cultures of Asia (and village and rural politics everywhere) follow the principle of *giri,* meaning moral reciprocation among family and friends. Obligations to friends, not references to issues or what candidates stand for, is the governing principle of their relatively new, often corrupt, but not unsuccessful democracies.[36] By Western standards, the claims of friendship are in conflict with the universal obligation to treat every human being as equal in worth and equal before the law.

John Stuart Mill, the author of many of our concepts of liberty and equal consideration of persons, concedes that people will be censured if they do not give special consideration to their families, but he believes that this special consideration applies only to private matters.[37] There lies a second point: the major problem for the Western advocates of fraternity is to preserve the distinction between public and private. This is especially important in Western societies because the norms of family justice and of public justice are different.[38] Although people do categorize and compartmentalize their thoughts and feelings, these thoughts tend not to follow the division of public and private. A common culture informs both, one that permits people to borrow concepts from the public domain for use in the private domain and vice versa.[39]

Indeed, one can argue that the public's relations with their leaders are largely reflections of their ideas of human relations more generally.[40] That is why interpersonal trust predicts democratic stability.

Inclusiveness and Heterogeneity

Democracy and the rule of law do not require equal treatment of all but rather equality of treatment within categories defined by criteria that are acceptable to universalistic principles, for example, age only when youth and seniority are functionally differentiated and sex only when related to biological functions; but never ethnicity or religion or race. Ethnicity and race are legitimate bases of political coalitions, but when they become legal categories, as in affirmative action, the public becomes restless.

Upon entering "the empire of law," however, ethnicity and race do not disappear as cognitive and affective categories but rather emerge in coded forms: in ethnically heterogeneous societies (and not just the United States) there is a tendency to scrimp on welfare because the welfare recipients are identified as ethnically different.[41] Compared to relatively homogeneous Michigan (outside of Detroit), multicultural Texas is more particularistic in its allocation of scholarships and rehabilitation programs, modifying the universalistic requirements of democratic principles.[42] The universalism of democratic justice is overridden by the cognitive and affective claims of particularistic (familistic) ethnic groups. Democracy and companionship, with its ethnic extensions, are once again at odds.

Empathy follows the categories of companionship through its affinity for the similar, sometimes defined by ideological and political as well as ethnic characteristics. At the extreme, people who are different may be defined not only as not like us but not even within the bounds of ordinary human treatment. The "good Germans" who went along with Nazi brutality to Jews salved their consciences by defining Jews out of the human community[43] — as the supporters of slavery did with African Americans in the United States. And school bond referenda tend to be more frequently defeated in heterogeneous communities; having a child in school is not a consideration[44] but having *our kind* of children in school is. Again, deprivation mobilizes when it is fraternal deprivation.

The familistic tropisms of companionship oppose in other ways the universalistic principle of democracy that invites individuality in heterogeneous settings. People tend to lose their individuality in heterogeneous groups: "Two experiments showed that when subjects believed a group to be heterogeneous, they based their liking for a particular group member on their liking for the group as a whole, independently of and in addition to the target's behavior, regardless of the target's typicality."[45] As "cognitive misers" people use the most easily available cues for assessing an individual, and heterogeneity encourages people to use stereotypes. Further, among strangers there is a tendency to combine so-called marked or less familiar characteristics (such as race) and marked or less conventional behavior (such as crime) so that racial minorities are stereotyped as, in this case, criminal or at least as deviant. This is not affective prejudice in the usual sense but rather cognitive economy. And it violates the norms of democracy.

The love of the familiar and similar comes into conflict with democratic principles on the issues of universal inclusion, equality of consideration, and, at the very least, equality before the law. It is "self-evident—that all men are created equal." Yes, but in preferring others like ourselves, especially kin, we bias our treatment of these equally created creatures, and we do not cease to want to do so—and in actually doing so—when we have a little power.

RELATION OF FRATERNITY TO LIBERTY AND EQUALITY

Setting aside the fact that for the Revolutionary French, *fraternité* meant solidarity with other revolutionary regimes,[46] one thinks of companionship in politics as part of the last item in the famous trinity Liberty, Equality, Fraternity. As we shall see in the next chapter, each of these three has an uncertain relation to SWB, but here one asks, Is it possible that liberty is antithetical to fraternity? Berlin thought that fraternity was not easily assimilated to concepts of liberty but was essentially "another good," more related, he said, to solidarity than to either positive or negative liberty.[47] But others find fraternity is the consequence of liberty and equality; indeed, fraternity is "an *end* in the relations of men; liberty and equality were only means."[48] In my opinion, however, liberty is no more a means to companionship than it is to anomie; at least the kinds of liberty recommended by libertarians do not recognize companionship as a good. In fact, the whole purpose of liberty is to permit people to define for themselves what ends to choose: say, among companionship, piety, and income.

Perhaps the answer to this riddle of the compatibility of liberty and companionship lies with the communitarian philosophy so popular in the 1990s. Alas, they unite by fiat what Berlin kept separate, defining communities as places in which the conflict between individuality and choice, on the one hand, and solidarity and affection, on the other, is minimized. That is to beg the question. Empirically, at least in the American South, the good ol' boys who value companionship do not value freedom[49] —although it is the companionship, not attitudes toward freedom, that drives this negative relation.

I must conclude that Berlin is nearer right: fraternity and community, the latter meaning a place marked by warm, intimate relations, are goods separate from the good of liberty and often incompatible with freedom of speech and heterodoxy of most kinds.

FAMILISTIC POLITICS VERSUS DEMOCRATIC POLITICS

Familistic principles in politics may be analyzed on two levels: as they apply to leaders and as they apply to citizens. Leaders first. In monarchies and aristocracies, leaders inherit their positions on the basis of family connections—ascription. In contrast, leaders in democracies achieve their positions by winning the support of an electorate (what Weber called the rational basis of authority). The grounds for legitimacy have moved from principles based on family and friendship (the cronyism of court politics makes Andrew Jackson look meritocratic) to principles that repudiate these particularistic grounds.

When a country retains familistic principles in politics, it may be said to return to the earlier, feudal ways of doing things. Reporting on rural and village politics in Japan, Nicholas Kristoff says, "Japanese politicians often inherit their seats in Parliament from their fathers or grandfathers, forming a modern aristocracy like the feudal lords of 150 years ago," a practice, he said, that is "becoming increasingly common." The feudal overtones appear salient when "commoners pay fealty in the form of votes—their own and those of people connected to them with bonds of *giri*."[50] But in Japanese cities, giri and inherited positions are less common; urbanization and its attendant modernization move societies closer to the Enlightenment concept of democracy and away from the classical ideal of a Republic. Urbanism erodes the ties of friends and family in politics.

Although not in the least feudal, something similar has occurred among voters in the individualistic West: families are no longer the kinds of political units they once were. The relatively high level of participation in the 1860–96 period is said to have been due to the "intense partisanship" created by family socialization in the predominantly rural and village nation.[51] Some fifty years later in the 1940s, family political unity still prevailed: at that time, 96 percent of married couples voted as a unit, and in the few cases in which the family was divided it was "cross-pressured" and had a tendency to show less interest in politics and to delay decisions about how to vote.[52] All that seems to have been changed in the recent period, as is witnessed by the so-called gender gap in politics. Children are similarly emancipated: when an adolescent's friends differ politically from his or her parents, the friends are more influential.[53] With some exceptions,[54] the overall picture is of atomistic urban politics rather than familistic politics of the village and rural world. The Montagues and the Capulets would no longer understand a political world in which, as in postwar

United States, almost three-quarters of the parents would not oppose their son's or daughter's marriage to a member of the opposite party. They would understand their native Italy better, where fewer than 15 percent were so politically lenient.[55]

The modern family has probably been greatly weakened by the separation of work and family life,[56] although that separation may have helped the economy by making individual workers more substitutable for each other. To a much lesser extent, the separation of family life from politics may have had a similar unfortunate effect on family coherence, but its effect on politics is more difficult to evaluate. On the one hand, political division within families may now, as in the 1940s, weaken political interest and lessen participation. On the other hand, separate decisions by each family member come closer to the democratic ideal of autonomous, discrete individuals making up their own minds on political matters. But what looked like family cohesion fifty years ago was the product of wives following their husbands' leads; if family cohesion were to depend on the subordination of women to their husbands, the principled democratic model of individual (atomistic) decisions would look more attractive and the model of family cohesion built on subordination would look less attractive. As for the independence of children, the repeal of what was once called the Mendelian law of politics is no loss.

The incompatibility of familistic values and the principles of democratic politics now seems reinforced. The family is, indeed, central to happiness, but so is the ability to control one's affairs. What democracy may have done is to create in one more setting the age-old conflict between these two sources of well-being: companionship and individual personal control (see chapter 13).

Social Capital and Political Capital

Consider the paradigmatic case of the uncivic society, one with minimal trust and meager memberships in voluntary associations, southern Italy.[57] One would not have said of that society that it was devoid of friendships or of the solidary family.[58] So much for solidarity without civics. In reverse, consider the fact that in the 1950s the United States, exemplifying the "civic culture," had the highest level of interpersonal trust and the most memberships in voluntary associations of any of the five countries Gabriel Almond and Sidney Verba studied.[59] But even then it also had the highest divorce rate of any Western society (much increased since then, of course) and, as Daniel Levinson said about the subjects of his study of the lives of American men, "In our interviews, friendship was largely noticeable by its absence."[60] A little earlier, Gorer noticed the strained relations between American male friends, something he attributed to their rivalry and their "panic" over homosexuality.[61] Was the United States then a case of civics without solidarity and only minimal companionship?

The point is that friendship and solidary families are social capital which underpin democracy, but they are not necessarily political capital. They are necessary for democracy but not part of democracy and not even implied by democratic processes. Could it be the case that a companionate democracy is an oxymoron?

Democracy Has Other Business to Do

Companionship may be the greatest boon to people's SWB, but that does not mean it should be the criterion for judging every institution, for example, the courts. Like the law, politics has other business. Following Edward Coke and William Blackstone, American constitutionalists often give priority to the rule of law. Madison said that governments must serve safety as well as happiness. Paine mournfully claimed that governments were necessary to regulate our vices. Jefferson would have agreed with Berlin: liberty is the first obligation of government, and, following market principles, many modern democratic theorists would say that provision of choice in how to conduct one's life is the first benefit of democratic government.[62] On the other hand, John Rawls, giving liberty a lexicographic priority, made justice the first virtue of government. Both Mill and Durkheim (and now Amartya Sen) have argued that the state's first business is to educate its citizens, a purpose which is essentially Aristotelian. The preeminent value of democracy, say others, is that it provides a consensual method of reconciling conflicts. Ideas about the public interest and "general will" refer to policies on everything but companionship. A normatively anemic group of American political scientists has argued that the main function of democracy is to provide a peaceful means of distributing the goods of society: *Politics: Who Gets What, When, How,* the implicit slogan of the earlier pluralists. It would be an uncertainly rewarding hedonic exchange to give up safety, freedom, peaceful reconciliation of conflicts, justice, and even a distribution system alternative to the market for closer relations with family and friends.

There are dangers to democracy in the thesis that the source of well-being derives only or mainly from companionship. Suppose that the companionate democracy has come to pass, and everyone is, *for that reason,* contented. One should then have to incite discontent because of defects in more or less objective circumstances that people deplore: persons happily integrated in a squalid slum, ill with a curable disease in the bosom of a loving family, popular in a school where students learn nothing—such persons are not to be abandoned because a utilitarian philosophy enriched by an understanding of the importance of companionship has ignored their other needs. As I said, democracy has other business to do.

15

Political Theory of Well-Being

"All our institutions," said Baron d'Holbach, "have nothing more for their object than to procure that happiness toward which our peculiar nature has made us [strive]."[1] If that were true, at what cost in other goods would governments concentrate on the happiness of their people? Utilitarians would say that there are no other goods, but, as mentioned in chapter 1, I think there are three competing ultimate goods: well-being, human development, and justice, no one of which is sufficient for a theory of democracy. Because every theory must have some criteria by which to judge the institutions it explicates, I offer these three as my candidates. As we shall see, they make a difference in the configuration of a political theory of well-being.

The Trinity of the Good

Start with an overarching good that implies the others, the "dignity" or ultimate worth of the human person.[2] But what is it about the human person that is so valuable? Following precedent, one would certainly say that capacity for thinking is essential, and so is some proper range of feeling that might be called emotional maturity. The person must also be able to carry thoughts and feelings into action; the older word for this quality was *conation* but let us call it will. Applied to moral questions, thinking and feeling and willing refer to virtue. But these qualities are static; I also mean the constant striving for improvement in these qualities, so the overall term for these components of dignity is human development.

The good, including these qualities of persons, must be fairly distributed: justice. Justice has an external quality—how one is treated and what one gets; and an internal quality—the will for justice, a prime element of human development. And virtue, the very disposition that recognizes and wills justice, must itself be fairly distributed. Human development and justice are inseparable but, of course, different.

Finally, following intuitionists and utilitarians, well-being (including both happiness and satisfaction with one's life) is an ultimate good. Well-being seems not to follow from the central idea of dignity, as does human development, but if one values the person one wishes him or her well, or "every happiness." Kant, from whom I borrowed the central idea of human dignity, makes happiness an instrumental good on the (correct) grounds that happy people will be more likely to follow the categorical imperative (treat everyone as an end).[3] If one acknowledges there are three primary goods, SWB, human development, and justice,[4] what happens to human development and justice and, indeed, to democracy itself if governments focus largely on SWB?

Toward a Political Theory of Well-Being

To round out the political theory of well-being, I want to revisit several points discussed briefly in earlier chapters. One might say that we already have a political theory of SWB or happiness: it is utilitarianism, however modified by contemporary philosophers.[5] But as the discussion of the limits to utilitarianism below reveals, the consequences of making happiness a single maximand are not promising. Like the economists' theory of utility, utilitarian theory suffers from a failure to operationalize its maximand, a failure that makes consequential thinking highly speculative. Bentham understood this; somewhere he complained, "Of pleasure and pain, we have no measure." My task is both to highlight a few of the political theoretical problems generated by the empirical analysis of well-being and then to treat directly the conceptual problems of SWB as the object of policy for democratic governments. But first a caution on what one can expect from government's address to SWB.

In addition to very great problems of measurement (see the Appendix), a political theory of well-being has many substantive obstacles: (1) unlike economic welfare, SWB is internal to persons, subject to temporary influences, often (but not always) inferred only from self-reports, and does not leave a public record. (2) We are dealing with matters whose main sources are the microworlds of home and workplace, not the public world of government. (3) The tendencies to respond to events with happiness or depression are partially given by genes and by personality traits that are more or less fixed at any one time. (4) The instruments available to governments are mainly law and bureaucracy—blunt instruments for so delicate a matter as mood and mental illness. Furthermore, (5) many scholars, including Mill, Jon Elster, and the psychologist Gordon Allport, believe that happiness can be approached only indirectly, en passant, as Mill said. And finally (6), happiness has an interactive effect: people are happier when their friends, family, or workmates are happier, partly because happiness is infectious and partly because happy people treat each other better. Happiness is not quite a public good like equality;[6] rather, satisfactions or utilities are interdependent. Thus, in ministering to the happiness of one, governments minister to the happiness of at least several and perhaps many.

Democracy and Well-Being

Democracy is not a good in itself but rather a device for maximizing the good, or, in this case, for optimizing the benefits of various goods and reconciling their differences.[7] My immediate concern, however, is not to justify democracy but to specify the relation between democracy and SWB.

DEMOCRACY AND SWB IN DEVELOPING AND ADVANCED SOCIETIES

In line with the general proposition that goods change their values according to their relative abundance (see chapter 1 and below), one is not surprised to learn that democracy is not related to well-being in developing countries $r = -.02$[NS].[8] but is related to it in advanced countries. In Europe: "Democratic institutions emerged earlier and persisted longer in nations with high levels of overall life satisfaction than in those characterized by relatively low levels."[9] Other evidence from advanced countries is supportive. For example, in the United States (1976): "The more positive were people's feelings about numerous life concerns, the less likely were they to desire major changes in their lives"[10] or in their societies. As I said in chapter 12, it is life satisfaction that drives political satisfaction and not the other way around.

Do we need two democratic theories of SWB, one for advanced countries and another for developing countries? It is a vexing question and one that has troubled a number of political economists.[11] Compared to (more or less) democratic India, undemocratic China has had higher growth rates, lower rates of infant mortality, longer life expectancy, and higher rates of literacy, each of which is associated with higher SWB in developed countries.[12] Inasmuch as economic development contributes a lot to SWB in developing countries but much less in advanced countries, whereas democracy contributes to SWB in advanced but not in developing countries, there seems to be a hedonic case for different priorities in societies according to their levels of development. Similarly, the reverse effect of SWB on democracy differs in the two kinds of society. The SWB/democracy relationship in the developed world is not dependent on income level, as it is in the developing countries. Indeed, in rich countries life satisfaction may take the place of per capita income in predicting democratic support. Economic development de-economizes support for democracy.[13]

EQUALITY AND SWB

An egalitarian theory of distributive justice may be clear in principle ("each person to count as one and no one as more than one") but is complicated by empirical findings. For one thing, as the principles of the economistic fallacy suggest, Americans are already much more equal in SWB than in their incomes.[14] For the same reason, there is almost no relationship between equality of income and average happiness across nations. Using the common *gini* measure of income inequality, a study mentioned in chapter 2 finds no relationship between inequality and happiness,[15] and another finds a relationship which, without controls, is marginally statistically significant ($-.48\ p < .05$) but the significance disappears when controlled for GDP per capita (.04).[16]

In my research on working-class men in Eastport, I found them horrified by the idea of social or income equality; the gain was not worth the loss, for they viewed with dismay the idea that the welfare cases in an adjoining housing project would be their equals.[17] There was more happiness in the current invidious distinctions than in income equality. Equality, it seems, is largely an ethical concept and finds almost no basis in any social theory of SWB that I have seen (but there is evidence that in the microworlds of families, where husbands and wives share decision making the spouses are happier than in families with a dominant partner).[18] General social equality does not have the pacifying effects egalitarians expect.[19] One reason is that social comparisons among equals increase invidiousness—a known detractor of SWB—whereas "downward comparisons" improve the morale of the unhappy.[20] As others have noted, this pattern suggests a skewness in which at least a few people are lower than others in the relevant respects.[21] As it turns out, across nations, a positively skewed income distribution is not related to the SWB score of the nation.[22] Fortunately, ethical theory rescues us from relying on such hedonic outcomes.

What kind of a democratic theory can at the same time give priority to the egalitarian principles so closely associated with the democratic theory of the

Left and also acknowledge that equality of income is not related to the happiness that democratic governments are pledged to facilitate? One horn of the dilemma is to divorce democracy from the idea of equality of condition; the other is to say that moral claims for equality take precedence over hedonic findings. Rightist democratic theorists will seize the first horn; Leftist theorists will seize the second.

RIGHTS AND SWB

There can be no democratic theory without provision for individual rights; it is the necessary complement to majority rule and popular sovereignty. But the idea of rights is an amorphous concept. Although Roscoe Pound wanted to limit rights to "legally enforceable claims" (which would have included the currently challenged entitlements), usage, from the Rights of Man (1789) to the Charter of the United Nation (1948),[23] includes moral claims along with legally enforceable claims: what ought to be as well as what is.[24] Is there anything in common between possessing rights and happiness?

On the surface, not much. In one cross-national study across all levels of GDP per capita a variety of rights were operationalized and found to fall in three clusters: (1) gross human rights violations (for example, disappearances, extrajudicial killings, detention without charge), (2) civil rights (for example, no searches without warrant, independent courts, innocent until proven guilty), and (3) political rights (for example, freedom of the press, freedom peaceably to assemble, multiparty elections by secret ballot). An overall score computed for the three kinds of rights was then used in a massive study of the correlates of happiness and life satisfaction in fifty-five nations. Without income controls, all three kinds of rights were equally and highly correlated with both happiness and life satisfaction (more highly with life satisfaction than with happiness). But with income controlled, the protection of rights (using the combined summary score) was not significantly correlated with SWB (−.01, NS).[25]

How can this be? A roundup of points made earlier might help. One answer is that people will and do fight to the death to gain these rights, but, as with income, once achieved, they adapt to their good fortune. They take their rights for granted. Another set of answers was illustrated in chapter 13 showing that people regard the right to vote as the right to engage in a time-consuming activity from which they think they, individually, gain no benefit. A third answer is inherent in the nature of a right: it is something owed to people because of their personhood or their citizenship; in that sense, it is ascriptive, not achieved or earned, and therefore does not yield the pleasure of personal control (see chapters 12, 13). A fourth answer is an unpleasant one: if tragedies happen to other people but do not involve me, they do not affect my happiness. Thus, countries with really poor records of civil rights like Malaysia can be and are above average in their levels of SWB.[26] Finally, the right to due process for the kinds of people one hates (criminals, homosexuals, atheists, communists) arouses mixed feelings, with support for the abstract right losing ground to the concrete objects of their hatred. For example, almost all Americans support the Bill of Rights in the abstract, but not the rights of atheists to teach in schools or communists to have their books available in school libraries.[27] This is not hypocrisy but rather the inability to bring cases within the rule of abstract concepts and the triumph of the concrete over the abstract.

The indirect effects of various kinds of individual rights on SWB are thought by democratic theorists to be quite different from the direct effects measured in the above studies: by allowing people to decide, without inappropriate legal constraints, how they shall pursue happiness, by providing a legal framework for freely choosing, by protecting minorities from discrimination by majorities, rights may be said to favor a more successful pursuit of happiness by more people than would have been possible under other political systems. I think this is true, but it must be squared with the high and growing levels of unhappiness (in the United States) and of depression in most market democracies protected by extensive rights.

Rights are essential to normative concepts of democracy, but that does not mean that the failure of rights to be associated with SWB is damaging to the concept of democracy. This is because the theory of democracy rests on two pedestals: first, normative and only secondarily prudential or felicific. If it is true that rights produce no gain in SWB (which is the main finding), two lines of defense are available: the normative pedestal stands without damage while the damaged prudential pedestal can be repaired by reference to unmeasured long-term effects. A realistic democratic theory, therefore, will be only marginally damaged by the gross evidence that, after level of development is taken into account, populations with rights are not happier than those without.

Given the amount of attention to rights by political philosophers and lawyers, I would be surprised if democratic rights were in any way threatened by these findings. But, as is often the case, the hedonic outcomes of this properly venerated feature of democracy may be out of joint with the glowing claims about their benefits.

FREEDOM AND SWB

Of course, freedom *must* make people happy; why else would there have been the long and painful struggle for freedom? But the struggle for freedom of speech, assembly, and thought (including religion) is relatively new. Setting aside an earlier beginning in fifth-century B.C. Greece, John Bury says the idea of freedom as autonomy starts with Jean Bodin and Francis Bacon; Isaiah Berlin says its origins lie in the Renaissance and the Reformation; Hegel says the French Revolution was the origin of the idea that man was free to change his institutions to serve his changing purposes (but for Hegel freedom is best exemplified by the Prussian state!); most scholars emphasize the Enlightenment. And of these sources, only the Enlightenment says freedom does or will or should make people happy.

Freedom is said to be a merit good, giving it ethical priority among other goods. Can one say that freedom is also justified because of its service to well-being? Are people who have more choices, or choices over more important issues, in any sense happier or more satisfied with their lives than those with fewer such choices? As we saw in chapter 13, Berlin emphasized the distinction between negative freedom and positive freedom, whereby negative freedom is the absence of constraints and positive freedom is the presence of opportunities for implementing choices. Negative freedoms have a clearer relation to SWB. It seems evident (see chapter 13) that people resist being told what to do and are distinctly unhappier when choices to which they have become accustomed are taken away;[28] they are happier when they feel generally more free and less tied down;[29] and their satisfaction with their own independence and freedom contributes more to their sense of well-being than do any of the economic measures (such as satisfaction with one's standard of living) but less than their satisfaction with their achievements and with their beliefs in their efficacy or their satisfaction with their family life.[30]

Positive freedom is harder to assess. In an objective sense, a person who is rich and powerful has more positive freedom than others. Indeed, William Graham Sumner said, "The resources of civilization are capital; and so it follows that the capitalists are free, or, to avoid ambiguities in the word capitalists, that the rich are free."[31] We already know that being poor is a source of unhappiness, partly because of limited choices, but being rich, with all its freedoms, is not much of a source of happiness, at least not when the rich man is compared to others who are somewhat less rich.

But the more relevant positive freedoms here are those that permit one to alter one's circumstances either through markets (*free* enterprise) or through political influence in democracies. As we have seen in the discussion of markets and democracies, both of these opportunities for influencing one's fate are only uncertainly related to SWB.

Also, as indicated in the discussion of rights, cross-national studies of the contribution to SWB of various rights, including political rights, show that when income is controlled the combined measure of rights is not significantly related to SWB (−.01). Illustratively, taking the available raw measure of civil rights by country in lieu of the unavailable comparable data for political freedoms, one finds that the people of Singapore, who have a much poorer rights record than the Japanese, nevertheless enjoy higher well-being; and Chileans (in the Pinochet period), with poorer civil rights than Panamanians (1980s), also enjoy higher well-being.[32] If these findings are right, or even partially right, why should this be?

The main reason, I think, is that the philosophical concepts of positive and negative freedom omit, or at least slight, a crucial third dimension: capacities and dispositions. When people are faced with freedom from constraint and with inviting positive opportunities, they must have the cognitive and conative capacities to make use of them. And they must desire to do so; the opportunities must appear attractive and not too costly. Some evidence suggests that when people believe they have a chance "to do what one likes," they rate their lives higher on a (ladder) measure of well-being.[33] But people do not usually want to do what political freedoms permit them to do, for example, to express heterodox opinions. We have seen (see chapter 13) that the sense of controlling one's destiny is closely and strongly associated with well-being,[34] but at the same time we saw that the exercising of political freedoms does not give people a sense of controlling their destinies; in that respect this exercise is not satisfying. In any event, in the absence of the belief that one *can* control events (internality), the opportunity to choose is not only meaningless but also frightening.[35] Freedom offers choices to minds that are often already overburdened. The contribution of freedom to SWB is not to be assumed, but rather it is another matter for investigation.

The problem for democratic theory is somehow to integrate the hedonic with the normative, the mixed hedonic record of freedom in both advanced and developing countries with the clear moral superiority of situations in which people both enjoy negative and positive freedom and have the capacities and desire for making free political and other choices. The easy solution is to say that democracies must educate their publics to the point where they can make use of the freedoms offered. In fact, democratic institutions do not prepare citizens for democratic practices.[36] (Civics courses help African-American but not white students.)[37] The "wish to be free"[38] and the capacities for free choice are not inherent (as is the desire for personal control); they must be learned and reinforced, probably in the microworlds of experience, where, to the extent that they are not fixed by one's genes, one learns those skills and attitudes necessary for democratic citizenship.

The Scope and Responsibilities of Government

Benthamite utilitarianism offered a goal for policy, but in spite of Bentham's efforts its causal theories were too weak to support valid policy recommendations. What might be called trinitarian utilitarianism (well-being as one of three goods) offers better causal theories, but because the trinitarian version has no maximand it can only be a guide to judgments about policy. Here, of course, I can do no more than explore a few of the relevant issues.

MARKETS OR GOVERNMENTS?

I think the evidence is clear that governments are economically (least monetary cost per unit of product) less efficient than markets,[39] but whether they are less efficient in terms of SWB (least pain per unit of SWB) is uncertain. Even with SWB criteria, however, the long-term and the short-term effects of the two agencies are so confounded that no decision emerges from any analyses that I have seen, especially since the hedonic effects are different for developing nations (governed by the affluence effect [see chapter 4]) compared to advanced countries (where the economistic fallacy takes hold).

THE WELFARE STATE

As we saw in chapter 9, people on welfare are not happy, but no one could conclude from this that a trinitarian utilitarian policy would do away with welfare. As I write, experiments in both Britain and the United States suggest that with a little help and encouragement, many welfare clients can, indeed, join the workforce. But some proportion remains scrounging on the streets or living as dependents on their relatives with, it must be supposed, a loss in felicity. The conclusion must be that by SWB criteria welfare is, at the maximum, a second-best solution.

Cross-national data support this inference: with income controlled, there was no relation between average SWB and proportion of GNP spent on welfare. Neither was there any correlated gain in SWB where governments increased their welfare payments compared to those who did not. This surprising finding is supported by a more objective measure: longevity is not improved by a higher proportion of per capita GNP devoted to welfare.[40] Because the poorly paid are happier than welfare clients, Milton Friedman is probably right: at least in developing countries, sweatshops are better than welfare. (But in advanced countries, upgrading of both jobs and people is even better, implying more, not less, government intervention in the economy!) General prescriptions across polities on the wisdom of more or less government are ideologically, not scientifically, inspired.

The other, and far less controversial, major component of the welfare state is social security, provision for the elderly financed by insurance principles sufficient to give recipients the illusion that they are paying their own way (which, however, is not the case). The elderly are, on the whole, more satisfied with their lives than other age groups, and, partly as a consequence, the growing incidence of major clinical depression has shifted from the old to the young.

But the cross-national studies again raise questions about the relationship between social security (pensions for the elderly) and SWB. The larger the proportion of national income spent on social security, the higher the SWB of its citizens (.57 $p < .05$), but this merely reflects the familiar fact that the richer the country, the more of its income it spends on social security. When this is taken into account, the relationship is still positive (.20), but not statistically significant.[41] Social security, the government program most popular and most sensitive to electoral rewards and punishments, is only tenuously related to SWB.

Political satisfaction is, as I have said more than once, driven by life satisfaction; accordingly, it is not at all clear that life satisfaction is influenced by public policy, what the government actually does. As has been found in connection with bureaucratic encounters in the United States (see chapter 12), the most favorable experiences are often trumped by a hostile ideology.[42]

Left and Right and SWB

If utilitarianism does not imply either conservative or liberal (social democratic) values, empirical studies of well-being offer clues for framing an ideology based on the greatest SWB for the greatest number. What would that look like?

The SWB reports are often Rightist in their implications, especially the findings that economic equality does not contribute to average SWB and that higher income and rising GDP per capita are what make democracy, freedom, and various rights fruitful sources of well-being. The economism of these findings is congenial to modern conservatives, if not to traditionalists, who prefer rectitude over felicity and believe that the perfectibility of man is a chimerical goal.[44] Further, the fact that in an economically inegalitarian society SWB is relatively equally distributed will relieve the Right of some moral pressure to favor redistribution of income, pressure against which it is already well protected.

The doctrine of minimal government finds other support in research suggesting that the things that make people happy are generated in people's private lives in their families and among their friends. Hedonic research is also socially conservative in the value given to religion. One might, falsely, infer that smaller taxes and fewer monetary transfers and regulations would follow: let families, churches, and communities take care of their human casualties. And from the power of self-attribution to raise SWB, one might further infer support for a policy of laissez-faire. Social conservatives might also have their values reinforced by the discovery that homogeneous communities are happier than heterogeneous ones, even though this relationship is, by cross-national studies, somewhat tenuous.[45]

The affluence effect is conservative, but the economistic fallacy is profoundly anticonservative. Is there other evidence of what informs the conservative and liberal (social democratic) mentalities?

For one thing, in the United States at least, conservatives have a higher sense of control over their environments than do liberals,[46] and that sense of control is highly correlated with SWB.[47] Should one be surprised that, irrespective of income, conservatives are more satisfied with their lives? Valuing happiness is itself a conservative trait; at least that value is inversely related (−.23) to valuing equality.[48]

But the findings that materialist motives are associated with unhappiness are liberal, for modern, if not traditional, conservatives are devoted to the overarching value of money. Findings favoring security over level of income and on the hedonic unfruitfulness of commodities are also liberal. Supporting the implications of the economistic fallacy are the findings that in advanced societies the relief of poverty is one certain method to relieve unhappiness, the one use of money and the one argument for economic growth in advanced countries that makes hedonic sense. The oddity in this situation is that market economics itself might have embraced these policies on the grounds of declining marginal utility of income.[49] Economists' escape through Pareto optimality, however, is invalidated by the common use of social comparisons.[50] Finally, the failure of hedonic (and other) research to show the value of extending the range of individual choices seems to undermine those conservative arguments (for example, Friedman's) that the extension of free choice in the voluntary exchanges of markets promotes utility (happiness?). The current level of unhappiness and evidence of rising depression suggest that in the U.S. market environment families and communities need help of kinds not available through markets.

If liberals focus on economic equality and conservatives on the value of choice, who speaks for fraternity, which, as I have said quite often enough, is a principal source of happiness? For that matter, given that utilitarians are caught up in the illusions of the economistic fallacy, who speaks for happiness? In the end, one has to wonder whether either liberal or conservative spokesmen care much about happiness, preferring instead to engage in moral argument.[51]

PATERNALISM AND SWB

Kant said that paternalism is "the greatest despotism imaginable," for, commented Berlin, it treats people as if they were not autonomous, but rather human material to be shaped by another.[52] On the other side of the globe, a specialist in Hindu culture reports, "What one finds in the reasoning of our Hindu informants is a preference for paternalism and asymmetrical interdependency, the idea that most people need to be protected against their own vulnerabilities, and a rejection of the idea of autonomous functioning and self-sufficient voluntarism."[53] In the light of these two views, consider the paternalism of the chicken farmer:

> It turns out that chickens allowed to choose their own diet vary widely in their ability to choose what is good for them. The good choosers become stronger, larger, more dominant than the poor choosers, which means that they get the best of everything. If then the diet chosen by the good choosers is forced upon the poor choosers, it is found that *they* now get stronger, bigger, healthier, and more dominant, although never reaching the level of the good choosers. That is, good choosers can choose better than bad choosers what is better for the bad choosers themselves.[54]

If he can, the poultry farmer, without scrupling about chicken autonomy or preference functions (but possibly with some reference to "their own good"), will limit the available choice of food to that which breeds stronger chickens. The study in a retirement home (see chapter 13) finding that residents actually lived longer if they were given more authority over their own welfare and given custody of a plant for which they took responsibility, seems to be a counter-poultry case — but the experimental authorities structured the situation so that the residents had new choices and responsibilities. Paternalism in the service of autonomy![55] I find this the central problem of framing a democratic theory of well-being: Can governments structure choices that help people choose their own well-being without substituting authoritative choices for free individual choices? But if this structuring is extended to the selection of information, the implications of paternalism are frightening.

Declining Marginal Utility for Happiness

Summarizing and expanding on some points made earlier, I find the following truths to be self-evident:

1. that people have multiple sources of happiness and satisfaction and will seek a variety of goods in their pursuits of happiness;

2. that as any one good becomes relatively more abundant, the satisfaction people get from that good usually [but not universally][56] wanes in relation to the satisfaction they get from other goods. (Schumpeter called this proposition of declining marginal utility an axiom rather than a psychological hypothesis);[57]
3. that, as historical and social circumstances change, the power of the various available goods (for example, income, companionship, work satisfaction) to yield satisfaction will change with the changes in the supply of each good (as well as with taste); and,
4. less self-evidently, that as people assess their lives to increase their SWB, they may find that their happiness is incomplete if there is not some purpose beyond that very happiness.

In line with the first and second propositions, I believe it has been shown (see chapters 4, 6) that both income and companionship have declining marginal utility or diminishing returns. Thus, increases in income produce large hedonic gains in developing countries, small and variable gains in Europe, and, at least over a fifty-year postwar period, negative gains in the United States. Cross-culturally, increases in income have declining marginal utility—as they do, except for the poor, among individuals in the United States.

Cross-culturally, companionship shows a similar pattern. Diener and Diener's findings show that companionship yields more happiness in individualistic societies, where it is scarce, than in collectivist societies, where it is abundant.[58] And for individuals, too, companionship has declining marginal utility where it is abundant (see chapters 5, 6). In both of these cases the return in diminishing returns was purely hedonic. Now I want to assess the value of that very criterion, happiness itself. By what standard might one say that happiness is overvalued or that there are diminishing returns to happiness? What would be the nature of such returns?

First, I propose to divide SWB into its two principal components, satisfaction with one's life and happiness, and then use life satisfaction as a criterion against which happiness is to be judged. Happiness is a mood; satisfaction with life is a more cognitive judgment. Because they are closely, but not perfectly, related, SWB includes both. Utilitarians often confound the two, as does the philosopher Wladyslaw Tatarkiewicz, who defined *happiness* as a relatively enduring, relatively comprehensive mood whose content is a "lasting, complete and justified satisfaction with life."[59] For example, emotions play a much larger role in assessing of life satisfaction in individualist cultures compared to collectivist cultures, where normative considerations are more important.[60] By separating the emotion of happiness from the judgments involved in life satisfaction, I believe I can show the declining marginal utility of happiness. In this sense, it is plausible to think of situations in which a person says, "I am happy but I am not satisfied with my life."

I can think of four reasons to justify this way of looking at happiness. First, the feeling of wanting more is part of the very concept of happiness. Thus Plato in the *Gorgias* (292B):

Socrates: Then the view that those who have no wants are happy is wrong.
Callicles: Of course; at that rate stones and corpses would be supremely happy.

Certainly wantlessness is a pathology incompatible with happiness. Second, as mentioned above, philosophers and psychologists point out more or less correctly that happiness cannot be pursued directly; it must be found en passant in the pursuit of another good.[61] So, perhaps the happy but dissatisfied person goes on to say, "I want to become a better person." Or, "I would like to help others become better persons." Implied in these statements are ideas of altruism and justice. In these situations happiness is not enough.

Third, there is the distinction between average and marginal happiness. In the case of the person who is happy but wants something more, one might say that her average happiness is high but not her marginal happiness; she is happy in one psychological sense (trait happiness) but something is missing; she is in an unhappy state — at the margin.

And fourth, because people's utilities are interdependent, it is not possible to focus exclusively on one's happiness without unintentionally reducing it. This point is not an ethical defense but rather an empirical observation: people's relationships with one another inevitably influence their pursuits of happiness. In this respect, market solutions, which generally assume independent utilities, are not relevant.

Economists' utility (the satisfaction derived from achieving one's ranked preferences) is a poor guide to the substantive feelings of SWB.[62] If one's feasible choices are themselves unsatisfactory, one can have one's preferences all satisfied in the preferred order and still feel unhappy. Would I rather drink the witches' brew in Macbeth or Socrates' hemlock?

In the early paragraphs of this chapter I identified two goods other than happiness: human development and justice. Here I rely on proposition (4) at the beginning of this section, which says that people have multiple desires, of which happiness is only one, and marry it to proposition (2), which states that as one good becomes more abundant, others, now relatively scarce, become more desirable. Economists, who require maximizing for their systems, will be unhappy with plural criteria, but most of us will find that our lives are, in fact, governed by more than one criterion or goal or value. Inasmuch as the value of happiness is itself culture-bound, there will be wide differences across history and the globe in the value assigned to happiness.[63]

Nonutilitarian philosophers generally agree that several ultimate goods can live happily together in a single philosophical system. Remember the classical trinity: the good, the true, and the beautiful. Among various other treatments, happiness, sometimes ambiguously called welfare,[64] is one of the goods—especially if merited (both Ross and Rescher make this condition); so, of course, is justice; and so are true knowledge, beauty, and, let it be noted, friendship (for example, by the Stoics and G. E. Moore).[65]

LIMITS TO UTILITARIANISM

If we identify a high quality of life exclusively with happiness, we jeopardize values that we cherish, not only justice and human development but also such instrumental values as freedom and human rights. There are four principal counts against pure utilitarian arguments,[66] but because my purpose is to show how happiness may have declining marginal returns, I will state the case without arguing it.

The first count is the infirm ethics of a strict SWB standard: "the greatest happiness of the greatest number" leaves open the exploitation of a minority by a majority (Bentham said that the doctrine of rights was "nonsense on stilts.") Thus, the utilities (including life itself) of individuals and minorities may be sacrificed to majorities because the slight preferences of the larger number outweigh the intense preferences of the minorities. In democracies these minorities are protected by rights, and "rights-based considerations . . . go against utilitarianism."[67]

On the second count, the utilitarian image of humanity, two eminent contemporary philosophers characterize this image in the following terms: "Essentially, utilitarianism sees persons as locations of their respective utilities—as the sites at which such activities as desiring and having pleasure and pain take place. Once note has been taken of the person's utility, utilitarianism has no further direct interest in any information about them. . . . [Utilitarianism especially shows] the neglect of a person's *autonomy*" and "lack of interest in a person's integrity."[68] (That is why human development is an additional good.)

The third count is the utilitarians' threat to freedom. For example, most Americans consider atheism to be an amoral and repulsive doctrine (Theodore Roosevelt called Thomas Paine "a dirty little atheist"). Silencing this offensive doctrine would, I think, marginally increase the happiness of the American people, unless, as in the case of Bolsheviks, there is more pleasure in hating them than pain in tolerating them. In a subtle analysis, Sen shows the way utilitarian thinking can justify the torture of an innocent person by a sadist and the denial by "Prude" of "Lewd's" decision to read *Lady Chatterley's Lover*.[69]

Finally, pleasures are not equal and require an additional criterion. "It is better to be a human being dissatisfied," said Mill, "than a pig satisfied; better to be Socrates dissatisfied than a fool satisfied. And if the fool, or the pig, are of different opinion, it is because they only know their own side of the question. The other party to the comparison [Socrates or someone who has experienced both "higher" and "lower" pleasures] knows both sides."[70]

Situating Happiness Among the Several Goods

In proposing plural coordinate goods, I am countering four traditions. (1) Aristotle believed that for clarity of thought a single-peaked set of *bonae* would be necessary, for then each good or virtue could be judged by how much it contributed to the single *summum bonum* (but he did not follow his own advice in this respect). (2) For the utilitarian, every individual has only one maximand, happiness, a good which could not suffer from diminishing marginal utility because it is all there is. For society there is also a single goal, the greatest happiness of the greatest number. (3) The economists' utility, whether as preference ordering or satisfaction, is a single maximand for both individuals and society.[71] And (4) the familiar procedure of many of the quality of life studies is to establish a single criterial measure for SWB and then assess the contribution of people's feelings about or resources for various domains of life according to how they add or subtract from that criterial measure.

If, however, happiness is only one of several criteria for assessing quality of life, we cannot follow these procedures. Instead, we must ask questions about the tradeoffs among unlike goods whose value has no single common measure or criterion, a procedure that we all follow all the time. We must ask: How much happiness should we give up to increase human development to the desired degree? Shall we shade justice here in order to get more human development there? This latter trade sounds fanciful until one thinks of the budgetary tradeoff between police and courts, on the one hand, and schools, on the other.

The first solution to these dilemmas I wish to propose is to follow consciously the procedures we unconsciously follow anyway: employ our models of the human person and our models of the good society as tests for assessing institutions and their practices, people and their behavior. Consciously use the three goods laid out above (or any other defining criteria of the good) for assessing people's behavior and institutional practices. This approach invites new questions about our institutions, for it implies that we ask of, say, our market institutions, What do people learn in the market? What does the market contribute to their enjoyment of life?[72] And how does the market facilitate justice? Happiness is an appropriate criterion for only the second of these questions.

Second, we might follow Aristotle, Epicurus, and Spinoza, who argue that only virtue leads to a true happiness. This is to establish by fiat what must be proved. Alternatively, one can show that a high quality of life, including well-being, necessarily implies certain matching qualities of persons.[73] This gives a research agenda: What qualities of persons shall we encourage to match the requirements of a high quality of life?

There is a third way in which SWB (for example, both happiness and life satisfaction) can be justified in a world of plural goods, namely, by distinguishing between being happy and pursuing happiness. As noted above, happiness is a by-product of doing something else. If, then, happiness is the by-product of some activity with moral status, at least two of the three goods are satisfied by a single act.[74] But the main point is the curious reinforcement of the value of plural goods; with a single good, even happiness, one risks losing it by too great a concentration on it.[75] Seek justice and you may be happier than if you pursue happiness. In this sense, too, summa bonae are better than a single summum bonum.

As we saw in chapter 13, happiness does contribute to other goods. Veenhoven suggests several ways that happiness contributes to human development: "Enjoyment of life seems (1) to broaden perception, (2) to encourage active involvement and thereby, (3) to foster political participation. It (4) facilitates social contacts, in particular, contacts with spouse and children. Further, happiness (5) buffers stress, thereby (6) preserving health and (7) lengthening life somewhat. There is no evidence of harmful effects."[76]

But this felicitous harmony is by no means universal. For example, if happiness is associated with conventionality and conservatism,[77] how much unhappiness is desirable to promote innovation and justice in a society? As mentioned in chapter 4, more than others, happy people tend to believe in a just world, a world in which victims deserve what they get.[78] To that extent happiness and humane justice are competing goods.

The good society is the society that optimizes human development, justice, and happiness. How will the right mix be decided upon? We need three things: science to get the causal connections sorted out; models of the good society and the good person to guide our choices; and responsive democratic institutions to create the frameworks for our working models. How will we judge the way democracy works? By the way it promotes happiness, human development, and justice. But that is circular — like a dictionary, which defines all words in terms of other words. We do not cease using a dictionary because of its circularity.

PART VI

Individualism

16

Are People the Best Judges of Their Own Well-Being?

A central tenet of the individualist doctrine dominant in the West is the belief that each person should decide for himself whether he is happy or sad, of course, but also why he feels that way and what to do about it.[1] This is the part of the Enlightenment's self-direction that Tocqueville said was "universally admitted in the United States." There, he said, "everyone is the best and sole judge of his own private interest, and . . . society has no right to control a man's actions unless they are prejudicial to the common weal."[2] The same idea is democratic theory's first premise: "In general, each adult person in the association is entitled to be the final judge of his or her own interests."[3] Are people the best judges of their own interests or well-being? Sometimes. The question asks if people are more likely than others to know (1) what they are feeling (I deal here more with feeling than thinking), a matter of introspection and the self-knowledge that may foster authentic information about the self; (2) why they feel that way, which depends on causal attribution and the relation between cognition and affect; and (3) how to make themselves feel better, again a question of causal analysis. In this chapter, I will deal chiefly with the first two questions, adding a section on avoiding ersatz, compensatory choices.

Because the implied defects are only partial handicaps, why do people not overcome them and choose the things that will likely maximize their utilities? I will explore some causes internal to the individuals involved and then the general reasons people experiencing dysfunctional cultural patterns do not correct them. The evidence in chapter 2 suggests that many have failed in their pursuit of well-being, some because they did not understand the what and the why of their own feelings, and many because societies' institutions designed to assist people in choosing do not help.

When the destructive work of the sappers and miners of our cherished beliefs in individual self-reliance is laid out before us, one may well ask what is left of the Kant–Mill idea of autonomy? But it was always a statement of an ideal without a plausible explanation to support it.[4]

What Am I Feeling?

What we are feeling may be something of a mystery, for, as we shall see, we do not have intimate knowledge of our internal emotional states, and what we are feeling often depends on their inferred causes. If people do not know either that or why they are happy or unhappy, the premises of prevailing analyses of markets and democracies have failed. I will give this failing a name: the hedonic fallacy. The fallacy is this: The belief that people know precisely what they are feeling, can explain why they are feeling that way, and, on the basis of this knowledge, can, within their means, maximize their own utilities. Most people at one time or another are victims of these fallacious beliefs, fallacious because they require qualities people rarely have. These qualities are capacities for introspection revealing to people the workings of their limbic systems; for authentic, ego-syntonic self-perceptions; for achieving unity of thought and feeling; and for avoiding compensatory pursuits that do not fulfill their promise. Lacking these capacities, people cannot maximize their well-being.

INTROSPECTION

One will not find ready acceptance of the idea that people frequently misinterpret what they are feeling or are ignorant of the sources of their happiness or of why they are dissatisfied with their lives. On the contrary, most people are confident that they do know what they are feeling and what gives them satisfaction. This is so much the stuff of life that people cannot believe there is not a direct line from the source of feelings to consciousness—even though research shows that some people demonstrably have no knowledge of their emotions except as they know their external causes.[5] Westerners are supported in their belief that they have access to their emotional life by the philosophical doctrine of "privileged information," information that outsiders cannot decently question. Neither the theory of a direct line nor reliance on privileged information is quite correct.[6]

True, there are grounds for believing that people have access to their moods and their causes. Self-reports of well-being are generally confirmed by the reports of teachers, workmates, and friends.[7] Almost no one has trouble answering questions about happiness or life satisfaction (there are almost no "don't know" responses). Satisfaction with the various domains of life (family, work, finances, and so forth) sum to satisfaction with life as a whole, high satisfaction in one area compensating for low satisfaction in another[8] — partly because people pool their experiences to achieve a running score of their satisfactions and dissatisfactions.[9] So far, it seems that people do make meaningful (reliable and valid) assessments of their moods.

The authenticity of these summary assessments, however, is somewhat modified by four considerations: First, people tend to find satisfactions in any choice after the event, partly because what is chosen is "mine," partly because it reflects their prized personal control (chapter 13), and partly because of "post-decision dissonance reduction,"[10] that is, having made a choice, one finds it easier to think that that choice must have been the right one than to suffer agonies of doubt or regret over something already done.

Second, although self-reports of satisfaction with life as a whole are too abstract and too vulnerable to distracting influences to be fully reliable, the assessment of a marriage, a job, a community is more concrete and generally reliable. Yet notice that the memory of an event can invoke a hedonic report different from that elicited during the event. Remembered pleasure and coincident pleasure can differ.[11]

Third, as Edward Wilson reports, "self-knowledge is constrained and shaped by the emotional control centers in the hypothalamus and limbic systems of the brain. These centers flood our consciousness with all the emotions — hate, love, guilt, fear, and others."[12] The centers in the brain reporting pain and pleasure do not carry much specific information. As the psychobiologist Keith Franklin reports (see chapter 3), it is hard to identify what these messages really mean.[13]

And fourth, there are physiological distortions in assessing one's feelings. For example, there is medical evidence of a pathological state, alexithemia (or alliesthesia), specifically defined as an "inability to identify one's own emotional state"; it is marked by failure of interhemisphere transfer of information and is frequently caused by trauma or a history of suppressed emotion.[14] The disconnection between actual experience and remembered experience is common. For example, experiences of pain are frequently misreported as people confuse intensity with frequency and duration.[15]

Thus, the assessment and interpretation of one's own emotions ("emotional intelligence") cannot be taken for granted in any particular case but rather vary greatly by individuals and by cultures.[16]

What else inhibits accurate self-assessments? Such assessments are painful and difficult. As Bentham remarked[17] and later research verified, stripping our reasons of their rationalizations and confronting one's ugly little secrets hurt and are rarely done. Even such self-awareness as that induced by mirrors and self-recordings is painful.[18] Then, too, introspection is difficult. Recall the biological origins of many moods (see chapter 3): It seems tautological to say, "I am happy because I was born with a cheerful disposition" — but that may be more important than the events that pleased and distressed a person.

It is usual to think that behavior follows moods, but some, William James, for example, claim that we know what we think or feel when we see what we do. "I must have been hungry; see what I ate"; or "I must have been afraid, I ran away" (but these cases depend on skipping over tacit, preconscious knowledge). Hormonal secretions *are* influenced by behavior. Finally, there are ambiguous feelings which are hard to interpret: People say, "I don't know whether to laugh or cry"; and their classic uncertainty about whether their fear or anger is dominant (fight or flight) has a physiological basis in the indistinguishable blood chemistry of the two states (although new research may have found differences). The stress-response fatigues partly because the source of the fatigue is unknown.

Unlike Plato, however, one should not make a shibboleth of self-knowledge, for self-focused attention, like self-consciousness, seems to increase vulnerability to depression, especially among women (but also among men).[19] Among the best adapted and most successful Harvard men studied by George Vaillant over almost fifty years, capacities for self-reflection were poor and had no relation to success in their careers or even in their marriages[20] (see chapter 3). Furthermore, the apparently genetically influenced belief that one's immediate environment is responsive to one's acts (self-attribution) is usually less true than one imagines — and yet that false belief serves both individuals and the species well[21] (see chapter 13). Unlike Plato's original noble lie (see chapter 12), a belief that one is the author of one's fate *because* it is unrealistically optimistic favors enterprise and self-help. Although it is sometimes said that the function of moods is to inform the person about the likely success or failure of his or her actions,[22] it is also true that the unrealistic nature of self-attribution associated with good moods is functional for the species and for some human institutions when it is not functional for an individual. In the absence of such beliefs, neither markets nor, especially, democracies would function as well as they do.

But let us return to the idea of a direct line from emotional sources to consciousness. In the following illustrations, I will be accused of confounding two separate levels of analysis: experiential and biological. But they come together when one does more than report one's mood and tries to *explain* it.

Biological Tropisms

Ask a chronic gambler why he is unhappy. He will likely say that it is his losses in gambling, but he may be more unhappy when he is not gambling. The current thinking about chronic gambling is that it represents "the need for arousal, . . . a need to increase the amount and frequency of behavior to achieve the desired excitement. [It] may even have a physiological basis. . . . [Researchers] have found high levels of norepinephrine and its breakdown products in the cerebrospinal fluid and urine of 17 pathological gamblers. Norepinephrine is a hormone produced by the adrenal glands and a central nervous system neurotransmitter with stimulant effects."[23]

Ask any man why he is happy in the company of a beautiful young woman. "She is charming," he may say, "fun to be with." What he cannot say is that appreciation of beauty has a cross-cultural evolutionary basis: "A built-in genetic tendency that evolved over millennia through natural selection seems to attract men to select as most attractive characteristics associated with youth and good health. . . . We have an innate mechanism that sees a certain geometry of the face as beautiful and attributes to that face other characteristics seen as most fit."[24]

Ask a woman who has just had a baby why she is pleased with the world. Of course she is; her baby accounts for that! She does not know that the newly manufactured oxytocin in her blood reduces anxiety and aggressiveness (see chapter 3). Pregnant women and lactating mothers "are much calmer, and more sensitive to the feelings of other people and to nonverbal communication."[25] Our body chemistry has a lot to do with our feelings — but we have no conscious access to body chemistry.

Assessing Well-Being

Subjectivity and physiology have a relation to each other which easily can be caricatured. I am happy because my left lobe is active; and the dopamine flow exceeds the flow of acetycholine. There are more fruitful ways of presenting and interpreting one's mood. The evidence presented in chapter 3 on the biological contributions to moods[26] helped us to understand the limited hedonic power of manipulating government policy. Here I draw attention to the effects of neural and biochemical influences on the power of introspection.

Introspection will tell a person what the body (ambiguously) reports and then construct a reason for those feelings that satisfies our need to explain our moods to ourselves. And if a person is perceptive, endowed with emotional intelligence and a good theory of human behavior, introspection contributes additional insights that add to the explanation. The explanatory model must avoid the human preference for disjunctive explanations (this or that) and use a conjunctive model, the layman's version of analysis of variance (this and that and that . . .). The explanatory model will then show how genetic endowments influence selection of environments and how environmental factors will enhance or dampen the genetically given.[27]

To return to the themes of the influence of self-assessed moods and satisfactions on markets and democracies, note how much these institutions rely for guiding information on people's assessment of their well-being. It is much more relevant to people's well-being that their preferences genuinely express their authentic values and the deepest, least conflicted elements of their personalities than that their choices in the market or anywhere else be consistent or meet other formal criteria for rationality.[28] But the inward-looking assessments of feelings are more complex and prone to error than seems apparent on the surface,[29] and probably more difficult to achieve than the assessments asked of rational economic man (and economic woman, of course). To serve the great institutions of market democracies, people must interpret their moods correctly and be able to explain what caused them so that they can take appropriate remedial action.

Separation of Thought and Feeling

Pavlovian associative learning is only one form of unconscious mental process; others include "learning without awareness of it, implicit memory, cognitive processing not explicitly accessible, and even forms of 'unconscious perception,'" which are all well known, but "unawareness of affect and emotion has been less recognized."[30] Here I focus on a small corner of that unawareness: false estimates of importance and inauthentic and ego-alien responses.[31]

Importance and inauthenticity. For reasons given above, if we relied on individuals to say what the main causes of their life satisfaction might be, we would often be wrong. Andrews and Withey report that there was a slight negative correlation between what people thought the important causes of their moods were and what the data revealed to be important; the finding has been duplicated in other studies.[32] The data show that, like the belief in the power of money to induce happiness, the belief that living under a benign government leads to happiness is similarly misleading. (Actually, living under a benign government may, indeed, foster well-being, but those who think that such circumstances are the source of their happiness are less happy than those who do not.) When housewives, who, compared to women with market work, "are much more likely to be anxious and worried, lonely, and to feel worthless," report themselves to be happy as often as working women do, one suspects inauthentic, but not consciously false, responses.[33] When most people speak of their unqualified delight with their children but in almost every survey married couples are happier before the children come and after they leave the home, one suspects that people are thinking of themselves as delighted with their children because they feel they should experience such delight.[34] These pressures to think of oneself as being happy, or even delighted, are strongest in the family domain and notably absent in comments on government in the United States. The difference reflects the tendency to invest more emotion in areas in which one can do something about an infelicitous situation, as well as the variation in social norms.

Two things stand out from this brief account: (1) the separation of thought and feeling is quite common and not necessarily a symptom of pathology, and (2) like ideologies (of which they are a part), accounts of satisfaction or happiness are not merely reports or neutral explanations but functional statements that further or retard so-called extraneous purposes.

Etzioni uses the concept of authenticity to mean the unity of thought and feeling; he says, "It is the fate of the inauthentic man that what he knows does not fit what he feels, and what he . . . [feels] is not what he knows or is committed to."[35] Without authenticity, the rationality of people's calculations can lead only to second-best states.[36] The knowledge of one's most genuinely satisfying preferences seems to refer to the selection of ends while rationality refers to means,[37] but in a more fundamental sense, choosing the best means to poorly selected ends can hardly be thought rational.

The ego-alien/ego-syntonic distinction is a useful supplement to the inauthentic/authentic distinction in relating choices to personality.[38] For example, the ego-alien includes choices based on the pursuit of neurotic gain, for example, the temporary and misleading advantages derived, say, by the agoraphobe from staying indoors. Fromm further illustrates this distinction between the ego-alien and the ego-syntonic. Prior to the rise of the Nazi movement in Germany, he says, the German working class held communist beliefs on the basis of what they conceived to be their interests, but these beliefs were not ego-syntonic, not resonant (*einklang*) with their own authoritarian personalities. The Nazi movement was quickly persuasive, therefore, not so much because of its ideological tenets as because of its appeal to something almost inarticulate, an emotional response to the authoritarianism of the movement.[39] No doubt for some people support of the market and democracy is, in the same sense, ego-alien.

The ego-alien is largely unconscious, but consciousness is an aid to intelligent and fruitful choice of goals. To pursue these unconsciously ego-alien goals is to fail to address the true sources of one's unhappiness. Because consciousness, like self-awareness, is often painful, ego-alien choices represent the flight from the immediate pain of consciousness toward goals that are likely to prove unsatisfying.

LABELING AND THE USE OF PRECONCEPTIONS

In market affairs people are easily labeled, not only as rich and poor, but also as stingy and generous, prudent and spendthrift, and, in what is called "psychographics," as family men, sportsmen, brand-conscious elites, and so forth. Politicians are, beyond all others, stereotyped.[40] We see ourselves as others see us—or as we think they see us.[41] As a consequence, people often accept stereotypical images of sex-linked traits (females are not good at statistics), of teacher or parental characterizations of their students and children (lazy, moody), or peer group definitions (jock, grind). The social labeling process shortcuts (and shortchanges) self-knowledge. Moreover, experiments show that once a person has accepted a self-schema, this view of the self is impervious to disconfirming evidence—following the general disposition to confirm rather than disconfirm observations and generalizations.[42] These self-schemas also distort and "bias [people's] memories or interpretations of events and thereby influence their expectations and subsequent behavior."[43] For example, although conventional theory holds that people learn to see themselves as helpless by lack of experience with contingent reinforcement (see chapter 13), other research shows that denigrating labeling and the experience of subordination can have this effect.[44]

COGNITION AND AFFECT AS TWO SYSTEMS

A further theory of the separation of thought from feeling is supported by considerable evidence. As mentioned in chapter 14, it is now thought probable that there are two evaluational systems, cognitive and affective, that are only partially in communication with each other. Judgments from the affective center, as in feelings of disgust, are made more quickly and with greater confidence than the slower, more reliable rational evaluation by the cognitive center.[45] The two most frequently used terms for SWB refer respectively to evaluations by these two systems: *happiness* for affective evaluation and *satisfaction* with life as a whole, implying cognitive appraisal. Although the two kinds of evaluations are closely related, when they are different they are out of touch with each other. In short, all kinds of evidence "contradict the common presupposition that emotional processes are by definition conscious states."[46] Under these circumstances people are very likely to be at least uncertain and often wrong about what they feel and why they feel that way.

Why Am I Feeling This Way?

Edward Everyman has recently bought an apartment that he likes very much; his son has graduated with honors from a university and, armed with a degree, has been promised a job. On the other hand, although Edward himself now has a good job that pays well, recently he has had to sell the business he had owned for many years; he has also recently been divorced from his wife and lives by himself in his new apartment. In spite of the good things that please him, he is deeply unhappy: Why? Because (a) he is no longer his own boss, has lost more or less absolute authority over a workforce, and is himself now subject to the authority of another? (b) Because he has lost the companionship and intimacy of his wife and feels rejected because his wife initiated the divorce? And/or (c) because the new apartment and his son's achievements are insufficient to compensate for his losses. Economic theorists, others who rely on the desire for power, and those who, like me, believe that interpersonal relations directly and through their effects on self-esteem are the main sources of joy and sorrow will all offer different answers; they all know the same facts, and all know Edward to the same degree. With others, I believe that the person with the best theories of human behavior, who may or may not be Edward, will be correct.[47]

FEELINGS DEPEND ON CAUSAL INTERPRETATION

We feel pity if a person receives injuries which are in no way that person's fault but, say, moral irritation if the person's injury was due to excessive drinking, and anger toward the injuring person if it was his or her malicious carelessness that caused the damage. We are pleased with our happy feelings if they come from earned rewards but ashamed of the same feelings if the rewards rightly should go to another. It is for these reasons that some psychologists say that one does not know what one feels until one knows why one feels that way.[48] To the extent that what one feels depends on causal attribution, then all of the difficulties of tracing causes beset our search: we are not very good at observing correlations; we easily drop out much of the information crucial to people's inferences on causation; our schemas are inadequate for many purposes and their default values are often mere stereotypes; our preferences override our observations—and so forth.[49] The cognitive demands of causal thinking are the same as those of scientific inference, but more difficult when applied to ourselves than when applied to, say, the expansion of gases.[50] Partly for this reason we tend to rely on conventional explanations—what would have been an appropriate explanation for anyone else in a similar situation. In this sense, we are to ourselves as outside observers.[51]

EXPLAINING AMBIGUOUS FEELINGS OF AROUSAL

Being human, we all understand to some extent the sources of behavior and feelings in ourselves and others. One test is this: Under what circumstances can people explain their behavior and feelings better than observers can? Compared to an actor's explanation, an observer's explanation of what an actor feels in a given situation may be better or worse depending, say Richard Nisbett and Lee Ross, on the relative validity of lay theories of emotion and behavior: "People's characterizations of themselves, like their characterizations of the objects and events that comprise their environment, are heavily based on prior theories and socially transmitted preconceptions."[52] Three related causal reports help to account for the way people explain their emotions and moods.

Physiological Arousal

With the exception of direct sensory experiences,[53] "once the individual becomes aware of his own state of physiological arousal, the labeling of that state — and the subjective experiences, self-reports, and emotionally relevant behavior that accompany such labeling — is the result of a search for a plausible cause of the arousal."[54] The sequence is this: one discovers first that one is aroused and then searches for a cause and, if that is not readily apparent in the situation, one searches further for something plausible to explain to the self why one experiences that arousal.

This process may be studied experimentally. "By holding constant subjects' emotional arousal but manipulating the source to which it may be plausibly attributed, experimenters have been able to produce either a heightening or lessening of many states, including fearfulness, aggressiveness, playfulness, and sexuality." In one experiment, male students rode an exercycle with sufficient vigor to induce a high state of physiological arousal. Although physiologically aroused (e.g., elevated pulse and adrenaline counts), after a few minutes this arousal was no longer recognized by the subjects and therefore not used to explain their feelings. "Nudes examined during this period [when a person was aroused but unaware of that fact] were rated as more attractive than those examined immediately after exercise [when subjects knew that they were still aroused from their exertions] or than those examined at a still later period [when there was no extraneous arousal to be misattributed]." Thus, "people's labeling of their emotional states [including happiness] depends on an analysis of evidence conducted in the light of preconceived theories about which antecedents produce which states — and which states are the product of which antecedents."[55] Market theory is rich in preconceived theories of which the misleading income maximization hypothesis is a prime example. Political and national symbols have powers of arousal whose effects are equally likely to lead to mistaken attributions, as when the national flag is linked to a commercial product.

Actor as Observer: Finding a Conventional Explanation

As mentioned above, theories of self-perception that rely on the conventional ideas of the culture[56] offer an alternative explanation of how people interpret their arousal. "It is clear," say Nisbett and Ross, "that people's ability to assess their feelings . . . will turn out to be largely dependent on their ability to perform . . . causal analysis."[57] But, unhappily, market economists' causal theory of behavior, often borrowed by politics, is a poor theory. (In both marketing and electoral studies, with explanatory theories drawn from other disciplines, analysts probably do know more about the causes of individual choices than do the individuals concerned.)

Assessing Why One Is Unhappy

But happiness and satisfaction with one's life may be something else. I offer here only one of the many available examples of the relevant research.

About twenty years ago J. Weiss and P. Brown studied the accuracy with which women subjects could identify influences on their mood states.[58] Subjects reported daily for a two-month period the quality of their moods and kept track of the various factors that they thought were influencing these moods, such as the amount of sleep they had the night before, their general state of health, sexual activity, stage of menstrual cycle, the day of the week, and the weather. At the end of the data-gathering period subjects filled out a final form assessing the importance of the various factors they had been monitoring. Subjects gave great weight to amount of sleep and almost none to day of the week. The investigators then correlated the co-occurrence of mood scores and alleged influencing factors and found that, in fact, day of the week was most important while amount of sleep had negligible influence. Indeed, as in Andrews and Withey's study of well-being reported above, there was a slightly negative correlation between what the participants thought was important and what turned out actually to be important: "The more subjects' mood covaries with the day of the week or weather, the less likely she was to give weight to these factors in her retrospective report. Thus, subjects erred in assessing the impact of various determinants of their mood fluctuations, mistaking strong influence for weak ones or vice versa, and even failing to distinguish between positive influences and negative ones." Later a different group of subjects acted as observers and was asked to make the same assessments of influences on moods, with the result that their ratings of likely influences on moods were nearly identical to those of the actors observing themselves. The evidence suggests again that actors behave as observers, using common theories and benefiting not at all from their privileged insight.[59] Asked why he or she was unhappy, a person brought up in a market culture would likely say it was because of insufficient income, but we know that this is likely to be wrong, for others with higher income would likely give the same answer in otherwise similar circumstances.

If it is the case "that actors' insights into the causes of their behavior and moods are best regarded as inferences rather than as privileged or 'direct' observation of the workings of their mental machinery," when are these inferences most likely to be accurate? In everyday life people are usually "right in their accounts of the reasons for their behavior" because of the obviousness of the relevant theory (hunger as a cause for opening the refrigerator door; a ringing doorbell as a cause for going to the door). Second, since only the actors know the special meanings for *them* of symbols or events (a familiar tune, resemblance to some hated person), only they can report how a particular stimulus will affect these special meanings. Third, people do have privileged information about their own goals and purposes (for example, saving for a vacation) and sometimes their own decision rules, (when in doubt, do nothing) which again will give crucial information on why they did what they did or believe what they believe—or feel happy or sad as they do. Fourth, there is privileged access to memory of similar circumstances in the past, which helps, at least, in predicting current behavior and, in a sense, in explaining that current action as well: "I do what I always do in such situations."[60] But no market experience will provide the insight that informs people that their arousal is stimulated by the flattery or slight received in negotiating a contract—and not by the terms of the contract itself.

Thus, the actor has clues to what the observer can only infer, but the clues are heavily freighted with emotion and may distract the individual from more straightforward, perhaps more rational, interpretations. Under these circumstances the actor might be a better observer of others than of the self:

> In short, the actor's unique ability to introspect will aid the goal of self-insight only to the extent that the products of such introspection are roughly as causally relevant as they are available and vivid, and only to the extent that they reflect accurate theories of why people like himself, or people in general, behave as they do. . . . When the actor's data and theories are superior [to those of an observer] he will be more accurate, when either is inferior he may be less accurate. . . . [But] on those occasions when the observer possesses a superior *theory*, it is normally the observer who has the advantage.[61]

(Note that the reference to theory here is to lay theory; it is not necessarily an advertisement for the superior explanatory power of psychologists, themselves.) Nisbett and Ross conclude from a variety of studies, "Simply put, [these studies] suggest that *people do not know what makes them happy and what makes them unhappy.*"[62] Under these circumstances, maximizing utility in the market or in politics is exceptionally difficult. Again, do you hear the peals of laughter from Olympus?

Compensatory Choices: Choosing the Lesser Good

In this section I will explain one of the devices employed by people who do not maximize their utilities in market democracies: they pursue money as a substitute or compensation for the loss of affection. Marx said it first: "Assume *man* to be *man* and his relationship to the world to be a human one: then you can exchange love only for love, trust for trust, etc." But if you cannot evoke love by your loving nature, in bourgeois society, you can exchange money for love, and "then your love is impotent—a misfortune."[63] The unhappy, socially awkward materialists described in chapter 8 seem to illustrate this world in which "man's relation to the world is not a human one."

Many people, however, derive genuine satisfactions from their standards of living, their income, and their material possessions or wealth. The choices they make are authentic and ego-syntonic. Although for some, the substitution of one good for another reveals a desirable flexibility of goals, others seek material things as compensations for the friendship and solidarity they fail to find.

What makes one object compensatory for another is a property of the person and not of the object,[64] but money may invite compensatory choices more than others: because it is the most salable of all goods (Schumpeter), because of its prominence in market democracies, its easy symbolization, and its glittering attractiveness. That particular compensatory substitution may be learned very early in life: research substantiates what we already know, namely, that parents unable to give love "use money as a substitute for affection."[65]

To the degree that money and possessions are sought as compensations for friendship or love, they are unlikely to provide ego-syntonic satisfactions, for they are not the ego's first choice. In K. A. Lancaster's theory of consumer choice, it is not the good itself that is wanted but its properties;[66] in this case the properties desired are affection and companionship.

In her research into the psychology of possessions, Lita Furby reports that "personal possessions provide substitutes where other needs or desires have not been met."[67] The consequences in childhood may be especially damaging. For example, children who are exceptionally acquisitive for material objects are distinguished by their poor linguistic and social development, a condition which tends to be fixed for the remainder of the child's life if not corrected by age six.[68] The material objects seem to be compensations for the childish play and social interactions that most normal children find more satisfying.

From the clinic comes other evidence. Stanley Isaacs says, "In the analysis of both adults and children, we find that their attitudes to material possessions frequently change a great deal during the course of analysis. This change is often in the direction of lessening the wish to own."[69] Relieved of their inner conflicts, these improving patients might then pursue the original and genuine objects of their desires, warm relations with others.

From the workplace it is reported that, compared to others, those marked by anxiety and low self-esteem are more interested in the pay than in other aspects of their jobs.[70]

Of the "money conscious" who fantasize about money and think about it more than about their work and families, Carin Rubenstein reports, "Such people are least likely to be involved in a satisfactory love relationship [many are unmarried and childless]. They also tend to be sexually unsatisfied, report worsening health, and almost half of them are troubled by constant worry, anxiety, and loneliness. They are dissatisfied with their jobs and feel they earn less than they deserve."[71]

This theme of substituting money for the lost or unattainable affection of friends or family is quite common. Irwin Sarason and his associates find that people with social support in their lives ("people you can count on") are less concerned about "achieving material success" than those without that support, that is, those with fewer and less satisfying friends.[72]

Markets and Compensatory Choices

Markets facilitate compensatory choices as they facilitate a variety of choices; their function is to make choices in economic transactions easy and inviting. Facilitating exchange, making it easy to substitute one commodity for another, is a virtue in most cases, including that of compensatory choices. The compensatory object is better than nothing. But if the market tempts or coerces people into substituting money for companionship, it undermines the well-being of its population.

Compensatory rewards serve neither market criteria of stable, transitive choices nor principles of SWB. Market information systems are not addressed to the problems of compensatory, inauthentic, and ego-alien desires. But whatever market and political institutions might do to ease these problems remains unexplored because they are currently blinded by the inadequacy of the disciplines that analyze them.

Why Do People Not Choose to Maximize Their Utilities?

As I have observed earlier, people in advanced societies are endowed with institutions, especially markets and democratic governments, that, compared to the institutions of most societies, offer abundant opportunities for choice. Why, then, do people not use these institutions to pursue happiness, as Adam Smith (with many doubts about their success) and Jefferson and Madison said they should do? There are a variety of reasons and causes for this perplexing obstinacy.

One reason is that when people in a market society must choose between money and happiness, they often choose money. This is nicely illustrated in an experiment by Amos Tversky and Dale Griffin in which subjects were given a choice between a job paying $35,000 while similar others are making $38,000 and a job paying $33,000 while similar others are making $30,000. Half of the subjects were asked which job they would choose and the other half were asked in which job they thought they would be happier. In the first group 84 percent said they would *choose* the higher absolute but lower relative salary; in the second group 62 percent said that in their *judgment* they would be happier in the job with the lower absolute but relatively higher salary. At the very least about a quarter of the sample chose a job with more income and less expected utility. On the basis of this and a parallel study, the authors comment, "These studies show that judgments of satisfaction and [actual] choice can yield systematically different orderings."[73] Apparently, under certain circumstances people maximize income at the anticipated cost of some lost happiness!

We are all quite certain that the one thing money will buy is relief from the pains associated with poverty. But physical pain is different. One experiment found that people will not endure longer periods of pain for increased payment, while they will permit the prolongation of pain in exchange for social approval.[74] Apparently, again, for the relief of pain, money is a less powerful incentive than the esteem of others.

SOCIETIES ARE NOT ENDOWED WITH SELF-CORRECTING MECHANISMS

Another reason or cause for people's failure to pursue well-being is the belief that markets and democracies offer alternatives permitting people to choose between, say, more income and more companionship in families, at work, and in friendship groups. For reasons given in parts IV and V of this book, markets and democracies, as they currently operate, are not good arenas for these kinds of choice, but as illustrated in this chapter we see a third explanation of why people do not maximize their (Benthamite) utilities:

People often do not know either what makes them happy or how to achieve that happiness. They think it is more money, but we know by now that for people above the poverty line this is not the case. What institutions or disciplines will come to the rescue?

As mentioned in chapter 1, neither "The Sorcerers of Dobu," whose mutual suspicion inhibited those friendly relations that make people happier and life more rewarding,[75] nor the Manus, whose debts incurred at marriage burdened the rest of their lives,[76] were able to see how to escape from their dysfunctional cultural patterns. Like the Dobus and the Manus and like the imaginary citizens of an imaginary "state of nature" who might not acknowledge that their lives were "nasty, brutish, and short," the enlightened citizens of market democracies may not know either *that* they are suffering or *why* they suffer. And like belief in sorcery and marital indebtedness, belief in market economics and current democratic practices may, without people's knowing it, create circumstances that invite unhappiness, dysphoria, and malaise. When scholars who have presided over the success of the current system share this pluralistic ignorance, the impetus for change is greatly weakened and the paths out of our malaise are obscured.[77]

The persistence of the maladaptive aspects of a system is reinforced when powerful elites profit from them. Along with Marxists one might think of this pattern as exploitation (not Marx's term), but this argument is greatly weakened if the cause of our unhappiness is, at least in part, a loss of social solidarity rather than insufficient income, especially if neither the exploiters nor the exploited know the source of their ill-being. If exploitation means to extract benefits for the self from others, the current malaise cannot be said to derive from exploitation.

In addition to pluralistic ignorance and exploitation the persistence of maladaptive social and economic patterns beyond their former usefulness may be explained by genuine differences in value. As Inglehart has pointed out, materialists and postmaterialists differ on the character of the good society; both are aware of alternative values; neither exploits or at least seeks to exploit the other, but each conscientiously promotes and pursues the values that their respective groups cherish. The materialists cherished institutions that have proved valuable (maximized Benthamite utility for most people) in the past while another group, the postmaterialists, glimpses possible alternatives that they think would make most people happier than they now are.[78] The reformers must cope with uncertainty, for, when the future comes, the fulfillment of its promise is uncertain. And it always comes dragging the past along with it.

Society is not a self-correcting organization. If people have great difficulties identifying the nature and sources of their unhappiness, and if the guiding disciplines share in the people's pluralistic ignorance, and if one cannot identify villains and exploiters in this scenario, and if most people would be better off under another scheme but enough people stand to gain from the way things are to make large-scale persuasion exceptionally difficult, whence cometh our help? Our help comes from investigation of the true sources of well-being and from the will to state, against the conventional wisdom of both scholars and their publics, what is wrong.

17

Self-Inspired Pain

Whence comes the pain of this world? The horsemen of the Apocalypse represented War, Death, Hell, and Hunger. The Giant Evils of William Beveridge were Want, Disease, Ignorance, and Squalor, evils which come upon us "not as enemies with whom each individual may seek a separate peace" but as social enemies to be defeated collectively.[1] Barrington Moore's *Causes of Human Misery* were "the ravages of war," poverty, hunger, disease, injustice and oppression, and persecution for dissident beliefs.[2] The horsemen are to be appeased by people's belief in Christ; thus relief lies within the power of each individual. But the evils listed by Beveridge and Moore were social evils with social solutions, "enemies" with which individuals might not negotiate "a separate peace."

Returning to the internal tradition of Revelation, Sigmund Freud saw the struggle with unhappiness as largely an individual matter—but not a struggle which people are likely to win. "Facing up to reality," he said, humanity had a set of options: it could "reduce its demands for happiness [or] withdraw from the world. . . . [Humanity could] annihilate instincts [as in the principles of Yogi] . . . seek to drug the body with intoxicants . . . [take] flight into neurotic illness," or seek sublimated gratification in beauty, where "aesthetics puts us beyond many troubles." His famous epigram on love and work as the business of life might offer areas of relief—but it doesn't. Devotion to work, he said, is promising, but "as a path to happiness, work is not valued very highly by men. The great majority work only when forced by necessity" and reveal a "natural aversion to work." Love offers "the greatest source of happiness. . . . [but] we are never so defenseless against suffering as when we love, never so forlornly unhappy as when we have lost our love-object or its love." As a consequence, "becoming happy is not attainable; yet we may not—nay, cannot—give up the effort to come nearer to realization of it by some means or other."[3] Life, itself, is a hedonic treadmill.

Adam Smith was not so pessimistic about life; it is ambition, the gift of an angry heaven, that makes men unhappy: "Through the whole of his life [the son of a poor man] pursues the idea of a certain artificial and elegant repose which he may never arrive at, for which he sacrifices a real tranquillity that is at all times in his power, and which, if in the extremity of old age he should at last attain, he will find to be in no respect preferable to that humble security and contentment which he had abandoned for it."[4]

Eight Kinds of Self-Inspired Pain

"The mind is its own place and in itself / Can make a heav'n of hell, a hell of heav'n." Milton took his own advice and did not complain (much) about the injustice of being blind. In what follows I wish to exemplify the ways in which people seem to create their own suffering or, at least, enlarge situational pains and magnify their suffering. They all reveal a failure of adaptation (means to ends), failed adaptation of ends to reality (Eros confronting "Ananke" in the Freudian drama). By *self-inspired* I do not mean to imply that situational forces are not at work or that in the S → O → R paradigm, *S* (stimulus) has been abandoned and that O (organism) does all the work. Rather, I mean unhappiness inspired by the acts and thoughts of those who construe situations in ways that make them unhappier than others who construe the same situation differently. In Milton's hyperbole, they "make a hell of heav'n" or, if not of heaven, at least of the earthly situations which for others would not be hell at all. Melvin Lerner was right: the idea of "a just world" is a "fundamental delusion,"[5] and I do not mean to imply otherwise.

The discussion of self-inspired pain has several purposes: not only does it reveal the limits of what markets and democracies can do to relieve pain, but it is also an appeal from utopia to the fallible humanity that we know. The concept of self-inspired pain reveals limits to the benefits which might be received from the adoption of my proposal: substituting companionship for money goals. No change in goals can do away with self-inspired unhappiness, although such a change may relieve some pain by inducing people to pursue goals that do, in fact, yield greater well-being. Furthermore, the idea of self-inspired pain reminds us that both wanting and wantlessness have their costs: there is no escape from pain in a world so constructed. There is no Nirvana (wanting wantlessness does not help). I will only sample the possibilities, slighting, for example, the problems of the pursuit of compensatory goods (see chapter 16) and omitting the failures of ingratiation (see chapter 5) and of persistence in the face of ceiling effects (see chapter 8) and the pernicious constancy of responses that are only intermittently rewarded (see chapter 13). Markets and democracies enter these pains peripherally, only as they structure society so as to make self-inspired pains more or less probable or more or less painful.

Finally, I want to show that there is more than one hedonic treadmill in our cosmos. Brickman and Campbell's version (see chapter 4), in which each new attainment is greeted by higher matching standards of satisfaction, is only one of several such treadmills[6] — or malign cycles or hedonic paradoxes.

WHEN IS A PERSON A CAUSE OF HER OWN UNHAPPINESS?

Recall (from chapter 3) the theory of stocks (family background, financial and educational endowments, age, and personality) and flows (psychic income, that is, sense of well-being). In this research, it was not the family background and certainly not the level of a respondent's income that accounted for most of the variance in well-being; rather it was personality (and age) that made the most difference, especially extroversion for positive affect and neuroticism for negative affect.[7] If an unhappy person is, say, an introvert and, because she does not enjoy social engagements, shuns the social participation that contributes to good moods for most people, does that person bring upon herself the unhappiness from which she suffers? If one divides causes between circumstances and dispositions, introversion is certainly a disposition. But one cannot blame her for bringing on herself her own suffering. Her friend says, "Why don't you go out and make some friends?" Could she not answer, "You can't blame me for my loneliness; I am an introvert"? Clearly, causal attribution and blame are separate matters. However Milton may have conceived the question, I shall treat the question of minds making their own heaven and hell as a matter of explanation and not of blame.

To go directly from trait to mood, however, leaves out a vital step in the way "the mind can make a heav'n of hell": "People with stable personality characteristics determine their own events; not exogenous circumstances."[8] That is, exogenous events that bring unhappiness are substantially caused by current and earlier choices precipitating these events. This introduces a historical dimension to the analysis, but when I say that unhappiness is often self-inspired,

I intend to call attention only to the variance explained by proximate dispositional factors. But when the road to "hell" starts very early shall one say that the infant's "mind is its own place and in itself can make a . . . hell of heav'n"? Yes, but one does not blame the infant.

I turn to eight examples of self-inspired (dispositionally influenced) unhappiness.

1. INSATIABILITY AND HEDONIC RELATIVISM

Is it the nature of human desire never to be satisfied? Aristotle thought so: "It is in the nature of desire to be infinite." Machiavelli was of the same opinion, as was Hobbes, whose view is more familiar: "Felicity is a continual progress of the desire, from one object to another; the attaining of the former, being still but the way to the latter."[9] Others have been less essentialist in their opinions, Rousseau holding that it was not the inherent essence of humans but only modern society that caused desires to be insatiable. Hamlet spotted one source of insatiability: "As if increase of appetite had grown / By what it fed on." More recent observers have returned to the insatiability theme without invoking its tragic overtones. Thus Lange, writing on the very nature of materialism, finds that receiving more tends to breed the desire for more again.[10] And by simple persistence forecasting, any benefit suggests the receipt of another like benefit in the future.[11]

There are cognitive roots to these psychologies: it takes a counterintuitive theory (which is rare) to discount the belief that what is seen to be rising will continue to rise further and what is falling will continue to fall further. A hedonic treadmill is a machine that thrives on these expectations of prosperity and alleged progress and grinds to a halt on disappointment. A rising level of aspiration in good times is one of its engines: "Levels of aspiration are not given and fixed for all time, but are raised by a sense of accomplishment and success and lowered by a sense of frustration and failure."[12] One must first be disappointed to be happy—later! (The necessity of contrasts is a constant theme in this literature.)

The operative mechanism in Brickman and Campbell's kind of hedonic treadmill is a special kind of insatiability: as circumstances improve, so do the standards required for the same level of satisfaction one had previously. Their adaptation level (AL) theory is the classic contemporary example. It has a physiological analogy: just as a ten-pound weight seems heavy when one has been lifting five-pound weights, so it seems light when one has been lifting twenty-pound weights. One adapts one's sense of pleasure and pain to what one has recently experienced. The authors describe their theory as follows: AL theory says that "the subjective experience of stimulus input is a function not of the absolute level of that input but the discrepancy between the input and past levels. As the environment becomes more pleasurable, subjective standards for gauging pleasurableness will rise, centering the neutral point of the pleasure-pain, success-failure continuum at a new level such that once again as many inputs are experienced as painful as are pleasurable."[13]

We have met the AL theory before: as mentioned in chapter 4, each new attainment, such as a promotion, leads to both expectations and aspirations of further promotions.[14] It is the gist of the theory of rising expectations: the more people get, the higher are their expectations of more.[15] Both hypotheses about rising expectations and rising aspirations are used to explain why increases in national income do not increase people's happiness.[16] The ominous clanking of the hedonic treadmill is brought closer when adaptation level theory is joined to the theory of rising levels of expectations and aspirations—and to Durkheim's fear of "fevered imaginations" without terminal facilities. Much follows from these premises.

If the standard by which one assesses one's satisfaction level is one's own previous experience, one is better off if one has a gradually ascending level of pleasant experiences; in contrast, a descending order of pleasure is painful at each step.[17] Thus, the life scheduling of a musician is better than that of an athlete and a historian's is better than a mathematician's.

Do past sorrows, then, increase current happiness? It depends on whether one contrasts one's current situation to those unhappy periods in the past (making one happier) or carries them along as current baggage, assimilating past moods to current ones (making one unhappier). In light of these alternatives, what would the effect of an unhappy childhood be? The matter is important only in retrospect: Which parents would make their children unhappy to benefit them later as adults? In any event, there is some evidence that the happiness of one's childhood is irrelevant to happiness as an adult[18]—and further evidence that hardship in adolescence (but not in childhood) in the Great Depression tempered adolescents to make them adaptable and happy adults.[19]

Abandoning socialization effects and sticking to well-being without benefit of AL and LA (level of aspiration) mechanisms, we see a larger point: in contrast to the adaptation level hypothesis, if one takes the sum total of happy years as the relevant criterion, one would have to weigh, Bentham-wise, the years of lost happiness against the gain, if there is any, in adult happiness. Some philosophers, notably Tatarkiewicz, say that assessing happiness requires just such an assessment of a whole lifetime,[20] and Solon reminds us, "Call no man happy until he dies."

Given that a person has both good and bad experiences throughout her life, she might enlist her memory to make an advantageous comparison between an unhappy spinsterhood and her current marriage so as to improve her failing sense of felicity in her current life. In this "playing with memory functions" the tendency to remember happy moments better than unhappy ones is a distinct disadvantage.[21] In any event, do not count on memories of an unhappy childhood to yield hedonic gains to an adult.

There is a codicil to theories of adaptation to pleasure: adaptation to physical pain (and to some kinds of physical pleasure) seems to be different: "Parts of the sensory pleasure system, especially those having to do with pain and some positive skin sensations, show remarkably little hedonic habituation."[22] Comparisons play little part in this form of pain.

Up to now I have focused largely on self-comparisons, but social comparisons (about which more later) are central to thinking about hedonic relativism. Brickman and Campbell hold that the "most potent mechanism for establishing hedonic AL is social comparison, or the comparing of the rewards accruing to oneself with the rewards accruing to a relevant other person [or persons]."[23] The hedonic treadmill is thus brought into play when the benefits one must receive to attain a given level of satisfaction rise to keep pace with the perceived benefits of others. A rising tide may lift all boats, but if my satisfactions depend on doing better than others, the rising tide will not bring a surge of joy to my boat.[24] To change the metaphor, the gold medal winner is happy because he won the race, the bronze medal winner, comparing himself to those who did not place, is happy because he did, but the silver medal winner is unhappy because he compares himself to the winner.

One of the most interesting facets of AL theory is its interpretation of the value of equality: "If we make all people equal, do we thereby destroy social comparison as a basis of satisfaction? Or do we thereby maximize satisfaction?"[25] There are two questions here that have been answered in earlier chapters: (1) except for downward comparison, social comparison is generally not as good a basis of life satisfaction as self-comparison; (2) as Tocqueville suggested, equality as a common standard for distribution tends to increase social comparison with its hedonic losses.

If, however, distributions are to be unequal, "should distribution be negatively skewed (so that most people lie above the mean, but a few lie far below it), positively skewed (so that most people lie below the mean, but a few lie far above it), or bimodal (haves and have-nots)?"[26] There are three answers to this question. First, as mentioned in chapter 15, across nations a positively skewed income distribution is not related to the SWB score of the nation.[27] Second, because almost all relevant comparisons are to adjacent others, the overall skewness does not matter; only microskewness matters. This suggests that a system of negative skewness in which, within each comparison group, most lie above the mean and a few below might maximize hedonic well-being. But,

Table 17.1. Comparisons with Mainstream Others in the United States

Where respondents say they stand in comparison with other Americans:		
Much higher	2%	62
Somewhat higher	17	
Slightly higher	43	
Same	25	
Slightly lower	10	13
Somewhat lower	3	
Much lower	<1	
Total	100%	

Source: Frank M. Andrews and Stephen B. Withey. 1976. *Social Indicators of Well-Being: Americans' Perceptions of Life Quality.* New York: Plenum, 317.

third, that may not matter either, for most people do the favorable skewing in their minds anyway. Andrews and Withey give this picture (table 17.1).

Germans are similarly, but slightly less self-protective: 46 percent believe their household income is higher than average, while only 29 percent think it is lower.[28] Yet the tendency of most people to see themselves as better off than the average does not offer an exit to the hedonic treadmill, for in this German study the most satisfaction with income came from those who had received a disproportionate raise—making their comparison group more dissatisfied. Thus, a rise in expectations following past rises in income created a "built-in dissatisfier."[29]

Without the aid of these data, Brickman and Campbell try to avoid pessimism—but they fail. They contemplate an end to evaluation on the grounds that happiness is unself-conscious and does not need it; they refer to the Stoic-Buddha-Thoreau solution of wantlessness (but slyly point out the perils of competitive asceticism or piety); they fear resignation (contentment?) as an invitation to oppression; and they even wonder if a new happiness drug (Prozac?) that allows its users to avoid relativism might be a solution. But in the end, they seem to believe that "evaluative judgments, and AL [adaptation level] and LA [level of aspiration] phenomena, are necessary to the restlessness and the searching that have made human life what it is." As a consequence, "the relativistic nature of subjective experience means there is no true solution to the problem of happiness."[30]

Given the unhappiness of this world, people may not be pleased with "human life [as] it is" and, in their "restlessness and searching," may seek a solution, not by abolishing relativistic thinking but by shifting our attention to domains in which the hedonic yield is greater.

2. REDUCING WANTS

If insatiability is a prescription for unhappiness, perhaps satiation, or at least a decline in desire, or, if not that, a waning of intensity of purpose is the answer. The premise of learning theory is that the goal of purposive action is "drive reduction," that is, a state of rest. But the answers of Callicles (see chapter 15) and Gracian[31] on the perils of wantlessness warn us about taking this route to happiness, as does research showing that the happiest people are active and purposeful. Mill's discussion of tranquillity and excitement as the two elements of a happy life includes the belief that these are substitutable for each other.[32] But Freedman's research on happy people finds that people are happiest when they have some measure of both. For example, he finds that without a variant of tranquillity, contentment (lack of worry), people are not fully happy.[33] Are, then, tranquillity and being content with your portion in life the answer to the problem of that threatening monster the hedonic treadmill?

For most people those two states would not produce a sense of well-being. Mill, whose ideal is the participant, active citizen, and Freedman, with his insistence on "active, dynamic experiences," would say tranquillity and contentment are an incomplete version of happiness.[34] So would Bertrand Russell, who says, "It is in [a] profound instinctive union with the stream of life that the greatest joy is to be found."[35] The reviews of empirical studies agree: "A direct influence on happiness has been found for social participation even when factors such as health and SES are controlled." Moreover, it is not so much the attainment of goals as their pursuit that makes people happy: "Being on the way to those goals and struggling to achieve them are more satisfying than is the actual attainment of the goals."[36] Happiness may be unself-conscious, as Brickman and Campbell said, but for the majority of people an active pursuit of something is a necessary condition for being happy.[37] Passivity, on the other hand, is a form of self-inspired unhappiness.

Do we care too much about these pursuits? No, because reducing the intensity of desire has other risks, for intensity is a general quality of some wanting persons and not a specific quality of a particular want.[38] Thus, given this quality, people cannot reduce their intensity of dissatisfaction without at the same time reducing their intensity of satisfaction, possibly lowering their hedonic level.

3. DECLINING (AND RISING) MARGINAL UTILITIES

If satiability were a quality of goods rather than of individuals, one could not speak of self-inspired unhappiness. And to some extent it is. Economists argue that because money buys so many kinds of goods, desire for money and the goods it buys is insatiable. But the economistic fallacy is a statement that levels of income *are* satiable: as frequently mentioned, beyond the poverty level, higher levels of income do not usually yield more life satisfaction or happiness. Following the distinction between utility from wanting and from liking (see chapter 15), this declining marginal utility for liking (outcome) utility does not at all imply a declining marginal utility for decisional or wanting utility. Thus, the idea that more money buys declining amounts of happiness is more than a restatement of the economists' theory of declining marginal utility; it restates the theory so that declining satisfaction is quite congruent with constant or increasing demand![39]

If money invites satiation, what goods are immune? Gordon Allport suggested self-respect,[40] a fair candidate. So is the sense of personal control which is the key to so much else. Among external goods, the goods people have themselves produced, literally "mixed with their labor," are also less likely than purchased goods to wear out their welcome.[41] In general, goods with personally significant symbolic values resist satiation more than others.[42]

Unlike commodities, skills have rising marginal utilities (see chapter 6). As one becomes more proficient in a skill, such as reading or making friends, one uses it more and enjoys its use more. This is one of the most important reasons for shifting our goals from commodity consumption to work "consumption" (obviously, challenging work never was a disutility, as claimed)[43] and to companionship, in which our social skills enjoy rising marginal outcome utilities — up to a point (see chapter 15). The payoff? There is no hedonic treadmill where goods have rising marginal outcome utilities. Self-inspired unhappiness is firmly attached to the selection of goods which are more easily sated and for which there is a declining marginal outcome utility.

Is there a need hierarchy such that the goods serving various needs are hierarchically organized (as in a Guttman scale)? Maslow suggests that the needs for physical nourishment and safety, sense of belonging, and, contra-Allport, social and self-esteem are deficiency needs which, if satisfied in childhood, are no longer urgent in adulthood. What are not satiable, he says, are goods that satisfy the need for what he calls "self-actualization," that is, personal growth, self-expression, extended learning for its own sake.[44] Maslow's need hierarchy theory cannot be accepted as a genuine scale with an irreversible order of satisfaction,[45] nor is it clear that the drive for self-actualization is insatiable. (Do not many people say or at least think, "I am satisfied with the kind of person I am"?) Rather, a non-Maslovian process is at work. As people make progress toward solving personality problems they give up their compensatory striving for money and prestige and shift their attention to goals with greater capacities for longer term hedonic yields (see chapter 16).

By choosing goals with more rapidly declining marginal utility; by avoiding goals with rising marginal utility; by choosing compensatory rather than ego-syntonic goals, people lower their SWB.

4. THE MALIGN CYCLE

Unto everyone that hath shall be given, and he shall have abundance; but from him that hath not shall be taken away even that which he hath.
—Matthew 25:39

A malign cycle is often associated with poverty: being poor, one cannot afford the education or telephone or (in the United States) the car necessary to get a job and so to climb out of poverty. And it has a psychological aspect that enlists the influence of personality that we have just examined: poverty breeds interpersonal distrust, and if one distrusts people and treats them with suspicion, they will respond with behavior that confirms that distrust. Similarly, helpless people create situations which increase their helplessness, whereas those with a sense of mastery "feel they can generally deal with (and benefit from) their relationships and interactions with others, even in situations where the threat of exploitation is present."[46] The poor who for some reason have a sense of personal control do not suffer more than others from unhappiness or psychological distress.[47] Thus, a malign cycle of poverty is both circumstantial and psychological: the poor have more problems, and they have fewer experiences of mastery or personal control, which, in turn, diminishes their capacity for self-help.

At every level of income, unhappiness is itself a source of malign cycles. It decreases sociability and cooperation, makes for delay and inefficiency in decision making, and reduces exploration of alternatives and prosocial behavior,[48] all of which create malign cycles of lack of reciprocal cooperation and help. Marriage contributes greatly to happiness, but "unhappiness is a handicap in love, both because it is a disadvantage in intimate encounters and because it is detrimental to the development of psychological characteristics that are crucial in modern marriage."[49] Happy Americans are generally less puritan than others; for the happy, "moral approval of pleasure adds to the enjoyment of life . . . not burdening the individual with notions of sin and . . . allowing full awareness of pleasurable experiences."[50] The bottom-up theory of happiness (daily pleasures make a person generally more happy) meets the top-down theory (overall happiness makes daily events seem more pleasurable) in a benign cycle. Reversed, it is a malign cycle.

At the level of societies, there are many familiar malign cycles: as Caesar explains to Cleopatra in Shaw's play, repression does not end with the crushing of rebels, but rather encourages more rebellion, which then requires even more repression; when people find a regime "illegitimate," they deprive it of the interstitial scope to address the problems which labeled it illegitimate in the first place; and the sensitive feedback system of markets makes a threat of a recession into an actual recession in a malign cycle of lost confidence and lost income.

Can these social cycles be called *self*-inspired cycles of unhappiness? It would be misleading, especially since an individual's acts in these cases may benefit the individual while distressing others. But we may call them *auto-generated* cycles in the sense that whole peoples unconsciously bring unhappiness on themselves—as in the cases of the Dobus and Manus (see chapters 1 and 16). Because they do not know the causes of their discontent, a dialectical solution (misery—revolt—relief of misery) is less likely than a malign cycle of discontent breeding further discontent.[51]

Happiness, goodness, and reform are intertwined in a way that embarrasses ethics. The pleasant cycle of Spinoza, in which goodness and happiness reinforce each other in a benign cycle under God's supervision, suggests a comfortable, ethically and hedonically progressive world. In contrast, there is the real world, in which the happiness of some is bought by the unhappiness of others. It is true that happy people engage in more prosocial behavior in the little worlds of their own vicinity, but beyond their immediate experiences happy people are, compared to others, more conventional and more likely to believe in a just world (see chapters 4 and 15) justifying misery (although more often the misery of others than of themselves).[52] The goodness of happy people is of the "brighten the corner where you are" variety. For a cosmopolitan theory of either self-inspired or auto-generated unhappiness, one must distinguish the local benign cycle from the malign cycle on the world stage that distressed Barrington Moore.[53] Like happiness, conventional goodness is not enough.

5. TRAPS: SHORT-TERM PLEASURE INHIBITS LONG-TERM HAPPINESS

A hedonic trap is a situation offering pleasure now (the bait) and triggering pain later (the closing of the trap). In the byways around the main route to the hedonic treadmill there are many traps that people fall into—or perhaps perversely select (self-inspired unhappiness, again). Addiction (drugs, nicotine, gambling) is the paradigm case, but any current indulgence followed by related pains is similar: impolitic angry rejoinders, impulsive but imprudent spending, or quitting school without a certificate. The obvious solution is a capacity for deferred gratification.[54] But it is not the only solution.

The problem with trap-avoidance is that it may itself involve systematic unhappiness: chronic self-denial lest some unforeseen peril befall, the over-controlled, buttoned-up personality. In itself, such puritanism is not a promising road to happiness, but it has its rewards. "Saving," say Robert Lynd and Helen Lynd, "ranks with 'hard work' in the central Middletown tradition, as one of the two joint keystones of the arch of a man's 'future.' " It is a "mark of character" and necessary for self-respect.[55] On the other hand, there is evidence (see chapters 13 and 16) that happy-go-lucky spenders are generally happier than prudent savers — and, incidentally, modest drinkers are happier than teetotalers, and they are less likely to become drunkards! It is a double trap: accept the pleasures of social esteem at the cost of a happier, more carefree way of life, or accept the pleasures of a preferred, less restricted way of life at the cost of losing the social esteem that yields satisfaction in many small preferments? In Middletown it is probably better to have character than to seek happiness, and, paradoxically, earning the social esteem associated with a self-denying character is probably the more efficient route to happiness. The double bind is not in itself a form of self-inspired unhappiness — except as one chooses for oneself that escape from the double bind that is less satisfying.

Distrust of others is a wary protection against entrapment — and distrust is generally associated with unhappiness. See how mistrust converts a trap of one kind (deceit) into a trap of another kind, failure to achieve a future good lest one be deceived. Arab children in Palestine choose one chocolate bar now rather than two chocolate bars later because they have learned to distrust promises, whereas, with greater trust, the Ashkenazi children of Israel choose two chocolate bars later, presumably with greater outcome utility.[56] Wariness against traps is itself a source of pain.

Is happiness, itself, a protection against traps as it is against trap-defeating puritan denial? Because happy people wish to hang on to their happiness, they indulge their appetites up to the point where they think indulgence will bring disapproval (including self-censure) and then frustrate these appetites when their indulgence seems threatening to their current mood.[57] Happiness is not normally thought of as encouraging wariness, but happy people are apparently wary of having "even that which they hath" taken away. It is not easy to avoid self-inspired unhappiness when one is beset by traps.

Digressing for a moment to social traps, I recall how the practice of devoting resources to current adult preferences at the expense of the future is a social trap. The most common example, of course, is the use of nonrenewable resources as though they were current income, but the worst case is the devaluation of children (see chapter 3), consuming the irreplaceable human capital with which nature has endowed us, underinvesting in children's education and public health, failing to give children and their nurturance priority — these are all social analogies of private indulgences of pleasure now for pain later.

6. ENDS WITHOUT MEANS

A person envies people who enjoy reading, but she does not like learning to read; she wants to play the piano but hates music lessons; she wants to be a doctor but detests organic chemistry. She is means-phobic and she suffers from self-inspired unhappiness. Puzzled by a failure to predict behavior from knowledge of what people wanted, Icek Azjen and Martin Fishbein found the main reason: liking or disliking the means necessary to obtain an object.[58] Whereas the trap involves short-term pleasure at the cost of long-term pain, means-phobia avoids short-term pain at the sacrifice of long-term pleasure.

The main loss for means-phobic persons is, of course, the loss of desired outcomes that are blocked by failure to pursue a goal. Means-phobias skew preference schedules away from that combination of goals that would be most satisfying. Furthermore, even lowly means often have the quality of ends, generally the potential intrinsic value of the activity itself or the learning value of the exercise of a skill. For example, research on process benefits suggests that the economic product should include the utilities of activities whether paid for or not: "People have preferences for what they do, and these preferences can be thought of as distinctly different from the satisfactions obtained from the tangible products of activity."[59] Thus, the intrinsic enjoyment of working at a job (often heavily influenced by the values of companionship) should be weighed as a source of private utility just as important as the utility of the pay earned and the commodities purchased with that pay. This line of thought on the intrinsic value of most means is given philosophical authority by Charles Fried, who says all means have some positive or negative intrinsic value.[60] The means-phobic person is insensitive to the positive values of the means that he avoids. The loss is a self-inspired loss.

In passing, note the parallel with the analysis of democracy in chapter 12: people want democracy but do not like the pains of participating in elections or of informing themselves about the issues. Tocqueville (echoing Rousseau) put it this way: "As the citizens who labor do not care to attend to public affairs, and as the class which might devote its leisure to these duties has ceased to exist, the place of the government is, as it were, unfilled. If at that critical moment some able and ambitious man grasps the supreme power, he will find the road to every kind of usurpation open before him."[61] Similarly, people want freedom of speech but do not like the pains of dissonance when that freedom is exercised by their enemies.

7. INTERNAL CONFLICTS AND AMBIVALENCE

Even if one did not have that gorgeous apparatus of internal conflict conceived by Freud in which the monstrous superego fights it out with the

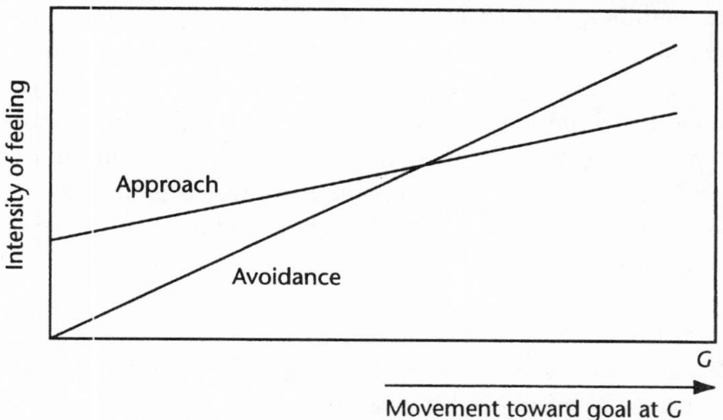

Figure 17.1. Approach–Avoidance Gradients
Source: Simplified version of figure in John Dollard and Neal E. Miller. 1950. *Personality and Psychotherapy.* New York: McGraw-Hill, 356. Reproduced with permission of The McGraw-Hill Companies.

equally monstrous id, the poor, fragile ego being caught in between, one could find plenty of evidence of painful inner conflicts. We desire and fear independence, resentfully clinging to our dependent status as long as we can.[62] In the American success culture, a fear of success might seem rare, but, at least for a time, it was common among women. A series of experiments in the 1970s showed that "women feared social rejection based on performance success much more than men did."[63] Women who did superlatively well in verbal tests before their school became coeducational did much worse afterward.[64] Similarly, the need for companionship that I have stressed is often undermined by a fear of rejection. In a set of experiments, those who scored high on a fear of rejection test (for example, "I prefer not to go to a place if I know that some of the people who will be there don't like me"), in contrast to those who scored low, preferred to meet and talk with lower status people compared to higher status people or equals.[65] Fear of intimacy creates similar conflicts among those seeking companionship. The power motive may be inhibited by a fear of power (also more common among women than men), whereas fear of weakness tends to lead to a grasping for power in both appropriate and inappropriate situations. Indeed, McClelland finds that "all social motives have avoidance aspects."[66] The consequence is a painful state of ambivalence.

There is a time sequence in this interplay of motive and avoidance that has been well studied.[67] You want to see your dentist, but as the appointment approaches you dread it more and more; you have been looking forward to having friends to dinner, but as the day approaches all the troubles of entertaining begin to overwhelm you. You suffer from a common form of approach–

avoidance pathology (fig. 17.1). This is neither a trap (pleasure now for pain later) nor a simple case of means-phobia; it is ambivalence of a time-ordered kind, getting worse along the way to the goal. Ambivalence is very common in economic life[68] and plays havoc with preference scheduling, inviting an Arrow-type cycling of preferences that makes utility maximization impossible. And because the sources of conflict, ambivalence, and the approach-avoidance pathology are internal to the person and not features of the goals, they induce self-inspired pain.[69]

8. UNATTAINABLE GOALS

"A man's reach should exceed his grasp." Why? Because he will never know the extent of his grasp, his possibilities, unless he explores their outer limits. But if he extends his reach, he takes risks of disappointment. The setting of standards so high that they may not be attained has several sources. Where individuals can set their own standards, "individuals are tempted to maximize rewards for minimum effort by lowering their standards. However, rewarding mediocre performance incurs self-esteem costs. [In one study]. . . . children apparently were willing to deny themselves rewards over which they had full control rather than risk self-disapproval for unmerited self-reward. Many of the children, in fact, set themselves goals that necessitated much effort at minimum material recompense."[70] Caught between self-disapproval, on the one hand, and a higher risk of failure, on the other, people (including very young people) often choose risk of failure. In the case of setting standards as in so many other cases, people cannot escape a risk of self-inspired pain and sensibly choose the risk of lesser pain, whether it be failure or self-criticism. One might say that wherever there is conscience, and therefore self-punishment, there is self-inflicted pain.

One sees here the compelling force of guilt compared to shame, probably a characteristic of more individualist societies. "In . . . communities in which the ethic of self-betterment predominates," says Albert Bandura (without much evidence), "people adhere to high self-demands and take pride and pleasure in their accomplishments."[71] The dark side is that they also suffer more intensely from their failures.

Standards are set in many ways: self-comparisons involving the person's own past achievements and experiences, comparisons with some ideal chosen from literature or social idols, concepts of equity (ratio of own costs to benefits compared to that of another), social comparison with "mainstream others" (see table 17.1 above) or, most often, adjacent others, such as relatives and coworkers or people in the same occupation everywhere.[72] It is not the relativism that is at stake here, it is the selection of standards and comparisons that imposes unattainable goals—the underside of Veblen's account of invidiousness.[73]

Strangely, striving for unattainable goals may be a solution for a person who fears failure, for failure is not then culpable. Persons who reveal in experiments that they are high on a test of fear of failure tend to avoid all tests, but if they have to choose they choose very easy ones which they can do or else very difficult ones in which their failure is excusable. Those without such a fear of failure choose challenging tasks that stretch their talents but at which they might or might not succeed.[74]

Literature is filled with sad stories of futile striving for unattainable goals: *An American Tragedy* is an account of unattainable love; unattainable religious standards sought by Jesuits among the Canadian Indians are reflected in *Black Robe; Macbeth's* search for secure power follows Hobbes's idea that one seeks "power after power" in a vain effort to find security. The success ethic invites chronic disappointment in business, as in *The Rise of Silas Lapham* (with redeeming self-knowledge) and, across the Atlantic in an account of literary striving, *Grub Street.* A man's reach should exceed his grasp—but misery may follow.

Returning to the question raised in the previous chapter: Should each person be the judge of her own best route to happiness? Usually yes, because that is good for society, and she probably knows what will give her the most satisfaction; but the perils of both insatiability and satiation, malign cycles and traps, of choosing goals that fail to satisfy, fear of the means necessary to obtain an end, and the dogged pursuit of unattainable goals all offer obstacles that cause many casualties along the way. Individualism licenses the exercise of these forms of self-inspired unhappiness. Can we discover a less painful way or are these self-inspired pains the necessary costs of a larger good?

PART VII

Conclusion

18

The Way Home

On the way home, one is entitled to look back as well as to look ahead to a safe harbor. The historical journey to modernity has been an extraordinary passage: from poverty to relative wealth, from ignorance to relative knowledge, from a short life to a relatively longer one, one which is increasingly free from disabling diseases. If, in the language of the 1960s, the United States is a sick society, its people are nevertheless emancipated from many of the hardships and burdens their fathers and grandfathers bore. Poverty in the midst of plenty? Some of that. Poverty of spirit in the midst of great social achievements? More of that. It is a mysterious puzzle that I am seeking to demystify.

Optimism and Pessimism, Nostalgia and Utopia

In our own time the "high IQ whimpering" (Maslow's term) of the French existentialists and the despair of the Frankfurt School are still vivid in recent memory. Outside this group, Hannah Arendt expressed her lament as follows: "It is quite conceivable that the modern age—which began with such an unprecedented and promising outburst of energy—may end in the deadliest, most sterile passivity history has ever known."[1] The editors of a then (1973) timely book on alienation sum up its contents and their own view in the following terms:

> Our present age of pessimism, despair, and uncertainty succeeds a quite different earlier period of optimism, hope and certainty. . . . Confused as to his place in the scheme of a world growing each day closer yet more impersonal, more densely populated yet in face-to-face relations more dehumanized; a world appealing ever more for his concern and sympathy with unknown masses of men, yet fundamentally alienating him from his next neighbor, today Western man has become mechanized, routinized, made comfortable as an object; but in a profound sense displaced and thrown off balance as a subjective creator and power.[2]

In the 1960s and early 1970s alienation was a fashionable theme: "People are dejected and disheartened by a vast meaninglessness that seems to have insinuated itself into their lives, a lack of purpose, irrelevancy. . . . We reach out and no one is there, turn inward and find nothing inside. There is a sense of nightmare, and there is real madness."[3] Is there pleasure in alienation? Some social scientists spoke of alienation as a source of relief, a "consolation prize" for marginal people who blame the system for their powerlessness. The theory was falsified in one study,[4] but there may, indeed, be private satisfaction for the messengers of despair in a smug world. I do not want to join either group.

Nostalgia is a powerful analgesic for the pain of modernity: the golden age, "the world of our fathers," happy days gone by. Nostalgia is especially appealing to Americans who glorify, say, the frontier and forget its pain, for example, *Son of the Middle Border*. "My argument," says Herbert Gans, the author of many community studies, is with "nostalgic critics who want to 'revive' a sense of community that never was save in their imagination."[5] My book is not nostalgic for *The World We Have Lost* described by Peter Laslett, and I do not share Tönnies's nostalgia for gemeinschaft and his view that in modern urban societies "everybody is by himself and isolated."[6] The ills I have documented and the idea of a "second relational bend in history" do not imply a return to any known past. The rediscovery of values more honored in the past than they are currently does not imply a return to the past. Cycle theories are not necessarily circular theories returning to origins; they can be spirals.

If nostalgia is tempting, especially for conservatives, utopia is even more inviting, for each can invent his or her own. Socialists do this, as in Marx's end of history, and sometimes it seems that such communitarians as Bellah and Etzioni dream the delightful dream of a pure and moral cooperative commonwealth. That capitalist organizer of a cooperative commonwealth Robert Owen actually created his own utopia—whose members were not, in the end, capable of the strains of utopia. Neither were the members of the original kibbutzim.[7] I am not cut to this pattern. Neither, again, are most Americans, whose vision of their future is only a little better than the present—and even that hopeful group comprised only about a sixth of a national sample.[8]

In place of nostalgia and utopia, the world offers a rich variety of social experiments from which one can learn. For example, in Britain only about a seventh of the population report themselves to be lonely; in France and the United States it is about a quarter[9]—what can the British teach the Americans? The Asian collectivist societies partially retain family solidarity in the midst of market success and failure; what can one learn from these diverse societies?

The recorded decline in happiness (and in trust and belief that life is getting better) which I have used as an occasion for exploring unhappiness and malaise in market democracies is likely to be ephemeral. The very theory of SWB tells us that unhappy people adapt to their circumstances so that any decline, even for a fifty-year period, will probably be reversed at some point, not so much because circumstances have changed or because we have learned a better way of living (which I hope we will) but because the baseline for assessing well-being has changed. The popular ignorance of the sources of people's own ill-being along with self-inspired unhappiness make institutional remedies difficult. We face adaptation without remedial change: "Although people may be happier if they live under improved conditions, the influence is likely to be large at first and then taper off."[10] Depression, however, offers no such self-initiated adjustments to fatigue, listlessness, and feelings of worthlessness, hopelessness, and helplessness. The depressed will not get well without companionship.

What Went Wrong?

Are people unhappy because their expectations of happiness are too high? Comparisons between the individualist cultures of the West and the collectivist cultures of Asia have found that happiness is not, at least explicitly, a conscious goal of collectivist cultures. Expecting less, Asians may be less disappointed or at least less involved in the pursuit of happiness—making comparisons of SWB across cultures difficult.

FAILED EXPECTATIONS

Over the long haul in the West the value of happiness (as measured by references to it in philosophy, history, and literature) has varied a great deal. P. A. Sorokin has traced three "ethical styles" over the long course of world history. The first of these is the "sensate ethics of happiness," which is sensory, pleasure loving, and wholly of this world; it is associated with hedonism,

Table 18.1. Sensate Ethics of Happiness and Absolute Ideational Ethics, 1400–1920

	Sensate Ethics of Happiness	Absolute Ideational Ethics
	(Percentages of Eminent Thinkers)	
1400–1500	8.7	91.3
1500–1600	43.5	56.5
1600–1700	38.4	61.6
1700–1800	36.3	63.7
1800–1900	38.0	62.0
1900–1920	43.0	57.0

Source: Pitirim A. Sorokin. 1941. *The Crisis of Our Age: The Social and Cultural Outlook.* New York: Dutton, 133–36 at 142.

utilitarianism, and relativism [Sorokin was not a philosopher]. The other two are "ideational ethics, [which] aims . . . at the union with the Absolute, which is supersensory" and a mixed "idealistic ethics," which is an "intermediate synthesis of ideational and sensate values."[11] Sorokin measured the dominance of these ethics by the proportion of the "partisans of each style . . . among all the eminent thinkers in each specified century." Taking the long sweep of recorded history from about 500 B.C.E. to 1920, he finds that the ethics of happiness was totally missing in 500 B.C.E., rose to a peak (75 percent of the eminent thinkers) in the period from 400 to 300, dropped again in a fluctuating manner to between 5 percent and 30 percent in the remaining centuries before Christ, and rocked along at under 10 percent until lost from sight at A.D. 400, when the absolute ideational ethics (union with the Absolute) dominates thought for a thousand years. In 1400–1500 happiness peeps through and then has a substantial popularity among "eminent thinkers" (table 18.1).

Recall that we are dealing here not with the way people feel or with whether or not they are happy, but with the value of happiness in given periods—as may be estimated from the work primarily of philosophers. This distinction between the value or goal of happiness and being happy opens a gap between the two modes of experience and thus suggests that the dominant utilitarian philosophy of our time, in which the greatest happiness of the greatest number is the stated aim of markets and the implicit premise of government policy, may in fact be marked more by unhappiness and depression than by the happiness that is the object of these institutions. There is, of course, superb irony in the idea that utilitarianism is associated with misery. But more important for our purposes is the possibility that the postwar decline in well-being is caused by falling short of these higher hedonic expectations, a possibility enhanced by the high value of happiness in the twentieth century, or at least in 1900–20, a value not approached since the Renaissance.

The feminist revolution in the West has raised women's expectations of well-being beyond possible attainment in the short period since the movement was launched; government attention to the welfare of African Americans in the United States has promised more well-being than it has delivered (accounting for their optimism in the 1960s and their pessimism at the turn of this waning century); in third world countries the novel idea of economic growth is said to have created a "revolution of rising expectations." Just as every promotion in a bureaucracy creates expectations of further promotions in a sequence that obviously must have a disappointing end, so every improvement in the circumstances of women, African Americans, and citizens of third world countries leads to disappointment. If this were true, increased unhappiness (of this relative kind) could be an indication of improved circumstances — a paradox and only minimally true.[12] In any event, this relativistic explanation could not account for the postwar decline in well-being of white males or the rise of depression, which has never been said to be relativistic in this fashion.

DECLINING MARGINAL UTILITY OF MONEY

Western societies kept on course too long. This sailing metaphor reflects the general tendency of sluggish cybernetic devices (Parsons calls culture the steering mechanism of society) to adapt too slowly to changed circumstances. As reported in chapters 5 and 6, the economic development that improved SWB over the millennia is no longer a major source of well-being in the United States. Like other goods, money income and the commodities it buys have declining marginal outcome utility while companionship has, at the moment, rising marginal utility. But the "self-evident truth" that the more one has of a good, the more relatively attractive other goods will become sooner or later applies to companionship. (Hence a return to gemeinschaft is unattractive.) It is not so much that human appetites per se are insatiable, as that human appetites are variable. In order to avoid the pain of wantlessness, desire itself *should be* insatiable, but particular desires for any one good are relatively satiable when another attractive good is available and relatively scarce. The urgent drive for commodities does more than deflect us from companionship: it deprives us of the relaxed atmosphere necessary for enjoying friends. (Time spent at the watercooler or on a coffee break, excoriated by management as detracting from productivity, is highly productive of outcome utility for workers.) As we move from a survival standard toward a well-being standard (see

Inglehart below), *efficiency* itself changes meanings: it means, as it should always mean, least cost in values given up for most benefit in values gained. If *utility* has any meaning at all, that is what the maximization of utility means. Preference schedules are only instruments to that end.

THE FAILURE OF THE GUIDING DISCIPLINES

What went wrong, then, is that the guiding disciplines failed to reconsider the ends that really mattered. It is not quite an accident of intellectual history that gave to economics the custody of how to think about well-being, for during the long period of its intellectual gestation the most important values were, first, survival and then deliverance from poverty. Thanks to technology as well as economics, the advanced countries of the world have solved the first problem and are hesitantly moving toward solving the second. It is this very success that raises to rival importance the value of the most urgent competing good, companionship. But this rival good is an externality to market economics; because it is not priced, the market is not sensitive to its fluctuating values (see chapter 9). It may be, as Ludwig von Mises said, that "modern economics makes no distinctions among ends because it considers all ends equally legitimate,"[13] but then the analysis of unpriced goods must find a "market" that does not rely on price, something not yet on the horizon.

Political and especially democratic theory suffers from some of the same problems as economic theory: it poses as ends what are really means. Maximizing choice (freedom) is valuable only as the choices contribute to well-being—or human development or justice. Democracy, itself, is a means which derives its value from its contribution to ends—but if the ends are not articulated, the value of democracy rests on uncertain grounds. In contrast to the means-phobia outlined in chapter 17, both economic and democratic theory exhibit a kind of means-philia, a fetishism of means at the sacrifice of ends.

Finally, all the considerations treated in chapter 12 imply a level of pain partially inherent in democratic processes, pain which is rarely acknowledged. In particular, the participationist arguments relying on civic duty (thus matching responsibilities to rights) ignore the pain of acting largely through a sense of obligation. If moralism is at one pole of the problem, economism is at the other. The very economism that infects political theory discourages participation for other reasons: what is the quid pro quo that makes politics an exchange process? Participation theory also greatly exaggerates both what people learn from political participation and the gain to feelings of self-determination from acting without direct contingent rewards (see chapter 13).

The problem goes deeper than the fetishism of means in the political and economic disciplines. Because of the failure to specify ends (except, among political theorists, for justice—an honorable exception), the means devised are often inappropriate. If the economistic fallacy (see chapter 4) is correct, neither contemporary schools of economics nor of political science can help us increase subjective well-being. I do not know what institutions will best serve SWB, nor do I know how markets and democracies may best go about optimizing well-being, let alone weighing well-being against human development and justice. This inadequacy is a direct consequence of the failure to incorporate into economics and political science what the behavioral, medical, and neurological sciences now know of the production functions of well-being and human development.[14] These other sciences are, indeed, working on the intricate relationships between the nervous system and experience, but they are doing so without an informed knowledge of the institutions that they must rely on. A collaborative effort is urgently required.

If one could count on nature to take a hand in giving reproductive success to those who discovered (and then taught by example) the best ways of achieving SWB, the guiding disciplines and their agents would need only be midwives to these evolutionary processes. But natural selection has no such agenda. Indeed, as mentioned in chapter 3, it is dissatisfaction, if not actual unhappiness, that "makes us productive."[15] As far as evolution is concerned, SWB is wholly an instrument for reproductive ends and not, as humans think, the other way around. Pain and pleasure are biological concepts; utility is not. But there is no reason to believe that the drive for pleasure directly undermines the importance of virtue or at least the recognition of moral obligation.[16] Indeed, even in the individualist West, sensitivity to moral norms is associated with fewer negative feelings.[17]

May I add a further note on philosophy, to which we turn for clarification of goals, especially ethical goals and standards of behavior? Philosophy deals with concepts and their implications, not with events and their causes. Except for deontology, philosophical treatments of the right and the good require consequential analysis. But philosophy has no endogenous expertise in causal analysis and must, therefore, borrow its causal analysis from science, both behavioral science and physical science. Of all disciplines, philosophy has the greatest claim to breadth of understanding—but it must substantiate that claim by paying attention to the inelegant world of behavioral consequences: what happens to individuals and society when happiness (or justice or human development) is pursued as an ultimate good?

The Failure of Individual Choice: Are There Immanent Forces to Help Us?

If people do not usually know the causes of their well-being, it seems that the institutions we have created to foster that felicitous state are impotent.

Both markets and democracies require individual decisions for guidance and change; both have, at least in theory, a bottom-up approach. This reliance on individuals for the initiatives of change, or at least assent to change, is the great achievement of post-Enlightenment civilization. But as that civilization unfolds, unhappiness does not diminish or die for lack of nourishment; it seems to be growing or at least maintaining an uncomfortable level of pain. Although companionship is a principal source of well-being, there is little general demand for more companionship, and although satisfaction with family life is the single greatest contributor to life satisfaction, there is an apparently endogenous self-inspired destruction of family life. The "rosy blush" of the Enlightenment pales under the withering stresses of life in market democracies.

Perhaps, however, there is an unfolding program in history that will assist the renewed emphasis on companionship, a program of which we are unaware. Hegel and Marx thought they had discovered such an immanent program in the laws of history, a discovery which, Hegel said "is humanity's leap from the realm of necessity into the realm of freedom."[18] If that were true, we would need only work with these known "historical laws" to hasten their destined achievement and to become the masters of our destinies. Are such immanent forces fanciful? This one was, but contemporary authors are reluctant to give up the idea that there is a logic to institutions which, at least in the short term, has predictive power: "Each of the most important institutional orders of contemporary Western societies has a central logic — a set of material practices and symbolic constructions — which constitutes its organizing principles and which is available to organizations and individuals to elaborate."[19]

Some find the immanence in human dispositions. Thus, the philosopher Alfred Whitehead and the historian Charles Beard believed that human curiosity guaranteed the march of science and technology, thus liberating us for more fruitful endeavors. Fromm claimed that because people have creative powers and wide-ranging talents and curiosities, they naturally seek mutual and cooperative relations with each other.[20] The evolutionary endowments mentioned in chapter 3 fall within this group — endowments whose frustration is said to lead to social tragedy.[21] Others find something with causal force in the nature of society itself, Parsons holding that there is an immanent trend in our society toward the rationalization of functions, a trend whose failure can be explained only by motivated resistance. Keynes came close to suggesting that the power of compound interest would inexorably relieve humankind of grubbing for a living so that we could, in the end, devote our talents to living well. Many believe, with some evidence, that increasing the level of education in a society forces social change in desired directions, but others find in Western individualism the force that will inevitably cause the "fragmentation" of society[22] with some of the dysfunctional features I have been examining. Is there anything here to indicate the movement of society toward more companionate forms?

The many failures of predictions based on so-called inevitable forces are cautions against placing too much reliance on this line of argument — as in capitalism's immanent trends for its self-destruction:

> "The more people accept the neoclassical paradigm as a guide for their behavior, the more the ability to sustain a market economy is undermined." (Etzioni)[23]

> "[Capitalism] exhibits a pronounced proclivity toward undermining the moral foundations on which any society, including the capitalist variety, must rest." (Hirsch)[24]

> "Capitalist motivation and standards have all but wilted away. The inference as to the transition to a socialist regime in such fullness of time is obvious." (Schumpeter)[25]

> "What the bourgeoisie, therefore, produces above all are its own gravediggers." (Marx and Engels)[26]

Given the thriving economic success of the U.S. version of individualist capitalism at the end of the twentieth century, there is an anachronistic quality to these accounts of capitalism's tendency to destroy itself. It is the theories of immanence and not capitalism that seem to destroy themselves. But the logic of institutions mentioned above may take us a little way toward understanding the direction of change. The idea of market equilibrium employs just such reasoning. Is there, then, something immanent in market forces that leads to unhappiness and depression in postindustrial societies — and then leads to their cures? (Or does the market generate its antithesis ready, at the appropriate time, to replace it?) And, second, do democracies offer some agency for repairing market damage? Or must they inevitably ignore all symptoms of dysphoria that cannot easily be aggregated in party programs or interest group agendas?

On the question about the market, the tentative answer is that it contains nothing within its incentive structure to ameliorate its hedonic failure, for, as we saw in chapters 9 and 10, the things that contribute most to SWB (family integrity, warm friendships, intrinsic work enjoyment) are externalities to markets. This deprives markets of any self-correcting tendencies. Let me emphasize once again that this pathology was not true of market economies for most of their existence when material welfare contributed more than did companionship to SWB. Over this period the commonsensical (though anti-Smithian) identification of economic welfare with SWB was right — and the justification of markets as the means for maximizing outcome utility was also right. It is not, therefore, the fault of the economists (except for their stubborn insularity) that their paradigm for (outcome) utility maximization should fail. They have done their work well, and the world, changed for the better because of that work, has moved on. "The end of history" is not the triumph of the market[27] but only the end of a particular history of one paradigm—and perhaps the beginning of the next.[28] The problem is to transcend the market culture, a leap for which there are few guides: of the three commonly mentioned, Marx, Freud, and Darwin, only Darwin remains.

The second question, asking whether the immanent features of democracy must inevitably ignore diffuse pain in the society, has a different kind of answer. Immanence lodges in systems, and, fortunately, democracy is not so coherent a system as are markets: equilibrium is more metaphorical; the tendencies of a political system to return to a norm when dislodged a degree or two from that norm cannot be counted on; even conceptually we do not speak of a perfect democracy as economists speak of a perfect market. Because the ends of democracy are plural, democratic theorists must optimize rather than maximize (in both systems, people actually satisfice). Unlike the market theory of justice, which says that whatever the perfect market decides is ipso facto the right distribution,[29] distributive justice in democracy is by no means defined by the processes which produce a distribution. For these reasons—and the failure of political demand to identify the most powerful sources of unhappiness—there is nothing immanent in a democratic system that serves to optimize well-being—or to prevent it.

Like all major transitions, the proposed transition will be painful, although, like the transition from agricultural to industrial society, that from an emphasis on the maximization of income to the enjoyment of companionship has a shared value: well-being in this world. Society has witnessed such pain before: rapid transitions to modernity in Micronesia and among African Americans leaving the rural South greatly increased the suicide rates in both cases.[30] And there is too much invested in intellectual and material property in the economistic system to hope for an easy birth.

What Will We Gain? What Will We Lose?

What we gain by shifting our goal from income to companionship is, of course, some relief from depression and from unhappiness. But there is more, because happiness and SWB lead, in turn, to many other benefits.

THE COSTS OF UNHAPPINESS AND DEPRESSION

Recall the summary account in chapter 13: positive moods "bring out our better nature," improve creativity and productive thinking, increase cooperativeness and generosity, improve health, and facilitate "personal growth."[31] Happy people make friends more easily than others, and the friends, in turn, make people more happy. A positive change in mood seems to decrease ethnic prejudice. (In contrast, bad moods impair people's judgments, leading them to self-defeating acts and high-risk behavior.)[32] Life satisfaction increases support for democratic government and decreases support for antidemocratic movements. Democracy, I said in chapter 13, is for happy people. On balance, good moods lead people to behaviors and sometimes to thoughts that are clearly beneficial to democratic society and to the happy person's family and associates. Any loss of these benefits is a substantial cost to advanced market democracies.

As one would expect, clinical depression, as contrasted to "mere" unhappiness, is even more costly (chapter 2). Not the least of these costs are those borne by the children of the depressed, who are more likely not only to suffer a disproportionate number of physical injuries,[33] but also, as adults, to be mentally disturbed. At work, coworkers enjoy their work less if they associate with depressed persons, and at school depressed students upset their friends—and often stimulate hostility to themselves.[34] Depressed persons also do less well in their studies than matched others who are not depressed. Like the effect of unhappiness on judgment, the effect of depression on judgment is severe,[35] incurring further costs at school and at work.

There are other behavioral costs: for example, depressed people are less capable of autonomous behavior than normals;[36] depressed children are more likely than normals to blame themselves for failure,[37] thus creating a malign cycle of pain and debilitation. Alcoholics who are also depressed engage in more fights and disturbances of the peace than alcoholics without depressive symptoms,[38] and, in the complex causal tangle of depression and alcoholism and drug dependency, depression has been found to be a contributing causal factor in both these unhappy addictions.[39] The quality of life of the depressed and of their associates and their children is, indeed, greatly reduced.

And there are, of course, substantial economic costs. An American study found that the mildly depressed have one and a half times the number of disability days as normal people, and the severely depressed have five times as many lost days as the mildly depressed,[40] an escalating curve. For a variety of reasons, including early death from heart attack[41] and especially from suicide, the depressed and the unhappy are likely to have shorter lives than others.[42]

It is enough that unhappiness and depression subtract from the quality of life and mock the idea of the good society, but we find also that they make people less cooperative, less good companions, less adequate parents, and less productive workers and that they drain the resources of the societies in which they live. If going from the money standard to the companionship standard reduced these human and financial costs, we would all be better off.

THE COSTS OF A SECOND RELATIONAL BEND IN HISTORY

If we sought to alter priorities so as to increase companionship even at the risk of reducing income, what, aside from the now-discounted pleasures of foregone commodities whose comparative yield in happiness has been shown to be low, would we lose in the process? The greatest loss, in my opinion, *might* be erosion of the belief that people control their own fates. Looking at the history of gemeinschaft and some of the current practices of collectivist societies of Asia, it seems that immersion in solidary groups, whether family or community or close networks of friends, tends to collectivize responsibility for an individual's outcomes. I have cited studies (see chapter 13) showing that there are two main, partially independent routes to well-being: developing a high sense of personal control and enjoying the security and warmth of companionship. In the collectivist societies, the first seems to be sacrificed to the second. But this disjunctive treatment is wrong.

In stressful situations people feel more in control of their destinies when they know they have social support,[43] that is, the normal additive relation among satisfactions is restored, a relation in which satisfaction in one domain cumulatively adds to satisfaction in other domains to predict well-being. And, second, people can achieve a feeling that they collectively control their destinies jointly with their families and friends, as among the Japanese.[44] At least one of the benefits of individualism can be found in modified form within collectivist societies. In any event, Westerners have exaggerated the degree to which people can control their destinies. I am not dismissing the criticism but only modifying it. I would be distressed if, for example, the idea of individual, as contrasted to collective, responsibility for a person's own acts were jeopardized; any drift toward guilt by association would be a genuine loss.

Justice. As noted in the discussion of companionate democracy, the costs of familism in society are high. The cost to justice and the sense of justice goes beyond the risk of loss of one's responsibility for one's own acts. For example, in Asian economies the chief executive officer of a firm is often a confidant and personal adviser to an employee. Good, the employee has a friend in power. But friendship of this kind risks partiality, and a sense of being fairly treated contributes substantially to life satisfaction, ranking fourth in one of Andrews and Withey's accounts.[45] As mentioned in chapter 14, applying particularistic norms of family justice to firms violates the logic of universalistic norms of justice that most ethicists endorse.

Justice in the larger society as well as in the firm is a problem for familistic cultures, as Yun-shik Chang's comments on the difficulty of developing an impersonal rule of law in a collectivist society illustrate.[46] In gemeinschaft as in individualistic gesellschaft, the very nature of judicial functions implies conflict between particularistic standards of a society and universalistic standards of justice.[47] Furthermore, when the onerous duties of governing and regulating behavior fall on the community and the family, the incompatibility of these duties may well erode affection as well as fairness.

Equality. Equality is often thought to be more characteristic of families than of societies (see chapter 15), but even in collectivist cultures equality within the family varies greatly: the Taiwanese family is relatively egalitarian but the South Korean family is patriarchal. And, as Peter Laslett remarks about the gemeinschaft we have lost, along with the mutual affection there are perils: "The worst tyrants among human beings . . . are jealous husbands . . . resentful wives, [and] possessive parents . . . [in] a scene of hatred."[48] Moreover, equal treatment of strangers and of group members is learned with difficulty in collectivist societies; it is more easily learned in market circumstances, as Robert Redfield observed when the Mayan village of Chan Kom converted to market crops.[49]

Cosmopolitanism. Tolerance toward differences, or cosmopolitanism, is also hindered by gemeinschaft's emphasis on ties of blood and place, ties that are broken by the strangeness of strangers.

Freedom of thought. Thought and action are probably less free in families than in societies, as suggested by Richard Sennett's work entitled "The Tyranny of Intimacy." Lewis Coser describes how household servants in nineteenth-century England welcomed the industrial discipline as a source of release from the more confining and unremitting (twenty-four hours a day) discipline of household duties.[50] Similarly, Edward Shorter describes how youth in nineteenth-century France fled the villages and the close surveillance they were under to work in the growing factories, where, in such spare time as they were allowed, they at least could be free of that surveillance.[51] Freedom for the thought we hate is uncongenial to familistic cultures. It is decreasingly true that the developed Asian collectivist societies are unfree or intolerant of heterodoxy, but their consensualism makes heterodoxy, especially in groups like families and small communities, a little less prevalent.

The enumeration of these costs of collectivist, affectionate patterns seems to imply an inevitability or immanence to the costs. But one must be cautious. Just as "the logic of collective action" can be overcome by rather small changes in publicizing behavior and assigning responsibility,[52] so the moral logic of collectivism can be overcome by the instituting of specific steps to create a counterlogic, a set of incentives whereby outsiders are treated with the same consideration given to insiders (the Muslim code for guests), heterodoxy is protected by group norms (as in sometimes incestuous schools of thought in academia), and professional codes restrain those in authority from favoring friends (as in the judicial profession). The self-reinforcing logic of "amoral familism" in southern Italy's peasant village of Montegrano[53] is easily matched by the "amoral individualism" currently at the forefront of some analyses in the West.[54] The roster of losses from familism merely cites risks against which countermeasures must be devised. My idea of a companionable society is not a formula for the good society, but rather a direction in which our individualistic societies should move to arrest their current decline in well-being.

INSTITUTIONAL COSTS

Like changes of beliefs in systems of ideas, changes in goals in a social system threaten a kind of social dissonance. (The pain of linking liked objects with disliked qualities: for example, my friend is a thief.)[55] As anthropologists know all too well, you cannot change just one thing. If one increasingly seeks companionship in place of greater income, what happens to the market (and not just market theory analyzed above) that brought us here? What happens to the way democracy works?

At first glance, the market is an anachronism in a world governed by the need for affiliation: in addition to the loss of equilibrating market mechanisms mentioned, the relation of supply of labor to demand for labor is problematic. When leisure for companionship becomes more highly prized than income from work, the labor supply curve slopes backward, as in the case of certain African communities in which increases in wages reduce the supply of labor. But there is an endogenous limit to this market erosion: because the replacement of the drive for income by the drive for solidary families and friends is contingent on a high level of income, any major reduction of income would seem to thrust us back to an income level at which the desire for more income again becomes dominant; that is, a cyclical movement develops whereby societies move from income scarcity to companionship scarcity and back again. Income maintenance is a condition for the full satisfaction of people's evident need for companionship — and this requires a successful market.

In the companionable society, the market is neither an anachronism nor a universal paradigm but rather a tool in a multipurpose society. And, as I have said, if the Asian collectivist societies can purge their economies of nepotism and cronyism (if this is not a contradiction), they may at least point in a direction which, bearing in mind the moral costs of gemeinschaft, offers a fragile signpost for our travels. Their lower rates of depression encourage us to believe that we have something to learn from Asia.

In chapter 14 I showed the tension between companionship and democracy. Does this imply that if we move to give companionship a higher priority compared to income that democracy itself would be threatened? We would ask the reverse question if we were a companionable society: might not a new emphasis on money corrupt our government—a worry, in fact, expressed by Tocqueville. In the event, money has corrupted democratic government, but no more in the individualist West than in the collectivist East. Corruption follows in the wake of any system that does not allocate its rewards according to universalistic roles and functions.

As for the analogous argument over erecting a wall between those areas in which ethics should dominate and those areas in which governmental purposes (defense as well as justice) properly dominate, I have always been skeptical of this kind of institutional protection,[56] preferring, instead, to rely on our capacities to compartmentalize our thoughts and create schemas in which ethical norms are definitionally associated with social and political concepts. Under temptation, the default values of these schemas then come to our rescue. But as we watch the Asian collectivist societies try to create schemas of meritocracy to replace cronyism, we appreciate how difficult cognitive solutions are when they require transcending a familiar culture.

By their very nature, democracies tend to respond to political demands—but not to needs. People need help, but democracies are not tuned to the voices of the unhappy, partly because private unhappiness does not aggregate and partly because unhappiness mutes these voices and inhibits participation—another malign minicycle to add to the malign cycles discussed in the previous chapter.

We know more about how well-being favors democracy than how democracy can or does favor well-being. Recall (chapter 15) Inglehart's research showing that "those nations characterized by high levels of life satisfaction, interpersonal trust, tolerance etc., would be likelier to adopt and maintain democratic institutions than those whose publics lacked such attitudes."[57] Does democracy contribute, in turn, to SWB? Political satisfaction has little effect on life satisfaction,[58] but that does not tell us much about how democracy fosters SWB. At the end of the next section I will suggest how democracies can lighten the shadows on the way home.

The Way Home

Perhaps Western societies are already on the way home. The economistic paradigm says we are traveling a road to ever greater wealth, a road made easier by our "spirit of rationality" (David Landes, Parsons). But it is an uncivic and almost autistic journey according to Robert Putnam's recent analysis of the effects of declining trust and withering participant norms, attributable, he says, to the effects of television.[59] But his theory needs sharp modification because of the rise of civic volunteering and the proliferation of small religious groups in the 1980s and 1990s (see chapter 7). What seems to have happened is that people, especially the young, have ceased joining formal organizations like the Girl Scouts and at the same time have increased their informal group membership and social action.[60] The deficit in companionship is mostly in family relations and the warmth of friendship. But perhaps help in the form of global shifts in values is on the way [61] — forces that defy Freud's claim that civilization itself makes us neurotic and Oswald Spengler's prophecy of the decline of the West.

THE ROAD WE ARE TRAVELING

Over the long haul represented by rising levels of economic and social development, new paradigms informed by new values claim to represent the future. For example, it seems that one can order world civilizations along two axes: (1) mode of authority — from traditional (priests, monarchs, and dictators) to secular-rational (democracies and bureaucracies) and (2) a value axis — from survival values (maximizing income and security) to well-being values (freedom and participation, humanistic ethics).[62] As might be expected, the richer and better educated nations (for example, those in Scandinavia and northern Europe) cluster in the well-being/secular-rational authority (northeast) quadrant. The United States is in this quadrant but is closer to the survival pole than are the northern European nations and more traditional than its wealth and educational levels would suggest. The well-being/secular-rational syndrome is called postmodernization: "In the postmodernization phase of development, emphasis shifts from maximizing economic gains — the central goal of modernization — to maximizing subjective well-being."[63] Good, but it is the traditional/survival cultures that treasure the family and the community, while postmodernizing cultures discount their value — an ominous, immiserating trend toward a relatively less happy future. The escape route from gemeinschaft has taken many wrong turnings, and postmodernization may be yet another one.[64] In any event, the United States is not traveling this route: interpersonal trust, characteristic of postmodernization and a condition for the companionate society we are seeking, has been declining in the United States (and in parts of Europe) for a quarter century.

In my opinion, the road the postmodernizing world is traveling will not lead to the increased well-being which Inglehart says is its destination. The discounting of family integrity and two-parent families by the postmodernizing nations (and, indeed, the postmaterialist syndrome) leaves an aching void in the pattern of things that comprise postmodernization. At least in our transitional period, all the evidence available suggests that a happy family life is the surest way to life satisfaction, while other evidence (see chapter 3) shows that delinquency, teenage suicide, child abuse, and other problems are demonstrably worse in families lacking a mother and a father. Moreover, the postmodernizing willingness to substitute sexual partnership without marriage for actual marriage is unpromising: "Those who live together before marriage have higher divorce rates, probably because they are self- and career-centered to begin with."[65] As also noted in chapter 3, in terms of their welfare and well-being, the current generation of children seems to be the first in a long time that is worse than that of their parents.[66] The happiness of postmoderns is both incomplete as far as they themselves are concerned and filled with tragic consequences for their children. The road Western societies are traveling is more lonely and less promising than that portrayed on Inglehart's postmodernizing road map.

CAN DEMOCRACY MAKE A DIFFERENCE?

I return to a question left unanswered above: Can democratic government improve well-being? The initial impression is that governments of any kind cannot do much, for, as mentioned, life satisfaction is forged in the microworlds of experience almost, but not quite, out of reach of governments. The strains of adjusting to demographic changes, globalization of markets, stress from rapid social change and its damaging stress-response, insecurity from obsolescence of skills, and even the "anomie of affluence" (Durkheim) all seem intractable to serious governmental intervention.

Then, too, there are the self-inspired forms of unhappiness that are difficult to modify through government action. Among these is the tendency to adapt to any change in circumstances that the government might promote: "Expectancies can outstrip reality even when an economy is growing rapidly—with a net loss in SWB." As a consequence, Diener and Suh, old hands in the study of SWB, recommend that the government use information on well-being only in the service of policies that have other justifications as well.[67] My purpose in this book is to diagnose the problem and not to offer remedies, but a few suggestions following Diener and Suh's caution come to mind.

In their analysis *The Social Causes of Psychological Distress,* Mirowski and Ross offer the following proven remedies: "(1) *education,* the headwaters of well-being; (2) *a good job:* providing an adequate income, a measure of autonomy, and a minimum of strain between the demands of work and family; and (3) *a supportive relationship:* fair and caring."[68] Most analysts find that education (and IQ) has only a minimal direct relationship to happiness and life satisfaction,[69] but Mirowski and Ross argue that education is related to intelligent problem solving and, not surprisingly, to finding and holding a good job, their second remedy. Others point out that, although above the poverty level income is almost irrelevant to SWB, education is a resource for finding and enjoying more enjoyable forms of leisure.[70] A large number of studies show that work satisfaction is related to life satisfaction (in a reciprocal manner),[71] and of course the absence of a job, unemployment, is a source of deep unhappiness. These two things, education and full employment are, indeed, amenable to government action.

But the third prescription, "a supportive relationship: fair and caring," representing the heart of my own thesis, is less sensitive to government action. Can the government do anything to preserve the integrity of the family? Perhaps, but the details are beyond my competence, except to say that any policy that (1) reduces the mobility of firms and individuals may help (the evidence is ambiguous), and (2) (again) policies that reduce unemployment—a source of intense family strain—are even more helpful. Redistribution of income is hedonically beneficial only when it reduces poverty—which also reduces mental illnesses of all kinds.

Mirowski and Ross's suggestions are really self-evident and require only that governments be willing to go beyond the prescriptions of economists and businesspeople—and, in truth, most people—to tolerate whatever reduction in economic growth may be required. As the experience with government promotion of self-esteem suggests,[72] governments cannot directly allocate or even foster the psychological components of SWB. Rather, the strategy must be to create life-frames, scaffolding supporting the microworlds of experience in a manner that protects those little worlds within which people can, mistaken as they may be, grow up without trauma, seek and find education, marry sensibly, enjoy their vocations, find and cherish their friends, achieve local respect, enjoy community life (in the communities that government can facilitate and protect), and pursue their dreams in peace. The American dream is about ever greater material possessions (and the status that they buy); the hard part for governments is to guide without coercing the content of these misaddressed dreams—a task of inspiration, not of Sorastro's sorcery. *Homo faber,* yes; *Homo consumens,* no—but where are *Homo ludens* and *Homo sapiens?*

Whence this inspiration? For culture change I turn to the originating agency of ideas (and ideologies), academia. Just as current economic teaching can make people less willing to give their money to group projects[73] and less willing to vote,[74] so, with a better theory of measured (and not just inferred) utility, divorcing decisional utility from outcome utility (see chapter 17), that magnificent apparatus of economic analysis might be turned to the purpose of improving well-being. It is not so much that economics should be more sensitive to ethical questions,[75] for ethical economics would probably concentrate on immediate justice at the expense of unfortunate long-term consequences like greater unemployment (a relation opaque to ethicists who lack models of economic cause and effect). Rather, economics should do what every other science does, specify a measurable criterion for the thing it is trying to explain and then maximize outcome utility and adjust its recommendations accordingly.

If political theorists could, for a moment, reduce their extended moralizing to make room for something as prosaic as well-being, their theories might influence lawyers and politicians to take into account the effects of policies on people's satisfaction with their lives. And if psychologists, biologists, and neuroscientists could join in seeking to understand how institutions influence pain and pleasure, we would be on our way home. Utilitarianism is the guiding philosophy of our time, but theories of what produces happiness have changed since Bentham. Both utilitarian philosophers and their critics speak in the language of the past. To be cheerful and happy, to have a sense that life is a satisfying undertaking is not enough. But if we understood how to bring these things about, we would have the beginning of a more humane science of the human enterprise.

Appendix. Measures of Well-Being and Depression

The purpose of this book is to give insight into the quality of life, especially its subjective components,[1] in market democracies, primarily the United States. In pursuing this purpose, I seek to do three things: (a) give empirical content to the utilitarian philosophy that dominates our thinking; (b) thus to modify the economic theory that reflects this utilitarian philosophy and the democratic theory that is informed by it; and (c) thereby to assess and also to improve the markets and democratic governments guided by these theories. How well do the measures of well-being and depression employed in this book serve these tasks?

Measures of Well-Being

In order to serve the purposes of a study, measures should accurately reflect the concepts they operationalize. Happiness is a mood (sometimes distinguished from an emotion, which has a more specific reference); it is affective. Because positive and negative affects are different from each other and not just obverses (they have different physiological sources), affect balance is often used in the literature to reflect the balance between these positive and negative feelings and emotions. To simplify the discussion and to connect with the utilitarian theories mentioned above, I have not used this concept or its measures here. A person's satisfaction with his or her life, taken as a whole, is more of a cognitive assessment, a judgment. Happiness and life satisfaction are related but sometimes assume different values; subjective well-being (SWB) refers to either (or both) happiness and life satisfaction (and may include affect balance, as well). Where I do not refer to SWB, with some license I have used the literary and philosophical term *happiness* to embrace these concepts and again to make connection with the looser traditions of utilitarianism and other political-economic doctrines.

As we shall see, each of the measures employed is flawed, sometimes seriously, sometimes in ways that only psychometricians will notice (for example, the number of response categories to questions on happiness is so few that much information is lost). These measures are employed because, in my opinion, they are better than the alternatives, principally to assume utility because a choice corresponds to a person's preference ordering or because a person chooses something a second time, or, alternatively, to beg the question by assuming that, say, level of income is a measure of well-being or that an increase in income increases levels of well-being. If the use of flawed measures is poor science, the use of assumptions without evidence or even the possibility of evidence is not science at all. Still, scientism, the pretense of science, a practice that gives the illusion of knowledge and therefore positively misleads may be still worse. For all their flaws, studies of SWB have not been accused of this defect. Rather, the questions about these studies are the usual ones: Are their findings reliable? Are they valid?

RELIABILITY

Questions asking whether respondents or subjects are happy and/or asking if respondents are more or less satisfied with their lives have been asked repeatedly, sometimes in panel studies in which the same subjects are asked the question more than once. Over time, of course, one would expect life events to change the happiness (or other measure of SWB) of some, but some lack of reliability is genuinely due to poor measurement. For example, in Campbell et al.'s study *The Quality of American Life,* after an eight-month period a retest of an "Index of Well-Being" found the reliability was only .53. Some of this variation is due to measurement error and some to genuine changed mood, but some of it is due to unreliability.[2] On the other hand, Headey and Wearing found that over a six-year period,[3] the reliability of their measures was an impressive .92 (higher for positive affect than negative affect), and the Oxford Happiness Inventory showed a reliability of .78 for a seven-week period and .67 for a five-month retest.[4] If a person is asked the same question at the beginning and end of an interview, no event other than the interview itself could affect the answers. Andrews and Withey sorted through a variety of tests in their massive surveys and decided that the single question (asked twice), "How do you feel about your life as a whole?" (scored "delighted" to "terrible") was the most informative of all the tests. They found that the scores from this repeated question gave them their standard criterial value.[5] Looking at the variation in several general surveys specifically addressed to the more variable question of happiness and comparing their variability with known invariant attitudes, Tom Smith reports that "happiness shows a high enough level of temporal stability to indicate that it is being meaningfully and consistently understood by respondents."[6]

Cutting across these questions of reliability is a more general substantive issue: Is what is being measured a trait, something that is persistent across situations, or a state, a mood or attitude that is the product of a specific situation? If the latter, low reliability is simply a matter of volatile moods; if the former, then the problem of reliability is genuine. Both traits and states are of interest, but for purposes of assessing quality of life, the more enduring trait is more relevant. In spite of Campbell et al.'s finding, most studies find that both happiness and life satisfaction are surprisingly persistent traits: across time, as in Headey and Wearing's Australian panel study over a six-year period,[7] and across situations, as in a study comparing the mood of a sample of persons at work and at leisure.[8] Although such ephemeral events as the day's weather and the fate of one's favorite football team make a difference in mood, people's moods and assessments of their lives cannot be dismissed as fleeting products of momentary emotion. Finally, single questions on happiness or life satisfaction in surveys are notoriously less reliable than are scales or multiple question syndromes. The answers to that criticism cannot rely on methodological criteria but must rely on testing experience. Here, the overwhelming experience of students of SWB is that the pattern is sensible.

VALIDITY

To say that responses are invalid means that people's answers do not reflect their true, authentic, ego-syntonic feelings. They may fail in this way for a variety of reasons:

1. People have no sense of their happiness or have never thought about whether their life is satisfying or not, that is, the questions have no meaning for them. Veenhoven, the Dutch archivist and analyst of measures of well-being, points out that the answers to simple questions on happiness and life satisfaction are prompt, and, like Andrews and Withey, he finds that people have usually given considerable thought to these issues.[9] In no study of Western individualist societies are there more than 1 or 2 percent "don't know" responses. But in collectivist or interdependent cultures: "If necessary, individuals are expected to subordinate their personal feelings and wishes to the goals of their in-group [and] . . . . individuals' thoughts and feelings acquire full meaning only in reference to the thoughts and feelings of others who are crucially important in the very definition of the self."[10] Not Kantian authenticity and autonomy, but heteronomy and harmony with others is the standard. As a consequence, questions about SWB take on a very different meaning or are essentially meaningless for respondents in collectivist societies. Nevertheless, based on within-nation and between-nation measures, Diener and Suh conclude that "the analyses of nation means is justified . . . based on the fact that certain factors have some influence on the majority of people within a nation."[11]
2. People have feelings of happiness and unhappiness and thoughts about the nature of their lives, but they can't get at them; they have no access to their inner emotions. This is a theme mentioned in chapter 16 emphasizing the difficulty

people may have in interpreting their feelings, the arcane promptings of their limbic systems and hypothalamuses. As also mentioned in chapter 16, this is apparently rare. Ready responses from respondents suggest that people know and understand the references to feelings of happiness and unhappiness, and the current research on how people can and do monitor and sum their (bottom-up) feelings of well-being seems to take care of this concern moderately well.[12]

3. A mood generalized from prior questions in a survey (or other contaminating stimuli) can influence responses; that is, people are then really responding to a particular series of questions and would (or do) respond differently when the order of questions is changed. For example, responses to a standard question on happiness in National Opinion Research Center surveys were regularly higher than responses to the same question in the National Election Studies surveys. The reason was that the NORC question was embedded in a series on family life with more favorable connotations than was the question context of the NEC question.[13] The point is more general: people's sense of well-being and particularly of life satisfaction is influenced by a set of stimuli of which the question on mood or life satisfaction is only one. For example, in experiments people's references can be changed by prior requests to think of happy events or sad events in their lives. We already know this from "the availability heuristic," which says that what is immediately available to consciousness colors attitudes. Although in their survey of methodological problems, Diener and Suh say that "measures of SWB are often not strongly influenced by people's current moods,"[14] in fact, they frequently are, as when a prior question on dating experiences increased reported levels of well-being.[15]

   One answer to this problem holds that in a national sample these prior influences largely cancel out. Because the influences that affect moods must be immediate, vivid, and personal, national events affecting large numbers of a population have only moderate effects. For example, as the authors of a study of public responses to the Cuban missile crisis of October 1961 observed, "When people assess their happiness they are more likely to be thinking of their personal successes and failures — the status of their married life and work life — than of events in the world community."[16] (A method for avoiding some of the problems of the test situation is to provide respondents with pagers and to ask them to record their answers when paged at random intervals.)

4. People are influenced by one or more of the many biases that devil all social judgments: the positivity bias (in the midst of misery, looking on the bright side), ambivalence (torn, perhaps chronically, between conflicting emotions or beliefs), dissonance repair (making all liked things go together and dissociating them from all disliked things), and ideological bias such that one is ("must be") happy when the ideologically "correct" outcome is implied. Some reassurance that these and other biases in self-reports of moods and life satisfaction are not damaging the validity of the responses is given by comparing self-reports to those of independent assessors: family, friends, teachers, and others who know the re-

spondent well—and of their interviewers. People who say they are happy smile more often than unhappy people.[17] Self-reported well-being is correlated with other feelings and thoughts that, intuitively, one would expect to be part of a well-being syndrome: self-esteem, sense of personal control, and optimism about their futures.[18] In my opinion, these measures independent of the respondent's self-report give strong support to the validity of self-reports.

5. One particular source of inauthenticity is troublesome: People give answers that they believe are more socially desirable than the true, authentic answers would be. As mentioned above, this is the norm in collectivist cultures, but it also occurs in individualist societies, as pointed out in chapter 16. Although Veenhoven has information suggesting that responses to questions on well-being are relatively free from contamination by social desirability (both from clinical reports and from the zero correlation between measures of well-being and a European "value hedonism scale"),[19] Diener and Suh report studies showing that young people report themselves happier and less depressed to interviewers than they do in self-administered tests.[20] Kant's detested heteronomy is a persistent problem, even within individualist cultures, where it is resisted by beliefs that people ought to know their own state of well-being without referring to a socially desirable response. But the next point, heavily supported by research, is an antidote to some of the problems of social desirability and other artifactual contaminants.
6. The search for inauthentic responses to self-reported well-being is frustrated by people's habitual adaptation both to adversity and to good luck and other favorable circumstances: "Because of biologically determined 'set-points' of reactivity to stimuli, people's reward and punishment systems adapt to the positive or negative stimuli, and the individual thereafter returns to his or her baseline of SWB."[21]

I have, of course, only touched on a few of the many measurement problems of self-reported accounts of well-being, but one thing is clear: these problems do not go unnoticed by empiricists blind to the flaws of what they are reporting. Both substantive critics and psychometricians within the ranks of students of well-being are far more effective critics than is the skeptical lay public, especially those comfortably lodged in the philosophical utilitarian tradition.

Measurements of Depression

Measures of depression raise even more questions than do measures of SWB, partly because people remember the time when psychiatry was dominated by the dramatic conflict among its three main characters, id, ego, and superego—but with only anecdotal evidence. Modern psychiatry has more or less repudiated this colorful past and, for purposes of epidemiology, employed specialists trained in disciplines with greater measurement sophistication. With Vienna almost forgotten (except in France), there is now a huge modern literature published in more than a hundred journals around the world on defining and measuring mental illnesses. I can do no more than offer brief, often inadequate answers to the many legitimate questions addressed to this literature. Referring back as necessary to the treatment in chapter 2, I shall divide this discussion into three parts: (1) the quality of the main measures of depression; (2) supporting and alternative measures of depression; and (3) most important for the idea of a rising tide of depression, assessment of evidence on the changing incidence and prevalence of depression.

Recall (see chapter 2) that we are dealing with illnesses that are estimated to strike from a fifth to a third of the U.S. population over the course of their lives, that seem to be increasing among children, and are most prevalent among adolescents and young adults, whose youthful illnesses predict probable later adult illnesses. Of mental illness in general, one source estimated that one-half of the U.S. population would experience at least a moderate form of psychiatric illness over their lifetimes.[22]

THE MEASUREMENT CONSTRUCT OF DEPRESSION

In a recent talk to a select audience of scholars, I was asked how it was possible to say that depression had increased over recent decades when only recently psychiatrists were talking about melancholia. It is not like that. In the early 1960s, two massive epidemiological studies of mental illness, one of midtown Manhattan and the other of Stirling County in Nova Scotia, used diagnoses of depression that mirror but are looser than contemporary usages.[23] Reporting in 1978 on the usages of the previous decade, the President's Commission on Mental Health never referred to melancholia but rather divided depression into two main kinds, "endogenous" (largely genetic) and "reactive" (produced by negative experiences).[24] Recognizing that verbal descriptions are inadequate for epidemiological and diagnostic uses, the American Psychiatric Association developed the kind of tests described in chapter 2: DSM-III, then revised (the one described), and most recently DSM-IV.[25]

There are problems with these tests. One fundamental criticism of the very way in which the concepts as well as the tests are devised argues that they use a Platonic epistemology: if there is a term, *depression,* there must be attributes to go with the term. Rather, say the sociologists Mirowski and Ross, one should first see what attributes are related to each other and give the cluster an appropriate name.[26] This is, indeed, what these authors do. Their clusters include most of those captured by DSM-III plus such others as alienation and authoritarianism (more as cause than a symptom). In my opinion, Mirowski and Ross have exciting results, but they do not easily connect with the concept of depression in an extensive literature. Other critics, in this case of the latest version of the standard test, DSM-IV, find it less conceptually crisp and more confusing than the tests it replaces.[27] I cannot evaluate these criticisms but offer this kind of evidence to show that methodological problems are taken very seriously by current epidemiological psychiatrists.

One special criticism seems to me germane: the tests following the DSM criteria are scored by the number of depression symptoms a patient has: one must have four of the eight symptoms to qualify for diagnosis of major depression; a lower score qualifies a person for the diagnosis of "dysphoria."[28] Thus, the measure is not a

(Guttman) scale such that any given score indicates just exactly what symptoms a person may have. For example, if listlessness counts as one and eating disorders also count as one but the two symptoms have different implications for future illness, then their equal scores are misleading. (For therapeutic purposes, of course, subcategories have been developed.)

Grounds for confidence in diagnosis and measurement come from much detailed work on three components of depressive illnesses. For example, worthlessness (low self-esteem) has been repeatedly found to be associated with other symptoms of depression.[29] So also have hopelessness[30] and helplessness.[31] In that sense, the depression construct has been validated and elaborated.

A major problem in psychiatric diagnoses and testing is the differentiation of various related mental illnesses. Comorbidity studies are used to test the relations among diseases.[32] How, for example, do anxiety, panic disorders and phobias relate to depressive illnesses? A German study, for example, reported that many individuals have both relatively high levels of happiness and relatively high levels of anxiety and worry.[33] Symptoms of various illnesses can thus coexist but be conceptually quite different. Special studies on the relations among these and other mental disorders again give reassurance that the depression construct is not a catchall for indiscriminate diagnoses of mental illnesses.[34] There is, therefore, reason to believe that psychiatry has joined the scientific community.

Finally, as in the case of SWB, one must be reassured that measures of depressive illness are reliable. One study showed that over a four-year period, "reliability of lifetime prevalence of major depression was excellent," better than that of other disorders measured (and apparently better than that of SWB reported above). Nor did this high reliability vary with sex or age.[35] Such high reliability will be an important consideration when I turn below to the analysis of changing incidence of depression.

OTHER TESTS AND CROSS-NATIONAL EVIDENCE

Relation of Low SWB to Depression

By definition, the dysphoria of depression is a measure of low SWB or unhappiness and low life satisfaction. At a crude level, the coincident decline of happiness and the rise of depression confirm this definitional relation. But the number of people reporting themselves as unhappy is smaller than the number identified as depressed and dysphoric in the epidemiological studies. This apparent anomaly has been explained by Ed Diener as the product of a tendency for people who are very happy at one time also to be very unhappy or depressed at another time: intensity of positive and negative emotions covary.[36] In any event, many studies find that both unhappiness and low life satisfaction are closely correlated with depression.[37] Thus, in one study measures of depression were the strongest predictors of SWB,[38] and in another depressive symptoms were very closely correlated with low life satisfaction.[39] In their classic study of depression in a London suburb, Brown and Harris report "a large overlap between our psychiatric categories and more traditional notions of happiness and dissatisfaction."[40]

If, however, measures of SWB and of depression conflict, I am inclined to believe the depression studies. The medical interviews are more thorough and less vulnerable to the kinds of artifactual contamination, such as adaptation to changing standards, discussed in connection with SWB. The ideas that the self is worthless, the world is meaningless, and the future hopeless are not to be changed by recent small victories—which, in any event, the depressed see as accidental and transient.[41] When physicians rely on *self*-reports of well-being they are often deceived.[42]

Depressive Symptoms Tested by Different Measures

Verbal, behavioral, and physiological measures tend to corroborate the psychiatric DSM series. For example, on a semantic differential test, depressed persons "rated all concepts significantly less potent, less active, and less evaluatively positive as compared to their nondepressed peers."[43] Behavioral measures include both suicide and attempts at suicide (as well as suicidal ideation), all of which are closely related to depression, as the definition of depression would predict.[44] Both brain waves and certain neurotransmitters (dopamine and noradrenaline) vary by level of depression.[45] The point is that depression is a disease with somatic indicators that can supplement and help to verify other forms of measurement.

Cross-Cultural Verification

As one might expect from the cross-cultural evidence of SWB, the meaning of depression and its symptomology do vary somewhat across cultures. In collectivist countries, where access to inner life has been found to be somewhat attenuated, depression is associated with environmental forces. For example, in describing their depressed feelings the Japanese use external referent words like "dark," "cloudy," "rain," while people in the United States use internal referents such as "sadness," "despair," and "loneliness."[46] The symptoms in Africa reflect more motor retardation than in the West, which, in contrast, reveals more evidence of guilt and self-blame. Depression among aboriginal peoples in both Australia and the United States is more associated with alcoholism, but otherwise quite similar.[47] As a disease requiring victims to account, at least to themselves, for their feelings, depressive symptoms must inevitably reflect the culture which is the source of these accounts. What is surprising, therefore, is that in four cultures (Canada, Iran, Japan, and Switzerland) the reported symptoms and etiology of depression have been found to be very similar.[48]

Other reasons for giving credence to the studies of depression are (1) the studies of depression do not rely on visits to therapists (which are contaminated by self-selection) but rather on massive surveys of the general public; (2) physical symptoms (fatigue, eating disorders), which are less vulnerable to so-called fashionable illnesses, support the diagnoses; (3) studies of children, who are less aware of what they "should" report, also support the diagnoses; and (4) instead of an overcount of cases of depression, there may well be an undercount owing to the prevalence of "masked depression."[49]

THE RISING TIDE OF DEPRESSION

The most controversial part of my analysis is the report of a rising tide of depression in the advanced and advancing countries of the globe. One reason why this trend is questionable is that the evidence requires baseline assessments that are not widely available prior to the creation of the DSM measures. Astonishingly, aside from the estimates and partial trends in the nine-nation survey of the Cross-National Collaborative Group (1996), summary data for the rising tide of depression are hard to find—at least (at my request in 1996) a supremely well qualified source found none in a search of the literature. That is, it is not enough to report that "people born after 1945 were 10 times more likely to suffer from depression than people born 50 years earlier,"[50] for that could be a cohort difference that did not reflect a general increase in depression. Are there reasons to think that whole populations are now more vulnerable to depression than they were, say, thirty years ago?

In a careful review of evidence of an increase in depression the *Harvard Mental Health Letter* (1994) reports,

> Twelve independent studies covering 43,000 people in several countries have found an overall rise in the rate of depression during the twentieth century, both for people born in each succesive five- or ten-year period and for the general population in each successive decade. The recent National Comorbidity Survey of more than 8,000 people aged 15 to 54 found a lifetime rate of 17% for major depression (21% among women and 13% among men) and a rate of 5% when people were asked whether they had been depressed in the previous month.[51]

The authors of this report then take up the various objections raised to these findings: changes in diagnoses partly due to the availability of new cures, failure of recall, age-related differences in willingness to report symptoms of depression, and selective mortality (the depressed in earlier periods died younger). They conclude, "Most experts do not believe these potential biases fully explain the findings."[52] Nevertheless, questions remain.

Rates of adult suicide (which have recently increased)[53] do not fully track reports of rising depression, and, in any event, suicides are more prevalent among males, whereas depression is more prevalent among females (an imbalance which, however, is changing). But suicide is a poor social indicator of depression, for it occurs in only a small proportion of the depressed and dysphoric population and, in fact, occurs more frequently in countries which, on other measures of well-being, rank rather high.[54] Nevertheless, the rising tide hypothesis is supported by evidence of increasing suicide attempts and of teenage suicides (the latter increasing in the United States by 40 percent from 1970 to 1990 and by similar amounts in other advanced countries).[55]

Longitudinal studies limited to single countries are also supportive. A Swedish study (1982) finds "an overall increase in depression during the last 15 years of the studies, and a 10-fold increase of depressive disorders with severe and medium impairment among men 20–39 years old."[56] A similar study in Greece also found evidence of increasing depressive symptoms.[57] The rise of depression among adolescents and young adults in the United States finds solid support.[58] And the idea that it is the advanced and not the less-developed countries or the collectivist countries of Asia that bear the brunt of this epidemic has been fairly well established.[59]

Depression studies also find support in other evidence. If the cause of the findings were a greater openness about psychological problems, there would have been as great an increase in phobic symptoms as of depression, but phobic symptoms did not increase. Although to some extent the measures of depression rely upon recall of depression earlier in life, as mentioned above, the reliability of self-reports of depressive episodes over a four-year period has been demonstrated in careful retests of depression assessments.[60] Weissman agrees that more accurate diagnoses might play a small part in explaining the rise of depressive illness,[61] but use of the same measure over time should relieve the longitudinal studies, at least, from contamination by the use of changing criteria. In any event, bipolar depression, used as a benchmark, is one of the least ambiguous psychiatric classifications, and this form of depression did not increase. In addition, some physiological changes seem to be ruled out. Martin Seligman holds that the data do not suggest a gene-environment interaction but rather "points to a purely environmental effect"[62]—including social environmental effects on alcohol and drug abuse. Together, these independent studies using different measures on widely differing populations come to the same conclusion: major depression and dysphoria have increased over the past few decades and will probably continue to increase.

Notes

Chapter 1. Shadow on the Land

1. Tjalling C. Koopmans. 1957. *Three Essays on the State of Economic Science.* New York: McGraw-Hill, 159

2. Ed Diener and Carol Diener. 1996. "Most People Are Happy." *Psychological Science* 7: 181–85.

3. Little pleads with welfare economics to say "happiness," when that is what they mean. I. M. D. Little. 1957. *A Critique of Welfare Economics,* 2d ed. Oxford: Oxford University Press.

4. Adam Smith. 1976 [1759]. *The Theory of Moral Sentiments,* ed. D. D. Rafael and A. L. Macfie. Oxford, Clarendon, 50.

5. Theodore Zeldin. 1995. *An Intimate History of Humanity.* London: Minerva, 61.

6. Ed Diener and Marissa Diener. 1995. "Cross-Cultural Correlates of Life Satisfaction and Self-Esteem." *Journal of Personality and Social Psychology* 68: 653–63.

7. Tocqueville, speaking of the effects of equality, said, "To these causes must be attributed that strange melancholy which often haunts the inhabitants of democratic countries in the midst of their abundance, and that disgust of life which sometimes seizes upon them in the midst of calm and easy circumstances." Alexis de Tocqueville. 1945. *Democracy in America,* Phillips Bradley, ed., vol. 1. New York: Knopf, 139. See also David M. Potter. 1954. *People of Plenty: Economic Abundance and the American Character.* Chicago: University of Chicago Press.

8. Ruut Veenhoven. 1993. *Happiness in Nations.* Erasmus University, Center for Socio-Cultural Transformation, RISBO Rotterdam, 76

9. A. L. Kroeber. 1944. *Configurations of Culture Growth*. Berkeley: University of California Press.

10. Francis Fukuyama. 1993. *The End of History and the Last Man*. New York: Avon.

Chapter 2. Unhappiness in Our Time

1. Sigmund Freud. 1930. *Civilization and its Discontents*. London: Hogarth, 141.

2. Erich Fromm. 1955. *The Sane Society*. New York: Rinehart, 102.

3. Jeremy Bentham. 1830. "The Rationale of Punishment." In W. Stark, ed. 1954. *Jeremy Bentham's Economic Writings*, vol. 3. London: Royal Economic Society for George Allen and Unwin, 254–55 at 437–38.

4. Albert O. Hirschman. 1982. *Shifting Involvements: Private Interest and Public Action*. Princeton: Princeton University Press.

5. Robert E. Lane. 1991. *The Market Experience*. New York: Cambridge University Press, 327–423.

6. Daniel Kahneman, Ed Diener, and Norbert Schwarz, eds. 1999. *Foundations of Hedonic Psychology: Scientific Perspectives on Enjoyment and Suffering*. New York: Russell Sage Foundation.

7. Frank M. Andrews and Stephen B. Withey. 1976. *Social Indicators of Well-Being: Americans' Perceptions of Life Quality*. New York: Plenum, 12.

8. John Stuart Mill. 1910 [1861]. *Utilitarianism*, in *Utilitarianism, Liberty, and Representative Government*. London: Dent, 12.

9. Jonathan Freedman. 1980. *Happy People*. New York: Harcourt, Brace, 30, 31–32.

10. Ibid, 31–32.

11. These are the criteria of well-being set forth in Partha Dasgupta. 1993. *An Inquiry into Well-Being and Destitution*. Oxford: Oxford University Press.

12. Ed Diener. 1984. "Subjective Well-Being." *Psychological Bulletin* 95: 542–75 at 555; Alex C. Michalos. 1986. "Job Satisfaction, Marital Satisfaction, and the Quality of Life: A Review and a Preview." In Frank M. Andrews, ed., *Research on the Quality of Life*. Ann Arbor: Institute for Social Research, 62.

13. Michael Argyle. 1993 [1987]. *The Psychology of Happiness*. London: Routledge; Lane, *The Market Experience*, chap. 26; Jonathan Freedman says, "Money matters a great deal to those who do not have enough to live on, but otherwise it is not very important. The rich are not likely to be happier than middle-income people." Freedman, *Happy People*, 136, 138. Almost all other quality of life studies confirm this general finding.

14. Ruut Veenhoven. 1993. *Happiness in Nations: Subjective Appreciation of Life in 56 Nations 1946–1992*. Rotterdam: Erasmus University, RISBO, 127.

15. Sheryl Zika and Kerry Chamberlain. 1987. "Relation of Hassles and Personality to Subjective Well-Being." *Journal of Personality and Social Psychology* 53: 155–62.

16. Reported in Kent C. Berridge. 1996. "Pleasure, Pain, Desire, and Dread: Some Biopsychological Pieces and Relations." In Kahneman et al., eds., *Foundations of Hedonic Psychology*.

17. From the many relevant papers at the conference "Enjoyment and Suffering," to be published as noted above, let me identify a few. In addition to Berridge mentioned above,

the following are relevant to the comments in the text: Howard Berenbaum, Chitra Raghavan, Huynh-Nhu Le, and Jose Gomez, "Disturbances in Emotion, Mood, and Affect"; Randolph Nesse, "Evolutionary Functions of Enjoyment and Suffering"; Daniel Kahneman, "Assessments of Individual Well-Being: A Bottom-Up Approach"; and Michael Kubovny, "On the Pleasures of the Mind."

18. Daniel Kahneman. 1996. "Assessments of Individual Well-Being: A Bottom-Up Approach." Paper presented to the Conference on Enjoyment and Suffering, Princeton University, Oct. 31–Nov. 3, 1996. For a contrary view, see Norbert Schwarz and Fritz Strack. 1991. "Evaluating One's Life: A Judgment Model of Subjective Well-Being." In Fritz Strack, Michael Argyle, and Norbert Schwarz, eds., *Subjective Well-Being: An Interdisciplinary Persopective.* Oxford: Pergamon, 27–48.

19. Ed Diener and Richard E. Lucas. 1996."Personality and Well-Being." Paper presented to the Conference on Enjoyment and Suffering, Princeton University, Oct. 31–Nov. 3, 1996.

20. Myrna M. Weissman, Martha Livingston Bruce, Philip J. Leaf, Louise Florio, and Charles Holzer III. 1991. "Affective Disorders." In *Psychiatric Disorders in America: The Epidemiological Catchment Area Study,* ed. Lee N. Robins and Darrel A. Regier. New York: Free Press, 54–80 at 54. A methodological appendix on measures of happiness and depression explains some of the problems of the assessments treated and reasons for believing they are generally accurate.

21. Aaron T. Beck. 1967. *Depression: Clinical, Experimental and Theoretical Aspects.* London: Staples Press.

22. Aaron T. Beck, Maria Kovacs, and Arlene Weissman. December 1975. "Hopelessness and Suicidal Behavior: An Overview." *Journal of the American Medical Association* 234: 1146–49.

23. Aaron T. Beck. 1974. "The Development of Depression: A Cognitive Model." In Raymond J. Friedman and Martin M. Katz, eds., *The Psychology of Depression.* Washington, D.C.: Wiley/Winston, 6.

24. Nesse, "Evolutionary Functions of Enjoyment and Suffering." But, as Nesse admits, the associated lack of initiative and self-confidence is a mystery.

25. Erik Erikson quoted in W. A. Scott. 1968. "Conceptions of Normality." In E. F. Borgatta and W. W. Lambert, eds., *Handbook of Personality Theory and Research.* Chicago: Rand McNally, 974.

26. T. A. C. Rennie and L. E. Woodward. 1948. *Mental Health in Modern Society.* New York: Commonwealth Fund, 334.

27. These questions and slight variations have been asked many times throughout the world; their correlates are known and fairly common to all settings; their validity is good, though not perfect (self-reported happiness changes with the weather!); and their reliability fairly well established. The happiness question is taken from the General Social Surveys (GSS); the question on feelings about life as a whole is taken from Andrews and Withey, *Social Indicators of Well-Being.* There are at least four literature reviews on various aspects of SWB: Ed Diener, "Subjective Well-Being"; Michalos, "Job Satisfaction, Marital Satisfaction, and the Quality of Life: A Review and a Preview"; Argyle, *The Psychology of Happiness;* and Veenhoven, *Happiness in Nations.*

28. This outcome corresponds to a major study of mental health in 1976 whose au-

thors reported that given the rising anxiety of the young, "we cannot expect a better future." Joseph Veroff, Elizabeth Douvan, and Richard Kulka. 1981. *The Inner Americans: A Self-Portrait from 1957 to 1976.* New York: Basic Books, 528.

29. Every now and then warnings of a declining morale in the United States have surfaced in the polls. In November 1973, for example, the Gallup Organization released a roundup of then-recent polls stating, "Surveys Find Pessimism, Dissatisfaction Growing." Gallup Opinion Index Number 101. I should also draw attention to the fact that although my thesis is growing unhappiness, I have chosen to index this by "very happy" responses. This is in line with other trend reports, e.g., those by Lipset and Schneider, Inglehart, etc. Ruut Veenhoven has kindly examined a part of the GSS evidence (1972–90) and written to me (March 1996) showing that the "not too happy" responses do not rise but rather tend to disappear into the middle category, "fairly happy." The net happiness, he says, tends to remain constant. Upon later examination of more recent (1994) data, Veenhoven concluded that net happiness figures do show a modest decline. At a minimum, all parties agree that there is a loss of joy in the United States in the postwar period.

30. Ed Diener and Carol Diener. 1996. "Most People in the United States are Happy." *Psychological Science* 7: 181–85.

31. Veenhoven, *Happiness in Nations,* 59.

32. "Across the varied people who fell within any of the social groups we have examined, the compensations were remarkably prevalent and account for our perhaps surprising finding that these social groups differed only rather modestly in *general* well-being." Andrews and Withey, *Social Indicators of Well-Being,* 306–07.

33. Sheena Ashford and Noel Timms. 1992. *What Europe Thinks: A Study of Western European Values.* Aldershot, U.K.: Dartmouth, 10, 128.

34. Ronald Inglehart. 1990. *Culture Shift in Advanced Industrial Societies.* Princeton: Princeton University Press, 25–29.

35. Daniel Goleman. December 8, 1992. "A Rising Cost of Modernity: Depression." *New York Times.* In this piece Goleman reviews the findings of a number of then-recent epidemiological studies of depression.

36. Martin E. P. Seligman. 1990. *Learned Optimism.* New York: Pocket Books, 10.

37. The Cross-National Collaborative Group report states at p. 3102, "The results show an overall trend for increasing rates of major depression over time for all sites." The multiple authors of this cross-national study were the first to use a standardized instrument (Diagnostic Statistical Manual of Mental Disorders — DSM-III) for large-scale cross-national work. See Cross-National Collaborative Group. December 2, 1992. "The Changing Rate of Depression: Cross-National Comparisons." *Journal of the American Medical Association* 268: 3098–3105. For a more recent analysis of gender differences in the same (augmented) data, see Myrna M. Weissman, Roger C. Bland, and fifteen others. July 24–31 1996. "Cross-National Epidemiology of Major Depression and Bipolar Disorder." *Journal of the American Medical Association* 276: 293–99.

38. George W. Brown and Tirril Harris. 1978. *Social Origins of Depression: A Study of Psychiatric Disorder in Women.* London: Tavistock, 274.

39. Norman Sartorius, H. Davidian, G. Ernberg, F. R. Fenton, I. Fujii, and nine others. 1983. *Depressive Disorders in Different Cultures.* Report of the World Health Organization Collaborative Study in Standardized Assessment of Depressive Disorders. Geneva: World Health Organization, 1.

40. Weissman et al. found that compared to samples in Germany, Canada, and New Zealand, U.S. figures were lower for both lifetime rates and one-year rates for both men and women. Myrna M. Weissman, Roger Bland, Peter R. Joyce, Stephen Newman, et al. 1993. "Sex Differences in Rates of Depression: Cross-National Perspectives. Special Issue: Toward a New Psychobiology of Depression in Women." *Journal of Affective Disorders* 29: 77–84.

41. Seligman in James Buie. October 1988. "'Me' Decades Generate Depression: Individualism Erodes Commitment to Others." *APA Monitor* 19: 18.

42. Weissman et al., "Affective Disorders," 78, 80. This finding corresponds to an earlier report of a six-year study tracking 956 American men and women: those under forty were three times more likely to become severely depressed than were older groups. Goleman, "A Rising Cost of Modernity," C3.

43. Weissman et al., "Affective Disorders," 64. "According to the epidemiological Catchment Area Survey of the National Institute of Mental Health, about 20% of the people report at least one depressive symptom in a given *month,* and 12% report two or more in a year." "Update on Mood Disorders — Part I. December 1944." *Harvard Mental Health Letter* 11:1–4 at 3.

44. Ronald C. Kessler, Katherine A. McGonagle, Nelson Shanyang, B. Christopher, et al. Jan. 1994. "Lifetime and 12-month Prevalence of DSM-III — R Psychiatric Disorders in the United States: Results from the National Comorbidity Study." *Archives of General Psychiatry* 51: 8–19.

45. Paul Lewis. 19 September 1993. "'Quarter of Children' Mentally Ill." (London) *Observer.* Lewis is quoting June McKerrow, director of the Mental Health Foundation.

46. Peter M. Lewisohn, Paul Rohde, John R. Seeley, and Scott A. Fischer. 1993. "Age-cohort Changes in the Lifetime Occurrence of Depression and other Mental Disorders." *Journal of Abnormal Psychology* 102: 110–20; Gerald L. Klerman. 1989. "The Current Age of Youthful Melancholia: Evidence for Increase in Depression among Adolescents and Young Adults." *Annual Progress in Child Psychiatry and Child Development.* New York: Brunner/Mazel, 333–54.

47. Myrna M. Weissman, Virginia Warner, Priya Wickramaratne, and Brigitte A. Prusoff. 1988. "Early-onset Major Depression in Parents and their Children. Special Issue: Childhood Affective Disorders." *Journal of Affective Disorders* 15: 269–77.

48. Angus Campbell, Philip E. Converse, and Willard L. Rodgers. 1976. *The Quality of American Life.* New York: Russell Sage; Andrews and Withey. *Social Indicators of Well-Being,* 116.

49. Diener, "Subjective Well-Being," 565.

50. Ruut Veenhoven. 1984. *Conditions of Happiness: Summary Print.* Dordrecht Holland: Reidel, Exhibit 9/1.1, p. 36.

51. See, for example, Andrews and Withey. *Social Indicators of Well-Being.*

52. Gabriel A. Almond and Sidney Verba. 1963. *The Civic Culture.* Princeton: Princeton University Press; Robert D. Putnam. 1993. *Making Democracy Work: Civic Tradition in Modern Italy.* Princeton: Princeton University Press; Francis Fukuyama. 1995. *Trust: The Social Virtues and the Creation of Prosperity.* New York: Free Press.

53. Eric M. Uslaner. 1995. "Trends in Comity in the United States." Draft paper privately circulated. Received February 1995.

54. Veenhoven, *Happiness in Nations,* 69.

55. Using the same ladder measurements as Glatzer, a special study commissioned by the *New York Times* came to the conclusion that American optimism evident from studies in the 1950s and 1960s had almost vanished. Robert Lindsey. October 26, 1975. "Economy Mars Belief in the American Dream." *New York Times,* 1, 48. Compare William Watts and Lloyd A. Free. 1973. *The State of the Nation.* Washington, D.C.: Universe/Potomac Associates, 23.

56. Alex Inkeles and Larry Diamond. 1980. "Personal Development and National Development: A Cross-Cultural Perspective." In Alexander Szalai and Frank M. Andrews, eds., *The Quality of Life: Comparative Studies.* Beverly Hills: Sage, 73–109 at 99.

57. W. N. Dember and J. Brooks. 1989. "A New Instrument for Measuring Optimism and Pessimism: Test-retest Reliability and Relations with Happiness and Religious Commitment." *Bulletin of the Psychonomic Society* 27: 103–57.

58. John Mirowski and Catherine E. Ross. 1989. *Social Causes of Psychological Distress.* New York: Aldine de Gruyter, 16.

59. Sartorius et al., *Depressive Disorders in Different Cultures,* 92. On the whole, however, this report finds few country differences, 86.

60. Paul Rozin. 1996. "Pleasures of the Body: The Puzzles and Properties of Pleasure." In Kahneman et al., eds., *Foundations of Hedonic Psychology*. Rozin quotes the Buddhist prayerbook, the *Dhanmmapada:* "From pleasure comes grief, from pleasure comes fear; he who is free from pleasure neither sorrows nor fears."

61. In his *America as a Civilization* [1957. New York: Simon and Schuster, 693], Max Lerner says, "If asked to reflect on what was their main aim in life, most Americans would probably shrug the question away, since they tend to take life goals as given; but if pressed, they would probably say, 'To be happy,' or 'To lead a happy life.' If asked what they want for their children, their answer would again be happiness."

62. Veenhoven, *Happiness in Nations,* 59, 76, 77.

63. David M. Potter. 1954. *People of Plenty: Economic Abundance and the American Character.* Chicago: University of Chicago Press.

64. Inglehart, *Culture Shift in Advanced Industrial Society,* 33.

65. See, for example, Daniel Lerner. 1958. *The Passing of Traditional Society.* New York: Free Press; Frederick W. Frey. 1973. "Communication and Development." In Ithiel de Sola Pool and Wilbur Schram, eds., *Handbook of Communication.* Chicago: Rand McNally.

66. Veenhoven, *Happiness in Nations,* 48.

67. Robert E. Lane. 1959. "The Fear of Equality." *American Political Science Review* 53: 35–51.

68. Alexander H. Leighton et al. 1963. *Psychiatric Disorder among the Yoruba.* Ithaca: Cornell University Press; Bruce P. and Barbara S. Dohrenwend. 1969. *Social Status and Psychological Disorder: A Causal Inquiry.* New York: Wiley-Interscience.

69. Ed Diener, Marissa Diener, and Carol Diener. 1995. "Factors Predicting the Subjective Well-Being of Nations." *Journal of Personality and Social Psychology* 69: 851–64.

70. Harry C. Triandis. 1995. *Individualism and Collectivism.* Boulder: Westview Press.

71. Mirowski and Ross. *Social Causes of Psychological Distress.*

72. John Mirowski and Catherine E. Ross. 1984. "Mexican Culture and Its Emotional Contradictions." *Journal of Health and Social Behavior* 25: 2–13; Catherine E. Ross,

John Mirowsky, and William C. Cockerham. 1983. "Social Class, Mexican Culture, and Fatalism: Their Effects on Psychological Distress." *American Journal of Community Psychology* 11: 383–99. I recognize that to generalize from Mexican to Puerto Rican culture on the ground that they are both Hispanic is somewhat perilous. Perhaps I could appeal to Inglehart's study showing the common culture on many dimensions among Latin Americans: Ronald Inglehart and Marita Carballo. 1997. "Does Latin America Exist? (And Is There a Confucian Culture?): A Global Analysis of Cross-Cultural Differences." *PS: Political Science and Politics* 30: 34–46.

73. Puerto Rican culture is different from Mexican culture: in Puerto Rico little of the original Indian culture remains and the impact of the United States has been much greater. Its economic advance has, until recently, also been much greater. But it shares the fatalism of the Mexicans. See Oscar Lewis. 1965. *La Vida: A Puerto Rican Family in the Culture of Poverty—San Juan and New York*. Vintage/Random House, esp. xlii–lii.

74. John G. Lang, Ricardo F. Muñoz, Guillermo Bernal, and James L. Sorensen. 1982. "Quality of Life and Psychological Well-Being in a Bicultural Latino Community." *Hispanic Journal of Behavioral Sciences* 4: 433–50 at 433. But even this modest support is controversial. See R. C. Kessler et al., "Lifetime and 12-month Prevalence of DSM-III-R Psychiatric Disorders," 8–19.

75. Seligman quoted in Buie, " 'Me' Decades Generate Depression," 18.

76. Barbara Crossette. May 16, 1995. "Mental Illness Found Rising in Poor Nations." *New York Times,* C9. These reports were based on Arthur Kleinman. 1995. *World Mental Health: Problems and Priorities in Low-Income Countries.* New York: Oxford University Press (for the United Nations).

77. J. Orley, D. M. Blitt, and J. K. Wing. 1979. "Psychiatric Disorders in Two African Villages." *Archives of General Psychiatry* 36: 513–21. Reported in a literature review by Frances M. Culbertson. 1997. "Depression and Gender: An International Review." *American Psychologist* 52: 25–31.

78. S. Nolen-Hoeksema. 1990. *Sex Differences in Depression.* Stanford: Stanford University Press.

79. An earlier study of mental hospital admissions over a century came to the conclusion that modern civilization, at least in Massachusetts, did not make people mentally ill. See Alfred Goldhamer and Andrew Marshall. 1953. *Psychosis and Civilization.* Glencoe, Ill.: Free Press. For a similar conclusion, see Sartorius et al., *Depressive Disorders in Different Cultures.* In contrast, see Crossette. "Mental Illness Found Rising in Poor Nations."

80. Max Weber. 1958 [1904–06]. *The Protestant Ethic and the Spirit of Capitalism,* trans. T. Parsons. New York: Scribner's, 181.

Chapter 3. Happiness as an Endowment

1. Neil McNaughton. 1989. *Biology and Emotion.* Cambridge: Cambridge University Press; Carroll E. Izard, Jerome Kagan, and Robert Zajonc, eds. 1989. *Emotions, Cognitions, and Behavior.* Cambridge: Cambridge University Press.

2. Bruce Headey and Alexander Wearing. 1989. "Personality, Life Events, and Subjective Well-Being: Toward a Dynamic Equilibrium Model." *Journal of Personality and Social Psychology* 57: 731–39.

3. Robert E. Lane. 1998. "Moral Blame and Causal Attribution." Paper delivered to the conference "Ethics in Practice." Darmstadt, July 9–11, 1998.

4. I ask the indulgence of neuroscientists and evolutionary psychologists for the following treatment. It is intended to persuade my colleagues in political science, sociology, economics, and philosophy that there is more to the body–mind problem than we find in *our* literatures.

5. Robert Plomin. May 1990. "Behavioral Genetics: Nature and Nurture." *Harvard Medical School Mental Health Letter* 8: 4–6 at 4.

6. A. Tellegen, D. T. Lykken, T. J. Bouchard, K. J. Wilcox, N. L. Segal, and S. Rich. 1988. "Personality Similarity in Twins Reared Apart and Together." *Journal of Personality and Social Psychology* 54: 1031–39.

7. Kenneth S. Kendler, Ellen E. Walters, Kim R. Truett, et al. July 1994. "Sources of Individual Differences in Depressive Symptoms: Analysis of Two Samples of Twins and Their Families." *American Journal of Psychiatry* 51: 1605–14. Reported in "Heredity vs. Environment in Depression." July 1995. *Harvard Mental Health Letter* 12: 7.

8. Colorado Adoption Project, John Defries, principal investigator, reported in Ruth Azar. May 1997. "Nature, Nurture: Not Mutually Exclusive." *APA Monitor* 25: 1, 28.

9. Research by David Reiss, Robert Plomin, and Mavis Heatherington at the University of Virginia, reported in ibid., 28.

10. Research by Ken Kendler, Medical College of Virginia, reported in ibid., 28. Note that some scholars still maintain that psychological distress has wholly environmental determinants: "Neither genetic nor biochemical factors have been shown to account for any substantial part of the differences in level of [psychological] distress in our society." John Mirowski and Catherine E. Ross. 1989. *Social Causes of Psychological Distress.* New York: Aldine de Gruyter, 18.

11. Edward O. Wilson. 1975. *Sociobiology: The New Synthesis.* Cambridge: Harvard University Press, 3, 4. See also: Jan Fawcett. 1975. "Biochemical and Neuropharmacological Research in the Affective Disorders." In E. James Anthony and Therese Benedek, eds., *Depression and Human Existence.* Boston: Little Brown, 21–52; Robert E. Thayer. 1989. *The Biopsychology of Mood and Arousal.* New York, Plenum.

12. Natalie Angier, the science reporter for the *New York Times,* responds, "While feeling tense and peevish may not be much fun, evolution cares nothing for our amusement, but only whether we survive long enough to breed." Angier, "Grumpy, Fearful Neurotics Appear to be Short on a Gene." November 26, 1996, B17.

13. Robert Wright. 1994. *The Moral Animal: Evolutionary Psychology and Everyday Life.* New York: Vintage/Random House, 298. Jerome Kagan disputes Wright's implied pleasure-seeking model, pointing out that, because of humans' unique symbolic capacities, much human behavior seeks "to maintain the belief that the agent is meeting his or her moral obligations." Jerome Kagan. 1996. "Three Pleasing Ideas." *American Psychologist* 51: 901–08 at 905.

14. A challenge to this idea comes from a strange source: "The capacity to be pleasant toward a fellow creature is in a sense hard work. It is not the default mode. Instead, affiliative behavior requires a hormonal and neural substrate, an activation of circuitry every bit as intricate as the mechanisms controlling the body's ability to fight an opponent or flee from danger." Natalie Angier. 1996. "Illuminating How Bodies Are Built for

Sociability." *New York Times,* April 30, 1996, C11. The report is from a conference at Georgetown University entitled "The Integrative Neurobiology of Affiliation," organized by the New York Academy of Sciences. But in the following paragraphs, see how this "default mode" is treated as exceptional by evolutionary biologists.

15. P. J. Livesey. 1986. *Learning and Emotion.* Hillsdale, N.J.: Erlbaum, 231, quoted in Randolph Nesse. 1996. "Evolutionary Functions of Enjoyment and Suffering." Paper presented to the Conference on Enjoyment and Suffering, Princeton University, Oct. 31–Nov. 2, 1996, p. 4.

16. Nesse, ibid., 8.

17. Ibid., 9–10.

18. Ibid., 4, 15. Brain specialists can locate certain emotions more specifically: "Happiness, sadness, and disgust were each associated with increases in activity in the thalamus and medial prefrontal cortex." Richard D. Lane, Eric M. Reiman, Geoffrey L. Ahern, Gary E. Schwartz, and Richard J. Davidson. 1997. "Neuroanatomical Correlates of Happiness, Sadness, and Disgust." *American Journal of Psychiatry* 154: 926–34 at 926.

19. Angier, "Illuminating How Bodies are Built for Sociability," C11. Susan Carter is a research scientist at the University of Maryland. For men, vasopressin serves (mutatis mutandis) similar functions.

20. Idem.

21. We cannot base this argument entirely on birthrates because these rates are also declining in the Asian, collectivist societies, in which affiliation remains high. But familistic economies, in which depression is still low by Western standards, may somehow enlist a competitive fight or flight hormonal system without losing the affiliative hormonal base.

22. McNaughton, *Biology and Emotion,* 171–72.

23. Angier, "Grumpy, Fearful Neurotics Appear to be Short on a Gene," B17. Research by Dennis L. Murphy of the National Institute of Mental Health, Dean H. Hamer of the National Institute of Cancer Research, and Klaus-Peter Lesch of the University of Würzburg in Germany. Original research report published in *Science,* November 29, 1996.

24. Lionel Tiger. 1979. *Optimism: The Biology of Hope.* New York: Simon and Schuster.

25. See Kent C. Berridge. 1998. "Pleasure, Pain, Desire, and Dread: Some Biopsychological Pieces and Relations." In Kahneman et al., eds., *Foundations of Hedonic Psychology.* New York: Russell Sage Foundation. The limited learning across settings is reported by Kagan, "Three Pleasing Ideas," 901.

26. David C. McClelland. 1985. *Human Motivation.* Glenview, Ill.: Scott, Foresman, 121; Michael Argyle and Maryanne Martin. 1991. "The Psychological Causes of Happiness." In Fritz Strack, Michael Argyle, and Norbert Schwarz, eds., *Subjective Well-Being: An Interdisciplinary Perspective.* Oxford: Pergamon, 77–100 at 80. See also Keith B. J. Franklin. 1993. "The Neural Basis of Pleasure and Pain." In Michael Hechter, Lynn Nadel, and Richard E. Michod, eds., *The Origin of Values.* New York: Aldine de Gruyter, 275.

27. Tina Adler. 1993. "EEGs Differ Widely for Those with Different Temperaments." *APA Monitor* 24: 7.

28. Tina Adler. 1993. "Shy, Bold Temperament? It's Mostly in the Genes." *APA Monitor* 24:1, 7. For the original research, see J. Kagan, N. Snidman, and D. M. Arcus. 1992. "Initial Reactions to Unfamiliarity." *Current Directions in Psychological Science* 1: 171–74.

29. John Medina. 1996. "Genetic Study of Human Behavior: Its Progress and Limitations." *Harvard Mental Health Letter* 12 (April): 4–5. Medina points out (5) that physiological determinants are broadly spread through the brain as in "the *glial cells* . . . which regulate groups of neurons by controlling the concentration of neurotransmitters and ions," and by genetic interaction.

30. Adrian Furnham. 1985. "Attitudes To, and Habits of, Gambling in Britain." *Human Individual Differences* 6: 493–502.

31. George W. Brown and Tirril Harris. 1978. *Social Origins of Depression: A Study of Psychiatric Disorder.* London: Tavistock/Cambridge University Press.

32. Ibid.; also Antonio Loa and Emilio Fava. 1992. "Provoking Agents, Vulnerability Factors and Depression in an Italian Setting: A Replication of Brown and Harris's Model." *Journal of Affective Disorders* 24:227–35; Charles G. Costello. 1982. "Social Factors Associated with Depression: A Retrospective Community Study." [Canada] *Psychological Medicine* 12: 329–39.

33. Research by Steven Suomi (National Institute of Child Health and Human Development), Dee Higley (NIH, Primate Center), and Markku Linnoila (National Institute on Alcohol Abuse and Alcoholism), reported in Ruth Azar. April 1997. "Environment Is Key to Serotonin Levels." *APA Monitor,* 26.

34. Research by Craig Ferris (Behavioral Neuropsychiatric Sciences Program, University of Massachusetts Medical Center), in ibid., 26.

35. M. Raleigh, M. McGuire, G. Brammer, D. Pollack, and A. Yuwiler. 1991. "Serotonergic Mechanisms Promote Dominance Acquisition in Adult Male Vervet Monkeys." *Brain Research* 559: 181–90; quoted in Nesse, "Evolutionary Functions," 20. Emphasis added.

36. In Azar, "Environment Is Key to Serotonin Levels," 26.

37. Research by Russell Fernald and others reported in Natalie Angier, *New York Times,* November 12, 1991, C1.

38. Research by Jay Weiss of Rockefeller University reported in Carol Turkington. October 1982. "Research Indicates Stress Induced Depression." *APA Monitor* 12: 17.

39. Michael Argyle and Maryanne Martin. 1991. "The Psychological Causes of Happiness." In Strack et al., *Subjective Well-Being: An Interdisciplinary Perspective,* 77–100 at 80.

40. Bruce Headey and Alexander Wearing. 1992. *Understanding Happiness: A Theory of Subjective Well-Being.* Melbourne: Longman Cheshire.

41. Bruce Headey and Alexander Wearing. 1991. "Subjective Well-Being: A Stocks and Flows Framework." In Strack et al., *Subjective Well-Being: An Interdisciplinary Perspective,* 49–73 at 49.

42. Ibid., 59, 61. The correlation between one favorable event and another was 0.50.

43. Ibid., 60.

44. Ibid., 64.

45. Angus Campbell, Philip E. Converse, and Willard L. Rodgers. 1976. *The Quality of American Life.* New York: Russell Sage, 368. The beta weight was .13 with all other sources controlled. In a literature review, Michalos reports two studies finding no significant relationship. Alex C. Michalos. 1986. "Job Satisfaction, Marital Satisfaction, and

the Quality of Life: A Review and a Preview." In Frank M. Andrews, ed., *Research on the Quality of Life*. Ann Arbor: Institute for Social Research, 62.

46. "Several studies have found that there is no significant effect [of education on SWB] when other factors are controlled." Ed Diener, 1984. "Subjective Well-Being." *Psychological Bulletin* 95: 542–75.

47. James R. Flynn. 1987. "Massive IQ Gains in 14 Nations: What IQ tests Really Measure." *Psychological Bulletin* 101: 171–91.

48. "Proceed with Caution." April 1997. *Harvard Health Letter* 22: 3. But note that the cheerful die younger than the "cautious and conscientious"! (See below.)

49. "Emotional reactions emerge early in life, are somewhat stable across time, and provide the building blocks for adult personality dimensions." Ed Diener and Richard E. Lucas. 1999. "Personality and Well-Being." In Kahneman et al., eds., *Foundations of Hedonic Psychology*, citing H. H. Goldsmith and J. J. Campos. 1986. "Fundamental Issues in the Study of Early Temperament: The Denver Twin Temperament Study." In M. E. Lamb and B. Rogoff, eds., *Advances in Developmental Psychology*. Hillsdale, N.J.: Erlbaum, 231–283.

50. A. E. Wessman and D. F. Ricks. 1966. *Mood and Personality*. New York: Holt, Rinehart, and Winston; Angus Campbell. 1982. *The Sense of Well-Being in America*. New York: McGraw-Hill, 217–18.

51. P. T. Costa and R. R. McCrae. 1980. "Influence of Extroversion and Neuroticism on Subjective Well-Being: Happy People and Unhappy People." *Journal of Personality and Social Psychology* 38: 668–78; Ed Diener, E. Sandvik, W. Pavot, and F. Fujita. 1992. "Extroversion and Subjective Well-Being in a U.S National Probability Sample." *Journal of Research in Personality*. 26: 205–15. Michael Argyle and Maryanne Martin. 1991. "The Psychological Causes of Happiness." In Strack et al., eds., *Subjective Well-Being: An Interdisciplinary Perspective*, 92–93.

52. But see Robert R. McCrae and Paul T. Costa, Jr. 1991. "Adding *Liebe und Arbeit*: The Full Five-Factor Model and Well-Being." *Personality and Social Psychology Bulletin* 17: 227–32.

53. Shelley Kichter, Karen Haye, and Richard Kammann. 1980. "Increasing Happiness Through Cognitive Retraining." *New Zealand Psychologist* 9: 57–64. See also Michael W. Fordyce. 1977. "Development of a Program to Increase Personal Happiness." *Journal of Counseling Psychology* 24: 511–21.

54. Michael Argyle. 1976. "Personality and Social Behavior." In R. Harre, ed., *Personality*. Oxford: Blackwell.

55. Lionel Tiger. 1993. "Morality Recapitulates Phylogeny." In Hechter et al., eds., *The Origin of Values*, 219–331 at 219. Tiger prudently skirts the problem of encoded instructions on women's role among the hunter gatherers.

56. Robert M. Sapolsky. 1999. "The Physiology and Pathophysiology of Unhappiness." In Kahneman et al., eds., *Foundations of Hedonic Psychology*.

57. Ibid., MS p. 1.

58. Ibid., MS pp. 6, 11.

59. Reported in Daniel Goleman. December 8, 1992. "A Rising Cost of Modernity: Depression." *New York Times*, C1.

60. Sapolsky, "The Physiology and Pathophysiology of Unhappiness," ms. 28. Given the strict hierarchy in many primate troops, it seems strange to say that humans invented societal stratification.

61. Albert Somit and Steven A. Peterson. 1995. "Darwinism, Dominance, and Democracy." *Research in Biopolitics* 3: 19–34 at 22.

62. Frans B. M. de Waal. 1993. "Sex Differences in Chimpanzee (and Human) Behavior: A Matter of Social Values." In Hechter et al., eds., *The Origin of Values,* 283–303.

63. Richard Wrangham and Dale Peterson. 1996. *Demonic Males: Apes and the Origins of Human Violence.* Boston: Houghton Mifflin.

64. Somit and Peterson, "Darwinism, Dominance, and Democracy," 27.

65. Stanley Coopersmith. 1967. *The Antecedents of Self-Esteem.* San Francisco: Freeman.

66. Natalie Angier. January 10, 1995. "For Baboons, Rising to the Top Has Big Cost in Fertility." *New York Times,* C1.

67. Mirowski and Ross, *Social Causes of Psychological Distress,* 150.

68. Sapolsky, "The Physiology and Pathophysiology of Unhappiness," ms 18. See also Hans Selye. 1956. *The Stress of Life.* New York: McGraw-Hill.

69. Wilson, *Sociobiology: The New Synthesis,* 8.

70. Wrangham and Peterson, *Demonic Males: Apes and the Origins of Human Violence.*

71. J. McVicker Hunt. 1979. "Psychological Development." *Annual Review of Psychology,* vol. 30. Palo Alto, Calif.: Annual Reviews, 103–43 at 126.

72. C. Z. Maletesta, P. Grigoryev, C. Lamb, M. Albin, and C. Culver. 1986. "Emotion Socialization and Expressive Development in Preterm and Full-term Infants." *Child Development* 57: 316–30. Reported in Diener and Lucas, "Personality and Well-Being," ms. 29.

73. Wagner Bridger. 1991. "Early Childhood and Its Effects." *Harvard Mental Health Letter* 8:(1) 4–6.

74. H. H. Goldsmith and J. J. Campos. 1986. "Fundamental Issues in the Study of Early Temperament: The Denver Twin Temperament Study." In M. E. Lamb and B. Rogoff, eds., *Advances in Developmental Psychology* [231–283), Hillsdale, N.J.: Erlbaum. Quoted in Diener and Lucas, "Personality and Well-Being" ms. 8.

75. Research by Glicksman (1995), reported in Ed Diener and Eunkook Suh, "National Differences in Subjective Well-Being." In Kahneman et al., eds., *Foundations of Hedonic Psychology.*

76. J. McVickers Hunt and Girvin E. Kirk. 1971. "Social Aspects of Intelligence: Evidence and Issues." In Robert Cancro, ed., *Intelligence: Genetic and Environmental Influences.* New York: Grune and Stratton, 262–306 at 270.

77. Philip E. Vernon. 1969. *Intelligence and Cultural Environment.* London: Metheun, 33.

78. Glen H. Elder, Jr., and Avshalom Caspi. 1988. "Human Development and Social Change: An Emerging Perspective on the Life Course." In Niall Bolger, Avshalom Caspi, Geraldine Downey, and Martha Moorehouse, eds., *Persons in Context: Developmental Processes.* Cambridge: Cambridge University Press, 77–113 at 81, 84.

79. Ibid., 87.

80. Norman M. Bradburn and David Caplovitz. 1965. *Reports on Happiness.* Chicago: Aldine.

81. Elder and Caspi, "Human Development and Social Change," 81.

82. Ronald Inglehart and Jacques-René Rabier. 1986. "Aspirations Adapt to Situations—But Why Are the Belgians so Much Happier than the French? A Cross-Cultural Analysis of the Subjective Quality of Life." In Frank M. Andrews, ed., *Research on the Quality of Life.* Ann Arbor: Institute for Social Research, 29. Later reviews of postmaterialism in Europe speak of the decline or possibly the end ("for now") of postmaterialism. See Elinor Scarborough. 1995. "Materialist-Postmaterialist Value Orientations." In Jan W. van Deth and Elinor Scarborough, eds., *The Impact of Values,* vol. 4 of *Beliefs in Government.* Oxford: Oxford University Press, 123–59.

83. The research is reported in George E. Vaillant and Caroline O. Vaillant. 1981. "Natural History of Male Psychological Health: Work as a Predictor of Mental Health." *American Journal of Psychiatry* 138: 1433–40. The quotation based on this research is from an interview with a reporter from the *New York Times,* 10 November 1981, 1, 4.

84. Jonathan Freedman. 1980. *Happy People.* New York: Harcourt, Brace. But because the sample for this study was drawn from relatively prosperous magazine readers, the study suffers from the tendency of upwardly mobile people to remember less favorable childhoods than do downwardly mobile people.

85. Adam Smith. 1939 [1776]. *An Inquiry into the Nature and Causes of the Wealth of Nations,* Edwin Cannan, ed. New York: Modern Library/Random House, 70–71.

86. In this section, a note of caution is in order: several longitudinal studies suggest that childhood socialization is not a good predictor of adult well-being. See George E. Vaillant and Caroline O. Vaillant reporting on the long-term longitudinal study of Harvard graduates in Daniel Goleman, "Men at 65: New Findings on Well-Being." *New York Times,* January 16, 1990, C1. The Vaillants found that when Harvard men were reinterviwed at age sixty-five there was "little evidence that being poor or orphaned in childhood, having parents who divorced (or were happily married) and having emotional problems in childhood or college" made any difference in their long-term life adjustments and satisfaction therewith. Note, however, that recollections of childhood at age forty-seven did predict happiness and adjustment at this point in middle life. In another study Wagner Bridger concludes (6) as follows: "To sum up, I believe that 30 to 40 percent of adult personality is due to environment, but there is no critical period in early childhood. Current and chronic life experience count for much more." Wagner Bridger. 1991. "Early Childhood and Its Effects." *Harvard Mental Health Letter* 8: 5. Finally, Michael Lewis has produced evidence that the quality of mother–child bonding does not predict disturbance at age eighteen. Michael Lewis. 1997. *Altering Fate—Why the Past Does Not Predict the Future.* Guilford, Conn.: Guilford Press.

87. David Popenoe. 26 December 1992. "The Controversial Truth: Two-Parent Families are Better." *New York Times,* 21. Popenoe is cochairman of the Council on Families in America and supports his statements with citations from the National Health Interview Survey of Child Health (1988). Lykkens reports, "Sons of single parents are at 7 times greater risk of incarceration than sons reared by two biological parents." D. T. Lykkens. 1994. "On the Causes of Crime and Violence: A Reply to Aber and Rappaport." *Applied and Preventive Psychology* 3: 55–58.

88. E. F. Zigler and E. P. Gilman. 1990. "An Agenda for the 1990s: Supporting Families." In D. Blankenhorn, S. Bayme, and J. B. Elshtain, eds., *Rebuilding the Nest: A New Commitment to the American Family.* Milwaukee: Family Service America. Cited by David G. Myers. 1996. "Close Relationships and the Quality of Life." In Kahneman et al., eds., *Foundations of Hedonic Psychology.*

89. Hillary R. Clinton. 1995. *It Takes a Village.* New York: Simon and Schuster. In Myers, ibid., 27.

90. John P. Robinson. 1985. "Changes in Time Use: An Historical Overview." In F. Thomas Juster and Frank P. Stafford, eds., *Time, Goods, and Well-Being.* Ann Arbor: Institute for Social Research, 299.

91. C. Russell Hill and Frank P. Stafford. 1985. "Parental Care of Children: Time Diary Estimates of Quantity, Predictability, and Variety." In ibid., 438.

92. Ronald M. Cohen. 1991. Reporting on National Commission on Children. *Beyond Rhetoric: A New American Agenda for Children and Families.* Washington, D.C.: U.S. Government Printing Office, reported in *New York Times,* October 13, 1991, Connecticut supplement, 3. See also Sylvia A. Hewlett. 1991. *When the Bough Breaks: The Cost of Neglecting Our Children.* New York: Basic Books; Viviana A Zelizer. 1985. *Pricing the Priceless Child: The Changing Social Value of Children.* New York: Basic Books.

93. Ruut Veenhoven. 1989 [1984]. *Conditions of Happiness: Summary Print.* Dordrecht: Reidel, 32.

94. Quoted in Victoria Brittain. June 22, 1994. "Poor Countries Shame U.S. in Care of Children." *The Guardian,* 24. Grant is basing his remarks on the then recently released report by UNICEF cited in the next footnote.

95. UNICEF. 1993. *The Progress of Nations: The Nations of the World Ranked According to their Achievements in Child Health, Nutrition, Education, Family Planning, and Progress of Women.* New York: United Nations, 11.

96. Brittain, "Poor Countries Shame U.S. in Care of Children," 4.

Chapter 4. Why Money Doesn't Buy Happiness

1. Tibor Scitovsky. 1977. *The Joyless Economy.* New York: Oxford University Press.

2. George H. Gallup. 1976–77. "Human Needs and Satisfaction: A Global Survey." *Public Opinion Quarterly* 40: 459–67.

3. Alex Inkeles and Larry Diamond. 1986. "Personal Development and National Development: A Cross-Cultural Perspective." In Alexander Szalai and Frank M. Andrews, eds., *The Quality of Life: Comparative Studies.* Ann Arbor: Institute for Social Research, 73–109.

4. Robert E. Lane. 1991. *The Market Experience.* New York: Cambridge University Press, 27–28.

5. Leonard W. Doob. 1960. *Becoming More Civilized: A Psychological Exploration.* New Haven: Yale University Press.

6. Yun-shik Chang. 1991. "The Personalist Ethic and the Market in Korea." *Comparative Studies in Society and History* 33: 106–29.

7. Margaret Mead, ed. 1955. *Cultural Patterns and Technical Change.* New York: Mentor; Doob, *Becoming More Civilized.*

8. For example, Ruth Benedict. 1959. *Patterns of Culture.* Boston: Houghton Mifflin; Florence R. Kluckhohn and Fred L. Strodtbeck. 1961. *Variations in Value Orientations.* Evanston, Ill.: Row, Peterson.

9. Ed Diener, Marissa Diener, and Carol Diener. 1995. "Factors Predicting the Subjective Well-Being of Nations." *Journal of Personality and Social Psychology* 69: 851–64 at 859.

10. Jeremy Bentham. 1954 [1830]. "The Rationale of Punishment." Reprinted in W. Stark, ed., *Jeremy Bentham's Economic Writings,* vol. 3. London: Royal Economic Society for George Allen and Unwin, 254–55.

11. Francis Fukuyama. 1989. "The End of History." *The National Interest,* Summer, 3–30.

12. Diener, Sandvik, et al. find that there is an attenuation of the happiness–income relation in the United States, but not a general curvilinear relation across nations or within nations. Ed Diener, Ed Sandvik, Larry Seidlitz, and Marissa Diener. 1993. "The Relationship between Income and Subjective Well-Being: Relative or Absolute?" *Social Indicators Research* 28: 195–223.

13. Ruut Veenhoven. 1993. *Happiness in Nations: Subjective Appreciation of Life in 56 Nations, 1946–1992.* Rotterdam: Erasmus University Press, Center for Socio-Cultural Transformation, RISBO, 127.

14. Ronald Inglehart and Jacques-René Rabier. 1986. "Aspirations Adapt to Situations — But Why Are the Belgians so Much Happier than the French? A Cross-Cultural Analysis of the Subjective Quality of Life." In Frank M. Andrews, ed., *Research on the Quality of Life.* Ann Arbor: Institute for Social Research, 46.

15. Veenhoven, *Happiness in Nations,* 76.

16. Inglehart and Rabier say that (in advanced countries) national cultural variation explains twice the variance of any other demographic category. Inglehart and Rabier, "Aspirations Adapt to Situations," 36. But Veenhoven's tests across nations of all stages of development seem to depreciate the influence of culture. Veenhoven, *Happiness in Nations,* 76.

17. Diener, Sandvik, et al., "The Relationship between Income and Subjective Well-Being: Relative or Absolute?" 195.

18. E. A. Wilkening and D. McGranahan. 1978. "Correlates of Well-Being in Northern Wisconsin." *Social Indicators Research* 5: 211–34; O. M. Amos, Jr., M. A. Hitt, and W. Larkin. 1992. "Life Satisfaction and Regional Development: A Case Study of Oklahoma." *Social Indicators Research* 11: 319–31. I am indebted to Paul L. Wachtel for these citations.

19. There can be little doubt that being unemployed is a disaster for well-being, but the effect on the morale of the general public is less certain. Lipset and Schneider show strong correlations between level of unemployment and confidence in government, but do not report on well-being. Their data on general optimism, however, suggest that there may well be an effect on SWB if the recession is prolonged. Seymour M. Lipset and William Schneider. 1983. *The Confidence Gap: Business, Labor, and Government in the Public Mind.* New York: Free Press, 73. On the other hand, Veenhoven finds that there is no relation between level of unemployment in a country and its average happiness. Veenhoven, 1989 [1984]. *Conditions of Happiness: Summary Print.* Dordrecht: Reidel, 56.

20. Speaking of this fall from felicity, Inglehart and Rabier say, "Unless our indicators are totally erroneous, this phenomenon, in its impact on human happiness, dwarfed most events that make world headlines." Inglehart and Rabier, "Aspirations Adapt to Situations," 47.

21. In a famous distinction, Hawtrey classified goods fulfilling basic needs as "defensive" and goods that satisfied more elegant tastes as "creative." See R. G. Hawtrey. 1925. *The Economic Problem* . New York: Longmans, Green.

22. Diener et al., "Factors Predicting the Subjective Well-Being of Nations." The study covered fifty-five nations and employed samples of adult as well as student populations. The mean size of the national samples was fourteen hundred. But note that in another study ("The Relationship between Income and Subjective Well-Being"), Diener, Sandvik, et al. generally fail to find a relativistic relation between income and SWB.

23. Diener et al., "Factors Predicting Well-Being."

24. Michael Pusey. 1997. "The Impact of Restructuring on Quality of Life in Middle Australia." Paper presented to the First Annual Meeting of the International Society of Quality of Life Studies, Charlotte, N.C., November 20–23, 1997, 1.

25. Silvana Schinfini D'Andrea. 1998. "Italian Quality of Life." *Social Indicators Research* 44: 5–39 at 31.

26. Robert E. Lane. 1955. "The Fear of Equality." *American Political Science Review* 53: 35–51.

27. Philip Shaver and Jonathan Freedman. 1976. "Your Pursuit of Happiness." *Psychology Today* 10: 27–32, 75.

28. Thomas Ashby Wills. 1981. "Downward Comparison Principles in Social Psychology." *Journal of Personality and Social Psychology* 90: 245–71.

29. R. A. Emmons. 1986. "Personal Strivings: An Approach to Personality and Subjective Well-Being." *Journal of Personality and Social Psychology* 51: 1058–68 at 1058; Nancy Cantor. 1994. "Life Task Problem Solving: Situational Affordances and Personal Needs." *Personality and Social Psychology Bulletin* 20: 235–43. I am indebted to Ed Diener and Richard E. Lucas for these citations.

30. Lane, *The Market Experience,* 524–47. Note that straight correlations of income and happiness show a more positive relationship than would be the case if only the nonpoor were measured.

31. Inglehart and Rabier, "Aspirations Adapt to Situations," 34.

32. Elemér Hankiss. 1980. "Structural Variables in Cross-Cultural Research on the Quality of Life." In Alexander Szalai and Frank M. Andrews, eds., *The Quality of Life: Comparative Studies.* Beverly Hills: Sage, 41–56.

33. Frank M. Andrews and Stephen B. Withey. 1976. *Social Indicators of Well-Being: Americans' Perceptions of Life Quality.* New York: Plenum, 287.

34. Jonathan Freedman. 1980. *Happy People* . New York: Harcourt Brace.

35. Angus Campbell. 1981. *The Sense of Well-Being in America.* New York: McGraw-Hill.

36. Inglehart and Rabier, "Aspirations Adapt to Situations," 3.

37. Michael Argyle. 1996. "Causes and Correlates of Happiness." In Daniel Kahneman, Ed Diener, and Norbert Schwarz, eds., *Foundations of Hedonic Psychology: Scientific Perspectives on Enjoyment and Suffering.* New York: Russell Sage. Others have

noted some exceptions to the general flat relationship between wealth and SWB in the United States. Thus, the informed journalist Robert Samuelson finds that above the poverty level the flat relationship prevails until the very rich, who do report themselves as happier. Robert J. Samuelson. January 17–23, 1994. "It's Not Just the Economy, Stupid." *D.C. Post National Weekly Edition,* 27.

38. Joseph Veroff, Elizabeth Douvan, and Richard Kulka. 1981. *The Inner Americans: A Self-Portrait from 1957 to 1976.* New York: Basic Books. 544.

39. Ed Diener and Carol Diener. 1996. "Most People Are Happy." *Psychological Science* 7: 181–85.

40. Lane, *The Market Experience,* chap. 6.

41. Ed Diener and F. Fujita. 1995. "Resources, Personal Strivings, and Subjective Well-Being: A Nomothetic and Ideographic Approach." *Journal of Personality and Social Psychology* 68: 926–35, reported in Ed Diener and Richard E. Lucas, "Personality and Subjective Well-Being." In Kahneman et al., eds., *Foundations of Hedonic Psychology.*

42. Louis Harris for the Lutheran Church, August 8, 1993, reprinted in *American Enterprise,* Nov./Dec. 1994, 98.

43. Princeton Research Associates, July 1994, reprinted in *American Enterprise,* Nov./Dec. 1994.

44. Gallup International (February 1996), reported in *The Guardian,* 18 August 1996.

45. Daniel Kahneman has developed a scheme for differentiating immediate pleasure (Benthamite utility), decisional pleasure (the economists' version of utility), and remembered and anticipated pleasure. For an exploration of the implications of this scheme, see Kent C. Berridge. 1998. "Pleasure, Pain, and Dread: Hidden Core Processes of Emotion." In Kahneman et al., eds., *Foundations of Hedonic Psychology.*

46. Adam Smith. 1976 [1759]. *The Theory of Moral Sentiments,* D. D. Rafael and A. L. Macfie, eds. Oxford, Clarendon, 50.

47. Mark Stein. 1997. "Money, Class, and Happiness." Yale University Ph.D program. The analysis used GSS data for 1993.

48. Melvin Kohn and Carmi Schooler. 1983. *Work and Personality: An Inquiry into the Impact of Social Stratification* . Norwood, N.J.: Ablex.

49. George Homans. 1961. *Social Behavior: Its Elementary Forms.* New York: Harcourt, Brace and World, 257.

50. Otis Dudley Duncan. 1975. "Does Money Buy Satisfaction?" *Social Indicators Research* 2: 267–74.

51. Campbell, *The Sense of Well-Being in America,* 217–18.

52. Andrews and Withey, *Social Indicators of Well-Being,* 135, 231, 303.

53. W. G. Runciman. 1966. *Relative Deprivation and Social Justice.* Berkeley: University of California Press; Faye J. Crosby. 1982. *Relative Deprivation and Working Women.* New York: Oxford University Press.

54. M. Joseph Sirgy. 1998, "Materialism and Quality of Life." *Social Indicators Research* 43: 227–60.

55. Sidney Verba and Gary R. Orren. 1985. *Equality in America: The View from the Top.* Cambridge: Harvard University Press.

56. Kay L. Schlozman and Sidney Verba. 1979. *Injury to Insult: Unemployment, Class, and Political Response.* Cambridge: Harvard University Press.

57. Richard T. Curtin. 1977. *Income Equity Among U.S. Workers: The Bases and Consequences of Deprivation.* New York: Praeger.

58. For a general statement of this position, see Jan Fawcett. 1975. "Biochemical and Neuropharmacological Research in the Affective Disorders." In E. James Anthony and Therese Benedek, eds., *Depression and Human Existence.* Boston: Little Brown, 21–52. The quotation is taken from an interview with Fawcett by Abby Avin Belson reported in the *International Herald Tribune,* 17 March 1983.

59. See, for example, Ellen J. Langer. 1983. *The Psychology of Control.* Beverly Hills: Sage. The positivity bias is treated in more detail in chapter 11.

60. The Gallup Organization. Oct.–Nov. 1981. *Public Opinion* 4: 35. The physiology of pleasure gives another clue to the failure of money to relate to SWB: many, if not most, types of pleasure depend on the presence of sensory organs with which all social classes are equally endowed.

61. Morris Rosenberg and Roberta G. Simmons. 1971. *Black and White Self-Esteem: The Urban School Child.* Washington, D.C.: American Sociological Association.

62. Lita Furby. 1978. "Possessions: Toward a Theory of Their Meaning and Function Throughout the Life Cycle." In P. B. Baltes, ed., *Life-Span Development and Behavior.* New York: Academic Press.

63. F. Thomas Juster. 1985. "Preferences for Work and Leisure." In Juster and Frank P. Stafford, eds., *Time, Goods, and Well-Being.* Ann Arbor: Institute for Social Research, 333–51.

64. Classical authors and the Stoics understood the dominance of the consciousness of pain over pleasure; more recently we have come to see that positive and negative affect are often separate feelings and not the two ends of a continuum. See, for example, Bruce Headey and Alexander Wearing. 1992. *Understanding Happiness: A Theory of Subjective Well-Being.* Melbourne: Longman Cheshire.

65. Andrews and Withey, *Social Indicators of Well-Being,* 332. Another study revealed that the less well paid and less educated worry about health and income and things they cannot easily control, whereas the worries of higher status and better educated people are more about their relations with their spouses and children and the more controllable features of their lives. Veroff et al., *The Inner Americans,* 98

66. John Mirowski and Catherine Ross. 1989. *Social Causes of Psychological Distress.* New York: Aldine de Gruyter, 163.

67. Burkhard Strumpel. 1976. "Economic Lifestyles, Values, and Subjective Welfare." In Strumpel, ed., *Economic Means for Human Needs.* Ann Arbor: Institute for Social Research. At the upper levels of income, people tend to worry more about the rate of increase in their incomes than their cessation. In this study, with comparable income levels, business managers were much more likely than professionals to worry lest their pay levels stop rising.

68. Thomas S. Langner and Stanley J. Michael. 1963. *Life Stress and Mental Health.* New York: Free Press. The findings reported in the text support the idea, discussed in chapter 17, that people often create their environments.

69. Stanley Lebergott. 1968. "Labor Force and Employment Trends." In Eleanor B. Sheldon and Wilbert E. Moore, *Indicators of Social Change.* New York: Russell Sage, 97–143.

70. Jean Piaget. 1973 [1947]. *The Psychology of Intelligence,* trans. M. Piercy and

D. E. Berlyne. Totowa, N.J.: Littlefield, Adams. We arrive at the same place by following Kahneman and Tversky's "availability heuristic," which says that what is vivid, immediate and *personal* dominates abstract backgrounds. See Daniel Kahneman and Amos Tversky. 1982. "Judgment under Uncertainty: Heuristics and Biases." In Kahneman, P. Slovic, and Amos Tversky, eds., *Judgment under Uncertainty: Heuristics and Biases*. New York: Cambridge University Press.

71. Andrews and Withey, *Social Indicators of Well-Being*, 191, 239.

72. Daryl J. Bem. 1972. "Self-Perception Theory." In Leonard Berkowitz, ed., *Advances in Experimental Social Psychology*, vol. 6. New York: Academic Press.

73. C. R. Snyder and Howard L. Fromkin. 1980. *Uniqueness: The Human Pursuit of Difference*. New York: Plenum; Andrews and Withey, *Social Indicators of Well-Being*, 164.

74. Princeton Research Associates, July 12–15, 1994, reprinted in *American Enterprise*, Nov./Dec. 1994, 99.

75. In 1994 the average amount estimated "just to get by" was $25,000, and the amount needed to "fulfill all your dreams" was $100,200, a fourfold increase. Roper Starch Worldwide Inc., April 16–23, 1994, reprinted in *American Enterprise*, Nov./Dec. 1994, 98. If these were the dreams of avarice, I doubt if they were a source of active discontent.

76. Randolph Nesse. 1996. "Evolutionary Functions of Enjoyment and Suffering." Paper presented to the Conference on Enjoyment and Suffering, Princeton University, Oct. 31–Nov. 2, 1996.

77. G. I. Olson and B. I. Schrober. 1993. "The Satisfied Poor." *Social Indicators Research* 28: 173–93.

78. Melvin J. Lerner. 1980. *The Belief in a Just World: A Fundamental Delusion*. New York: Plenum.

79. Isaac M. Lipkus, Claudia Dalbert, and Ilene C. Siegler. 1996. "The Importance of Distinguishing the Belief in a Just World for Self Versus for Others: Implications for Psychology of Well-Being." *Personality and Social Psychology Bulletin* 22: 666–77.

80. Charles E. Lindblom. 1977. *Politics and Markets: The World's Politico-Economic Systems*. New York: Basic Books, chap. 13.

81. *Jeremy Bentham's Economic Writings*, W. Stark, ed., 427–28.

82. Lane, *The Market Experience*, chaps. 18, 19.

83. Andrews and Withey, *Social Indicators of Well-Being*, 124.

84. Juster, "Preferences for Work and Leisure," 336.

85. Karl Polanyi. 1971. "Our Obsolete Market Mentality." In his *Primitive, Archaic, and Modern Economies*, G. Dalton, ed. Boston: Beacon.

86. Angus Campbell, Philip E. Converse, and Willard L. Rodgers. 1976. *The Quality of American Life: Perceptions, Evaluations, and Satisfactions*. New York: Russell Sage, 28.

87. Ronald Inglehart. 1982. *The Silent Revolution*. Princeton: Princeton University Press. Idem. 1990. *Culture Shift in Advanced Industrial Society*. Princeton: Princeton University Press.

88. Elinor Scarborough. 1995. "Materialist-Postmaterialist Value Orientations." In Jan W. van Deth and Elinor Scarborough, eds., *The Impact of Values*, vol. 4 of *Beliefs in Government*. Oxford: Oxford University Press, 123–59.

89. Alexander W. Astin, Kenneth C. Green, and William S. Korn. 1986. *The American*

Freshman: Twenty Year Trends. Los Angeles: Cooperative Institutional Research Program sponsored by the American Council on Education. Supplemented for later years from the *Chronicle of Higher Education,* January 12, 1996. I am indebted to David G. Myers for the graph and the reference.

90. Fred Hirsch. 1976. *Social Limits to Growth.* Cambridge: Harvard University Press.

91. Thomas E. Patterson. 1980. *The Mass Media Election.* New York: Praeger, chaps. 3, 11; Doris A. Graber. 1980. *Mass Media and American Politics.* Washington, D.C.: CQ Press, 178–80.

92. Norman M. Bradburn and David Caplovitz. 1965. *Reports on Happiness.* Chicago: Aldine.

93. Richard Morin. Aug. 30–31, 1997. "America's Blues: Prosperity Is No Cure." *International Herald Tribune,* 1, 4. The story deals with concerns about the American family, crime, television violence and sex, divorce, and out-of-wedlock births.

94. Samuelson, "It's Not Just the Economy, Stupid," 27.

95. Philip Brickman and Donald T. Campbell. 1971. "Hedonic Relativism and Planning the Good Society." In M. H. Appley, ed., *Adaptation-Level Theory: A Symposium.* New York: Academic Press. But later physiological research by Daniel Kahneman suggests that there is no reason to believe that sustained affective states must become "hedonically neutral." Daniel Kahneman. "Assessment of Individual Well-Being: A Bottom-Up Approach." Paper presented to the Conference on Enjoyment and Suffering, Princeton University, Oct. 31–Nov. 2, 1996.

Chapter 5. Companionship or Income?

1. Frank M. Andrews and Stephen B. Withey. 1976. *Social Indicators of Well-Being: Americans' Perception of Life Quality.* New York: Plenum, 124, 262, 265. In this study the question was: "How do you feel about . . . your children, . . . your husband/wife, . . . your marriage, . . . etc." In a field of thirty domains "a sense of achievement" ranked first and "the things you do with your family" ranked sixth; Angus Campbell, Philip E. Converse, and Willard L. Rodgers. 1976. *The Quality of American Life.* New York: Russell Sage; in Campbell et al. satisfaction with leisure activities ranked first. The national sample was 2,164, and the date of the survey was 1971

2. For example, "marriage and family satisfaction is one of the most important predictors of SWB"; satisfaction with one's love life is "the most important" contributor to life satisfaction. Ed Diener. 1984. "Subjective Well-Being." *Psychological Bulletin* 95: 542–75 at 556, 557.

3. In Andrews and Withey, *Social Indicators of Well-Being,* the friendship item ranked twenty-first out of thirty items, 124; in Campbell et al., *The Quality of American Life,* friendship ranked seventh out of seventeen items, 76.

4. Ed Diener and Marissa Diener. 1995. "Cross-Cultural Correlates of Life Satisfaction and Self-Esteem." *Journal of Personality and Social Psychology* 68: 653–63 at 656. The betas are friendship satisfaction .21 and family satisfaction .15. A somewhat exotic explanation of U.S.–European differences is offered by Geoffrey Gorer, who believes that American men tend to avoid close relations with other men because of what he calls a panic over homosexuality. Geoffrey Gorer. 1948. *The American People: A Study in*

National Character. New York: Norton, 125. Daniel J. Levinson observes that few of his respondents had close male friends; 1978. *The Seasons in a Man's Life.* New York: Knopf, 335.

5. Andrews and Withey, *Social Indicators of Well-Being,* 262.

6. Bruce W. Headey, E. L. Holmstrom, and Alexander Wearing. 1985. "Models of Well-Being and Ill-Being." *Social Indicators Research* 17: 211–34. I am indebted to Michael Argyle for this reference.

7. Myrna M. Weissman, Martha Livingston Bruce, Philip J. Leaf, Louise Florio, and Charles Holzer III. 1991. "Affective Disorders." In Lee N. Robins and Darrel A. Regier, eds., *Psychiatric Disorders in America: The Epidemiological Catchment Area Study.* New York: Free Press, 54–80 at 64. Inglehart and Rabier report that although women in most marital circumstances are happier than men, widowed and divorced men are happier than women in these circumstances. Ronald Inglehart and Jacques-René Rabier. 1986. "Aspirations Adapt to Situations—But Why Are the Belgians so Much Happier than the French? A Cross-Cultural Analysis of the Subjective Quality of Life." In Frank M. Andrews, ed., *Research on the Quality of Life.* Ann Arbor: Institute for Social Research, 26.

8. For example, David G. Weeks, John L. Michela, Letitia A. Peplau, and Martin E. Bragg. 1980. "Relation Between Loneliness and Depression: A Structural Equation Analysis." *Journal of Personality and Social Psychology* 39: 1238–44. Martin Eisemann. 1984. "The Availability of Confiding Persons for Depressed Patients." *Acta Psychiatrica Scandinavica* 70: 166–69; Ed Diener and Richard E. Lucas. 1996. "Personality and Well-Being." In Daniel Kahneman, Ed Diener, and Norbert Schwarz, eds., *Foundations of Hedonic Psychology: Scientific Perspectives on Enjoyment and Suffering.* New York: Russell Sage; Shelley Lichter, Karen Haye, and Richard Kammann. 1980. "Increasing Happiness Through Cognitive Retraining." *New Zealand Psychologist* 9: 57–64. On the one hand "it has been shown that as depressives recover, their social relations improve, and when they relapse, their social relations deteriorate." Eugene S. Paykel and Myrna W. Weissman. 1973. "Social Adjustment and Depression: A Longitudinal Study." *Archives of General Psychiatry* 28: 659–63. But another study shows that social networks are somewhat independent of depression. See Lawrence A. Palinkas, Deborah L. Wingard, and Elizabeth Barrett Connor. 1990. "The Biocultural Context of Social Networks and Depression among the Elderly." *Social Science and Medicine* 30: 441–47.

9. Ruut Veenhoven. 1989 [1984]. *Conditions of Happiness: Summary Print.* Dordrecht: Reidel, 25. Diener and Diener, "Cross-Cultural Correlates of Life Satisfaction and Self-Esteem," 657.

10. For example, a cross-national study found that British pregnant mothers suffered less from bad moods than Greek pregnant mothers because, the evidence showed, British mothers received and strongly benefited from better emotional support (mostly from their husbands) in their time of trial. Karen J. Thorpe, Thalia Dragonas, and Jean Golding. 1992. "The Effects of Psychosocial Factors on the Emotional Well-Being of Women During Pregnancy: A Cross-Cultural Study of Britain and Greece." *Journal of Reproductive and Infant Psychology* 10: 191–204.

11. Andrews and Withey, *Social Indicators of Well-Being,* 119.

12. Louis Harris for the Lutheran church, Aug. 8, 1993. Reprinted in *The American Enterprise,* Nov./Dec. 1994, 98.

13. If marriage is thought to be—and found to be—a major source of happiness, how shall one interpret the minority report of marriage as a source of unhappiness? But one knows the answer: "Marriage is the relationship which is the greatest source of conflict, violence is not uncommon, and divorce is increasingly common; it is a complex and intense relationship, quite different from friendship, for example, and has more powerful effects." Michael Argyle and Adrian Furnham. 1983. "Sources of Satisfaction and Conflict in Long-Term Relationships." *Journal of Marriage and the Family* 45: 481–93.

14. Campbell et al., *The Quality of American Life*, 364. 368. Another study found that among a variety of factors, number of friends had a beta weight of .15. M. A. Okun, W. A. Stock, M. J. Haring, and R. A. Witten. 1984. "Health and Subjective Well-Being." *International Journal of Aging and Human Development* 19: 111–32. I am indebted to Michael Argyle for this citation.

15. Michael Argyle. 1996. "Causes and Correlates of Happiness." In Kahneman et al., eds., *Foundations of Hedonic Psychology*.

16. George W. Brown and Tirril Harris. 1978. *The Social Origins of Depression: A Study of Psychiatric Disorders*. London: Tavistock/Cambridge University Press, 176. This finding is confirmed by a study comparing depressive with nondepressive patients. Eisemann, "The Availability of Confiding Persons for Depressed Patients." Also see Palinkas et al., "The Biocultural Context of Social Networks and Depression among the Elderly," 441.

17. Harry T. Reis. 1990. "The Role of Intimacy in Interpersonal Relations." *Journal of Social and Clinical Psychology* 9: 15–30 at 19.

18. Harry T. Reis, Yi-Cheng Lin, M. Elizabeth Bennett, and John B. Nezlek. 1993. "Change and Consistency in Social Participation during Early Adulthood." *Developmental Psychology* 29: 633–45.

19. R. Larson. 1990. "The Solitary Side of Life: An Examination of the Time People Spend alone from Childhood to Old Age." *Developmental Review* 10: 155–83. I am indebted to Michael Argyle for this citation.

20. *The American Enterprise*, Nov./Dec. 1991, 102.

21. "We conclude from these analyses that living alone is often a preferred arrangement for which compensating mechanisms of social support often exist, rather than an isolating situation." Duane F. Alwin, Philip E. Converse, and Steven S. Martin. 1986. "Living Arrangements and Social Integration." In Frank M. Edwards, ed., *Research on the Quality of Life*. Ann Arbor: Institute for Social Research, 271.

22. "Hearts and Minds—Part II." (August 1997) *Harvard Mental Health Letter* 14: 1–4 at 1.

23. Mihalyi Csikszentmihalyi and Maria Mei-Ha Wong. 1991. "The Situational and Personal Correlates of Happiness: A Cross-National Comparison." In Fritz Strack, Michael Argyle, and Norbert Schwarz, eds., *Subjective Well-Being: An Interdisciplinary Perspective*. Oxford: Pergamon, 193–212.

24. Michael Argyle and M. Henderson. 1985. *The Anatomy of Relationships*. Harmondsworth: Penguin.

25. Barry Gruenberg. 1980. "The Happy Worker: An Analysis of Educational and Occupational Differences in Determinants of Job Satisfaction." *American Journal of Sociology* 86: 247–71 at 269.

26. James S. House. 1986. "Social Support and the Quality and Quantity of Life." In Andrews, ed., *Research on the Quality of Life,* 255.

27. Andrews and Withey, *Social Indicators of Well-Being,* 302.

28. Charles Horton Cooley. 1912. *Human Nature and the Social Order.* New York: Scribner's, 152.

29. Robert E. Lane. 1965. "The Need to be Liked and the Anxious College Liberal." *Annals of the American Academy of Political and Social Science* 361: 71–80; Eugenia Hanfman. 1957. "Social Perception in Russian Displaced Persons and an American Comparison Group." *Psychiatry* 20: 135–36.

30. Ann P. Ruvolo and Caroline Jobson Brennan. 1996. "What's Love Got to do with It? Close Relationships and Perceived Growth." *Personality and Social Psychology Bulletin* 23: 814–23.

31. Angus Campbell. 1981. *The Sense of Well-Being in America.* New York: McGraw-Hill, 217–19.

32. Michael Argyle and Adrian Furnham. 1983. "Sources of Satisfaction and Conflict in Long-Term Relationships." *Journal of Marriage and the Family* 45: 481–93.

33. For some insight into this distinction, see Karen S. Rook. 1987. "Social Support versus Companionship: Effects of Life Stress, Loneliness, and Evaluations by Others" *Journal of Personality and Social Psychology* 52: 1132–47.

34. Robert E. Lane. 1962. *Political Ideology: Why the American Common Man Believes What He Does.* New York: Free Press.

35. Argyle, "Causes and Correlates of Happiness."

36. Gina Kolata. May 3, 1993. "Family Aid to Elderly is Very Strong" *New York Times,* 16. The quoted comment is by Douglas Wolff, demographer at Syracuse University.

37. Natalie Angier. January 10, 1995. "For Baboons, Rising to the Top Has Big Cost in Fertility." *New York Times,* C1.

38. Edward O. Wilson. 1975. *Sociobiology: The New Synthesis.* Cambridge: Harvard University Press, 7.

39. The bonding is generally reinforced by the need for protection by males not only from predators of other species but more especially from the aggressive, warlike predations of neighboring troops of the same species, at least among most (but not all) primates. Wilson. ibid., 351–352.

40. Richard Wrangham and Dale Peterson. 1996. *Demonic Males: Apes and the Origins of Human Violence.* Boston: Houghton Mifflin. The main exception are the bonobos, a pacific subspecies of apes.

41. "What Is Social Support?" *Harvard Mental Health Letter* 14, 6–7 June 1998. This report is based substantially on Kenneth S. Kendler. October 1997. "Social Support: A Genetic-Epidemiological Analysis." *American Journal of Psychiatry* 154: 1398–1404. Emphasis added.

42. Allen H. Stix. 1974. "Chlordiazepoxide (Librium): The Effects of a Minor Tranquilizer on Strategic Choice Behavior in the Prisoner's Dilemma." *Journal of Conflict Resolution* 18: 373–95.

43. Instinctual territoriality is still an unsettled question. Wilson, *Sociobiology,* 565. Were it not for the counterclaims of Christian fundamentalists and the eighteenth-century theories of a social contract among isolated individuals in a state of nature, the biological

foundations of the sources of well-being in family and friends would hardly need to be mentioned. Freud's idea that sexual stimulation evolved from olfactory to visual excitation—and hence a noncyclical attraction—finds little support in current evolutionary psychology.

44. Martin Reite, Robert Short, Conny Seiler, and Donald J. Pauley. 1981. "Attachment, Loss, and Depression." *Journal of Child Psychology and Psychiatry and Allied Disciplines* 22: 141–69.

45. John Bowlby. 1969. *Attachment and Loss,* vol. 1, *Attachment.* New York: Basic Books, 207, 209. Bowlby was influenced by Konrad Lorenz's theory of imprinting, which now may be out of date, 209. But Bowlby's further extensions to include attachment to the sovereign (e.g., the British monarch) and hence to the state and to the community so far have not been substantiated. See Wolfgang Stroebe and Margaret Stroebe, Georgios Abakoumkin, and Henk Schut. 1996. "The Role of Loneliness and Social Support in Adjustment to Loss: A Test of Attachment versus Stress Theory." *Journal of Personality and Social Psychology* 70: 1241–49. The study supported attachment theory in its narrower form.

46. For example, Kim Bartholomew and Leonard M. Horowitz. 1991. "Attachment Styles Among Young Adults: A Test of a Four-Category Model." *Journal of Personality and Social Psychology* 61: 226–44; Mario Mikulincer and Orrioa Nachshon. 1991. "Attachment Styles and Patterns of Self-Disclosure." *Journal of Personality and Social Psychology* 61: 321–31. For a review of this literature, see Tiffany Field. 1996. "Attachment and Separation in Young Children." In *Annual Review of Psychology,* vol. 47. Palo Alto, Calif.: Annual Reviews Inc., 541–61. Recent research, however, finds that twelve-month-old infants judged by standard tests to be securely attached were not less likely to be maladjusted at age eighteen years. Michael Lewis. 1997. *Altering Fate—Why the Past Does Not Predict the Future.* Guilford, Conn.: Guilford Press.

47. Brown and Harris, *The Social Origins of Depression,* 103.

48. Theodore Zeldin. 1995 [1994]. *An Intimate History of Humanity.* London: Minerva, 60.

49. Leo Srole, Thomas S. Langner, Stanley T. Michael, Marvin K. Opler, and Thomas A. C. Rennie. 1962. *Mental Health in the Metropolis: The Midtown Manhattan Study,* vol. 1. New York: McGraw-Hill, 285.

50. Herbert J. Gans. 1967. *The Levittowners.* New York: Random House, 230–34; Lord Taylor and Sidney Chave. 1964. *Mental Health and Environment.* Boston: Little, Brown. There is evidence from a national study confirming Gans's findings. Campbell et al.'s study *The Quality of American Life* included a semantic differential question asking, among other things, whether people found life "lonely" or "friendly." The responses showed a general tendency to think of lives as friendly, 38, 41, 48.

51. L. Wheeler, H. T. Reis, and J. Nezlek. 1983. "Loneliness, Social Interaction, and Sex Roles." *Journal of Personality and Social Psychology* 45: 943–53.

52. Zeldin, *An Intimate History of Humanity,* 60–61; Wolfgang Glatzer. 1991. "Quality of Life in Advanced Industrialized Countries: The Case of West Germany." In Strack et al., *Subjective Well-Being: An Interdisciplinary Perspective.* 272. See also M. Hojat. 1989. *Loneliness: Theory, Research, and Applications.* Berkeley: Sage.

53. Weeks et al., "Relation Between Loneliness and Depression," 1238–44.

54. Andrew M. Forman and Ven Sriram. 1981. "The Depersonalization of Retailing: Its Impact on the 'Lonely' Consumer." *Journal of Retailing* 67: 226–43; R. S. Weiss. 1975. *Loneliness: The Experience of Emotional and Social Isolation.* Cambridge: MIT Press.

55. Joseph Veroff, Elizabeth Douvain, and Richard A. Kulka. 1981. *The Inner American: A Self-Portrait from 1957 to 1976.* New York: Basic Books, 57. From 1957 to 1976 fathers' worries about "affiliative problems" increased substantially (from 16 percent to 26 percent), and whereas in 1960 only 7 percent of a national sample worried about loneliness and relations with others, by 1976 this kind of worrying had nearly doubled, 215, 240–41. The change in the nature of worrying is further indicated in table 5.1 above: whereas economic and material problems (which are volatile) were nine times as distressing as interpersonal problems in 1957, they were only about one and a half times as distressing in 1976.

56. Norman Sartorius, H. Davidian, G. Ernberg, F. R. Fenton, I. Fujii, and nine others. 1983. *Depressive Disorders in Different Cultures: Report of the World Health Organization Collaborative Study in Standardized Assessment of Depressive Disorders.* Geneva: WHO, 1.

57. Philip Shaver and Jonathan Freedman. 1976. "Your Pursuit of Happiness." *Psychology Today,* 10 (August), 27–32, 75.

58. The measure is explained in David McClelland. 1985. *Human Motivation.* Glenview, Ill.: Scott, Foresman.

59. John W. Atkinson, Roger W. Heyns, and Joseph Veroff. 1958. "The Effect of Experimental Arousal of the Affiliation Motive on Thematic Apperception." In Atkinson, ed., *Motives in Fantasy, Action, and Society.* Princeton: Van Nostrand, 95–104 at 97.

60. Patricia Lunneborg and Linda Rosenwood. 1972. "Need Affiliation and Achievement: Declining Sex Differences." *Psychological Reports* 3: 795–98.

61. David C. McClelland. 1978. "Managing Motives to Expand Human Freedom." *American Psychologist* 33: 201–10.

62. See D. E. Entwhistle. 1972. "To Dispel Fantasies about Fantasy Based Measures of Achievement Motivation." *Psychological Bulletin* 77: 377–91.

63. David C. McClelland. 1971. *Motivational Trends in Society.* Morristown, N.J.: General Learning Press, 7–10.

64. Nancy M. Henley. 1967. "Achievement and Affiliation Imagery in American Fiction, 1901–1961." *Journal of Personality and Social Psychology* 7:208–10; James A. Beshair. 1972. "Content Analysis of Egyptian Stories." *Journal of Social Psychology* 87: 197–233.

65. For further discussion of compensatory choices, see Robert E. Lane. 1991. *The Market Experience.* New York: Cambridge University Press, 553–56.

66. Campbell et al., *The Quality of American Life,* 358–50, 380.

67. Argyle and Martin, "The Psychological Causes of Happiness."

68. Philip Brickman, D. Coates, and R. Janoff-Bulman. 1978. "Lottery Winners and Accident Victims: Is Happiness Relative?" *Journal of Personality and Social Psychology* 36: 917–27.

69. "Hearts and Minds—Part II." 1, emphasis added. "In a study of 500 Californians, people were more than twice as likely to die over a nine-year period, even after correction for their physical condition, when they had limited social affiliations," 1.

70. These correlations are for very large, multiple-year national samples gathered by the NORC General Social Survey for the years 1972–94.

71. Andrews and Withey, *Social Indicators of Well-Being,* 124.

72. Campbell et al., *The Quality of American Life,* 380–381.

73. Tibor Scitovsky. 1977. *The Joyless Economy.* New York: Oxford University Press.

74. Andrews and Withey, *Indicators of Well-Being,* 277. But styles of marital attachment (secure versus avoidant) have a very modest relation to financial adversity. Kristin D. Mickelson, Ronald C. Kessler, and Phillip R. Shaver. 1997. "Adult Attachment in a Nationally Representative Sample." *Journal of Personality and Social Psychology* 73: 1092–1106.

75. Robert Pear. 15 January 1992. "Poverty Termed a Divorce Factor: Poor couples are twice as likely as others to split up, U.S. Report says," *New York Times,* A10.

76. Brown and Harris, *The Social Origins of Depression,* 252–53. The authors compare the incidence of depression in their study with that in a crofting village in the Hebrides and find that something about the poverty in London makes the poor more depressed than in the village in the Hebrides. Urbanism, rather than the market economy, is indicted here. (But see chapter 7 below.)

77. Lane, *The Market Experience,* 553–56.

78. Campbell et al., *The Quality of American Life,* 85, 91.

79. Tim Kasser and Richard M. Ryan. 1996. "Further Examining the American Dream: Differential Correlates of Intrinsic and Extrinsic Goals." *Personality and Social Psychology Bulletin* 22: 280–87.

80. Elchanan I. Meir and Samuel Melamed. 1986. "The Accumulation of Person–Environment Congruences and Well-Being." *Journal of Occupational Behaviour* 7: 315–23.

81. R. F. Fortune. 1963 [1932]. *The Sorcerers of Dobu: The Social Anthropology of the Dobu Islanders of the Western Pacific.* Rev. ed. London: Routledge and Kegan Paul.

82. Michael Argyle and L. Lu. 1990. "The Happiness of Extroverts." *Personality and Individual Differences* 11: 1011–17.

83. "The product moment correlation between the perception that the pay is good and reported earnings is about .30, certainly not very impressive." Campbell et al., *The Quality of American Life.*, 304.

84. Richard A. Easterlin. 1974. "Does Economic Growth Improve the Human Lot?" In Paul A. David and Melvin W. Reder, eds., *Nations and Households in Economic Growth: Essays in Honor of Moses Abramovitz.* Stanford: University of Stanford Press. Recently Easterlin has returned to the argument; see his (1995) "Will Raising the Incomes of All Increase the Happiness of All?" *Journal of Economic Behavior and Organization* 27: 35–47.

85. I do not have the figures to support this relative judgment, but the contributions to SWB of friendship satisfaction and of number of friends are closer to each other than is satisfaction with income and actual income. As a consequence, income satisfaction (beta .29) has a stronger influence on SWB than friendship satisfaction (beta .20) whereas, as we saw, actual income makes a weaker contribution to SWB than actual friendships. Campbell et al., *The Quality of American Life,* 374.

86. Or, as Sumner said, "in reality the thirst for wealth is the thirst for independence." William Graham Sumner. 1934. "Who Is Free?" In *Essays of William Graham Sumner,* ed. Albert G. Keller and Maurice Davie, vol. 1. New Haven: Yale University Press, 301. Compare Adam Smith's idea that the "thirst for wealth" is actually a thirst for social esteem.

87. Robert E. Lane. 1994. "The Road Not Taken: Friendship, Consumerism, and Happiness." *Critical Review* 8(4): 521–54.

88. Christopher Jencks, Lauri Perman, and Lee Rainwater. 1988. "What Is a Good Job? A New Measure of Labor-Market Success." *American Journal of Sociology* 93: 1322–57.

89. Daryl Bem. 1972. "Self-Perception Theory." In Leonard Berkowitz, ed., *Advances in Experimental Social Psychology,* vol. 6. New York: Academic Press.

90. This would seem to make sense because the difference in importance rating, mentioned in chapter 2, was relatively small in l973, and in the 1969 study there was no difference between importance ratings of friends and of income. Furthermore, as a kind of check on the validity of self-reported importance measures, Sheppard and Herrick report that the correlations of these two importance ratings with reported job satisfaction are almost equal. Harold L. Sheppard and Neal Q. Herrick. 1972. *Where Have All the Robots Gone?* New York: Free Press, l97.

91. Campbell et al., *The Quality of American Life,* 358, 382.

92. George Katona. 1975. *Psychological Economics.* New York: Elsevier.

93. Ibid., 71–74, 203.

94. Frank H. Knight. 1947. *Freedom and Reform: Essays in Economics and Social Philosophy.* New York: Harper, 66.

95. Paul Diesing. 1962. *Reason in Society.* Urbana: University of Illinois Press, 23–24.

96. Alfred Marshall. 1938. *Principles of Economics,* 8th ed. London: Macmillan, 15, 16. Along similar lines, John R. Hicks reports that "the econometric theory of demand does study human beings, but only as *entities* having certain patterns of market behaviour; it makes no claim, no pretense, to be able to see inside their heads." John R. Hicks. 1956. *A Revision of Demand Theory.* Oxford: Oxford University Press, 6.

97. Lane, *The Market Experience,* chaps. 11, 12.

98. J. J. La Gaipa, and H. D. Wood. 1981. "Friendship in Disturbed Adolescents." In S. Duck and R. Gilmour, eds., *Personal Relationships,* vol. 3: *Personal Relationships in Disorder.* London: Academic Press. Reported in Michael Argyle. 1991. *Cooperation: The Basis of Sociability.* London: Routledge, 166.

99. Stanley S. Guterman. 1970. *The Machiavellians.* Lincoln: University of Nebraska Press, 59–62.

100. Shaver and Freedman, "Your Pursuit of Happiness," 75.

101. See George Levinger. 1974. "A Three-Level Approach to Attraction: Toward an Understanding of Pair Relatedness." In *Foundations of Interpersonal Attraction,* Ted L. Huston, ed. New York: Academic Press, 118.

102. See Uriel Foa. 29 January 1971. "Interpersonal and Economic Resources." *Science* 171: 345–51.

103. Norman M. Bradburn and David Caplovitz. 1965. *Reports on Happiness.* Chicago: Aldine, 43.

104. Nicholas Babchuk and Alan P. Bates. 1963. "The Primary Relations of Middle-Class Couples: A Study in Male Dominance." *American Sociological Review* 28: 377–84.

105. R. B. Hays. 1985. "A Longitudinal Study of Friendship Development." *Journal of Personality and Social Psychology* 48: 909–24; reported in Argyle, *Cooperation: The Basis of Sociability,* 166.

Chapter 6. Searching for Lost Companions

1. Henry Sumner Maine. 1931 [1861]. *Ancient Law.* Oxford: Oxford University Press, 139–40, 141.

2. Ferdinand Tönnies. 1957 [1887]. *Community and Society* (*Gemeinschaft und Gesellschaft*), trans. C. P. Loomis. East Lansing: Michigan State University Press, 35.

3. Ibid., 43.

4. Ibid., 65.

5. Ibid., 77.

6. I am relying here on Talcott Parsons, ed. 1947. *Max Weber: The Theory of Social and Economic Organization.* New York: Oxford University Press, and Robert A. Nisbet. 1966. *The Sociological Tradition.* New York: Basic Books. The quotations are in Weber's words extracted by these two authors.

7. James S. House. 1986. "Social Support and the Quality and Quantity of American Life." In Frank M. Andrews, ed., *Research in the Quality of Life.* Ann Arbor: Institute for Social Research, 267.

8. In a study of changes in interaction between 1965 and 1975, there was, indeed, an increase in the use of the telephone at the same time that there was a marked decline in visiting patterns. Compared to earlier periods, of course, there was also a marked drop in letter writing. John P. Robinson. 1985. "Changes in Time Use: An Historical Overview," chap. 11 in Thomas F. Juster and Frank P. Stafford, eds., *Time, Goods, and Well-Being.* Ann Arbor: Institute for Social Research, 299

9. Harry T. Reis. 1990. "The Role of Intimacy in Interpersonal Relations." *Journal of Social and Clinical Psychology* 9: 15–30 at 18.

10. Robert D. Putnam. 1995. "Bowling Alone: America's Declining Social Capital." *Journal of Democracy* 6: 65–78.

11. Mihalyi Csikszentmihalyi and R. Kubey. 1981. "Television and the Rest of Life: A Systematic Comparison of Subjective Experiences." *Public Opinion Quarterly* 45: 317–28.

12. Alex Inkeles and Larry Diamond. 1986. "Personal Development and National Development: A Cross-Cultural Perspective." In Alexander Szalai and Frank M. Andrews, eds., *The Quality of Life: Comparative Studies.* Ann Arbor: Institute for Social Research, 73–109 at 97.

13. Since trust is only modestly correlated (+.05, $p > 001$) with the number of friends a person has (or claims) it is unclear whether this general suspiciousness would tend to isolate people from their friends and family, as Tönnies believed. Note that between 1981 and 1990 in Europe interpersonal trust increased in Germany, Italy, and the Netherlands, but that overall there was no change. Sheena Ashford and Noel Timms. 1992. *What Europe Thinks: A Study of Western European Values.* Aldershot, U.K.: Dartmouth, 12–13.

14. The detailed demographics are from Floris W. Wood, ed. 1990. *An American Profile—Opinions and Behavior, 1972–1989.* Detroit: Gale, as well as directly from GSS data.

15. Curiously, the pattern among the other vulnerable demographic group, the young, is just the opposite: an actual increase in neighboring (which was always high among the young) and a decline in isolation over the twenty-year period, perhaps, again in contrast to women, to compensate for their decline in visiting with friends (see below).

16. Of the elderly, it seems that retirement is more important than aging in accounting for the falloff in socializing in this older group. For example, although there is no marked decline in the 60–64 group, there is in the 65+ group.

17. Compared to women, men were slightly more likely to visit with friends. At the same time, the young (ages eighteen to twenty-three) decreased their socialization for ten years and then increased it for eleven for a net gain over the period. Also they steadily, if very modestly, decreased their isolation from their friends over the twenty-one-year period. Because socializing promotes happiness and isolation promotes depression, the source of these moods and illnesses among the young does not seem to be loss of friends.

18. Christopher Lasch. 1977. *Haven in a Heartless World: The Family Besieged.* New York: Basic Books. The GSS data show only a trivial overall decline in satisfaction with family life—which could reflect the tendency to underplay family dissatisfaction.

19. A. Vadher and D. M. Ndetei. 1981. "Life Events and Depression in a Kenyan Setting." *British Journal of Psychiatry* 139: 134–37.

20. Joseph Veroff, Elizabeth Douvan, and Richard Kulka. 1981. *The Inner Americans: A Self-Portrait from 1957 to 1976.* New York: Basic Books, 57, 529, 533. Concern about the future is partly attributable to growing anxiety among the young, 528.

21. The GSS data do not show any decline in satisfaction, but a Harris report finds that "those pleased with their friendships has declined" over the 1972–86 period, although the satisfaction remains high and the decline is modest: from 70 percent to 65 percent satisfied. Louis Harris. 1987. *Inside America.* New York: Random House/Vintage, 40.

22. This aggregate constant level of satisfaction seems to be a reversal of the trends in an earlier twenty-year period (1957–76), which showed an increase in the unhappiness attributed to interpersonal relations. Veroff et al., *The Inner Americans,* 537.

23. Ibid., 545, 546.

24. Ibid., 549.

25. Putnam, "Bowling Alone: America's Declining Social Capital." Putnam's data, however, show only that people bowl less often in leagues or teams.

26. Robinson, "Changes in Time Use," 300.

27. Ed Diener, Marissa Diener, and Carol Diener. 1995. "Factors Predicting the Subjective Well-Being of Nations." *Journal of Personality and Social Psychology* 69: 851–64.

28. Ruut Veenhoven. 1993. *Happiness in Nations: Subjective Appreciation of Life in 56 Nations, 1946–1993.* Rotterdam: Erasmus University: RISBO Press, 42. In certain richer countries (e.g., in Europe), however, rural and village residents are slightly happier than residents of cities, although the longer one lives in a city, the happier one becomes. Ronald Inglehart and Jacques-René Rabier. 1986. "Aspirations Adapt to Situations—But Why Are the Belgians so much Happier than the French? A Cross-Cultural Analysis of the Subjective Quality of Life." In Frank P. Andrews, ed., *Research on the Quality of Life.* Ann Arbor: Institute for Social Research, 20.

29. The general rule is that depression is higher in urban areas than in rural areas or villages, but in the United Sates, while the rule applies to the area around Durham, North Carolina, it does not apply to the area around St. Louis, Missouri. Myrna M. Weissman, Martha Livingston Bruce, Philip J. Leaf, Louise Florio, and Charles Holzer III. 1991. "Affective Disorders." In Lee N. Robins and Darrel A. Regier, eds., *Psychiatric Disorders in America: The Epidemiological Catchment Area Study.* New York: Free Press, 76. But note that in Taiwan, with income and migration controlled, dysphoria is higher in rural areas than in Taipei, whereas in Quebec, urban areas have higher rates of depression than rural or small town areas. T. A. Cheng. 1989. "Urbanization and Minor Psychiatric Morbidity." *Social Psychiatry and Psychiatric Epidemiology* 24: 309–16.

30. Ted L. Huston, ed. 1974. *Foundations of Interpersonal Attraction.* New York: Academic, passim; George Levinger. 1974. "A Three Level Approach to Attraction: Toward an Understanding of Pair Relatedness," 100–20. In Huston, ed., ibid; Pitirim A. Sorokin. 1937. *Social and Cultural Dynamics.* New York: American Book Company, vol. 3; William C. Schutz. 1966. *The Interpersonal Underworld.* Palo Alto, Calif.: Science and Behavior Books.

31. For example, the liking–loving distinction, who controls whom, kinds of exchange, mutual investment, feelings of intimacy, and other features of companionship. And many studies addressed specifically to the quality versus quantity of the relationships studied stress the importance of intimacy. See Lawrence A. Palinkas, Deborah L. Wingard, and Elizabeth Barrett-Connor. 1990. "The Biocultural Context of Social Networks and Depression among the Elderly." *Social Science and Medicine* 30: 441–47 at 441; M. S. Clark and H. T. Reis. 1988. "Interpersonal Processes in Close Relationships." *Annual Review of Psychology,* vol. 39: 609–872.

32. Harry T. Reis. 1990. "The Role of Intimacy in Interpersonal Relations." *Journal of Social and Clinical Psychology* 9: 15–30 at 18.

33. Ibid., 19.

34. L. Wheeler, H. T. Reis, and J. Nezlek. 1983. "Loneliness, Social Interaction, and Sex Roles." *Journal of Personality and Social Psychology* 45: 943–53.

35. S. E. Asch. 1946. "Forming Impressions of Personality." *Journal of Abnormal and Social Psychology,* 41: 258–90; Harold H. Kelley. 1949–50. "The Warm–Cold Variable in First Impressions of Person." *Journal of Personality* 18: 431–39.

36. "Support comes when people's engagement with one another extends to a level of involvement and concern, [but] not when they merely touch at the surface of each other's lives. . . . The qualities that seem to be especially critical involve the exchange of intimate communications and the presence of solidarity and trust." Leonard I. Pearlin, Morton A. Lieberman, Elizabeth G. Menaghan, and Joseph T. Mullan. 1981. "The Stress Process." *Journal of Health and Social Behavior* 22: 337–356 at 340, quoted in John Mirowski and Catherine E. Ross. 1989. *Social Causes of Psychological Distress.* New York: Aldine de Gruyter, 143.

37. Karen S. Rook. 1987. "Reciprocity of Social Exchange and Social Satisfaction Among Older Women." *Journal of Personality and Social Psychology* 52: 145–154.

38. Veroff et al., *The Inner Americans,* 117.

39. "Many more people in the 1976 population look at their own independence as a

source of their well-being. . . . Seeking self-sufficiency [is regarded] as a crucial life value for well-being." Ibid., 535.

40. Wheeler, Reis, and Bond. (1989) reported in Harry S. Triandis. 1995. *Individualism and Collectivism.* Boulder: Westview Press, 111.

41. Van Tilburg and associates argue that "reciprocity of social support is the source of feelings of well being," and if this is violated a strain develops between the exchanging parties. Theo Van Tilburg, Eric van Sonderen, and Johan Ormel. 1991. "The Measurement of Reciprocity in Ego-Centered Networks of Personal Relationships: A Comparison of Various Indices." *Social Psychology Quarterly* 54: 54–66 at 54.

42. Peter M. Blau. 1964. *Exchange and Power in Social Life.* New York: Wiley; George Homans. 1961. *Social Behavior: Its Elementary Forms.* New York: Harcourt, Brace and World.

43. Peter P. Ekeh. 1979. *Social Exchange Theory: The Two Traditions.* London: Heinemann.

44. Marcel Mauss. 1954. *The Gift: Forms and Functions of Exchange in Archaic Societies,* trans. I. Cunnison. London: Cohen and West.

45. Triandis, *Individualism and Collectivism,* 43–44. The four measures of the individualism–collectivism dimension correlate .40, which is substantial because reliabilities tend to be low (around .70), so correlations above .49 are impossible. But the measures do converge. The reliabilities are low because there are different kinds of individualism and collectivism. See also Geert Hofstede. 1984. *Culture's Consequences: International Differences in Work-Related Values.* Abridged ed., Beverly Hills, Calif.: Sage. Hofstede's measures of individualism/collectivism correlate .83 with Triandis's measures. For a criticism of this dichotomy, see Shalom H. Schwartz. 1990. "Individualism–Collectivism: Critique and Proposed Refinements." *Journal of Cross-Cultural Psychology* 22: 139–57.

46. Charles Korte, Ido Ypma, and Anneke Toppen. 1975. "Helpfulness in Dutch Society as a Function of Urbanization and Environmental Input Level." *Journal of Personality and Social Psychology* 32: 996–1003; David C. Glass and Jerome E. Singer. 1972. *Urban Stress: Experiments on Noise and Social Situations.* New York: Pantheon.

47. Richard Christie and Florence Geis. 1970. *Studies in Machiavellianism.* New York: Academic, 3–4.

48. Stanley S. Gutterman. 1970. *The Machiavellians: A Social Psychology of Moral Character and Organizational Milieu.* Lincoln: University of Nebraska Press.

49. Christie and Geiss, *Studies in Machiavellianism,* 315–21.

50. Triandis, *Individualism and Collectivism,* 2; Hofstede, *Culture's Consequences.* For a critique of these measures, see Schwartz, "Individualism-Collectivism," 139–57.

51. U.S. Bureau of the Census. 1995. *Statistical Abstract of the United States: 1995.* Washington, D.C., table 1391. The figures are leading, not coincident, "international economic composite indexes." These figures are generally higher than normal growth rates (e.g., U.S. 1993 7.7 vs 3.2). Barrell and Pain report that for the two decades up to 1998, Singapore and South Korea grew at an average rate of almost 10 percent per annum, while Thailand, Malaysia, and Indonesia also grew at "rapid rates." Ray Barrell and Nigel Pain. 1998. "Developments in East Asia and Their Implications for the U.K. and Europe." *National Institute Economic Review,* no. 163 (January) 64–70 at 64, 65.

52. Marco Orrú, Nicole Woolsey Biggart, and Gary G. Hamilton. 1991. "Organizational Isomorphism in East Asia." In Walter W. Powell and Paul J. DiMaggio, eds., *The New Institutionalism.* Chicago: University of Chicago Press, 361–89 at 386–89. See also Yun-shik Chang. 1991. "The Personalist Ethic and the Market in Korea." *Comparative Studies in Society and History* 33: 106–29.

53. Cross-National Collaborative Group. Dec. 2, 1991. "The Changing Rate of Depression: Cross-National Comparisons." *Journal of the American Medical Association* 268: 3098–3105; Myrna M. Weissman, Roger C. Bland, and fifteen others. July 24–31, 1996. "Cross-National Epidemiology of Major Depression and Bipolar Disorder." *Journal of the American Medical Association* 276: 293–99.

54. Ed Diener, Marissa Diener, and Carol Diener. 1995. "Factors Predicting the Subjective Well-Being of Nations." *Journal of Personality and Social Psychology* 69: 851–64 at 858. A curious datum: cross-culturally, divorce is not significantly related to SWB, 859.

55. David I. Hitchcock. 1997. *Factors Affecting East Asian Views of the United States: The Search for Common Ground.* Washington, D.C.: Center for Strategic and International Studies, 12.

56. Max Weber. 1946. "The Social Psychology of the World Religions." In H. H. Gerth and C. Wright Mills, eds., *From Max Weber: Essays in Sociology.* New York: Oxford University Press.

57. Chang, "The Personalist Ethic and the Market in Korea," 106, 120, 121, 122. The real challenge to the Confucian code, he says, is not in the market but in the imperatives of an impersonal rule of law, n. 5, p. 125.

58. Doh C. Shin. 1980. "Does Rapid Economic Growth Improve the Human Lot? Some Empirical Evidence." *Social Indicators Research* 8: 199–221.

59. The conflict between family roles and economic roles takes many forms. Margaret Mead describes the injury to father–son relations when a son learns skills unknown to the father and earns more as a youth than the father has ever earned. Margaret Mead, ed. 1955. *Cultural Patterns and Technical Change.* New York: Mentor. In a cross-cultural study John Whiting found that mothers with economic roles are less indulgent toward their children than mothers whose sole job is family related. John M. Whiting. 1961. "Socialization Process and Personality." In Francis L. K. Hsu, ed., *Psychological Anthropology: Approaches to Culture and Personality.* Homewood, Ill.: Dorsey, 355–80 at 373–74.

60. Diener, Diener, and Diener, "Factors Predicting the Subjective Well-Being of Nations," 851–64 at 859. Oddly, the rate of growth had a low, nonsignificant (.17) relation to level of income, 851.

61. . Weissman et al., "Cross-National Epidemiology of Major Depression and Bipolar Disorder," 295, 297.

62. *The Economist,* August 1–7, 1998. Vol. 345, no. 8079, 700.

63. Barrell and Pain, "Developments in East Asia and Their Implications for the U.K. and Europe," 65.

64. E. B. Ayal. 1963. "Value Systems and Economic Development in Japan and Thailand." *Journal of Social Issues* 19: 35–51.

65. (London) *Guardian,* 29 August 1987, 16.

66. Henry Sumner Maine. 1931 [1861]. *Ancient Law.* Oxford: Oxford University Press, 139–40.

67. James R. Lincoln and Kerry MacBride. 1987. "Japanese Industrial Organization in Comparative Perspective." *Annual Review of Sociology.* Palo Alto, Calif.: Annual Reviews, 13: 289–312 at 291.

68. Hitchcock, *Factors Affecting East Asian Views of the United States,* 17–18.

69. Ibid., 20.

70. Daniel T. L. Shek. 1996. "The Value of Children to Hong Kong Chinese Parents." *Journal of Psychology* 30: 561–70.

71. Leonard Doob. 1960. *Becoming More Civilized: A Psychological Explanation.* New Haven: Yale University Press.

72. Economic "choices were not guided exclusively by economic needs, but rather by the interaction of economic and cultural factors. Individuals and families in the past did not always respond to economic conditions strictly in economic terms." Tamara K. Hareven. 1990. "A Complex Relationship: Family Strategies and the Processes of Economic and Social Change." In Roger Friedland and A. F. Robertson, eds., *Beyond the Marketplace: Rethinking Economy and Society.* New York: Aldine de Gruyter, 219.

Appendix to Chapter 6

1. Stanley Milgram. 1970. "The Experience of Living in Cities: A Psychological Analysis." In Frances F. Korten, Stuart W. Cook, and John I. Lacey, eds., *Psychology and the Problems of Society.* Washington, D.C.: American Psychological Association, 152–73.

2. Charles Korte, Ido Ypma, and Anneke Toppen. 1975. "Helpfulness in Dutch Society as a Function of Urbanization and Environmental Input Level." *Journal of Personality and Social Psychology* 32: 996–1003. The evidence eliminates the effect of more bystanders discovered by Latané and Darley.

3. Claude S. Fischer. 1973. "On Urban Alienation and Anomie, Powerlessness and Social Isolation." *American Sociological Review* 38: 311–26.

4. Jonathan L. Freedman. 1975. *Crowding and Behavior.* San Francisco: Freeman, 135.

Chapter 7. Gaining Felicity While Losing Income?

1. Karl Marx and Friedrich Engels. 1932. *Manifesto of the Communist Party.* New York: International Publishers, 12.

2. It seems that the effect of affiliative behavior on productivity is logistic: a little affiliation on the job increases productivity (and the affiliator's salary) but a little more and productivity declines. Put differently, sociability is compatible with high productivity (and pay) but the *need* for affiliation is not. Randall Filer. 1981. "The Influence of Affective Human Capital on the Wage Equation." In Ronald G. Ehrenberg, ed., *Research in Labor Economics,* vol. 3. Greenwich, Conn.: JAI Press.

3. Barry Gruenberg. 1980. "The Happy Worker: An Analysis of Educational and Occupational Differences in Determinants of Job Satisfaction." *American Journal of*

Sociology 86: 247–71; Christopher Jencks, Laura Perman, and Lee Rainwater. 1988. "What is a Good Job? A New Measure of Labor-Market Success." *American Journal of Sociology* 93: 1322–57. But compare Melvin L. Kohn and Carmi Schooler. 1983. *Work and Personality: An Inquiry into the Impact of Social Stratification.* Norwood, N.J.: Ablex, 66.

4. Glen H. Elder, Tri Van Nguyen, and Avshalom Caspi. 1985. "Linking Family Hardship to Children's Lives." *Child Development* 85: 361–75.

5. Tibor Scitovsky. 1977. *The Joyless Economy.* New York: Oxford, 104.

6. Stein Ringen and Brendan Haplin. 1995. *The Standard of Living of Children.* Oxford: Department of Applied Social Studies and Social Research of the University of Oxford, 32.

7. John Mirowski and Catherine E. Ross. 1989. *Social Causes of Psychological Distress.* New York: Aldine de Gruyter, 142.

8. Ed Diener and Eunkook Suh. 1999. "National Differences in Subjective Well-Being." In Daniel Kahneman, Ed Diener, and Norbert Schwarz, eds. *Foundations of Hedonic Psychology: Scientific Perspectives on Enjoyment and Suffering.* New York: Russell Sage.

9. George W. Brown and Tirril Harris. 1978. *The Social Origins of Depression.* London and Cambridge: Tavistock/Cambridge University Press, 293.

10. Denise B. Kandel, Mark Davies, and Victoria H. Raveis. 1985. "The Stressfulness of Daily Social Roles for Women: Marital, Occupational and Household Roles." *Journal of Health and Social Behavior* 26:64–78.

11. For example, Ruut Veenhoven. 1989. *Conditions of Happiness: Summary Print.* Dordrecht: Reidel, 25.

12. David Birch and Joseph Veroff. 1966. *Motivation: A Study of Action.* Belmont, Calif.: Brooks/Cole, 69.

13. Abraham Maslow. 1968. *Toward a Psychology of Being,* 2d ed. Princeton, N.J.: Van Nostrand, 26, 401–02

14. Israel Adler and Denise B. Kandel. 1982. "A Cross-Cultural Comparison of Sociopsychological Factors in Alcohol Use Among Adolescents in Israel, France, and the United States." *Journal of Youth and Adolescence* 111: 89–113.

15. Clyde Z. Nunn, Harry J. Crockett, Jr., and J. Allen Williams, Jr. 1978. *Tolerance for Nonconformity.* San Francisco: Jossey-Bass.

16. Everett E. Hagen. 1962. *On the Theory of Social Change: How Economic Growth Begins.* Homewood, Ill.: Dorsey; Robert K., Merton, ed. 1973. *The Sociology of Science: Theoretical and Empirical Investigations.* Chicago: University of Chicago Press.

17. Leonard Doob. 1960. *Becoming More Civilized: A Psychological Investigation.* New Haven: Yale University Press. Malcolm Browne. April 10, 1977. *New York Times,* F9; Daniel Lerner. 1959. *The Passing of Traditional Society.* New York: Free Press.

18. Thomas Nagel. 1979. *Mortal Questions.* Cambridge: Cambridge University Press, 132.

19. Philip Brickman and Donald T. Campbell. 1971. "Hedonic Relativism and Planning the Good Society." In M. H. Appley, ed., *Adaptation-Level Theory: A Symposium.* New York: Academic Press.

20. Philip Brickman, D. Coates, and R. Janoff-Bulman. 1978. "Lottery Winners and

Accident Victims: Is Happiness Relative?" *Journal of Personality and Social Psychology* 36: 917–27.

21. Ed Diener, Marissa Diener, and Carol Diener. 1995. "Factors Predicting the Subjective Well-Being of Nations." *Journal of Personality and Social Psychology* 69: 851–64 at 861.

22. L. Wheeler, H. T. Reis, and M. H. Bond. 1989. "Collectivism-Individualism in Everyday Social Life: The Middle Kingdom and the Melting Pot." *Journal of Personality and Social Psychology* 57: 79–86. Reported in Harry C. Triandis. 1995. *Individualism and Collectivism.* Boulder: Westview Press, 111. Americans will be startled to find that an Asian group engages in more self-disclosure than they do.

23. Robert Wuthnow. 1994. *Sharing the Journey: Support Groups and America's New Quest for Community.* New York: Free Press, passim and 53, 170, 172, 199.

24. Edward O. Wilson. 1975. *Sociobiology: The New Synthesis.* Cambridge: Harvard University Press, 7.

25. Sigmund Freud. 1951. *Civilization and its Discontents,* trans. J. Riviere. London: Hogarth Press, 126.

26. Erich Fromm. 1947. *Man for Himself.* New York: Rinehart.

27. Guy Oakes. 1990. *The Soul of the Salesman: The Moral Ethos of Personal Sales.* New York: Humanities Press; Susan Porter Benson. 1986. *Counter Cultures: Saleswomen, Managers, and Customers in American Department Stores, 1890–1940.* Urbana, Ill.: University of Illinois Press.

28. D. Miller, M. F. R. Kets de Vries, and J-M. Toulouse. 1982. "Top Executive Locus of Control and its Relationship to Strategy-Making, Structure, and Environment." *Academy of Management Journal* 25: 237–53.

29. Christopher Jencks, Susan Bartlett, et al. 1979. *Who Gets Ahead? The Determinants of Economic Success in America.* New York: Basic Books, 222.

30. Immanuel Kant. 1920. *Preface to the Fundamental Principles of the Metaphysic of Morals,* ed. and trans. T. K. Abbott and published as *Kant's Theory of Ethics.* London: Longmans, Green, 6th ed. Reprinted in T. M. Greene, ed., *Kant: Selections.* New York: Scribner's Sons, 35.

Chapter 8. Materialism in Market Democracies

1. Although materialists tend to be unhappier than others, there is no evidence that the less intelligent (or at least the less well educated) tend to be materialists. The correlation between a test of materialism and education is +.06 and not significant. Marsha L. Richins and Scott Dawson. 1992. "A Consumer Values Orientation for Materialism and Its Measurement: Scale Development and Validation." *Journal of Consumer Research* 19: 303–16 at 311. There is, however, some evidence that the very effort to be rational makes people unhappy. Robert E. Lane. 1991. *The Market Experience.* New York: Cambridge University Press, 74–77.

2. Asked "When you think about happiness, which one of these things comes to mind as most important?" the postmaterialist emphasizes "interesting and socially useful activities, being esteemed by others, getting along with friends, and leisure activities." The materialist, on the other hand, is much "more likely to emphasize the importance of good

health and having enough money." Ronald Inglehart and Jacques-René Rabier. 1986. "Aspirations Adapt to Situations — But Why Are the Belgians so Much Happier than the French? A Cross-Cultural Analysis of the Subjective Quality of Life." In Frank M. Andrews, ed., *Research on the Quality of Life*. Ann Arbor: Institute for Social Research, 32.

3. Ibid., 32. In later publications Inglehart finds that people in countries with higher proportions of postmaterialists are happier than others. By another measure ("desire for less emphasis on money"), there was no change in the 1981–90 period. Sheena Ashford and Noel Timms. 1992. *What Europe Thinks: A Study of Western European Values*. Aldershot, U.K.: Dartmouth, 134.

4. Inglehart's main critic on this score is A. Marsh. 1975. "'The Silent Revolution,' Value Priorities and the Quality of Life in Britain." *American Political Science Review* 69:21–30. For a rebuttal, see Inglehart. 1977. "Values, Objective Needs, and Subjective Satisfaction Among Western Publics." *Comparative Political Studies* 9: 429–58.

5. Aaron Ahuvia and Nancy Wong. 1997. "Three Types of Materialism: Their Relationships and Origins," working paper delivered at the First Annual Meeting of the Society for Quality of Life Research, Charlotte, N.C., October 1997, 12–15. Aaron Ahuvia, University of Michigan Business School, Ann Arbor, MI 48109–1234. The student sample N was 287, interviewed in 1995–96.

6. Trust other people (r^2 = .02), believe others try to he helpful (r^2 = .03), believe others likely to take advantage of you (r^2 = .05) — all NS. General Social Survey (NORC), National Sample Survey. N various (1,500+), 1994. Historically the love of gain was often extolled. Hume thought that the substitution of "the love of gain over the love of pleasure [is] a great advantage"; Henri Pirenne identified the love of gain with the love of adventure; and the historian Habbakuk believed that it was British acquisitiveness that launched the development of modern economic progress. On the other hand, Schumpeter believed that the great entrepreneurs were not so much interested in gain as in "creating a private kingdom."

7. Marsha L. Richins and Scott Dawson. 1992. "A Consumer Values Orientation for Materialism and Its Measurement: Scale Development and Validation." *Journal of Consumer Research* 19: 303–16 at 308. Strumpel finds that achievement orientation does not imply materialism. Burkhard Strumpel. "Economic Lifestyles, Values, and Subjective Welfare." In Strumpel, ed., *Economic Means for Human Needs*. Ann Arbor: Institute for Social Research, 41.

8. Tim Kasser and Richard M. Ryan. 1993. "A Dark Side of the American Dream: Correlates of Financial Success as a Central Life Aspiration." *Journal of Personality and Social Psychology* 65: 410–22 at 411. Kasser and his associates focus on the goal of "financial success . . . aspirations to attain wealth and material success."

9. Leo Srole. 1956. "Social Integration and Certain Corollaries." *American Sociological Review* 21: 709–16.

10. Gallup Poll, May 17–20, 1990. N = 1,255. Reported in James K. Glassman, "For Most People, Real Wealth Doesn't Come in a Wallet." *Washington Post,* Oct. 22, 1993, B1, B2. As an aside, note that in another poll, those who said they would be willing to sacrifice happiness for a higher paying job were overwhelmingly the young — those whose job status was most precarious. Lutheran Brotherhood Reports. July 1996, reported in *USA Today*.

11. Robert E. Lane. 1962. *Political Ideology: Why the American Common Man Believes What He Does.* New York: Free Press, 259–61.

12. Kasser and Ryan found a similar social desirability factor in their antimaterialism answers, but controlling for this human foible, their main findings held. Tim Kasser and Richard Ryan. 1996. "Further Examining the American Dream: Differential Correlates of Intrinsic and Extrinsic Goals." *Personality and Social Psychology Bulletin* 22(5): 280–87 at 285.

13. Lane, *The Market Experience,* 58–78.

14. Max Weber. 1958 [1904–08]. *The Protestant Ethic and the Spirit of Capitalism,* trans. T. Parsons. New York: Scribner's. But Weber also thought that "the mass of men" were more likely to be motivated by material interests. 1947. *The Theory of Social and Economic Organization,* trans. and ed. T. Parsons. 2d ed. New York: Oxford University Press, 319.

15. D. Collard. 1978. *Altruism and Economy: A Study in Non-Selfish Economics.* Oxford: Martin Robertson; Howard Margolis. 1982. *Selfishness, Altruism, and Rationality: A Theory of Social Choice.* Cambridge: Cambridge University Press; Robert H. Frank. 1988. *Passions Within Reason: The Strategic Role of the Emotions.* New York: Norton.

16. Richins and Dawson, "A Consumer Values Orientation for Materialism," 313. All of the correlations mentioned in the text were at or less than $p < .01$.

17. Kasser and Ryan, "A Dark Side of the American Dream," 415–16. Tocqueville comments, "It is strange to see with what feverish ardor the Americans pursue their own welfare, and to watch the vague dread that constantly torments them lest they should not have chosen the shortest path which may lead to it." *Democracy in America,* Phillips Bradley, ed. New York: Knopf, 2:136.

18. H. W. Perkins. 1991. "Religious Commitment, Yuppie Values, and Well-Being in Post-College Life." *Review of Religious Research* 32: 244–51. I am grateful to David Myers for this summary.

19. Richins and Dawson, "A Consumer Values Orientation for Materialism," 312–13.

20. Ibid., 304. Ahuvia and Wong, however, find a modest relationship between feeling materially deprived in childhood and materialist values, "Three Types of Materialism," 15. Materialism does have a relation to income, but, as we shall see, that relation is to GDP per capita, not specifically the income of the materialist.

21. Kasser and Ryan, "The Dark Side of the American Dream," 421.

22. Kasser and Ryan, "Further Examining the American Dream," 283; Richins and Dawson, "A Consumer Values Orientation for Materialism," 311.

23. Kasser and Ryan, "Further Examining the American Dream," 285.

24. E. L. Deci and R. M. Ryan. 1985. *Intrinsic Motivation and Self-Determination in Human Behavior.* New York: Plenum.

25. Mark R. Lepper and David Greene, eds. 1978. *The Hidden Costs of Rewards: New Perspectives on the Psychology of Human Motivation.* Hillsdale, NJ: Erlbaum.

26. Lita Furby. 1978. "Possessions: Toward a Theory of Their Meaning and Function Throughout the Life Cycle." In P. B. Baltes, ed., *Life-Span Development and Behavior.* New York; Academic Press, 322.

27. Edward E. Lawler III. 1971. *Pay and Organizational Effectiveness.* New York: McGraw-Hill.

28. Kasser and Ryan, "A Dark Side of the American Dream," 415–16. The idea that working with things is less rewarding than working with ideas or people has received only moderate support. See Melvin L. Kohn and Carmi Schooler. 1983. *Work and Personality: An Inquiry into the Impact of Social Stratification.* Norwood, N.J.: Ablex, 64.

29. Richins and Dawson, "A Consumer Values Orientation for Materialism," 308. My emphasis.

30. M. Joseph Sirgy. 1998. "Materialism and Quality of Life." *Social Indicators Research* 43: 227–60 at 228.

31. Harold Laski (1948) believed that Americans are notably "troubled in their consciences" because of the conflict between their dominant materialism and the "American dream of equal opportunity which is always challenging the values of a *business civilization.*" *The American Democracy.* New York: Viking, 12.

32. Daniel K. Yankelovich. 1974. *Changing Values in the 1970s: A Study of American Youth.* New York: John D. Rockefeller 3rd Fund, 16; the same proportion of national samples of adults in Europe (1981 and 1990) agreed. Ashford and Timms, *What Europe Thinks,* 134–36. Reports on the *meaning of money* also suggest conflict and ambivalence. Some accounts refer to the following money problems: obsession with money, anxiety about money, conflict between retentiveness (saving, niggardliness) and spending binges, distrust, shame, self-punishment, money as moral evil, and money as security. Lane, "Money Symbolism and Economic Rationality," chap. 6 of *The Market Experience.*

33. Jeremy Bentham commented: "Under another name, the *desire for wealth* has been furnished with a sort of *letter of recommendation,* which under its own name could not have been given to it." *Jeremy Bentham's Economic Writings,* W. Stark, ed. 1954. vol. 3. Royal Economic Society by George Allen and Unwin, 427.

34. Russell W. Belk. 1984. "Three Scales to Measure Constructs Related to Materialism: Reliability, Validity, and Relationships to Measures of Happiness." In *Advances in Consumer Research* 11, ed. Thomas Kinnear. Provo, Utah: Association for Consumer Research, 291–97; and Russell W. Belk. 1985. "Materialism: Trait Aspects of Living in a Material World." *Journal of Consumer Research* 12: 265–80.

35. Jane Loevinger. 1976. *Ego Development.* San Francisco: Jossey-Bass, 19. Emphasis added. Maturity is here measured by indicators of ego-development, in which at a rather early "conformist stage" people are concerned with "social acceptance and reputation, and . . . *material things.*" As a caveat, however, note that the rejection of material values by youth in the 1960s occurred just at the time a higher incidence of depression and increased unhappiness prevailed among the young.

36. Kasser and Ryan, "A Dark Side of the American Dream," 420.

37. Richins and Dawson. "A Consumer Values Orientation for Materialism," 303; Kasser and Ryan, "Further Examining the American Dream," 284.

38. Kasser and Ryan, "Further Examining the American Dream," 283. With social desirability controlled, the findings still reached statistical significance.

39. Sirgy, "Materialism and Quality of Life," 228.

40. F. Thomas Juster. 1985. "Preferences for Work and Leisure." In Juster and Frank P. Stafford, eds., *Time, Goods, and Well-Being.* Ann Arbor: Institute for Social Research, 333–51 at 336.

41. Kasser and Ryan, "Further Examining the American Dream," 286; K. M. Sheldon

and T. Kasser. 1995. "Coherence and Congruence: Two Aspects of Personality Integration." *Journal of Personality and Social Psychology* 68: 531–43.

42. Sirgy, "Materialism and the Quality of Life." "These equity comparisons generate feelings of inequity, injustice, anger, or envy," 228.

43. Tim Kasser, R. Ryan, M. Zax, and A. Sameroff. 1995. "The Relations of Maternal and Social Environments to Late Adolescents' Materialistic and Prosocial Values." *Developmental Psychology* 31: 907–14.

44. Ahuvia and Wong, "Three Types of Materialism," 14.

45. George P. Moschis. 1987. *Consumer Socialization: A Life-Cycle Perspective.* Lexington, Mass.: Lexington Books.

46. Kasser et al., "The Relations of Maternal and Social Environments to Late Adolescents' Materialistic and Prosocial Values," 907. The subjective experience of recalled "felt deprivation" is even more closely related to adult materialism. Ahuvia and Wong, "Three Types of Materialism," 14.

47. Ronald Inglehart. 1982. "Changing Values in Japan and the West." *Comparative Political Studies* 14: 447–79 at 465.

48. In chapter 7 I found that markets taught much that favored good human relations. The second half of the lesson is that when markets teach materialism, the learning is likely to be situation specific.

49. Teodor Ayllon and Nathan Azrin. 1968. *The Token Economy: A Motivational System for Therapy and Rehabilitation.* New York: Appleton-Century-Crofts.

50. Daryl J. Bem. 1972. "Self-Perception Theory." In Leonard Berkowitz, ed., *Advances in Experimental Social Psychology,* vol. 6. New York: Academic Press.

51. Jeylan T. Mortimer and Jon Lorence. 1985. "Work Experience and Occupational Value Socialization: A Longitudinal Study." *American Journal of Sociology* 84: 1361–85.

52. Ellen Greenberger and Laurence Steinberg. 1986. *When Teenagers Work.* New York: Basic Books.

53. Deborah S. Freedman and Arland Thornton. 1990. "The Consumption Aspirations of Adolescents: Determinants and Implications." *Youth and Society* 21: 259–81.

54. Ron Lesthaeghe and Dominique Meekers. 1986. "Value Changes and the Dimensions of Familism in the European Community." *European Journal of Population* 2: 225–68. Given the role of Protestantism in fostering materialism, I doubt that Western religion resists materialism, although Hinduism may do so. I am indebted to Ahuvia and Wong for this and the two citations just above.

55. For further discussion, see Lane, *The Market Experience,* 563–68.

56. Robert B. Textor. 1967. *A Cross-Cultural Summary.* New Haven: HRAF Press.

57. Furby, "Possessions: Toward a Theory of Their Meaning and Function Throughout the Life Cycle," 304–05.

58. Somewhere Margaret Mead suggests that when toddlers begin to reach for things that do not belong to them, they are told, "That is not yours." Robert White's study of children in play groups found that "a disproportionately high amount of time spent procuring objects is negatively related with good development." Robert W. White. April 1976. "Exploring the Origins of Competence" *APA Monitor,* 40–45.

59. Ernest Beaglehole. 1931. *Property: A Study in Social Psychology.* London: Allen and Unwin.

60. Stephen E. G. Lea, Roger M. Tarpy, and Paul Webley. 1987. *The Individual in the Economy.* Cambridge: Cambridge University Press, 165.

61. Lawrence D. Becker. 1980. "The Moral Basis of Property Rights." In J. R. Pennock and J. W. Chapman, eds., *Property,* NOMOS, vol. 22. New York: New York University Press, 201.

62. See, for example, M. A. Wahba and L. G. Bridewell. 1976. "Maslow Reconsidered: A Review of Research on the Need Hierarchy." *Organizational Behavior and Human Performance* 15: 210–40.

63. See, for example, in a growing literature on evolutionary psychology, Richard Wrangham and Dale Peterson. 1996. *Demonic Males: Apes and the Origins of Human Violence.* Boston: Houghton Mifflin; Albert Somit and Steven A. Peterson. 1997. *Darwinism, Dominance, and Democracy: The Biological Basis of Authoritarianism.* Westport, Conn.: Praeger.

64. The quotations from Thurnwald and Malinowski and the last quotation from Polanyi are all from Karl Polanyi. 1971. "Our Obsolete Market Mentality." In George Dalton, ed., *Primitive, Archaic, and Modern Economies: Essays of Karl Polanyi.* Boston: Beacon Press, 66.

65. Alex Inkeles and David H. Smith. 1974. *Becoming Modern.* Cambridge: Harvard University Press.

66. Leonard W. Doob. 1960. *Becoming More Civilized: A Psychological Exploration.* New Haven: Yale University Press.

67. Ed Diener and Marissa Diener. 1995. "Cross-Cultural Correlates of Life Satisfaction and Self-Esteem." *Journal of Personality and Social Psychology* 67: 653–63 at 661. See also Russell W. Belk. 1988. "Third World Consumer Culture." In *Research in Marketing,* Suppl. 4, Erdogan Kumcu and A. Fuat Firat, eds. Greenwich, Conn.: JAI Press.

68. Irvin L. Child. 1968. "Personality in Culture." In Edgar F. Borgata and William W. Lambent, eds., *Handbook of Personality Theory and Research.* Chicago: Rand McNally, 82–145.

69. "In the postmodernization phase of development, emphasis shifts from maximizing economic gains—the central goal of modernization—to maximizing subjective well-being." Ronald Inglehart and Marita Carballo. 1997. "Does Latin America Exist? (And Is There a Confucian Culture?): A Global Analysis of Cross-Cultural Differences." *PS: Political Science and Politics* 30: 34–46 at 39.

70. John Maynard Keynes. 1972 [1930]. "Economic Possibilities for Our Grandchildren." *Essays in Persuasion.* In *Collected Works of John Maynard Keynes,* vol. 9. London: Macmillan for the Royal Economic Society, 321–34 at 329. Keynes went on to say, "All kinds of social customs and economic practices, affecting the distribution of wealth and economic rewards and penalties, which we now maintain at all costs, because they are tremendously useful in promoting the accumulation of capital, we shall then be free, at last, to discard." What will happen to Keynes's discipline when acquisitiveness declines? Hirschman proposes that "the main impact of *The Wealth of Nations* was to establish a powerful *economic* justification for the untrammeled pursuit of individual self-interest"—as contrasted to the previous political justifications. Albert O. Hirschman. 1977. *The Passions and the Interests: Political Arguments for Capitalism Before Its Triumph.* Princeton: Princeton University Press, 100.

71. Elinor Scarborough. 1995. "Materialist-Post-materialist Value Orientations." In Jan W. van Deth and Elinor Scarborough, eds., *The Impact of Values,* vol. 4 of *Beliefs in Government.* Oxford: Oxford University Press, 123–59.

72. Fuchs and Klingeman report that "the post-materialist age has, for the moment at least, come to a halt." Dieter Fuchs and Hans Dieter Klingeman. 1995. "Citizens and the State: A Relationship Transformed." In Hans Dieter Klingeman and Dieter Fuchs. 1995. *Citizens and the State: Beliefs in Government,* vol. 1. Oxford: Oxford University Press, 419–43 at 439.

73. Ahuvia and Wong, "Three Types of Materialism," 12–15.

74. Scarborough, "Materialist-Post-materialist Value Orientations," 156.

75. Levy found that in Israel two orthogonal values accounted for most of the ideological pattern: wanting "to be rich" or wanting "to be religious." Shlomit Levy. 1986. *The Structure of Social Values,* trans. H. Gratch. Jerusalem: Guttman Institute of Applied Social Research.

76. Ronald Inglehart. 1977. *The Silent Revolution: Changing Values and Political Styles Among Western Publics.* Princeton: Princeton University Press, 38; idem. 1981. "Post-Materialism in an Environment of Insecurity." *American Political Science Review* 75: 880–900 at 888. (By 1980, these ranks had changed hardly at all, and the U.S. figures not at all.) Because of the large group of people with mixed responses, these data account for less than half of the population.

77. Geoffrey Gorer says that Americans talk more about money than Europeans (giving the impression of greater materialism), but in fact they value money less than others. He refers to the "symbolic value of money" as something like school grades and contrasts that with valuing money for what it will buy. Geoffrey Gorer. 1948. *The American People: A Study in National Character.* New York: Norton, 174.

78. Eric L. Dey, Alexander W. Astin, and William S. Korn. 1991. *The American Freshmen: Twenty-Five-Year Trends.* Los Angeles: Higher Education Research Institute, Graduate School of Education UCLA; Alexander Astin and others. 1991–95. *The American Freshmen: National Norms for Fall 1991* (and ensuing volumes through 1995). Los Angeles: High Education Research Institute, UCLA. The graph and citation are copied from a manuscript kindly sent to me by David Myers, Hope College. A confirming study that pinpoints the period of greatest change is offered by the pollster and savant Daniel Yankelovich, who found an extraordinary shift toward goal materialism. Over the three years from 1970 to 1973, the students in his national college sample drastically shifted their concept of "most important goals" to emphasize "the money you earn" from 36 percent in 1970 to 61 percent in 1973. An account in the *New York Times* of January 1, 1987, gives a report of a similar survey of California freshmen: over the decade 1976 to 1986, the proportion of freshmen reporting that it is important "to promote racial understanding" declined from 36 percent to 27percent, while the proportion believing that it is important "to be very well off financially" increased from 53 percent to 73 percent. (Yankelovich, *Changing Values,* 16.) The evidence of a rise in materialist values among the young is overwhelming. For further evidence, see Frank Levy. 1985. "Happiness, Affluence, and Altruism in the Postwar Period." In Martin David and Timothy Smeeding, eds., *Horizontal Equity, Uncertainty, and Economic Well-Being.* Chicago: University of Chicago Press, 7–34.

79. Scarborough, "Materialist-Post-materialist Value Orientations," 138.

80. The trouble with this theory is that occupation is not closely linked to policy materialism in Europe (ibid., 149, 150) or to goal materialism in the United States (at least it is not related to income or closely related to education). Kasser and Ryan, "Further Examining the American Dream," 383; Richins and Dawson, "A Consumer Values Orientation for Materialism," 311.

81. Inglehart and Rabier, "Aspirations Adapt to Situations," 22.

82. Strumpel, "Economic Life-Styles, Values, and Subjective Welfare," 27.

83. Frank Knight. 1935, *The Ethics of Competition and Other Essays.* New York: Augustus Kelley, 44.

84. Inglehart and Rabier, "Aspirations Adapt to Situations," 32.

85. "More emphasis on family life": 1981 = 85 percent%; 1990 = 87 percent. Ashford and Timms, *What Europe Thinks,* 134, 136. A somewhat similar pattern prevails in the United States: asked (1986) about the areas of improvement and decline in American life, 64 percent of an American national sample said family life had declined (and 8 percent said it had improved) while 54 percent said our standard of living had declined (and 14 percent said it had improved). Of the solutions offered, 44 percent said society should put less emphasis on money and material things. *The Public Perspective,* Feb.–March 1997. 8: 10.

86. Richins and Dawson, "A Consumer Values Orientation for Materialism," 303, 308.

87. Lane, *The Market Experience,* 74–77.

Chapter 9. Is Well-Being a Market Externality?

1. Randall Bartlett. 1989. *Economics and Power: An Inquiry into Human Relations and Markets.* Cambridge: Cambridge University Press, 3.

2. Ed Diener, Marissa Diener, and Carol Diener. 1995. "Factors Predicting the Subjective Well-Being of Nations." *Journal of Personality and Social Psychology* 69: 851–64 at 861. For a balanced account of the costs of growth in South Korea, see Doh C. Shin. 1980. "Does Rapid Economic Growth Improve the Human Lot? Some Empirical Evidence." *Social Indicators Research* 8: 199–221.

3. Richard A. Easterlin. 1995. "Will Raising the Incomes of All Increase the Happiness of All?" *Journal of Economic Behavior and Organization* 27: 35–47 at 41.

4. Myrna M. Weissman and seventeen others. July 24–31 1996. "Cross-National Epidemiology of Major Depression and Bipolar Disorder." *Journal of the American Medical Association* 275: 293–99 at 295.

5. Joseph A. Schumpeter. 1936 [1911]. *The Theory of Economic Development: An Inquiry into Profits, Capital, Credits, Interest, and the Business Cycle,* trans. R. Opie, 2d ed. Cambridge: Harvard University Press.

6. Ed Diener and F. Fujita. 1995. "Resources, Personal Strivings, and Subjective Well-Being: A Nomothetic and Ideographic Approach." *Journal of Personality and Social Psychology"* 68: 926–35.

7. Diener et al., "Factors Predicting the Subjective Well-Being of Nations," 861.

8. Karl Polanyi. 1944. *The Great Transformation.* New York: Rinehart.

9. As Schor points out, employers do not offer their workers a choice between more

income or more leisure; except for the roughly 18 percent who are represented by unions, these choices are decided unilaterally by the employer. Juliet B. Schor. 1991. *The Overworked American: The Unexpected Decline of Leisure.* New York: Basic Books, 1, 3.

10. Robert E. Lane. 1991. *The Market Experience.* New York: Cambridge University Press, 309, 334.

11. Robert E. Lane. 1992. "Work as 'Disutility' and Money as 'Happiness': Cultural Origins of a Basic Market Error." *Journal of Socio-Economics* 21: 43–64.

12. C. Brown. 1980. "Equalizing Differences in the Labor Market." *Quarterly Journal of Economics* 94: 113–34. Adam Smith (1937 [1776]) said, "The wages of labor vary with the ease or hardship, the cleanliness or dirtiness, the honourableness or dishonourableness of employment." *The Wealth of Nations,* Edwin Cannan, ed. New York: Random House, 100.

13. Schor, *The Overworked American.* Other studies (whose data Schor challenges) disagree. See John P. Robinson. 1985. "Changes in Time Use: An Historical Overview." In F. Thomas Juster and Frank P. Stafford, eds., *Time, Goods, and Well-Being.* Ann Arbor: Institute for Social Research. Also Juster, "A Note on Recent Changes in Time Use," chap. 12. In ibid., 318–19. Schor and the U.S. Bureau of the Census disagree, e.g., 1990. *Statistical Abstract of the United States, 1990.* Washington, D.C. Although it seems to be true that women, with their dual responsibilities, are overworked, among men only the better educated are (1994) working longer than they were twenty years ago, while those with high school or less education are working fewer hours now than in 1975. Data from 1981–82 show that if one adds household work to market work, men in the 25–44 age group worked 61.4 hours, while women in the same age group worked 56.4 hours. But it is certainly true that Americans have shorter vacations and fewer holidays than Europeans. Sylvia Nasar. December 1, 1994. "More Men in Prime of Life Spend Less Time Working." *New York Times,* Al, D15.

14. "Reserve Board Officials Say the Economy Wasn't Braked Too Heavily." *New York Times,* March 15, 1995, 23.

15. Melvin L. Kohn and Carmi Schooler. 1983. *Work and Personality: An Inquiry into the Impact of Social Stratification.* Norwood, N.J.: Ablex, 142.

16. Angus Campbell, Philip E. Converse, and Willard L. Rodgers. 1976. *The Quality of American Life: Perceptions, Evaluations, and Satisfactions.* New York: Russell-Sage, 356. The figure is from page 357.

17. Schor, *The Overworked American,* 11.

18. In a somewhat hyperbolic statement (not accounting for the one hundred capitalist years during which hours were shortened or for the greater leisure time in Europe), Schor says, "In the starkest terms, my argument is this: Key incentive structures of capitalist economies contain biases toward long working hours. As a result of these incentives, the development of capitalism led to the growth of what I call 'long hour jobs,' " ibid., 7. For other theories of the sources and meaning of the tradeoff between work and leisure, see Gary Becker. 1965. "A Theory of the Allocation of Time." *Economic Journal* 75: 493–517; Steffan Linder. 1970. *The Harried Leisure Class.* New York: Columbia University Press.

19. R. D. Caplan, A. Abbey, D. J. Abramis, F. M. Andrews, T. L. Conway, and R. P. French. 1984. *Tranquilizer Use and Abuse.* Ann Arbor: Institute for Social Research.

20. Antonia Abbey and Frank M. Andrews. 1986. "Modeling the Psychological Deter-

minants of Life Quality." In Frank M. Andrews, ed., *Research on the Quality of Life*. Ann Arbor: Institute for Social Research, 108. Louis Harris (1987) reports that 74 percent of those with low stress say they are satisfied with their lives, 55 percent with moderate stress, and only 32 percent of those reporting high stress. *Inside America*. New York: Vintage, 42

21. David Brindle. 30 May 1994. "GPs Report Rise in Stress." *The Guardian*, 3.

22. Harris, *Inside America*, 8–10.

23. Schor, *The Overworked American*, 11.

24. Harris, *Inside America*, 10. Stress increases the level of serotonin in the blood, a useful nonmanipulable measure which, so far as I know, has not been used to verify alleged increases in the stress levels of a population over time.

25. John P. Robinson. 1990. "The Time Squeeze." *American Demographics* 12: 30–33; Jeremy Rifkin. 1987. *Time Wars*. New York: Henry Holt, 14–15; Schor, *The Overworked American*, 11; Harris, *Inside America*, 8–10.

26. Ruut Veenhoven. 1989 [1984]. *Conditions of Happiness: Summary Print*. Dordrecht: Reidel, 56. Veenhoven found that unemployment decreases happiness only for those who want to work, that is, the retired, housewives happy in their homemaking role, and the unemployed who have given up are no less happy than working people. But most of what we think of as the unemployed do want to work.

27. Norman M. Bradburn and David Caplovitz. 1965. *Reports on Happiness*. Chicago: Aldine, 72–73.

28. Michael Argyle. 1992. *The Social Psychology of Everyday Life*. New York: Routledge, 264. That unemployment is more the cause than the consequence of depression is confirmed by other studies: see Ronald C. Kessler, James S. House, and J. Blake Turner. 1987. "Unemployment and Health in a Community Sample." *Journal of Health and Social Behavior* 28: 51–59.

29. Michael Frese and Gisela Mohr. 1987. "Prolonged Unemployment and Depression in Older Workers: A Longitudinal Study of Intervening Variables." *Social Science and Medicine* 25: 173–78.

30. Olafur Olafson and Per-Gunnar Svensson. 1986. "Unemployment-Related Lifestyle Changes and Health Disturbances in Adolescents and Children in the Western Countries." *Social Science and Medicine* 22: 1105–13 at 1105.

31. Norman T. Feather and P. R. Davenport. 1981. "Unemployment and Depressive Affect: A Motivational and Attributional Analysis." *Journal of Personality and Social Psychology* 41: 422–36.

32. James N. Morgan, Ismail S. Sirageldin, and Nancy Baerwaldt. 1966. *Productive Americans: A Study of How Individuals Contribute to Economic Progress*. Ann Arbor: Institute for Social Research.

33. Before events in the 1990s overtook the idea of a "natural rate" of unemployment necessary to prevent inflation, Samuelson and Nordhaus observed, "The natural rate of unemployment seems tragically high—far above the rate necessary for frictional migration of young workers searching for jobs. This sober finding must restrain the most enthusiastic defender of mixed capitalism." Paul A. Samuelson and William D. Nordhaus. 1985. *Economics*, 12th ed. New York: McGraw-Hill, 206–07.

34. Ibid., 258. The European pattern of high wages, high taxes, high welfare provi-

sions—and high unemployment (compared to U.S. standards in these respects) reflects a market equilibrium that distributes well-being in a curiously selective way.

35. Ralph Catalano and David C. Dooley. 1977. "Economic Predictors of Depressed Mood and Stressful Life Events in a Metropolitan Community." *Journal of Health and Social Behavior* 18: 292–307. Nor does inflation influence political choices: Sears and Funk's exhaustive analysis of self-interest in politics finds "the personal impact of inflation quite consistently has had no influence on voters' choices." David O. Sears and Carolyn L. Funk. 1991. "The Role of Self-Interest in Social and Political Movements." *Advances in Experimental Social Psychology,* vol. 24. New York: Academic Press, 1–91 at 44.

36. Ruut Veenhoven. 1993. *Happiness in Nations: Subjective Appreciation of Life in 56 Nations 1946–1992*. Rotterdam: Erasmus University, RISBO, 127.

37. Robert J. Schiller. March 1996. "Why Do People Dislike Inflation?" Cowles Foundation Discussion Paper No. 1115. New Haven: Yale University.

38. The security offered by money has political consequences as well. Georg Simmel puts it this way: "The feeling of personal security that the possession of money gives is perhaps the most concentrated and pointed form and manifestation of confidence in the social-political organization and order." Georg Simmel. 1978 [1907]. *The Philosophy of Money,* trans. T. Bottomore and D. Frisby. London: Routledge and Kegan Paul, 179.

39. Frank M. Andrews and Steven B. Withey. 1976. *Social Indicators of Well-Being: Americans' Perceptions of Life Quality.* New York: Plenum, 253.

40. Alex C. Michalos. 1986. "Job Satisfaction, Marital Satisfaction, and the Quality of Life." In Frank M. Andrews, ed., *Research on the Quality of Life.* Ann Arbor: Institute for Social Research, 75; my emphasis.

41. "Robert Reich calls salaried people with a growing sense of insecurity, 'the anxious class . . . consisting of those Americans who no longer can count on having their jobs next year, or next month, and whose wages have stagnated or lost ground to inflation.'. . . 'Over and over people tell us they are concerned about their jobs, that they don't feel secure, that the economy is doing badly. . . . For most people, if the economy is not synonymous with jobs, it is at least highly coordinated with jobs.' (From Louis Harris polls). . . 'The Michigan Consumer Survey and the University of Chicago's NORC . . . describe the anxiety and insecurity that emerge from life without this safety net, and even among people with good jobs at good pay.'. . . 'For the first time in 50 years, we are recording a decline in people's expectations and their uncertainty and anxiety grows the farther you ask them to look into the future.'. . . 'Over the last decade or so, layoffs have spread from blue-collar workers and the less educated across the income and education stratum.'" (Richard Curtin, director of Michigan Consumer Surveys.) These quotations are taken from Louis Uchitelle, "The Rise of the Losing Class," *New York Times,* November 20, 1994, Section 4, 1, 5.

42. Mark Tran. 30 August 1997. "Job Insecurity Haunts U.S. Workers Despite Boom." *The Guardian,* 3. The same article reports a then-recent survey of the U.S. workforce reporting widespread feelings of insecurity.

43. In 1996, 85 percent of a national sample said they liked their jobs. *The Public Perspective,* vol. 8, Feb.–March 1997, 9. An earlier study showed that work commitment ("I'm fully committed to my work") was higher in the States (68 percent) than any of the

six nations measured except for Israel. Daniel Yankelovich, Hans Zetterberg, Burkhard Strümpel, and Michael Shanks. 1985. *The World at Work: An International Report on Jobs, Productivity, and Human Values*. New York: Octagon, 393–97. The correlation of work satisfaction with happiness is a modest but respectable +.29 (as reported in table 2.2) and seems to fit with the majority of studies dealing with the contribution of work satisfaction to SWB.

44. Jeylan T. Mortimer. 1979. *Changing Attitudes Toward Work: Highlights of the Literature*. New York: Pergamon for American Institute Studies in Productivity, 10. One review of twenty-three studies found that "for more than 90 percent of the cases, the direction of this relationship [between job satisfaction and overall well-being] was positive; none of the scattered negative relationships was statistically reliable." R. W. Rice, R. G. Hunt, and J. P. Near. 1980. "The Job-Satisfaction/Life-Satisfaction Relationship: A Review of Empirical Research." *Basic and Applied Social Psychology* 1: 37–64 at 37, cited in Michalos, "Job Satisfaction, Marital Satisfaction, and the Quality of Life," 62.

45. Linder, *The Harried Leisure Class*.

46. Kohn and Schooler, *Work and Personality*, 87, 117–18.

47. Frederick Herzberg. 1973. *Work and the Nature of Man*. New York: Mentor/New American Library.

48. Harry Braverman. 1974. *Labor and Monopoly Capital: The Degradation of Work in the Twentieth Century*. New York: Monthly Review Press.

49. Kenneth I. Spenner. 1979. "Temporal Change in Work Content." *American Sociological Review* 44: 968–75. For a fuller treatment see my *The Market Experience*, 283–88.

50. Richard T. Curtin. 1977. *Income Equity Among U.S. Workers: The Bases and Consequences of Deprivation*. New York: Praeger.

51. Faye J. Crosby. 1982. *Relative Deprivation and Working Women*. New York: Oxford University Press.

52. Sidney Verba and Gary R. Orren. 1985. *Equality in America: The View from the Top*. Cambridge: Harvard University Press.

53. Christopher Jencks, Lauri Perman, and Lee Rainwater. 1988. "What Is a Good Job? A New Measure of Labor-Market Success." *American Journal of Sociology* 93: 1322–57 at 1343.

54. Barry Gruenberg. 1980. "The Happy Worker: An Analysis of Educational and Occupational Differences in Determinants of Job Satisfaction." *American Journal of Sociology* 86: 247–71 at 269. Juster and Courant report that "enjoying people one works with" is most important for work satisfaction, but nearly twice as important for women as for men. For those who dislike work, "dislike people [I] work with" is the most important reason. F. Thomas Juster and Paul N. Courant. 1986. "Integrating Stocks and Flows in Quality of Life Research." In Frank M. Andrews, ed., *Research on the Quality of Life*. Ann Arbor: Institute for Social Research, 156–57.

55. Joseph Veroff, Elizabeth Douvan, and Richard A. Kulka. 1981. *The Inner Americans: A Self-Portrait from 1957 to 1976*. New York: Basic Books, 546.

56. Tibor Scitovsky. 1977. *The Joyless Economy*. New York: Oxford University Press.

57. Yankelovich et al., *The World at Work*, 393.

58. The relative pay of professors may be high or low, according to one's standards, but

there is no question about their liking their work: asked if they would choose the same career if they had a second chance, 93 percent of urban university professors said they would repeat their choices, more than the members of any other occupation. United States Department of Health, Education, and Welfare, Task Force. ca. 1972. *Work in America.* Cambridge: MIT Press, 16. Professors were followed in close order by mathematicians, physicists, biologists, and chemists. Then came lawyers (83–85 percent), journalists, and then, at 77 percent, church university professors. White-collar workers (43 percent) were far above blue-collar workers (24 percent).

59. Daniel Yankelovich and John Immerwahr. 1983. *Putting the Work Ethic to Work.* New York: Public Agenda Foundation. The interesting and complex effect of pay on intrinsic enjoyment of work is developed in my *The Market Experience,* 364–425 and in some detail in Mark R. Lepper and David Greene, eds. 1978. *The Hidden Costs of Rewards: New Perspectives on the Psychology of Human Motivation.* Hillsdale, N.J.: Erlbaum.

60. Rosabeth Moss Kanter. 1977. *Work and Family in the United States.* New York: Russell Sage.

61. Karl Polanyi. 1971. "Our Obsolete Market Mentality." In Polanyi, *Primitive, Archaic and Modern Economies.* Boston: Beacon, 70.

62. Glen H. Elder, Tri Van Nguyen, and Avshalom Caspi. 1985. "Linking Family Hardship to Children's Lives." *Child Development* 85: 361–75.

63. Arlie Hochschild. 1989. *The Second Shift: Working Parents and the Revolution at Home.* New York: Viking Penguin. Quoted in Schor, *The Overworked American,* 12.

64. Compared to women in market work, housewives "are much more likely to be anxious and worried (46% to 28%), lonely (44% to 26%), and to feel worthless (41% to 24%)." Philip Shaver and Jonathan Freedman. 1976. "Your Pursuit of Happiness." *Psychology Today* 10 (August), 27–32, 75 at 29. See also P. Newberry, M. M. Weissman, and J. K. Myers. 1979. "Working Wives and Housewives: Do They Differ in Mental Status and Social Adjustment?" *American Journal of Orthopsychiatry* 49: 282–91.

65. Robinson, "Changes in Time Use: An Historical Overview," 299.

66. Sylvia A. Hewlett reports that "child neglect has become endemic to our society." See her [1991] *When the Bough Breaks: The Cost of Neglecting Our Children.* New York: Basic Books, 1. But time use studies find that time spent in child care by college-educated women with market jobs is as great as that of housewives without market jobs. C. Russell Hill and Frank P. Stafford. "Parental Care of Children: Time Diary Estimates of Quantity, Predictability, and Variety." In Juster and Stafford, eds., *Time, Goods, and Well-Being,* 425.

67. Olafur Olafsson and Per-Gunnar Svensson. 1986. "Unemployment-Related Lifestyle Changes and Health Disturbances in Adolescents and Children in the Western Countries." *Social Science and Medicine* 22: 1105–13.

68. Victor H. Vroom. 1964. *Work and Motivation.* New York: Wiley. For some exceptions, see Edward E. Lawler III. 1982. "Strategies for Improving the Quality of Work Life." *American Psychologist* 37: 486–93.

69. Randall Filer. 1981. "The Influence of Affective Human Capital on the Wage Equation." In Ronald G. Ehrenberg, ed., *Research in Labor Economics,* vol. 3. Greenwich, Conn.: JAI Press. For some unhappy consequences of the need for affiliation, see chapter 5.

70. "By and large . . . the norm of treatment in the factory emphasizes just, humane, respectful treatment of subordinates, at least compared to what goes on in many other settings in underdeveloped countries." Alex Inkeles and David H. Smith. 1974. *Becoming Modern.* Cambridge: Harvard University Press, 65.

71. David C. McClelland and David G. Winter. 1971. *Motivating Economic Achievement.* New York: Free Press, 15.

72. Raymond Firth. 1968. "The Social Framework of Economic Organization." In E. E. Clair and H. K. Schneider, eds., *Economic Anthropology.* New York: Holt, Rinehart and Winston, 79.

73. Michael Buroway. 1979. *Manufacturing Consent: Changes in the Labor Process under Monopoly Capitalism.* Chicago: University of Chicago Press.

74. "Constructive work . . . lead[s] on indefinitely from one success to another without ever coming to an end." Bertrand Russell. 1930. *The Conquest of Happiness.* London: G. Allen and Unwin, 214. But the evidence that people use their free time to work on problems that interest them comes from the psychologists' laboratory. See, for example, Richard de Charms. 1968. *Personal Causation: The Internal Affective Determinants of Behavior.* New York. Academic Press.

75. John Maynard Keynes. 1972 [1931]. "Economic Possibilities for Our Grandchildren." In his *Essays in Persuasion.* In *Collected Works of John Maynard Keynes,* vol. 9. London: Macmillan for the Royal Economic Society, 321–34 at 332.

Chapter 10. Pain and Loneliness in a Consumers' Paradise

1. I thank for their help and absolve from blame Michael Argyle, Patrick Dunleavy, Stephen Edgel, and Stein Ringen, who commented on an earlier version of this chapter, "The Road Not Taken."

2. James F. Engel, Roger D. Blackwell, and David T. Kollat. 1978. *Consumer Behavior,* 3d ed. Hinsdale, Ill.: Dryden Press, 3.

3. Stanley Diamond. 1974. *In Search of the Primitive.* New Brunswick, N.J.: Transaction, 11.

4. Erich Fromm. 1968. *The Revolution of Hope.* New York: Rinehart, 1, 28. Along lines similar to mine, Fromm then advises a more humanistic form of consumption (120). For a rejoinder to this and other criticisms of consumption, see George Katona. 1975. *Psychological Economics.* New York: Elsevier, 376.

5. Michael E. Sobel. 1981. *Lifestyles and Social Structure.* New York: Academic Press, 32.

6. Juliet Schor. 1991. *The Overworked American: The Unexpected Decline of Leisure.* New York: Basic Books, 3, 107.

7. Martha S. Hill. 1985. "Patterns of Time Use." In F. Thomas Juster and Frank P. Stafford, eds., *Time, Goods, and Well-Being.* Ann Arbor: Institute for Social Research, 133–76 at 151. After retirement the sex difference almost disappears. It is notable that the total population spends about twice as much time on shopping as on child care (ibid., 136).

8. George Katona, Burkhard Strumpel, and Ernest Zahn. 1971. *Aspirations and Affluence: Comparative Studies in the United States and Western Europe.* New York: McGraw-Hill, 37. These authors contrast the American assimilationist class model to the

failure of the working class in Germany to aspire to middle-class status—but things may have changed since 1972.

9. Engel et al., *Consumer Behavior,* 99, 101.

10. Vicky Robin. 1991. "Sustainable Lifestyles: Must We Shop 'Till We all Drop?" *TOES/Americas* 8 (Fall/Winter), 22–23 at 22.

11. Alvin Haddock. 1974. "Use of Demographics in Analysis of Channels of Distribution." In William D. Wells, ed., *Life Style and Psychographics.* Chicago: American Marketing Association, 215.

12. Frank M. Andrews and Stephen B. Withey. 1976. *Social Indicators of Well-Being: Americans' Perceptions of Life Quality.* New York: Plenum, 124, 132.

13. F. Thomas Juster. 1981. "Preferences for Work and Leisure." In Juster and Stafford, eds., *Time, Goods, and Well-Being,* 333–51 at 336.

14. John P. Robinson. 1977. *How Americans Use Their Time.* New York: Praeger; quoted in Michael Argyle, *The Psychology of Happiness.* London: Methuen, 67. Out of eighteen activities a national sample ranked shopping fifteenth, about the same as television watching and scoring far lower than that generally disliked activity, housework (eleventh).

15. Theo B. C. Poiesz and Jaspar von Grumbkow. 1988. "Economic Well-Being, Job Satisfaction, Income Evaluation and Consumer Satisfaction: An Integrative Attempt." In W. Fred Van Raaij, Gery M. Van Veldhoven, Karl-Erik Wärneryd, eds., *Handbook of Economic Psychology.* Dordrecht: Kluwer, 570–93 at 580.

16. Alice M. Isen. 1987. "Positive Affect, Cognitive Processes, and Social Behavior." In L. Berkowitz, ed., *Advances in Experimental Social Psychology,* vol. 20. New York: Academic Press. 103–253.

17. "Money transforms the *real essential powers of man and nature* . . . into tormenting chimeras—just as it transforms . . . chimeras—and essential powers which are really impotent, which exist only in the imagination of the individual—into *real powers and faculties.*" Karl Marx. 1964 [1844] "The Power of Money in Bourgeois Society." In *Economic and Philosophical Manuscripts of 1844,* trans. M. Milligan, ed. Dirk Struik. New York: International Publishers, 169. Emphasis in the original.

18. Joan Robinson. 1969. *The Economics of Imperfect Competition,* 2d ed. London: Macmillan, xi–xii. Engels et al. argue that consumer sovereignty follows from the highly limited control by advertising of consumer choices: only a third of the commercials to which a person is exposed make an impression on active memory and of those attended to only 6 percent can be recalled twenty-four hours later. This kind of "minimal influence" argument has been undermined by research on "priming," putting things on the agenda. See Engel et al., *Consumer Behavior,* 6. Put more forcefully, "the essential element [of marketing thinking] is that the *consumer* is central to both the design and the delivery responsibility of marketing managers." F. Stuart DeBruicker and Scott Ward. 1980. *Cases in Consumer Behavior.* Englewood Cliffs: Prentice-Hall, 1.

19. Milton Friedman. 1962. *Capitalism and Freedom.* Chicago: University of Chicago Press. Friedman points out that economic transactions are such that both parties must be relatively satisfied in order for the transaction to take place. Friedman translates this to mean an enhancement of freedom, but of course all acts are freely chosen or they would not have been undertaken. (I freely choose to hand over my wallet to the robber who

threatens my life if he freely chooses to accept my wallet in exchange for not shooting me.) The crucial question is whether the costs of not accepting an offer are in some sense acceptable, e.g., the opportunity costs are not penury and destitution but rather a less well-paying job. Friedman's point must be stripped of its ideology to be useful.

20. Joseph Plummer. 1974. "Applications of Life Style Research in the Creation of Advertising Campaigns." In Wells, ed., *Life Style and Psychographics,* 166.

21. "Today, . . . people seem to use their consumption styles as a way of expressing their identity and social position." Milton Moss. 1968. "Consumption: A Report on Contemporary Issues." In Eleanor B. Sheldon and Wilbert E. Moore, eds., *Indicators of Social Change: Concepts and Measurements.* New York: Russell Sage, 164; Berkely Rice. 1988. "The Selling of Life-Styles." *Psychology Today* 22(3): 48–50; M. J. Sirgy. 1982. "Self-Concept in Consumer Behavior: A Critical Review." *Journal of Consumer Research* 9: 287–300.

22. Leo Lowenthal. 1969. *Literature, Popular Culture, and Society.* Palo Alto, Calif.: Pacific Books.

23. Engels et al., *Consumer Behavior,* 214.

24. Sobel, *Lifestyles and Social Structure,* chap. 9.

25. Brian Mullen and Craig Johnson. 1990. *The Psychology of Consumer Behavior.* Hillsdale, N.J.: Erlbaum, 80.

26. T. A. Wills. 1981. "Downward Comparison Principles in Social Psychology." *Psychological Bulletin* 90: 245–71.

27. In her more general attack on consumerism, Schor makes this point. *The Overworked American,* 119.

28. Ibid.

29. R. W. Belk and R. W. Pollay. 1985. "Images of Ourselves: The Good Life in Twentieth-Century Advertising." *Journal of Consumer Research* 11: 887–97.

30. Katona, *Psychological Economics,* 388.

31. Max Weber. 1958 [1904–06]. *The Protestant Ethic and the Spirit of Capitalism,* trans. T. Parsons. New York: Scribner's, 181.

32. Robert Kuttner. 1997. *Everything for Sale: The Virtues and Limits of Markets.* New York: Knopf. When large firms substitute contract labor for in-house labor, says Kuttner, workers and managers lose their security and sense of well-being (as well as their loyalty to the firm); in matters of health, whenever business criteria are substituted for professional medical criteria, patients suffer longer illnesses and sometimes accelerated death.

33. Hannah Arendt. 1958. *The Human Condition.* Chicago: University of Chicago Press, 100.

34. Gary A. Steiner. 1963. *The People Look at Television.* New York: Knopf.

35. John Ward, letter to *The Observer,* 15 May 1983. Ward was responding to a letter from Martin Amis reporting that he found the broadcast advertising offensive. Responding to a variety of complaints, President Kennedy set forth a Consumers' Bill of Rights in the early 1960s, and claims that consumerism reduced well-being have become increasingly prevalent: C. Droge, M. Agrawal, and R. Mackoy. 1993. "The Consumption Culture and Its Critiques: A Framework for Analysis." *Journal of Macromarketing* 13: 32–45. In 1997, at least four organizations make less consumption, if not asceticism, their

main message: "The Other Economic Summit" (TOES), Center for a New American Dream, the Karl Polanyi Institute (Concordia University), and the Global Development and Environment Institute (Tufts University). For the last of these, see Neva R. Goodwin, Frank Ackerman, and David Kiron, eds. 1997. *The Consumer Society.* Washington, D.C.: Island Press, produced by the institute.

36. Joel B. Cohen and Dipankar Chakravarti. 1990. "Consumer Psychology." *Annual Review of Psychology, 1990.* Palo Alto, Calif.: Annual Reviews, 243–88 at 251.

37. See, for example, James G. March. 1978. "Bounded Rationality, Ambiguity, and the Engineering of Choice." *Bell Journal of Economics* 9: 578–608 at 597.

38. E. J. Mishan. 1971 [1967]. *The Costs of Economic Growth.* Harmondsworth, U.K.: Penguin, 159–60.

39. Steven H. Chafee and Jack M. McLeod. 1973. "Consumer Decisions and Information Use." In Scott Ward and Thomas S. Robertson, eds., *Consumer Behavior: Theoretical Sources.* Englewood Cliffs: Prentice-Hall, 387.

40. F. T. Marquez. 1977. "Advertising Content: Persuasion, Information, or Intimidation." *Journalism Quarterly* 54: 3.

41. Jacob Jacobs, Donald E. Speller, and Carol A. Kohn. 1974. "Brand Choice Behavior as a Function of Information Load." *Journal of Marketing Research* 11: 63–69.

42. Harold M. Schroder, Michael J. Driver, and Siegfried Streufert. 1967. *Human Information Processing.* New York: Holt, Rinehart and Winston.

43. Jacob Jacobs. 1976. "Perspectives on a Consumer Information Program." In Michael L. Ray and Scott Ward, eds., *Communicating with Consumers.* Beverly Hills, Calif.: Sage, 21–22.

44. Joseph A. Schumpeter. 1950. *Capitalism, Socialism, and Democracy,* 3d ed. London: George Allen and Unwin, 259.

45. For example, Engel et al., *Consumer Behavior;* Katona, *Psychological Economics;* Cohen and Chakravarti, "Consumer Psychology"; R. W. Belk, K. D. Bahn, and R. N. Mayer. 1982. "Developmental Recognition of Consumption Symbolism." *Journal of Consumer Research* 9: 4–17; and Peter Earl. 1983. *The Economic Imagination: Towards a Behavioural Analysis of Choice.* Armonk, N.Y.: Sharpe.

46. Reported in Kent C. Berridge. 1996. "Pleasure, Pain, Desire, and Dread: Some Biopsychological Pieces and Relations." In Daniel Kahneman, Ed Diener, and Norbert Schwarz, eds. 1999. *Foundations of Hedonic Psychology: Scientific Perspectives on Enjoyment and Suffering.* New York: Russell Sage.

47. Walter Mischel. 1974. "Processes in Delay of Gratification." In L. Berkowitz, ed., *Advances in Experimental Social Psychology,* vol. 7. New York: Academic, 217.

48. Dennis W. Rook. 1987. "The Buying Impulse." *Journal of Consumer Research* 14: 189–99 at 189.

49. Katona, *Psychological Economics,* 237.

50. Adrian Furnham. 1985. "Attitudes To, and Habits of, Gambling in Britain." *Human Individual Differences* 6: 493–502. Note that Scitovsky's criticism of American consumption was that it was guided too much by a policy of minimal arousal (comfort) and not enough by arousing challenges (pleasure). Tibor Scitovsky. 1977. *The Joyless Economy.* New York: Oxford University Press.

51. Kurt W. Fischer and Louise Silvern. "Stages and Individual Differences in Cognitive

Development." *Annual Review of Psychology,* vol. 36. Palo Alto, Calif.: Annual Reviews, 639.

52. "Stimuli that are moderate in intensity, complexity, and novelty should be more likely to hit the optimal level." Michael L. Ray. 1973. "Psychological Theories and Interpretations of Learning." In Ward and Robertson, eds., *Consumer Behavior: Theoretical Sources,* 45–75 at 75.

53. Adam Smith. 1939 [1776]. *An Inquiry into the Nature and Causes of the Wealth of Nations,* Edwin Cannan, ed. New York: Modern Library/Random House, 14.

54. As a caveat, note that in the United States, where the largest proportion of the GDP is spent on advertising, the public also spends the most on philanthropy, both in volunteering time and in contributing money to charity. Helmut K. Anheier, Lester Salamon, and Edith Archambault. March–April 1994. "Participating Citizens: U.S.–Europe Comparisons in Volunteer Action." *The Public Perspective* 5: 16–17, 34. For example, whereas the proportion of people who volunteered their time was 19 percent in France and 13 percent in Germany, 49 percent of the people in the States volunteered. Also whereas about 44 percent of the French and Germans (eliminating the voluntary religious tax) contributed money in the previous twelve months, 73 percent of the Americans did so, 17. This is not just a reflection of the higher claim religious organizations make on Americans, for those who gave to churches were also more likely to give to secular organizations. Robert Wuthnow. 1994. *Sharing the Journey: Support Groups and America's New Quest for Community.* New York: Free Press, 66, 326.

55. Kenneth Boulding. 1967. "The Basis of Value Judgments in Economics." In Sidney Hook, ed., *Human Values and Economic Policy.* New York: New York University Press, 68. For the importance of trust in developing countries, see George M. Guthrie. 1977. "A Social Psychological Analysis of Modernization in the Philippines." *Journal of Cross-Cultural Psychology* 8: 177–206.

56. Alex Inkeles and Larry Diamond. "Personal Development and National Development: A Cross-Cultural Perspective." In Alexander Szalai and Frank M. Andrews, eds., *The Quality of Life: Comparative Studies.* Ann Arbor: Institute for Social Research," 73–109 at 97.

57. James S. House and Sharon Wolf. 1978. "Effects of Urban Residence on Interpersonal Trust and Helping Behavior." *Journal of Personality and Social Psychology* 36: 1029–43.

58. Morris Rosenberg and Leonard E. Pearlin. 1978. "Social Class and Self-Esteem among Children and Adults." *American Journal of Sociology* 84: 53–77.

59. Joseph Luft. 1957. "Monetary Value and the Perception of Persons." *Journal of Social Psychology* 46: 245–51.

60. Robert Goodin has argued that because the market corrupts moral values, one should erect a wall between activities that require moral norms and those commercial activities that do not and which must be preserved because of the usefulness of the more or less naked pursuit of self-interest. Robert E. Goodin. 1982. *Political Theory and Public Policy.* Chicago: University of Chicago Press. I doubt if that is possible; and certainly not in economic life—as in the case of a family business.

61. Kuttner, *Everything for Sale: The Virtues and Limits of Markets.*

62. Allen Silver. 1990. "Friendship in Commercial Society: Eighteenth-Century Social Theory and Modern Sociology." *American Journal of Sociology* 95:1474–1504 at 1474.

63. Leonard Berkowitz and P. Friedman. 1967. "Some Social Class Differences in Helping Behavior." *Journal of Personality and Social Psychology* 5: 231–42.

64. Robert B. Hays. 1985. "A Longitudinal Study of Friendship Development." *Journal of Personality and Social Psychology* 48: 909–24.

65. Georg Simmel. 1950. "The Metropolis and Mental Life." In *The Sociology of Georg Simmel,* trans. and ed. Kurt H. Wolff. Glencoe, Ill.: Free Press, 412.

66. Geoffrey Gorer. 1948. *The American People.* New York: Norton.

67. Leonard J. Pearlin and Melvin L. Kohn. 1966. "Social Class, Occupation, and Parental Values: A Cross-Cultural Study." *American Sociological Review* 31: 466–79.

68. Belk et al., "Developmental Recognition of Consumption Symbolism." E. C. Hirschman and M. B. Holbrook, eds. 1981. *Symbolic Consumer Behavior.* Ann Arbor: Association for Consumer Research.

69. A. Braithwaite. 1983. "Situations and Social Action: Applications for Marketing of Recent Theories in Social Psychology." *Journal of the Market Research Society* 25: 19–38 at 33. For a glimpse at comparable problems in Germany, see Susanne C. Grunert and Gerhard Scherhorn. 1990. "Consumer Values in West Germany: Underlying Dimensions and Cross-Cultural Comparison with North America." *Journal of Business Research* 20: 97–107.

70. While it might be objected that income, rather than the availability of time, determines how much time one shops, the fact is that nationally, time spent shopping has declined as per capita income has increased; and, in any event, time spent shopping is unrelated to level of income.

71. John P. Robinson, "Changes in Time Use: An Historical Overview." In Juster and Stafford, eds., *Time, Goods, and Well-Being,* 305. While such gross figures are important, a more careful analysis would break down the figures by social group. For example, for the 1975–81 comparison, elderly men increased their television watching by eight hours and decreased their "services shopping" by half an hour, whereas young husbands did not increase their television watching at all and *increased* their shopping by about half an hour.

72. F. Thomas Juster. "A Note on Recent Changes in Time Use." In Juster and Stafford, *Time, Goods, and Well-Being,* 318–19. For men, the new time released by marginally declining work hours — about one hour per week — was, after a general increase in household work is accounted for, devoted about equally to television, shopping, and socializing. In contrast, the increased time women spent on their jobs came from decreasing housework and from watching less television (about fifty minutes per week), rather than from reductions in social entertainment or conversation. And women with jobs spend almost as much time shopping as do housewives. Incidentally, there was a modest decline in television exposure in the United States during the 1975–82 period, mostly among young adults and more often among men than women. There was also a British decline, with an estimated average exposure of 27.0 minutes per day in 1985 declining to 25.1 minutes in 1990. *The Independent,* 25 June 1992, 3.

73. Michael Argyle. 1996. *The Social Psychology of Leisure.* London: Penguin, 185–86.

74. Ibid., 187.

75. In 1994, Roper asked the following question: "Please tell me if you think each of the following explains your use of television very well, sometimes, or hardly at all." Almost half agreed that television entertained and informed them about the news; a third agreed that it was a form of relaxation; 26 percent said it helped to fill their spare time; and 23 percent said "for companionship when alone." Roper. Nov. 5–12, 1994. In *The Public Perspective,* 6 (Aug.–Sept. 1995): 47

76. Michael Argyle and Maryanne Martin. 1991. "The Psychological Causes of Happiness." In Fritz Strack, Michael Argyle, and Norbert Schwarz, eds., *Subjective Well-Being: An Interdisciplinary Perspective.* Oxford: Pergamon, 77–100 at 92.

77. Robert D. Putnam. 1996. "The Strange Disappearance of Civic America." *The American Prospect* 24 (Winter): 34–48 at 47.

78. Albert Bandura. 1977. *Social Learning Theory.* Englewood Cliffs: Prentice-Hall, 184.

79. Argyle and Martin, "The Psychological Causes of Happiness," 92. The authors are reporting on research by Csikszentmihalyi and Kubey (1981).

80. Brian Swimme. 1966. *The Hidden Heart of the Cosmos.* Maryknoll, N.Y.: Orbis. Reprinted in "How Do Our Kids Get So Caught up in Consumerism?" *Enough* (Center for the New American Dream), November 1997, 1.

81. Scott Ward, Daniel B. Wackman, and Ellen Wartella. 1977. *How Children Learn to Buy.* Beverly Hills: Sage. Engel et al. also report that the effect of advertising on children "often adds to parent–child conflict by stimulating repeated purchase requests." *Consumer Behavior,* 272.

82. Grant Noble. 1975. *Children in Front of the Small Screen.* Beverly Hills: Sage, 76.

83. Sara Rimer. May 1, 1996. "With TV Off, Real Life Reasserts Itself." *New York Times,* A12.

84. Engel et al., *Consumer Behavior,* 279–80. Interpersonal recommendations rely on opinion leaders whose salient quality was "gregariousness," not expertise. 285.

85. Ibid., 12–13.

86. Plummer, "Applications of Life Style Research in the Creation of Advertising Campaigns," 166.

87. Engel et al., *Consumer Behavior,* 135–36.

88. Anat Rafaeli and Robert I. Sutton. 1990. "Busy Stores and Demanding Customers: How Do They Affect the Display of Positive Emotion?" *Academy of Management Journal* 33: 623–37. Similarly in banking: "The more crowded the bank, the less satisfied was the customer." Richard S. Cimbalo and Patricia M. Mousaw. 1975. "Crowding and Satisfaction in a Banking Environment, an Ethological Approach." *Psychological Reports* 37: 201–02. The authors explain this dissatisfaction as resentment about the violation of personal space.

89. Andrew M. Forman and Ven Sriram. 1991. "The Depersonalization of Retailing: Its Impact on the 'Lonely' Consumer." *Journal of Retailing* 67: 226–43.

90. Martha S. Hill and F. Thomas Juster. 1986. "Constraints and Complementarities in Time Use." In Juster and Stafford, *Time, Goods, and Well-Being,* 461. Hill and Juster believe that the force of gender roles found in their study is changing, but that the current pattern still reflects a major division between the sexes. Married women who work for

wages average between three and eighteen more hours per week in total work than married men.

91. It has been alleged that "the number of products that an individual always buys for individual consumption must certainly represent a very small proportion of consumer expenditures." Engel et al., *Consumer Behavior,* 151. Conflicts over consumer preferences are negatively related to well-being. See also Lyman E. Ostland. "Role Theory and Group Dynamics." In Scott Ward and Thomas S. Robertson, eds., *Consumer Behavior.* Englewood Cliffs: Prentice-Hall, 230–64. Because spending money on collectively consumed goods requires extensive family discussion, this allegation implies extensive socializing. Hill, "Patterns of Time Use," 151–52, 160–61.

92. In discussions of politics, there was a certain deference to the wife of someone who might be expected to be informed, but regarding commodities, everyone was her own expert. Elihu Katz and Paul Felix Lazarsfeld. 1955. *Personal Influence: The Part Played by People in the Flow of Mass Communications.* Glencoe, Ill.: Free Press.

93. Peter H. Reingen, Brian L. Foster, Jacqueline L. Brown, and Stephen B. Seidman. 1984. "Brand Congruence in Interpersonal Relations: A Social Network Analysis." *Journal of Consumer Research* 11: 771–83.

94. There is a large literature on "collective consumption" which I cannot discuss here. This literature deals in part with the public–private dimension and the government regulation of consumption, but not with the way collective consumption encourages companionship. I am greatly indebted to Dunleavy for drawing my attention to this literature. See Patrick Dunleavy. 1992. *Democracy, Bureaucracy, and Public Choice.* Englewood Cliffs: Prentice-Hall.

95. Robinson, "Changes in Time Use," 299.

96. U.S. Bureau of the Census, *Statistical Abstract of the United States, 1990.* Washington, D.C.: G.P.O., tables 699 and 713. Comparisons for earlier periods do not always confirm the thesis advanced.

97. Mihalyi Csikszentmihalyi and Eugene Rochberg-Halton. 1981. *The Meaning of Things: Domestic Symbols and the Self.* Cambridge: Cambridge University Press, 129.

98. Peter Laslett. 1971. *The World We Have Lost,* 2d ed. New York: Scribner's, 22.

99. Richard A. Musgrave. "When Is the Public Sector Too Large?" In Charles Lewis Taylor, ed. 1983. *Why Governments Grow: Measuring Public Sector Size.* Beverly Hills: Sage, 20.

Chapter 11. Rising Malaise

1. Ronald Inglehart. 1997. *Modernization and Postmodernization: Cultural, Economic, and Political Change in 43 Societies.* Princeton: Princeton University Press.

2. Ed Diener, Ed Sandvik, and William Pavot. 1991. "Happiness Is the Frequency, Not the Intensity, of Positive versus Negative Affect." In Fritz Strack, Michael Argyle, and Norbert Schwarz, eds., *Subjective Well-Being: An Interdisciplinary Perspective.* Oxford: Pergamon, 119–40; Richard R. Lau, David Sears, and R. Centers. 1979. "The 'Positivity Bias' in Evaluations of Public Figures: Evidence Against Instrumental Artifacts." *Public Opinion Quarterly* 43: 347–58.

3. "Psychologists have long been aware that human subjects, asked to make ratings of

almost anything, tend to use the positive side of the rating scale more heavily than the negative side." Angus Campbell, Philip Converse, and Willard L. Rodgers. 1976. *The Quality of American Life*. New York: Russell Sage, 99.

4. Margaret Matlin and David J. Stang. 1978. *The Pollyanna Principle: Selectivity in Language, Memory, and Thought*. Cambridge, Mass.: Schenkman; Darlene E. Goodhart. 1985. "Some Psychological Effects Associated with Positive and Negative Thinking about Stressful Outcomes: Was Pollyanna Right?" *Journal of Personality and Social Psychology* 48: 216–32.

5. Jean Piaget. 1977. *The Origins of Intelligence in the Child,* trans. M. Cook. New York: Norton, 17; Michael I. Posner. 1973. *Cognition: An Introduction.* Glenview, Ill.: Scott Foresman, 116.

6. Ruut Veenhoven. 1991. "Questions on Happiness: Classical Topics, Modern Answers, Blind Spots." In Strack et al., eds., *Subjective Well-Being: An Interdisciplinary Perspective,* 14.

7. Ed Diener. 1984. "Subjective Well-Being." *Psychological Bulletin* 95: 542–75; Michael W. Fordyce. 1977. "Development of a Program to Increase Personal Happiness." *Journal of Counseling Psychology* 24: 511–21.

8. Ed Diener and Carol Diener. 1996. "Most People Are Happy." *Psychological Science* 7: 181–85.

9. Ed Diener and Marissa Diener. 1995. "Cross-Cultural Correlates of Life Satisfaction and Self-Esteem." *Journal of Personality and Social Psychology* 68: 653–63.

10. Richard A. Brody and Paul M. Sniderman. 1977. "From Life Space to Polling Place: The Relevance of Personal Concerns for Voting Behavior." *British Journal of Political Science* 7: 337–60 at 359.

11. Richard R. Lau. 1985. "Two Explanations for Negativity Effects in Political Behavior." *American Journal of Political Science* 29: 119–38 at 119.

12. Jill G. Klein. 1991. "Negativity Effects in Impression Formation: A Test in the Political Arena." *Personality and Social Psychology Bulletin* 17: 412–18 at 412.

13. Arthur H. Miller. 1974. "Political Issues and Distrust in Government: 1964–1970." *American Political Science Review* 68: 951–72 at 952.

14. William A. Gamson. 1968. *Power and Discontent.* Homewood, Ill.: Dorsey. Lipset and Schneider use the virtual synonym, "confidence." Seymour M. Lipset and William Schneider. 1983. *The Confidence Gap: Business, Labor, and Government in the Public Mind.* New York: Free Press.

15. Ronald Inglehart. 1990. *Culture Shift in Advanced Industrial Societies.* Princeton: Princeton University Press, 31–33.

16. Humphrey Taylor. 1992. "The American Angst of 1992." *The Public Perspective* 3:3.

17. Lipset and Schneider, *The Confidence Gap,* 61–66.

18. Unless otherwise specified, these data are from the National Election Studies CD-ROM, analyzed by Soo Yeon Kim of the Yale Social Science Statistical Laboratory. Supplementary comments are based on National Election Studies. 1994. *1952–1992 Cumulative Data File: Codebook*. Ann Arbor: Center for Political Studies; and Warren Miller and Santa A. Traugott. 1989. *American National Election Studies: Data Sourcebook, 1952–1986.* Cambridge: Harvard University Press. Over this period, all age

groups increased their distrust, although women were less trusting of government than men; and college education was something of a protection against distrust.

19. More detailed graphs—not shown—portray the negative, distrustful answers peaking in 1980 and again in 1990, a pattern for which political explanations are, at best, strained.

20. A. Miller, "Political Issues and Distrust in Government: 1964–1970"; E. J. Dionne, Jr. 1991. *Why Americans Hate Politics.* New York: Simon and Schuster.

21. Jack Citrin. 1974. "Comment: [on A. Miller "Political Issues and Distrust in Government: 1964–1970"] Political Relevance of Trust in Government." *American Political Science Review,* 68: 973–88; Everett C. Ladd. 1992. "Who Says Americans Are 'Mad as Hell'?" *The Political Perspective,* July/August, 6–7; Lipset and Schneider, *The Confidence Gap.*

22. Citrin, "Comment," 975.

23. Alexis de Tocqueville. 1945 [1835]. *Democracy in America,* Phillips Bradley, ed. New York: Knopf, 2:330.

24. James Bryce. 1910. *The American Commonwealth.* New York: Macmillan, 2:352.

25. A. Lawrence Lowell. 1913. *Public Opinion and Popular Government.* New York: Longmans, Green, 130–31.

26. Geoffrey Gorer. 1948. *The American People.* New York: Norton, 225.

27. Lipset and Schneider, *The Confidence Gap,* 159.

28. Donald J. Treiman. 1977. *Occupational Prestige in Comparative Perspective.* New York: Academic.

29. Eric Anderson and Donald Granberg. 1991. "Types of Affective Evaluators in Recent U.S. Presidential Elections." *Polity* 24: 147–55.

30. For example, Leonard Silk. April 17, 1992. "Is Liberalism Back in the Saddle?" *New York Times,* D2. Silk is reporting on an article by William G. Mayer showing that between 1980 and 1989 there was a dramatic decrease in popular beliefs that the "government in Washington" was "too big" (from about a half to about a third) and a decline in those claiming that taxes were too high (58 percent to 55 percent).

31. Lowell, *Public Opinion and Popular Government,* 131.

32. James Boswell. 1906 [1791]. *The Life of Samuel Johnson,* vol. 2. New York: E. P. Dutton, 149.

33. Hugo Young goes on to say that Parliament "impedes rather than advances questions that transcend politics but require a political solution; and instead of a consensus for action, Parliament's great modern achievement is consensus for a style of politics that prevents action. Parliament is in low water" ("The Down-Your-Throat Politics that Chokes Debates." *The Guardian,* 15 July 1993, 20). Also, the leader of the Liberal Democrats, Paddy Ashdown, referred (*The Guardian,* 13 July 1993, 8) to a "public disenchantment with the political process" and went on to say that members of the public "see the House of Commons as a political soap opera . . . good for entertainment but not of much relevance to their real lives."

34. Eric Jacobs and Robert Worcester. 1990. *We British: Britain under the MORI-scope.* London: Weidenfeld and Nicolson, 67–68. The survey question was, "Now looking at this list of people and organizations, which, if any, would you say you are satisfied with in how it is performing its role in society? And which, if any, are you dissatisfied with

in how it is performing its role in society?" "Government ministers" ranked fourth from the bottom (26 percent satisfied; 47 percent dissatisfied), and Parliament itself ranked only a little better (28 percent satisfied; 45 percent dissatisfied).

35. Inglehart, *Culture Shift in Advanced Industrial Societies,* 38; and Inglehart. 1977. "Values, Objective Needs, and Subjective Satisfaction Among Western Public." *Comparative Political Studies* 9: 429–58. The papers at the First Europaeum Conference (1993) on the question "Are Elites Losing Touch With their Publics?" suggested considerable concern about the loss of trust in European publics. See Jack Hayward, ed. 1996. *Élitism, Populism, and European Politics.* Oxford: Clarendon Press.

36. Ronald Inglehart and Jacques-René Rabier. 1986. "Aspirations Adapt to Situations — But Why Are the Belgians so Much Happier than the French? A Cross-Cultural Analysis of the Subjective Quality of Life." In Frank M. Andrews, ed., *Research on the Quality of Life.* Ann Arbor: Institute for Social Research, 54; Sheena Ashford and Noel Timms. 1992. *What Europe Thinks: A Study of European Values.* Aldershot, U.K.: Dartmouth, 92.

37. Dieter Fuchs and Hans Dieter Klingeman. 1995. "Citizens and the State: A Relationship Transformed." In Hans Dieter Klingeman and Dieter Fuchs, eds., *Citizens and the State: Beliefs in Government,* vol 1. Oxford: Oxford University Press, 419–43 at 430.

38. Dieter Fuchs, Giovanna Guidorossi, and Palle Svensson. 1995. "Support for the Democratic System." In ibid. 323–53 at 334. For a contrary interpretation, see Robert D. Putnam. 1995. "Bowling Alone: America's Declining Social Capital." *Journal of Democracy* 6: 18–19.

39. James Sterngold. 1995. "In Japan the Clamor of Change Runs Headlong into Old Groove." *New York Times,* January 3, A6. In Indonesia (hardly a democracy), Malaysia, and Thailand the principal stated sources of malaise among one hundred selected leaders were corruption and inefficiency. David I. Hitchcock. 1997. *Factors Affecting East Asian View of the United States: The Search for Common Ground.* Washington, D.C.: Center for Strategic and International Studies, 10–11. In Thailand the urban population opposed corruption while the rural population saw it as simply a continuation of the familiar patron–client relation.

40. For some historical periods in the United States, both the alternative and alternating theories may be correct, since the all-time high for antibusiness feeling in the United States was in the Populist period of the 1890s (higher than during the New Deal), when people turned to government for redress of their economic grievances. Louis Galambos. 1975. *The Public Image of Big Business in America, 1880–1940.* Baltimore: Johns Hopkins University Press, 275.

41. In explaining this parallelism, I have shown how the public confound the two domains (asked about the economy, the public responds in terms of government regulation, taxes, and welfare), how, because information is stored in the memory by mood, feelings generalize from one domain to another, and how the public holds government responsible for economic performance, especially inflation and unemployment. Robert E. Lane. 1979. "The Legitimacy Bias: Conservative Man in Market and State." In Bogdan Denitch, ed., *The Legitimation of Regimes.* London: Sage.

42. A. D. Lindsay. 1943. *The Modern Democratic State.* Oxford: Oxford University Press.

43. Angus Campbell. 1981. *The Sense of Well-Being in America.* New York: McGraw-Hill.

44. M. Margaret Conway. 1991. *Political Participation in the United States,* 2d ed. Washington, D.C.: Congressional Quarterly Press, 51–52.

45. In 1988 the NES added a middle term, "neither agree nor disagree," which is invariably attractive to the less interested and involved. With that term added, measures for 1988, 1990, and 1992 reveal a modest reversal of the decline, with a very flat line showing a modest increase in disagreement. By and large, the old were more efficacious; efficacy increases with education and even more with income; and men were more efficacious than women.

46. A. Miller. "Political Issues and Trust in Government: 1964–1970."

47. Each of the two questions used here forms a part of a broader index; since the indices do not cover the long-term periods that concern us, I have used the longest-running single question, instead. Some confidence that internal political efficacy measures the more general personality trait of personal control is suggested by the correlation of the efficacy question with a more general "personal competence" question asked only in the 1968–76 period. The correlation of 0.286 may not seem high by some standards, but it is higher than any of the eight other correlations measured, except for external efficacy as given in the text.

48. Icek Ajzen and Martin Fishbein. 1980. *Understanding Attitudes and Predicting Social Behavior.* Englewood Cliffs: Prentice-Hall.

49. Virginia Held. 1989 [1984]. *Rights and Goods: Justifying Social Action.* Chicago: University of Chicago Press; C. R. Sunstein. 1991. "Preferences and Politics." *Philosophy and Public Affairs* 20: 3–34.

50. Robert E. Lane. 1996. "'Losing Touch' in a Democracy: Demands vs. Needs." In Hayward, ed., *Élitism, Populism, and European Politics,* 33–66.

51. "A few big interests" had its highest sustained rating under Carter, peaking in 1980 (Reagan–Carter campaign), dropped for four years, and then, through Reagan's second term and Bush's term, rose again to its previous high (almost 80 percent) in the Bush–Clinton campaign.

52. This question is part of a general citizen duty index including such items as the following: Do people think it important to vote "when so many other people vote," "when your party doesn't have a chance to win," and voting in relatively "unimportant" local elections. In the early 1980s from 86 to 91 percent of the public affirmed the importance of voting.

53. See William H. Riker and Peter C. Ordshook. 1973. *An Introduction to Positive Political Theory.* Englewood Cliffs: Prentice-Hall, 62–63.

54. David O. Sears and Carolyn L. Funk. 1991. "The Role of Self-Interest in Social and Political Movements." *Advances in Experimental Social Psychology,* vol. 24. New York: Academic Press, 1–91; Dale T. Miller and Rebecca K. Rattner. 1998. "The Disparity Between the Actual and Assumed Power of Self-Interest." *Journal of Personality and Social Psychology* 74: 53–62.

55. Patrick A. Pierce. 1993. "Political Sophistication and the Use of Candidate Traits in Candidate Evaluation." *Political Psychology* 14: 21–35.

56. I do not believe that this can be described as a flight from guilt; there are positive

pleasures in collective ceremonies of civic duty. Robert E. Lane. 1965. "The Tense Citizen and the Casual Patriot: Role Confusion in American Politics." *Journal of Politics* 27: 735–60.

57. Sears and Funk, "The Role of Self-Interest," 14.

58. In addition to Brody and Sniderman, Citrin, Dionne, Lau, A. Miller, and Taylor, all cited above, see Michael Crozier, Samuel P. Huntington, and Joji Watanuki. Nov.–Dec. 1993. "The Ungovernability of Democracy." *The American Enterprise* 4: 26–41; Jeffrey C. Goldfarb. 1991. *The Cynical Society: The Culture of Politics and the Politics of Culture.* Chicago: University of Chicago Press; Donald L. Kanter and Philip H. Mirvis. 1989. *The Cynical American: Living and Working in an Age of Discontent and Disillusion.* San Francisco: Jossey-Bass.

59. David Watson, James W. Pennebaker, and Robert Folger. 1986. "Beyond Negative Affectivity: Measuring Stress and Satisfaction in the Workplace." *Journal of Organizational Behavior and Management* 8: 141–57. Batson and associates distinguish between negative *affect* (irritation, fear, anger), which leads to remedial action, and negative *mood* (unhappiness, dysphoria, depression), which tends to inhibit action. It seems to me that political negativity is more of a negative affect than a negative mood, helping to explain why cynicism or even alienation does not have more effect on turnout. See C. Daniel Batson, Laura L. Shaw, and Kathryn C. Oleson. 1992. "Differentiating Affect, Mood, and Emotion: Toward Functionally Based Conceptual Distinctions." In Margaret S. Clark, ed., *Emotion.* Review of Personality and Social Psychology, vol. 13. Newbury Park, Calif.: Sage, 294–326.

60. Ruut Veenhoven. 1993. *Happiness in Nations: Subjective Appreciation of Life in 56 Nations 1946–1992.* Rotterdam: Erasmus University, RISBO, 69.

61. Inglehart, *Culture Shift in Advanced Industrial Societies,* 30, 33.

62. On a seven-point scale, in which a score of 5.0 is average, respondents to a national survey ranked their feelings about "the way our national government is operating and what it is doing" at 4.0, almost the lowest, while ranking "your standard of living—the things that you have like housing, car and furniture" at 5.1, and "your family life—your wife/husband, your marriage, your children, if any" at 5.7. In addition to "the way our national government is operating;" the questions (early 1970s) included "what our government is doing about the economy"; "our national military activities"; "the way our political leaders think and act"; and "how the United States stands in the eyes of the rest of the world." Frank M. Andrews and Steven B. Withey. 1976. *Social Indicators of Well-Being: Americans' Perceptions of Life Quality.* New York: Plenum, 124, 127–28.

63. If the method of calculation used is a stepwise regression, evaluation of national government adds slightly more to the predictive power of these political items. Ibid., 127–28.

64. John Mirowski and Catherine E. Ross. 1989. *Social Causes of Psychological Distress.* New York: Aldine de Gruyter, 131.

65. Ibid., 13.

66. Ibid.

67. Veenhoven, *Happiness in Nations,* 50.

68. Hadley Cantril. 1965. *The Pattern of Human Concerns.* New Brunswick, N.J.: Rutgers University Press.

69. Veenhoven, *Happiness in Nations,* 69. It is important to control for level of income, for interpersonal trust is highly correlated with GDP per capita. In Europe this correlation was .53. Inglehart, *Culture Shift in Advanced Industrial Societies,* 37.

70. Robert D. Putnam. Winter 1996. "The Strange Disappearance of Civic America." *American Prospect* 24: 34–48 at 41. The original "misanthropy scale" which included the trust item was devised to assess political attitudes. See Morris Rosenberg. 1956. "Misanthropy and Political Ideology." *American Sociological Review* 6: 690–95.

71. This is not surprising because trust is, as these things go, relatively closely linked to internal political efficacy (+.28) and with a participation scale (+.20). Asked, "Do you think most people try to take advantage of you if they get a chance, or would they try to be fair?" a little over a third think others would take advantage of them, with the highest answers of this kind in the most recent years measured, 1993–94, and a steady decline in "try to be fair" from 1980 to 1994. See table 2.4.

72. Putnam's research also emphasizes the decline in interpersonal trust in accounting for the decline in civic participation and social capital. Robert D. Putnam. 1993. *Making Democracy Work: Civic Tradition in Modern Italy.* Princeton: Princeton University Press; and Putnam, "Bowling Alone;" NES data also show that trust in people is strongly related to political participation.

73. Albert O. Hirschman. 1977. *The Passions and the Interests: Political Arguments for Capitalism Before its Triumph.* Princeton: Princeton University Press.

74. Harold Laski. 1948. *The American Democracy.* New York: Viking, 34; emphasis added.

75. Andrews and Withey, *Social Indicators of Well-Being,* 315.

76. In 1975 the *New York Times* commissioned a study of American views of the future using the Cantril self-anchoring ladder scale. Their findings were reported in Robert Lindsey. 1975. "Economy Mars Belief in the American Dream." *New York Times,* October 26, 1, 48. The study found a "substantial decline in optimism about the future," which was attributed in part to a belief that "the rules of the game" had changed so that hard work no longer paid off and a college education was no longer a passport to success. A little later (1984), a German study found that Germans, too, experienced (1978–84) a declining sense that the future would be better. Wolfgang Glatzer. 1991. "Quality of Life in Advanced Industrialized Countries: The Case of West Germany." In Strack, Argyle, and Schwarz, eds., *Subjective Well-Being,* 261–79.

77. Sara Staats. 1987. "Hope: Expected Positive Affect in an Adult Sample." *Journal of Genetic Psychology* 148: 357–64.

78. David G. Myers and Ed Diener. 1995. "Who Is Happy?" *Psychological Science* 6: 10–19.

79. Glatzer, "Quality of Life in Advanced Industrialized Countries: The Case of West Germany."

80. Neil D. Weinstein. 1980. "Unrealistic Optimism About Future Life Events." *Journal of Personality and Social Psychology* 39: 806–20. The unrealistic optimism of the poor is reported in Don R. Bowen, Elinor Bowen, Sheldon Gawiser, and Louis H. Masotti. 1968. "Deprivation, Mobility, and Orientation Toward Protest of the Urban Poor." In Louis H. Masotti and Don R. Bowen, eds., *Riots and Rebellion: Civil Violence in the Urban Community.* Beverly Hills: Sage, 187–200.

81. Lionel Tiger. 1979. *Optimism: The Biology of Hope.* New York: Touchstone/Simon and Schuster. In his treatment, Tiger points to a benign, reinforcing cycle in which optimists act to create the circumstances that justify their optimism. Beyond that, there is some evidence that Nature, for its own purposes of improving genetic advantages, endowed the human species with a disposition toward optimism.

82. "In short, we find greater optimism about the economic future in the less developed countries, whereas in the wealthier nations there is some expectation of a tailing-off of the personal and national progress previously experienced." Alex Inkeles and Larry Diamond. 1980. "Personal Development and National Development: A Cross-Cultural Perspective." In Alexander Szalai and Frank M. Andrews, eds. 1980. *Quality of Life: Comparative Studies.* Beverly Hills: Sage, 73–109 at 99.

83. Cantril, *The Pattern of Human Concerns.*

84. Lindsey, "Economy Mars Belief in the American Dream," 48.

85. The trend is quite general across population groups: both men and women and young and old increase their pessimism. But there is a difference by education and income with the less well educated and the poor increasingly tending to agree that the world is getting worse for the average person. National Data Program for the Social Sciences at NORC, University of Chicago, 1994. *General Social Surveys: Cumulative Codebook.* Distributed by the Roper Center, University of Connecticut. Data analyzed by Soo Yeon Kim of the Yale Social Science Statistical Laboratory. This has been supplemented by reference to Floris W. Wood, ed. 1990. *An American Profile—Opinions and Behavior, 1972–1989.* New York: Gale.

86. The demographic data and associated trends are partly from the NES CD-ROM and partly from Miller and Traugott, *American National Election Studies: Data Sourcebook, 1952–1986.*

Chapter 12. Do Democratic Processes Contribute to Ill-Being?

1. Almond and Verba have a somewhat similar division, but their "input affect" refers both to feelings about the electoral and legislative process and to feelings about people's own efficacy. Their "output affect" refers to feelings about whether or not people like themselves receive attention and policies that satisfy them. Gabriel A. Almond and Sidney Verba. 1965. *The Civic Culture.* Princeton: Princeton University Press, 63–64.

2. Amos Tversky and Daniel Kahneman. 1981. "The Framing of Decisions and the Psychology of Choice." *Science* 211 (January 30): 453–58.

3. Daniel Kahneman and Amos Tversky. 1982. "Judgment Under Uncertainty: Heuristics and Biases." In Kahneman, P. Slovic, and Amos Tversky, eds., *Judgment Under Uncertainty: Heuristics and Biases.* New York: Cambridge University Press.

4. Susan Moses-Zirkes. August 1993. "Pleasure, Pain Evaluation not Always Rooted in Logic." *APA Monitor* 24: 30.

5. E. Allen Lind and Tom R. Tyler. 1988. *The Social Psychology of Procedural Justice.* New York: Plenum.

6. Robert E. Lane. 1988. "Procedural Goods in a Democracy: How One Is Treated Versus What One Gets." *Social Justice Research* 2: 177–92.

7. F. Thomas Juster and Frank P. Stafford, eds. 1985. *Time, Goods, and Well-Being.* Ann Arbor: Institute for Social Research.

8. Icek Ajzen. 1988. *Attitudes, Personality, and Behavior.* Chicago: Dorsey Press.

9. Joseph Veroff, Elizabeth Douvan, and Richard Kulka. 1981. *The Inner Americans: A Self-Portrait from 1957 to 1976.* New York: Basic Books, 57.

10. Karl R. Popper. 1963. *Conjectures and Refutations: The Growth of Scientific Knowledge.* London: Routledge and Kegan Paul, 380–83.

11. Peter L. Berger and Thomas Luckman. 1967. *The Social Construction of Reality.* Garden City, N.Y.: Doubleday Anchor, 380–87.

12. E. J. Dionne, Jr. 1991. *Why Americans Hate Politics.* New York: Simon and Schuster, 343.

13. Dionne says that politics suffers from public contempt because the issues at the forefront of political attention are not the issues whose solution would make most people's lives better; but he forgets that even more than the economic issues that he favors these symbolic or even "irrational" issues are symbols of important values that arouse emotion and challenge the *rightness* of people's world views. Ibid., 322. Similarly, Edelman mourns the way the general public is granted only symbolic rewards while organized interests receive material rewards, but he, too, forgets that symbolic rewards may be the most important. Murray Edelman. 1964. *The Symbolic Uses of Politics.* Urbana: University of Illinois Press.

14. Robert E. Lane. 1991. *The Market Experience.* New York: Cambridge University Press, 524–47.

15. "Of the 12 domains [measured], satisfaction with *financial security* has the greatest relative impact on satisfaction with life as a whole." Alex C. Michelos. 1986. "Job Satisfaction, Marital Satisfaction, and the Quality of Life: A Review and a Preview." In Frank M. Andrews, ed., *Research on the Quality of Life.* Ann Arbor: Institute for Social Research, 75.

16. Tom R. Tyler, K. Rasinski, and N. Spodick. 1985. "The Influence of Perceived Injustice on Support for Political Authorities." *Journal of Personality and Social Psychology* 48: 72–81.

17. Ruut Veenhoven. 1989 [1984]. *Conditions of Happiness: Summary Print.* Dordrecht: Reidel, 30.

18. Bert Klandermans. 1989. "Does Happiness Soothe Political Protest? The Complex Relation Between Discontent and Political Unrest." In Ruut Veenhoven, ed., *How Harmful is Happiness?* Rotterdam: University Pers Rotterdam, 61–78 at 75.

19. Douglas A. Hibbs, Jr. 1987. *The American Political Economy: Macroeconomics and Electoral Politics.* Cambridge: Harvard University Press; compare Edward R. Tufte. 1978. *Political Control of the Economy.* Princeton: Princeton University Press.

20. David O. Sears and Carolyn L. Funk. 1991. "The Role of Self-Interest in Social and Political Movements." *Advances in Experimental Social Psychology,* vol. 24. New York: Academic Press. On the other hand, the gratitude of the beneficiaries of firm-specific or industry-specific benefits is different, for, in exchange for benefits or anticipated benefits, beneficiaries give campaign money. There is no economistic fallacy in the political process of money raising and spending.

21. Robert A. Dahl. 1992. "Why Free Markets Are Not Enough." *Journal of Democracy* 3: 82–89.

22. Richard A. Brody and Paul M. Sniderman. 1977. "From Life Space to Polling Place: The Relevance of Personal Concerns for Voting Behavior." *British Journal of Political Science* 7: 337–60.

23. Michael Pusey. 1997. "The Impact of Restructuring on Quality of Life in Middle Australia." Paper presented to the First Annual Meeting of the International Society of Quality of Life Studies, Charlotte, N.C., November 20–23, 1997.

24. Harvey Liebenstein. 1976. *Beyond Economic Man: A New Foundation for Microeconomics.* Cambridge: Harvard University Press; see also George J. Stigler. 1967. "The Xistence of X-efficiency." *American Economic Review* 66: 213–16; Liebenstein. 1978 "Inefficiency Xists—Reply to an Xorcist." *American Economic Review* 68: 203–11.

25. Robert E. Lane. 1986. "Market Justice, Political Justice." *American Political Science Review* 80: 383–402.

26. Ruut Veenhoven. 1993. *Happiness in Nations: Subjective Appreciation of Life in 56 Nations 1946–1992.* Rotterdam: Erasmus University, RISBO, 127.

27. Sears and Funk,"The Role of Self-Interest in Social and Political Movements," 44.

28. Frank M. Andrews and Stephen B. Withey. 1976. *Social Indicators of Well-Being: Americans' Perceptions of Life Quality.* New York: Plenum, 124, 254.

29. Humphrey Taylor. 1992. "The American Angst of 1992." *Public Perspective,* July/August, 5.

30. Lane, "Procedural Goods in a Democracy."

31. Some economists (e.g., Musgrave) have suggested that the solution to the problem of achieving the right size public sector, at least conceptually, lies in offering the public only those goods that the public would buy if the goods were priced on the market. But this fails to take into account the problem of aggregation of individual demands into group demands whereby these individual preferences are changed by the group references and identifications which characterize *political* choices. Richard A. Musgrave. 1959. *The Theory of Public Finance.* New York: McGraw-Hill.

32. Daniel Katz, Barbara A. Gutek, Robert L. Kahn, and Eugenia Barton. 1975. *Bureaucratic Encounters: A Pilot Study in the Evaluation of Government Services.* Ann Arbor: Institute for Social Research.

33. Sears and Funk, "The Role of Self-Interest in Social and Political Movements," 35, 37.

34. David Lowery and Lee Sigelman. 1981. "Understanding the Tax Revolt: Eight Explanations." *American Political Science Review* 75: 963–74 at 972.

35. Seymour Martin Lipset and William Schneider. 1983. *The Confidence Gap: Business, Labor, and Government in the Public Mind.* New York: Free Press, 343–46.

36. S. Briar. 1966. "Welfare from Below: Recipients' View of the Public Welfare System." In J. TenBroek, ed., *The Law of the Poor.* San Francisco: Chandler, 53.

37. Robert E. Lane. 1996. "'Losing Touch' in a Democracy: Demands vs. Needs." In Jack Hayward, ed., *Élitism, Populism, and European Politics.* Oxford: Clarendon Press, 33–66.

38. Popper, *Conjectures and Refutations,* 381–83.

39. Lane, *The Market Experience,* chap. 27; Lane. 1994. "Quality of Life and Quality of Persons: A New Role for Government?" *Political Theory* 22: 219–52.

40. Taylor, "The American Angst of 1992," 4.

41. John Bowlby. 1969. *Attachment and Loss,* vol. 1, *Attachment.* New York: Basic Books, 211.

42. "Religious faith, importance of religion, and religious traditionalism generally relate positively to SWB." Ed Diener. 1984. "Subjective Well-Being." *Psychological Bulletin* 95: 542–75 at 556. Freedman finds that although religious faith contributes to happiness, agnostics are no less happy. Jonathan Freedman. 1980. *Happy People.* New York: Harcourt, Brace. Catherine E. Ross (1990) agrees with Freedman: "Religion and Psychological Distress." *Journal for the Scientific Study of Religion* 29: 236–45.

43. Martin Seligman, commenting on the erosion of this commitment to one's nation, said, "To the extent that it is now difficult for young people to take seriously . . . their relationship to their country, . . . meaning in life will be very difficult to find. The self, to put it another way, is a very poor site for meaning." James Buie (quoting Martin Seligman). October 1988. " 'Me' Decades Generate Depression: Individualism Erodes Commitment to Others." *APA Monitor* 19: 18.

44. Survey by the Center for Applied Research in the Apostolate, reported in *New York Times,* May 19, 1982, A1. The sample sizes were twelve hundred in each country.

45. In the postwar 1950s, Americans and British reported the most pride in their political system (85 percent and 46 percent, respectively); the Germans emphasized the "characteristics of the people" (36 percent); the Italians, their contribution to the arts (16 percent); and the Mexicans also their political system (30 percent). Almond and Verba, *The Civic Culture,* 102. The question in 1996 was, "To what extent are you proud to live under our political system?" In a numerical scoring system, 76 percent were scored as proud and only 13 percent as not proud. *Public Perspective,* Feb.–March, 1997, 8: 7. There was an increase with age in pride, but almost no difference by race or sex.

46. Stephen White. 24 August 1991. "Soviet Union/Stephen White has Second Thoughts on His Risky Choice of Title: 'Gorbachev in Power." *The Independent,* 26.

47. Dionne, Jr., *Why Americans Hate Politics;* Taylor, "The American Angst of 1992," 5; Donald Granberg and Sören Holmberg. 1989. *The Political System Matters: Social Psychology and Voting Behavior in Sweden and the United States.* New York: Cambridge University Press.

48. David R. Mayhew. 1991. *Divided We Govern: Party Control, Lawmaking, and Investigations, 1946–1990.* New Haven: Yale University Press.

49. The U.S. government was quicker to pass antimonopoly legislation and to regulate the securities industry, to police food and drugs and ban lead in gasoline, to establish effective safety rules in mines and industry, to initiate affirmative action, to establish universal primary and secondary education, and to enlarge tertiary education. It was slower to provide universal health care, decent child care (still backward in all advanced English-speaking nations), environmental amenities (e.g., greenbelts), and public housing.

50. D. Watson and L. A. Clark. 1992. "On Traits and Temperaments: General and Specific Factors of Emotional Experience and Their Relation to the Five-Factor Model." *Journal of Personality* 60: 441–76.

51. See, for example, Michael Walzer. 1970. *Obligations: An Essay on Disobedience, War, and Citizenship*. Cambridge: Harvard University Press.

52. John H. Flugel. 1945. *Man, Morals and Society: A Psychoanalytic Study*. New York: International Universities Press.

53. Lawrence Kohlberg. 1969. "Stage and Sequence: The Cognition-Developmental Approach to Socialization." In D. Goslin, ed., *Handbook of Socialization Theory and Research*. Chicago: Rand-McNally.

54. "For the present, it appears that advocates of both sides of major controversial policy issues are represented among voters in proportion to their numbers in the general population." Raymond E. Wolfinger and Steven J. Rosenstone. 1980. *Who Votes?* New Haven: Yale University Press, 114.

55. Russell Hardin. 1988. *Morality Within Limits of Reason*. Chicago: University of Chicago Press, 182–84.

56. On happiness, see Hans J. Kelsen. 1957. *What Is Justice?* Berkeley: University of California Press. On obligation, see Ronald Dworkin. 1986. *Law's Empire*. Cambridge: Harvard University Press. But moral obligation may imply quite the reverse of conventional citizen duty; see Walzer, *Obligations: Essays on Disobedience, War, and Citizenship*.

57. See, for example, Keith B. J. Franklin. 1993. "The Neural Basis of Pleasure and Pain." In Michael Hechter, Lynn Nadel, and Richard E. Michod, eds., *The Origin of Values*. New York: Aldine de Gruyter, 273–84.

58. M. E. P. Seligman and J. L. Hager. 1972. *Beyond Biological Boundaries of Learning*. New York: Appleton-Century-Crofts. Evolutionary theory has evolved: today, instead of survival, evolutionary psychology would make proliferation of genes the criterion.

59. C. Daniel Batson, Laura L. Shaw, and Kathryn C. Oleson. 1992. "Differentiating Affect, Mood, and Emotion: Toward Functionally Based Conceptual Distinctions." In Margaret S. Clark, ed., *Emotion*. Review of Personality and Social Psychology, vol. 13. Newbury Park, Calif.: Sage, 294–326.

Chapter 13. The Pain of Self-Determination in Democracy

1. Isaiah Berlin. 1969. "Two Concepts of Liberty." In his *Four Essays on Liberty*. London: Oxford University Press, 138.

2. Russell Hardin. 1988. *Morality Within Limits of Reason*. Chicago: University of Chicago Press, 202.

3. Douglas P. Crowne and David Marlowe. 1964. *The Approval Motive*. New York: Wiley.

4. Jean Piaget and Barbara Inhelder. 1969. *The Psychology of the Child*, trans. H. Weaver, New York: Basic Books.

5. John Stuart Mill. 1944 [1859]. "On Liberty." In Mill, *Utilitarianism, Liberty, and Representative Government*, A. D. Lindsay, ed. New York: Dutton Everyman, 116. Similarly, in his essay *Self-Reliance*, Emerson said, "I appeal from your customs. I would be myself"—as though responding to the norms of one's society were to give up the self. Ralph Waldo Emerson. 1951. "Self-Reliance." In Irwin Edman, ed., *Essays of Ralph Waldo Emerson*. New York: Crowell, 53. Emersonian self-reliance has been said to be the

most important cause of the historic lack of socialism in the United States. Irving Howe. 1985. *Socialism and America.* New York: Harcourt, Brace, Jovanovich. Emerson frames the idea of self-reliance as the independence of mind to resist appeals to charitable feelings, putting self-reliance in the worst possible light.

6. Richard Nisbett and Lee Ross. 1980. *Human Inference: Strategies and Shortcomings of Social Judgment.* Englewood Cliffs: Prentice-Hall, 31.

7. Herbert M. Lefcourt. 1976. *Locus of Control: Current Trends in Theory and Research.* Hillsdale, N.J.: Erlbaum/Wiley, 31. For the difference between attribution of one's own acts and the acts of others, see E. E. Jones, D. E. Kanouse, H. H. Kelley, R. E. Nisbett, S. Valins, and B. Weiner, eds. 1972. *Attribution: Perceiving the Causes of Behavior.* Morristown, N.J.: General Learning Press; Harold H. Kelley. 1967. "Attribution Theory in Social Psychology." In *Nebraska Symposium on Motivation.* Lincoln: University of Nebraska Press, 192–238.

8. Alexis de Tocqueville. 1945. *Democracy in America,* Phillips Bradley, ed. New York: Knopf, 2:99.

9. George Katona, Burkhard Strumpel, and Ernest Zahn. 1971. *Aspirations and Affluence: Comparative Studies in the U.S. and Western Europe.* New York: McGraw-Hill. This difference may be changing, however, for in the decade up to 1990, Europeans, with the exception of France, have *increased* their sense of control over their own lives. Sheena Ashford and Noel Timms. 1992. *What Europe Thinks: A Study of Western European Values.* Aldershot, U.K.: Dartmouth, 8–9.

10. Lee Ross. 1977. "The Intuitive Psychologist and His Shortcomings." In L. Berkowitz, ed., *Advances in Experimental Psychology,* vol. 10. New York: Academic, 174–220. Applying more perspective, most psychologists believe that the *interaction* between dispositions and circumstances explains the way people respond to the events in their lives. See Daryl J. Bem and David C. Fundor. 1978. "Predicting More of the People More of the Time: Assessing the Personality of Situations." *Psychological Review* 85: 485–501.

11. Berlin, "Two Concepts of Liberty," 131, 138.

12. In his review of research with animals and children, White finds exploratory and manipulative behavior in the absence of tissue needs and infers a common cross-species desire for "competence," activated by an "effectance" motive, and gratified by "a feeling of efficacy." Robert W. White. 1959. "Motivation Reconsidered: The Concept of Competence." *Psychological Review* 66: 297–333 at 329.

13. Ellen J. Langer. 1983. *The Psychology of Control.* Beverly Hills: Sage.

14. Lefcourt, *Locus of Control,* passim; Julian B. Rotter. 1966. "Generalized Expectancies for Internal Versus External Control of Reinforcement." *Psychological Monographs* 80, #609.

15. White, "Motivation Reconsidered: The Concept of Competence," 323.

16. Martin E. P. Seligman. 1975. *Helplessness: On Depression, Development, and Death.* San Francisco: W. H. Freeman, 98.

17. Ibid.

18. Ellen J. Langer. 1975. "The Illusion of Control." *Journal of Personality and Social Psychology* 32: 331–28.

19. Jerry M. Burger. 1985. "Desire for Control and Achievement-Related Behavior." *Journal of Personality and Social Psychology* 48: 1520–33.

20. John Condry and James Chambers. 1978. "Intrinsic Motivation and the Process of Learning." In Mark R. Lepper and David Greene, eds., *The Hidden Costs of Rewards: New Perspectives on the Psychology of Human Motivation.* Hillsdale, N.J.: Wiley/Erlbaum, 73, 79.

21. If, for example, *A* is preferred to *B,* which is preferred to *C*—but then one is told one cannot have *C,* suddenly one prefers *C* to the two others—a response called "reactance." Jack W. Brehm. 1972. *Responses to the Loss of Freedom: A Theory of Psychological Reactance.* Morristown, N.J.: General Learning Press.

22. Melvin Kohn and Carmi Schooler. 1983. *Work and Personality: An Inquiry into the Impact of Social Stratification.* Norwood, N.J.: Ablex. One of Terkel's respondents illustrates this theme: "I'd rather work my ass off for eight hours a day with nobody watching me than five minutes with a guy watching me." Studs Terkel. 1975 [1972]. *Working.* New York: Avon, xxxii.

23. Angus Campbell. 1981. *The Sense of Well-Being in America.* New York: McGraw-Hill, 214.

24. White, "Motivation Reconsidered."

25. Albert Somit and Steven A. Peterson. 1995. "Darwinism, Dominance, and Democracy." *Research in Biopolitics* 3: 19–34; idem. 1997. *Darwinism, Dominance, and Democracy: The Biological Bases of Authoritarianism.* Westport, Conn.: Praeger. Note that Milgram's "agentic state" relies on the evolutionary advantages of behavior controlled by another. Stanley Milgram. 1974. *Obedience to Authority: An Experimental View.* New York: Harper and Row. See also Herbert C. Kelman and V. Lee Hamilton. 1989. *Crimes of Obedience: Toward a Social Psychology of Authority and Responsibility.* New Haven: Yale University Press.

26. Erich Fromm. 1941. *Escape from Freedom.* New York: Rinehart; E. R. Dodds. 1957. *The Greeks and the Irrational.* Boston: Beacon Press.

27. John Mirowski and Catherine E. Ross. 1989. *Social Causes of Psychological Distress.* New York: Aldine de Gruyter, 13. See also Richard Nisbett and Lee Ross. 1980. *Human Inference: Strategies and Shortcomings of Social Judgment.* Englewood Cliffs: Prentice-Hall, 30.

28. See, for example, Douglas J. Needles and Lyn W. Abramson. 1990. "Positive Life Events, Attributional Style, and Hopefulness: Testing a Model of Recovery from Depression." *Journal of Abnormal Psychology* 99: 156–65; John Mirowski and Catherine E. Ross. 1984. "Mexican Culture and Emotional Contradictions." *Journal of Health and Social Behavior* 25: 2–13.

29. M. Margaret Conway. 1991. *Political Participation in the United States,* 2d ed. Washington, D.C.: Congressional Quarterly Press, 159–60.

30. Arthur H. Miller says measures of political efficacy correspond closely to Seeman's powerlessness dimension of alienation. "Political Issues and Trust in Government: 1964–1970." *American Political Science Review* 68: 951–72, n. 9, p. 952

31. Peter Gay. 1973. "Introduction" to his edited book *The Enlightenment: A Comprehensive Anthology.* New York: Simon and Schuster, 23.

32. In the nineteenth century Mill (again) said, "It is desirable that in things which do not concern others, individuality should assert itself." Where custom requires confor-

mity, he said, "there is wanting one of the principal ingredients of human happiness, and quite the chief ingredient of individual and social progress." Mill, "On Liberty," 115.

33. Milton Rokeach and Sandra J. Ball-Rokeach. 1989. "Stability and Change in American Value Priorities, 1968–1981." *American Psychologist* 44: 775–84. This ranking of independence as free choice is apparently in conflict with responses to the "instrumental value" described as "independent, self-reliant, self-sufficient" which, among eighteen instrumental values ranks only twelfth and thirteenth, just ahead of "politeness" and just behind "self-restrained."

34. Emerson, "Self-Reliance," 53.

35. Sniderman and Brody found that only one-sixth of an American national sample believed that "government ought to provide any help whatsoever to them. By contrast, if they feel anything can be done, more than 80 percent believe it is up to themselves or others around them to do it, and more than 80 percent of these feel they should rely on themselves rather than others. Paul M. Sniderman and Richard A. Brody. 1977. "Coping: The Ethic of Self-Reliance." *American Journal of Political Science* 21: 501–21 at 507. See also Brody and Sniderman. 1977. "From Life Space to Polling Place: The Relevance of Personal Concerns for Voting Behavior." *British Journal of Political Science* 7: 337–60. The opposite of self-reliance, dependency, is abhorred, at least according to the impressionistic evidence of Hsu's account of the American character. Francis L. K. Hsu, ed. 1961. *Psychological Anthropology.* Homewood, Ill.: Dorsey. The fear of dependency has a long history. In opposing poor relief, John Bright, one of the early Manchester liberals, declared, "Mine is that masculine species of charity, which would lead me to inculcate in the minds of the working classes the love of independence, the privileges of self-respect, the disdain of being patronized or petted, the desire to accumulate and the ambition to rise." Guido de Ruggiero. 1927. *The History of European Liberalism,* trans. R. G. Collingswood. London: Oxford University Press, 126.

36. Theodore Caplow and Howard Bahr. 1979. "Half a Century of Change in Adolescent Attitudes: Replication of a Middletown Survey by the Lynds." *Public Opinion Quarterly* 43: 1–17.

37. "Survey of American Culture." Feb.–March 1997 [1996]. *The Public Perspective* 8: 90. The survey runs from 1972 (65 percent agree) to 1994 (70 percent agree).

38. Berlin, "Two Concepts of Liberty," 129.

39. Herbert M. Lefcourt and Carl Sordoni. 1973. "Locus of Control and the Expression of Humor." *Proceedings of the 81st Annual Convention of the American Psychological Association* 8: 185–86.

40. Condry and Chambers, "Intrinsic Motivation and the Process of Learning."

41. Lefcourt, *Locus of Control,* 55.

42. Ibid., 65.

43. Ibid., 44–45, 48. The findings on cheating applied more to girls than boys.

44. Herbert C. Kelman and Lee H. Lawrence. 1972. "Assignment of Responsibility in the Case of Lt. Calley: Preliminary Report on a National Survey." *Journal of Social Issues* 28: 177–212.

45. Lefcourt, *Locus of Control,* 49.

46. Ellen J. Langer and Judith Rodin. 1976. "The Effects of Choice and Enhanced

Personal Responsibility for the Aged: A Field Experiment in an Institutional Setting." *Journal of Personality and Social Psychology* 34: 191–98; and Judith Rodin and Ellen J. Langer. 1977. "Long-Term Effects of a Control-Relevant Intervention with the Institutionalized Aged." *Journal of Personality and Social Psychology* 35: 897–902.

47. Susan T. Fiske and Shelley E. Taylor. 1984. *Social Cognition.* New York: Random House, 63–64. See also Sanford Golin, Paul D. Sweeney, and David E. Shaeffer. 1981. "The Causality of Causal Attributions in Depression: A Cross-Lagged Panel Correlational Analysis." *Journal of Abnormal Psychology* 98:14–22.

48. Anatol Rapoport. 1982. "Prisoners Dilemma — Recollections and Observations." In Brian Barry and Russell Hardin, eds., *Rational Man and Irrational Society? An Introduction and Sourcebook.* Beverly Hills: Sage, 71–83.

49. Fred Hirsch. 1976. *Social Limits to Growth.* Cambridge: Harvard University Press.

50. Thomas Ashby Wills. 1981. "Downward Comparison Principles in Social Psychology." *Journal of Personality and Social Psychology* 90: 245–71.

51. Charles Lewis Taylor and David A. Jodice. 1983. *World Handbook of Political and Social Indicators,* 3d ed. New Haven: Yale University Press, table 2.6.

52. The inequality data are from the Center for Budget and Policy Studies and reported in the *New York Times,* December 17, 1887, B6. Turnout figures are from table no. 444, *Statistical Abstract of the United States: 1990.* The controls for education are from the same source, table no. 219. Unfortunately, only the fifteen most populous states were included in this table. I hereby express my thanks to Daniel Dowd of the Yale Social Science Statistical Laboratory. The interpretation of the findings, of course, is wholly mine.

53. Ronald Inglehart. 1990. *Culture Shift in Advanced Industrial Societies.* Princeton: Princeton University Press, 40.

54. Conway, *Political Participation in the United States,* 187–93. See also James W. Button. 1989. *Blacks and Social Change.* Princeton: Princeton University Press; Earl Black and Merle Black. 1987. *Politics and Society in the South.* Cambridge: Harvard University Press.

55. Conway, *Political Participation in the United States,* 186–87.

56. Raymond E. Wolfinger and Steven J. Rosenstone. 1980. *Who Votes?* New Haven: Yale University Press.

57. Peter F. Nardulli, Jon K. Dalager, and Donald E. Greco. 1996. "Voter Turnout in U.S. Presidential Elections: An Historical View and Some Speculations." *PS: Political Science and Politics* 29: 480–90.

58. Sidney Verba and Norman H. Nie. 1972. *Participation in America: Political, Democratic, and Social Equality.* New York: Harper and Row, 333.

59. "The largest single drop in nonvoting in Germany actually occurred in the last election of March 1933. Nonvoting dropped from 19 per cent in 1932 to 11 per cent in 1933, a drop of 8 percentage points, while the Nazi vote increased from 33 per cent to 43 per cent." Note, however, that the decks were stacked by President Paul von Hindenburg's appointment of Hitler. Seymour Martin Lipset. 1981. *Political Man: The Social Bases of Politics.* Expanded ed. Baltimore: Johns Hopkins University Press, 151.

60. Fritz Stern. 1965. *The Politics of Cultural Despair.* Garden City, N.Y.: Doubleday/Anchor; Fromm, *Escape from Freedom.*

61. Benjamin Barber. 1984. *Strong Democracy: Participatory Politics for a New Age.* Berkeley: University of California Press; Carole Pateman. 1970. *Participation and Democratic Theory.* Cambridge: Cambridge University Press.

62. Robert E. Lane. 1988. "Procedural Goods in a Democracy: How One Is Treated Versus What One Gets." *Social Justice Research* 2: 177–92.

63. For example, Frank M. Andrews and Stephen B. Withey. 1976. *Social Indicators of Well-Being: Americans' Perceptions of Life Quality.* New York: Plenum; Angus Campbell, Philip E. Converse, and Willard L. Rodgers. 1976. *The Quality of American Life.* New York: Wiley; Fritz Strack, Michael Argyle, and Norbert Schwarz, eds. 1991. *Subjective Well-Being: An Interdisciplinary Perspective.* Oxford: Pergamon.

64. John P. Robinson and Philip E. Converse. 1972. "Social Change Reflected in the Use of Time." In Angus Campbell and Converse, eds., *The Human Meaning of Social Change.* New York: Russell Sage, 17–86 at p. 70. The "little visibility in time budget diaries" is reflected by the estimated six minutes per day spent on organizational work (including politics) in the mid-1960s. Is the U.S. less political than other countries? Among the other nationalities studied at the same time, the French, West Germans, and Peruvians each spent about two minutes per day, one-third of the American time devoted to a broad category which included political activity. Alexander Szalai, ed. 1972. *The Use of Time.* The Hague: Mouton, 580.

65. John P. Robinson. 1977. *How Americans Use Their Time.* New York: Praeger.

66. W. Dean Burnham. 1955. *Presidential Ballots: 1836–1892.* Baltimore: Johns Hopkins University Press, 21, 26.

67. Robert E. Lane. 1965, "The Tense Citizen and the Casual Patriot: Role Confusion in American Politics." *Journal of Politics* 27: 735–60.

68. Alex C. Michalos. 1986. "Job Satisfaction, Marital Satisfaction, and the Quality of Life: A Review and a Preview." In Frank M. Andrews, ed., *Research on the Quality of Life.* Ann Arbor: Institute for Social Research, 60.

69. Antoni Z. Kaminski. 1991. "The Public and the Private: Introduction." *International Political Science Review* 12: 263–66; idem. 1991. "Res Publica, Res Privata." *International Political Science Review* 12: 337–51.

70. Philip E. Converse. 1964. "The Nature of Belief Systems in Mass Publics." In David Apter, ed., *Ideology and Discontent.* New York: Free Press, 206–61.

71. Harold M. Schroder, Michael J. Driver, and Siegfried Streufert. 1967. *Human Information Processing.* New York: Holt, Rinehart and Winston.

72. Mihalyi Csikszentmihalyi and Maria Mei-Ha Wong. 1991. "The Situational and Personal Correlates of Happiness: A Cross-National Comparison." In Strack et al., eds., *Subjective Well-Being: An Interdisciplinary Perspective,* 193–212.

73. Tocqueville, *Democracy in America,* 99. Tocqueville also said that "the most democratic country in the world now is that in which men have in our time carried to the highest perfection the art of pursuing in common the objects of common desires and have applied this new technique to the greatest number of purposes." *Democracy in America,* J. P. Meyer, ed., trans. George Lawrence. Garden City, N.Y.: Anchor, 1969, 516–17.

74. S. Kagan and M. C. Madsen. 1971. "Co-operation and Competition of Mexican, Mexican-American, and Anglo-American Children of Two Ages under Four Instructional Sets." *Developmental Psychology* 5: 32–39. Later cross-cultural studies in many

settings found that urbanization, more than capitalism, most influenced the exclusively *self-oriented* pattern of self-determination.

75. Yun-shik Chang. 1991. "The Personalist Ethic and the Market in Korea." *Comparative Studies in Society and History* 33: 106–29; E. B. Ayal. 1963. "Value Systems and Economic Development in Japan and Thailand." *Journal of Social Issues* 19: 35–51.

76. Elizabeth Mutran and Donald G. Reitzes. 1984. "Intergenerational Support Activities and Well-Being Among the Elderly: A Convergence of Exchange and Symbolic Interaction Perspectives." *American Sociological Review* 49: 117–30. Diener's literature review shows that the effects reported here are not limited to the elderly. See Ed Diener. 1984. "Subjective Well-Being." *Psychological Bulletin* 95: 542–75 at 557.

77. Blair Wheaton. 1980. "The Sociogenesis of Psychological Disorder: An Attributional Theory." *Journal of Health and Social Behavior* 21: 100–24.

78. Andrews and Withey, *Social Indicators of Well-Being,* 132.

79. Lefcourt, *Locus of Control;* Rotter, "Generalized Expectancies for Internal versus External Control of Reinforcement," 80.

80. Seligman, *Helplessness: On Depression, Development, and Death.*

81. Richard DeCharms. 1968. *Personal Causation: The Internal Affective Determinants of Behavior.* New York: Academic Press, 269

82. Seligman, *Helplessness: On Depression, Development, and Death,* 13–20. Environmental responses are not likely to be so invariably contingent as this; they are probabilistic and people are not very good at estimating probabilities or perceiving covariances. "Extinction," the decline of a learned response, occurs more slowly when sometimes the environment responds and sometimes does not in a fashion the individual cannot fathom.

83. Maxwell J. Elden. 1981. "Political Efficacy at Work: The Connection between More Autonomous Forms of Workplace Organization and a More Participatory Politics." *American Political Science Review* 75: 43–58.

84. William M. Lafferty. 1989. "Work as a Source of Political Learning Among Wage-Laborers and Lower-Level Employees." In Roberta S. Sigel, ed., *Adult Political Socialization.* Chicago: University of Chicago Press, 102–42. In *The Civic Culture* (1963), Almond and Verba report similar findings. For a review of the literature, see Robert A. Dahl. 1985. *A Preface to Economic Democracy.* Berkeley: University of California Press.

85. Kohn and Schooler, *Work and Personality: An Inquiry into the Impact of Social Stratification,* 32.

86. H. J. Reitz and G. K. Groff. 1974. "Economic Development and Belief in Locus of Control Among Factory Workers in Four Countries." *Journal of Cross-cultural Psychology* 15: 344–55.

87. The European evidence comes from a standard question about one's success in making plans taken from the Rottter scale. The averages increased and all countries, except France, increased their sense of personal control. Ashford and Timms, *What Europe Thinks,* 8–9. In the United States between 1957 and 1976 the proportion of people disagreeing with the question "I have always felt pretty sure that my life would work out the way I wanted it to" declined from 25 percent to 16 percent. Joseph Veroff, Elizabeth Douvan, and Richard Kulka. 1981. *The Inner Americans: A Self-Portrait from 1957 to 1976.* New York: Basic Books, 59.

88. Peter M. Blau and Otis Dudley Duncan. 1967. *The American Occupational Structure,* New York: Wiley, 170. Another assessment of occupational attainment found that teacher ratings of "industriousness" predicted occupational success better than years of schooling, but, of course, industriousness is part of prior family culture. Christopher Jencks, Susan Bartlett, et al. 1979. *Who Gets Ahead?* New York: Basic Books, 222–23.

89. Recall the findings reported in chapter 3: the stocks, or relatively fixed resources, employed in each engagement with the world included not only education, parental background, and social networks but also, and most important, "endowed" personality characteristics, such as cheerfulness and "negative affect."

90. Gerald Gurin and Patricia Gurin. 1976. "Personal Efficacy and the Ideology of Individual Responsibility." In Burkhard Strumpel, ed., *Economic Means for Human Needs.* Ann Arbor: Institute for Social Research.

91. C. Daniel Batson, Laura L. Shaw, and Kathryn C. Oleson. 1992. "Differentiating Affect, Mood, and Emotion: Toward Functionally Based Conceptual Distinctions." In Margaret S. Clark, ed., *Emotion.* Review of Personality and Social Psychology, vol. 13. Newbury Park, Calif.: Sage, 294–326 at 299, 300.

92. David V. Sheslow and Marilyn T. Erickson. 1975. "Analysis of Activity Preference in Depressed and Nondepressed College Students." *Journal of Counseling Psychology* 22: 329–32.

93. Norma D. Feshbach and Seymour Feshbach. 1987. "Affective Processes and Academic Achievement." *Child Development; Special Issue on Schools and Development* 58: 1335–47.

94. Steven J. Morris and Frederick H. Kanfer. 1987. "Altruism and Depression." *Personality and Social Psychology Bulletin* 9: 567–77.

95. Kenneth K. Miya. 1976. "Autonomy and Depression." *Clinical Social Work Journal* 4: 260–68.

96. Andreas Knapp and Margaret S. Clark. 1991. "Some Detrimental Effects of Negative Mood on Individuals' Ability to Solve Resource Dilemmas." *Personality and Social Psychology Bulletin* 17: 678–88.

97. John S. Gillis. 1993. "Effects of Life Stress and Dysphoria on Complex Judgments." *Psychological Reports* 72, Pt. 2: 1355–63. On the other hand, depressed subjects make more accurate estimates of the effects of their actions on events because, with their sense of helplessness, they are less infected by the illusion of control. Carmelo Vázquez. 1987. "Judgment of Contingency: Cognitive Biases in Depressed and NonDepressed Subjects." *Journal of Personality and Social Psychology* 52: 419–31.

98. Alice Isen. 1988. "Feeling Happy, Thinking Clearly." *APA Monitor* 19 (4): 6–7.

99. Bert Klandermans. 1989. "Does Happiness Soothe Political Protest? The Complex Relation Between Discontent and Political Unrest." In Ruut Veenhoven, ed., *How Harmful Is Happiness?* Rotterdam: Universitaire Pers, 74.

100. Ruut Veenhoven. 1984. *The Conditions of Happiness.* Dordrecht: Reidel, 30.

Chapter 14. Companionate Democracy

1. Aristotle. 1908. *Politics.* Jowett trans. Oxford: Clarendon Press, 119–20 [1280b].

2. Among the first of these pluralists was the sociologist William Kornhauser. 1959.

The Politics of Mass Society. Glencoe, Ill.: Free Press. The importance of these intermediary groups has recently been revived under the heading of "social capital" by Putnam. Robert D. Putnam. 1993. *Making Democracy Work: Civic Tradition in Modern Italy.* Princeton: Princeton University Press; idem. 1996. "The Strange Disappearance of Civic America." *American Prospect* 24 (Winter): 34–48.

3. Robert A. Nisbet. 1966. *The Sociological Tradition.* New York: Basic Books, 80.

4. Eric M. Uslaner. 1993. *The Decline of Comity in Congress.* Ann Arbor: University of Michigan Press; and "Trends in Comity in the United States." Draft paper privately circulated. Received February 1995.

5. Leo Srole. 1956. "Social Integration and Certain Corollaries." *American Sociological Review* 21: 709–16; see also Herbert McClosky and John H. Schaar. 1965. "Psychological Dimensions of Anomy." *American Political Science Review* 30: 14–40.

6. David Easton. 1953. *The Political System.* New York: Knopf.

7. Joseph Rothschild. 1979. "Political Legitimacy in Contemporary Europe." In Bogdan Denitch, ed., *The Legitimation of Regimes.* London: Sage, 37–54.

8. Donald R. Kinder and David O. Sears. 1985. "Political Opinion and Political Action." In *Handbook of Social Psychology,* 3d ed., 659–741 at 703.

9. Stephen Knack. 1992. "Civic Norms, Social Sanctions, and Voter Turnout." *Rationality and Society* 4: 133–56 at 133.

10. Melvin Seeman. 1972. "Alienation and Engagement." In Angus Campbell and Philip E. Converse, eds., *The Human Meaning of Social Change.* New York: Russell Sage, 467–527.

11. Bert Klandermans. 1989. "Does Happiness Soothe Political Protest? The Complex Relation Between Discontent and Political Unrest." In Ruut Veenhoven ed., *How Harmful Is Happiness?* Rotterdam: University Pers Rotterdam, 61–78 at 66.

12. C. Daniel Batson, Laura L. Shaw, and Kathryn C. Oleson. 1992. "Differentiating Affect, Mood, and Emotion: Toward Functionally Based Conceptual Distinctions." In Margaret S. Clark, ed., *Emotion.* Review of Personality and Social Psychology, vol. 13. Newbury Park, Calif.: Sage, 294–326.

13. Edward O. Wilson. 1975. *Sociobiology: The New Synthesis.* Cambridge: Harvard University Press, 3, 7, 8.

14. Marvin Ember and Carol R. Ember. 1 February 1995. "Democracy in the Anthropological Record." Remarks for a Symposium on New and Restored Democracies. Sponsored by United Nations Studies at Yale.

15. Seymour M. Lipset and William Schneider. 1983. *The Confidence Gap: Business, Labor, and Government in the Public Mind.* New York: Free Press, 82.

16. David O. Sears. 1983. "The Person-Positivity Bias." *Journal of Personality and Social Psychology* 44: 233–50.

17. Paul B. Sheatsley and Jacob J. Feldman. 1965. "A National Survey on Public Reactions and Behavior." In Bradley S. Greenberg and Edwin B. Parker, eds., *The Kennedy Assassination and the American Public: Social Communication in Crisis.* Stanford: Stanford University Press, 163.

18. Ibid., 162.

19. David G. Winter. 1973. *The Power Motive.* New York: Free Press.

20. Robert B. Zajonc. 1980. "Feeling and Thinking: Preferences Need No Inferences." *American Psychologist* 35: 151–75.

21. For a political illustration of this pain, see Robert P. Abelson, Donald R. Kinder, Mark D. Peters, and Susan T. Fiske. 1982. "Affective and Semantic Components in Political Person Perception." *Journal of Personality and Social Psychology* 42: 619–30.

22. Vernon L. Allen. 1975. "Social Support for Nonconformity." In Leonard Berkowitz, ed., *Advances in Experimental Social Psychology.* New York: Academic Press, 1–43.

23. "Individuals who tend to respond in socially desirable ways are truly happier individuals" (even when measured by nonself-report measures). Ed Diener, Ed Sandvik, and William Pavot. 1991. "Happiness Is the Frequency, Not the Intensity, of Positive versus Negative Affect." In Fritz Strack, Michael Argyle, and Norbert Schwarz, eds., *Subjective Well-Being: An Interdisciplinary Perspective.* Oxford: Pergamon, 119–40 at 136.

24. Irving L. Janis. 1972. *Victims of Groupthink.* Boston: Houghton Mifflin.

25. Lyman E. Ostlund. 1973. "Role Theory and Group Dynamics." In Scott Ward and Thomas S. Robertson, eds., *Consumer Behavior: Theoretical Sources.* Englewood Cliffs: Prentice-Hall, 250.

26. Eunkook Suh, Ed Diener, Shifehiro Oishi, and Harry C. Triandis. 1998. "The Shifting Basis of Life Satisfaction Judgments Across Cultures: Emotions versus Norms." *Journal of Personality and Social Psychology* 74: 482–93 at 483.

27. In his *Homo Ludens,* Johan Huizinga (1955) mourned the passing of the good humor of American pre–Civil War politics reflected in the "log cabin and cider campaign." Trans. R. F. C. Hull. Boston: Beacon Press.

28. Gabriel A. Almond. 1954. *The Appeals of Communism.* Princeton: Princeton University Press.

29. Graham Wallas. 1909. *Human Nature in Politics.* Boston: Houghton Mifflin, 236–37.

30. Ember and Ember, "Democracy in the Anthropological Record."

31. Lionel Tiger. 1987. *The Manufacture of Evil: Ethics, Evolution, and the Industrial System.* New York: Harper and Row.

32. Lawrence Kohlberg. 1981. *The Philosophy of Moral Development: Moral Stages and the Idea of Justice.* New York: Harper and Row.

33. Carol Gilligan, Janie Victoria Ward, and Jill McLean Taylor, eds. 1989. *Mapping the Moral Domain.* Cambridge: Harvard University Press. In my opinion, this is the kind of quarrel in which each party wants to appropriate a valued term for his or her own concept of what is important. Kohlberg's use of the term is more conventional, and Gilligan means something other than what we have conventionally meant by *justice.*

34. Robert E. Lane. 1988. "Procedural Goods in a Democracy: How One Is Treated versus What One Gets." *Social Justice Research* 2: 177–92.

35. Cross-cultural research presents the competing moral claims in terms of universal vs. familistic justice. See Joan G. Miller and David M. Bersoff. 1992. "Culture and Moral Judgment: How Are Conflicts Between Justice and Interpersonal Responsibilities Resolved?" *Journal of Personality and Social Psychology* 62: 541–54; Richard A. Schweder, Manamohan Mahapatra, and Joan G. Miller. 1990. "Culture and Moral Development." In James W. Stigler, Richard A. Schweder, and Gilbert Herdt, eds., *Cultural Psychology: Essays on Comparative Human Development.* New York: Cambridge University Press, 130–204. In my opinion, gemeinschaft, or familistic "justice," confounds two goods.

36. Nicholas D. Kristoff. October 13, 1996. "Family and Friendship Guide Japanese Voting." *New York Times,* 1, 10

37. John Stuart Mill. 1910 [1861]. *Utilitarianism*. In *Utilitarianism, Liberty, and Representative Government*. London: Dent, 1–60 at 37–39.

38. Melvin J. Lerner. 1975. "The Justice Motive in Social Behavior." *Journal of Social Issues* 31: 1–19.

39. It was once said that (middle-class) children projected their ideas of their father onto political leaders: "The Benevolent Leader" (who lasted as long as did Eisenhower's presidency and disappeared with Nixon). Fred I. Greenstein. 1965. *Children and Politics*. New Haven: Yale University Press.

40. Robert E. Lane. 1978. "Interpersonal Relations and Leadership in a 'Cold Society'." *Comparative Politics* 10: 443–59.

41. Martin Gilens. 1992. "Racial Attitudes and Opposition to the American Welfare State." Ph.D. diss. Department of Sociology. University of California, Berkeley.

42. Philip Brickman, Robert Folger, Erica Goode, and Yaacov Schul. 1981. "Microjustice and Macrojustice." In Melvin J. Lerner and Sally C. Lerner, eds. 1981. *The Justice Motive in Social Behavior: Adapting to Times of Scarcity and Change*. New York: Plenum, 173–202.

43. G. M. Gilbert. 1950. *The Psychology of Dictatorship*. New York: Ronald Press.

44. David O. Sears and Carolyn L. Funk. 1991. "The Role of Self-Interest in Social and Political Movements." *Advances in Experimental Social Psychology*, vol. 24. New York: Academic Press, 1–91.

45. Alan J. Lambert and Robert S. Wyer. 1990. "Stereotypes and Social Judgment: The Effects of Typicality and Group Heterogeneity." *Journal of Personality and Social Psychology* 59: 664–75 at 664.

46. R. R. Palmer. 1959–64. *The Age of Democratic Revolution: A Political History of Europe and America*, 2 vols. Princeton: Princeton University Press.

47. Isaiah Berlin. 1969. "Two Concepts of Liberty." In his *Four Essays on Liberty*. London: Oxford University Press, 157–59. But Berlin had in mind the demand for rule by a compatriot instead of by an outsider.

48. Wilson Carey McWilliams. 1973. *The Idea of Fraternity in America*. Berkeley: University of California Press, 5. Perhaps he is right about equality, for there is evidence (or at least argument) that among the forms of justice, equality is chosen by societies that put a premium on cooperative, rather than competitive, relations. Morton Deutsch. 1975. "Equity, Equality, and Need: What Determines Which Value Will be Used as the Basis of Distributive Justice?" *Journal of Social Issues* 31: 139–49. I am doubtful of Deutsch's thesis, for where equality is an overriding norm, envy of small differences spoils human relations. At least this was reported to be the case in the Soviet Union.

49. Clyde Z. Nunn, Harry J. Crockett, Jr., and J. Allen Williams, Jr. 1978. *Tolerance for Nonconformity*. San Francisco: Jossey-Bass.

50. Kristoff, "Family and Friendship Guide Japanese Voting," 10.

51. M. Margaret Conway. 1991. *Political Participation in the United States*, 2d ed. Washington, D.C.: Congressional Quarterly Press, 73–74.

52. Paul F. Lazarsfeld, Bernard Berelson, and Hazel Gaudet. 1948. *The People's Choice*. New York: Columbia University Press, 63, 155.

53. Conway, *Political Participation in the United States*, 56.

54. Ideologies, in Australia at least, may be different. One scholar finds that analysis of

the individual ideologies of married couples adds nothing to the analysis of the ideology of the couple taken as a unit. Arthur L. Stinchcombe. June 1988. "Married Couples as Units in Analysis of Ideology." Paper distributed to Yale's Complex Organization Workshop, November 19, 1991, 1.

55. Gabriel A. Almond and Sidney Verba. 1963. *The Civic Culture.* Princeton: Princeton University Press, 234–35.

56. Rosenblatt comments that the "average level of love is high" in the United States because there are few economic interests that enter into the marriage contract. Paul C. Rosenblatt. 1974. "Cross-Cultural Perspective on Attraction," 79–95 at 82. In Ted L. Huston, ed., *Foundations of Interpersonal Attraction.* New York: Academic Press. But I would argue, in words used for other purposes, that "love is not enough": ties are improved, not diluted, when there is something that people do in common; common work is a great adhesive.

57. Putnam, *Making Democracy Work.*

58. In Montegrano, a town in southern Italy, Banfield said the moral code could be expressed as follows: "Maximize the material, short-run advantage of the nuclear family; assume that all others will do likewise." Edward Banfield. 1958. *The Moral Basis of a Backward Society.* Glencoe, Ill.: Free Press, 131.

59. Almond and Verba, *The Civic Culture.*

60. Daniel J. Levinson. 1978. *The Seasons in a Man's Life.* New York: Knopf, 335.

61. Geoffrey Gorer. 1948. *The American People: A Study in National Character.* New York: Norton, 125, 128.

62. See, for example, Robert A. Dahl. 1985. *Democracy and Its Critics.* New Haven: Yale University Press.

Chapter 15. Political Theory of Well-Being

1. Baron d'Holbach. 1973 [1770]. *Système de la Nature.* Reprinted in Peter Gay, ed. *The Enlightenment.* New York: Simon and Schuster, 374.

2. David Ross, who thought of (merited) happiness as one of the ultimate goods, once said that if you imagine a world without mind "you will fail to find anything in it that you can call good in itself." W. David Ross. 1930. *The Right and the Good.* Oxford: Clarendon Press, 140.

3. Immanuel Kant. 1920. *Preface to the Fundamental Principles of the Metaphysic of Morals,* ed. and trans. T. K. Abbott, and published as *Kant's Theory of Ethics.* London: Longmans, Green, 6th ed. Reprinted in T. M. Greene, ed., *Kant: Selections.* New York: Scribner's Sons, 277. In quite another sense, the evolutionary biologists also make happiness an instrumental good (happiness is valued by nature only so far as it serves the reproduction of our genetic heritage). "Emotions had their origins in the evolution systems that enable the animal to perceive the outcomes of actions as affects or feelings, pleasurable or painful, i.e., 'the 'reward' and 'punishment' effects." J. Livesey, 1986. *Learning and Emotion,* Hillsdale, N.J.: Erlbaum, 231. I am indebted to Randolph Nesse for this reference.

4. In my opinion other goods commonly held to be ultimate are best (and most economically) treated as embraced by these three, especially human development. *Free-*

dom is valuable only as opportunities which people are capable of using and lack of constraints preventing them from using such opportunities. Freedom also facilitates the search for happiness. *Knowledge* is not valuable in itself (as Ross suggests) but only as it is used and only because it reflects the thinking person (cf. Plato and Aristotle). *Beauty* (G. E. Moore) is not exclusively a property of objects but rather is found in an interaction with persons who can appreciate the objects. *Self-respect* and *autonomy* are more obviously features of human development.

5. See, for example, Nicholas Rescher. 1969. *Introduction to Value Theory.* Englewood Cliffs: Prentice-Hall; Ross, *The Right and the Good.*

6. J. E. Meade. 1976. *The Just Economy,* vol. 4 of *Principles of Political Economy.* London Allen and Unwin.

7. See, for example, Jane Mansbridge. 1990. "Hard Decisions." *Philosophy and Public Affairs* 10: 1–5.

8. Ruut Veenhoven. 1993. *Happiness in Nations: Subjective Appreciation of Life in 56 Nations 1946–1992.* Rotterdam: Erasmus University, RISBO, 50. The measure of democracy was an index assessing the presence of regular elections, opposition parties, a functioning parliamentary system, and lack of military coups.

9. Among these European nations the overall correlation "between life satisfaction and the number of continuous years a given nation has functioned as a democracy is .85. This relationship is translated into politics in Europe, where life satisfaction is an inoculant against antidemocratic political groups of both Right and Left. Ronald Inglehart. 1990. *Culture Shift in Advanced Industrial Societies.* Princeton: Princeton University Press, 41.

10. Frank M. Andrews and Stephen B. Withey, 1976. *Social Indicators of Well-Being: Americans' Perceptions of Life Quality.* New York: Plenum, 167

11. See, for example, T. N. Srinivasan. 1994. "Destitution: A Discourse." *Journal of Economic Literature* 32: 1842–55.

12. For what it is worth, the standardized average of all relevant surveys (1980s) shows SWB in India as −1.13 and in China as − 1.92. But the N for the Chinese sample was a trivial 149. Ed Diener, Marissa Diener, and Carol Diener. 1995. "Factors Predicting the Subjective Well-Being of Nations." *Journal of Personality and Social Psychology* 69: 851–64 at 856.

13. Inglehart finds that an axis with survival orientation at one end and concern for quality of life at the other end helps to organize masses of world survey data. The above interpretation seems congruent with this point of view. See Ronald Inglehart and Marita Carballo. 1997. "Does Latin America Exist? (And Is There a Confucian Culture?): A Global Analysis of Cross-Cultural Differences." *PS: Political Science and Politics* 30: 34–46. The article is based on Ronald Inglehart. 1997. *Modernization and Postmodernization: Cultural, Economic, and Political Change in 43 Societies.* Princeton: Princeton University Press.

14. Angus Campbell. 1981. *The Sense of Well-Being in America.* New York: McGraw-Hill.

15. Veenhoven, *Happiness in Nations,* 48. But a weaker measure of economic differences, dispersion, is related to dispersion of happiness. 132–34.

16. Ed Diener et al., "Factors Predicting the Subjective Well-Being of Nations," 861.

17. Robert E. Lane. 1962. *Political Ideology: Why the American Working Man Believes What He Does.* New York: Free Press.

18. John Mirowski and Catherine E. Ross. 1989. *Social Causes of Psychological Distress.* New York: Aldine de Gruyter, 89.

19. I think Tocqueville is right when he says, "When . . . social conditions differ but little, the slightest privileges are of some importance; as every man sees around himself a million people enjoying precisely similar or analogous advantages, his pride becomes craving and jealous, he clings to mere trifles and doggedly defends them." Alexis de Tocqueville. 1945. *Democracy in America,* Phillips Bradley, ed., vol. 2. New York: Knopf, 226.

20. Thomas Ashby Wills. 1981. "Downward Comparison Principles in Social Psychology." *Journal of Personality and Social Psychology* 90: 245–71.

21. Philip Brickman and Donald T. Campbell. 1971. "Hedonic Relativism and Planning the Good Society." In M. H. Appley, ed., *Adaptation-Level Theory: A Symposium.* New York: Academic Press, 285–301.

22. Diener et al., "Factors Predicting the Subjective Well-Being of Nations," 859.

23. "Everyone has the right to a standard of living adequate for the health and well-being of himself and of his family, including food, clothing, housing and medical care and necessary social services." Universal Declaration of Human Rights, Article 25. Adopted December 10, 1948, by the General Assembly of the United Nations.

24. It was, however, the Declaration of Independence (and *Federalist* 45 and 47), not the Bill of Rights, that declared that people have a *right* to life, liberty, and the pursuit of happiness.

25. Diener et al., "Factors Predicting the Subjective Well-Being of Nations," 861. Note that a low score means higher level of rights.

26. Ibid., 856. Similarly, although we know that if a person is unemployed he or she will suffer a great deal, high national levels of unemployment do not affect national average SWB. Ruut Veenhoven. 1989 [1984]. *Conditions of Happiness: Summary Print.* Dordrecht: Reidel, 56.

27. Samuel A. Stouffer. 1955. *Communism, Conformity, and Civil Liberties.* New York: Doubleday; Clyde Z. Nunn, Henry J. Crockett, Jr., and J. Allen Williams, Jr. 1978. *Tolerance for Nonconformity.* San Francisco: Jossey-Bass.

28. Jack W. Brehm. 1972. *Responses to the Loss of Freedom: A Theory of Psychological Reactance.* Morristown, N.J.: General Learning Press.

29. Angus Campbell, Philip E. Converse, and Willard L. Rodgers. 1976. *The Quality of American Life: Perceptions, Evaluations, and Satisfactions.* New York: Russell Sage, 48.

30. The "independence and freedom" questions were, "How do you feel about . . . 'your independence or freedom—the chance you have to do what you want'; and 'the variety and diversity of your life?' " Andrews and Withey, *Social Indicators of Well-Being,* 114–15.

31. William Graham Sumner. 1934 [1889]. "Who Is Free?" In Albert G. Keller and Maurice Davie, eds., *Essays of William Graham Sumner,* vol. 1. New Haven: Yale University Press, 301.

32. Diener et al., "Factors Predicting the Subjective Well-Being of Nations," 856.

33. Hadley Cantril. 1965. *The Pattern of Human Concerns*. New Brunswick, N.J.: Rutgers University Press, 267; Campbell, *The Sense of Well-Being in America*, chap. 13.

34. R. Lawson. 1989. "Is Feeling 'in Control' Related to Happiness in Daily Life?" *Psychological Reports* 64: 775–84.

35. Suzanne C. Thompson and Shirlynn Spacapan. 1991. "Perceptions of Control in Vulnerable Populations" *Journal of Social Issues* 47: 1–21.

36. Mark Warren. 1992. "Democratic Theory and Self-Transformation." *American Political Science Review* 86: 8–23; Carol Gould. 1988. *Rethinking Democracy: Freedom and Social Cooperation in Politics, Economy, and Society*. Cambridge: Cambridge University Press.

37. M. Kent Jennings and Richard G. Niemi. 1974. *The Political Character of Adolescence: The Influence of Families and School*. Princeton: Princeton University Press.

38. Fred Weinstein and Gerald M. Platt. 1969. *The Wish to Be Free*. Berkeley: University of California Press.

39. Charles Wolf, Jr. 1988. *Markets or Governments: Choosing Between Imperfect Alternatives*. Cambridge: MIT Press; Thomas E. Borcherding, Werner Pommerehne, and Friedrich Schneider. 1982. *Comparing the Efficiency of Private and Public Production: The Evidence from Five Countries*. Zurich: Institute for Empirical Research in Economics, University of Zurich.

40. Ruut Veenhoven and Piet Ouweneel. 1994. "Livability of the Welfare State: Appreciation-of-Life and Length-of-Life in Nations Varying in State-Welfare Effort." Paper presented to the 13th World Congress of Sociology, Bielfeld, Germany, July 1994.

41. Veenhoven, *Happiness in Nations*, 50.

42. Daniel Katz, Barbara A. Gutek, Robert L. Kahn, and Eugenia Barton. 1975. *Bureaucratic Encounters: A Pilot Study in the Evaluation of Government Services*. Ann Arbor: Institute for Social Research.

43. Veenhoven, *Conditions of Happiness*, 30.

44. Russell Kirk. 1956. *Beyond The Dreams of Avarice*. Chicago: University of Chicago Press.

45. E. Seidman and B. Rapkin. 1983. "Economics and Psychosocial Dysfunction: Toward a Conceptual Framework and Prevention Strategies." In R. D. Felner, L. A. Jason, J. N. Mortisugu, and S. S. Farber, eds., *Preventive Psychology*. New York: Pergamon Press, 175–89; Diener et al., "Factors Predicting the Subjective Well-Being of Nations," 858–59.

46. John Clayton Thomas. 1975. *The Decline of Ideology in Western Political Parties: A Study of Changing Policy Orientations*. Beverly Hills: Sage; Adrian Furnham and Maria Rose. 1987. "Alternative Ethics: The Relationship Between Wealth, Welfare, Work, and Leisure Ethic." *Human Relations* 40: 561–73. In the latter study conservatism is measured by a "wealth ethic" indicator. Social, but not economic, conservatives are less intelligent than liberals, but intelligence is not related to SWB. S. K. Harvey and T. G. Harvey. 1970. "Adolescent Political Outlooks as an Independent Variable." *Midwest Journal of Political Science* 14: 565–95.

47. Recall the longitudinal study of Harvard men (chapter 3) finding that those who were most satisfied with their lives (and most successful in their occupations and mar-

riages) were also most marked by their conventional attitudes toward society and American values. George E. Vaillant. 1977. "The 'Normal Boy' in Later Life: How Adaptation Fosters Growth." *Harvard Magazine* 80: 46–51, 60–61 at 60.

48. Milton Rokeach. 1973. *The Nature of Human Values.* New York: Free Press.

49. Schumpeter argued that a progressive income tax was not implied by the axiom (Schumpeter's term) of declining marginal utility; all that doctrine implied was that in some degree the rich had more utility than the poor—but the degree was unknown. "Pareto optimality," he said, "saved the situation." Joseph A. Schumpeter. 1954. *History of Economic Analysis.* Edited from manuscript by Elizabeth Boody Schumpeter. New York: Oxford University Press, 1072–73.

50. Tversky and Griffin's research showed that although Pareto optimality increases well-being if there are no social comparisons, because there are social comparisons and because individuals compare any given situation with previous situations, "welfare policy derived from Pareto optimality could result in allocations that make most people less happy because it ignores the effect of social comparison." Amos Tversky and Dale Griffin. 1991. "Endowment and Contrast in Judgments of Well-Being." In Fritz Strack, Michael Argyle, and Norbert Schwarz, eds. 1991. *Subjective Well-Being: An Interdisciplinary Perspective.* Oxford: Pergamon, 101–18 at 117.

51. In his *Beyond the Dreams of Avarice,* Kirk argues that the fear of happiness stems largely from a view of humans as highly imperfect; their regeneration comes first.

52. Isaiah Berlin. 1969. "Two Concepts of Liberty." In his *Four Essays on Liberty.* London: Oxford University Press, 137. Berlin said that paternalism is what the early utilitarians offered.

53. Richard A. Schweder, Manamohan Mahapatra, and Joan G. Miller. 1990. "Culture and Moral Development." In James W. Stigler, Richard A. Schweder, and Gilbert Herdt, eds., *Cultural Psychology: Essays on Comparative Human Development.* New York: Cambridge University Press, 130–204 at 199. If we turn to Hinduism for enlightenment on happiness, we will find the following in the *Dhammapada* (Buddhist prayerbook): "From pleasure comes grief, from pleasure comes fear; he who is free from pleasure neither sorrows nor fears." I. Babbitt. 1936. *The Dhammapada.* Translated from the Pai with an Essay on Buddha and the Occident. New York: New Directions. 212.

54. Abraham Maslow. 1970 [1959]. "Psychological Data and Value Theory." In Maslow, ed., *New Knowledge in Human Values.* Chicago: Regnery, 121.

55. Like the poultry farmer, the welfare state sometimes offers goods in kind (food, housing, medical care, education), rather than money or freely convertible vouchers, in order to guide the poor choosers to those things that will make them (and especially their children) stronger. There are ethical defenses for this preselection of goods in such cases. See Michael Walzer. 1983. *Spheres of Justice.* Oxford: Robertson, 75ff. The argument over paternalism engages partisans of China and India, where (as mentioned above) paternalistic China increases the literacy and longevity of its citizens far beyond the levels in India, still under the influence of British values of autonomy.

56. Not only do skills show rising marginal utility as people master them, but the well-supported theory of the love of the familiar (chapter 14) is a powerful drag on the decline of marginal utility in many cases.

57. Schumpeter, *History of Economic Analysis,* 1073.

58. Ed Diener and Marissa Diener. 1995. "Cross-Cultural Correlates of Life Satisfaction and Self-Esteem." *Journal of Personality and Social Psychology* 68: 653–63 at 657. The finding applies to friendship satisfaction but not to satisfaction with family life.

59. Wladyslaw Tatarkiewicz. 1976. *Analysis of Happiness,* trans. Edward Rothert and Damuta Zielinskn. Warsaw: Polish Scientific Publishers, 16. In general, philosophy imposes moral criteria on both happiness and satisfaction: happiness, if merited, and satisfaction, if one is satisfied with morally acceptable things. But happiness or by some interpretations, *eudaimon,* can be an ultimate good, whereas satisfaction cannot.

60. Eunkook Suh, Ed Diener, Shifehiro Oishi, and Harry C. Triandis. 1998. "The Shifting Basis of Life Satisfaction Judgments Across Cultures: Emotions versus Norms." *Journal of Personality and Social Psychology* 74: 482–93.

61. John Stuart Mill. 1969. *Autobiography.* Oxford: Oxford University Press, 86. See also Jon Elster. 1983. *Sour Grapes: Studies in the Subversion of Rationality.* Cambridge: Cambridge University Press, 91–100; Gordon Allport. 1985. *Becoming.* New Haven: Yale University Press, 68.

62. See Daniel Kahneman and Carol Varey. 1991. "Notes on the Psychology of Utility." In Jon Elster and John Roemer, eds., *Interpersonal Comparisons of Well-Being.* Cambridge: Cambridge University Press, 127–64.

63. Two papers at the Conference on Enjoyment and Suffering (1996) make this point: Ed Diener and Eunkook Suh. "National Differences in Subjective Well-Being," and Paul Rozin, "The Puzzles and Properties of Pleasure." Conference on Enjoyment and Suffering, Princeton University, October 30–November 3, 1996. Diener and Suh point out that happiness has much more salience in individualist than in collectivist societies.

64. Little pleads with welfare economists to say "happiness," when that is what they mean. I. M. D. Little. 1957. *A Critique of Welfare Economics,* 2d ed. Oxford: Oxford University Press.

65. For example, Ross. *The Right and the Good;* G. E. Moore. 1903. *Principia Ethica.* Cambridge: Cambridge University Press; Nicholas Rescher. 1969. *Introduction to Value Theory.* Englewood Cliffs: Prentice-Hall; " 'The Stoics:' from Diogenes Laertius." *Lives of Eminent Philosophers* (c. 230 A.D.), trans. R. D. Hicks. Reprinted in Richard B. Brandt. 1961. *Value and Obligation: Systematic Readings in Ethics.* New York: Harcourt, Brace and World, 87–92. Money or wealth is never entered in these lists except by Bentham, who believes that "money . . . [is] the most accurate measure of the quantity of pain or pleasure a man can be made to receive." Jeremy Bentham. 1830. "The Rationale of Punishment." In W. Stark, ed. 1954. *Jeremy Bentham's Economic Writings,* vol. 3. London: Royal Economic Society for George Allen and Unwin, 437–38.

66. For a defense of utilitarian ethics, see Peter Singer. 1993. *Practical Ethics,* 2d ed. Cambridge: Cambridge University Press; essays by J. J. C. Smart and others in Smart and Bernard Williams, eds. 1973. *Utilitarianism, For and Against.* Cambridge: Cambridge University Press.

67. Amartya Sen and Bernard Williams. 1982. "Introduction" to Sen and Williams, eds., *Utilitarianism and Beyond.* Cambridge: Cambridge University Press, 7.

68. Ibid., 4, 5–6.

69. Amartya Sen. 1979. "Utilitarianism and Welfarism." *Journal of Philosophy* 76: 463–88.

70. John Stuart Mill. 1910. *Utilitarianism* [1861]. In *Utilitarianism, Liberty and Representative Government.* London: Dent, 32.

71. "The economic approach . . . now assumes that individuals maximize their utility from basic preferences that do not change rapidly over time." Gary S. Becker. 1976. *The Economic Approach to Human Behavior.* Chicago: University of Chicago Press, ix.

72. These are the questions addressed in Robert E. Lane. 1991. *The Market Experience.* New York: Cambridge University Press.

73. Robert E. Lane. 1994. "Quality of Life and Quality of Persons: A New Role for Government?" *Political Theory* 22: 219–52.

74. Rawls misses a moral justification of happiness in claiming only that happiness is that state which follows from having one's life plans on their way to success. John Rawls. 1971. *A Theory of Happiness.* Cambridge: Harvard University Press. Empirical research shows that "being conscientious may . . . imply being honest to oneself. . . . norm oriented people run less often into troubles, thus often feeling better than their counterparts on the other side of the scale." Hermann Brandstätter. 1991. "Emotions in Everyday Life Situations: Time Sampling of Subjective Experience." In Strack et al., eds., *Subjective Well-Being,* 173–92 at 189–90.

75. There is something of the Dodson-Yerkes principle here: trying *too* hard for something or wanting it *too* much is self-defeating. See a summary of this principle in John C. McCullers. 1978. "Issues in Learning and Motivation." In Mark R. Lepper and David Greene, eds. *The Hidden Costs of Rewards: New Perspectives on the Psychology of Human Motivation.* Hillsdale, N.J.: Erlbaum, 6.

76. Ruut Veenhoven. 1988. "The Utility of Happiness." *Social Indicators Research* 20: 333–54 at 333.

77. Veenhoven, *Conditions of Happiness,* 30.

78. Michael E. Hyland and Peter L. Dann. 1987. "Exploratory Factor Analysis of the Just World Scale Using British Undergraduates." *British Journal of Social Psychology* 26: 73–77; Isaac M. Lipkus, Claudia Dahlbert, and Ilene D. Siegler. 1996. "The Importance of Distinguishing the Belief in a Just World for the Self versus for Others: Implications for Psychological Well-Being" *Personality and Social Psychology Bulletin* 22: 666–77.

Chapter 16. Are People the Best Judges of Their Well-Being?

1. For further analysis of the way people misunderstand their feelings of well-being, see Robert E. Lane. 1991. *The Market Experience.* New York: Cambridge University Press, chap. 27. I have borrowed some portions of that chapter in the discussion below.

2. Alexis de Tocqueville. 1945 [1845 French edition]. *Democracy in America.* Phillips Bradley, ed., New York: Knopf, 1:64.

3. Robert A. Dahl. 1985. *A Preface to Economic Democracy.* Berkeley: University of California Press, 57. Dahl goes on to say (58), "All are equally well qualified to decide which matters do or do not require binding collective decisions."

4. Isaiah Berlin, "Two Concepts of Liberty." In his *Four Essays on Liberty.* London: Oxford University Press, 138. Russell Hardin. 1988. *Morality Within Limits of Reason.* Chicago: University of Chicago Press, 202.

5. R. W. Levenson, P. Ekman, K. Heider, and W. V. Friesen. 1992. "Emotion and

Autonomic Nervous System Activity in the Minangkabau of West Sumatra." *Journal of Personality and Social Psychology* 62: 977–88.

6. Richard Nisbett and Lee Ross. 1980. *Human Inference: Strategies and Shortcomings of Social Judgment.* Englewood Cliffs: Prentice-Hall, 204.

7. Ed Diener. 1984. "Subjective Well-Being." *Psychological Bulletin* 95: 542–75.

8. Frank M. Andrews and Stephen B. Withey. 1976. *Social Indicators of Well-Being: Americans' Perceptions of Life Quality.* New York: Plenum, 110; Angus Campbell, Philip E. Converse, and Willard L. Rodgers. *The Quality of American Life.* New York: Russell Sage.

9. Daniel Kahneman. 1998. "Assessments of Individual Well-Being: A Bottom-Up Approach." Paper presented to the Conference on Enjoyment and Suffering. Princeton University, Oct. 31–Nov.2, 1996.

10. Leon Festinger. 1957. *A Theory of Cognitive Dissonance.* Stanford: Stanford University Press.

11. Kent C. Berridge. 1999. "Pleasure, Pain, Desire, and Dread: Some Biopsychological Pieces and Relations." In Daniel Kahneman, Ed Diener, and Norbert Schwarz, eds., *Foundations of Hedonic Psychology: Scientific Perspectives on Enjoyment and Suffering.* New York: Russell Sage.

12. Edward O. Wilson. 1975. *Sociobiology: The New Synthesis.* Cambridge: Harvard University Press, 3, 4.

13. Keith B. J. Franklin. 1993. "The Neural Basis of Pleasure and Pain." In Michael Hechter, Lynn Nadel, and Richard E. Michod, eds., *The Origin of Values.* New York: Aldine de Gruyter, 273–84 at 276.

14. Howard Berenbaum, Chitra Raghavan, Huynh-Nhu Le, and Jose Gomez. 1999. "Disturbances in Emotion, Mood, and Affect." In Kahneman et al., eds., *Foundations of Hedonic Psychology.*

15. Berridge. "Pleasure, Pain, Desire, and Dread." Here Berridge is reporting the work of Thomas and Diener (1990); Kahneman, Frederickson, Schreiber, and Redelmeier (1993); and Kahneman (1994).

16. Eunkook Suh, Ed Diener, Shifehiro Oishi, and Harry C. Triandis. 1998. "The Shifting Basis of Life Satisfaction Judgments Across Cultures: Emotions versus Norms." *Journal of Personality and Social Psychology* 74: 482–93 at 481.

17. "By interest, a man is continually prompted to make himself completely and as correctly acquainted as possible with the springs of action by which the minds of others are determined. . . . But by interest he is at the same time diverted from any close examination into the springs by which his own conduct is determined. From such knowledge he has not, in any ordinary shape, anything to gain — he finds not in it any source of enjoyment." Jeremy Bentham. 1954. *Jeremy Bentham's Economic Writings,* ed. W. Stark. London: Royal Economic Society by George Allen and Unwin, 3:456.

18. Robert A. Wicklund. 1975. "Objective Self-Awareness." In L. Berkowitz, ed., *Advances in Experimental Social Psychology,* vol. 8. New York: Academic Press. Note that the authoritarian personality is not the only personality syndrome that is "anti-introceptive," that is, resists looking inward at his or her own contaminated soul. T. W. Adorno, E. Frenkel-Brunswick, D. J. Levinson, and R. N. Sanford. 1950. *The Authoritarian Personality.* New York: Harper.

19. Rick E. Ingram, Debra Cruet, Brenda R. Johnson, and Kathleen S. Wisnicki. 1988. "Self-focused Attention, Gender, Gender Role, and Vulnerability to Negative Affect." *Journal of Personality and Social Psychology* 55: 967–78.

20. George E. Vaillant. 1977. "The 'Normal Boy' in Later Life: How Adaptation Fosters Growth." *Harvard Magazine* 80: 46–51, 60–61 at 51.

21. Herbert M. Lefcourt. 1976. *Locus of Control: Current Trends in Theory and Research.* Hillsdale, N.J.: Erlbaum/Wiley, 97–104.

22. William N. Morris. 1992. "A Functional Analysis of the Role of Mood in Affective Systems." In Margaret S. Clark, ed., *Emotion.* Review of Personality and Social Psychology, vol. 13. Newbury Park, Calif.: Sage, 256–93.

23. Sheila B. Blume. February 1991. "Compulsive Gambling: Addiction Without Drugs." *Harvard Mental Health Letter* 8: 4–5.

24. Jane E. Brody. March 21, 1994. "Notions of Beauty Transcend Culture, New Study Suggests." *New York Times,* A14. Brody is quoting Nancy L. Etcoff, a neuropsychologist at Massachusetts General Hospital.

25. Natalie Angier. November 2, 1993. "What Makes a Parent Put up with It All?" *New York Times,* C1, 14. Research by Kerstin Uvnas Moberg, Karolinska Institute (Stockholm).

26. A convenient summary is available in Ed Diener and Richard E. Lucas. 1999. "Personality and Well-Being." In Kahneman et al., *Foundations of Hedonic Psychology.*

27. Ruth Azar. May 1997. "Nature, Nurture: Not Mutually Exclusive." *APA Monitor* 25: 1, 28.

28. Robin M. Hogarth and Melvin W. Reder, eds. 1987. *Rational Choice: The Contrast Between Economics and Psychology.* Chicago: University of Chicago Press; Donald P. Green and Ian Shapiro. 1994. *Pathologies of Rational Choice Theory: A Critique of Applications in Political Science.* New Haven: Yale University Press. "Consistency," say Tversky and Kahneman, "is only one aspect of the lay notion of rational behavior. . . . [T]he common concept of rationality also requires that preferences as utilities for particular outcomes should be predictive of satisfaction or displeasure, associated with their occurrences. Thus, a man could be judged irrational either because his preferences are contradictory or because his desires and aversions do not reflect his pleasures and pains." Amos Tversky and Daniel Kahneman. 30 January 1981. "The Framing of Decisions and the Psychology of Choice." *Science* 211: 453–58 at 458.

29. The psychiatrist Paul Wachtel reports, "People are not clear about what really makes them happy or what the consequences are of various patterns that are central to their lives." See his (1983) *The Poverty of Affluence: A Psychological Portrait of the American Way of Life.* New York: Free Press, 288.

30. Berridge, "Pleasure, Pain, Desire, and Dread," MS p. 8.

31. For a specification of the questions, see chapter 2. In my opinion, the analysis that follows here does not undermine the survey data I have reported but rather (1) helps to account for the remainder of the variance, and (2) offers a possible prior set of variables, influencing and perhaps contaminating but not invalidating, both the specific and the general questions asked.

32. Andrews and Withey, *Social Indicators of Well-Being,* 242–43; Campbell et al., *The Quality of American Life,* 83.

33. Philip Shaver and Jonathan Freedman. August 1976. "Your Pursuit of Happiness." *Psychology Today* 10: 27–32, 75 at 29.

34. Andrews and Withey, *Social Indicators of Well-Being,* 265–67.

35. Amitai Etzioni. 1968. *The Active Society.* New York: Free Press, 619–20.

36. James G. March goes beyond the usual concepts of "bounded rationality" to suggest that to the various forms of rationality there should be added concepts of choice mechanisms embracing future as well as current preferences. See his (1978) "Bounded Rationality, Ambiguity, and the Engineering of Choice." *Bell Journal of Economics* 9: 578–608. This fruitful discussion, however, does not come to grips with the intrapsychic processes that give insight into "ego-syntonic" concepts of happiness.

37. "Rationality should probably include whether values specified are worth pursuing. . . . Rationality is not limited to a choice of means." Abraham Kaplan. 1963. "Some Limits on Rationality." In Carl J. Friedrich, ed., *Rational Decision,* NOMOS 7. New York: Atherton, 57. Compare Karl P. Popper. 1963. *Conjectures and Refutations: The Growth of Scientific Knowledge.* London: Routledge and Kegan Paul, 380–83.

38. Ego-syntonic choices are similar to authentic choices but more related to concepts of personality. Ego-syntonic choices are: (1) congruent with the most stable and firmly held *beliefs* of the individual; (2) resonant with the individual's long term *interests;* (3) they express the individual's deepest and most keenly felt *emotions;* and (4) they serve the individual's dominant *values.* The ego-syntonic has other, nondefinitional characteristics: it is (5) congruent with the self-concept; (6) generally self-referential (not relying on social comparisons), and (7) the product of experience rather more than of tuition. On the last point, see Robert P. Abelson. 1981. "The Psychological Status of the Script Concept." *American Psychologist* 36: 715–29 at 722.

39. Erich Fromm. 1941. *Escape from Freedom.* New York: Rinehart, Appendix, "Character and the Social Process."

40. Susan T. Fiske. 1982. "Schema-Triggered Affect: Applications to Social Perception." In Margaret S. Clark and S. T. Fiske, eds., *Affect and Cognition: The Seventeenth Annual Carnegie Symposium on Cognition.* Hillsdale, N.J.: Erlbaum.

41. Charles Horton Cooley. 1912. *Human Nature and the Social Order.* New York: Scribner's, 152.

42. Susan T. Fiske and Shelley E. Taylor. 1984. *Social Cognition.* New York: Random House, 321 and chap. 11 passim.

43. Nisbett and Ross, *Human Inference,* 198. The depressed, however, are more realistic in their assessments of how others see them than are nondepressed or normal people—their depression correcting for normal tendencies to exaggerate the positive.

44. Ellen J. Langer and Anne Benevento. 1978. "Self-Induced Dependence." *Journal of Personality and Social Psychology* 36: 886–93.

45. Robert B. Zajonc. 1980. "Feeling and Thinking: Preferences Need No Inferences." *American Psychologist* 35: 151–75.

46. Berridge, "Pleasure, Pain, Desire, and Dread."

47. Nisbett and Ross, *Human Inference.*

48. B. Weiner, I. Frieze, A. Kukla, L. Reed, S. Rest, and R. M.. Rosenbaum. 1972. "Perceiving the Causes of Success and Failure." In E. E. Jones, D. E. Kanouse, H. H. Kelley, R. E. Nisbett, S. Valins, and B. Wiener, eds., *Attribution: Perceiving the Causes of Behavior.* Morristown, N.J.: General Learning Press, 95–120.

49. Nisbett and Ross, *Human Inference,* passim.

50. Harold H. Kelley. 1967. "Attribution Theory in Social Psychology." In *Nebraska Symposium on Motivation.* Lincoln: University of Nebraska Press, 192–238.

51. Daryl J. Bem. 1972. "Self-Perception Theory." In L. Berkowitz, ed., *Advances in Experimental Social Psychology,* vol. 6. New York: Academic, 2.

52. Nisbett and Ross, *Human Inference,* 197. The following discussion relies heavily on chap. 9, "The Lay Scientist Self-Examined," 195–227. See also Alice M. Tybout and Carol A. Scott. 1983. "Availability of Well-Defined Internal Knowledge and the Attitude Formation Process: Information Aggregation versus Self-Perception." *Journal of Personality and Social Psychology* 44: 474–91.

53. Tybout and Scott hypothesize that "immediately available sensory data" will give a person access to his judgmental processes whereas other data are interpreted by reference to conventional behavior. They confirm their hypothesis by experiments comparing taste data to social consensus data. Tybout and Scott, "Availability of Well-Defined Internal Knowledge and the Attitude Formation Process."

54. Nisbett and Ross, *Human Inference,* 199. There is evidence that a person may find reasons for an emotional state and then reject them, preferring to rely on affective "conclusion" without cognitive support. Fiske and Taylor, *Social Cognition,* 334. And it is not infrequent that people do not know *that* they are aroused. Ibid., 2.

55. Nisbett and Ross, *Human Inference,* 200. This discussion is based on the work of Stanley Schacter.

56. "To the extent that internal cues are weak, ambiguous, or uninterpretable, the individual is functionally in the same position as an outside observer who must necessarily rely upon those same external cues to infer the individual's inner states." Bem, "Self-Perception Theory," 2.

57. Nisbett and Ross, *Human Inference,* 202.

58. The reference is to J. Weiss and P. Brown. 1977. *Self-Insight Error in Explanation of Mood,* [then] unpublished manuscript, Harvard University, cited in Nisbett and Ross, *Human Inference,* 221.

59. Nisbett and Ross, *Human Inference,* 221–22.

60. Ibid., 211–12.

61. Ibid., 223–25.

62. Ibid., 223, emphasis added.

63. Karl Marx. 1964 [1844]. "The Power of Money in Bourgeois Society." In *Economic and Philosophical Manuscripts of 1844,* trans. M. Milligan, ed. Dirk Struik. New York: International Publishers, 169.

64. Kenneth Burke points out that "in the economy of one man, monetary power may be *compensatory* to some other kind of power (physical, sexual, moral, stylistic, intellectual, etc.). That is, he may seek by the vicarage of money, to 'add a cubit to his stature.' But in the economy of another man, monetary power may be *consistent* with one or all of these." Kenneth Burke. 1969. *A Grammar of Motives.* Berkeley: University of California Press, 114–15.

65. Edith Neisser. 1960. "Emotional and Social Values Attached to Money." *Marriage and Family Living* 22: 132–38 at 133.

66. K. A. Lancaster. 1971. *Consumer Demand: A New Approach.* New York: Columbia University Press.

67. Lita Furby. 1978. "Possessions: Toward a Theory of Their Meaning and Function Throughout the Life Cycle." In P. B. Baltes, ed., *Life Span Development and Behavior,* vol. 1. New York: Academic Press, 320, 329.

68. Robert White. April 1976. "Exploring the Origins of Competence." *APA Monitor,* 40–45.

69. Stanley Isaacs. 1967 [1949]). "Property and Possessiveness." In T. Talbot, ed., *The World of the Child.* Garden City, N.Y.: Doubleday/Anchor, cited in Furby, "Possessions," 324.

70. Edward E. Lawler III. 1971. *Pay and Organizational Effectiveness: A Psychological View.* New York: McGraw-Hill.

71. Carin Rubenstein. May 1981. "Money and Self-Esteem, Relationships, Secrecy, Envy, Satisfaction." *Psychology Today* 15: 29–44 at 42.

72. Irwin Sarason, Henry M. Levine, Robert B. Basham, and Barbara Sarason. 1983. "Assessing Social Support: The Social Support Questionnaire." *Journal of Personality and Social Psychology* 44: 127–39.

73. Amos Tversky and Dale Griffin. 1991. "Endowment and Contrast in Judgments of Well-Being." In Fritz Strack, Michael Argyle, and Norbert Schwarz, eds., *Subjective Well-Being: An Interdisciplinary Perspective.* Oxford: Pergamon, 101–18 at 114–15.

74. Diane G. Symbaluk, C. Donald Heth, Judy Cameron, and W. David Pierce. 1997. "Social Modeling, Monetary Incentives, and Pain Endurance." *Personality and Social Psychology Bulletin* 23: 258–69.

75. R. F. Fortune. 1963. *Sorcerers of Dobu,* rev. ed. London: Routledge and Kegan Paul.

76. Margaret Mead. 1956. *New Lives for Old.* New York: Morrow.

77. Robert E. Lane. 1991. *The Market Experience.* New York: Cambridge University Press, 612.

78. Ronald Inglehart. 1990. *Culture Shift in Advanced Industrial Society.* Princeton: Princeton University Press.

Chapter 17. Self-Inspired Pain

1. William H. Beveridge. 1945. *Full Employment in a Free Society.* New York: Norton, 254–55.

2. Barrington Moore, Jr. 1972. *Reflections on the Causes of Human Misery, and Upon Certain Proposals to Eliminate Them.* Boston: Beacon, 2.

3. Sigmund Freud. 1951. *Civilization and its Discontents,* trans. J. Riviere. London: Hogarth Press, 34–42. In some ways Freud was a negative utilitarian: "avoiding pain forces seeking pleasure into the background."

4. Adam Smith. 1976 [1759]. *The Theory of Moral Sentiments,* ed. D. D. Raphael and A. L. Macfie. Indianapolis: Liberty Press, 181.

5. Melvin J. Lerner. 1980. *The Belief in a Just World: A Fundamental Delusion.* New York: Plenum.

6. Philip Brickman and Donald T. Campbell. 1971. "Hedonic Relativism and Planning the Good Society." In M. H. Appley, ed., *Adaptation-Level Theory: A Symposium.* New York: Academic Press. In contrast, Daniel Kahneman holds that there is no necessity for each new level of satisfaction to replace the previous (zero) level so that the "strong

version of the hedonic treadmill" is not implied by the adaptation process. Kahneman. 1999. "Assessment of Individual Well-Being: A Bottom-up Approach." In Kahneman, Ed Diener, and Norbert Schwarz, eds., *Foundations of Hedonic Psychology: Scientific Perspectives on Enjoyment and Suffering.* New York: Russell Sage.

7. Bruce Headey and Alexander Wearing. 1991. "Subjective Well-Being: A Stocks and Flows Framework." In Fritz Strack, Michael Argyle, and Norbert Schwarz, eds., *Subjective Well-Being: An Interdisciplinary Perspective.* Oxford: Pergamon, 49–73 at 59.

8. Ibid., 60

9. Thomas Hobbes. 1911. *Leviathan.* London: Dent, chap. 11.

10. Frederick A. Lange. 1925 [1865]. *The History of Materialism,* trans. E. D. Thomas. 3d ed. rev. London: Routledge and Kegan Paul.

11. George Caspar Homans. 1961. *Social Behavior: Its Elementary Forms.* New York: Harcourt, Brace and World, 276. Homans (267) says, "The greater the amount the individual gets, the greater his satisfaction and, at the same time, the more the individual still desires, the less his satisfaction." Homans is here quoting Nancy Morse. 1953. *Satisfactions in the White-Collar Job.* Ann Arbor: University of Michigan Press, 28. On the first (what he gets), the reward may be discretion or reputation as well as money.

12. George Katona. 1975. *Psychological Economics.* New York: Elsevier, 15.

13. Brickman and Campbell, "Hedonic Relativism and Planning the Good Society," 287.

14. Homans, *Social Behavior,* 269–75

15. Ibid., 268, 272–73.

16. Otis Dudley Duncan. 1975. "Does Money Buy Satisfaction?" *Social Indicators Research* 2: 267–74; Richard Easterlin. 1973. "Does Money Buy Happiness?" *Public Interest,* no. 30 (Winter), 3–10.

17. Brickman and Campbell, "Hedonic Relativism and Planning the Good Society," 280–81.

18. Philip Shaver and Jonathan Freedman. 1976. "Your Pursuit of Happiness." *Psychology Today* 10 (August): 27–32, 75.

19. Glen H. Elder, Tri Van Nguyen, and Avshalom Caspi. 1985. "Linking Family Hardship to Children's Lives." *Child Development* 85: 361–75.

20. Wladyslaw Tatarkiewicz. 1876. *Analysis of Happiness,* trans. Edward Rothert and Damuta Zielinskn. The Hague: Martinus Nijhoff and Warsaw: Polish Scientific Publishers, 8.

21. Brickman and Campbell, "Hedonic Relativism and Planning the Good Society," 293. I have borrowed from this source the idea that people forget unhappy events quicker than happy ones but reversed its implication.

22. Paul Rozin. 1999. "Pleasures of the Body: Preadaptation and the Puzzles and Properties of Pleasure." In Kahneman et al., eds., *Foundations of Hedonic Psychology.*

23. Brickman and Campbell, "Hedonic Relativism and Planning the Good Society," 294.

24. One should adjust the metaphor further: people do not compare themselves with *all* boats; they compare their situations only with those in the adjacent boats, suggesting that insofar as social comparisons create the relevant standards, adaptation level theory must explain stratified, rather than aggregate, levels of discontent

25. Brickman and Campbell, "Hedonic Relativism and Planning the Good Society," 299.

26. Ibid.

27. Ed Diener, Marissa Diener, and Carol Diener. 1995. "Factors Predicting the Subjective Well-Being of Nations." *Journal of Personality and Social Psychology* 69: 851–64 at 859.

28. The upward skewing is further shown by the fact that 28 percent of the lowest quintile believe their income is about average while only 14 percent of the highest quintile believe that their income is about average. The consequence is socially important: "The relative position in respect to the imagination of an average German household influences satisfaction with income significantly." Wolfgang Glatzer. 1991. "Quality of Life in Advanced Industrialized Countries: The Case of West Germany." In Strack et al., eds., *Subjective Well-Being,* 268.

29. Ibid., 269.

30. Brickman and Campbell, "Hedonic Relativism and Planning the Good Society," 299, 300.

31. Tatarkiewicz cites Gracian to express a similar view: "There must always be some desire unfulfilled if we are not to be unhappy in our felicity." Tatarkiewicz, *Analysis of Happiness,* 10.

32. John Stuart Mill. 1910 [1861]. *Utilitarianism.* In *Utilitarianism, Liberty, and Representative Government.* London: Dent, 35.

33. Jonathan Freedman. 1980. *Happy People.* New York: Harcourt, Brace, 31–32.

34. Ibid., 30

35. Bertrand Russell. 1930. *The Conquest of Happiness.* London: G. Allen and Unwin, 248.

36. Ed Diener. 1984. "Subjective Well-Being." *Psychological Bulletin* 95: 542–75 at 557, 562. Compare: "We may think of a person as being happy when he is on the way of a successful execution (more or less) of a rational plan of life drawn up under (more or less) favorable conditions, and he is reasonably confident that his plans can be carried through. Someone is happy when his plans are going well, his more important aspirations are being fulfilled, and he feels sure that his good fortune will endure." John Rawls. 1971. *A Theory of Justice.* Cambridge: Harvard University Press, 409.

37. "'Hormism' . . . is the theory that pleasure occurs when a conation, i.e., some striving for an object or goal, is being successful, while displeasure occurs when a conation is being frustrated." K. Duncker. 1941. "Pain, Pleasure, Emotion, and Striving." *Philosophy and Phenomenological Research* 1:391–430 at 392. I am indebted to Paul Rozin for this reference.

38. Ed Diener, Ed Sandvik, and William Pavot. 1991. "Happiness Is the Frequency, Not the Intensity, of Positive versus Negative Affect." In Strack et al., eds., *Subjective Well-Being,* 119–40. Compare the Yerkes-Dodson hypothesis that caring too much about an outcome is a prescription for poorer performance.

39. Daniel Kahneman and Carol Varey. 1991. "Notes on the Psychology of Utility." In Jon Elster and John Roemer, eds., *Interpersonal Comparisons of Well-Being.* Cambridge: Cambridge University Press, 127–64. The research and theory in this area are at early stages of development and the domains where "wanting" and "liking" may differ

have been so little explored that the economic implications of the distinction are still speculative.

40. "The individual's desire for personal status is apparently insatiable. Whether we say that he longs for *prestige,* for *self-respect, autonomy,* or *self-regard,* a dynamic factor of this order is apparently the strongest of his drives." Gordon Allport. 1945. "The Psychology of Participation." *Psychological Review* 52: 122. Confounding status and prestige, on the one hand, with self-respect, on the other, is misleading.

41. Richard DeCharms. 1968. *Personal Causation: The Internal Affective Determinants of Behavior.* New York: Academic Press.

42. See Mary Douglas and Baron Isherwood. 1980 [1978]. *The World of Goods: Towards An Anthropology of Consumption.* Harmondsworth: Penguin. These authors point out that "some goods possess holistic symbolic significance and thus cannot be treated as bundles of technical characteristics." Hence one cannot assume the stability of preferences for these goods over time, 126

43. Robert E. Lane. 1991. *The Market Experience.* New York: Cambridge University Press, part V.

44. Abraham Maslow. 1970. *Motivation and Personality,* rev. ed. New York: Harper and Row.

45. See M. A. Wahba and L. G. Bridewell. 1976. "Maslow Reconsidered: A Review of Research on the Need Hierarchy." *Organizational Behavior and Human Performance* 15: 210–40. Inglehart, however, believes these self-actualizing needs are those that postmaterialists seek to satisfy. Ronald Inglehart. 1972; *The Silent Revolution.* Princeton: Princeton University Press; and 1990. *Culture Shift in Advanced Industrial Society.* Princeton: Princeton University Press.

46. John Mirowski and Catherine E. Ross. 1989. *Social Causes of Psychological Distress.* New York: Aldine de Gruyter, 137.

47. "Objective powerlessness is a condition in which the individual is unable to achieve desired goals. It leads to subjective powerlessness, the sense that important outcomes are beyond one's control — the consequences of chance, fate, or powerful others." Ibid., 12.

48. Alice M. Isen. 1987. "Positive Affect, Cognitive Processes, and Social Behavior." In L. Berkowitz, ed., *Advances in Experimental Social Psychology.* vol. 20. New York: Academic Press, 203–53; Michael Carlson, Ventura Charlin, and Norman Miller. 1988. "Positive Mood and Helping Behavior: A Test of Six Hypotheses." *Journal of Personality and Social Psychology* 55: 211–29.

49. Ruut Veenhoven. 1989. "Does Happiness Bind? Marriage Chances of the Unhappy." In Veenhoven, ed., *How Harmful Is Happiness?* Rotterdam: University Pers Rotterdam. 44–60 at 44.

50. Ruut Veenhoven. 1989 [1984]. *Conditions of Happiness: Summary Print.* Dordrecht: Reidel, 31

51. Veenhoven reports a malign outcome: "Widespread dissatisfaction with life tends to act as a bomb under the social system. . . . A willing public for radical reformers may thus cause upheaval and violence." Ibid., 62. It might happen that way, but over the long course of history a different sequence is more likely: low life satisfaction creates political dissatisfaction, which, in turn, promotes withdrawal and not protest.

52. Isaac M. Lipkus, Claudia Dahlbert, and Ilene D. Siegler. 1996. "The Importance of

Distinguishing the Belief in a Just World for the Self versus for Others: Implications for Psychological Well-Being." *Personality and Social Psychology Bulletin* 22: 666–77.

53. B. Moore argues that although capitalism is not necessarily exploitative, democratic openness makes exploitation easier: "The openness has been for some time mainly in one direction. It is vastly easier . . . to promote inhumane and cruel polities than others." *Reflections on the Causes of Human Misery,* 146.

54. See Walter Mischel. 1974. "Processes in Delay of Gratification." In L. Berkowitz, ed., *Advances in Experimental Social Psychology,* vol. 7. New York: Academic.

55. Robert S. Lynd and Helen M. Lynd. 1963 [1937]. *Middletown in Transition: A Study in Cultural Conflicts.* New York: Harcourt Brace, 476.

56. Shlomo Maitel. 1982. *Minds, Markets, and Money.* New York: Basic Books, chap. 3.

57. Louise C. Perry, David G. Perry, and David English. 1985. "Happiness: When Does It Lead to Self-Indulgence and When Does it Lead to Self-Denial?" *Journal of Experimental Child Psychology* 39: 203–11.

58. Icek Ajzen and Martin Fishbein. 1980. *Understanding Attitudes and Predicting Social Behavior.* Englewood Cliffs: Prentice-Hall.

59. F. Thomas Juster and Paul N. Courant. 1986. "Integrating Stocks and Flows in Quality of Life Research." In Frank M. Andrews, ed., *Research on the Quality of Life.* Ann Arbor: Institute for Social Research, 150.

60. Charles Fried. 1970. *The Anatomy of Values.* Cambridge: Harvard University Press.

61. Alexis de Tocqueville. 1945. *Democracy in America.* Phillips Bradley, ed., New York: Knopf, 2:140.

62. Ellen J. Langer and Anne Benevento. 1978. "Self-Induced Dependence." *Journal of Personality and Social Psychology* 36: 886–93.

63. David C. McClelland. 1985. *Human Motivation.* Glenview, Ill.: Scott, Foresman, 398.

64. Ibid., 399.

65. Ibid., 395.

66. Ibid., 404–10. Quotation at 410.

67. For example, see John Dollard and Neal E. Miller. 1950. *Personality and Psychotherapy.* New York: McGraw-Hill, 355–63.

68. James G. March. 1978. "Bounded Rationality, Ambiguity, and the Engineering of Choice." *Bell Journal of Economics* 19: 587–608 at 601–03.

69. Higgins suggests that hedonic calculations should be viewed as having two basic dimensions: a promotion focus (approach) and a prevention focus (avoidance). Each focus, then, would have its own sources of pain and pleasure. E. Tory Higgins. 1997. "Beyond Pleasure and Pain." *American Psychologist* 52: 1280–1300.

70. Albert Bandura. 1977. *Social Learning Theory.* Englewood Cliffs: Prentice-Hall, 143. As Bandura comments, this makes a hash of economists' utility theory.

71. Ibid., 138. But Bandura has in mind the contrast between Puritan cultures compared to "self gratification patterns [in which] people reward themselves freely regardless of how they behave."

72. See Alex C. Michalos. 1986. "Job Satisfaction, Marital Satisfaction, and the Qual-

ity of Life: A Review and a Preview." In Andrews, ed., *Research on the Quality of Life,* 66; Theo B. C. Poiesz and Jaspar von Grumbkow. 1988. "Economic Well-Being, Job Satisfaction, Income Evaluation, and Consumer Satisfaction: An Integrative Attempt." In W. Fred Van Raaij, Gery M. Van Veldhoven, Karl-Erik Wärneryd, eds., *Handbook of Economic Psychology.* Dordrecht: Kluwer, 570–93.

73. "The end sought by accumulation is to rank high in comparison to the rest of the community in point of pecuniary strength. . . . However widely, or equally or 'fairly,' it may be distributed, no general increase of the community's wealth can make any approach to satiating this need, the grounds of which is the desire of every one to excel every one else in the accumulation of goods." Thorstein Veblen. 1994. *The Theory of the Leisure Class.* Mineola, N.Y.: Dover, 20–21.

74. McClelland, *Human Motivation,* 383.

Chapter 18. The Way Home

1. Hannah Arendt. 1958. *The Human Condition.* Chicago: University of Chicago Press, 322.

2. Eric and Mary Josephson,. 1973. "Introduction" to their edited *Man Alone.* New York: Dell, 11.

3. Burt Alpert. 1973. *Inversions: A Study of Warped Consciousness.* Ann Arbor: Edwards Brothers, 1–2.

4. John Mirowsky and Catherine E. Ross. 1990. "The Consolation-Prize Theory of Alienation." *American Journal of Sociology* 95: 1505–35.

5. Herbert J. Gans. 1967. *The Levittowners.* New York: Random House, 146.

6. Ferdinand Tönnies. 1957 [1887]. *Community and Society* (*Gemeinschaft und Gesellschaft*) trans. C. P. Loomis. East Lansing: Michigan State University Press, 65.

7. Avner Ben-Ner. 1982. "Changing Values and Preferences in Communal Organizations: Economic Evidence from the Experience of the Israeli Kibbutz." In D. Jones and J. Svejnar, eds., *Participatory and Self-Managed Firms: Evaluating Economic Performance.* Lexington, Mass.: Lexington/Heath.

8. Although more people thought the future would be better than thought it would be worse, only 17 percent anticipated substantial improvements in their situations. Moreover, "their sense of past progress was unrelated to their expectations about future progress . . . [and] we concluded that the measure named 'progress past and future' probably did not represent any thoughts that were real to most respondents and that it should be discarded." Frank M. Andrews and Steven B. Withey. 1976. *Social Indicators of Well-Being: Americans' Perceptions of Life Quality.* New York: Plenum, 106.

9. Theodore Zeldin. 1995 [1994]. *An Intimate History of Humanity.* London: Minerva, 60.

10. Ed Diener and Eunkook Suh. 1999. "National Differences in Subjective Well-Being." In Daniel Kahneman, Ed Diener, and Norbert Schwarz, eds., *Foundations of Hedonic Psychology: Scientific Perspectives on Enjoyment and Suffering.* New York: Russell Sage.

11. Pitirim A. Sorokin. 1941. *The Crisis of Our Age: The Social and Cultural Outlook.* New York: Dutton, 133–36.

12. Marylee C. Taylor. 1982. "Improved Conditions, Rising Expectations, and Dissatisfaction: A Test of the Past/Present Relative Deprivation Hypothesis." *Social Psychology Quarterly* 45: 24–33.

13. Ludwig von Mises. 1960. *Epistemological Problems of Economics,* trans. G. Reisman. Princeton: Van Nostrand, 61.

14. This failure of political theory to specify the production functions of human development is all the stranger because of the leads in the classical authors. In *The Statesman,* Plato argues that the purpose of political philosophy is to develop character. In *Politics,* Aristotle [1280b] says, "Virtue must be the serious care of a state which truly deserves that name." And *eudäimon* is the object of elaborate (if confused) discussion in both authors. See, for example, J. C. B. Gosling and C. C. W. Taylor. 1982. *The Greeks on Pleasure.* Oxford: Oxford University Press.

15. Robert Wright. 1994. *The Moral Animal: Evolutionary Psychology and Everyday Life.* New York: Random House, 298.

16. Jerome Kagan. 1996. "Three Pleasing Ideas." *American Psychologist* 51: 901–08 at 904.

17. Hermann Brandstätter. 1991. "Emotions in Everyday Life Situations: Time Sampling of Subjective Experience." In Fritz Strack, Michael Argyle, and Norbert Schwarz, eds., *Subjective Well-Being: An Interdisciplinary Perspective.* Oxford: Pergamon, 173–92 at 189–90. In the Asian collectivist societies, however, this sensitivity to social norms is much stronger and takes the place of reference to a person's internal feelings. Eunkook Suh, Ed Diener, Shifehiro Oishi, and Harry C. Triandis. 1998. "The Shifting Basis of Life Satisfaction Judgments Across Cultures: Emotions versus Norms." *Journal of Personality and Social Psychology* 74: 482–93.

18. Quoted in Friedrich Engels. n.d. c. 1933 [1890]. *Socialism: Utopian and Scientific.* In V. Adoratsky, ed., *Karl Marx: Selected Works.* New York: International Publishers Press, 186.

19. Roger Friedland and Robert R. Alford. 1991. "Bringing Society Back In: Symbols, Practices, and Institutional Contradictions." In Walter W. Powell and Paul J. DiMaggio, eds., *The New Institutionalism in Organizational Analysis.* Chicago: University of Chicago Press, 285.

20. Erich Fromm. 1961. "Marx's Concept of Man," in his edited volume by the same name. New York: Ungar, 1–69.

21. Lionel Tiger. 1993. "Morality Recapitulates Phylogeny." In Michael Hechter, Lynn Nadel, and Richard E. Michod, eds., *The Origin of Values.* New York: Aldine de Gruyter, 291–331.

22. Orbell and associates ran a computer simulation showing that where individual encounters are governed by individualistic assumptions, given inequality, society tends to fragment. John Orbell, Langche Zeng, and Matthew Mulford. 1996. "Individual Experience and the Fragmentation of Societies." *American Sociological Review* 61: 1018–32.

23. Amitai Etzioni. 1988. *The Moral Dimension: Toward a New Economics.* New York: Free Press, 251.

24. Fred Hirsch. 1976. *Social Limits to Growth.* Cambridge: Harvard University Press, 12.

25. Joseph A. Schumpeter. 1950. *Capitalism, Socialism, and Democracy,* 3d ed. London: Allen and Unwin, 219.

26. Karl Marx and Friedrich Engels. 1848 [1932]. *Manifesto of the Communist Party.* New York: International Publishers, 12.

27. Francis Fukuyama. 1993. *The End of History and the Last Man.* New York: Avon.

28. It is ironic that just as the power of market economics begins to fail to account for well-being, it should seek to extend its empire to other fields. See, for example, Gary S. Becker. 1976. *The Economic Approach to Human Behavior.* Chicago: University of Chicago Press; James Buchanan and Gordon Tullock. 1962. *The Calculus of Consent.* Ann Arbor: University of Michigan Press.

29. For economists, a fair remuneration is defined by whatever the perfect market delivers, something that appears to be pure procedural justice, but since, unlike due process, the procedures are devised for purposes other than justice, this "procedural justice" of the market is of uncertain value. See John Rawls. 1971. *A Theory of Justice.* Cambridge: Harvard University Press, 86.

30. Dante Cichetti and Sheree L. Toth. 1998. "The Development of Depression in Children and Adolescents." *American Psychologist* 53: 221–41.

31. Alice M. Isen. 1988. "Feeling Happy, Thinking Clearly." *APA Monitor* 19: 4, 6–7.

32. Karen Pezza Leith and Roy F. Baumeister. 1996. "Why Do Bad Moods Increase Self-Defeating Behavior? Emotion, Risk Taking, and Self-Regulation." *Journal of Personality and Social Psychology* 71: 1250–67. See also Noel Murray, Harish Sujan, Edward R. Hurt, and Mita Sujan. 1990. "The Influence of Mood on Categorization: A Cognitive Flexibility Interpretation" *Journal of Personality and Social Psychology* 59:3, 411–25; D. M. Taylor and J. Brown. 1988. "Illusions and Well-Being: A Social Psychological Perspective of Mental Health." *Psychological Bulletin* 103: 195–210.

33. George W. Brown and Tirril Harris. 1978. *Social Origins of Depression: A Study of Psychiatric Disorder.* London and Cambridge: Tavistock/Cambridge University Press, 283.

34. Jack E. Hokanson and Andrew C. Butler. 1992. "Cluster Analysis of Depressed College Students' Social Behaviors." *Journal of Personality and Social Psychology* 62: 273–80; Juliet Harper and Elizabeth M. Kelly. 1985. "Anti-Social Behaviour as a Mask for Depression in Year 5 and 6 Boys." *Mental Health in Australia* 1: 14–19.

35. John S. Gillis. 1993. "Effects of Life Stress and Dysphoria on Complex Judgments." *Psychological Reports* 72 [pt. 2): 1355–63.

36. Kenneth K. Miya. 1976. "Autonomy and Depression." *Clinical Social Work Journal* 4: 260–68

37. Nancy E. Meyer, Dennis G. Dyck, and Ron J. Petrinack. 1989. "Cognitive Appraisal and Attributional Correlates of Depressive Symptoms in Children." *Journal of Abnormal Child Psychology* 17: 325–36.

38. Richard C. Fowler, Barry I. Liskow, and Vasantkumar L. Tanna. 1980. "Alcoholism, Depression, and Life Events." *Journal of Affective Disorders* 22: 127–35.

39. Charles P. Cummings, Charles K. Prokop, and Ruth Cosgrove. 1985. "Dysphoria: The Cause or the Result of Addiction?" *Psychiatric Hospital* 16: 131–34.

40. Daniel Goleman. December 30, 1993. "Costs of Depression on a Par with Heart Disease, a Study Says." *New York Times,* A25.

41. Bernard Lubin, Marvin Zuckerman, Linda M. Breytspraak, Neil C. Bull, et al. 1988. "Affects, Demographic Variables, and Health." *Journal of Clinical Psychology* 44: 131–41.

42. Ruut Veenhoven. 1993. *Happiness in Nations.* Erasmus University, Center for Socio-Cultural Transformation, RISBO Rotterdam, 47. The medical costs of treating anxiety and depression are substantial; in Britain, for example, the cost was estimated to be £4.6 billion in 1992, a sum representing about a seventh of the total inpatient cost of the health service. And in the United States, the annual costs of depression were estimated to be $44 billion, with the costs of alcoholism almost double that amount. Howard Berenbaum, Chitra Raghavan, Huynh-Nhu Le, and Jose Gomez. 1999. "Disturbances in Emotion, Mood, and Affect." In Kahneman et al., eds., *Foundations of Hedonic Psychology.*

43. Brenda Major, Catherine Cozzarelli, Anne M. Sciacchitano, M. Lynne Cooper, et al. 1990. "Perceived Social Support, Self-Efficacy, and Adjustment to Abortion." *Journal of Personality and Social Psychology* 59: 452–63 at 452.

44. Richard W. Brislin. 1983. "Cross-Cultural Research in Psychology." *Annual Review of Psychology* 34. Palo Alto, Calif..: Annual Reviews, 363–400 at 375.

45. Andrews and Withey, *Social Indicators of Well-Being,* 135.

46. Yun-shik Chang. 1991. "The Personalist Ethic and the Market in Korea." *Comparative Studies in Society and History* 33: 106–29. The real challenge to the dominant Confucian code of mutual help, he says, is not in the market but in the imperatives of an impersonal rule of law, n. 5, p. 125.

47. See, for example, the "pattern variables" defining some of these differences in Talcott Parsons and Edward A. Shils. 1962 [1951]. "Values, Motives, and Systems of Action." In Parsons and Shils, eds., *Toward a General Theory of Action: Theoretical Foundations for the Social Sciences.* New York: Harper Torchbook, 80–84. These patterns, in fact, were derived from Tönnies.

48. Peter Laslett. 1971. *The World We Have Lost,* 2d ed. New York: Scribner's, 4.

49. Robert Redfield. 1950. *A Village That Chose Progress: Cham Kom Revisited.* Chicago: University of Chicago Press.

50. Lewis A. Coser. 1974. *Greedy Institutions.* New York: Free Press.

51. Edward Shorter. 1975. *The Making of the Modern Family.* New York: Basic Books. The situation was a little different in Puritan New England, where factory girls were required to live in dormitories where they could be supervised.

52. Lane, *The Market Experience,* 47–49.

53. Edward C. Banfield. 1958. *The Moral Basis of a Backward Society.* Glencoe, Ill.: Free Press.

54. For example, William Ophuls, 1997. "Requiem for Representative Democracy." *The Good Society,* Committee on the Political Economy of the Good Society, (Winter) 7: 1–10.

55. Leon Festinger. 1957. *A Theory of Cognitive Dissonance.* Stanford: Stanford University Press.

56. Robert E. Lane. 1989. "Market Choice and Human Choice." *Markets and Justice,* NOMOS 31. New York: New York University Press, 226–49.

57. Ronald Inglehart. 1990. *Culture Shift in Advanced Industrial Societies.* Princeton: Princeton University Press, 41. This inference is supported by the fact that the relationship between *political* satisfaction and tenure of democracy in Europe is small (.21) compared to the strong relationship of .85 between life satisfaction and democratic duration, 33.

58. Andrews and Withey, *Social Indicators of Well-Being,* 43.

59. Robert D. Putnam. 1995. "Bowling Alone: America's Declining Social Capital." *Journal of Democracy* 6: 65–78.

60. Barbara A. Burk, S. M. Zdep, and H. Kushmer. 1973. "Affiliation Patterns Among American Girls." *Adolescence* 8: 542–46.

61. In the current (1998) atmosphere of economic insecurity, "the end of history" has a clammy feel about it. As I write, two clippings from British newspapers lie before me: "Job Insecurity Haunts U.S. Workers Despite Boom," by Mark Tran. *The Guardian,* 30 August 1997, 3; and "The Happiness Gap: Capitalism . . . Makes You Miserable," by Oliver James, *The Guardian,* 15 September 1997, D2, 2.

62. Ronald Inglehart and Marita Carballo. 1997. "Does Latin America Exist? (And Is There a Confucian Culture?): A Global Analysis of Cross-Cultural Differences." *PS: Political Science and Politics* 30: 34–46 at 39. The basic source is Inglehart. 1997. *Modernization and Postmadernization: Cultural, Economic, and Political Change in 43 Societies.* Princeton: Princeton University Press. Empirically, the survival values are associated with traditional views of the role of women, rejection of outgroups, dogmatic morality, orthodox religious adherence, a high value for money, and trust in science. Associated with well-being values are: valuing freedom, tolerance of heterodoxy, favoring smaller families, equality for women, tolerance of homosexuality, higher degrees of life satisfaction, and a relatively low value assigned to national pride. The traditional authority/survival cluster (southwest quadrant on Inglehart's map) includes low interpersonal trust, whereas the secular-rational/well-being cluster reflects high interpersonal trust.

63. Inglehart and Carballo, "Does Latin America Exist?" 39.

64. The theory of postmodernization depends to some extent on Inglehart's theory of policy-postmaterialism and shares its premises. As mentioned in chapter 8, a thorough review of European value trends finds that "the proportion of postmaterialists relative to materialists has either ceased to increase or has even declined in several West European countries." Dieter Fuchs and Hans Dieter Klingeman. 1995. "Citizens and the State: A Relationship Transformed." In Klingeman and Fuchs. 1995. *Citizens and the State: Beliefs in Government,* vol. 1. Oxford: Oxford University Press, 419–43 at 439. In any event, "postmaterialism is not much more widespread among the post-war cohorts than it would have been had there been no post-war years of 'unprecedented' peace and prosperity." See Elinor Scarborough. 1995. "Materialist-Postmaterialist Value Orientations." In Jan W. van Deth and Elinor Scarborough, eds., *The Impact of Values,* vol. 4 of *Beliefs in Government.* Oxford: Oxford University Press, 123–59 at 138, 141.

65. Jennifer Steinhauer. April 19, 1995. "Big Benefits in Marriage, Studies Say." *New York Times,* A10. In addition, the children of divorced parents die younger and themselves have more divorces than others. Joan S. Tucker, Howard S. Friedman, Joseph E. Schwartz, Michael H. Criqui, Carol Tomlinson-Keasey, Deborah L. Wingard, and Leslie R. Martin. 1997. "Parental Divorce: Effects on Individual Behavior and Longevity." *Journal of Personality and Social Psychology* 73: 381–91.

66. David Popenoe. 26 December 1992. "The Controversial Truth: Two-Parent Families Are Better." *New York Times,* 21. Popenoe is cochairman of the Council on Families in America.

67. Diener and Suh, "National Differences in Subjective Well-Being," 28

68. John Mirowski and Catherine E. Ross. 1989. *Social Causes of Psychological Distress*. New York: Aline de Gruyter, 181. Emphasis added.

69. Alex C. Michalos. 1986. "Job Satisfaction, Marital Satisfaction, and the Quality of Life: A Review and a Preview." In Frank M. Andrews, ed., *Research on the Quality of Life*. Ann Arbor: Institute for Social Research, 62.

70. Michael Argyle. 1999. "Causes and Correlates of Happiness." In Kahneman et al., eds., *Foundations of Hedonic Psychology*.

71. Michalos, "Job Satisfaction, Marital Satisfaction, and the Quality of Life," 60–61.

72. Terry P. London. 1997. "The Case Against Self-Esteem: Alternate Philosophies Toward Self that Would Raise the Probability of Pleasurable and Productive Living." *Journal of Rational-Emotive and Cognitive Behavior Therapy* 15: 19–29.

73. Gerald Marwell and Ruth E. Ames. 1981. "Economists Free Ride, Does Anyone Else?" *Journal of Public Economists* 15: 295–310.

74. Gregory G. Brunk. 1980. "The Impact of Rational Participation Models on Voting Attitudes." *Public Choice* 35: 549–64. See Etzioni, *The Moral Dimension,* passim.

Appendix. Measures of Well-Being and Depression

1. A very short bibliography of works treating measurement problems of SWB is available in nn. 12, 13, chap. 2. The following is a tiny sample of more recent work: Ed Sandvik, Ed Diener, and Larry Seidlitz. 1993. "Subjective Well-Being: The Convergence and Stability of Self-Report and Non-Self-Report Measures." *Journal of Personality* 61: 317–43; Eunkook Suh, Ed Diener, Shifehiro Oishi, and Harry C. Triandis. 1998. "The Shifting Basis of Life Satisfaction Judgments Across Cultures: Emotions versus Norms." *Journal of Personality and Social Psychology* 74: 482–93; W. Pavot and Ed Diener. 1993. "Review of the Satisfaction with Life Scale." *Psychological Assessment* 5: 164–72; Ed Diener and Richard E. Lucas. 1996. "Personality and Well-Being." Paper presented to the Conference on Enjoyment and Suffering, Princeton University, Oct. 31–Nov. 3, 1996, 34. Richard E. Lucas, Ed Diener, and Eunkook Suh. 1996. "Discriminant Validity of Well-Being Measures." *Journal of Personality and Social Psychology* 71: 616–28. Assessments of measures of depression are treated in the section on depression, below.

2. Angus Campbell, Philip E. Converse, and Willard L. Rodgers. 1976. *The Quality of American Life*. New York: Russell Sage, 50.

3. Bruce Headey and Alexander Wearing. 1991. "Subjective Well-Being: A Stocks and Flows Framework." In Fritz Strack, Michael Argyle, and Norbert Schwarz, eds., *Subjective Well-Being: An Interdisciplinary Perspective*. Oxford: Pergamon, 49–73 at 55.

4. Michael Argyle and Maryanne Martin. "The Psychological Causes of Happiness." In ibid, 77–100 at 78.

5. Frank M. Andrews and Stephen B. Withey. 1976. *Social Indicators of Well-Being: Americans' Perceptions of Life Quality*. New York: Plenum.

6. Tom W. Smith. 1979. "Happiness: Time Trends, Seasonal Variations, Intersurvey Differences, and Other Mysteries." *Social Psychology Quarterly* 42: 18–30 at 20. If the test–retest reliability is only moderately good, it may be argued that people's levels of satisfaction do change. In Andrews and Withey's study cited above the within-test reliability was .70. The global measures tend to be context dependent, whereas those focus-

ing on such specific areas of life as work and marriage are not—yet the measures of these specific areas sum rather nicely to predict the global measures. See National Research Council of the National Academy of Science. 1981. *Surveys of Subjective Phenomena: Summary Report.* Washington, D.C.: National Academy Press; Robert E. Lane. 1991. "Misinterpreting Happiness and Satisfaction in a Market Society." Chapter 27 of *The Market Experience.* New York: Cambridge University Press.

7. Headey and Wearing, "Subjective Well-Being: A Stocks and Flows Framework," 49–73. Diener and Lucas report that measures of life satisfaction over a four-year period correlated .52.

8. David G. Myers and Ed Diener. August 1997. "The New Scientific Pursuit of Happiness." *Harvard Mental Health Letter* 14: 4–7 at 7. The correlation was 0.70.

9. Ruut Veenhoven. 1993. *Happiness in Nations: Subjective Appreciation of Life in 56 Nations 1946–1992.* Rotterdam: Erasmus University, RISBO Press, 11.

10. Suh et al., "The Shifting Basis of Life Satisfaction Judgments Across Cultures: Emotions versus Norms," 483.

11. Ed Diener and Eunkook Suh. 1999. "National Differences in Subjective Well-Being." In Daniel Kahneman, Ed Diener, and Norbert Schwarz, eds., *Foundations of Hedonic Psychology: Scientific Perspectives on Enjoyment and Suffering.* New York: Russell Sage.

12. Daniel Kahneman. 1996. "Assessment of Individual Well-Being: A Bottom-Up Approach." Paper presented to the Conference on Enjoyment and Suffering, Princeton University, Oct.31–Nov. 3. As Kahneman knows, there is also a top-down effect where, say, a cheerful disposition colors the interpretation of life events. Diener and Lucas, "Personality and Well-Being."

13. C. F. Turner and E. Martin. 1984. *Surveying Subjective Phenomena.* New York: Russell Sage.

14. Diener and Suh, "National Differences in Subjective Well-Being."

15. Norbert Schwarz and Fritz Strack. 1991. "Evaluating One's Life: A Judgment Model of Subjective Well-Being." In Strack et al., eds., *Subjective Well-Being: An Interdisciplinary Perspective,* 28–29.

16. Ibid., 84–85. My emphasis.

17. "People who describe themselves as happy seem happy to their friends, their families, and [their] interviewers. Compared to very unhappy people, they smile more. They are more loving, hopeful, and helpful. They are even less vulnerable to illness." Myers and Diener, "The New Scientific Pursuit of Happiness," 5.

18. Lucas et al., "Discriminant Validity of Well-Being Measures," 616–28.

19. Veenhoven, *Happiness in Nations,* 59, 76, 77.

20. Diener and Suh, "National Differences in Subjective Well-Being," 9–10.

21. Diener and Lucas, "Personality and Well-Being," 20.

22. Ronald C. Kessler, Katherine A. McGonagle, Nelson Shanyang, B. Christopher, et al. Jan. 1994. "Lifetime and 12-month Prevalence of DSM-III—R Psychiatric Disorders in the United States: Results from the National Comorbidity Study." *Archives of General Psychiatry* 51: 8–19.

23. Dorothea C. Leighton, John S. Harding, David B. Mocklin, Allister M. MacMillan, and Alexander H. Leighton. 1963. *The Character of Danger.* The Stirling County Study

of Psychiatric Disorder and Sociocultural Environment, vol. 3. New York: Basic Books; Leo Srole, Thomas S. Langner, Stanley T. Michael, Marvin K. Opler, and Thomas A. C. Rennie. 1962. *Mental Health in the Metropolis: The Midtown Manhattan Study,* vol 1. New York: McGraw-Hill.

24. President's Commission on Mental Health. 1978. *Report.* Washington, D.C.: U.S. Government Printing Office.

25. For a roundup of recent diagnostic and measurement problems, see a two-part analysis beginning with *Harvard Medical School Mental Health Letter,* vol 6: 12 (June 1990), 1–3; Paul Willner. 1985. *Depression: A Psychobiological Synthesis.* New York: Wiley.

26. John Mirowski and Catherine E. Ross. 1989. *Social Causes of Psychological Distress.* New York: Aldine de Gruyter, 36–37.

27. Herb Kutchins and Stuart A. Kirk. May 1995. "DSM-IV: Does Bigger and Newer Mean Better?" *Harvard Mental Health Letter* 11: 4–6.

28. Thus, Weissman reports that a diagnosis for dysthymia would be appropriate if a person's "depressed mood lasted over two years but they had too few associated symptoms to meet criteria for major depression, and if they had no psychotic symptoms such as delusions or hallucinations." Myrna M. Weissman, Martha Livingston Bruce, Philip J. Leaf, Louise Florio, and Charles Holzer III. 1991. "Affective Disorders." In Lee N. Robins and Darrel A. Regier, eds., *Psychiatric Disorders in America: The Epidemiological Catchment Area Study.* New York: Free Press, 54–80 at 55.

29. G. W. Brown, B. Andrews, Antonia T. Bifulco, and H. O. Veiel. 1990. "Self-Esteem and Depression: I. Measurement Issues and Prediction of Onset." *Social Psychiatry and Psychiatric Epidemiology* 25: 200–09.

30. Aaron T. Beck, Maria Kovacs, and Arlene Weissman. Dec. 1975. "Hopelessness and Suicidal Behavior: An Overview." *Journal of the American Medical Association* 234: 1146–49; Grant N. Marshall and Eric L. Lang. 1990. "Optimism, Self-mastery, and Symptoms of Depression in Women Professionals." *Journal of Personality and Social Psychology,* 59: 132–39.

31. Frank D. Fincham, Carol I. Diener, and Audrey Hokoda. 1987. "Attributional Style and Learned Helplessness: Relationship to the Use of Causal Schemata and Depressive Symptoms in Children." *British Journal of Social Psychology* 26: 1–7.

32. Kessler et al., "Lifetime and 12-month Prevalence of DSM-III—R Psychiatric Disorders in the United States: Results from the National Comorbidity Study," 8–19.

33. Wolfgang Glatzer. "Quality of Life in Advanced Industrialized Countries: The Case of West Germany." In Strack, Argyle, and Schwarz, eds., *Subjective Well-Being,* 264.

34. For example, Robert A. Steer, Aaron T. Beck, John H. Riskind, and Gary Brown. 1986. "Differentiation of Depressive Disorders from Generalized Anxiety by the Beck Depression Inventory." *Journal of Clinical Psychology* 42: 475–78; Murray B. Stein, Manuel E. Tancer, and Thomas W. Uhde. 1990. "Major Depression in Patients with Panic Disorder: Factors Associated with Course and Recurrence." *Journal of Affective Disorders* 19: 287–96.

35. Brigitte A. Prusoff, Kathleen R. Merikangas, and Myrna M. Weissman. 1988. "Lifetime Prevalence and Age of Onset of Psychiatric Disorders: Recall 4 Years Later." *Journal of Psychiatric Research* 22: 107–17.

36. Private communications Jan. 17, 1995; Ed Diener, Ed Sandvik, and William Pavot. 1991. "Happiness Is the Frequency, Not the Intensity, of Positive versus Negative Affect." In Strack, Argyle, and Schwarz, eds., *Subjective Well-Being: An Interdisciplinary Perspective,* 119–40.

37. Peter M. Lewisohn, Julie E. Redner, and John R. Seeley. 1991. "The Relationship between Life Satisfaction and Psychosocial Variables: New Perspectives." In ibid, 141–69.

38. Antonia Abbey and Frank M. Andrews. 1986. "Modeling the Psychological Determinants of Life Quality." In Frank M. Andrews, ed., *Research on the Quality of Life.* Ann Arbor: Institute for Social Research, 87–88.

39. William E. Snell, Raymond C. Hawkins, and Sharyn S. Belk. 1990. "Measuring Depressive Life Experiences." *Personality and Individual Differences* 11: 605–13.

40. George W. Brown and Tirril Harris. 1978. *Social Origins of Depression: A Study of Psychiatric Disorder in Women.* London: Tavistock, 283.

41. I do not think it is fruitful or correct to explain the discrepancy between the two measures by referring to the "masked depression" of those who possess all the other symptoms but who will not face their own feelings. There is very little evidence of "faking happy" in the survey studies.

42. "According to psychiatrists and geriatricians, this scenario [in which an older patient reports to his physician that 'other than reporting a few aches and pains, he says he feels fine'] illustrates how depressive illness is typically overlooked in the elderly: patients don't mention it and doctors often neglect to ask, attending instead to physical complaints." "Late-Life Depression: Let There Be Light." 1995. *Harvard Health Letter* 20 (March), 6–8.

43. Paul Karoly and Linda Ruehlman. 1983. "Affective Meaning and Depression: A Semantic Differential Analysis." *Cognitive Therapy and Research* 7: 41–49.

44. Beck et al., "Hopelessness and Suicidal Behavior: An Overview," 1146. Chapter 2 gave confirming evidence on the rise of suicide among adolescent and young adults.

45. Reported in Argyle and Martin, "The Psychological Causes of Happiness," 77–100; the location of happy and depressed feelings by analysis of brain waves in infants is described by Richard Davidson and Nathan Fox as reported in Daniel Goleman, "TV's Power to Teach." *New York Times,* 22 Nov. 88, C1.

46. Richard W. Brislin. 1983. "Cross-Cultural Research in Psychology." *Annual Review of Psychology* 34. Palo Alto, Calif.: Annual Reviews, 363–400 at 383.

47. Marvin W. Kahn. 1986. "Psychosocial Disorders of Aboriginal People of the United States and Australia." *Journal of Rural Community Psychology* 7: 45–59.

48. A. Jablensky, N. Sartorius, W. Gulbinat, and G. Ernberg. 1981. "Characteristics of Depressive Patients Contacting Psychiatric Services in Four Cultures: A Report from the WHO Collaborative Study on the Assessment of Depressive Disorders." *Acta Psychiatrica Scandinavica* 63: 367–83.

49. Joseph H. Talley. 1986. "Masks of Major Depression." *Medical Aspects of Human Sexuality* 20: 16–25.

50. Martin Seligman in James Buie. October 1988. "'Me' Decades Generate Depression: Individualism Erodes Commitment to Others." *APA Monitor* 19: 18.

51. "Update on Mood Disorders—Part I." *Harvard Mental Health Letter* 11: (Dec. 1994), 1–4 at 4.

52. Ibid.

53. In nine out of the past eleven years (1980–91) suicides increased in Great Britain. *Observer,* 27 Sept. 1992, 4. As reported in chapter 2 above, suicides among youth from ages fifteen to twenty-four have increased in most Western countries in the 1970–90 period. For example, in the United States youth suicides per 100,000 increased during that brief period from 8.0 to 13.2. UNICEF. 1993. *The Progress of Nations.* New York: United Nations, 45.

54. Ronald Inglehart and Jacques-René Rabier. 1986. "Aspirations Adapt to Situations — But Why Are the Belgians so Much Happier than the French? A Cross-Cultural Analysis of the Subjective Quality of Life." In Frank M. Andrews, ed., *Research on the Quality of Life.* Ann Arbor: Institute for Social Research, 51. One anomaly that invites further study is the report that suicidal tendencies may have a genetic base. Part of the evidence for this is the evidence that depression is itself based on inheritable factors. Thus, "twenty percent of the monkeys [studied] are predisposed to becoming seriously depressed — roughly the same as the human lifetime risk of the disorder — when they lose a relative or close partner, or suffer a drop in social status." See Natalie Angier, "Quest for Evolutionary Meaning in the Persistence of Suicide." *New York Times,* April 5, 1994, C1, C10.

55. Maria Kovacs, David Goldston, and Constantine Gatsonis. 1993. "Suicidal Behaviors and Childhood-Onset Depressive Disorders: A Longitudinal Investigation." Special Section of "Longitudinal Studies of Depressive Disorders in Children." *Journal of the American Academy of Child and Adolescent Psychiatry* 32: 8–20.

56. Olle Hagnell, Jan Lanke, Birgitta Rorsman, and Leif Ojesjo. 1982. "Are We Entering an Age of Melancholy? Depressive Illnesses in a Prospective Epidemiological Study over 25 Years: The Lundby Study, Sweden." *Psychological Medicine* 12: (May) 279–89.

57. M. G. Madianos and C. N. Stefanis. 1992. "Changes in the Prevalence of Symptoms of Depression across Greece." *Social Psychiatry and Psychiatric Epidemiology* 27: 211–19.

58. Gerald L. Klerman. 1989. "The Current Age of Youthful Melancholia: Evidence for Increase in Depression Among Adolescents and Young Adults." *Annual Progress in Child Psychiatry and Child Development: 1989,* 333–54.

59. Gerald L. Klerman and Myrna M. Weissman. April 1989. "Increasing Rates of Depression." *Journal of the American Medical Association* 261 (no. 15): 2229.

60. Prusoff et al., "Lifetime Prevalence and Age of Onset of Psychiatric Disorders: Recall 4 Years Later," 107–17.

61. Myrna M. Weissman, Roger Bland, Peter R. Joynce, Stephen Newman, J. Elisabeth Wells, and Hans-Ulrich Wittchen. 1993. "Sex Differences in Rates of Depression: Cross-National Perspectives." *Journal of Affective Disorders* 29: 77–84.

62. Martin Seligman quoted in James Buie, "'Me' Decades Generate Depression," 18.

Index